Wells, Fargo & Co.
Stagecoach and Train
Robberies, 1870–1884

Wells, Fargo & Co. Stagecoach and Train Robberies, 1870–1884

The Corporate Report of 1885 with Additional Facts About the Crimes and Their Perpetrators

JAMES B. HUME *and*
JOHN N. THACKER

Edited and expanded by
R. MICHAEL WILSON

REVISED EDITION

McFarland & Company, Inc., Publishers
Jefferson, North Carolina, and London

LIBRARY OF CONGRESS CATALOGUING-IN-PUBLICATION DATA

Hume, James B., 1827–1904.
Wells, Fargo & Co. stagecoach and train robberies, 1870–1884 :
the corporate report of 1885 with additional facts about the crimes
and their perpetrators / James B. Hume and John N. Thacker ;
edited and expanded by R. Michael Wilson. — Rev. ed.
            p.   cm.
Previously published: Las Vegas, Nev. : Stagecoach Books, c2007, under the title Wells, Fargo & Co.
report of losses from stagecoach and train robbers, 1870 to 1884.
Original report published in 1885 under title: Report of Jas. B. Hume and Jno. N. Thacker,
special officers, Wells, Fargo & Co.'s express.
Includes bibliographical references and index.

ISBN 978-0-7864-4855-5
softcover : 50# alkaline paper ∞

1. Stagecoach robberies — West (U.S.) — History — 19th century. 2. Train robberies —
West (U.S.) — History — 19th century. 3. Brigands and robbers — West (U.S.) — History — 19th century.
4. Criminals — West (U.S.) — Identification — History — 19th century. 5. Wells, Fargo & Company —
History — 19th century. 6. Express service — West (U.S.) — History — 19th century. 7. West (U.S.) —
History — 1860–1890. 8. Stagecoach robberies — West (U.S.) — History — 19th century — Sources.
9. Train robberies — West (U.S.) — History — 19th century — Sources. 10. West (U.S.) — History —
1860–1890 — Sources. I. Thacker, John N. II. Wilson, R. Michael, 1944– III. Hume, James B.,
1827–1904. Wells, Fargo & Co. report of losses from stagecoach and train robbers, 1870 to 1884.
IV. Hume, James B., 1827–1904. Report of Jas. B. Hume and Jno. N. Thacker, special officers, Wells, Fargo
& Co.'s express. V. Title. VI. Title: Wells, Fargo and Co. VII. Title: Wells, Fargo & Company.
HV6661.W47H86 2010   364.15'52097809034 — dc22   2009051627

British Library cataloguing data are available

©2010 R. Michael Wilson. All rights reserved

*No part of this book may be reproduced or transmitted in any form
or by any means, electronic or mechanical, including photocopying
or recording, or by any information storage and retrieval system,
without permission in writing from the publisher.*

Front cover: *top left* Henry Wells, founder; William G. Fargo, founder;
Wells Fargo Express Co. Deadwood Treasure Wagon and Guards with $250,000 gold
bullion from the Great Homestake Mine, Deadwood, South Dakota (Library of Congress)

Manufactured in the United States of America

*McFarland & Company, Inc., Publishers
Box 611, Jefferson, North Carolina 28640
www.mcfarlandpub.com*

Table of Contents

Preface 1
Introduction 3
   Stagecoaching 6
   Report Summary 9

THE ROBBERS' RECORD 13

Appendix: Additional Robbers
   and Their Crimes 241
Bibliography 265
Index 267

Preface

Wells, Fargo's chief detective James B. Hume was hired in 1871, and 14 years later he and detective John N. Thacker published a report of the losses to the company during Hume's tenure. The summary takes up only three pages and, like the rest of the 91-page report, consists mostly of a listing of events rather than a presentation of details. This is not surprising when one considers that the report covers 313 stagecoach robberies, 23 burglaries, and four train robberies involving Wells, Fargo & Company property.

A glance at the report reveals that the detectives had an underlying motive because it is better considered as a textual "mug book" of road agents (robbers) arrested, convicted and sent to prison. The listing of their exploits seems almost incidental. The report was widely circulated to western lawmen to help them identify these robbers should they again engage in robbing stagecoaches or trains or burglarizing businesses. For decades this report served as the only treatment of stagecoach robbery and thereafter was addressed piecemeal, first in Old West magazines and then as chapters in books of general interest.

Hume and Thacker organized the bulk of the report, the 83-page "Robber's Record," alphabetically by the last name of the robber. For those men still alive by late 1884 the physical descriptions are precise. The section begins with the caveat: "Note — The age, as given in describing robbers, is fixed at the date of this publication —1885." What Hume and Thacker failed to include was a detailed account of each robbery or burglary so that lawmen could identify a specific *modus operandi* from future crimes, something we know today is an important part of an investigation.

This book expands upon the original Wells, Fargo report and provides the details of each crime for which a road agent went to prison or was killed in the act. The primary source for researching stagecoach and train robberies and burglaries are contemporary newspapers, and we are indebted to the many editors who saw that the thrilling details of a crime caught the attention of the public. The more thrilling, fascinating, and mysterious the story the greater the readership of that edition, and all the better for subscriptions. There were a few instances for which personal diary entries or personal accounts were found, and court records sometimes provided important information on a crime and trial. Even then many of these sources were also found in the local newspapers of the time. When more than one culprit was involved the details are found under the name of the first or main criminal, and the names of his partners in crime will refer the reader back to that case history.

The entries in the Appendix detail stagecoach robberies which were excluded in the original Robbers' Record; they were only listed in the summary pages at the beginning of the report under such headings as "Number of Wells Fargo Guards Killed," "Number of Passengers seriously wounded," etc. Rather than disrupt the flow of the original Robbers' Record these events were addressed in alphabetical order in the Appendix.

Of course there were far more stagecoach and train robberies and burglaries in the West between 1856, when the first stagecoach was robbed in California, and 1916, when the last stagecoach was robbed in Nevada, than the Wells, Fargo report documents. Since these crimes did not involve Wells, Fargo property, they did not make it into the report.

Introduction

Before 1849 express companies were active throughout the East and Midwest, but there was only one small concern operating on the Pacific Coast, and C. L. Cady's Express was announced in the *Californian* newspaper on April 24, 1847. The need for express businesses changed dramatically when gold was discovered at Sutter's Mill on January 24, 1848. There was an immediate need for expanded operations to bring in the mail to miners in isolated gold camps and to bring out the gold to a place from which it could be processed or shipped. Several express companies sprang up quickly, but the Adams Express Company, by 1852, had established itself as the major express company in California and by 1854 dominated the Pacific Coast. The men behind Wells, Fargo & Company, Henry Wells and William G. Fargo, carefully watched the situation in California and finally opened their Pacific express business in 1852. Their first public notice appeared in the *New York Times* on May 20, 1852:

> WELLS FARGO & CO. CALIFORNIA EXPRESS
> Capital $300,000
> A joint stock company. Office 16 Wall Street
> ... This company having completed its organization as above is now ready to undertake the general forwarding agency and commission business; the purchase and sale of gold dust. Bullion and specie, also packages, parcels and freight of all description in and between the City of New York and the City of San Francisco, and the principal cities and towns in California ...

A similar notice appeared in the *Alta California* in early 1852, before the company had opened an office and even before its representative arrived on the Pacific Coast. Once established, the company quickly grew and soon adopted a policy of acquiring its smaller competitors. As early as November 1852 it bought Gregory & Company Express; in September 1853 it acquired Reynolds, Todd & Company Express; and in July 1854 it added Hunter & Company Express. That left it with only one major competitor in the West, Adams Express.

In California the drought of 1854 brought mining to a halt. Water was necessary for placer mining so, with a drought at hand, many miners sat about idly during much of that year. Consequently there was far less gold to be shipped by express while merchants and financial concerns overextended credit to the miners. The Adams Express Company concentrated upon its waning express business in association with Page, Bacon & Company, a banking firm which was located in the same building. The parent bank of Page, Bacon was in St. Louis, and it had invested heavily in the Ohio & Mississippi Railroad. When that venture failed the parent bank was forced to close its doors. The San Francisco branch had just sent $1 million in assets to the parent bank, so, when word of the St. Louis closure reached San Francisco on February 23, 1855, the local bank was unable to meet the demand and had to close its doors. Adams Express Company at San Francisco followed suit, never to reopen.

The founders of Wells, Fargo & Company: Henry Wells, left, and William G. Fargo (used with permission from Wells Fargo Bank N.A.).

By the end of the Civil War, Wells, Fargo & Company had expanded its transportation of treasure and express operations to include stagecoach lines, the pony express, wagons and buckboards, as well as sleighs and dog sleds in colder climes. The company also contracted for shipments on railroads and ships owned by other companies. When gold and silver was discovered in Nevada, Wells, Fargo & Company, now the dominant express com-

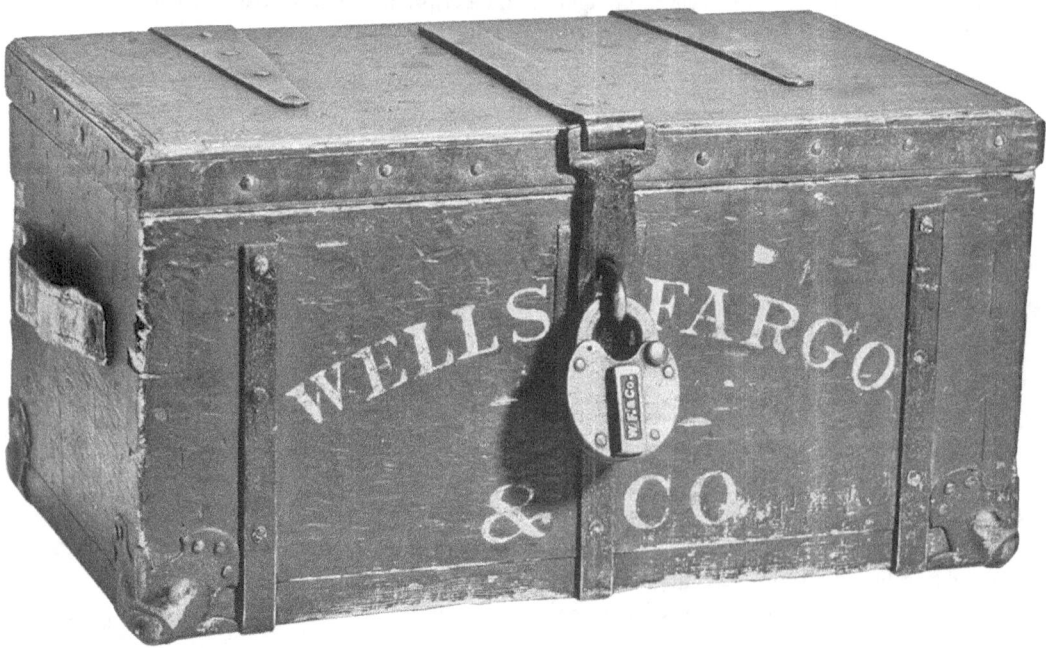

Wells, Fargo's "little green treasure box," built with Ponderosa pine, oak rims and iron strapping by J.Y. Ayers of San Francisco (used with permission from Wells Fargo Bank N.A.).

Two of Wells, Fargo's best detectives were James B. Hume, left, and John N. Thacker (used with permission from Wells Fargo Bank N.A.).

pany in the West, added stagecoach lines to its operations. It purchased the Pioneer Stage Line in 1864 and on November 1, 1866, added the Holladay Overland Mail & Express Company. Within a few weeks all interests were combined under one banner. In 1869 Wells, Fargo & Company, realizing that the operation of stage lines was not its business, sold its stage line interests and thereafter contracted the handling of express in its "green treasure boxes" on whichever stage line operated regionally.

Those little green treasure boxes became the standard for carrying express, and other companies included making up boxes as part of their process of "stocking the road." The treasure boxes used by Wells, Fargo & Company were manufactured by J. Y. Ayers of San Francisco. He used Ponderosa pine for the body which he reinforced with oak rims and iron strapping. A box measured 20 inches long by 12 inches high by 10 inches deep and weighed nearly 25 pounds empty. At first the boxes were loaded in the office and deposited into the driver's boot or inside the passenger compartment. But the oft-heard command of "Throw down that box" led to its being bolted into the boot or chained to the coach in later years, and in some cases it was replaced with an iron safe riveted to the floor of the passenger compartment.

The scourge of the road agent was the Wells, Fargo & Company detective, and two of the best were James B. Hume and John N. Thacker. James B. Hume (January 23, 1827–May 18, 1904) went west in 1850 and in 1860 became the tax collector for El Dorado County, California. In 1864 he became the city marshal at Placerville, California, and soon afterward was appointed undersheriff of El Dorado County. He was such an effective lawman that he was hired as a Wells, Fargo & Company detective in 1871, but took a one-year leave of absence to serve as warden of the Nevada State Prison. He returned and served as Wells, Fargo & Company's chief detective until his death in 1904. John N. Thacker (1838–January 3, 1913) was elected sheriff of Humboldt County on November 3, 1868, and in 1875 he was hired as a Wells, Fargo & Company detective. He stayed with the company until November 1, 1907, and retired after 32 years of service. In November 1884 Hume and Thacker compiled their famed report of company losses covering the previous 14 years, and they published their report on January 1, 1885.

Stagecoaching

The stagecoach is one of the icons of the Old West, and the stagecoach played a key role in opening the western frontier to settlement. Conestoga wagons could take months to travel from the Mississippi River to the Pacific Ocean, and trains did not become an important form of transportation until the late nineteenth century, but stagecoaches made the trip between St. Louis and San Francisco in less than a month. The word "stage" in stagecoach was, in the beginning, a measure of distance as a "coach" traveled from one place to another in stages of about 15 miles. But with continued misuse the term "stage" replaced "coach" for the average westerner. At each end of a stage was a station, a "swing" or "way" station, where teams of horses were changed. At intervals there were "home" stations where the horses were changed but also a meal was provided, and a home station might also offer a store, a saloon, lodging, and a livery. Every third or fourth station on a stagecoach route would be a home station, and a stagecoach route consisted of as many "stages" as it took to get from the point of departure to the point of destination, and proportionately as many swing and home stations. Locating a station on any route depended upon finding the necessities, or arranging to have them hauled in by wagon, and these necessities included grass for the stock; water for the stock, farm animals, personnel and travelers; game to feed the personnel and travelers; and wood for heating, cooking, and building. In addition, stations stocked grain and various spare parts and other items for repair or replacement of the stagecoaches, including king pins, harness, grease, wheels or wheel parts, horseshoes and nails, and the tools needed to keep the coaches in good repair and the horses properly shoed. Stagecoaches traveled at the approximate rate of eight miles per hour so the time between stations generally was about a two-hour ride, and between home stations about six to eight hours.

The "coach" in stagecoach was any four-wheeled vehicle pulled by horses or mules. To qualify as a stagecoach the vehicle had to be a public conveyance, run on an established route and on a regular schedule. A stagecoach had to be able to carry passengers, express, mails, and freight, though on any particular trip the coach might be empty. Even if empty it had to make the trip on schedule as there might be a full load on the return run. Stagecoach vehicles included spring wagons or dead axle wagons, surplus army ambulances, celerity coaches or mud wagons, and of course the deluxe Concord coach. The mud wagon (known also as the celerity wagon) was used to carry passengers in the mountains and on soft roadways as these wagons were lighter and the wheels were three inches wide, as opposed to Concord's two-inch wide wheels. Selection of the type of vehicle might be determined by availability, the terrain to be traversed (mud or soft sand), and the load to be carried in each direction, and the stage line owner made those decisions. The size of a team depended on a variety of circumstances such the type of vehicle used; the terrain to be covered; the weather; and the load anticipated in each direction. In the mountains or on the desert a team of six horses (a six-up) might be employed but in level country on good roads a four-up might suffice, and when there was a light load a buckboard or other wagon with a two-horse team might be substituted.

The horses or mules changed out at a station one day might be used on the return trip the following day or, if there were sufficient horses at a station, they might sit out one or two trips before they returned to the previous station. Teams often went from one station to another and returned to the previous station for years, so they came to know every detail of that small piece of roadway. Teams were made up of two, four or six animals, and the hostlers and drivers often had a relationship with a team that lasted many years. They harnessed the animals to get the most efficient, humane, and safest use and kept efficient teams intact whenever possible. The animals on the left of a team, or farthest from the driver, were called the "nigh" horses, and those on the right or nearest the driver were called the "off" horses. The front two animals in a team were the "leaders," and these were usually the smallest, smartest, and most alert of the animals, while the rear animals in a team were the "wheelers" and were the largest and strongest to give the greatest stability near the coach. If the team had six horses, the middle two were called "swingers," and these were generally mid-sized horses so they were more easily controlled by the other two pairs as they did their work leading or stabilizing.

A stage line refers to a line of "stages" of 12 to 15 miles comprising a route. A stage line, except during the earliest days of a boom town, could not survive on passenger service alone. The express contract made a stage line successful, and the mail contract made it quite profitable. Private freight shipments were usually too irregular to do more than add a little extra profit from time to time. Stage lines operated on a regular schedule and route so when the schedule changed newspapers gave advance notice. Stage lines were established between towns or between a town and a railroad depot or a port. When the railroads began crossing into the West it was generally thought that this would spell the end of stagecoaches but, in fact, more stage lines were established because of the railroads. The railroads made it possible to build towns all along a rail line and develop new areas some distance from these rail towns or depots, and of course stagecoaches were needed to operate between the depots and those towns established some distance away. However, while there was a growth in stagecoach operations the distances they traveled grew shorter and in some cases there were no "stages" to a route, as the coach went from its point of origination to its destination and back without a change of horses.

The primary persons associated with stagecoach operations, after the owners, were the driver and the shotgun messenger or guard, and the primary person associated with stagecoach robberies was the road agent. Stagecoach drivers were known by many sobriquets including Knight or Knight of the Lash, Whip, Sagebrush Navigator, or by the biblical reference Jehu. Drivers were a hardy lot representing a cross-section of the nation's citizenry, and many chewed or smoked tobacco or drank to excess, and some cussed mercilessly, but others were kind and gentle, especially toward the ladies riding in their coaches. Drivers were the captains of their vessels and commanded all who boarded, and they were always respected, usually appreciated, and often admired. Not every man could handle the ribbons of a four-up or six-up and many times it was only a driver's iron will and bravado which brought the coach, passengers, and contents through bad weather, across swollen rivers, over treacherous roads, with poor stock, while surviving attacks by Indians or highwaymen. Shotgun messengers sat beside the driver and shared the discomfort and danger, more so in those rare instances of a robbery because the messenger was the first target of a road agent's bullets. Putting a messenger on a stagecoach was a sure sign that there was substantial treasure aboard because a stage line operator would not pay a messenger to ride along if there was nothing significant to protect. Many lawmen, when not engaged in their primary vocation, worked as messengers, and men such as Wyatt and Morgan Earp worked for Wells, Fargo in that capacity at Tombstone.

The term "road agent" originated with a station keeper after two men stopped at his station and later the stagecoach arrived and reported a robbery. The description of the robbers matched the two men who had stopped, and the station keeper, in his report to the head office, referred to them as "agents of the road." Wells, Fargo & Company adopted the term "road agent." Road agents shared a *modus operandi* which varied only slightly except in a few instances, and it was based upon common sense. Road agents usually worked in parties of two to four men since it took more than one to watch everything going on during a robbery, but too many men meant the plunder had to be split into many shares. Even when acting alone, a road agent often made it appear that there were other robbers in hiding by deploying one or more dummies with sticks as gun barrels. One of the advantages in robbing stagecoaches was that the work was done at some isolated location allowing the road agents time to escape before a posse could be organized. The scene of the robbery was a place where the stagecoach would naturally travel at a slower pace, such as when the coach was ascending a steep or long grade, driving across soft sand, crossing a narrow bridge, or where there was a sharp curve in the road. A coach could be stopped by almost any obstruction, or by nothing more than a man stepping in front of the horses, pointing his gun at the driver, and ordering him to halt. Other methods included placing something in the roadway such as a log, a brush pile, rocks, or a long tree limb propped at waist level, or tying a rope across the road. The road agent would appear suddenly, masked and well armed, and often he would muffle his feet to avoid leaving distinctive boot tracks. Road agents would tie their horses out of sight since animals were easier to identify than a disguised road agent, and weapons included shotguns, rifles and pistols. A road agent gang might use a spy to watch whether the loading of the treasure box at the express office indicated it was heavy, or look for a shotgun messenger, which would signal there was substantial treasure aboard. At the scene of a robbery, once the driver, messenger and passengers were covered by firearms, a road agent would order the driver to throw out the treasure box. Sometimes the mail sacks would also be demanded, but often road agents did not want to involve federal authorities and would not take the mail bags. Occasionally the passengers would be "stood-up" and ordered to "pungle" for their money and valuables, or the road agent would search them himself. If the robbers got nothing for their trouble it was called a "water haul," indicting the value of the plunder was no more than water. If road agents had limited their work to the money in the pockets of the passengers few would have been caught, but their constant demand for the Wells, Fargo & Company express treasure box was their undoing as evidenced by the hundreds of men put in prison by such capable detectives as Hume and Thacker.

However, many stagecoach robberies were not solved because there was no motivation to pursue the robbers and lawmen had no budget to finance a posse. The lawmen had to put up the funds themselves to pay the cost of a pursuit so there were many instances where a posse numbered only one or two men. Lawmen relied on the rewards for "arrest and conviction" or the rewards for recovered treasure to reimburse them for their expenses, so if there was no reward posted, there was no pursuit. Still, lawmen were relatively effective and, if there was a pursuit, the road agents were usually caught. It was quite common in the Old West that, upon capture, criminals confessed and often informed, or "peached," on their partners-in-crime. Those who were jailed would have an examination before a justice of the peace, who would weigh the evidence and determine if it was adequate to hold the prisoners for the grand jury, and set bail. The grand jury would indict the men by returning a true bill and the prisoners would then be arraigned. Road agents often pled guilty because by cooperating they might earn a lighter sentence. Road agents were sent to prison, and sentences typically ranged from five years to fifteen years. Often when road agents turned state's evidence and testified against their fellow road agents, they were released or received a very short sentence. Stagecoach robbers were not legally executed, though once in Del Norte, Colorado, two young brothers were lynched for the crime. But stagecoach robbery sometimes led to murder, and first-degree murder was a capital crime in all parts of the Old West.

When trains began to operate between major population centers of the West, treasure was accumulated and periodically sent in one large shipment. Frustrated stagecoach robbers might then mature into train robbers, and they adopted a similar commonsense approach. Train robbers would wait for the train to stop or slow in some isolated location before boarding and taking control, or cause it to stop by signaling danger ahead or by derailment. They would come prepared with explosives because the "way-safe," the one carrying valuables for distribution at points along the route, could be opened by the express messenger, but the "through-safe" contained the greatest treasure and had to be blown open. It could only be opened by the agents at the point of departure and the point of destination.

Report Summary

The following comprises the original report's first three pages.

REPORT
JAS. B. HUME and JNO. N. THACKER,
SPECIAL OFFICERS,
WELLS, FARGO & CO'S EXPRESS,
Covering a Period of Fourteen Years,
Giving Losses to
Train Robbers, Stage Robbers and Burglaries,
AND A FULL DESCRIPTION AND RECORD OF ALL
NOTED CRIMINALS
CONVICTED OF OFFENSES AGAINST WELLS, FARGO & COMPANY
SINCE NOVEMBER 5TH 1870.

SAN FRANCISCO
H.S. CROCKER & CO., STATIONERS AND PRINTERS, 215–219 BUSH STREET
1885

WELLS, FARGO & CO'S EXPRESS

Report of Special Officers concerning Robberies, etc.

Mr. Jno. J. Valentine,
    Vice-Pres. And Gen'l Manager of Wells, Fargo & Company
        San Francisco

Dear Sir:—

We have compiled from the records in our Department the following data, extending over a period of fourteen years—from November 5th, 1870, to November 5th, 1884. The amounts taken, attendant expenses, pay of guards and special officers, may not be exact, but are not overstated. The data giving the number and character of offenses committed, names of offenders, the number of convictions secured, lives lost, etc., are substantially correct.

Total amount taken from W. F. & Co's Express by stage robbers,
    train robbers and burglars during the fourteen years beginning
    November 5, 1870 .... $415,312.55
Rewards paid for arrest and conviction of said robbers, etc., and
    percentage paid on treasure recovered 73,451.00
Attorney's fees and legal expenses of prosecution 22,368.00
Incidental expenses incurred in arrests and convictions 90,079.00
Salary of Guards and Special Officers 326,517.00
Total loss $927,726.55

Number of Stage Robberies during the fourteen years named 313
   "   Attempted Stage Robberies 34
   "   Burglaries 23
   "   Train Robberies 4
   "   Attempted Train Robberies 4
   "   Convictions for Robbery and Attempt at Stage Robbery 206
   "   Convictions for Train Robbery and attempt at same 20
   "   Convictions for Burglary 14

Number of W. F. & Co's Guards killed while in discharge of duty,
    by stage robbers 2
        Andy Hall, August 20, 1882, on route Florence to Globe, A. T. [*see entry for* Grimes, Cicero]
        John H. Collins, August 10, 1883, on route Florence to Globe, A. T. [*see* Appendix]

Number of W. F. & C's Guards wounded while in discharge of duty,
    by stage and train robbers 6
        James Miller, December 3, 1874, on route Eureka to Palisade, Nev. [*see* Curran, John]
        Jimmy Brown, September 3, 1877, on route Eureka to Tybo, Nev. [*see* Davis, A. J.]
        Wm. Blankenship, July 11, 1879, on route Maricopa to Phoenix, A. T. [*see* Appendix]
        Mike Tovey, September 5, 1880, on route Bodie to Carson, Nev. [*see* Sharp, M. A.]
        George W. Hackett, July 13, 1882, on route Laporte to Oroville, Cal. [*see* Appendix]
        A. Y. Ross, January 22, 1883, on route San Francisco to Ogden (train) [*see* Anderson, Rais]

Number of Stage Drivers killed by robbers during the fourteen years 4
        Billy Mann, April 27, 1873, on route Hamilton to Pioche, Nev. [*see* Appendix]
        Charlie Phelps, July 30, 1883, on route Corinne, U. T. To Montana [*see* Appendix]
        Budd (Eli) Philpott, March 15, 1881, on route Tombstone to Benson, A. T. [*see* Appendix]
        Senor Romero, June 19, 1884, on route Railroad depot to Leone, Mex. [*see* Appendix]

Number of Stage Drivers seriously wounded by robbers 4
    L. C. Woodworth [sic], February 17, 1871, on route Petaluma to Cloverdale, Cal. [see Andrus, W.E.]
    Jerry Culverhouse, February 16, 1875, on route Shasta to Redding, Cal. [see Appendix]
    George H. Smith, March 9, 1877, on route Anaheim to San Diego, Cal. [see Appendix]
    Richard Richards, December 14, 1881, on route Tombstone to Benson, A. T. [see Appendix]

Number of Passengers killed by stage robbers during the fourteen years 4
    Henry P. Benton, February 17, 1871, on route Petaluma to Cloverdale, Cal. [see Andrus, W.E.]
    John T. Lloyd, February 14, 1877, on route Mojave to Darwin, Cal. [see Appendix]
    Peter Roerig, March 15, 1881, on route Tombstone to Benson, A. T. [see Appendix]
    Dr. W. T. Vail, August 20, 1882, on route Florence to Globe, A. T. [see Grimes, Cicero]

Number of Passengers seriously wounded by stage robbers 2
    A. Kaufman [sic], February 17, 1871, on route Petaluma to Cloverdale, Cal. [see Andrus, W.E.]
    Henry Scammon, November 13, 1876, on route Downieville to Marysville, Cal. [see Brown, Tom]

Number of Stage Robbers killed while in the act of robbing or attempting to
rob the express on stages, by W.F.&Co's Guards 5
    H. S. Hunt, by Guard McNamara [sic], Oct. 24, 1876, on route Weaver to Shasta, Cal. [see Appendix]
    John Carlo, by Guards Jimmy Brown and Eugene Blair, February 27, 1877, on route Eureka to Ward, Nev. [see Crawford, James]
    Jack Davis by Guards Jimmy Brown and Eugene Blair, September 3, 1877, on route Eureka to Tybo, Nev. [see Davis, A. J.]
    Andy Marsh, by Guard J. E. Reynolds, September 7, 1878, on route Yreka to Redding, Cal. [see Jackson, Tom]
    W. C. Jones, alias Frank Dow, by Guard Mike Tovey, September 5, 1880, on route Bodie, Cal., to Carson, Nev. [see Sharp, M. A.]

Number of Robbers killed while resisting arrest 11
    Joe Brown, alias, Foster, Nov. 18, 1876 [see Brown, Tom]
    Joe Blanchard, July 18, 1877 [see Barber, William]
    John [sic] Brazelton, August 19, 1878 [see Appendix]
    Thomas Francis, November 19, 1879 [see Morgan, William A.]
    Jack Brown, alias O'Neill, April 26, 1881 [see Brown, John]
    Bill Leonard, June 1, 1881 [see Appendix]
    Harry Head, June 1, 1881 [see Appendix]
    Jim Crane, June 13, 1882 [see Appendix]
    Jack Almer, Oct. 3, 1883 [see Appendix]
    Charles Hensley, October 3, 1882 [see Appendix]
    George W. Cleveland, March 10, 1884 [see Joy, Kit]

Number of Robbers hanged by citizens in the fourteen years 7
    Leander Morton, near Aurora, Nev., September 27, 1871 [see Baker, Daniel Boone]
    Lafayette Grimes, Globe, A. T., August 25, 1882 [see Grimes, Cicero]
    C. B. Hawley, Globe, A. T., August 25, 1882 [see Grimes, Cicero]
    Len Redfield, Florence, A. T., September 3, 1883 [see Appendix]
    Joe Tuttle, Florence A. T., September 3, 1883 [see Appendix]
    Mitch Lee, Silver City, N. M., March 10, 1884 [see Joy, Kit]
    Frank Taggart, Silver City, N. M., March 10, 1884 [see Joy, Kit]

You will notice by the foregoing that the number of lives lost, as a result of the above enumerated robberies and attempted robberies, amounts to thirty-three.

There have also been seven horses killed and thirteen stolen from the various stage teams in time of robberies and attempted robberies during the fourteen years included in our report.

Your attention is invited to the details connected with these extensive operations, which follow this summary.

>Respectfully submitted,
>J. B. Hume,
>J. N. Thacker,
>>Special Officers

San Francisco, December 19, 1884

The Robbers' Record

Adams, George

Nativity, New York; Age 25 years; Occupation, Laborer; Height 5 feet 6¼ inches; Complexion, Light; Color of Eyes, Blue; Color of Hair, Light; Square features, high forehead, eyes deep-set, small scar left thumb, do pit of stomach, mole back of left shoulder, slim built.
Robbed W. F. & Co's Express on stage from San Luis Obispo to Soledad, alone, December 3, 1879.
Received at California State Prison December 15, 1879. No. of commitment, 9148. Crime Robbery; Term 5 years; County sent from, Monterey.
Discharged upon expiration of sentence July 15, 1883.

On December 3, 1879, the Coast Line stagecoach, when approaching Soledad in Monterey County, was stopped by a lone highwayman. He demanded the Wells, Fargo & Company treasure box and, once it was delivered, he ordered the coach to continue into Soledad. He broke open the box and took out $160 and a check for $140 drawn on a bank in San Luis Obispo. As soon as the coach reached town Sheriff Franks went to the scene and followed a clear trail into San Francisco where he arrested the road agent and identified him as Salinas resident George Adams. Adams was only nineteen years old and had never been in any trouble but he readily admitted to being the road agent. The sheriff bought his prisoner back to Salinas by train the following day and lodged him in jail. The grand jury was in session at the time so there was no delay in beginning the criminal proceedings. Adams, at his examination, again admitted that he was the road agent. He was quickly indicted and on December 18, only two weeks after he had stopped the stagecoach, Adams pled guilty. He was sentenced the same day to serve five years at San Quentin and was immediately transported to the prison and registered as prisoner No. 9148. Adams served out his entire term and was released, by expiration of sentence, on July 15, 1883.

Salinas City Index [CA]: December 11, 1879; December 18, 1879.

Adams, William

Robbed W. F. & Co's Express on stage from Kelton, U. T. to Albion, I. T. July 25, 1882, in company with Jack King, Dave Francis, and Francis Hawley.
Robbed W. F. & Co's Express on stage from Kelton U. T. To Albion, I. T., July 30, 1882, in company with King Francis and Hawley.
Received at Territorial Prison, Boise, I. T. June 12, 1883. No. of Commitment, 32. Crime, Robbery; Term, Life.

On July 25, 1882, the overland stagecoach was stopped and robbed by four masked, heavily armed road agents when it was between Cassia and Raft River, thirty-five miles from

Kelton in the Idaho Territory. The work was done with such precision that the *Wood River Times* of July 27 said, "it reads like the performances of the old-time Nevada agents on the Geiger Grade." The road agents were cinching their saddles, seemingly oblivious to the approaching stagecoach, until it came upon them and then they suddenly turned and ordered the driver to halt as they pointed their six-shooters at him. The driver was ordered to raise his hands and he and the passenger riding with him were told to disembark and the two passengers riding inside, a man and a woman, were ordered out. The leader of the robbers kept guard over the passengers while the others took out two treasure boxes and the mail sacks.

The boxes were quickly broken open and they were about to cut open the mail sacks when the leader told them to wait, and had them thoroughly search the coach. The two male passengers were also searched but the lady, who was identified as the wife of the other inside passenger, was not molested and they missed $400 she had with her. The robbers took $800 from the two men but passed over the driver when he said he had no money. The passenger who had been riding atop managed to hide his wallet with $200, but $7.50 was taken from his pockets. The robbers collected two watches but returned one. When all was done they ordered everyone aboard and told the driver to continue, and he hurried to the next stop and sent back an alarm.

On July 30 the same stagecoach, Kelton to Albion, was robbed when only eighteen miles from Kelton or a dozen miles before the place where it had been robbed several days earlier. The party of four were the same men that had robbed the previous stagecoach and they were well armed and mounted. The amount they obtained in the second robbery was later reported as "$2,000 in money and valuable jewelry, two stagecoach horses and the contents of the treasure boxes." There were seven men and one woman on the stagecoach and a Frenchman from Leadville, Colorado contributed $500, while D. C. Sprague lost $350, G. H. Search contributed $135, and W. S. Hunt put in $110 and a gold watch and chain, but Miss Sallie Clinetop, an actress from Leadville, saved $1,000 by hiding it in her skirts.

The four masked road agents were cool, taking nearly two hours in searching the coach and passengers to be sure they had everything of value before sending the coach on its way. After the second robbery the four men fled south into Nevada. James Hume was put on the case and he tracked down two of the men, arrested them, and brought them back to Idaho for trial.

The two men, identified as William Adams and Jack King, admitted their guilt in both Idaho stagecoach robberies and were taken to Boise and lodged in jail. The other two road agents, David Francis and Francis Hawley, eluded capture until they took part in an attempted train robbery at Montello, Nevada, on January 22, 1883 [see Francis, David]. They were never tried for stagecoach robbery but received terms of fourteen years in Nevada's state prison for attempting to rob the Overland Express train from San Francisco to Ogden, Utah.

Adams and King were indicted for robbery and tried at the summer 1883 session. They were found guilty and sentenced to serve life terms at the Territorial Prison in Boise, I. T. as federal prisoners, because they had molested the mails. They both arrived at the prison on June 12, 1883, and both men were transferred to the Detroit House of Corrections in Michigan in February 1884.

Territorial Enterprise [Virginia City, NV]: August 1, 1882; August 8, 1882; August 13, 1882.

Allen, John—*alias* Sheet Iron Jack

Nativity, New York; Age, 37 years; Occupation, Barber; Height, 5 feet 6⅜ inches; Complexion, Fair; Color of eyes, Gray; Color of hair, Brown. Long features, nose leaning to the right, eyes deep-set, scar center of forehead edge of hair, do. left side of forehead, do. on chin, woman's head on right forearm, second finger of right hand off at knuckle joint, flag and blue streak in ink left forearm; medium built.

No. of first commitment, 6395. Received at California State Prison, February 18, 1875. Crime, assault with deadly weapon; Term, 2 years; sent from Shasta County; discharged by order of court for a new trial, July 13, 1875.

Robbed W. F. & Co's Express on stage from Shasta to Redding, November 6, 1876, in company with John A. Toney and Frank Chapman.

Robbed W. F. & Co's Express on stage from Shasta to Redding, November 8, 1876, in company with John A. Toney and Frank Chapman.

Robbed W. F. & Co's Express on stage from Yreka to Redding, November 11, 1876, in company with John A. Toney and Frank Chapman.

Received at California State Prison, December 25, 1876. No. of commitment, 7313. Crime, Robbery; Term, 24 years, on three convictions; County sent from Shasta.

Conditionally commuted by Governor George C. Perkins, December 9, 1882, to a term of ten years, and that he leave the State immediately upon his release; discharged June 25, 1883.

Received at California State Prison at Folsom, April 22, 1884. No. of commitment 781. Crime, grand larceny; Term 6 years; County sent from San Francisco.

John Allen, alias "Sheet-iron Jack," although possibly his real name was John D. Gundlack, reportedly served in the Army during the Civil War and had many distinctive scars which he claimed were from wounds inflicted during the conflict. When discharged from the military he went west and tried a number of jobs, not all of which were legal employment, and in February 1875 he was convicted of "assault with a deadly weapon" and sentenced to serve two years. On July 13, 1875, after only a few months imprisonment he was granted a new trial and this time he was convicted only of "assault," sentenced to pay a fine, given credit for the time he had already served, and released. In late 1876 Allen rendezvoused with John A. Toney, a man he had met during his brief stay in prison, and Frank Chapman, a man with no criminal record. A lone road agent had been operating in the Shasta area, and this would later confuse lawmen in their search for road agents and prompt the *Shasta Courier* to comment, "Four stage robberies within fifteen miles of Shasta inside of four weeks is pretty rough." The first robbery by this lone road agent was on October 16, 1876, when the stagecoach from Scott's Bar in Siskiyou County bound for Fort Jones was stopped and robbed of $1,250 in gold belonging to A. B. Carlock. The robber was armed with a double-barreled shotgun and had his face blackened so identification would have been difficult. However, on Tuesday, October 24 the stagecoach from Shasta to Weaverville in Trinity County was coming around a curve above the Tower House when the same lone road agent jumped from behind a bush and aimed a Spencer rifle at Wells, Fargo's messenger John McNemar. The robber got the box but McNemar returned to the scene and killed the road agent [see Appendix: H. S. Hunt].

John Allen, at the same time, was planning several stagecoach robberies. On Friday, November 3 three masked, heavily armed men stopped the mail coach between Reid's Ferry and Buckeye in Shasta County. They demanded the treasure box and mail sacks, smashed open Wells, Fargo & Company's treasure box and took out $1,100, then slashed open the mail sacks and took a considerable amount of money from the registered mail. Allen would not take part in any further robberies but did the planning and had Toney and Chapman do the work at the scene, but still demanded an equal share for his contribution to the conspiracy. On Monday, November 6, 1876, the stagecoach from Shasta to Weaverville, when near Redding in Shasta County, was stopped by two masked road agents wielding shotguns. They appeared suddenly from a stand of willows near the road, pointed their weapons at the driver, and called for the coach to halt. They demanded the Wells, Fargo & Company treasure box and it was thrown down, and then the coach was allowed to continue on. When the box was opened the two road agents found it was empty of valuables so on Wednesday, November 8 the same two road agents, Toney and Chapman, determined to overcome their "water haul" from two days earlier, stopped the same coach at approximately the same place and this time took $1,100 from Wells, Fargo's Express box. On November 11 the same road agents stopped the stagecoach traveling between Yreka in Siskiyou County and Redding when it was near Ross's Station, though three road agents were reported. Their faces were blackened and they were well armed so when the demand was made for the treasure box it was thrown down immediately and the coach was ordered to move on. Deputy sheriff Whiting and Constable Eckles went to the scene and recovered the treasure box but could find no clues to the identity of the robbers nor a good trail to follow. The box, it was later learned, was empty so there was little motivation to pursue the road agents.

Allen doubted the men were telling him the truth about their lack of plunder on two robberies, and felt certain they were cheating him out of his share so he went to local lawmen to inform on Toney and Chapman and take his cut from their rewards. However, in order to explain how he knew of the details and identities of the road agents he had to confess to his part in planning the robberies, and he was arrested. Since his part came before the robberies he was charged as a principal as if he had been at the scene, rather than as an accessory-after-the-fact. Chapman was arrested at Chico on November 16 and lodged in the Shasta jail with Allen, and Toney was arrested by R. Kennedy and L. D. Bickford at Rising River on November 23 and he joined his two fellow road agents behind bars. On December 2 the grand jury indicted the three road agents. On December 12, while awaiting trial, Toney, Chapman, Allen, and two other prisoners tried to dig their way out of jail but were discovered and thereafter were heavily ironed. On December 23, 1876, Allen pled guilty to three robbery charges and he was sentenced to serve eight years on each charge, or twenty-four years in total. He arrived at the California State Prison on Christmas day and registered as prisoner No. 7313. His term was conditionally commuted to ten years by Governor George C. Perkins and, after agreeing to leave the state, he was discharged on June 25, 1883. Allen not only reneged on his promise to leave California but committed a grand larceny in San Francisco County and was returned to prison on April 22, 1884, to serve six years on a new commitment. Toney had been in prison for grand larceny for seven years when pardoned on October 18, 1872, and he served another term of twenty-one months for an "assault to rob," remaining in prison between November 1873 and August 1875. On December 23, 1876, he also pled guilty to three stagecoach robbery charges and was sentenced to serve seven years on each conviction, a total of twenty-one years. Toney arrived at the California State Prison on Christmas day 1876 and registered as prisoner No. 7312. He served thirteen years and was released on November 25, 1889. Chapman had no prison record in California so he was allowed to turn state's evidence and testify against the other two men. He pled guilty to three robbery charges and was sentenced to serve sixteen months imprisonment on each conviction, or four years total. He arrived at San Quentin Prison on December 25, 1876, and registered as prisoner No. 7314. Chapman was conditionally pardoned by Governor William Irwin and discharged on May 4, 1877. He was required to leave the state and lost no time in booking passage to return to England.

Republican Free Press [Redding, CA]: April 5, 1884. *San Francisco Examiner [CA]*: September 17, 1882; September 27, 1882. *San Francisco Chronicle [CA]*: April 1, 1884. *Shasta Courier [CA]*: November 11, 1876; November 18, 1876; November 25, 1876; December 23, 1876; December 30, 1876. *Yreka Union [CA]*: November 11, 1876.

Allen, S. A.—*alias* Ned Allen, Sol White

Nativity, Ohio; Age, 52 years; Occupation, Farmer; Height, 5 feet 8½ inches; Complexion, Light; Color of eyes, Gray; Color of hair, Fair; Vaccine marks on right and left arms, scar base of right thumb, cupping marks on right breast, 2 scars center of back, scar center of forehead, and slim built; bald head.
No. of first commitment 4443. Received at California State Prison April 27, 1870. Crime, grand larceny; Term, 2 years; County sent from Yolo.
Pardoned by Gov. H. H. Haight, February 18, 1871.
Robbed W. F. & Co's Express on stage from Lone Pine to Bakersfield [Cal] January 15, 1875, in company with Charlie Cooper, alias Williamson.
Turned State's evidence against Cooper and was released.
Stole W. F. & Co's treasure box from the Visalia depot at Goshen, March 30, 1875, and fled to San Luis Obispo County, where he robbed W. F. & Co's Express on stage.
Was arrested under name Sol White; and while in jail awaiting the action of the Grand Jury, made a murderous assault on Jailer Ross, and escaped, leaving Ross for dead.
Robbed W. F. & Co's Express on stage from Oroville to Laporte, June 27, 1876, in company with James Jones, alias Texas.
Robbed W. F. & Co's Express on stage from Carson City, Nev., to Aurora, October 3, 1876, in company with Jones, alias Texas.
Was arrested in Jackson, Cal., and taken to Douglass County jail at Genoa, Nev., by W. F. & Co's special officer.
Escaped from jail, December 17, 1876, and was recaptured same day.
Received at Nevada State Prison, December 19, 1876. No. of commitment, 147. Crime, robbery; Term 8 years; County sent from, Douglass.
Discharged upon expiration of sentence December 5, 1883.

On January 15, 1875, the stagecoach from Lone Pine to Bakersfield was stopped by two road agents after leaving Havilah near Stark's Station in Kern County, California. Following the robbery the road agents fled to San Francisco with Sheriff Bowes and deputy H. Bludworth close on their trail. The lawmen captured the two fugitives and by February 27 they were on their way to Bakersfield. The two prisoners arrived by stagecoach on Sunday February 28 but their examination was postponed until Wednesday because of the distance one key witness had to travel. At 10:00 A.M., when the court convened, the two men were brought before Justice Wilkinson and gave their names as Ned Allen and Charles Williamson. They were arraigned, waived examination, and were remanded to the custody of the Sheriff to await action by the grand jury. While awaiting indictment Allen agreed to turn state's evidence against Williamson and on March 13 the *Kern County Weekly Courier* reported that Williamson was brought into court and, after pleading guilty, said he was the least guilty of the two men and that "the same offers and inducements were made to me that induced my companion 'to peach.'" He was sentenced to serve ten years in San Quentin Prison and then the Judge listened to the district attorney who said that a conviction of Williamson would not have been possible without Allen's testimony, so the judge ordered Allen's release "but did so with great reluctance." Williamson arrived at San Quentin Prison on March 13, 1875, and registered as prisoner No. 6430. His sentence was commuted to nine and one half years by Governor William Irwin on April 23, 1878, and he was discharged, by expiration of sentence, on August 6, 1881.

Allen stole a treasure box from a stagecoach on March 30, 1875, and was arrested, but he escaped after a murderous assault on the jailor. He robbed the stagecoach from Oroville in Butte County bound for Laporte in Plumas County on June 27, 1876, before moving his operations into Nevada. On October 3, 1876, at 9:30 A.M. the stagecoach from Aurora in Esmeralda County to Carson City, Nevada, was one mile from Kilgore's Station and the Mountain House, and in plain view from those establishments, when two masked road agents armed with double barreled shotguns and six-shooters halted the coach. One road agent was tall while the other was medium sized, and both were noticeably slim. They demanded the Wells, Fargo & Company treasure box and sawed it open, taking out $228, checks and papers. On board were five passengers and nine bars of gold bullion but the robbers did not molest the passengers nor take the bullion, possibly because of its heavy weight to transport. Wells, Fargo & Company's chief detective James Hume was soon on their trail and he traced them to Jackson, California, where they were arrested within a week following the robbery. Hume was familiar with both men, and identified one as a California stagecoach robber, S. A. "Ned" Allen and the other road agent was identified as James "Texas" Jones, a man involved in a number of robberies from Chinese workers. He took his prisoners to Sacramento where he booked passage on the stagecoach for Carson City. On October 13, 1876, the men arrived in Nevada, bound for the Douglas County jail at Genoa. They had their preliminary examination that same day and were held to answer to the grand jury. They were both indicted, held for trial, and in December both men were convicted of stagecoach robbery. Allen arrived at the Nevada state prison on December 19, 1876, sentenced to serve eight years. He served out his entire sentence and was released on December 5, 1883. Jones was sentenced to serve five years and arrived at the state prison on December 20, 1876. Jones escaped from the prison in December 1880, at the age of sixty-four, and was not heard of again.

Kern County Weekly Courier [Bakersfield, CA]: February 27, 1875; March 6, 1875; March 13, 1875. *Territorial Enterprise [Virginia City, NV]*: October 4, 1876; October 14, 1876.

Anderson, John

Nativity, Kansas; Age, 25 years; Occupation, Laborer; Height, 5 feet 7 inches; Complexion, Sallow; Color of eyes, Hazel; Color of hair, Dark. Square features, high forehead, curly hair, small round ears, lobes attached, rather small nose, round nostrils, pouting lips, two moles near left collar bone, scar back of right shoulder, do. Back of left forearm; stout built.

No. of first commitment, 7954. Received at California State Prison, January 19, 1878. Crime, burglary second degree; Term, 3 years; County sent from San Francisco.

Discharged by expiration of sentence, May 19, 1880.

Burglarized W. F. & Co's office at Galt, Cal., November 18, 1881, in company with Charles Mills and Michael Sheehan, but was convicted of burglary of a later date in Alameda County.

Received at California State prison, March 24, 1882. No. of commitment 10340. Crime, burglary; Term, 10 years; County sent from Alameda.

John Anderson lived in San Francisco and in late 1877 he committed a burglary and was soon arrested and lodged in jail. In January 1878 he was indicted, convicted on a charge of second degree burglary, and sentenced to serve three years at San Quentin. He arrived at the prison on January 19, 1878, and registered as prisoner No. 7954. On April 24, 1878, Michael Sheehan, also from San Francisco, arrived at San Quentin Prison, convicted of an "assault to rob" and sentenced to serve a term of four years. He registered as prisoner No. 8166. On May 23, 1878, Charles Mills, also from San Francisco, arrived at San Quentin Prison serving a term of four years for first degree burglary, and Mills registered as prisoner No. 8237. It is not known if these three men were friends in San Francisco, or had met while spending time in a San Francisco jail cell, but in prison they started to make plans to work together when they were released. Anderson was the first to be released, by expiration of sentence on May 19, 1880, and during the next eighteen months he stayed out of trouble, or at least was not identified for any crimes he committed. On September 6, 1880, Sheehan was moved to Folsom prison where he registered as prisoner No. 139 and was the next man to be released, by expiration of sentence, on April 24, 1881. On May 23, 1881, Mills was released, also by expiration of sentence and the three men rendezvoused to make plans for their first crime, the burglary of the Wells, Fargo depot at Galt in Sacramento County on November 18, 1881. They burglarized the depot and managed to avoid detection and identification, and soon were on their way to Alameda County where they had plans to burglarize another business, but this time the target of the crime did not involve Wells, Fargo property. After their second burglary they were arrested and at their examination the evidence, though circumstantial, was so strong that they were held for action by the grand jury. The three men were indicted and pled not guilty but at trial the evidence proved too strong to overcome and all three men were convicted. When brought into court the judge noted that each had a prior conviction for a felony, and then sentenced them each to serve terms of ten years. Wells, Fargo & Company acquiesced, being entirely satisfied with the conviction and sentence of the three men for the other burglary committed in Alameda County. Charles Mills, Michael Sheehan and John Anderson arrived at San Quentin Prison on March 24, 1882: Mills registered as prisoner No. 10338; Sheehan as prisoner No. 10339; and Anderson as prisoner No. 10340. All three men were released on September 24, 1888, after serving six years, six months.

Anderson, Rais

Nativity, Denmark; Age, 22 years; Occupation, Farmer; Height, 5 feet 5 inches; Complexion, Light; Color of eyes, Gray; Color of hair, Light. Single, drinks moderately, weight 140 pounds, does not use opium, size of foot No. 3, uses tobacco, scar over right and left eye, small scar on middle finger of right hand, web-toed both feet first and second toes, scar on front of right shin, scar on first joint of little finger left hand, left eye crossed.

Attempted to rob Overland Express train from San Francisco to Ogden at Montello, January 22, 1883, in company with Sylvester Earl, Francis "Frank" Hawley, Orrin Nay and David Francis.

Montello is a water-tank station 109 miles east of Elko, Nevada. When the train reached that point at 1:30 A.M., January 22, 1883, a "danger signal" was discovered just ahead, the train was stopped and a train-man advanced to learn the cause of the trouble, when he was met by five armed men named above, who took him and the other train-men, including the conductor, and locked them in the lower part of the water-tank. They then went to the car of W. F. & Co. and ordered A. Y. Ross, messenger of W. F. & Co., in charge, to "hop out," as they were going to rob the Express. This Ross very manfully refused to do. They then fired a volley of shots into the car, three of which took effect upon the person of Ross.

Ross "stood them off" for three hours and twenty minutes, firing at them through the car from time to time until daylight, when they mounted their horses and rode away.

They were arrested at Deep Creek, Utah on the 30th of January, Nay and Hawley being seriously wounded while resisting arrest.

Received at Nevada State prison, March 2, 1883. No. of commitment 247. Crime, Assault to commit robbery; Term, 12 years; County sent from, Elko.

On January 22, 1883, at 1:30 A.M. two men stepped onto the tracks at Montello, a Nevada rail station near the Utah border in Elko County, and waived a red light, a signal of danger ahead no engineer could ignore. When the train came to a stop seven gunmen appeared and captured the engineer, his fireman, and his brakemen and took them to the water tower where they were bound and guarded. Aaron Y. Ross, the express messenger, though wounded fought off the robbers for more than three hours and later received a reward of $150 from the railroad for his bravery. Wells, Fargo & Company paid his medical bill and after he recovered from his wounds they rewarded Ross with $1,000 and a gold watch. Ross had been a stagecoach driver in Montana and he had been "jumped" by road agents twice before, and in one incident he traded shots wounding several robbers before he got away and saved the treasure box. Ross was an imposing figure for those times at six foot three inches and two hundred fifty pounds, and when interviewed about this latest road agent adventure he said:

> We left Toano on time, and I checked the way-bills received at that station, lay down, and went to sleep. The next thing which I was aware of was a rap on the car door, as if an agent had called, and supposing the train was at Tecoma, I got up and went to the door, opened it and looked out, when a man pointed a gun at me and said, "Hop out — we are going through you." I jumped back, pulled the door to and hooked it. They then went over to the opposite side of the car and said, "Open up the door and jump out. We are going to rob the train."
>
> I replied, "Just wait until I get my boots on."
>
> "Never mind your boots. Hop right out here and we will get through with you and then you can get your boots on."
>
> After pulling my boots on I drew my kit chest around, and threw my blankets on top of it. Again the men said, "Open up or we'll burn you out and murder you."
>
> I then got into position and shot through the side of the car. Nothing was said or done for a few minutes, until one of the robbers asked, "Ain't you going to open up the door and come out?"
>
> I told them I was not coming out. Then I heard them walk under and around the car, and another demand was made for me to hop out. I made no reply to that. They then stationed one man at each corner of the car, between me and the baggage car, and five shots were fired simultaneously from different quarters, all ranging toward the center of the car. These were the shots that struck me — one on the finger, one on the hip, and one just below the breast, near the watch pocket. They then got up on the end of the car to uncouple the train. There-upon I fired two shots through the end of the car.
>
> At this time they heard No. 2, the west-bound express train, coming. They backed our train up and went on the side track and sent two men down to meet No. 2. When it came up I heard Conductor Clement ask Cassin, "What are you doing here? I want to speak to you." The robbers pointed their guns at Clement's head and told him to pull out, and he pulled out.
>
> The robbers then returned to the train, and one of them tried to get on the front end of the car and upon the roof. I fired in that direction as near as I could calculate where he was, and he dropped down on the platform. Then all was quiet for a few minutes. They went down to the water tank, got the engineer and the brakeman, brought them back and made the brakeman uncouple my car from the baggage car. I thought I would save my ammunition, so did not fire. They dropped the express car down about two car lengths from the train, uncoupled the mail car from the express and drew it away about two lengths, then came back again and asked me if I wasn't coming out. I made no reply, whereupon they commenced breaking in both doors with

coal picks, besides firing several shots into the car. I never moved or said a word, but kept waiting for them to come in. Presently they gave up the attempt to get in by the use of coal picks, and left and went down to the engine.

They ordered the engineer to back down on the express car as hard as he could. When the mail car struck the express car, both doors of the latter sprung open the length of the chain. That left me unprotected in my rear, and I got up and went to the other end of the car to pile up some boxes, but thinking it would take too much time, I closed the doors instead, and hooked them. They then backed down on me again, and again the doors flew open. I immediately closed them. They now left my car and went down to get some wood from the engine. The fireman told them that there was no wood, or only two or three sticks.

They then went to the section house, and on coming back for the third time said, "Ain't you going to hop out?" They then backed down on my car again, but it was not a very hard bump, as the engine did not have much steam. They then asked Cassin how long it would be before another train would arrive. He told them that another train from the East would be in thirty minutes. Then they left us and rode off.

The gang numbered seven and they had nine horses. The number of passengers on board in sleeping cars and coaches was very small, and the money in the express car amounted to but about $600.

The gang avoided a "water haul" by taking a mere $10 from the wallet of the conductor and then fled east into Utah where they hid in Millard County. Rewards continued to grow to nearly $6,000 so there was little difficulty in organizing posses. In Utah a posse of seventeen men was organized from Nevada and Utah forces and on January 28 they cornered Orrin Nay, sometimes spelled Ormus Nay, and Frank Hawley, alias Jack Todd, at Deep Creek, Utah but these men were desperate and decided to die game. They were both wounded in the shooting that followed, captured alive, and they recovered from their wounds. As soon as Nay and Hawley were in the custody of lawmen they informed on their fellow train robbers, named them and told where they could be found. The posse, then armed with a small cannon and dynamite, went to the hide-out on January 30 and surrounded Sylvester Earl, Erastus "Rais" Anderson, and David Francis, sometimes given as Daniel Francis. Seeing that resistance was futile, and probably fatal, the fugitives surrendered without a fight. It was later reported that John Brently was the man shot by Ross during the robbery and he had died, but the seventh man had separated from the gang at some time before they were captured, fled in a different direction, and he was never captured or named. The five prisoners were returned to Elko County in early February, indicted, tried and by the end of the month they were convicted of "assault to commit robbery." On March 2, 1883, the five men arrived at the prison near Carson City: Anderson and Earl were sentenced to serve twelve years; while Francis, Hawley and Nay were sentenced to serve fourteen years. Earl, after serving only four years, four months, and eleven days, was discharged on July 13, 1887. Next to be released was Anderson who was pardoned on September 24, 1887, and released. Francis, Hawley and Nay, the three men with the longest sentences, were discharged on January 2, 1893.

Chicago Tribune [IL]: January 24, 1883. *Daily Nevada State Journal [Reno, NV]*: January 26, 1883. *Weekly Elko Independent [NV]*: January 28, 1883; February 4, 1883; March 4, 1883.

Andrus, W. E.—*alias* Big-Foot

In 1869 and early 1870 robbed W. F. & Co.'s Express on several stages in Sonoma and Mendocino Counties, [California] in company with Lodi Brown and John Houx.

Attempted to rob W. F. & Co.'s Express on stage from Petaluma to Cloverdale, August 16, 1871, in company with Brown Houx, and a John Doe. W. F. & Co.'s guard, Charles Upton, fired at them without effect and the driver, C. L. Woodworth, put the whip to his team, without having made any halt whatever. The robbers opened fire on the stage, and continued to fire at the fleeing stage until it was beyond their reach, yelling and whooping, at the same time, like demons. The result of their fusillade was the serious wounding of Woodworth, the driver, and A. Kaufman, a passenger, and the killing of Henry Peek Benton. Mr. Benton had been East and had his aged mother on the stage, whom he was bringing out to spend her declining years with him in his comfortable home in Ukiah.

Andrus and Brown were allowed to plead guilty to murder in the second degree; Houx turned State's evidence and escaped punishment.

Received at California State Prison, February 29, 1872. No. of commitment, 5157. Crime, murder in second degree; Term, 30 years.

Commuted by Governor William Irwin, May 30, 1876, to 25 years.

Killed in State Prison by a fellow prisoner, August 6, 1879. He had been promised a further commutation to 10 years before he was killed.

During the early months of 1871 there had been a rash of stagecoach hold-ups in Sonoma and Mendocino County. The coach on the Cloverdale to Healdsburg route in Sonoma County had been stopped eight times in six months. While the loot from any individual robbery was small, the largest being only $1,500, the accrued plunder was a staggering loss for Wells, Fargo & Company. The robbers followed the generally accepted plan of selecting a spot where the coach would naturally be moving at a slow pace, such as a steep grade, and would step out from the side of the road with guns in hand. Brown Houx was suspected, arrested several times and lodged in the Ukiah, Mendocino County jail, but the lawmen could not work up a case against him so each time he was released. His "gang" consisted of Elisha "Big Foot" Andrus, brothers Lodi and Johnny Brown, Tom Jones and Billy Curtis. Houx, Andrus, and Lodi Brown were badmen with reputations to match, but Johnny Brown, Jones and Curtis had good reputations despite their continued association with bad company. On August 12, 1871, Brown Houx and several members of the gang stopped the Cloverdale to Healdsburg stagecoach but found it was occupied by four heavily armed hunters so they declined to make any demands and rode off. On the evening of August 16, 1871, the southbound coach from Cloverdale to Petaluma in Sonoma County, with C. L. "Sandy" Woodworth at the reins, left Cloverdale with messenger Charles D. Upton atop and fourteen passengers aboard, nine inside and five on top, and several of the passengers were armed as they anticipated another robbery. At 9:00 P.M. the stagecoach had slowed for a steep grade north of Healdsburg when four masked men—Houx, Andrus, Lodi Brown, and one unidentified gang member—suddenly appeared from both sides of the road and covered those on top with shotguns, rifles, and pistols. They called for the driver to stop and fired once into the air. Without a moments hesitation Woodworth whipped up his team and the coach lurched forward at a rapid pace. The robbers fired after the fleeing coach and one buckshot hit the driver in the cheek and another cut his whip but he continued to urge on the team. Upton returned fire at the robbers and passenger Myers F. Truett shoved his shotgun out a window and fired both barrels. Lodi Brown and the unnamed robber were wounded, the latter seriously. Another passenger riding atop, B. S. Coffman, tried to pull his pistol but was shot in the arm and slumped back against Woodworth. Then, as the robbers continued a withering fusillade after the coach, Coffman was hit in the face with eighteen buckshot and Henry P. Benton, another passenger riding atop, was shot through the stomach with a rifle ball. The coach was soon out of rifle range so the robbers hurried to their horses and fled. The badly wounded robber only made it a short distance before he declared that he was dying and begged to be killed, so Houx and Andrus accommodated their partner, and then put a noose around his neck so it would appear he had been lynched and threw the body in the Russian River. The stagecoach continued to the first ranch they encountered and had the wounded passengers taken inside. Benton died the following day but Coffman, whose wounds were thought fatal, fully recovered. Wells, Fargo posted a $3,500 reward and the state added $1,000 and Steve Venard, the renowned road agent killer, was sent to Sonoma County to investigate. He met with Healdsburg deputy William B. Reynolds who said he was certain the guilty parties were Houx and his gang, but he cautioned that there was not enough evidence and Houx would again elude indictment. Venard went undercover and learned that Billy Curtis had recently withdrawn from the gang, and when the lawmen gave him a promise of immunity he rejoined the gang as an agent for Venard and Reynolds.

On October 10 Houx, Curtis and several others robbed the coach at McDonald's House and took $925 from Wells, Fargo's treasure box. Curtis then got word to Reynolds that Houx and company were going to rob Sheriff D. C. Crockett of Mendocino County's taxes when the lawman took them to Ukiah. Houx, for some reason, was suspicious and rode from Colverdale to Healdsburg to see what Reynolds was doing but found him at home with his family. Houx decided that everything was in place for his plan to rob the Sheriff so he headed for Cloverdale. However, as soon as Houx left Reynolds telegraphed Venard at Cloverdale and then, with his brother Hedge Reynolds, started north. When Houx reached Cloverdale he was met by Curtis and Venard who invited him for a drink. Just as he raised his glass he found himself looking down the barrel of Venard's pistol, who announced, "You are arrested. Throw up your hands or you're a dead man." The Reynolds brothers arrived a few minutes later and the town was sealed, to prevent any of Houx' friends from riding out to warn the other gang members. Venard told Houx of the evidence against him and offered him immunity if he would identify the murderer of Benton. Houx put the blame on Lodi Brown and Andrus but would not disclose the name of the dead road agent, and also implicated Johnny Brown and Tom Jones in several robberies, and he told Venard where Andrus could be found. Curtis and the Reynolds boys rode to the Jones farm and arrested Tom Jones. Both road agents were then placed under a strong guard and all the lawmen and Curtis rode to the home of Houx's ex-wife. They arrived at 10:00 P.M. and surrounded the house to await daylight, but when they went in at dawn Andrus was not there. The ex-Mrs. Houx told them that he and Lodi Brown were at a deserted cabin on the headwaters of Dry Creek, ten miles north of Cloverdale, and that Johnny Brown was at the home of Houx's father. At the Houx ranch a dog barked so Lodi Brown appeared at the door heavily armed, but Reynolds approached and said, "I will have to disarm you," and then did so without incident.

In Cloverdale the three road agents were loaded into a coach and taken to McDonald's Station while Venard, Curtis and William Reynolds started for Andrus' cabin, and along the way met a rancher familiar with the country who took them within a mile of their destination. They went up the canyon afoot until they saw fresh sign and heard voices. In a few minutes Lodi Brown walked down the trail and was captured. Venard asked "Where is Bigfoot?" and Brown answered "He's up the canyon about three hundred yards getting dinner," and then warned, "You'll never take him unless you kill him." Venard and Reynolds hid while Curtis walked Brown down the canyon, fired his rifle into the air and, threatening Brown, forced him to call out, "Bill, I've killed a big buck. Come and help me pack him in." As Andrus came down the trail he was suddenly confronted by two lawmen armed with shotguns and ordered to "Unbuckle your pistol, drop it, and step aside." They secured their prisoners and then went to their camp to search for plunder and evidence. They found the ax used to break open the treasure boxes, Bigfoot's over-sized shoes, and a mask. They took their prisoners to McDonald's and then continued on with the five road agents to the jail at Ukiah, arriving just before midnight November 10, 1871. The prisoners were then removed to Sonoma County's jail at Santa Rosa. Houx, the leader and worst of the lot, turned state's evidence and was released in consideration of his cooperation and testimony. After his release he returned to Missouri where he died of smallpox several years later. The case against Tom Jones was weak as he was only charged with informing the gang when there were large Wells, Fargo shipments, and he was released after his preliminary hearing. Johnny Brown was indicted for several robberies, pled guilty, and received a sentence of three years. Andrus and Lodi Brown were charged with Benton's murder but they were both allowed to plead guilty to second degree murder and each received a sentence of thirty years. Lodi Brown served eight years before he was pardoned, on the condition he leave the state. He went to New Mexico where he became involve in a fracas and was killed. Andrus, in May 1876, had his sentence commuted to twenty-five years, sometimes a precursor to an early pardon, and he had been promised a further commutation to ten years. However, on August 6, 1879, he had a disagreement with cellmate Tim McGrath who cut his throat from ear to ear with a shoe knife taken from the prison's shoe factory. Andrus bled to death almost instantly.

Marin County Journal [CA]: November 25, 1871; March 9, 1872. *Mendocino Democrat [Ukiah, CA]*: November 17, 1871; November 24, 1871; February 29, 1872; May 16, 1872. *Mendocino Press [Ukiah, CA]*: November 16, 1871. *Russian River Flag [Healdsburg, CA]*: May 16, 1872; January 1, 1880; January 15, 1880. *San Francisco Chronicle [CA]*: August 6, 1880. *San Francisco Daily Alta [CA]*: August 18, 1871; July 12, 1872. *San Francisco Examiner [CA]*: December 29, 1889. *Territorial Enterprise [Virginia City, NV]*: November 24, 1871.

Arthur, Stonewall Jackson

Nativity, California (half-breed Indian); Age, 18 years; Occupation, Farmer; Height, 5 feet 9⅝ inches; Complexion, very Sallow; Color of eyes, Brown; Color of hair, Black; Size of foot, 8½. Square features, low forehead, pointed chin, rather flat nose, round nostrils, small round ears, small lobes attached, circular scar above inner corner of right eye extending up to the forehead, hair mole left cheek (about 1½ inches from corner of mouth), hair mole ¼ inch from left nostril, two moles between nipples near center of breast, scar outer edge of left forearm, right index finger and middle finger deformed from gunshot wound, large scar right side of head; do. left side in front.

No. of first commitment, 10444. Received at California State Prison, June 9, 1882. Crime, burglary second degree; Term, 1½ years; County sent from Shasta County

Discharged, by expiration of sentence, September 8, 1883.

Robbed W. F. & Co.'s Express on stage from Alturas to Redding [Cal.] May 26, 1884, in company with T. C. Arthur (his brother).

Received at California State Prison, July 11, 1884; No. of commitment 11314; Crime, robbery; Term, 9 years; County sent from, Shasta.

On Monday, May 26, 1884, a "half-breed Indian" named Stonewall Jackson Arthur stopped and robbed the stagecoach from Alturas in Modoc County bound for Redding in Shasta County. The southbound coach, driven by Edward Brackett, was between Morley's Station and Round Mountain when the lone, masked and armed road agent appeared. He pointed his six-shooter at the driver and demanded the Wells, Fargo treasure box and Brackett, who was unarmed, had no choice but to deliver. In the box was a pair of shoes of an unusually large size and $125 in currency, and the robber left the shoes behind. After the treasure box was thrown down the road agent gestured to Brackett to continue and the driver hurried into Redding where he reported the robbery. Constable McComber organized a posse of three men and they were soon on the track of the fugitive, and found where he had camped to await the arrival of the coach. The lawmen continued on the trail and the following day, Tuesday, arrived at Predmore's Ranch and surrounded the house. Soon a young man appeared carrying supplies and they followed him, and after going a short distance the fugitive road agent came out of the brush to collect his food. The posse men confronted him and he began to struggle with them but they knocked him to the ground and took his pistol, so he was forced to surrender without further resistance. He was taken to Millville and from there deputy sheriff Reynolds took him to Shasta and lodged him in the county jail. He gave his name as Stonewall Jackson Arthur and confessed all the details of the robbery. He was well known to lawmen and for the past six months, since his return home from San Quentin Prison, he had been committing petty crimes and annoying his neighbors but a case could not be worked-up against him. They identified the prisoner's brother as the man who was aiding him in eluding arrest by bringing supplies, so Thomas Chamberlain Arthur soon joined his brother in jail charged with being an accessory-after-the-fact. The two prisoners had their examinations and were held for action by the grand jury. They were indicted, Stonewall for the robbery and Thomas as an accessory, they were tried, and convicted of the charges on July 8, 1884. Stonewall was sentenced to serve a term of nine years and Thomas a term of two years. On Wednesday, July 9, Undersheriff Reynolds left for San Quentin with the two prisoners and they arrived on July 11, Thomas registering as prisoner No. 11313 and Stonewall registering as prisoner No. 11314. Thomas was discharged on March 11, 1886, after serving one year and seven months and his brother, Stonewall, was discharged four years later on June 11, 1890.

Republican Free Press [Redding, CA]: May 31, 1884. *Shasta Courier [CA]*: July 12, 1884.

Arthur, T. C.

Nativity, California (half-breed Indian); Age, 14 years; Height 5 feet 2⅝ inches; Complexion, Sallow; Color of eyes, Brown; Color of hair, Black; Size of foot, 6. Square features, low forehead, small ears, flat nose, thick lips, two scars on right side of forehead above right eye, two scars on left cheek-bone under left eye, mole left side of throat, small scar on right breast, scar from chicken pox left side of left upper arm, black mole under right breast, black mole between shoulders, pockmarked on back; stout built.

Robbed W. F. & Co.'s Express on stage from Alturas to Redding [Cal.] May 26, 1884, in company with Stonewall Jackson Arthur (his brother).

Received at California State Prison, July 11, 1884; No. of commitment 11314; Crime, robbery; Term, 9 years; County sent from, Shasta.

[See Arthur, Stonewall Jackson]

Baker, Charles—*alias* Charles Hanlin *or* Hanlon

Nativity, Ohio; Age 32 years; Occupation, Stove Moulder; Height, 5 feet 10⅝ inches; Complexion, Florid; Color of eyes, Blue; Color of hair, Light. Square features, high forehead, small scar on chin,

Goddess of Liberty inside left forearm, scar base left thumb, Dancing Girl inside of right forearm, scar base of right thumb, do. on back of left shoulder, small scar over left eye on forehead, 2 flesh moles right side of neck, small round scar left jawbone about 1¼ inches from ear, stout built.
No. of first commitment 7768. Received at the California State Prison, September 29, 1877. Crime, embezzlement; Term, 1 year; sent from Mono County.
Discharged by expiration of sentence, July 29, 1878.
Robbed W. F. & Co's Express on stage from Benton to Darwin, [Cal.] December 11, 1880, alone.
Received at California State Prison, April 5, 1881. No. of commitment 9842; Crime, robbery; Term, 10 years; County sent from, Inyo.

Charles Baker was twenty-four years old when he served his first sentence at California's State Prison for embezzlement. The ten months he spent behind the prison walls served as an opportunity to learn from California's "worst" desperadoes. Baker listened with interest and after his release he spent a few months acclimating to his new found freedom before taking up arms and stopping a stagecoach. On December 11, 1880, Baker, working alone and masked, stepped onto the road between Benton in Mono County and Darwin in Inyo County and stopped the stagecoach. He demanded the Wells, Fargo Express box and the driver had no alternative but to deliver. Baker was soon captured and he was tried in March, convicted of robbery, and sentenced to serve ten years in San Quentin Prison. He registered as prisoner No. 9842 on April 5, 1881. Baker was released in February 1885 and soon he was interested in robbing another stagecoach. In late 1885 he found a willing partner in Charles Manning and Baker, using the alias H. W. Hanlon, decided to stop both the up and down coaches on the route between Cloverdale and Mendocino City. Baker chose for their location the point in Anderson Valley where the two coaches passed and on January 5, 1886, the two men positioned themselves in the brush along the roadway within two miles of one another, and they dressed similarly and were approximately the same size. When the southbound coach arrived at 10:30 P.M. one of the road agents stepped out and, covering the driver with his gun, demanded the treasure box and as soon as it was delivered the driver was ordered to continue. The southbound coach came abreast of the northbound coach in less than a mile and the northbound driver reported that he had been robbed, and the southbound driver then said he, too, had been robbed and the manner and descriptions were so similar that it was at first believed to be the same man. The two road agents fled, buried their plunder, and tried to remain inconspicuous for nearly two months.

Sheriff J. Standley listened intently to the reports of the two drivers and concluded that the work had to be done by two men, as the two coaches had been stopped almost simultaneously some distance apart. There were no clues at the scene so he sent out descriptions of the road agents as provided by the drivers and passengers and in late February received word that two men matching the description were on the coach from Cloverdale to Anderson Valley. He went out after his quarry and captured Baker, still using his alias, and Manning soon after they had dug up their plunder. He lodged them in the jail at Ukiah and returned the plunder to Wells, Fargo & Company. There was some delay in getting the prisoners to trial but in April 1889 they were both convicted of the robbery and sentenced to serve seventeen years in San Quentin Prison. Baker, as Hanlon, registered as prisoner No. 13524 and Manning registered as prisoner No. 13523. They arrived at San Quentin prison on April 11, 1889. Manning wanted to escape, and arranged to have guns hidden near a work site outside the prison walls, and the two road agents and one other convict made their move but their attempt was immediately met with gun fire from rifles and then from the prison's Gatling gun. Still, they managed to flee three miles before being cornered where the fight went on for hours before the convicts, after being assured they had not killed anyone, surrendered. Baker was involved in another escape attempt in 1891 but it was also foiled. He caused no more trouble and was released on November 11, 1899. Baker did not appear on California's criminal rolls again. Manning was released on the same day as Hanlon, each serving ten years of their sentences, and he also disappeared from the criminal rolls of California.

Mendocino Beacon [CA]: January 12, 1889; March 2, 1889; April 13, 1889. *Mendocino Dispatch Democrat [CA]*: August 15, 1890. *San Francisco Examiner [CA]*: September 6–7, 1891; September 10, 1891; September 26–27, 1891. *San Francisco Chronicle [CA]*:August 12–13, 1890; August 26, 1891; August 28, 1891.

Baker, Daniel Boone

Nativity, Kentucky; Age, 37 years; Height, 5 feet 6 inches; Complexion, Dark; Color of eyes, Dark; Color of hair, Black. Mark on left arm.

Robbed overland express train from San Francisco to Ogden near Pequop November 7, 1870, in company with Dan F. Taylor, Leander Morton and John Doe.

Received at Nevada State Prison, January 19, 1871. No. of commitment, 73; Crime, robbery; Term, 30 years; County sent from, Elko.

Escaped in "Big Break," September 17, 1871, and fled to Oregon

Captured in 1874, by W. F. & Co's special officer, and returned to prison.

Pardoned, July 15, 1879.

> *[The so-called "Big Break" at the Nevada State prison occurred at "lock-up" time, Sunday evening, September 17, 1871, in which 29 of the 73 prisoners confined therein escaped. The break was planned and executed by twelve of the most desperate, who broke into the guard-room, and got possession of all the prison arms and ammunition. In efforts to prevent the escape, Lieut.-Gov. Frank Denver (ex-officio Warden) and two of the guards were seriously wounded and two guards mortally. Matt Pixley, a worthy citizen living outside the walls, rushed in to assist the officers, and was instantly killed by the outlaws. The twelve then opened all the prison doors, and invited the other prisoners to join them in their flight, seventeen of whom availed themselves of the opportunity to obtain their freedom.]*

On October 13 soldier Edward Carr was at Sallie Whitmore's bordello located two miles south of Camp Halleck in Elko County, Nevada. He became embroiled in an affray with a sergeant and was badly beaten. He hurried back to camp for his carbine and returned to Sallie's place where he fired a single round at his antagonist, but hit the madam in the groin inflicting a fatal wound. Carr was arrested for murder and taken to Camp Halleck where he was to be turned over to Constable William Baugh. The lawman planned to take his prisoner to the city of Elko but soldiers threatened to rescue Carr and the constable, fearing for his safety, left his prisoner at the camp and returned to town for a posse. When Baugh returned the next morning Carr and his five friends were gone. A post muster revealed that six soldiers had deserted and, when a train was robbed three weeks later, they would be suspected and this would lead to delays and confusion over the identities of the guilty parties.

On November 4, 1870, Central Pacific's train No. 1 left San Francisco heading eastbound for Salt Lake City. Just after midnight the train crossed into Nevada when it was robbed by a gang of seven men at Verdi. With telegraph wires cut the train had to proceed to Reno to make the report, and was delayed for several hours while lawmen were notified. The train took on more treasure at Reno and then continued on its way. An hour before midnight on the same day the train had traveled three hundred eighty-five miles and was approaching Nevada's border with Utah, east of Pequop Siding and west of Toano but still fifteen miles from the more prominent town of Independence. Only twenty-one hours had elapsed since Central Pacific's train No. 1 had experienced the first train robbery in America's west when two men jumped onto the engine and two more onto the rear platform of the express car. The crew was quickly captured and the engine, tender and express cars were uncoupled and pulled westward to Pequop Siding. One robber was left to guard the trainmen while four others approached the express car. Frank Minch, the same messenger who had been robbed at Verdi, managed to hide $10,000 in newly minted gold coins behind a rack of lanterns, and he also hid twenty-three packets of mail. He then admitted the robbers and they took all they could find, money totaling only $3,100. They immediately fled into the desert leaving the engine to back down the line and pick up the passenger coaches. As soon as the train arrived at Toana, Division Superintendent Gillett sent an engine with several men to Wells to form a posse and also to gather intelligence regarding the robbers. By daylight he had three different posses on their trail and also started an engine and boxcars from Carlin, which stopped at Elko to pick-up Elko's county sheriff J. B. "Ben" Fitch and a posse of nine men with fresh horses. Sheriff Fitch and Wells, Fargo detectives went to Pequop Siding, the site of the second train robbery, to search for clues. A glove was found with the name of Edward Carr on it and a brass compass engraved with the name "William H. Harvey" was found on the floor of the express car. It was learned that Carr and Harvey were two of the six soldiers who had deserted from the Third Cavalry unit posted at Camp Halleck and the deserters then became the prime suspects in the second robbery. The robbery at Verdi was the first time Wells, Fargo & Company had suffered a loss in a train robbery and now there was a second loss on the same day, and the company was outraged. Company superintendent John J. Valentine quickly issued a notice of reward:

$5,000 Reward,
The express car on the eastern bound passenger train of the Central Pacific Railroad was forcibly entered near Pequop, Nevada, last evening, and robbed of our treasure. We will pay $2,500 reward for the arrest and conviction of the robbers, or proportionately for each and $2,500 reward for the recovery of the treasure, or proportionately for any part of it.
Wells, Fargo & Co.
Elko, November 6, 1870.

Wells, Fargo & Company offered a similar reward for the robbers of the train at Verdi, the U. S. post office offered another $500, and the State of Nevada added $20,000 to the reward fund. After the robbery at Pequop various dispatches reported sightings of the robbers: "Toano, Nevada, Nov 7th. Two suspicious characters with jaded horses, without blankets or provisions, were seen about ninety miles south of here this morning, and were supposed to be two of the parties who robbed the Express car on the night of the 5th. Parties are now in pursuit of them." Two telegrams dated November 8 were received at Toano: "A mining camp ninety miles south of this place [Deep Creek, Utah], two suspicious characters had passed there on horse-back in an easterly direction avoiding the camp;" and "Two more came on horse back, heavily armed, and stopped long enough to purchase provisions and then left, going in an easterly direction. They displayed a number of $20 [gold] pieces, coined at San Francisco and dated 1870, and large rolls of greenbacks. No doubt these are the men who committed the deed. Deputy Sheriff Moffitt and party have left in pursuit of them. Lieut. King, with a detachment of thirty cavalry, left Toano on the 8th inst." Two of the men seen were wearing army uniforms, which added to the mistaken belief they were deserters. The men were easily tracked across the desert by five posses, one a troop of U. S.

cavalry from Camp Halleck. A dispatch to the *Ogden Junction* [Utah] dated November 12 said: "H. P. Kimball and J. L. Knowlton were dispatched on Wednesday last by the agent of Wells, Fargo & Co., in pursuit of four suspicious characters, about whom he had received a telegram. On their way out west, they obtained the assistance of Mr. Judd, and soon after came up with two men on horseback, Baker & Morton, who answered to the description furnished them. They captured one without resistance, but the other tried to make his escape, being pursued by Mr. Knowlton, and was finally taken after a sharp chase, but his saddle bags were gone, and he said he had thrown them in the water—$100 in greenbacks and 50 ounces of gold were found on their persons. They were taken to Salt Lake on Thursday, and locked up in jail. The stream near the woolen factory at Grantsville, was subsequently dragged and two bags of gold, and $1200 in greenbacks fished up and handed over to the proper officers." Leander Morton and Daniel Boone Baker were captured in a desolate area eighty-five miles south of the Great Salt Lake. Morton, when apprehended, had on a pair of buckskin gloves marked in ink, "W. H. Harvey" and marked with Harvey's company. This connected these men to the train robbery and to the deserters; but these men were not among the deserters but had, at some time, acquired the items from the deserters. Kimball and Riley Judd later captured a third member of the gang who gave the name Daniel F. Taylor and he was brought into town on the evening of November 22, 1870. It was reported that a fourth robber, whose name was George Lee, was taken by officers about the same time but later it turned out that it was only his name that was learned and he had eluded capture, and the fifth robber was never identified. The three prisoners, after being lodged in jail at Elko, confessed their guilt and in the November 30, 1870, edition of the *Elko Independent* [Nevada] it was reported that "Daniel Taylor, Daniel Baker and Leander Morton have been indicted for robbing the Wells, Fargo & Company express car and the U.S. Mail." On January 14, 1871, the *Independent* reported: "The Railroad Robbers,—The three railroad robbers, Dan Taylor, Leander Morton and Daniel Baker, have been on trial during the present week in the District Court, and the case, after argument of counsel, reached the jury at 4 o'clock P.M. yesterday who, after being out a few minutes, returned a verdict of guilty. They will probably receive the full extent of the law provided for such offences; after which a United States Court will take them in hand, and if found as charged in the indictment by the U.S. Grand Jury, recently in session in Carson City, they will be hanged. Rather a gloomy prospect for the boys." The Elko County jury had deliberated only a few minutes before returning the guilty verdict and on January 17, 1871, Daniel Taylor, Daniel Baker and Leander Morton were sentenced to serve thirty years each in the Nevada State Penitentiary. On January 19 they started their long prison terms: Taylor registering as prisoner No. 70, Morton as No. 71, and Baker as No. 72.

On Sunday evening, September 17, 1871, twenty-nine of Nevada's most desperate outlaws broke out of the Nevada State Penitentiary at Carson City, well armed from the prison armory. Daniel Baker and Leander Morton were among those who escaped but Daniel Taylor failed to join them. Some of the convicts went their own way while others split into smaller groups, and one of these parties consisted of Morton, Tilton Cockerell, Charley Jones, Moses Black, John Burke, and J. Bedford Roberts. This party of six convicts fled south through Esmeralda County and on September 20 captured William Poor, a young man carrying mails between Aurora and Carson. They murdered him, stole his clothes and boots, and continued southwest toward California. Posses from Bodie and Aurora went after the six escapees and picked up their trail. On September 25 the posse came across Morton, Roberts and Black on the slopes of the Sierras and, in a brief exchange of shots, posseman Morrison was killed and convict Roberts was seriously wounded. The posse retreated a short distance to regroup while the escapees made their way upwards to the place where Paiute Indian tracker Mono Jim was holding his and deputy sheriff Hightower's horses. Black murdered the Indian and they took the fresh horses to make their escape. Two days later, exhausted by their flight across hard country, Morton and Black were run to ground in the sand hills five miles southeast of Round Valley. Morton gave up without a fight but, as Black raised his hands, an Indian tracker thought he was raising a gun and fired, causing a mortal head wound. The two men were taken to town and left there while the lawmen went after Roberts, his location disclosed by Morton and Black. Black soon died of his wound and, since the farmers had to dig one grave they hanged Morton and buried both men. When the lawmen returned with Roberts the farmers told the lawmen that both prisoners had died but refused to tell where they were buried. They made no attempt to lynch Roberts due to his young age, only eighteen at the time, and because of his willingness to tell all he knew, which disclosed that he had not been involved in the murder of Poor, Morrison, or Mono Jim nor of Matt Pixley during the break-out.

Daniel Baker made good his escape and it was not until three years later, in 1874, that Wells Fargo's detectives tracked him down and arrested him in Corvallis, Oregon. He had been in that city for two years, had married, and had earned a reputation as an honest, sober and industrious citizen. He was returned to Carson City where he served two years more before being granted a pardon on July 15, 1879. Baker returned to his wife and child who, in the meantime, had moved to Idaho. Daniel Taylor, who failed to join his fellow train-robbers in the "Big Break-out," was pardoned on January 15, 1878, and discharged within a few days. A dispatch, dated December 19, reported that: "The post office Department offered a reward of $25,000 for his [Lee's] arrest concerning his role in the robbery of the Central Pacific train near Pequop, Elko County, Nevada, on November 5, 1870. The Central Pacific Company offered $1,000, gold coin, additional, and Wells, Fargo & Co., $500. A handbill was issued giving his description in full." George Lee, alias Lee Morgan, eluded capture and the fifth robber was never identified.

Daily State Record [Reno, NV]: September 29, 1870; September 19, 1871; September 29, 1871: October 8, 1871. *Deseret News [Salt Lake City, UT]*: November 23, 1870. *Elko Independent [NV]*: November 9, 1870; January 14, 1871; November 18, 1871. *Gold Hill Daily News [NV]*: November 7–8, 1870; December 16, 1870; December 19, 1870; October 7–8, 1871; November 16, 1876. *Humboldt Register [NV]*: November 12, 1870; November 19, 1870, January 4, 1871. *New York Herald [NY]:*, November 23, 1870. *Reno Evening Gazette [NV]*: March 4, 1901. *Territorial Enterprise [Virginia City, NV]*: October 6, 1871. *Weekly Nevada State Journal [Reno, NV]*: November 18, 1876; December 22, 1940.

Barber, William

Nativity, New York; Age, 38 years; Occupation, Laborer; Height, 5 feet 6⅜ inches; Complexion, Florid; Color of eyes, Brown; Color of hair, Brown. Small features, eyes deep-set, slightly bald, high cheek-bones, scar inside of left forearm, slim built.

Robbed W. F. & Co's Express on stage from Redding to Yreka, July 18, 1877, in company with William Blanchard [*sic*].

Blanchard was killed in resisting arrest.

Received at California State Prison, October 17, 1877; No. of commitment, 7831; Crime, robbery; Term 15 years; County sent from, Siskiyou.

On July 11, 1877, two men robbed a sheep ranch on the McCloud River and took $300 in property, including a needle gun and a double-barreled shotgun. On Wednesday, July

18 the northbound California & Oregon stagecoach from Redding in Shasta County, driven by Tom Tyndall, was one and a half miles north of Soda Springs when two road agents stepped out of the brush and halted the coach. They were masked and wielding a needle gun and double-barreled shotgun.

There was only one passenger aboard and he was riding atop with the driver. The road agents ordered them to throw off the express box and mail sacks. The passenger threw out the mail sacks while the driver controlled his team, and Tyndall then informed the road agents that the box was chained to the coach and could not be thrown down. They next ordered the driver and passenger to alight and had Tyndall take his place at the heads of the leaders to control the team. They demanded the tool sack but found nothing inside they could use, so one robber took the ax belonging to the coach and chopped open the box while the other guarded the driver and passenger with the shotgun. They took out everything of value, including some letters and $600, then decided they had done well enough with the treasure box and had the passenger put the mail sacks back onto the coach without opening them. They asked for nothing from the passenger except his labor and cooperation and finally ordered the two men to board and continue on their way. The driver hurried into Sisson's Station and reported the robbery. Siskiyou County deputy sheriff John Hendricks of Yreka, Charles Carroll, and Richard Hubbard, with two Indian trackers, went to the scene of the robbery and took the trail of the two robbers "through some of the roughest country ever traveled." The Indians, Sisson's "Indian Jim" and Bob Pitt's "Indian Charley" trailed the two men for forty miles to a point six miles from Trinity Center, near Bard and Morton's ranch on the fork of the Trinity River. The two men had concealed their camp in a deep brushy gulch where, on Saturday afternoon, July 21 the two road agents were cornered. The lawmen got the drop on them but one, later identified as Joe Blanchard, immediately turned and started to run. He was ordered to halt but when he continued to make his escape Carroll shot him with a load of buckshot, and the pellets struck Blanchard in the small of his back and traveled to his hips. The wound was thought to be a mortal one so Blanchard was left in the care of Carroll while Hendricks took the other prisoner, who gave the name William Barber, to Marysville and lodged him in jail. All the money from the stagecoach hold-up was recovered, except $6, and the guns stolen from the sheep ranch and used in the robbery were also found with the two men. Barber said he first met Blanchard at Reno, Nevada, a year earlier and they had been together, robbing and stealing, ever since.

Wells, Fargo's chief detective, James Hume, interrogated the prisoners and Blanchard claimed to be a French-Canadian while Barber said he was a long time resident of Ventura County, California, and each man confessed all the details of the robbery. Four days after Blanchard was wounded his condition had improved and it was thought he would recover, but he suddenly took a turn for the worst and died on the evening of July 25. Barber was examined before a Justice of the Peace and held for action by the grand jury. He was indicted and tried in Siskiyou County in October and easily convicted on the evidence, testimony, and his confession.

He was sentenced to serve a term of fifteen years at San Quentin Prison, arriving on October 17, 1877, and registering as prisoner No. 7831. Barber was discharged on March 17, 1887, after serving less than ten years.

Shasta Courier [CA]: July 23, 1877; August 4, 1877. *The Daily Appeal [Marysville, CA]*: July 20, 1877; July 24, 1877; July 26, 1877.

Barker, Frank—*alias* Frenchy

Nativity, New York; Age, 31 years; Occupation, Laborer; Height, 5 feet 8 inches; Complexion, Fair; Color of eyes, Brown; Color of hair, Dark. Prominent forehead, nose inclining to the left, mole under right ear, mole below left shoulder, mole on left side of neck, mole above left arm-pit, 2 scars on right wrist, stout built.

Burglarized W. F. & Co's office at Quincey May 24, 1875, in company with Johnny Sansome.

Received at California State Prison, October 7, 1875; No. of commitment, 6708; Crime, burglary; Term, five years; County sent from, Plumas.

Commuted by Governor William Irwin, March 5, 1877, to 4½ years.

Discharged, upon expiration of sentence, January 23, 1879.

The store of C. T. Kaulback on Main Street in Quincy, Plumas County was closed as usual on Monday evening, May 24, 1875, and the money belonging to the proprietor together with Wells, Fargo & Co.'s express money and other funds were secured in the safe. On Tuesday morning, when Kaulback's clerk, P. L. Hallsted, went to the store he discovered the safe was missing. An examination proved that burglars had entered by forcing open the back door, unlocking the second, or middle, door and carrying off the safe which was a Tilton & McFarland weighing about eleven hundred pounds. In getting the safe down the backstairs, eight steps, it had apparently gotten away from them and fallen and the stairs were shattered and the floor boards at the bottom were split and broken. The burglars took the safe into a back shed and commenced operations on the side of the safe by cutting through with some sharp instrument, and then inserting a bar of iron and wrenching the thin iron until a hole was made ten inches in diameter. The lining was "punched out with a bar in a bungling sort of a way, the wooden lining on the inside being broken and shattered, and the contents rifled." The amount taken from the safe was a little over $3,000, with Wells Fargo & Co.'s loss estimated at $2,666. Wells, Fargo also had some packages which were on the way to Greenville, the value of which was not known. Quincy's "Plumas Lodge of Odd Fellows" had $180 deposited in the safe and of course it was taken, as was a package of old letters and a gold ring belonging to a Mr. Hallsted were taken, and also the waybills directed to Greenville. A can of gold dust belonging to Kaulback was "bursted open, its contents strewn through the rubbish, and nearly all recovered by panning it out." Some fifty or sixty dollars in coin was also left in the safe, being overlooked by the burglars. The full amount left in the safe was $132, including one package in charge of the express company sent by Rosenburg & Bro. of Taylorville containing a new American silver watch, a round package of retorted amalgam weighing twenty-two and one half ounces, and fourteen ounces of fine dust, and a ring belonging to Kaulback was left on the counter. The papers in the safe seemed to have been examined carefully and most of them, which could be of no value to thieves, were found scattered near the safe in the morning. The burglars next went through the store's money drawers but only succeeded in finding a few bits which they appropriated, but they also took the express pockets, but the merchandise in the store was not disturbed. Several townspeople heard the noise made by the burglars in getting out the safe and breaking into it but no one thought to report the suspicious noises. From the tracks, which were traced from the rear of the store through Major Haun's field, it appeared that there were three men concerned in the burglary. Wells, Fargo & Co. offered a reward of $250 each for the arrest and conviction of the three persons who stole the safe from Kaulback's and removed its contents. They also offered one-fourth of the amount of treasure recovered and provided a more detailed description of the treasure taken, in the hope it could be identified and the culprits apprehended as a result: "$1,296 coin, $270 dust;

quick-silvered and very dark colored, grain dust, in buck purse, marked 'J.R. Wyatt, Quincy,' $400, package of dust from Greenville, 14 oz., fine dust from Taylorville, 22½ oz., retorted gold, round shaped, new. A new 5-oz., silver watch, New England Watch Co., Providence, Rhode Island, Maker's No ..., $60 check drawn by C. G. Rodgers, on C. J. Pillsbury, payable to T. F. Emmons, No. 41 plain gold ring — weight about $3.00: 'H.' engraved inside. Purse, marked 'I.O.O.F., No. 88,' containing $180, coin."

The *Plumas National*, on May 29, 1875, reported: "Only one clew [*sic*] to the robbery has been obtained as far as heard from. For particulars ask Edwards of Kellogg...." Apparently there was more than a single clue because on June 5 James B. Hume, Wells, Fargo & Co.'s chief detective, swore out a warrant against two parties suspected of being connected with the burglary of Kaulback's safe. They were arrested at Stockton, where they had "invested in good clothes." and were spending money very freely. On Monday, June 14 Sheriff Boring received a dispatch from Hume announcing that he had arrested the two men he suspected and stated that he would be at Oroville with them on Tuesday. The Sheriff went down on Tuesday's coach and got back on Wednesday evening, having the men in charge. They gave their names as John Sansome and Frank Barker, alias "Frenchy." Sansome was a rather heavy-set man, about forty years of age, with a dark complexion and a rather a pleasant look. He was said to be "an old operator in this line of business, and one of the best in the State." Barker was a tall, slim young fellow not over twenty years of age, "but little seems to be known of him until within the past year, though it is said he is quite expert in the business for a youngster." A preliminary examination was set for Thursday morning but postponed until Saturday, June 19. District Attorney Variel was to be assisted by J. D. Goodwin in the prosecution and W. W. Kellogg was employed by the prisoners for their defense. After considerable argument by counsel bail was fixed by the Court in the sum of $5,000 each and they were again confined in the jail. The examination of John Sansome and Frank Barker commenced before Justice T. F. Hersey on Saturday but was continued until Wednesday noon when a very large number of witnesses were examined, several having been brought from Stockton and other towns in the lower country. Hume, assisting the prosecution, proved that he was "thoroughly posted in his business and had worked up the evidence, even to the smallest particulars, in a manner that evinced an unusual degree of sagacity."

The defense attorneys made a spirited fight but the evidence was conclusive enough to satisfy Justice Hersey that the men should be held for trial. The two defendants were bound over to await the action of the grand jury and bail was again fixed at $5,000 each. The two men, in default of bail, were remanded to the County jail and special measures were taken to keep them confined, but neither man would peach on the third burglar. The prisoners were indicted in the fall and tried in early October. They were convicted on the overwhelming evidence and on October 7, 1875, Barker and Sansome arrived at San Quentin Prison, Barker registering as convict No. 6708 serving a five year term and Sansome registering as prisoner No. 6707 serving fifteen years. Sansome's long sentence was in consideration of his four previous prison terms — two for grand larceny and two for burglary. Barker's sentence was commuted to four and one half years by Governor William Irwin on March 5, 1877, and he was discharged, upon expiration of sentence, on January 23, 1879. Sansome was transferred to Folsom Prison on December 4, 1880, and managed to escape on December 27, 1881, but remained free for only two weeks before being returned to Folsom. Sansome was discharged on June 29, 1886.

Plumas National [Quincy, CA]: May 29, 1875; June 5, 1875; June 12, 1875; June 19, 1875; June 26, 1875.

Bassett, Charles

Nativity, Michigan; Age, 55 years; Occupation, Laborer; Height, 5 feet 8 inches; Complexion, Light; Color of eyes, Blue; Color of hair, Brown. Small white scar close to right nipple, small scar on outside of knee-cap of left leg, one vaccination mark on left arm, his entire body very hairy, nearly bald-headed, very bad set of teeth.

Robbed W. F. & Co's Express on stage from Grant's Pass to Jacksonville, Oregon, in company with William Briscoe and Charles Keeton.

Escaped from Jackson County Jail, August 27, 1884; recaptured, September 4, 1884.

Received at Oregon State Prison, December 4, 1884; Commitment, —; Crime, robbery; Term, 8 years; County sent from, Jackson.

On Friday, January 18, 1884, the southbound stagecoach from Grant's Pass to Jacksonville, Oregon, driven by Ab Giddings was ascending a hill near the "23 Mile House" when stopped by two road agents, masked and armed with six-shooters. The coach had only traveled three miles from Grant's Pass when the road agents stepped out onto the roadway and covered the driver with their pistols, then kept one six-shooter pointed at the driver's head as Giddings was ordered to throw down the Wells, Fargo treasure box. The other road agent kept his pistol trained on the coach and as soon as Giddings threw out the treasure box he was ordered to drive on. There were passengers aboard but they were not molested, and the road agents did not ask for, nor receive, the U.S. mail sacks, and the box contained $600 belonging to W. G. Kenney and other currency. Detective Hogan and Sheriff Jacobs investigated but could find no clues until, on January 29, the sheriff found the broken express box. The box contained the way bills, Postmaster Muller's money order stamp, and the letters which had been mutilated, so only the money had been taken. It was not long before several desperadoes found their way behind bars and the first of these was Frank Settle, arrested by Detective Hogan at Lebanon, Idaho. He had gone there to be with his parents during a severe illness and was brought back to Jacksonville by train. It seemed he knew something of the robbery as he implicated several men in the affair. Soon Newt Yocum was arrested at Myrtle Creek and he joined Settle behind bars, and at their examination they were held over for action by the grand jury. Next to be jailed was Charles W. Keeton who had been arrested by Sheriff Jacobs and Wells, Fargo detective J. N. Thacker in Douglas County on April 12. Keeton had his examination in Judge Huffer's court on April 14 and he was also held for action by the grand jury, bail set at $1,000. The remaining three fugitives were thought to have fled the country and the description of Frank Howard, William Briscoe and Charles Bassett were circulated widely.

Thacker was on the trail of another road agent and tracked him to Redding, California, where he arrested Frank Howard and lodged him in the local jail to await a requisition. Meanwhile Sheriff Jacobs continued his search and arrested William Briscoe, an ex-deputy sheriff, at Grant's Pass. Briscoe arrived in Jacksonville in early May and had his examination in Judge Huffer's court where, by the 9th, he was held to answer to the grand jury, bail set at $1,500. When Briscoe arrived behind bars Keeton decided to turn state's evidence and thereby gain his release. He informed on his fellow robbers and implicated all of the parties in custody, and also John M. Jarrett and Charles Bassett. After being named by Keeton, Jarrett was behind bars by mid–May and held to answer at his examination, bail set at $1,000. Meanwhile Sheriff Jacobs had gone to Redding and started back with Howard but at Castle Rock Station the lawman dozed-off while the horses were being changed and when he awoke his prisoner had disembarked with the other passengers and bolted. Jacobs was immediately on his trail and soon had him in custody again and on his way to the Jacksonville jail. The grand jury in mid–June returned indictments against Charles Keeton, William Briscoe, John M. Jarrett, Frank Howard, and Charles Bassett. William Briscoe's trial lasted one day — June 27, 1884, the primary witness being Keeton, and after an hour and a half in deliberations the jury found him guilty of stagecoach robbery. Judge Webster sentenced Briscoe to serve eight years at San Quentin. On July 20 Constables C. J. Sullivan, Skinner, and Hennerson arrested a man who gave his name as Russell but was identified as Marion D. Lockwood, a man sought by California authorities. Hennerson recognized him as the man wanted for a stagecoach robbery near Sweet Briar Ranch in Shasta County, California, which occurred on April 24, 1884. He traced him from Durham to a saloon in Grainland, Butte County, California, and there the three lawmen made the arrest. They took their prisoner to Chico and lodged him in the county jail, and it was not long before Lockwood was identified as Charles Bassett. A requisition was delivered to California's Governor for his extradition but the case in Oregon was so strong that California's Governor approved that extradition and Bassett was taken to Jacksonville.

On Wednesday night, August 27 four prisoners in the Jacksonville jail broke out by picking the cell door locks with a wire. Prisoners Watkins and Culp decided to stay and returned to their cells, prisoner Justus left a note saying he would return in a few days after attending to some business, but Bassett took "French leave" with no intention of returning to his cell again. Lawmen were soon on the trails of the escapees and Justus was back behind bars the next morning, after going only a few miles to his mother's house. Bassett was trailed to the "Jump-off-Joe" precinct and on September 4 he was captured and returned to his cell. In late November Basset was indicted, tried for stagecoach robbery and convicted, with Briscoe and Keeton testifying against him and he was sentenced to a term of eight years. Only two men had committed the robbery, and they were Bassett and Briscoe, so Settle, Yocum, Howard and Jarrett were released. Keeton, who had not been at the scene, was released in consideration of his cooperation and testimony against Briscoe and Bassett. William Briscoe was received at the Oregon State Prison on July 2, 1884, registering as prisoner No. 1547. His sentence was commuted to three years by Governor Z. F. Moody and he was discharged, by expiration of sentence, on January 29, 1887. Charles Bassett was also sentenced to serve eight years and he arrived at the prison on December 4, 1884, registering as prisoner No. 1605. Bassett was discharged, by expiration of sentence, on April 24, 1889.

Baker County Reveille [OR]: January 31, 1884. *Democratic Times [Jacksonville, OR]*: January 25, 1884; February 1, 1884; April 14, 1884; April 18, 1884; May 2, 1884; May 9, 1884; May 16, 1884; July 4, 1884; July 25, 1884; August 29, 1884; September 5, 1884.

Bell, W. T.—*alias* Doc Bell

Nativity, London, England; Age at present 40 years; Occupation, Druggist; Height 5 feet 11 inches; Complexion, Dark; Color of eyes, Brown; Color of hair, Dark Brown.
Robbed W. F. & Co's Express and U.S. Mail on stage from Wells to Cherry Creek, Nevada, November 21, 1877, in company with George Wilson and Felix Donnelly.
Tried at Carson in United States Court for mail robbery, W. F. & Co. prosecuting and furnishing assistant counsel, etc. Convicted.
Received at Albany Penitentiary, New York, February 3, 1879. No. of commitment, —; Crime, mail robbery. Term, Life; County sent from, Elko.

On Friday evening, November 23, 1877, the Woodruff & Ennor stagecoach from Wells to Cherry Creek, Nevada, was nearing its destination when it was stopped by four masked road agents. They robbed the passengers, who contributed $150 in coin, and they took the U.S. mail sacks. Wells, Fargo & Company had installed an iron treasure safe which the robbers would have to blow with explosives, but the up-stagecoach from Cherry Creek to Wells appeared on the road and scared off the robbers. Within hours four men were arrested at Cherry Creek and they included W. T. "Doc" Bell, George Wilson, Mose Watkins, and Felix Donnelly. These four men were tried twice on the territorial charge but the jury could not bring in a verdict so they were taken to Carson City to be tried in the U. S District Court on the federal charge of robbing the U.S. Mail. George Wilson was first to be tried while Donnelly and Bell were to be tried together later. The evidence against Mose Watkins was not strong so he was released. Wilson was found guilty in early December and the following week, as the other two defendants began their trial, he was sentenced to serve a term of life in prison. Within a week Bell was also convicted, but Donnelly was acquitted; and Bell was also sentenced to a life term. On February 3, 1882, both men were received at the Albany Prison in New York to finish out their federal sentences.

Territorial Enterprise [Virginia City, NV]: November 29, 1877; October 9, 1878; November 20, 1878; December 5, 1878.

Benson, James

Nativity, Ohio; Age, 33 years; Occupation, Laborer; Height, 5 feet 10½ inches; Complexion, Light; Color of eyes, Blue; Color of hair, Light. Square features, high forehead, scar over left eye, small ears, mole inside left forearm, shoulders freckled, stout built.
Robbed W. F. & Co's Express on stage from Milton to Sonora, in company with John Benson (brother) and Ab Bryant [*sic*], August 31, 1877.
Received at California State Prison, January 30, 1878. No. of commitment, 7991; Crime, robbery; Term, 12 years; County sent from, Calaveras.
Commuted conditionally to 10 years to leave the State, by Governor George Stoneman.
Discharged upon expiration of sentence, June 30, 1884.

On Friday, August 31, 1877, the down-stagecoach from Milton to Sonora, driven by Sam Smith, was halted by three masked road agents when four miles beyond Copperopolis in Calaveras County. They stepped into the road in front of the horses and pointed their arms at Smith, who reined in his team. The road agents then had the passengers disembark and march a short distance away where one robber stood guard while Smith was required to unhitch his team. They made short work of the wooden Wells, Fargo express box but there was nothing inside. They next tackled the iron safe bolted inside the passenger compartment and had brought with them the necessary hammers and cold chisels. Once the safe was opened they removed $1200 in coin, including a sack containing $600 in silver coins. The two road agents who worked on the safe then helped Smith hitch his team while the other man brought back the passengers, who were ordered to board the coach, and as soon as all was in readiness the three men ordered Smith to continue. As the stagecoach passed out of view the three men could be seen sitting in the middle of the road dividing their plunder. As soon as the robbery was reported ex-sheriff Ben K. Thorn went to the scene and took up their trail. He was joined by Wells, Fargo's chief detective James Hume and by the following day they had identified two of the road agents as the Benson brothers, James and Patrick of Central Hill. When express messenger Thomas Magee heard of the warrant he enlisted G. F. Wesson and they arrested the Bensons at Junction, and the prisoners were taken to San Andreas and lodged in jail. Patrick quickly proved an alibi and was released but that same day, Saturday, September 1 two men were arrested near the Stanislaus River, eight miles from Modesto, by Hume, Calaveras County undersheriff Garvey, and Stanislaus County undersheriff Lane. They gave the names W. H. Odum and John Benson, another brother of James Benson. They were brought to San Andreas and joined James in jail, but Odum was soon cleared and released. Hume continued his investigation and soon identified a third man believed involved in the stagecoach robbery — Ab Bryan of San Andreas. He went to Carson City, Nevada, with a requisition for Bryan and a warrant was issued for his arrest and surrender to Hume. Douglas County deputy sheriff J. C. Lupton received word of the warrant and on September 6 he found Bryan and arrested him. On September 8 Hume started for San Andreas with his prisoner and two days later he joined the other two prisoners in the San Andreas jail. Meanwhile Thorn, who was then in the employ of Wells, Fargo, trailed a fourth man to St. Louis, Missouri and, with a requisition from Governor Irwin, arrested Daniel "Dave" Parks and returned him to San Andreas. Parks was well known to Thorn as he had been sent to prison for ten years in 1864 for a robbery in Calaveras County. The prisoners had their examination in San Andreas and were held to answer to the grand jury. On Friday, November 2 the Sonora to Milton stagecoach, driven by J. D. Gibbons, was hailed by one man who looked inside at the single passenger and then summoned the two others to join him. After a brief discussion they sent the stagecoach on its way. The actions and comments of the men suggested they were looking for those who had testified against the Bensons, Parks and Bryan at their examination, but none of the witnesses were aboard so the intentions of the three "road agents" was never determined.

In early December each of the men was indicted, arraigned and given until December 6 to plead. They pled not guilty and trial was set for December 7 for Parks, Bryan, John Benson and December 8 for James Benson, but they all asked for and were granted separate trials. Ab Bryan turned state's evidence in time for the trial of John Benson, which commenced on schedule and the trial took four days, and the following day, December 13 the jury returned a guilty verdict. On Monday, January 11, 1878, Judge Ira H. Reed set the date for sentencing John Benson for January 26 and also permitted James Benson to withdraw his not guilty plea and plead guilty. On the date of sentencing John was given a term of sixteen years and James a term of twelve years at San Quentin. The brothers arrived at the prison on January 30, John registering as convict No. 7990 and James registering as convict No. 7991.

James Benson was pardoned by Governor Washington Bartlett on May 3, 1887, and he was discharged. John Benson was pardoned and discharged on May 5, 1887, serving just two more days than his brother. The cases of Bryan and Parks dragged on until the next court session in April. The trial of Daniel Parks finally commenced on Thursday, April 18 and concluded on April 20 with the Benson brothers and Bryan testifying against him. The jury returned a guilty verdict the following day and sentencing was scheduled for April 27. Bryan, in consideration of turning state's evidence, had his case continued and was released on his own recognizance, never to be tried for the robbery. Parks was finally sentenced to a term of eighteen years and he arrived at the prison on April 29, 1878, where he registered as convict No. 8188. Parks was discharged on June 29, 1889, after serving just over eleven years.

Calaveras Chronicle [CA]: September 8, 1877; September 15, 1877; October 5, 1877; November 17, 1877; December 8, 1877; December 15, 1877; January 8, 1878; January 11, 1878; January 19, 1878; February 2, 1878; April 6, 1878; March 30, 1878; April 20, 1878; April 27, 1878; May 4, 1878.

Benson, John

Nativity, Ohio; Age, 37 years; Occupation, Engineer; Height 5 feet 6¾ inches; Complexion, Dark; Color of eyes, Gray; Color of hair, Black. Heavy eyebrows, nose crooked, mole on the right side of nose, vaccine mark right upper arm, spare features, slim built.

No. of first commitment, 4695. Received at the California State prison, December 28, 1870; Crime, assault to rape; Term, 2 years; County sent from, Calaveras.

Pardoned by Governor Newton Booth, May 23, 1872.

Robbed W. F. & Co's Express on stage from Milton to Sonora, August 3, 1877, in company with Dave Parks and Ab. Bryant.

Robbed W. F. & Co's Express on stage from Milton to Sonora, August 31, 1877, in company with Jim Benson and Ab. Bryant [*sic*].

Convicted of robbery of August 3.

Received at California State Prison, January 30, 1878; No. of commitment, 7990; Crime, robbery; Term, 16 years; County sent from, Calaveras.

[*See* Benson, James]

Berry, Benjamin

Nativity, Kentucky; Age 41 years; Occupation, Stage Driver; Height, 5 feet 4½ inches; Complexion, Sandy; Color of eyes, Blue; Color of hair, Auburn. Scar on left hand from knife, small scar on left cheek.

Robbed W. F. & Co's Express on stage from Pendleton to Umatilla, Oregon, October 21, 1875, in company with J. H. Maxon.

Received at Oregon State Prison, May 3, 1876; No. of commitment 666; Crime, robbery; Term, 10 years; County sent from, Umatilla.

Pardoned, May 29, 1879.

On October 21, 1875, the regular stagecoach from Pendelton to Umatilla was halted and robbed by two masked, heavily armed road agents. They demanded the Wells, Fargo treasure box and as soon as it was delivered the stagecoach driver was told to continue on. When the robbery was reported the men and their horses were described and the information was widely circulated. A posse went to the scene and, because it had rained recently, they were able to follow the tracks of the robbers for some distance but the trail was lost in the mountains not far from Meacham. A few days later two Pendleton men went to Weston to investigate the report of strangers there and as soon as they arrived they saw a horse in the livery barn that was identical to one ridden by one of the road agents. One of the men hid in a stall to await the owner's return while the other man went on to Walla Walla to follow a clue that the second road agent had gone there. It was not long before the owner of the horse appeared and he was captured. His description fit exactly one road agent and as soon as he was under close guard he let slip that his partner was still in town, and at that moment at the hotel having a meal. It was not long before the second robber was also detained and a man was sent to Pendleton to obtain warrants for their arrest. A deputy sheriff was dispatched with the warrants and he brought the prisoners to Pendleton and lodged them in jail. They gave their names as J. H. "Billy" Maxon and Benjamin Berry. Both men were indicted, tried and convicted, and each received a sentence of ten years at the prison in Salem, Oregon. As the men were about to be transferred to the prison Maxon offered to tell where the treasure had been hidden, as it had not been recovered when they were arrested, but only if it would mean a reduced sentence for both convicted road agents. No promises were made but Maxon was told that if he cooperated everything would be done on his behalf. Both men arrived at the prison on May 6, 1876, Maxon registering as prisoner No. 665 and Berry as No. 666.

Wells, Fargo was notified of Maxon's offer and several months later Lot Livermore, their agent at Pendleton, and H. C. Page, the agent at Boise, Idaho, with detailed instructions in hand went to the robber's camp near Meachum but could not find the buried treasure. Page then visited the penitentiary where Maxon provided step-by-step directions and the two agents returned to the camp in the mountains near Meacham. The new instructions said the treasure was beneath a downed tree, not buried as previously related, and the convict described the tree in detail. The two Wells, Fargo agents found the downed tree and scratched at the ground beneath until they had unearthed a baking powder tin containing $2,800 in currency and two buckskin sacks, one with $800 and the other $900 in gold dust. They continued to search and found the gold brick valued at $2,500. After they recovered all $7,000 of the stolen treasure it was returned to the Wells, Fargo office at Boise, Idaho. As agreed the sentences of both men were shortened and Maxon, because he had cooperated more fully, was pardoned and released on August 30, 1878, after serving only twenty-eight months; and Berry was pardoned and released on May 29, 1879, after serving just over three years.

Oregon Historical Quarterly: v. 58, 1957; v. 99, 1998. *Oregon Journal*: October 20, 1946. *Oregon Historical Society scrapbook*, 132, p. 229.

Bixler, John S.

Nativity, Nebraska; Age, 25 years; Occupation, Laborer; Height, 5 feet 5 inches; Complexion, Dark; Color of eyes, Brown; Color of hair, Black. Small features, high forehead, large scar over left eye, do. between eyes, do. top of stomach, very large vaccine mark right upper arm, stout built.
Robbed W. F. & Co's Express on stage from Soledad to Newhall, alone, August 27, 1877.
Received at California State Prison, April 6, 1878; No. of commitment, 8118; Crime, robbery; Term, 2 years; County sent from, San Diego.
Discharged upon expiration of sentence, December 6, 1879.

The southbound coach from Los Angeles bound for the city of San Diego was waylaid by a lone highwayman at 10:00 A.M. on August 27, 1877. The Wells, Fargo & Company treasure box was demanded and the unarmed driver, Frank Shaw, had no choice but to "throw down that box!" As soon as the box was in the roadway Shaw was told to continue on, and he hurried to the next station and reported the robbery. The following morning Ned Bushyhead, Constable James Russell and driver Shaw started from San Diego for the scene of the robbery. Bushyhead returned to town that evening and reported that the robber was well mounted and headed toward Smith's Mountain [now Mount Palomar] forty-five miles northeast of San Diego, but the small posse had not yet overtaken him. Soon after Bushyhead left the posse the trail turned south and headed directly for San Diego. Shaw and Russell followed it right into town and Shaw began searching for the road agent. It was not long before he located and positively identified the wanted man walking on Fifth Street, and he and Russell arrested him without resistance. Their nineteen year old prisoner gave the name John S. Bixler but denied taking any part in a stagecoach robbery, even though the small amount of plunder taken from the coach was recovered from his pockets, and Bixler was lodged in jail. At his examination Bixler was held to answer to the grand jury but the grand jury had finished its work for the fall session when Bixler was arrested, and the gravity of his crime did not warrant convening a special grand jury. He was held in jail, unable to post bail, until early March 1878 when he was indicted. He continued to deny any part in the robbery and, though the evidence was mostly circumstantial it was very strong, especially the testimony of Shaw. On March 1 the jury was seated and sworn and the following day the case was tried, concluded and the jury started deliberations. The jurors quickly returned a verdict of guilty but on application of the defendant the judgment was postponed to Monday, March 25, at 10 A.M. On the day of sentencing Bixler was brought into court and was surprised to receive only two years at San Quentin. The short sentence might have been due to his young age, his clean record prior to the robbery, or the full recovery of the minuscule plunder. Bixler arrived at San Quentin on April 6, 1878, and registered as prisoner No. 8118. He was discharged, upon expiration of sentence, on December 6, 1879, and, with good time credits, served only twenty months.

San Diego Union Tribune [CA]: August 29, 1877.

Black, J. S.

Nativity, Maryland; Age, 41 years; Height, 5 feet 10 inches; Complexion, Dark; Color of eyes, Hazel; Color of hair, Dark Brown.
Robbed W. F. & Co's Express on stage from Baker City to Boise, I. T., October 2, 1871, in company with Al Priest.
Received at Territorial Prison, Boise, I. T., December 19, 1971; No. of commitment —; Crime, robbery; Term, 15 years; County sent from, Boise.
Pardoned, December 1, 1874.

The stagecoach between Umatilla, Oregon, and Boise, Idaho, was stopped when it was two miles east of Old's Ferry. The robbers laid in wait in the sagebrush, just where the road came up out of a gully, with both men on the same side. When the horses came abreast one of them jumped up causing the horses to shy and the driver to yell out, "What are you doing?" The robber who first exposed himself replied, "We want Wells, Fargo's treasure box." The driver took but a moment to consult passenger J. R. V. Witt, who was riding next to him, and they decided to deliver the box. Witt rummaged around in the boot and finally located the box. One robber squatted in the road and kept his shotgun pointed at Witt and the driver while the other indicated where he wanted the box thrown. Witt threw it out and then the driver asked, "Where will you leave it?" However, instead of answering, the robber asked how many passengers were aboard and the driver replied, "Three." The robber than asked, "Have you any Jews along?" and when the driver answered, "No," he ordered, "drive on then." They did not ask for the mail sacks nor did they molest the passengers. The *Statesman* noted that "the road agents are probably green at the business" as they "chose a stage least likely of any in the territory to be transporting treasure of any value." The box, when hefted to be thrown down, was noticeably light leading Witt to later say that the men made a "water haul," but the manifests were in the box so there was no way to be certain what they had obtained. Witt had $2,500 on his person and there was no way to know what the other two passengers might have been carrying, nor what the robbers missed in the mails. As soon as the two robbers let the coach continue the driver hurried to the next point where he could report the robbery and soon Sheriff Bryon, with a small posse, was in pursuit. It was not long before both men, who gave the names J. S. Black and Al Priest, were captured and lodged in jail to await their examination. They were held for the grand jury and indicted in December.

The trial commenced on Saturday, December 16, 1871, and in one day a jury was empaneled, they were tried and found "guilty as charged" with a recommendation to the mercy of the court, and three days later they were brought into court for sentencing. Judge Hollister emphasized the enormity of the crime and complimented the District Attorney and Sheriff before sentencing each man to serve fifteen years at hard labor. He went on to express the hope that there would be no executive clemency granted the two road agents and that they would serve out their full terms. He said he had letters which showed these two men were in a conspiracy with others for the purpose of lawlessness and they had threatened violence towards the officers as soon as they were freed. In order to give them the stiffest of penalties the Judge had ignored the recommendation for mercy made in the jury's verdict.

Black, after serving less than three years, was pardoned on December 4, 1874. Priest, however, did not fare as well as Black as he managed to escape on April 25, 1872. Priest was working in the yard picking up stones while On Gow, a Chinese prisoner, was working in the kitchen when Priest asked permission to go into the kitchen for a drink. Priest was gone too long so guard Woolf went to investigate and found that he had raised the window in the end of the hall and climbed over to freedom, the bars on the window not going all the way to the top leaving a two foot gap. On Gow, seeing Priest leave, had followed and then fled in a different direction, which divided the pursuing force. All the other prisoners and guards were at work in the ditch so it took a while to organize a large posse. On April 26 U.S. Marshal Joseph Pinkham offered a $100 reward for Priest's capture, but Priest had shed his shackles soon after he escaped and apparently had some help in getting supplies and eluding capture.

In early May Priest was heard of near Isaac's Bridge where he stole a span of horses belonging to Mr. Rynearson and two riding saddles, using one horse and saddle for his pack animal. At Canyon Creek he stole an old wagon sheet and black smith tools to fix the horses' shoes. Rynearson went in pursuit of the horse thief, not knowing it was Priest, and when he reached Rock Creek he learned he was close behind his horses. He acquired fresh horses and was soon gaining on Priest but the road forked at several places and Priest took the Basin Road, but at some point got lost and doubling back lost the pursuers. However, they were soon back on his track and kept him in view through a telescope and, by rushing forward whenever Priest was around a bend or over a hill, they managed to catch up with him before he knew they were closing in. When they were within a dozen yards Priest finally turned and saw them but before he could make a break Rynearson dismounted and took careful aim with his rifle. He placed his first bullet in Priest's forehead, just over the right eye but under his hat brim, passing entirely through and coming out on the back side just above the hat's brim. Priest fell to the ground, instantly dead. The posse went into camp to rest the horses and men but could not bury Priest because they had no shovel, and the next day the posse returned to Rock Creek with the stolen animals, wagon, tack, and other items. They left Priest's body at the scene of his death and it was two days before anyone with a shovel came along, and John Boise buried the dead prison escapee.

Idaho Tri-Weekly Statesman [Boise, ID]: October 5, 1871; December 19, 1871; December 21, 1871; April 27, 1872; April 30, 1872; May 11, 1872; May 25, 1872.

Bolton, Charles E.—*alias* C. E. Boles, Black Bart, the P. O. 8

Nativity, New York; Age, 55 years; Occupation, Miner; Height, 5 feet 7½ inches; Complexion, Light; Color of eyes, Blue; Color of hair, Gray; Size of foot, 6. High forehead, points running well up on each side of head, high cheek-bones, heavy eyebrows, chin square — rather small, two upper front teeth on right side gone, two lower center teeth gone, small mole on left cheek bone, scar on top of forehead right side, scar on left side of wrist, shield in India ink on right upper arm, gunshot wound on right side of navel.

Robbed W. F. & Co's Express on stages on the routes and dates enumerated below:

Sonora to Milton	July 26, 1875
San Juan to Marysville	December 28, 1875
Roseburg to Yreka	June 2, 1876
Point Arenas to Duncan's Mills	August 3, 1877
Quincy to Oroville	July 25, 1878
Laporte to Oroville	July 30, 1878
Cahto [sic] to Ukiah	October 2, 1878
Covelo to Ukiah	October 3, 1878
Laporte to Oroville	June 21, 1879
Roseburg to Redding	October 25, 1879
Alturas to Redding	October 27, 1879
Point Arenas to Duncan's Mills	July 22, 1880
Weaverville to Redding	September 1, 1880
Roseburg to Yreka	September 16, 1880
Roseburg to Redding	November 20, 1880
Roseburg to Yreka	August 31, 1881
Lakeview to Redding	October 11, 1881
Downieville to Marysville	December 15, 1881
North San Juan to Smartville	December 27, 1881
Ukiah to Cloverdale	January 26, 1882
Little Lake to Ukiah	June 14, 1882
Attempt to rob stage from Laporte to Oroville	July 13, 1882
Yreka to Redding	September 17, 1882
Lakeport to Cloverdale	November 24, 1882
Lakeport to Cloverdale	April 12, 1883
Jackson to Ione	June 23, 1883
Sonora to Milton	November 3, 1883

He committed all the foregoing robberies alone, and in nearly every instance robbed the U.S. Mail. Plead guilty to the robbery of November 3, 1883, and was received at California State Prison, November 21, 1883; Commitment 11-046; Crime, robbery; Term, 6 years; County sent from, Calaveras.

Since the conviction and incarceration of Charles E. Bolton for robbing Wells, Fargo & Co's Express, numerous inquiries have been received from Sheriffs and other officers, inquiring as to the identity of Bolton, alias "Black Bart." This inquiry has doubtless been occasioned by the statement of the prisoner when pleading guilty before the Court, to a particular robbery, that it was his first offence, and that he was not "Black Bart." All officers will readily understand the reason of such a statement, viz.: To excite judicial clemency. The identity is certain; and he had confessed to all the robberies above enumerated. He is a person of great endurance, a thorough mountaineer, and a remarkable walker, and claims that he cannot be excelled in making quick transits over mountains and grades; when reading without glasses, holds paper of at arms' length; is comparatively well educated, a general reader, and is well informed on current topics; cool, self-contained, a sententious talker, with waggish tendencies; and since his arrest has, upon several occasions, exhibited genuine wit under most trying circumstances. Has made his headquarters in San Francisco for past eight years; has made but few close friends, and those of first-class respectability; is neat and tidy in dress, highly respectable in appearance, and extremely proper and polite in behavior, chaste in language, eschews profanity, and has never been known to gamble, other than buying pools on horse races and speculating in mining stocks.

On the morning of July 26, 1875, the celerity stagecoach, or "mud wagon," from Sonora in Tuolumne County bound for Milton in Calaveras County carrying ten passengers driven by John Shine was three hours out from Sonora and an hour from Copperopolis. The coach carried a Wells, Fargo Express box and U.S. mail bags but the treasure box contained only a few hundred dollars in currency, so there was no shotgun guard aboard. The horses were slowly ascending a steep grade approaching the summit of Funk Hill when a man suddenly appeared from behind a boulder on the side of the road, stepped in front of the leaders, crouched to keep the horses between him and the driver, and ordered Shine to rein in his team. The road agent was masked with a flour sack with eye holes cut in it which was pulled over his hat and face, and he brandished a modern-style double-barreled shotgun. He said, "Please, throw down that box." Shine struggled with the box so the road agent called out, "If he makes a move, give him a volley, boys." Shine looked to where the robber had directed his instruction and saw the barrels of two guns pointed at him. Once the box was thrown down the demand for the mail sacks followed and as they struck the roadway one of the female passengers also threw out her purse. The road agent bowed as returned it to her, saying, "I don't want your money, only the express box and mail," and he then gestured Shine to drive on. A second stagecoach appeared on the road also bound for Copperopolis, but when the driver told the road agent he had no treasure aboard he was told to continue. A short distance beyond the scene the stagecoach drivers rendezvoused and, with a small party, returned to the scene where they found the gun barrels of the robber's confederates to be a ruse — just sticks positioned to appear as gun barrels. They recovered the broken box and cut mail sacks and hurried into Copperopolis to notify the authorities. There had been several stagecoaches robbed in the vicinity in the recent past and the northeastern part of the state had been active for road agents for more than a decade, but this was the first robbery for this agent with his unique *modus operandi*. This road agent wore a distinctive mask and a soiled linen duster over typical miner's clothing, and his boots were muffled to disguise his tracks. He leaped from hiding in front of the horses and used the leaders for cover so that he was barely exposed to the driver or anyone else who might be riding atop. It later became apparent that he avoided stagecoaches with messengers, which meant his plunder would always be moderate at best. He cut the mail sacks open with a distinctive "T," and was overwhelmingly polite in his remarks to the driver and female passenger.

Wells, Fargo agent J. M. Pike notified Calaveras County Sheriff Benjamin Thorn and related the details of the robbery and the lawman was soon on the trail of the robber. He found evidence at the scene, including a 12 gauge shotgun — a breech-loading side-hammer with barrels cut to twenty-four inches which made it a close range weapon of formidable firepower. There was nothing, however, to identify the robber nor a trail sufficient to track him. Within a week Wells, Fargo issued a reward poster stating that the road agent had gotten only $160 from their box, but offered a reward of $250 for his capture and one fourth of any money recovered. The road agent laid low for five months before reappearing in the hills north of Smartsville in Nevada County. Although this was the second robbery of the North San Juan to Marysville stagecoach within two weeks this robber, unlike the first, was unusually polite but let his shotgun speak for him. There was but one confederate aiming a gun barrel at the driver this time, but it was later presumed it was a stick positioned similar to the ruse he used on July 26. Driver Mike Hogan delivered the treasure box and mail sacks before he was waved on. He hurried into Marysville and organized a posse. They hurried to the scene and recovered the broken box and mail sacks, cut open with a "T," but could find no clue to the robber's identity. Once again the road agent disappeared from the highways for months before reappearing on June 2, 1876. This time he stopped the stagecoach from Roseburg, Oregon, to Yreka, Siskiyou County, California, when it was five miles north of Cottonwood. His *modus operandi* was the same, excepting this time he worked at night for the first time but chose a night with bright moonlight to aid in his work. Driver A. C. Adams was ascending a steep grade, driving his six-up at a slow pace, when a masked man stepped in front of the team, pointed his shotgun at Adams, politely demanded the express box and mail sacks, and then waved him on. The stagecoach hurried into Cottonwood and at first daylight a posse went to the scene. They were joined by deputy sheriff John Halleck but they could find no clue nor a continuous trail to follow. The State of California added $300 to the reward of $250 offered by Wells, Fargo but no one came forward to collect, and Wells, Fargo refused to quantify their losses so the amount taken was never documented, though it must have been substantial as the road agent took off an entire year.

At 6:00 A.M. on August 3, 1877, the stagecoach driven by Ash Wilkinson left Point Arenas in Mendocino County bound for Duncan's Mills in Sonoma County. By mid-afternoon the coach was ascending a steep grade near the Russian river and still several hours from its destination when a masked road agent wielding a shotgun stepped in front of the leaders. He politely demanded the express box and mail sacks and they were thrown out. There was no further delay and Wilkinson was waved on. The road agent took from the box $300 in coin and a check, which was later destroyed because cashing it could identify the robber. This was the robbery where the road agent first left that famed note for the lawmen and newspaper editors, and the one where he established his alias:

> I've labored long for bread,
> For honor and for riches,
> But on my corns too long you've tread,
> You fine haired Sons of Bitches.
>   Black Bart, the P O 8

The road agent had adopted the sobriquet "Black Bart" used by Bartholomew Graham, a fictional desperado created in 1871 by William H. Rhodes for his tale "The Summerfield Case." Beneath this brief poem Black Bart wrote, "Driver, give my respects to our old friend, the other driver. I really had a notion to hang my old disguise hat on his weather eye."

Once again lawmen were clueless and the road agent disappeared from the highways again for nearly a year. Then, on July 25, 1878, Black Bart stopped the stagecoach from Quincy to Oroville in Butte County when it was a mile from the Berry Creek Sawmill. He held steadfastly to his *modus operandi* except for failing to muffle his boots, and the tracks were thought to be size 6 or 8, and he left another poem which extended his literary contributions—the last poem he would leave at a robbery scene. From the express box he took $379 in coin, a $25 silver watch, and a $200 diamond ring. On July 30 just after sunrise Black Bart robbed the stagecoach from Laporte to Oroville driven by Dan Barry when it was six miles from Laporte, and still in Plumas County. Black Bart stepped out of heavy timber in front of the horses and followed the familiar pattern of robbery, and Wells, Fargo reported that he got only $50 in gold nuggets and another cheap watch. Sheriff James H. Yeates organized a posse and went to the scene but found only a few boot tracks he thought to be size 8. On October 2, 1878, Alex Fowler was driving the stagecoach from Arcata in Humboldt County [Hume reports Cahto] to Ukiah in Mendocino County and ten miles from its destination it was stopped and robbed of the mail sacks and express box, which contained only $40 in coin and a gold watch. Mendocino County Sheriff James R. Moore organized a posse and went to the scene but again there were no clues of significance. Sixteen hours later the stagecoach from Covelo in Mendocino County to Ukiah, driven by Nathan Waltrip was robbed near Centerville, only twenty miles from the robbery the previous day, and from the detailed report it was clearly Black Bart again. The road agent got more than $400 on this outing so after this eighth robbery Wells, Fargo increased their reward to $300 and the post office added another $200, bringing this sum with the state's $300 to a total reward of $800 for the capture of Black Bart.

Once again Black Bart laid low for months but then on June 21, 1879, he stopped the stagecoach from Laporte to Oroville when three miles west of Forbestown in Butte County. He demanded the express box and mail sacks from driver Dave Quadlin. He took $50 and a silver watch from the express box but as was the usual case there was no way to determine what was taken from the mails. Sheriff Yeates made every effort to track him down but returned to town empty-handed. On October 25, 1879, the stagecoach from Redding in Shasta County left for Roseburg, Oregon, at dusk and as the team ascended the grade to the summit of Bass Hill, near Buckeye, Black Bart suddenly appeared from the roadside and ordered driver James Smithson to rein in his team. When the express box was demanded Smithson told the road agent that he could not throw out the box as it was chained inside the coach. Black Bart ordered the driver to dismount and hold the leaders' harness. He ordered the only passenger, a woman, to dismount and stand away while he broke open the box and removed the contents, nearly a "water haul," but the robber then went through the registered mail which newspapers reported contained more than $1,000. Black Bart then had the passenger and driver board and continue on their way and two days later, on October 27, Black Bart robbed the stagecoach from Redding to Alturas in Modoc County. The celerity wagon, driven by Ed Payne, was traveling slowly along a particularly narrow and winding portion of the road twenty-five miles east of Redding and as it came around a sharp turn he found Black Bart standing in the middle of the road. As soon as the mail sacks and express box were delivered the road agent ordered Payne to continue. He hurried into Millville where a posse of three lawmen was organized. They went to the scene and took up the robber's trail at daylight but soon lost it in rough country. The treasure box, it was reported, again yielded nearly a "water haul" but the mails reportedly contained $1,300.

On July 22, 1880, stagecoach driver Martin McClennan, on the Point Arenas to Duncan's Mills run, was stopped by a masked road agent brandishing a double-barreled shotgun when four miles from Henry's Hotel. The robber demanded the express box but, when he found it securely bolted into the coach floor, settled for the mail sacks and gestured for McClennan to continue. On September 1, 1880, Black Bart stopped the stagecoach from Weaverville in Trinity County to Redding driven by Charley Creamer after it crossed the line into Shasta County, but before reaching the Last Chance Station. He demanded and received the wooden treasure box and the mail sacks, but then demanded the second box. Creamer told him it was bolted inside the coach and made of iron. The road agent ordered out the only passenger, a woman, and tried to chop it open with an ax but finally gave up. He had the woman board and sent the coach on its way. From the wooden box he realized $100 but the amount found in the mails was unknown. As soon as the coach reached town a posse was organized and they followed the robber's trail for some distance before losing it. On September 16, 1880, Black Bart crossed the line into Oregon and stopped the stagecoach from Roseburg bound for Yreka, Siskiyou County, California. He chose that date as he had a bright moon to work under and had planned the robbery for the nighttime hours. When the coach was still two miles north of the state border the road agent halted driver Nort Eddings, pointed his shotgun at the driver, and demanded the express box and mail sacks. Eddings threw out the mail but said the box was bolted in the rear boot. This time the robber was prepared and, with the proper tools, broke open the box without removing it and extracted more than $1,000 in gold dust and coin, and also a considerable amount of currency. Black Bart had done so well in Oregon he repeated the robbery on September 23, this time stopping driver George Chase and again finding more than $1,000. As usual, there were no clues to help identify the road agent. On November 20 Black Bart closed out his 1880 endeavors with the robbery of the stagecoach traveling from Redding in Shasta County to Roseburg, Oregon, perhaps hoping for another good haul from an Oregon coach. Driver Joe Mason was halted and the mail sacks and treasure box were demanded. The mail was thrown out but Mason said the box was too heavy for one man to lift. When the road agent mounted the wheel to help lift the box Mason took a swing with a hatchet and nearly hit Black Bart in the head. The robber fell and fled and Mason hurried on, leaving the mail behind. Later another stagecoach recovered the slashed mail sacks and the mail Black Bart had not taken. The post office, in a rare disclosure, reported that the mail contained little of value.

Perhaps the close call in November 1880 had its effect because Black Bart did not appear again until August 31, 1881, when he stopped the stagecoach from Roseburg, Oregon, bound for Yreka, California, when it was nine miles from its destination. There was a small fire beside the road, providing enough light for the nighttime work, and when driver John Sullaway came abreast of it a masked road agent wielding a shotgun stepped into the road and ordered him to stop. The mail bags were thrown out on demand but the box was fastened to the coach so Sullaway was ordered to dismount and hold the leaders. The robber broke open the box with an ax and found very little for his trouble, and then Sullaway was sent on his way. On October 8 Black Bart returned to Bass Hill, near Buckeye in Shasta County, and stopped the stagecoach from Redding to Yreka driven by Horace Williams. After the mail sacks were thrown out he learned that the treasure box was bolted inside the coach so he had the three passengers get out and walk some distance down the road while Williams was ordered to hold the leaders. He broke open the box and got just enough to avoid a "water haul," about $60. Three days later Black Bart found driver Lewis Brewster, who was driving south from Lakeview, Oregon, to Redding in Shasta County, California, stopped two miles north of Round Mountain and engaged in making some repair. The road agent made him climb aboard, throw out the mail sacks and treasure box, and then continue on. Brewster stopped after traveling a short distance and returned to the scene with rifle in hand but Black Bart had already secured his booty and fled. When Hume and Thacker compiled their report of company losses they had failed to list the robbery of October 8 but reluctantly listed two robberies in December 1881. Their reluctance stemmed from the belief that the robber was a copycat — a very poor caricature of the real Black Bart. Two months after the October 11 robbery, on December 15, a road agent in Yuba County stopped the stagecoach from Downieville to Marysville when it was four miles north of Dobbins Ranch. The man stepped from behind a tree and then stepped back to keep partly concealed, pointed his shotgun at driver George Sharpe, and commanded, "Throw down that box or I'll blow your damned head off!" The polite request was absent but there were other discrepancies in the *modus operandi* as the robber used a different style of shotgun, used profanity rather freely throughout the affair, and wore a different type of mask. The road agent must have been disappointed when he found the box was empty and there was very little in the mails. The only thing consistent with Black Bart's methods was that he did not molest the passengers, five Chinese men riding inside, nor the small boy riding atop. On December 27, 1881, this same copycat "Black Bart" robbed the stagecoach from North San Juan to Smartsville when four miles north of its destination. The robber again made a "water haul." These were the only robberies in December that Hume attributed to Black Bart as he had otherwise ended his campaigns in late November at the latest.

On the afternoon of January 26, 1882, the real Black Bart reappeared in Mendocino County and stopped the stagecoach coming from Ukiah to Cloverdale, Shasta County. The road agent stepped into the road in front of the horses only a mile from the toll station operated by J. A. Lance, reportedly wielding a rifle but masked and dressed in his customary attire, and politely requested the Wells, Fargo express boxes and mail sacks. Driver Harry Forse delivered two boxes and the mails before he hurried to the station. He organized a small posse and returned to the scene but when they arrived they found only the two boxes broken open and the mail sacks slashed with a distinctive "T." The posse followed a clear trail for some distance before darkness ended the pursuit and the following day they lost the trail, so two larger posses were organized but they could not capture the road agent. Wells, Fargo reported that the box held only $300, but by then they were inclined to under-report their losses and there was probably a substantial sum found in the mails. Once again Black Bart took a long hiatus but on June 14, 1882, he stopped the stagecoach traveling from Little Lake, near Willits, to Ukiah in Mendocino County when three miles from the former place. The road agent stepped into the road in front of the horses and pointed his shotgun at driver Thomas Forse. When the polite request came to "Please, throw down that box," Forse replied that he couldn't because the iron box was bolted down. The road agent had Forse dismount, searched him for weapons, then had him unhitch the team and take the horses a distance down the road. Black Bart had brought the correct tools and within an hour he had emptied the iron box and fled. One month later, on July 13, Black Bart stepped from the side of the road in front of the leaders when the stagecoach from Laporte to Oroville was nine miles from Strawberry. The coach was carrying $23,000 and this large sum warranted a shotgun messenger. George Hackett rode on the seat next to driver George Helm and when Black Bart appeared Hackett grabbed his rifle and shot once at the road agent. The round creased the robber's right temple and sent him running for the trees. Hackett gave chase but only managed to capture the robber's blood-stained hat and mask. The road agent did not return fire and later, after his capture, claimed his weapon was never loaded while engaged in the business and this was the only time Black Bart tried to take in a stagecoach with a messenger aboard. Black Bart did not try for another stagecoach for two months but on September 17, 1882, he set up his operation fourteen miles from Redding to stop the down-coach from Yreka. Driver Horace Williams, whom he had robbed two years earlier, delivered the box and mail sacks before continuing on to his destination. On November 24 Black Bart, in his final adventure for the year, stopped the stagecoach from Lakeport to Cloverdale driven by Dick Crawford. He ordered the driver to unhitch the team and escort his passengers down the road a safe distance while he attacked the iron box bolted inside the stagecoach. There was probably little plunder realized in either of his last two robberies for 1882 since the amount stolen was not even sufficient to report.

Once again Black Bart took off the winter months and reappeared on April 12, 1883. The stagecoach from Lakeport to Cloverdale driven by Bill Connibeck was five miles from its destination when Black Bart appeared and followed his well established protocol in securing two treasure boxes and the mail sacks, reportedly profiting less than $50 in all. On June 23 Black Bart stopped the stagecoach from Jackson to Ione in Amador County driven by Clint Radcliff. The boxes and mail bags were thought to contain a substantial sum as the area was thriving at the time and the amount taken gave Black Bart the opportunity to take another six month hiatus. Just after sunrise on November 3, 1883, the stagecoach from Sonora in Tuolumne County to Milton in Calaveras County driven by Reason E. McConnell left Reynolds Ferry and within an hour was making its way up the Funk Hill grade. Just before reaching the summit Black Bart stepped into the road in front of the horses wielding his shotgun and reenacting the exact scenario he had used during his first outing on July 26, 1875. When told that the box was bolted inside the coach Black Bart ordered the driver to dismount and unhitch the horses. There were no passengers aboard but a young man from the Ferry had hitched a ride and, shortly before the robbery, had dismounted and took his rifle into the hills to hunt deer. McConnell, stalling for time, said the brakes were bad and the coach would roll backward but the robber ordered him to block the wheels with rocks. McConnell suggested the robber do it and was surprised when Black Bart placed rocks behind the wheels. McConnell then got down, unhitched the horses, and led them up the hill while Black Bart started working on the metal treasure box. After traveling two hundred yards McConnell saw the lad from the Ferry, James Rolleri, and summoned him. McConnell explained the situation, took the rifle, and the two men then started back down the hill. When they were still one hundred yards from the stagecoach Black Bart spotted them and started to run and McConnell fired twice, missing. Rolleri then took his rifle and, just before the road agent entered the brush, he fired once deeply grazing the left hand of the robber. They followed a trail of letters the robber dropped, and found several spotted with blood, but the robber had managed to hold onto the sack containing his shotgun, $550 in coin, and twenty pounds of amalgam. Rolleri then said that he was certain it was the same man who had stayed at the Reynolds' Ferry Hotel the previous week, a man who had inquired about stagecoach schedules. This proved the case and for the first time lawmen had a detailed description of Black Bart. McConnell hitched his team and hurried into Copperopolis where he reported the robbery.

A posse of citizens was headed for the scene within an hour and Sheriff Ben Thorn was at the scene before dusk, and Wells, Fargo's special agent James Hume was on his way. The sheriffs of San Joaquin and Tuolumne Counties were notified and were asked to watch for the robber. Even though the posse had contaminated the scene and obliterated most of the boot tracks, Sheriff Thorn began to collect evidence: a black derby hat, size 7¼; an old leather valise which contained a variety of items including bags of food items stamped with a logo from an Angel's Camp store, but most importantly a handkerchief. On the handkerchief was a laundry mark, "F. X. O. 7." The proprietor of the Angel's Camp store gave a detailed description of the man who had purchased the food items and it tallied with the description of the man who had stayed at the ferry hotel. Thorn tracked the robber to the cabin of trapper Thomas Martin, a mile from the robbery scene but the trail was lost there, though Martin confirmed the description once again. The robber traveled as fast as he could and finally, to speed his escape, hid his shotgun and the amalgam keeping only the coin. He went to Sacramento, then to Reno, Nevada, before returning to San Francisco on November 10. James Hume had also returned to San Francisco and there he turned over all the evidentiary items to Harry Morse, an ex-Sheriff of Alameda County hired specifically to work on the Black Bart case. Morse compiled a list of the ninety-one laundries in San Francisco, the place he decided to start his investigation, and canvassed them trying to match the laundry mark. On November 12 Morse learned that the laundry mark was from the Ferguson & Biggs California Laundry and was a mark used by their agent Thomas Ware, who operated a tobacco shop and laundry service. Ware identified the mark and said it was assigned to Charles E. Bolton. Morse said he was a mining man and wanted to meet Bolton, a well known and successful mining man, and wanted Ware to introduce him to Bolton. Ware told him Bolton lived at the Webb House, 37 Second Street so detectives were dispatched from the police station to watch for Bolton. Morse went to Ware's shop to request him to accompany him to the Webb House to make the introduction so Ware locked his shop and the two men started, but they met Bolton on the street after walking a short distance. Bolton agreed to accompany this "fellow mining man" to discuss a mining matter and they walked to the Wells, Fargo Office where Bolton was introduced to James Hume. Bolton kept his composure as he was questioned but became somewhat flustered when confronted with inconsistencies, became evasive, and finally refused to answer any further questions. After some coaxing Bolton began answering questions again and after several more hours of questioning, and many inconsistencies, the Wells, Fargo agents and a police captain took Bolton to his room in the Webb House and found a large body of incriminating evidence. In the room was also found a bible inscribed with the prisoner's true name — Charles E. Boles. Questioning continued and by midnight Bolton, who now refused to answer any further questions, was arrested and jailed. The next morning Bolton agreed to accompany them to Calaveras County. He was officially in the custody of police captain Appleton W. Stone and John N. Thacker, and Morse joined the party as they boarded the boat to Stockton. They were met by Sheriff Ben Thorn on their arrival, who had come to the city with trapper Thomas Martin to identify Black Bart. Martin immediately picked out Charles Bolton from a large crowd of curious citizens who had gathered at the dock and Bolton was jailed overnight. The next day the party started for Milton where they would meet stagecoach driver Reason McConnell, but the driver could not identify the man by sight as the road agent had been masked, but when the two men were introduced McConnell positively identified Bolton's voice. Bolton was next taken to San Andreas and lodged in the county jail. Although everyone was exhausted by a full day of travel Morse decided to begin a course of relentless questioning, confronting the prisoner with a chronological list of the evidence against him. Bolton filibustered, talking about everything from his mining expertise to his civil war experiences, until 1:00 A.M. when he suggested he might make a confession in return for some concessions. Morse offered to charge him with a single crime and, if he cooperated with a detailed confession and returned the plunder, he would receive a reduced sentence. However if he did not cooperate Morse threatened that he would be tried with as many offenses as could be proved and receive maximum, consecutive sentences on each. Bolton offered restitution if he could escape a prison sentence but Morse told him that could not happen. Morse then brought in Sheriff Thorn and Captain Stone, and Bolton confessed to the Funk Hill stagecoach robbery of November 3, 1883, and agreed to take them to the hidden treasure. They took their rented buggy and started for the scene of the final robbery and on the way Bolton began relating the details of other stagecoach robbing adventures. On November 16 Charles Bolton appeared before San Andreas Justice of the Peace P. H. Kean for his examination and entered a plea of guilty to the November 3 stagecoach robbery. He was held over for trial in the Superior Court and the following day he waived a jury trial, again entered a plea of guilty, and was sentenced by Judge C. V. Gottschalk to serve a term of six years in San Quentin Prison. Bolton arrived at the prison on November 21 and registered as prisoner No. 11046. On January 21, 1888, Bolton was discharged, by expiration of sentence, after being credited with good time as required under the Goodwin Act.

Amador Dispatch [CA]: June 30, 1883. *Calaveras Chronicle*: July 31, 1875; November 9, 1883. *Calaveras Weekly Citizen [CA]*: November 17, 1883; November 24, 1883. *Daily Alta California [San Francisco]*: November 14, 1883. *Daily Appeal [Marysville, CA]*: December 16, 1881. *Daily Evening Expositor [Fresno, CA]*: August 6, 1889. *Evening Mail [Stockton, CA]*: November 24, 1883. *Marysville Daily Appeal [CA]*: December 15–17, 1881. *Mendocino Democrat [CA]*: August 10, 1877; October 4, 1878; July 23, 1880; January 27, 1882; June 16, 1882. *Mountain Messenger [Sierra Co., CA]*: November 24, 1883; December 1, 1883. *Transcript [Nevada City, CA]*: December 30, 1875; December 29, 1881. *Oroville Weekly Mercury [CA]*: July 26, 1878; August 2, 1878; June 27, 1879; July 14, 1882. *Plumas National [CA]*: August 3, 1878; June 28, 1879; July 15, 1882. *San Francisco Call [CA]*: November 16–21, 1883. *San Francisco Chronicle [CA]*: January 6, 1884. *San Francisco Examiner [CA]*: April 3, 1887; December 3, 1888. *Shasta Courier [CA]*: November 1, 1879; September 4, 1880; November 27, 1880; October 15, 1881; *Yreka Union [CA]*: June 3, 1876; September 18, 1880; September 3, 1881; September 23, 1882.

Bouldin, George

Nativity __; Age, 47; Occupation, Teamster; Height, 6 feet; Complexion, Dark; Color of eyes, Blue; Color of hair, Brown.
Robbed W. F. & Co's Express on stage from Boise to Silver City, I. T., in company with J. M. Saunders, November 10, 1875.
Charles Downey, driver John Lee and J. W. Trask, accessories.
Received at Territorial Prison, Boise, I. T., December 26, 1876; No. of commitment —; Crime, robbery; Term, 8 years; County sent from, Ada.
Pardoned, December 31, 1879.

Stagecoach robbery was usually chosen as a crime because the coach could be stopped some distance from any population center, thus allowing time for the robbers to flee before a posse could take the field, so it was peculiar to have a stagecoach jumped within sight of town. The Silver City coach was robbed repeatedly at about 3:30 A.M. near the old ferry house because three coaches were leaving Boise at the same hour and each drove in rotation the seventy-five yards from the post office in the Overland House where they picked up the mail and then to the Northwestern Stage Company Office to pick up their passengers. The Umatilla coach went first at 3:00 A.M. and then departed, and in about ten minutes the Silver City coach, the one usually carrying treasure, finished loading and started out. Next came the Overland coach which started about ten minutes after the Silver City coach and this, it was thought, would not give the robbers time to accomplish their work. The robbers, however, knew of the schedule and were game to try robbery anyway. On November 10, 1875, the Silver City coach driven by Charley Downey was stopped at 3:30 A.M. not more than a mile and a half south of Boise City. Three road agents, disguised and carrying double-barreled shotguns, demanded and received Wells, Fargo & Company's treasure box, and the mails were also taken. They got $7,069.19 in gold bullion, dust, and greenbacks. The driver, however, lost the advantage because he went on to the Sixteen Mile House before he sent someone back with a report of the robbery, which wasted more than seven hours. It rained hard between the time of the robbery and its report in the city so no tracks were visible when the lawmen arrived at the scene and there seemed no leads. Wells, Fargo & Company's detective John N. Thacker was put on the case but it was not until May 1876 that Thacker was able to arrest five men, including the three highway men named George Bouldin, John Souder, and John Lee. Driver Charles W. Downey was arrested for complicity in the crime and James M. Trask was jailed as an accessory before and after the fact for "running" (melting) the bullion to change its appearance. The men were indicted and tried for stagecoach robbery in December but the jury could not arrive at a verdict. A motion was filed for a new trial and on December 19, 1876, the grand jury returned indictments against the prisoners for grand larceny, a lesser charge.

On February 2, 1876, before the arrest of the November 10 robbers, the Silver City stagecoach driven by Tom Huston was stopped south of the city at about 3:30 A.M., this time just before crossing the first bridge which was only a half mile below the city. The highwaymen demanded the treasure box, but this time refused to take the mail. The box contained $35 in gold coin and $240 in currency, and the express mail. Like the first robbery the *Idaho Statesman* reported this to be "the boldest robbery in this part of the country." Within two days Sheriff Agnew and Marshal Pinkham, and their deputies, had arrested the Henderson brothers and four others they thought involved. Eventually all the prisoners were released except Steve J. Henderson, who was twice tried for stagecoach robbery and finally acquitted in December. The third in the series occurred on April 19, 1876, when the Silver City stagecoach was again driven by Charley Downey. This time the robbers would be caught and sentenced to terms in prison [*see* Miller, John W.]. Strangely, none of the road agent gangs knew of one another, except as the later robbers read the accounts in the *Statesman*.

Idaho Statesman [Boise, ID]: November 11, 1875; November 16, 1875; February 3–5, 1876; February 8, 1876; February 10, 1876; December 16, 1876.

Bragg, Calvin—*alias* Hampton

Received at the California State Prison, September 22, 1874; No. of first commitment, 6161; Crime, grand larceny; Term, 1 year; County sent from, Calaveras.
Discharged by expiration of sentence, August 2, 1875.
Received at California State Prison, April 12, 1877. No. of second commitment, 7515; Crime grand larceny; Term, 5 years; County sent from, Calaveras.
Discharged by expiration of sentence, November 12, 1880.
Robbed W. F. & Co's Express on stage from Chinese Camp to Milton, February 2, 1882, in company with Frank Rolfe.
Received at California State Prison, Folsom, May 3, 1882; No. of commitment, 467; Crime, robbery, Term, 5 years.
Died in Prison, October 8, 1882.

On February 2, 1882, during the early morning hours the stagecoach "which plies between Sonora, Chinese Camp, and Copperopolis" was halted when it was five miles from Chinese Camp in Tuolumne County, California. Two masked road agents with feet muffled to cover their tracks appeared suddenly from the roadside, covered the driver with double-barreled shotguns, and ordered him to rein in his team. The robbers demanded the Wells, Fargo treasure box and it was handed down. One robber took a sledge hammer and cold chisel and opened the box taking out $286, but there were no passengers aboard. When told to continue on the driver whipped up his team and hurried to the next stop. County Sheriff Ben Thorn was notified and he was soon on the trail of the robbers. Thorn, with deputy William Hendricks of Milton, returned on February 10 without prisoners but reported that Sheriff Yaney of Tuolumne County, with a large posse, was trailing the robbers and, if he had no better luck, Thorn would again take the trail. However, neither Thorn nor Yaney found the robbers. On February 16 Captain Aull and deputy sheriff Whitlock of Fresno got onto the track of the robbers after they learned the two men had stopped two days at Jim White's place near the Fresno slough, but had left for Hollister via Big

Pinoche and Tres Pinos Canyons. The lawmen followed and that night were joined by L. C. Davis of Los Banos. They arrived at the Big Pinoche store at daybreak and found that the fugitives were only a few hours ahead of them so they hurried over the ridge into Tres Pinos canyon and, after going ten miles, overtook their quarry heading toward Hollister in a light wagon. They were taken completely by surprise and, though heavily armed, were arrested without resistance. Captain Aull, who had worked as a guard at San Quentin, recognized both as ex-convicts, one giving the name Frank Rolfe and the other Joe Hampton, though it was later learned his real name was Calvin Bragg. On February 25 at 1:00 P.M. the two prisoners were safely lodged in the jail at Sonora. The men had their examination and were held over for action by the grand jury. They were indicted and Rolfe was tried in late March, with Bragg testifying against him. He was easily convicted and Rolfe, who had a long prison record, was sentenced to serve a life term. He managed to escaped from the Sonora jail during the first days of April but was recaptured the same day and arrived at San Quentin Prison on April 8, 1882. On July 17, 1908, Rolfe's life sentence was commuted and he was discharged. Bragg was tried in late April and also convicted of the robbery, but his previous prison record was not as impressive as Rolfe's, he had cooperated in testifying against Rolfe, and he was sickly so he was only sentenced to serve five years. Bragg arrived at the California State Prison at Folsom, to keep him away from Rolfe, on May 3, 1882. Bragg died in the prison hospital on October 8, 1882, probably of consumption contracted during his previous imprisonment, which was epidemic in such close confinement.

Calaveras Chronicle [CA]: February 11, 1882; February 25, 1882.

Brannan, John M.—*alias* Johnny Behind the Rocks

Nativity, Maryland; Age, 37 years; Occupation, Laborer; Height, 5 feet 3¼ inches; Complexion, Dark; Color of eyes, Gray; Color of hair, Black. Small features, scar over right eye, scar over right cheek bone, 3 scars on each shoulder near neck, pit-scars all over body, scar inside lf right forearm, end of third finger right hand crooked, scar on index , second and little finger of right hand, both little fingers crooked, two scars on left thumb, scar on middle finger left hand near nail; medium built.
Robbed W. F. & Co's Express on stage from Sumner to Bakersfield, alone, October 4, 1875.
Received at California State Prison, November 1, 1875; No. of commitment 6735; Crime, robbery; Term, 15 years; County sent from, Kern.
Removed to Folsom Prison, August 23, 1880.
Sentence commuted to eleven years by Governor George C. Perkins.
Discharged, upon expiration of sentence, December 4, 1882.

On Monday night, October 4, 1875, the "Omnibus" stagecoach driven by A. P. Bernard was on its way from Bakersfield to Sumner in Kern County to connect with the train for San Francisco. On board was the U.S. mail, the Wells, Fargo & Company Express box, and five passengers — one lady and four gentlemen. At 11:00 P.M. the coach had only gone as far as north Third Street, about four hundred yards beyond the Bakery, when a lone highwayman stepped out of the weeds and bushes by the roadside and, wielding a double-barreled shotgun, demanded the treasure box. He was wearing a bandage about his head and the rest of his face had been blackened. There were three lights on the stagecoach and they all shined directly onto the robber. As soon as the box was delivered he ordered the driver to continue on so Bernard hurried back into Bakersfield and reported the robbery. A search was conducted the following day and tracks were found from the scene to the rear of the brewery, and by noon the box was found smashed open and empty with $324 missing. Suspicion immediately attached to a well known character about town known as Johnny-behind-the-rocks, though his real name was John Brannan. His boot tracks were observed and they corresponded exactly in size and design to the tracks found at the scene of the robbery, the tracks trailed to the rear of the brewery, and the tracks found about the area where the empty Wells, Fargo box was found, so he was arrested. He was searched and, though he had been "hard up" he was found to have a $10 coin in his pantaloons, a $10 coin in his coat pocket, $240 in gold coins in his left boot, and $11 dollars in change. In all, $311 of the $324 stolen was finally recovered. On Wednesday, October 6 the prisoner was brought before Judge Adams for his examination and it was learned that he had borrowed a shotgun from John Lake between 9 and 10 o'clock the evening of the robbery, saying he wanted to go hunting in the morning, but returned it shortly after 11:00 P.M. saying he did not need it any longer; and the next day he loaned Lake $10. When Brannan had first appeared in town after the robbery several persons noticed that he had blackened his face, had partially washed off the black, but had left traces about his eyes. This evidence was deemed conclusive and Brannan was held for action by the grand jury, bail set at $1,500. Brannan was indicted and tried within weeks. He was easily convicted by the overwhelming evidence and at 3:00 P.M. on October 30 he was sentenced to serve fifteen years in California's State Prison. He arrived on November 1, 1875, and registered as prisoner No. 6735, but was removed to the more secure facility at Folsom Prison on August 23, 1880. His sentence was commuted to eleven years by Governor George C. Perkins and he was discharged, upon expiration of sentence, on December 4, 1882.

Kern County Weekly Courier [Bakersfield, CA]: October 9, 1875; October 30, 1875.

Briscoe, William, a deputy sheriff

Nativity, Missouri; Age, 37 years; Occupation, Deputy Sheriff; Height, 5 feet 7¾ inches; Complexion, Dark; Color of eyes, Gray; Color of hair, Black. Small mole center of small of back, ankle of right leg badly crippled, very large scar on shin bone of left leg; quick, nervous action

Robbed W. F. & Co's Express on stage from Grant's Pass to Jacksonville, Oregon, in company with Charles Keeton and Charles Bassett., January 18, 1884.

Received at Oregon State prison, July 2, 1884; Commitment, 1547; Crime, robbery; Term, 8 years; County sent from, Jackson.

[*See* Bassett, Charles]

Brown, John—*alias* J. W. Marshall, O'Neill, Old Jack Brown the Cell-tender

No. of first commitment, 373. Received at the California State Prison, May 8, 1854; Crime, grand larceny; Term 5 years, County sent from, Sacramento.

Escaped, September 28, 1856.

No. of second commitment, 1858. Received at the California State Prison, April 9, 1860; Crime, grand larceny; Term, 4 years; County sent from, Siskiyou.

Discharged, by expiration of sentence, January 21, 1864.

No. of third commitment, 5728. Received at the California State Prison, September 7, 1873; Crime, grand larceny; Term, 9½ years.

Discharged, by expiration of sentence, November 22, 1879.

Robbed W. F. & Co's Express on stage from Laporte to Oroville, November 30, 1880 — alone.

Robbed W. F. & Co's Express on stage from Igo to Anderson, April 18, 1881—alone.
Killed while resisting arrest, April 25, 1881.

The stagecoach from Laporte in Plumas County to Oroville in Butte County was stopped and robbed by a lone highwayman on Tuesday, November 30, 1880. The coach was one mile from Forbestown at a point called Garden Ranch Ravine when the road agent appeared from the brush, masked and wielding a shotgun. He demanded that the Wells, Fargo treasure box be thrown out and the driver had no choice but to comply. The box contained only a few hundred dollars so there was no shotgun guard, but there were two female passengers aboard and they were not molested. As soon as the road agent had the box the driver was ordered to continue, so he whipped up his team and hurried to the next place with a telephone, and the robbery was called in to Sheriff Sprague in Oroville. Sprague immediately contacted Captain Aull, a Wells, Fargo detective who happened to arrive in town that morning, and they started for the scene. They had no luck trailing the robber and the following day they were joined by J. B. Hume, chief detective for the express company. Wells, Fargo did not want to spare any expense as there had been a number of robberies in the vicinity recently, but the lawmen were not able to work up a case against anyone for six months.

In April 1881 the *Shasta Courier* reported that Igo was one of the most pleasant towns in Shasta County and among its many residents of "stamina, wealth, honesty, courage and enterprise" was Warren "Doc" Dunham. Dunham managed the post office and contracted for handling express operations out of Igo. He convinced Wells, Fargo & Company to establish an office and had a "fine stage built on the new and improved pattern" before he established the schedule for a stage line to make daily runs to the railroad connection at Anderson. The Dunham & Leiter Stage Line began operations in September 1879 and on Monday, April 18, 1881, the Igo to Anderson stagecoach driven by Watt Gage left Igo at 4:00 P.M. and had traveled four miles to the old Champion house when it was halted by a lone highwayman. The road agent, masked and with pistol in hand, stepped out from the roadside, stopped the horses, and commanded, "give up that box!" As soon as the box was on the roadway the road agent ordered Gage to drive on toward Anderson. A mile from the scene of the robbery Gage met Thad Jones, gave him the details of the robbery, and sent him back to Igo to report to the authorities, and he made the trip into Anderson in less than an hour. Dunham, with a man named Conger, went to the scene and two hundred yards off the roadway they found the broken box, a sledge hammer, and an axle used as a pry bar, along with the waybills from which they learned that the road agent had removed $1,100 in currency, 10,000 shares of Chicago Mine stock, and some letters. From the detailed description of the road agent it was believed he was the same man who had broken into the home of N. Beeves the previous Sunday, rifled a trunk for some coins, and then slept the night in the carpenter shop; and also matched the description of the road agent who stopped the stagecoach from Laporte to Oroville on November 30, 1880. Sheriff J. W. Smiley received the description of the man who had robbed the Igo stagecoach and learned that the fugitive had been seen at the cabin of John Day and James Moore. On April 25 Smiley, with James Moore, traveled all night and most of the next day arriving at Moore's cabin at 4:00 P.M. They found Day at home and Smiley sent him out to find and decoy the robber to the cabin while he and Moore lay down to rest, but they fell asleep. A noise awoke Smiley and he raised up to find the fugitive seated at the table, and the fugitive said, "Come here, I want to see you." However, he immediately ran outside while trying to draw his revolver and Smiley commanded him to halt. The man continued to run and managed to free his pistol from its scabbard as Smiley, Day and Moore rushed out and the sheriff commanded a second time for the fleeing fugitive to halt, and when he would not comply the lawman ordered Day to shoot. Day fired one round but it did not hit its target so Sheriff Smiley said, "shoot him, for God's sake!" Day fired a second time and the man fell onto his elbows with his revolver still in his hand. The Sheriff then advanced on his quarry and the man said, "I didn't think you s__s of b___s would murder me." Smiley then commanded, "disarm yourself or I will blow your brains out!" He had to repeat the order a second time before the man threw the revolver aside and said, "for God's sake, don't murder me. I am killed anyway." The man, who refused to identify himself, was carried to the cabin and Smiley sent Day for the doctor while Moore gathered up the man's coat, the pockets of which contained some gold dust and $13.10 in coin. The doctor arrived and cut out the bullet, which had entered on the left side in the small of his back and perforated the bowels of the prisoner. The men constructed a litter and took their prisoner to the hospital at Weaverville, but he died at 11:00 P.M. on April 27 after lingering in excruciating pain for hours. The body was put in charge of Shasta County Sheriff Hull for identification and burial. At the inquest the jury identified the deceased as Ed Wilson, but later it was determined by James B. Hume that he was John Brown, alias Ed Wilson, J. W. Marshall, O'Neill, or "Old Jack Brown, the Cell-tender." Brown was well known to lawmen as he had served three terms at San Quentin between 1854 and 1879: for larceny from May 8, 1854, to September 28, 1856, when he escaped; for larceny from April 9 to, 1860, to January 21, 1864; and for grand larceny from September 7, 1873, to November 22, 1879. He had been free less than one year when he robbed his first stagecoach and less than two years when he was killed while resisting arrest.

Plumas National [CA]: December 11, 1880. *Shasta Courier [CA]*: May 7, 1881.

Brown, Lodi

Nativity, Missouri; Age, 34 years; Occupation, Farmer; Height, 5 feet 4½ inches; Complexion, Light; Color of eyes, Gray; Color of hair, Light Brown. Mole on left of nose, scar left eye, mole on muscle of left arm, mole on right arm, small scar on left index finger, small mouth, small chin, small face, medium built.

In 1869 and early 1870 robbed W. F. & Co.'s Express on several stages in Sonoma and Mendocino Counties, [California] in company with W. E. Andrus and John Houx.

Attempted to rob W. F. & Co.'s Express on stage from Petaluma to Cloverdale, August 16, 1871, in company with Andrus, Houx, and a John Doe.

Received at California State Prison, February 29, 1872. No. of commitment, 5156. Crime, murder in second degree; Term, 30 years; County sent from, Sonoma.

Conditionally pardoned, provided he leave the state, by Governor William Irwin January 3, 1880, and *Discharged*, January 6, 1880.

[*See* Andrus, W. E.]

Brown, Mitchell—*alias* Little Mitch

Nativity, Austria; Age, 40 years; Occupation, Laborer; Height, 5 feet 4¾ inches; Complexion, Florid; Color of eyes, Hazel; Color of hair, Dark. Broad features, small chin, nose turned slightly to the right, eyes deep-set, high forehead, hair thin on top, small mole left cheek, full hairy breast, scar base of left thumb, two moles near right elbow, small scar back of right wrist, hairy back, two scars above left elbow under arm, scar back of right shoulder blade; very stout built.

Robbed W. F. & Co's Express on stage from Sonora to Milton, November 2, 1874, in company with "Big Mitch," Ramon Ruiz, and "Old Joaquin."
Robbed W. F. & Co's Express on stage from Mokelumne Hill to Lodi, in company with "Big Mitch," March 1, 1875.
Robbed W. F. & Co's Express on stage from Sonora to Milton, March 23, 1875, in company with "Big Mitch," Ramon Ruiz, and "Old Joaquin."
Attempted to rob W. F. & Co's Express on stage from Sonora to Milton, October 12, 1875, in company with "Big Mitch," Ramon Ruiz, and "Old Joaquin."
Received at California State Prison, May 5, 1876; Commitment No. 7010; Crime, robbery; Term, 15 years; County sent from, Calaveras.
[*See* Ruiz, Ramon]

Brown, Tom—*alias* Tom Foster

Nativity, Missouri; Age, 31 years; Occupation, Laborer; Height, 5 feet 5½ inches; Complexion, Fair; Color of eyes, Gray; Color of hair, Hair. Long features, large nose, large ears, several moles on right fore-arm, scar across inside of right wrist, 2 moles on left fore-arm, 1 mole on left shoulder blade, slim built.
No. of first commitment, 6204. Received at California State Prison, October 16, 1874; Crime, grand larceny; Term 2 years; County sent from, Sutter.
Discharged, by expiration of sentence, July 5, 1876.
Robbed W. F. & Co's Express on stage from Yreka to Redding, November 3, 1876, in company with Joe Brown (brother) and Dave Tye.
Robbed W. F. & Co's Express on stage from Downieville to Marysville, in company with his brother, Joe Brown, November 13, 1876. In committing this robbery they shot and killed a stage horse, and very seriously wounded Henry Scammon, a banker of Downieville, who was a passenger.
(They also robbed the U.S. Mail and passengers. On November 24, 1876, in resisting arrest, Joe Brown was mortally wounded, and died in jail at Chico a few days later.) Plead guilty to last robbery
Received at California State Prison, January 13, 1877; No. of commitment, 7336; Crime, robbery; Term, 10 years; County sent from, Yuba.
Was taken from the State Prison to Marysville April 12, 1877, to testify against Charles Frazier, who was indicted for being an accessory to the above robberies.
Escaped April 24, 1877, from Marysville jail, stole the Sheriff's horse and fled the region.

Tom Brown, Joe Brown, and Dave Tye were stealing horses in central California in 1874 when Tom and Joe were caught, lodged in the Sutter County jail, convicted on separate charges, and sent to prison. Tom partnered with Dave Tye after he left prison and by the end of October 1876 his brother Joe had escaped from San Quentin and the three men rendezvoused. They decided to rob a stagecoach and set their sights on the coach running from Yreka in Siskiyou County to Redding in Shasta County, but missed the coach on November 1 and 2. On November 3 they stopped the coach and demanded the mail sacks and Wells, Fargo treasure box before ordering the coach to continue on. From the mail sacks the three men took $1,230 in currency, a gold bar valued at $275, and $130 in gold notes; and from the treasure box they got $1,060 in gold dust and $45 in gold notes. The brothers were disappointed with Tye's performance through-out the robbery and decided to find another man to replace him. Tom and Joe recruited Charles "Red" Frazier, who worked on a ranch in the vicinity, and when he agreed to provide fresh horses the Brown's planned their next robbery for the coach from Downieville in Sierra County to Marysville in Yuba County. The Browns hid along the road to Marysville on November 13 and stepped out of the brush when the coach came into view. They were masked with guns in hand as they ordered the driver to halt. They were about to demand the treasure box and mail sack as the coach came to a halt but Henry Scammon, a Downieville banker, stuck his pistol out the window and fired at the two robbers. He missed them but he was seriously wounded by the return fire and several shots killed a stagecoach horse. Once the shooting ceased the Brown brothers demanded the treasure box and mails and, upon receiving them, immediately broke open the box with an ax and, seeing it contained treasure, left it until they concluded their business. They went through the passengers taking all their money and jewelry, getting about $450. They then allowed the dead horse to be cut free and sent the coach on its way with a three horse team. The take was not large so they supplemented it with gold dust from the Shasta robbery in making their escape to Norco, California, where they stole fresh horses and headed into Nevada. The son of the horses' owner, Charles Wilson, with a Mexican tracker and deputy Sheriff Alonzo Dolliver, followed the two road agents to Susanville where they organized an eleven man posse and continued in pursuit. They cornered the horse thieves in a corral near Deep Holes Springs in Nevada and, blockading the exit, forced the two men to abandon the stolen stock and flee on foot. Joe Brown, after running one hundred yards, was shot through the calf of his leg by a bullet from Wilson's Henry rifle and he collapsed from the wound, and Tom surrendered to avoid the same fate. Once both brothers were arrested they were searched and the plunder from the stagecoach was found: $170 in dust and $100 in coin — the first time the posse men knew they were after bigger game than horse thieves. Although the brothers begged to be released and offered bribes to allow them to escape they were taken to Chico and lodged in jail. Joe was in terrible agony as a serious infection had set in, and he begged to be killed. On December 5, 1876, he died from the infection.

James Hume was brought in and he told Tom of the overwhelming evidence against him and he then informed on Dave Tye and Charles Frazier to get a reduced sentence. Brown was indicted and in January 1877 he was tried and convicted. He was sentenced to serve a ten year term at San Quentin, arriving on January 13, 1877, and registering as prisoner No. 7336. Dave Tye was also convicted of the November 3 robbery and sentenced to serve seven years, arriving on March 8, 1877, and registering as prisoner No. 7431. Tye served out his entire term and was released by expiration of sentence on December 5, 1881, and was then pardoned to restore his rights. Frazier was convicted of being an accessory to both robberies and sentenced to serve seventeen years in prison, arriving on April 6, 1878, where he was registered as prisoner No. 8121. Frazier's late arrival was due to several escapes from the Marysville jail — first on June 1, 1877, and again on February 26, 1878. Frazier was pardoned by Governor George Stoneman on March 16, 1883, after serving only five years.

Tom Brown was taken out of prison to testify against Frazier on April 24, 1877, and, while in the Marysville jail, he managed to escape. He headed north and met two old friends, Tom Connor and Martin Myers, and they robbed the stagecoach between Roseburg and Redding on the night of May 27, 1877. Brown fled into Oregon with deputy sheriff John Hendricks and Wells, Fargo messenger John Reynolds close on his trail. They captured Brown at Ashland, Oregon, when he stopped to replace a horseshoe. He was first taken to Yreka and then to Redding where he was tried and convicted of his latest stagecoach robbery. This time the judge sentenced him to seventeen years in prison and on September 22, 1877, Brown arrived at San Quentin. He was once again brought to Marysville to testify against Frazier and he nearly escaped from the jail through a tunnel, but he was returned to prison after testifying. He was once again taken out in April 1878 to testify against Connors and again made several attempts at escape, and upon his return to San Quentin he was quickly transferred to the more secure facility at Folsom. Brown became a model prisoner for several years, but all the better to find another opportunity to escape and this came on June 15, 1886. Brown "stepped out for a smoke" and took off at a run. He hid the rest of that day and spread pepper on his trail to foil the dogs, then made his way to Ione before heading for Big Trees in Calaveras County. County Sheriff Ben Thorn was on his trail and captured the fugitive after knocking his semi-conscious during a desperate struggle. By mid–July Brown was back in prison and once again tried the "model prisoner" dodge, but this time it worked only because he got his good time credits restored and was discharge on April 3, 1891, before he could devise another escape plan. Tom Brown was not heard of again on California's criminal roll. Thomas Connor was found guilty of robbing a stagecoach in Shasta County on April 27, 1877, and sentenced to serve seven years at San Quentin prison. He arrived on April 25, 1878, and registered as prisoner No. 8173. Connor was released, by expiration of sentence, on January 25, 1883. Myers does not appear on the criminal record so he either turned state's evidence and was released, or managed to flee the region and was never captured.

Calaveras Chronicle [CA]: March 6, 1880. *Calaveras Prospect [CA]*: June 2, 1886. *Folsom Weekly Telegraph [CA]*: July 3, 1886; July 17, 1886. *Marysville Daily Appeal [CA]*: November 5, 1876; November 14–15, 1876; November 23, 1876; November 28, 1876; December 3, 1876; December 21, 1876; December 23–25, 1876. *Sacramento Daily Record-Union [CA]*: June 16–17, 1886; June 30, 1886; November 18, 1905. *Shasta Courier [CA]*: December 9, 1876; December 30, 1876; October 6, 1877; February 16, 1878; April 27, 1878. *Stockton Daily Evening Herald [CA]*: November 17, 1874; November 27–28, 1874; November 30, 1874. *Yreka Journal [CA]*: December 6, 1876; July 11, 1877. *Weekly Appeal [Marysville, CA]:* July 20, 1877; February 15, 1878; March 15, 1878; January 18, 1879; February 1, 1879; March 15, 1879. *Yreka Union [CA]*: July 14, 1877; September 22, 1877.

Buckner, J. B.

Nativity, Missouri; Age, 33 years; Occupation, Vaquero; Height; 5 feet 8 inches; Color of eyes, Light; Color of hair, Light Brown; Weight, 154 lbs. Mole on each arm above elbow, scar on left knee, does not drink, is single.
Robbed W. F. & Co's Express on stage from Boise [I. T.] to Winnemucca [Nev.], September 10, 1873, in company with Harry [Hiram] McComas.
Received at Nevada State Prison, December 15, 1873; No. of commitment, 182; Crime, robbery; Term, 5 years; County sent from, Humboldt.
Pardoned, and *released* July 13, 1877.

The stagecoach from Boise, Idaho Territory, to Winnemucca, Nevada, when five miles west of Buffalo Springs, or about forty miles north of its destination, was stopped by three masked men armed with a shotgun, a Spencer rifle, and a six-shooter. They demanded and broke opened the express box and found only $12.50 inside, from the mail bags they took nothing, from the driver they obtained $5, and from passenger F. P. Brougham they took a watch, so they went through the luggage and took a number of clothing items. They cut the harness from the leaders and then had the stagecoach continue on, pulled only by the wheelers, which delayed the report of the robbery. One of the robbers made for Winnemucca while the other two made plans to rendezvous at San Jose, California, but one of the robbers had been recognized. Within days of the robbery David Ebi was captured at Winnemucca and, according to Carson City's *Daily Appeal*, "being apprehended he 'blowed' like a coward and thief, and turned State's evidence against them [the other two robbers]." He named Hiram McComas and J. B. Buckner as the two men involved in the robbery. Hiram McComas, who was well known to lawmen in California, was soon captured at San

Jose and lodged in the Humboldt County jail. On November 10 a Sacramento deputy sheriff received a dispatch saying Buckner was on a westward-bound train so he boarded but failed to capture his man. He rode along to Brighton and there captured Buckner, who had evaded him at the Sacramento depot. Buckner then, learning that Ebi had informed, confessed the details of the robbery and said that Ebi had "put up the job." However, lawmen had already made their deal with Ebi and would not renege. A baggage claim ticket was found on Buckner and, when retrieved, his bundle included items stolen from the stagecoach including a buffalo robe, shawl, and overcoat, all bound-up with harness from the stagecoach team. Buckner also said that the watch found in McComas' possession, when arrested, belonged to passenger Brougham. The three men were indicted in Humboldt County, brought to trial at the fall 1873 term of the district court, and Buckner and McComas were found guilty of robbery while Ebi was released in consideration of his cooperation with the authorities and his testimony. Buckner and McComas were sentenced to serve terms of five years at the state's prison and both men arrived there on December 15, 1873. Buckner and McComas were pardoned on July 13, 1877, and were not heard of again on the criminal rolls of Nevada.

Territorial Enterprise [Virginia City]: December 16, 1873. Sacramento [CA] *Union*: November 19, 1873.

Campbell, T. Z.

Nativity, __; Age, 36 years; Occupation, Telegraph Operator, Height, 5 feet 9 inches; Complexion, Very Dark; Color of eyes, Brown; Color of hair, Dark Brown and Gray; Weight, 150 lbs. Deep-set eyes, heavy dark brown beard, usually wears only mustache — very heavy, always wears a frown, 4 upper teeth false.

Stole $500 from W. F. & Co's office Carbondale, Kansas, May 30, 1882, and fled region.

Was arrested and returned in 1884, and October 26th convicted and sentenced to a term of 18 months in State Prison.

Escaped from Sheriff of Osage County while en route to Prison. Still at large, January 1, 1885.

Z. T. Campbell (Hume and Thacker mistakenly called him T. Z.) was a clerk in the Carbondale, Kansas, office of Wells, Fargo & Company. On the evening of May 29, 1882, Campbell finished his paperwork, appeared to secure in the safe the valuables he received during his shift, and left the office as usual. However, Campbell did not report for work the following morning and a review of his accounts showed that a package containing $500, which he received the previous day, was missing. Campbell was neither young nor irresponsible so another employee was sent to his rooms to check on the employee. He found that Campbell had packed all his belongings, checked out, and saddled his horse and, with all his baggage, had left town without leaving a forwarding address. No one seemed to know which direction he had gone. Wells, Fargo & Company immediately replaced the stolen money but was reluctant to publicize a theft by a trusted employee. They did, however, circulate Campbell's description throughout Kansas and to lawmen and detective agencies in nearby states. In the fall of 1884, more than two years after the theft, a man in St. Louis, Missouri raised the suspicions of a detective named Dustan. He "shadowed" his suspect for some time before he realized he was following a wanted man and finally identified him as Z. T. Campbell, even though the fugitive had lost a considerable amount of weight. Dustan arrested Campbell and notified Wells, Fargo & Company and the Kansas authorities. In early October Governor George W. Glick issued a requisition to have Campbell returned to Kansas for prosecution. As Campbell was being brought back to Osage County the grand jury was being convened and following his examination he was quickly indicted. He pled not guilty but the evidence, though circumstantial, was strongly linked and he was convicted at trial. He was sentenced to serve eighteen months at the Kansas State Prison, but while en route he managed to escape from the Osage County sheriff and was never seen again.

Osage County Chronicle [Burlingame, KS]: October 2, 1884; November 11, 1884.

Carr, Peter

Nativity, West Virginia; Age, 35 years; Occupation, Hostler; Height 5 feet 6½ inches; Complexion, Fair; Color of eyes, Gray; Color of hair, Dark. Round features, face freckled, powder marks on right cheek, dent on right cheek, scar near left temple, large scar on right forearm; scar and a dim ink mark on left forearm.

Robbed W. F. & Co's Express on stage from Santa Clara to Santa Cruz, April 1, 1874, in company with A. P. Hamilton, alias Albert Tarlton.

Received at California State Prison, May 26, 1874; No. of commitment, 6021; Crime, robbery; Term, 10 years, County sent from, Santa Clara.

Pardoned by Governor William Irwin, August 15, 1878.

Second commitment, 8661. Received at the California State Prison, February 4, 1879; Crime, burglary second degree; Term, 5 years, County sent from, San Francisco.

Discharged, by expiration of sentence, September 4, 1882.

[*See* Hamilton, A. P.]

Casey, James

Nativity, New York; Age, 25 years; Occupation, Steward; Height 5 feet 4 inches; Complexion, Florid; Color of eyes, Black; Color of hair, Black; Size of foot, 5. Broad features, small chin, wide jaws, small ears, sharp nose slightly turned up, high forehead, heavy black eyebrows, small mole on throat, vaccine mark left upper arm, small mole back of left forearm, small scar base of right thumb, square shoulders; stout built.

Robbed W. F. & Co's Express on stage from Grayson to Bantas, October 23, 1884, in company with Peter Smith and Eugene Murphy.

Received at California State Prison, October 29, 1884; No. of commitment, 11434, Crime, robbery; Term, five years; County sent from, San Joaquin.

On October 23, 1884, at 7:00 A.M. the southbound Ferry Hill stagecoach, driven by Frank Grimes, was approaching a small bridge on the road between Banta in San Joaquin County and Grayson in Stanislaus County, which required the coach to move at a slow pace. The driver noticed three roughly dressed men near the bridge, but they were not masked so he paid them little attention. As the stagecoach neared one of the men, who had been carelessly leaning over the railing of the bridge, straightened himself and commanded the driver to halt and at the same time the other two emphasized the command by aiming guns at the driver. There was one passenger aboard, J. J. Sweeney, who was riding atop with the driver and he was covered by a double-barreled shotgun while the other two men pointed their revolvers at Grimes as they demanded the Wells, Fargo treasure box. After the box was delivered one of the men, noticing Sweeney's watch and chain, asked him to hand it over. Sweeney later claimed that he replied the watch was a present from his mother and the robber, if he wanted it, would have to "take it from my dead body." Sweeney said that the robbers, apparently, did not want to go to that extreme over a watch so they ordered the driver to continue on. Grimes drove a mile and a half to Kasson's Ranch and from there messengers were sent to San Joaquin City, where Constable Finch and Joe Nye were notified of the robbery. From there telegrams were sent to the Wells, Fargo office in San Francisco and to San Joaquin County's Sheriff Cunningham. Grimes reported that the robbers were "green at the business" as they were terribly nervous and could not hold the muzzles of their guns steady; and he gave a good description of the three men. By noon of the same day the Sheriff had left Stockton to investigate the robbery and track the road agents and he was joined by Wells, Fargo's detective John N. Thacker. The robbers were trailed, by deputy sheriff Fulkerth, from the scene of the robbery to Gerlach's Ranch in the mouth of Lone Tree Canyon, eight miles distant. The three men stopped for lunch at noon and then left for Ingram Canyon where they stopped at the ranch of a widow and had another meal at 3:00 P.M. Instead of striking into the foothills they continued to skirt along the edge of the valley and arrived at Ed Thomas' ranch at 6:00 P.M. where they ate supper. After eating their third meal in six hours they went down the canyon a short distance, found a haystack, and settled in for the night. Fulkerth found them asleep in the haystack and captured them without resistance. Sheriff Cunningham and detective Thacker were a mile and a half away when the three road agents were captured by Fulkerth, having been delayed when their horses gave out and they could not obtain fresh animals. When they joined the deputy and his prisoners Thacker questioned them and they admitted their guilt. They declined counsel and gave their names as James Casey, Peter Smith, and Eugene Murphy, and Murphy said of Sweeney's story, of refusing to surrender his watch, "He is a liar. He sat on his seat as limp as a rag and almost scared to death." They said they had missed a "water haul" by ten cents, all that was in the box excepting three letters written in Chinese. The well-fed road agents said they were motivated to rob the stagecoach "out of hunger." The prisoners were taken to Modesto and lodged in jail and their examination before Judge Treatwell was scheduled for Monday, October 27. When they appeared they waived examination and were held over for the grand jury, bail set in the sum of $5,000 each. Their arraignment was set for 3:30 that afternoon in Department 2 of the Superior Court, but was delayed to the following day when they pled guilty and were sentenced to serve five years in San Quentin Prison. They arrived at the prison on October 29, 1884, only six days after robbing the coach: Casey registering as prisoner No. 11434, Murphy as No. 11435, and Smith as No. 11436. Eugene Murphy was the first to be released when he was pardoned and released on August 19, 1886. James Casey was also pardoned and he was released on December 31, 1886. Peter Smith served out his entire sentence and was released upon expiration of sentence on May 29, 1888.

Stockton Daily Independent: October 24, 1884; October 26, 1884; October 28–29, 1884.

Castle, Charles

Nativity, England; Age, 36 years; Occupation, Miner; Height 5 feet, 6¼ inches; Complexion, Fair; Color of eyes, Gray; Color of hair, Light. Spare features, slightly cross-eyed, scar over and under right eyebrow, scar on right side of upper lip, scar on back of right thumb, Eagle and "In God we trust" on left forearm, second joint of left index finger stiff.

Robbed W. F. & Co's Express on stage from Bakersfield to Panamint, March 17, 1875, in company with James Wellock.

Received at the California State Prison, May 8, 1875; No. of commitment, 6516; Crime, robbery; Term, 10 years; County sent from, Kern.

Removed to Folsom prison, September 30, 1880.
Discharged, upon expiration of sentence, November 8, 1881.

On March 17, 1875, the northbound stagecoach from Bakersfield in Kern County to Panamint Springs in Inyo County, driven by W. J. Ladd, was stopped at 3:00 P.M. when two and one half miles beyond Canebreak Station, still inside Kern County. On board were two Wells, Fargo treasure boxes, one filled and the other empty. When the two road agents demanded the box the driver threw out the empty box and, when ordered to move along, he hurried to Coyote Holes Station and recruited P. Cline to go with him and arrest the robbers. En route they met two men but had no reason to suspect they were the robbers. At the scene they found many boot tracks of the type known as "O. K." with heavy nailed heels, and realized these were the tracks of the men they had met on the road who were wearing "O. K." boots. They were quickly on their trail but the men had stopped and extracted the "tell-tale nails." Ladd and Cline hurried on to Coyote Holes Station and in about an hour the two suspected road agents, who had been traveling by a more circuitous route, arrived there. Ladd pulled his revolver and put the barrel to the head of one road agent demanding he surrender and the man said, "Don't hurt me, we didn't hurt you." They were taken into Bakersfield and given their examination before Justice Wilkinson, where they gave the names Charles Castle and James Wellock. The evidence was strong enough to hold them for the grand jury and the sheriff, concerned for the security of his jail, took them to Visalia and lodged them in the jail there. In May the Kern County grand jury convened and when Wellock turned state's evidence a true bill [indictment] was returned against Castle. Castle first pled not guilty but, facing the testimony of his fellow road agent, he soon changed it to a guilty plea. When court convened on Friday Castle was brought in and sentenced to ten years at San Quentin Prison. He arrived at the prison on May 8, 1875, and registered as prisoner No. 6516. He was removed to the more secure facility at Folsom prison on September 30, 1880, and thirteen months later, on November 8, 1881, he was discharged upon expiration of his sentence.

Kern County Weekly Courier [Bakersfield, CA]: March 20, 1875; March 27, 1875; May 8, 1875.

Chambers, Charles—*alias* James Jackson

Nativity, Arkansas; Age, 27 years; Occupation, Laborer; Height, 5 feet 9½ inches; Complexion, Sallow; Color of eyes, Gray; Color of hair, Brown; Size of foot, 8. Square features, high broad and retreating forehead, slight indented scar near outer corner of right eye, four moles outer edge of left forearm, vaccine mark on right arm, small gunshot wound one inch from left shoulder blade, small, round scar at lower point of left shoulder, hair inclined to be curly.

Robbed W. F. & Co's Express on stage from Boise, I. T., to Kelton, Utah, January 3, 1881.

Received at Territorial Prison, Boise, I. T, November 10, 1881; No. of commitment —; Crime robbery; Term, 9 years.

Escaped, July 6, 1882; recaptured at Portland, Oregon, and returned to Prison, August 22, 1882.

Escaped, March 22, 1883, and fled to California.

The evening of August 1, 1883, he robbed the Hon. John Lynch in a street in Benicia. In resisting arrest soon after he shot and seriously wounded Deputy Sheriff John Ferrin and slightly wounded Officer Murphy. Officer Ferrin shot and seriously wounded Chambers and took him into custody. He gave the name of James Jackson.

Received at the California State Prison, November 1, 1883; No. of commitment, 11012; Crime, assault to murder and robbery; Term, 20 years, County sent from, Solano.

The overland stagecoach left Boise, Idaho, at six o'clock on Friday, July 22, 1881, bound for Kelton, Utah, with six passengers aboard, including a family of husband, wife and three children, and a hostler in the employ of the stage line. At 1:00 A.M. the stagecoach was slowly making its way over the high hills north of Soul's Rest when all of a sudden the driver saw the head of a man rise up from behind a big rock, the muzzle of a shotgun was pointed at his face, and a hoarse voice called put, "throw out that box you s__ of a b___." The driver did not wait for a second demand, got hold of the Wells Fargo box for Wood River, threw it down and drove on. There was no attempt to molest the passengers and there was no demand for the mail sacks. Five hundred yards from that point the down-coach driver met the incoming stagecoach and informed the driver of what had occurred so that he could be on his guard. However, when the up-coach got to the place where the robbery had occurred the robber had already disappeared in the darkness with the box. It was later determined that the box held $600 for N. Falk & Bros., consisting of twenty-six $20 gold pieces and $80 in ten dollar coins, and some other very small amounts of coin. The up-coach continued into Boise and reported the robbery so Mr. Hailey and Boise's City Marshal Robbins started for the scene. Only one man had been seen and the posse, by Monday, had recovered the broken box and was on the trail of the road agent, who had been heading in the direction of the South Fork of the Boise River. A. H. Boomer, Wells Fargo's agent, on July 27 posted a reward of $300 for the arrest and conviction of the robber and $150 for the recovery of the stolen money. John Danskin came forward and reported that on the night prior to the robbery he met a man on the road and stopped to talk with him for a few minutes. After the robbery he returned to the place he saw the man, traced his steps and found where he had gone behind the robber's rock and lay in wait for the coach, but the trail died out after a short distance from that place. Danskin gave a detailed description and Boomer published a good description of the robber and his horse: About 25 or 26 years old; complexion rather fair than otherwise; rather sharp features, brown hair and eyes, wore chin whiskers and moustache; beard scattering of thin, light brown in color; height about 5 feet 8 or 9 inches, rather slim build, weight about 140 or 150 pounds; voice rather soft; talks slow; grins somewhat after speaking; evidently cool and self-possessed under all circumstances; wore dark pants, a pair of old boots, about No. 8, badly run over at the sides; a very dirty shirt, originally white and blue checks, an old brown blouse, dark slouch hat, originally tall, had a seamless sack in which he carried some food; carried a new Winchester rifle, sits considerably bent over when riding, rode a slim built bay horse, about fifteen hands high, branded diamond L or E on near stifle; old saddle, bridle was of new black leather, nickel plated mountings.

Circulars were sent out, particularly to men along the major thoroughfares where the road agent might pass and Frank Ward, a cattle rancher on the Camas Prairie, met a man answering the description. However, the man was riding a dun horse and he gave the name Charles Chambers. Ward learned that Chambers was heading for Bellevue so he notified Messrs. Gil, Bixby and Poe and put them on the trail. In Bellevue Chambers tried to change his appearance by taking a bath, getting a shave and haircut, and donning a new set of clothes, throwing away his old clothes. He then went for a good meal at the Virginia Chop Stand but thought he was being watched so after he ate he returned to the place he threw his old clothes and found them gone. After some time, with no action taken, he dismissed the coincidence and went to the Eureka House to rent a bed for the night. A few minutes after his arrival at the hotel deputy sheriff Trav Johnson arrested Chambers who, the deputy learned, was from a prominent family and well known in Bellevue. The prisoner was cool and quiet, even when they found $530 in coin in his pockets which, along with the three $10 and two $20 coins he had spent, corresponded exactly to the missing money in specie and amount. Chambers had his examination in early August and, though the evidence was circumstantial, it was strong and he was held over for the grand jury, bail set at $2,500. He did not have the funds to post bond so he remained behind bars. Chambers was indicted, tried at the fall term of the court, and convicted of robbery. He was sentenced to serve nine years at the prison in Boise, Idaho Territory, and arrived on November 10, 1881. Chambers managed to escape from prison on July 6, 1882, but six weeks later he was recaptured in Portland, Oregon, and returned to the prison on August 22, 1882. On March 22, 1883, he again escaped and this time made his way to Benecia, Solano County, California, where, on August 1, he robbed the Honorable John Lynch. During his arrest he shot and seriously wounded deputy sheriff John Ferrin and slightly wounded officer Murphy. Ferrin returned fire and wounded Chambers, who then surrendered. Chambers gave the name James Jackson but it was soon learned that he was Charles Chambers. He was tried as James Jackson for robbery and assault to murder, was convicted as charged, and sentenced to serve twenty years at San Quentin Prison, arriving on November 1, 1883, as prisoner No. 11012. He was released, upon expiration of sentence, on March 1, 1896.

Idaho Tri-Weekly Statesman [Boise, ID]: July 26, 1881; July 28, 1881; August 2, 1881; August 5, 1881.

Chapman, Frank

Nativity, England; Age, 31 years; Occupation, Laborer; Height, 5 feet 5 inches; Complexion, Light; Color of eyes, Blue; Color of hair, Brown. Small features, bridge of nose low, nose slightly turned to the left, high forehead, blue dot back of left forearm, F. C. back of left forearm, scar on first knuckle of left hand, scar on first joint of right forefinger; medium built.
Robbed W. F. & Co's Express on stage from Shasta to Redding, November 6, 1876, in company with John A. Toney and John Allen.
Robbed W. F. & Co's Express on stage from Shasta to Redding, November 8, 1876, in company with John A. Toney and John Allen.
Robbed W. F. & Co's Express on stage from Yreka to Redding, November 11, 1876, in company with John A. Toney and John Allen.
Received at California State Prison, December 25, 1876. No. of commitment, 7314. Crime, robbery — three commitments; Term, 4 years; County sent from, Shasta.
His light sentence was in consideration of his having testified against John A. Toney and their accessory John Allen, alias "Sheet Iron Jack."
Pardoned, conditionally, to leave the State, May 4, 1877, by Governor William Irwin.
[*See* Allen, John]

Chapman, J. E.

Nativity, Canada; Age, 40 years; Height, 5 feet 8 inches; Complexion, Dark; Color of eyes, Brown; Color of hair, Brown. Scar on left foot, ten large scars on right leg, small scar on back of neck.
Robbed Overland Express train from San Francisco [Cal.] to Odgen [U. T.] near Verdi [Nev.], November 6, 1870, with Tilton P. Cockrell, A. J. Davis, John Squires, R. A. Jones, E. B. Parsons, and James Gilchrist.
Received at the Nevada State Prison, December 25, 1870; No. of commitment, 68; Crime, robbery; Term, 18 years; County sent from, Washoe.
Escaped in "Big Break" of September 17, 1871; recaptured and returned to prison, September 28, 1882 [*sic*].

Pardoned, July 13, 1877.
[*See* Davis, A. J.]

Clark, B. F.—*alias* B. F. Claughton

Nativity, Missouri; Age, 35 years; Occupation, Farmer; Height 5 feet 9¼ inches; Complexion, Fair; Color of eyes, Hazel; Color of hair, Auburn. Round features, scar on forehead at base of the hair, heavy eyebrows, two moles on the left cheek, mole on the left ear, scar on top of the head, mole on the left shoulder, three moles on left upper arm, mole on back of neck, numerous moles on the back, large mole on the belly; stout built.

No. of commitment, 4627. Received at the California State Prison, October 27, 1870; Crime, attempt to rob U.S. Mail; Term, 4 years; County sent from, San Francisco.

Discharged, by expiration of sentence, March 18, 1874.

Attempted to rob W. F. & Co's Express on stage from Spadra to San Bernardino, August 29, 1874, in company with Richard Johnson, alias McMahon. After arrest he seized the Deputy Sheriff's pistol and wounded him in an effort to escape.

Received at the California State Prison, October 15, 1874; No. of commitment, 6199; Crime, assault to murder and rob; Term, 12 years; County sent from, San Bernardino.

Discharged, per Act, June 15, 1882.

At 10:00 P.M. on Saturday, August 29, 1874, the stagecoach westbound for Los Angeles had left Spadra in San Bernardino County and was four and one half miles from the latter place when a man suddenly sprang from the brush and tried to grab the harness of the off-leader, the right front horse. At the same time he yelled to driver Tommy Peters, "Halt!" The horses were at a trot and the fast gait prevented him from getting hold of the harness so the road agent fired a shot at the horse attempting to drop him and thereby stop the coach, but this "spooked" the horses and they hurried forward. Peters yelled at the horses, whipped up the team, and dropped into the boot just as the road agent fired a second shot at him. As Peters proceeded toward town he saw, from the labored breathing of the off-leader, that the horse was seriously wounded so he pushed the team to get as close to town, and as far from the road agent, as he could before the horse collapsed. The stagecoach was just at Fabron's place on the outskirts of San Bernardino when the horse collapsed and died of loss of blood from a neck wound. None of the passengers—two men, three women and two children—were injured by the shots or the harrowing rush to town. As soon as the coach reached town the attack was reported and Sheriff Mayfield and deputy Yager formed a posse, deputizing James Stewart, Eugene Lander and Gus Starke. They hurried to the scene of the robbery and found a clear trail of boot tracks from two men. As soon as there was enough light Mayfield, Yager and Lander took up the trail of boot tracks and followed it toward the Cajon Pass. The trail was circuitous but the lawmen were tenacious and after following the tracks all day they came upon the fugitives at Vincent's house in the pass, where they had just ordered something to eat. They were disarmed, arrested without resistance, and placed under guard. The posse was very tired so they decided to start back the next morning. Lander was put on guard during an early hour and one of the prisoners, patiently awaiting the opportunity, made a desperate attempt to escape by attacking Lander. Somehow he managed to get possession of his own gun, taken from him when arrested. The prisoner pointed the cocked pistol at Lander but quick as thought Lander jumped him and a terrible struggle ensued. The prisoner managed to fire one round which missed Lander and struck Yager in the hip, causing a minor grazing wound. Yager came to Lander's aid and received a severe blow to the head, but the prisoner was then overpowered and, again, disarmed. The prisoners, who gave the names B. F. Clark and Richard McMahon, were taken into San Bernardino the following day and lodged in jail to await their examination.

On Tuesday, September 1, the prisoners were taken before Justice Mathews where bail was set at $1,500 for Clark, who tried to escape, and $1,000 for McMahon who had cooperated. They were remanded to the sheriff to await action by the grand jury, which was then in session. The grand jury returned indictments against the two prisoners, and McMahon gave his true name as Richard Johnson, and they were tried in early October. Both men were convicted, Clark of an assault to murder and rob and Johnson of attempted robbery only. Johnson was sentenced to serve six years and arrived at the prison on October 15, 1874, registering as prisoner No. 6200. During his transportation to the boat in San Francisco, to be taken across the bay to the prison, he tried to escape. He had filed off one of his shackles the previous night and would have gotten away from his guard except for the presence of a San Francisco policeman. Johnson, who had been in San Quentin three times previously, was discharged by expiration of sentence on December 14, 1878. Clark was sentenced to serve a term of twelve years and also arrived on October 15, 1874, registering as prisoner No. 6199. He was discharged by expiration of sentence, with good time credits under the Goodwin Act, on June 15, 1882.

San Bernardino Guardian [CA]: September 5, 1874; October 24, 1874.

Clark, John—*alias* Jake Clark, Connub

Nativity, Massachusetts; Age, 39 years; Occupation, Laborer; Height, 5 feet 7½ inches; Complexion, Dark; Color of eyes, Blue; Color of hair, Brown. Heavy eyebrows, long features, mole on left cheek, do. right side of neck, vaccine mark left upper arm, star at base of left thumb, large mole on back.
Received at the California State Prison, October 9, 1869. No. of commitment, 4237; Crime, burglary; Term, 2 years; County sent from, Butte.
Discharged, upon expiration of sentence, June 24, 1871.
Received at the California State Prison, October 9, 1871. No. of commitment 5010; Crime, robbery; Term, 2 years; County sent from, Sonoma.
Discharged, upon expiration of sentence, June 28, 1873.
Robbed W. F. & Co's Express on stage from Forest Hill to Auburn, September 12, 1873, in company with John "Shorty" Hays and Eddie Lee.
Robbed W. F. & Co's Express on stage from Yreka to Redding, October 10, 1873, in company with John "Shorty" Hays and Charlie Thompson.
Received at the California State Prison, February 16, 1874; No. of commitment, 5886; Crime, robbery; Term, 21 years; County sent from, Shasta.
Taken out by order of court to be tried on additional charge in Placer County, March 7, 1874. Returned to prison March 17, 1874, under a new commitment, viz.:
Received at California State Prison, March 17, 1874; No. of commitment, 5930; Crime robbery; Term, 30 years; County sent from, Placer.
Escaped, January 14, 1881.

John Clark, alias Jake Clark or "Connub," was convicted of a burglary in Butte county in 1869 and arrived at San Quentin on October 9. Over the next twenty-one months he received an extensive "jail-house" education on the techniques of criminal activity and met John "Shorty" Hays, who was serving a term of five years for a grand larceny in Yuba County. The two men also befriended Eddie Lee, alias Thomas Martin, who was serving a term of six years for a burglary in San Francisco County. Lee was pardoned and released on February 22, 1872, Hays was released on October 31, 1872, and Clark was released on June 28, 1873. As soon as all three men were free they rendezvoused and prepared to rob stagecoaches. There seemed to be no reason to delay so within three months they set their trap along the Forest Hill to Auburn stagecoach route in Placer County. On September 12, 1873, three masked, heavily armed road agents stepped out and called for the driver of the Auburn-bound coach to halt. They demanded the Wells, Fargo & Company treasure box and it was delivered without any show of resistance. It seemed so easy that the three men, as they moved north, easily recruited a fourth man interested in making fast money, and the recently released convict gave the name Charles Thompson. The four men made their way to the Yreka to Redding stagecoach route and made camp near Buckeye, just north of Redding in Shasta County. On October 10, 1873, they stopped the southbound stagecoach and, after securing the Wells, Fargo treasure box, made the passengers disembark and line up. They went through them, including a reporter for the *Sacramento Record* who later complained, "Here I want to enter a protest against green men undertaking such close work. Their hands trembled so I was fearful they would shoot accidentally and hurt someone." The robbers went through a total of eight passengers, all men, and from five Chinese men they took a total of $1,460 and from the other three they got $460—a total of $1,960. They next broke open the Wells, Fargo treasure box and took out $2,000. As soon as they had all the loot they fled south, and the passengers quickly boarded and the coach hurried into Buckeye to report the robbery. The four road agents separated with Lee and Thompson staying in Sacramento, but after a few days Thompson was arrested and he quickly informed on his fellow road agents. Hays and Clark had gone on to San Francisco and, not knowing that they had been identified and described, made little effort to remain inconspicuous. Hays, well known to lawmen in the city, was next to be arrested and he had used $800 of his share of the plunder to buy an interest in a restaurant at the foot of Jackson Street on the wharf, where he was found and captured. Clark was soon in custody and he joined Hays in the San Francisco County Jail, but Lee managed to elude the authorities for several weeks.

The three men first arrested, Clark, Hays and Thompson, were taken to Shasta County and charged in the robbery of the stagecoach near Buckeye. They were indicted on a large body of evidence but, on December 14, 1873, the three men were in the jail's exercise room without supervision just before supper. They pried open a door, armed themselves, and when their food arrived they captured the undersheriff and cook and locked them in a cell. As they worked on their shackles the sheriff arrived and was also captured and locked in a cell. Hays could not break his chains so, when the three men were outside, they separated. Hays hid near the jail while the other two men went into the nearby woods and soon Clark and Thompson were led back to their cells. Once the lawmen were occupied with the two fugitives Hays fled into the woods. He made his way south walking through deep snow as he followed the railroad tracks and after several days he went to a cabin to warm himself, and was nearly captured but managed to pull his gun and warn off his attacker. He went on to Red Bluff and broke into a blacksmith shop where he finally broke his chains. In ten days he made it to Marysville and on Christmas eve he walked into the United States Hotel and had his first good meal since breaking jail, later bedded down, and was sleeping soundly when arrested. Hays was returned to jail and, with his two confederates, was tried in February 1874 for the October stagecoach robbery. Each man received a sentence of twenty-one years to be served at San Quentin prison. Thompson received no credit for his cooperation in informing on his fellow robbers. The men were taken together to the prison, arriving on February 16, and Hays was registered as prisoner No. 5884, Thompson as No. 5885, and Clark as No. 5886.

Hays and Clark were taken out prison on March 7, 1874, by court order to be tried in Placer County for robbing the Forest Hill to Auburn stagecoach on September 12, 1873. They were both convicted and sentenced to serve terms of thirty years and returned to prison, Hays now prisoner No. 5929 and Clark prisoner No. 5930. Hays escaped from prison twice: once in May 1876 and again in December 1884 and lost one hundred thirty-seven months of good time credit but it was later restored and he was released on October 17, 1891. Clark escaped from prison on January 14, 1881, and was not heard of again. Thompson had his sentenced commuted and all rights restored by Governor George C. Perkins and he was discharged on September 24, 1881. Eddie Lee was captured a few weeks after the other three road agents but a case could not be made against him in Shasta County. He was taken to Placer County and charged with the robbery of the Forest Hill to Auburn stagecoach on September 12, 1873. He was indicted, tried, and convicted in early March 1874 and sentenced to serve a term of only four years. He arrived at the prison on March 21, 1874, and registered as prisoner No. 5933. He was discharged, upon expiration of his sentence, on August 13, 1877.

Daily Alta California [San Francisco, CA]: October 31, 1873. *Daily Morning Call [San Francisco, CA]*: June 5, 1881; January 9, 1885. *Marysville Appeal [CA]*: December 25, 1873. *Sacramento Record [CA]*: October 11, 1873. *Sacramento Bee* [CA]: November 13, 1873. *San Francisco Chronicle [CA]*: October 31, 1873; *San Francisco Examiner [CA]*: October 18, 1891; November 1, 1891. *Shasta Courier [CA]*: January 20, 1877. *Yreka Journal [CA]*: February 18, 1874, June 7, 1876. *Yreka Union [CA]*: June 10, 1876.

Clifford, Frank—*alias* Charles G. Ames, Frank Marrion, Chatfield

Nativity, Maryland; Age, 42 years; Occupation, Carpenter; Height, 5 feet 8 inches; Complexion, Light; Color of eyes, Dark; Color of hair, Light Brown. Scar ¾ inch long below left shoulder-blade, lump on left of spine between shoulders, 3 small vaccine marks, bullet wound near pit of stomach, broad high forehead, weight 157 lbs.

Received at California State Prison, December 7, 1869, from Los Angeles County; Crime, robbing U.S. Mail; Term, 15 years.

Granted a new trial and taken out for second trial, May 9, 1870. Prosecuting witness had "skipped" and the indictment was dismissed.

Received at Nevada State Prison April 22, 1870; Crime, robbery; Term, 10 years. County sent from, White Pine.

Escaped September 9, 1870. Recaptured and returned same day.

Escaped in "Big Break" September 17, 1871. Recaptured and returned to prison October 1871.

Escaped from Carson City Jail with John Burke, alias "Frank Harker," while awaiting trial for prison-breaking, and the two fled to Eureka County and robbed W. F. & Co's Express and passengers on stage from Mineral Hill to Eureka. Recaptured and returned to Nevada State Prison, as escapes, without trial for the stage robbery.

Pardoned August 30, 1878, at the instance of Senator Cleveland of White Pine.

February 26, 1878, stole a bar of W. F. & Co's bullion from Pioche stage.

Received at Nevada State Prison, May 6, 1879. No. of commitment, 91; Crime, grand larceny; Term, 11 years; County sent from, White Pine.

Frank Clifford burst onto the western criminal scene with the robbery of the eastbound stagecoach at Pilot's Knob near Los Angeles, California. An account of the robbery stated that the coach for Gilroy left at its usual hour, about sundown, with eight passengers aboard.

When two miles out the coach was stopped by four highwaymen with cocked pistols and the passengers were relieved of their valuables. The leader ordered one of the passengers to deliver a belt filled with coin, which contained $1,000, and it was clear that he knew of its existence, and B. C. Truman contributed $180. The express boxes were broken open but only a small amount of treasure was found inside so in all the robbers secured a total of $1,500 for their trouble. The mail bags, which were not molested, reportedly contained several hundred thousand dollars in greenbacks. The four road agents returned to Los Angeles and began to spend their plunder and this raised suspicions, as they had no money before the robbery and had no means to earn it. They were arrested and identified as Charles G. Ames, D. Warren, D. Harrington, and Frank Clifford. Clifford, to take advantage of the situation, quickly informed on his fellow thieves and agreed to testify against them at trial, and in return he was released. After he testified Clifford fled to White Pine County, Nevada, either as a stipulation in his agreement with authorities or to avoid being killed by other criminals.

By mid–February Clifford, who was a carpenter by trade, was already figuring on some opportunity to rob another stagecoach. He recruited a youngster named John Moore and, through tales of adventure and untold wealth, convinced the gullible boy to aid him in his next robbery. On February 19, 1870, they stole the milkman's horses and left the city. Two days later, at 6:30 P.M. Clifford and Moore stopped the Beachy, Wines & Company stagecoach seven miles south of Telegraph Station, which was twelve miles south of Cherry Creek. They gave the impression there was a third road agent taking aim at the driver as they demanded the treasure box. They opened the box and removed two bars of bullion weighing ninety-three pounds and valued at $1,696.66. Within hours Len Wines, Tom Andrews and Joe Demars were on their trail and they traveled one hundred five miles in sixteen hours to overtake the robbers, and captured them fifteen miles from Diamond Springs. The two road agents were brought into Pioche and lodged in jail. They were indicted and on March 7 Clifford and Moore were taken before Judge W. H. Beatty and they pled not guilty. The following day the two prisoners nearly escaped so they were moved to an inner cage within the jail, and this gave the jailor the opportunity to encourage Moore to confess, but the boy said he was afraid of Clifford. When he was assured he would be guarded against harm he informed on his partner. Meanwhile, though Clifford did not know the boy had confessed all the details of the robbery, he sent for County Attorney Frank Kennedy and said he would confess, plead guilty, and accept whatever sentence the court deemed appropriate if Moore was not charged and released. He assumed the entire blame for the robbery and told Kennedy that the boy would never have robbed the stagecoach without his influence and inducement. Moore was released and Clifford kept his word, pled guilty, and was sentenced to serve ten years at the Nevada State Prison near Carson City. He arrived there on April 22, 1870, and registered as prisoner No. 32.

Clifford escaped on September 9, 1870, but was captured within hours and returned to the prison. Clifford helped plan and execute the "Big Break-out" on September 17, 1871, when twenty-nine convicts escaped and several people were killed. He partnered with John Burke alias Francis Harker, convicted of manslaughter in Esmeralda County and sentenced to serve five years, and George Roth, convicted of second degree murder in Washoe County and sentenced to serve forty-three years. Clifford was only free eleven days and by October 23, 1871, they were all back in custody, facing an additional criminal charge for breaking prison, and they were housed at the county jail in Carson City awaiting trial. On March 1, 1872, Clifford, Burke and Roth, with six other prisoners, broke out of the county jail. The escapees had been confined in the south cells which had the western wall in common with the Magnolia Saloon and one of them obtained a file and removed their irons, then removed the flagstone floor and tunneled under the bars until all were in the last cell. They broke through the wall into a rear card room of the saloon and escaped into the alley. The nine escapees divided into smaller parties, with Clifford, Burke and Roth remaining together and heading toward Eureka. The three fugitives eluded the authorities for a month but needed a stake, so they decided to rob a stagecoach.

It was a little after 7:00 P.M. on March 28 when the Woodruff & Ennor stagecoach from Austin bound for Eureka was three miles from Hay Ranch Station, or about eighteen miles southwest from Palisade in Eureka County. Four masked road agents were lying on the ground along the roadside and the first the driver saw of them was when they sprang up all at once, three with shotguns and the fourth with two pistols all pointed toward the driver. The leader ordered him to stop and then, while one man remained behind a bush and covered the driver with his shotgun, the other three approached the coach. There were several passengers on board from Eureka and White Pine, including Mr. Cromer of the firm of Maupin & Cromer with his wife and children. All the window curtains were down except on the window next to Mrs. Cromer and she was the first to notice the robbers as the man with two pistols thrust them in the window nearly into her face. The passengers were assured that if they did not resist they would not be hurt. The Wells, Fargo treasure box was demanded and as soon as it was passed down they chopped it open with an ax. When it was determined that the box contained only $500 in currency and $90 in coin the robbers decided to go through the passengers so they were ordered out of the coach one at a time and their valuables collected, including about $200, four watches, and a derringer. They were then lined up along the road at the rear of the coach and covered by one robber with a shotgun, though Mrs. Cromer was allowed to remain in the coach. The robbers then unlashed the rear boot and went through the trunks and other baggage, the ax being used freely to smash items to bits. One trunk was supposed to contain a sack of money and after some effort one robber said to another, "I have struck it!," and the searching ceased. The robbers, who had two horses tied nearby, cut the harness to pieces and took the swing horses from the six-up, then the four men rode off eastward.

The driver and passengers believed that the party included the escaped prisoners Clifford and Parsons, but two of the passengers were so badly frightened that they hid their heads beneath the seats until dragged out by the robbers. Two of the robbers also seemed frightened and trembled for some time after the stagecoach was first stopped. The leader of the robbers was described as tall and slim with striped prison-looking pants and a large, broad-brimmed white felt hat. He did most of the heavy work and all of the talking. A few days later two more horses were stolen from the Hay Ranch Station but the *Sentinel* complained that no track of the robbers had been found "for the reason, we suppose, that no one has been out to look for them." On Saturday, March 30 deputy sheriff John Nicholson of White Pine was on his way to Steptoe Valley and while at Hercules Gap he noticed three men on the side of the road, and immediately recognized one as Clifford but took no action. A man nearby was repairing the road and the deputy asked him to keep a watch on the movements of the three fugitives and then the deputy rode on to the next settlement for assistance. Nicholson deputized Messrs. Cowder, Douglass and Brockman and asked for more men to join them later and the posse returned to Hercules Gap, went into camp, and set out pickets to guard the Gap and the camp. At daybreak Sunday three more men joined Nicholson's posse and then the road worker informed them that the three fugitives had gone into the canyon and had not come out, so he concluded they had camped there. The posse found the three men asleep in their camp and arrested them without resistance, although they had a shot gun, three revolvers and a derringer near at hand. They also had the stagecoach horses stolen from the coach and other plunder and, when questioned about the fourth man, said it was a dummy put up behind the bush with a stick to resemble a gun. The three men were brought into town on the next stagecoach and a crowd of nearly one thousand people were on hand. There was sudden rush to see them, among them the Cromers. Mrs. Cromer could not identify the men as the robbers but Mr. Cromer identified his watch, which had been taken from one of the prisoners. Sheriff Patterson took the prisoners to Carson City and they were returned to the prison. None of the men were tried for stagecoach robbery because they were already serving long sentences, but apparently Burke forfeited his good time credits earned under the Goodwin Act because he was not released until February 1, 1876, upon expiration of his sentence. Burke went to Utah where he robbed the eastbound and westbound coaches between Salt Lake City and Pioche on May 31, 1876. He was captured on June 2 and, after several escapes and recaptures, he was tried, convicted of mail robbery and sentenced to a life term at the Detroit House of Corrections. He arrived in Detroit in October 1877 but escaped from the House of Corrections on November 2, 1877, and was not heard of again. Roth was pardoned on April 10, 1882, and was not heard of again in the criminal records of Nevada. Clifford remained in prison until March 6, 1887, when his sentence expired and he was released.

Eureka Sentinel [NV]: March 30, 1872; April 2, 1872; April 4, 1872; April 6, 1872; April 9, 1872. *Territorial Enterprise [Virginia City, NV]*: December 10, 1870; March 15, 1872; April 2, 1872; April 3, 1878; July 3, 1878; May 1, 1879. *White Pine Daily News [Hamilton, NV]*: February 24–27, 1870; March 4, 1870; March 7, 1870; March 9, 1870; March 31, 1870; April 13, 1870.

Cockrell, Tilton P.

Nativity, Illinois; Age, 52 years; Occupation, Laborer; Height 5 feet 1½ inches; Complexion, Dark; Color of eyes, Gray; Color of hair, Black; Weight, 170 lbs. High forehead, scar on left eye, two scars on outside left thigh, scar on left knee, top of head bald.

Robbed Overland Express train from San Francisco [Cal.] to Odgen [U. T.] near Verdi [Nev.], November 6, 1870, with J. E. Chapman, A. J. Davis, John Squires, R. A. Jones, E. B. Parsons, and James Gilchrist.

Received at the Nevada State Prison, December 25, 1870; No. of commitment, 67; Crime, robbery; Term, 22 years; County sent from, Washoe.

Escaped in "Big Break" of September 17, 1871; recaptured and returned to prison, October 23, 1871.

Pardoned, July 12, 1882.

[*See* Davis, A. J.]

Collins, George [Negro]

Nativity, Maryland; Age, 38 years; Occupation, Laborer; Height 5 feet 8 inches; Complexion, Dark; Color of eyes, Brown; Color of hair, Black. Long features, high forehead, scar on left jaw, stomach badly scarified; slim built.

Stole W. F. & Co's Express box from steamer Julia,

Received at the California State Prison, January 24, 1879; No. of commitment, 8646; Crime,. Grand larceny; Term, 1 year; County sent from, San Francisco.

Discharged, per Act, and *pardoned*, November 24, 1879.

In late 1878 George Collins stole a Wells, Fargo & Company Express treasure box from the steamer Julia while she was docked at San Francisco. He did not "break-in," which would have been a burglary, nor was anyone present so it could not be a robbery. He was soon suspected of the theft, arrested, and lodged in jail. The prisoner was held, following his examination, to answer to the grand jury and on December 4 they returned an indictment against Collins charging him with grand larceny. When Collins was brought into court on January 10, 1879, he cooperated and pled guilty, to reduce his prison term, and he was sentenced to serve one year. He arrived at San Quentin Prison on January 24, 1879, registering as prisoner No. 8646. Collins served ten months and, with good time credit afforded under the Goodwin Act, he was released by expiration of sentence on November 24, 1879.

San Francisco Chronicle [CA]: December 4, 1878, January 10, 1879.

Collins, P.—*alias* Punch Collins [Negro]

Nativity, Texas; Age 26 years; Occupation, Cattle-man; Height, 6 feet; Complexion, Black; Color of eyes, Black; Color of hair, Black and kinky. Scar on line of hair on left side of forehead, scar one inch long on left wrist.

Attempted to rob W. F. & Co's Express on train No. 102 on A. T. & S. F. R. R. at a point about five miles north of Socorro, N. M. in company with Edward [*sic*] White, J. W. Pointer, Bill Allen, and Jefferson Kerkendall [*sic*].

On the night of October 30, 1884, the five men came to the point on the railroad selected for the robbery, and with a large monkey-wrench which they had brought from Punch Collin's ranch they tried to unscrew the splice-taps, hoping thereby to ditch the train by displacing a rail. Failing in this they placed rocks on the rail its entire length. They then disguised themselves by means of handkerchiefs with eye-holes cut in them. Punch Collins was detailed to take in and hold the fireman and engineer, and Pointer and Allen were to keep the passengers and trainmen from coming out of the cars, while White and Kerkendall were going through the Express matter. Failing to obtain what they wanted in the Express car, they were either to rob the mail or passengers, but which, they had not decided upon. Mr. Skuse, the engineer, seeing the obstruction on the track brought the train to a sudden stop, and the fireman, who got down to remove the obstructions, was confronted by Kerkendall and White, who ordered him to hold up his hands and get back upon the engine, which he did without parley. During this time Collins, on the opposite side of the train, brought his pistol down on the engineer, saying, "Hold up, now, for I have got you." The engineer said, "Don't shoot, and I will get down."

The brakes having at this time become released, the engineer and fireman squatted down on the footboard and pulled the engine throttle wide open, and she plowed her way through the obstructions and took the train away in safety. About twenty shots were fired at the train, only five of which took effect, one hitting the gong on top of the cab. No one was hurt.

[William Allen eluded capture and fled the region, but the other four train robbers were captured, tried and convicted.]

Received at Kansas State Prison, November 21, 1884; No. of commitment, 3396; Crime, assault to commit robbery, Term, 7 years; County sent from, Socorro.

On the night of October 30, 1884, the Atchison, Topeka, & Santa Fe train No. 102 left Socorro, New Mexico with engineer James Skuse at the throttle and conductor J. D. Hedrick in charge of the passenger cars. The train had only gone a few miles when it came to an abrupt stop and then, after a brief delay, started up again at full throttle as more than fifty shots were fired into the engine and cars, every car being hit and many windows broken. One bullet passed through a sleeping car just missing two ladies asleep in their bunk and Hedrick, who stepped onto a platform to investigate the stoppage, was nearly killed.

The passengers lay down on the floor and looked for weapons to return fire, but the only guns present were two pistols, one in the satchel of H. D. Ferguson and the other without cartridges, and neither was deployed in time. The engineer later told the passengers what had happened:

> I saw ahead of me an obstruction on the right side, which consisted of a pile of stones fully twelve inches above the track. I stopped, of course, and then told the fireman to get down and remove the stones. It was moonlight so that I could see plainly. At the moment I stopped I saw three men jump from behind a clump of trees and pointing their guns at me they said, "Stop! We want you. We've got you!" Quick as lighting I saw our predicament and decided what to do. I told them, "all right, don't shoot," and then to the fireman "drop down." I gave the throttle a jerk wide open and dropped down myself. As I jerked they fired into the cab. I didn't know whether we should jump the track or not, but I wasn't going to have my passengers robbed. The obstruction damaged the cow catcher considerably. I saw three men on my right, two on the left, and one on horseback.

A combined reward of $2,000 was offered for each man so it was not long before lawmen went to the scene of the robbery to investigate and search for the aspiring train robbers. They found, among other evidence, one exceptionally large boot track and immediately suspected the man who had made it, but lawmen were certain they knew who all the robbers were and were soon on their trail and circulating their names and descriptions throughout the region. It was not long before deputy sheriff Rose found Edwin White at "old man Scott's cabin" fifty miles from the railroad and arrested him without resistance. On November 10 deputy sheriff Harry J. Franklin and Wes Bruton cornered Punch S. Collins, alias Punch Brockman, at his ranch on the Hilosa above the old Fowler place and arrested him. Franklin and Bruton took both prisoners into Soccoro where Sheriff Pete Simpson lodged them in jail. White was anxious to improve his situation and needed little coaxing before he informed on his fellow train robbers.

The *Las Vegas Daily Optic* published an interview with Collins, whom they described as "a massive specimen of his [Negro] race, who, until recently, enjoyed the good opinion of his employers." The *Optic* noted that Collins claimed to be innocent, but then "added in a harmonious way, looking at his canal boat shoes, 'Well, boss, I guess dose big feet gabe me away. De been always gettin' me into trouble!' " The newspaper learned that the gang of five had spent October 29 in a canyon northeast of Socorro and rode down to the tracks about dark on the day of the robbery attempt. By the aid of a monkey wrench, which they stole from Bruton's ranch, they tried to remove a fish plate and then remove a rail, but when this failed they piled rocks on the track to wreck the train. The wrench was found at the scene and taken for evidence. On November 17 the *Daily Optic* reported that deputy sheriff Stocking had arrested another train robber and took him to Albuquerque, and also reported that Wes Bruton had arrested Jeff Kirkendall, sometimes spelled Kukendall, at the old Joe Fowler horse ranch west of Socorro. The first prisoner mentioned was either J. W. Pointer or Lon Bass, the latter believed to be the fifth man or at least an accomplice or accessory. The arrest of Bass delayed the search for the fifth robber, Bill Allen, who managed to flee from the region. Bass was cleared by White's confessions and later released but based on the information from White the search for Bill Allen continued. On November 22 the *Optic* reported that the robbers were taken to Santa Fe and then returned to Socorro to be arraigned in the district court. White had named four other men involved in the attempted train wrecking, apparently in the hope of being released for his continued cooperation, and they were being investigated but none of these men were ever implicated in the train wrecking scheme. When the four defendants were brought into court for their arraignment they pled guilty to the charge of "assault to commit robbery," hoping to reduce their sentences by cooperating, and each was given a term of seven years to be served in the Kansas State Prison, excepting White who received a reduced sentence of five years for informing on his fellow train wreckers. Collins, Pointer and Kirkendall arrived at the prison on November 21, 1884, registering as prisoners No. 3396, 3397 and 3398 respectively; while White arrived on December 1, 1884, and registered as prisoner No. 3407. On March 8, 1885, Allen was found in Rio Pecos, New Mexico eighteen miles below Fort Sumner and within twenty-two days he had been examined, indicted, tried and convicted of "obstructing a railroad track." He joined the other four convicts in the same prison in Kansas. On February 28, 1886, Governor Edmund G. Ross ordered the five bungling train robbers removed to the New Mexico State Prison at Santa Fe, and they arrived on March 2, 1886. Edwin White, who had attempted to escape on November 27, 1886, died of consumption in the prison hospital on March 17, 1887; on January 21, 1889, Jefferson Kirkendall was pardoned by Governor Ross; on August 21, 1889, Collins and Pointer were released, by expiration of sentence, with good time credits allowed by the Goodwin Act; and on August 8, 1889, Governor L. Bradford Prince declined to pardon Allen, but on December 27, 1889, he granted a pardon for the last of the train robbers.

Journal [Albuquerque, NM]: October 31, 1884; November 1, 1884. *Las Vegas Daily Optic [NM]*: November 11–13, 1884; November 17, 1884; November 21–22, 1884; March 4, 1886. *Silver City Enterprise [NM]*: November 7, 1884. *Kansas State Prison Records*: convict No. 3396, 3397, 3398, and 3407. *New Mexico State Prison Records:* Convict No. 107, 108, 109, 110, 111.

Connor, Thomas

Nativity, Ireland; Age, 65 years; Occupation, Laborer; Height, 5 feet 7⅞ inches; Complexion, Florid, Color of eyes, Blue; Color of hair, Gray. Square features, heavy eyebrows, sharp nose, scar under lip, scar on first knuckle of left hand; stout built.

Robbed W. F. & Co's Express on stage from Yreka to Shasta, May 27, 1877, with Tommy Brown.

Received at the California State Prison, April 25, 1878; No. of commitment, 8173; Crime robbery; Term, 7 years; County sent from, Shasta.

Discharged, upon expiration of sentence, January 25, 1883.

[*See* Brown, Tom]

Corbett, William

Nativity, California; Age, 19 years; Occupation, Laborer; Height 5 feet 4 inches; Complexion, Light; Color of eyes, Blue; Color of hair, Brown; Size of foot, 6. Thin, spare features, retreating forehead, long sharp nose, small ears, small mouth and chin, heavy eyebrows, large vaccine mark left upper arm, scar bade left thumb, scar first knuckle fore finger left hand, mole point left shoulderblade, drooped shoulders; slim built.

Robbed W. F. & Co's Express on stage from Cloverdale to Mendocino, October 9, 1884, with John Dwyer.

Escaped from County Jail at Ukiah, November 8, 1884. Recaptured November 13, 1884.

Received at the California State Prison, November 14, 1884; No. of commitment, 11449; Crime, robbery; Term, 5 years; County sent from, Mendocino.

On October 9, 1884, at 3:00 A.M. the stagecoach from Cloverdale and Anderson Valley to Mendocino, when it was three miles from Booneville in Mendocino County, was stopped by two masked, heavily armed road agents. They demanded and received the Wells, Fargo Express treasure box and the local mail bag. After the box and mail bag was delivered the robbers told the driver to continue on. The box was reported to contain $3,664 but the amount taken from the mails was not known, but being only the local mail it would have been an insignificant sum. The driver hurried into Anderson and reported the hold-up. The citizens of Anderson, knowing the sheriff was away electioneering, organized a posse consisting of John Burger, E. K. Jones, Charles Rector, John Ingram, Nute Ornbaum, and Hugh Hereford and they went to the scene of the robbery. They were soon on the trail of the robbers and captured them. The two road agents identified themselves as nineteen year old William Corbett of San Francisco and twenty-two year old John Dwyer of Missouri. They were captured so soon after the robbery they still had all the plunder with them, and it was recovered to the cent. At first it was thought that parties from Anderson had lynched the two road agents but they soon arrived at Ukiah and were lodged in jail. By the first week of November the prisoners had been examined, indicted, tried and convicted of stagecoach robbery. On November 8, the night before they were to depart for the prison to begin their five year terms, they escaped from the jail. Undersheriff Seawell had no notion that the boys were planning or preparing for an escape when he went to supper but when he returned he noticed that the iron shutter over the barred window of the jail was ajar. On examination he found that the bars had been sawed through and the lock for the shutter had been pried off with one of those iron bars. He checked the prisoner population and found all present excepting the two convicted road agents, and the other prisoners feigned ignorance of the entire affair. Sheriff Standley formed a posse and they traced the men to the Seven-mile House, but the escapees had continued on and were next heard of east of Colverdale. The men were finally cornered and captured in Napa County on November 13 and jailed there to await transfer to San Quentin. Mendocino officers took their prisoners directly from the Napa County jail to the prison on November 14, 1884. Corbett registered as prisoner No. 11449 and Dwyer as prisoner No. 11450. Dwyer had his sentence commuted and he was released on January 6, 1887, while Corbett was released, by expiration of sentence, on June 14, 1888.

Territorial Enterprise [Virginia City, NV]: October 10–11, 1884; October 16, 1884. *Ukiah City Press [CA]*: November 14, 1884; October 17, 1884.

Crawford, James

Attempted to rob W. F. & Co's Express on stage from Eureka to Pioche, February 27, 1877, with John Carlo. Eugene Blair, W. F. & Co's Guard on stage at the time killed Carlo.
Received at Nevada State Prison, June 6, 1877; No. of commitment, 55; Crime, robbery; Term, 7 years.
Died in prison, January 18, 1881.

At 8:00 P.M. on February 27, 1877, the stagecoach from Hamilton to Pioche was climbing the steep grade into Ward and was about two and one half miles from town when a masked man stepped out from behind a tree on the right and said, "Hold up!" A shotgun was immediately fired by the first road agent seen but the direction of the shot was not certain. Messenger Eugene Blair, riding next to the driver, returned fire at the man who had stepped out and Blair jumped down from the coach, then saw a second man. The second road agent shot at the messenger with one barrel at a time from his double barreled shotgun — two separate blasts. Blair returned fire as the man fled and Blair followed him seventy-five yards but lost sight of him. Blair returned to the stagecoach and heard a man calling out that he would surrender and was in a dying condition, so he was taken aboard the stagecoach. Blair then discovered that passenger Stanfield had been struck by three buckshot pellets in his legs and one pellet in his stomach and passenger Conover was also shot once in the leg, but the third passenger named Guyer was not hit by the road agent's buckshot. The wounds suffered were not serious and both men recovered. The stagecoach continued into Ward and, while en route to town, the captured road agent requested to be shot to death. When Blair declined to oblige him the prisoner said, "You won the fight, but if you had come an hour earlier we would have got you." He gave his name as John Carlo, sometimes spelled Carlow, but he would not disclose the name of the other road agent. In Ward Carlo was treated by Dr. M. Rockman, who reported that Carlo had two bullet holes on his right side, one between the fifth and sixth rib and the other near the breast bone in line with the nipple, and one of the balls had passed into his thorax. Carlo's right arm had been shattered near the shoulder so the doctor ordered cold applications applied to the wound, but by midnight it was clear that he had to amputate the arm and did so at midnight. Carlo, during the next hours, was visited by an acquaintance named William Peters and Carlo told him that he had been waiting for the coach at 4:30 P.M. but it did not come until after dark. He said, "I was on my knee when I leveled and fired my gun, which was to my disadvantage, or else I'd fetched him." Peters understood he meant Blair and asked him why he wanted to kill the messenger. Carlo answered, "I have been in the business before. If I had not been coppered and my arm broken, I would have killed the whole outfit." Carlo later called for Peters, and asked him, "Bill, do you think I will have to die?" and Peters replied, "I think you will." Carlo then requested that Peters write to his brother in Ohio and gave him the address, but still he would not inform on his fellow robber. Carlo died at 7:00 A.M. on March 1 and during the autopsy Dr. Rockman found the thorax filled with blood and also found that the ball entering at the ribs had broken the sixth rib and passed through the right lung, and two balls were lodged in Carlo's liver as well. The cause of death was determined to be internal hemorrhaging in the thorax.

As soon as the stagecoach reached town Blair gave a detailed description of the second road agent as a tall, slender, stoop-shouldered man with a moustache. He was immediately identified as James Crawford, a close acquaintance of Carlo who had been seen in his company just prior to the robbery. Posses took the field in search of the fugitive while Blair and stage line owner Jack Gilmer followed Crawford's trail across the mountains from Pony Springs and found the fugitive near Bristol. They rode up on their quarry, their intentions obvious, and the road agent seeing Blair surrendered without resistance even though had a shotgun, a pistol and a knife. He begged them not to take him to Ward City, where he feared he might be lynched, so he was taken into Pioche and lodged in jail. Crawford had his examination before a Justice of the Peace who ordered him held on $5,000 bail to await action by the grand jury. He was indicted, tried, and convicted at the summer term of the district court and sentenced to serve a term of seven years at the state prison. He arrived at Nevada's state prison on June 6, 1877. Crawford died in prison on January 18, 1881. The cause of death is not recorded but consumption [tuberculosis] was common and very contagious in such close quarters and many prisoners died during prison terms or soon after release.

White Pine Daily News [Hamilton, NV]: March 3, 1877; March 10, 1877; March 13, 1877.

Crum, James

Nativity, Missouri; Age, 47 years; Occupation, Laborer; Height, 5 feet 6¾ inches; Complexion, Sallow; Color of eyes, Gray; Color of hair, Black. Square features, high full forehead and retreating, prominent nose, long nostrils, rather deep-set eyes, heavy eyebrows, ears rather small, small lobes slightly detached, square-cut chin and mouth, flesh mole left side of neck neat the base, slight scar near base of third finger left hand, vaccine mark left upper arm, numerous small scars back of neck, breast and belly very hairy, hair on arms and back; medium built.

Received at the California State Prison, December 16, 1871. No. of first commitment, 5061; Crime, grand larceny; Term, 10 years; County sent from, Sacramento.

Commuted by Governor William Irwin, March 38, 1877, to 9½ years and *discharged*, by expiration of sentence, June 8, 1878.

Robbed W. F. & Co's Express on stage from Sonora to Milton, November 27, 1881, in company with William A. "Billy" Miner, William A. Miller and S. C. Jones.

Received at the California State Prison, December 21, 1881; No. of commitment, 10192; Crime, robbery; Term, 12 years County sent from, Tuolumne.

Pardoned conditionally by Governor George Stoneman, June 15, 1884, in consideration of testimony given against his associates in the robbery, and against Dorsey and Patterson, who murdered Cummings, a passenger on the stage from Moore's Flat to Nevada City, September 1, 1879.

[*See* Miner, William]

Cullen, William

Nativity, Canada; Age, 39 years; Occupation, Butcher; Height, 5 feet 11 inches; Complexion, Fair, Color of eyes, Gray, Color of hair, Dark. Square features, large Roman nose, large mouth, pleasant countenance, dim scar center of forehead, two small scars across right cheek, small scar on left upper arm, full breast; straight and stout built.

Robbed W. F. & Co's Express on stage from Red Bluff to Shasta, September, 30, 1871, in company with J. H. Grant, Milton Shepardson, Ziska Calmez, and Billy Fugate.

Received at the California State Prison, April 2, 1872; No. of commitment, 5261; Crime, robbery; Term, 7 years, County sent from, Shasta.

Pardoned by Governor Romualdo Pacheco, April 6, 1875.

[*See* Shepardson, Milton]

Cummings, James H.

Nativity, Ireland; Age, 53; Occupation, Laborer; Height, 5 feet 10 inches; Complexion, Light, Color of eyes, Gray; Color of hair, Black. Bushy eyebrows, sharp, prominent nose, scar over left corner upper lip, mole near lower point right ear, mole right corner mouth, four moles on left forearm, vaccine mark on both arms, points of both little fingers deformed, raw-boned; stout built.

Convicted of forging the name of Captain Dwyer to a "shipping receipt" and drawing the money at W. F. & Co's office, Marysville, California, in 1879.

Received at the California State Prison, January 15, 1881; No. of commitment, 9745; Crime, forgery; Term, 3 years; County sent from, Yuba.

Discharged, upon expiration of sentence, May 14, 1883.

James H. Cummings, during the early days of 1879, created a shipping receipt in the name of "Captain Dwyer" for the payment of money, went to the Marysville, Yuba County office of Wells, Fargo & Company, uttered [cashed-in] the forged document, and collected the amount stated. The forgery was quickly discovered and Cummings was arrested. He was examined, held over for the grand jury, and indicted. The prisoner was given an extension of his time to plead but, failing to do so, a plea of not guilty was entered on his behalf in late April and his trial was set for May 12. On May 15, 1879, the court spent the entire day trying to empanel a jury but only managed to seat six men from the first venire. A special venire was ordered and a jury of twelve men was finally chosen and the indictment was read. A. G. Severance, Cummings' attorney, stated he was not ready so all witnesses were ordered to return on Friday. When the case resumed the courthouse was filled with spectators and the prosecution, led by District Attorney Davis, introduced thirteen witnesses who testified to the facts of the case, including Captain T. Dwyer and also several expert witnesses on hand written signatures. Seventeen exhibits of paper were also introduced and the case was still going strong at 9:30 P.M., but the evidentiary portion of the trial was concluded.

The next morning the case resumed with arguments by counsel, and by 5:00 P.M. the case went to the jury. On the first vote the jury stood eleven for conviction and one undecided, but within a half hour the last man was convinced and the jury returned a guilty verdict. Cummings was sentenced to serve a three year prison term but was not immediately taken to the California State Prison. He was delivered to San Quentin on January 15, 1881, and registered as prisoner No. 9745. He was discharged, upon expiration of sentence, on May 14, 1883.

Weekly Appeal [Marysville, CA]: April 25, 1879; May 16, 1879; May 23, 1879.

Curran, John—*alias* Patsey Marley No. 2

Nativity, Pennsylvania; Age, 35 years; Occupation, Laborer; Height, 5 feet 7½ inches; Complexion, Light; Color of eyes, Blue; Color of hair, Light Brown; Weight, 163 lbs. Bullet scar on right cheek bone, scar on point of right shoulder, scar on right breast above nipple, vaccine mark on left arm, mole on right buttock, scar on right instep, birth marks on inside of left thigh, large face, very flat nose, cat-like teeth in front.

Robbed W. F. & Co's Express on stage from Eureka to Pioche, Nev., December 3, 1874.

Escaped from Pioche Jail, January 20, 1875.

Recaptured and returned to jail, January 24, 1875.

While en route to the Prison, jumped from the train while at full speed, with his leg irons on. He was captured by Indians a few days later.

Received at the Nevada State Prison, February 27, 1875; No. of commitment, 27; Crime, robbery; Term 9½ years; County sent from, Lincoln.

Escaped, October 29, 1877.

Recaptured and returned to prison the same day. Tried and convicted of Prison-breaking and given another year.

Discharged, upon expiration of sentence, June 2, 1883.

On December 3, 1874, Eureka's stagecoach for Palisade left town at 9:00 P.M. driven by Ira Van. When the coach reached Diamond Wells, eight miles south of town, a man stepped into the road and ordered the driver to "Hold on!" The team was a particularly spirited one and it took some effort for Van to bring them to a standstill, but he did accompanied by several threats from the road agent. As soon as the coach was stopped another road agent stepped out of the darkness and commanded the driver to "pass down that box." Van passed down Wells, Fargo & Company's treasure box and the robber immediately began to work on it, trying to burst it open or at least knock off the lid. While the second robber worked at the box messenger James Miller, seated beside the driver, was sizing up the situation. He first thought to bring his six-shooter into play but wanting to make a "sure shot" he decided to go for his shotgun, which was on the roof behind the driver. The first road agent, the one who ordered the halt, was watching Miller and, seeing his movements, ordered him to "sit quiet." Miller ignored the order and managed to get his shotgun and take aim but he chose to fire at the robber working on the treasure box. The other robber, who was on guard, then fired both barrels at Miller. The driver narrowly escaped being riddled with buckshot but Miller was wounded in his right arm and left hand, which left him unable to continue the gun battle. The robber laboring over the treasure box then drew his six-shooter and fired one shot in Miller's direction, but he did not hit anyone. Van and his four passengers, one female and three males, were not hurt. Van did not see that Miller was wounded when he, shouted, "Jim, go after them with your revolver!" and at that same moment started the team, which had become too restless to hold. Hardly had the horses moved then they were halted as the leaders plunged to the ground. The robbers had taken the rope from a nearby well and stretched it across the road from the granary to the station, but it had not been visible in the dark and the robbers had not mentioned it. Now the horses were frantic, the swingers and wheelers becoming entangled with the leaders. The team thrashed about until the leaders broke the swing pole, freed themselves, and ran off. In the excitement the road agents fled leaving the treasure box behind. The remaining four horses slowly stepped over the rope and took the coach a short distance ahead and then one of the passengers named John Lambert went back and got the treasure box, which had not been opened. He removed the rope, the stagecoach was turned around, and Lambert was picked up on the way back into Eureka. The stagecoach arrived at midnight and Miller was rushed to the International Hotel where the town's doctors were summoned. Drs. A. C. Bishop, W. B. Williams, and J. J. Callahan found that Miller's wounds were more serious than had first been suggested. The wound to the right arm was superficial but the wound to left hand was so serious that the little finger and part of Miller's palm had to be amputated, and he was recovering but still in a critical condition several days later. His arm had become swollen and he seemed to be "sinking" but he rallied on Sunday, about the time Dr. Daniel L. Deal of Pioche passed through town, and he examined the patient. He approved of the treatment by Eureka's doctors and Miller was already showing signs of a full recovery.

The driver and passengers related the details to Sheriff John D. Sullivan and he organized a posse, and when they came to the fork in the road they divided with the sheriff heading toward Devil's Gate while Zeph King and George Gilmore kept to the main road searching for a trail. As the pursuit continued it became clear that the men had planned the operation for days in advance, and had laid down a number of false trails in the vicinity of the robbery and around the regular station which was four miles beyond Diamond Wells. Once they started toward Devil's Gate there were several false trails leading in other directions and the posse had to eliminate each before continuing forward. It was finally determined that the two fugitives were generally heading toward Robert's Creek Mountains and the search focused on that region. The posse had acquired fresh horses and believed the fugitives animals were jaded, and so were confidant of an early capture, but soon they found the men had eluded them and they returned to town empty-handed. Meanwhile Sheriff John Emery had started from Austin with another posse and followed several trails before they gave up. Mart Packard, road superintendent for W. L. Pritchard, had been sent from Eureka in an entirely different direction, on the chance the men were circling around, and he back tracked the direction he believed they would flee. He found the two leaders which had escaped from the coach and they were only a quarter mile from the scene of the robbery, and badly tangled in their harness. "Old Reilly," the weaker of the two animals, had died when the bit cut through his jaw almost severing it, and he bled to death. The other horse received a severe cut in his nether lip but Packard sutured it closed, cut the harness away, and brought the horse to town. It recovered and was ready for service within a week.

Wells, Fargo & Company's chief detective, James B. Hume, had been in Austin on company business when the robbery occurred so he started for Monitor and Spring Valleys to watch for the fugitives by that route. Hume had been investigating three men suspected of robbing stagecoaches going to or from Eureka on June 28, August 11 and 13, 1874, though only two were seen at these robberies, and he had worked up a good case. He was keeping track of their whereabouts and believed they were in the area of Eureka "for the purpose of doing work." He warned the stage line owners, drivers and messengers, but there was little concern that they would rob the down coach. While the robbery of December 3 was taking place Hume was in Austin meeting with the county's district attorney, discussing the case against the three suspected road agents. Wells, Fargo & Company was quick to offer a reward of $500 for the arrest and conviction of the two men named by Hume — Jack McDonald and George Small. As days passed and there was no sign of the fugitives their descriptions were sent to an ever widening region. On January 22, 1875, District Attorney George W. Merrill sent a dispatch to Carson: "Send a copy of the indictment or complaint against Small and McDonald for robbing the Eureka stagecoach. They have been captured in Oregon."

McDonald and Small, however, proved to be the wrong men; but Hume, all along, had been investigating that third man. Hume was "a complete detective" so even though everyone was certain that McDonald and Small "were the right birds" and there were only two road agents involved, Hume continued to track and build a case against a third man — John Curran. This road agent was well known to the authorities and had served a prison term under his alias Patsey Marley. When he arrived at the prison there was already a Patsey Marley serving time, so he was registered as "Patsey Marley No. 2." When released he resumed using his real name but at every encounter with lawmen or newsmen the numbered alias came back to haunt him. Hume tracked Curran into Utah and arrested him, even before McDonald and Small had been found. He lodged Curran in the jail at Pioche and charged him as being the smaller of the road agents, being 5 feet 7 inches tall and weighing 163 pounds. Curran managed to escape from the jail on January 20 but was recaptured four days later. He was tried at the spring term of the court and convicted of the December 3, 1874, robbery. He had not been the road agent who shot Miller, would not plead guilty to any of the stagecoach robberies, and would not inform on his fellow bandit, so his sentence was set at seven and one half years. While en route to the state prison in Carson City on December 25 Curran jumped from the train. Sheriff A. Fife, when the train was between Oreana and Lovelock, let Curran go onto the platform confident that he would not jump from a train moving at full speed. However, Curran jumped and the train was halted, but the escapee eluded capture. Curran managed to remain free for only a few days before Indian trackers cornered him and he was delivered to the prison on February 27, 1875. Curran, prisoner No. 27, managed to escape prison on October 29, 1877, but was captured the same day, tried for prison breaking, and given an additional year. He served out his entire sentence, less good time accredited under the Goodwin Act, and was released on June 2, 1883.

Elko Independent [NV]: February 27, 1875. *Reese River Reveille [Austin, NV]:* December 5, 1874. *Territorial Enterprise [Virginia City, NV]:* December 8–9, 1874; February 26, 1875; March 2, 1875.

Davis, A. J.—*alias* Big Jack Davis

Robbed Overland Express train from San Francisco [Cal.] to Odgen [U. T.] near Verdi [Nev.], November 6, 1870, with J. E. Chapman, Tilton P. Cockrell, John Squires, R. A. Jones, E. B. Parsons, and James Gilchrist.
Prior to this train robbery, Davis, Squires and Cockrell had robbed W. F. & Co's Express three times on stages between Reno and Virginia City, Nevada.
Received at the Nevada State Prison, December 25, 1870; No. of commitment, —; Crime, robbery; Term, 10 years; County sent from, Washoe.
Pardoned, February 16, 1875.
Was killed September 3, 1877, by W. F. & Co's guards Jimmy Brown and Eugene Blair—while attempting to rob the Express on stage between Eureka and Tybo in company with Bob Hamilton, Bill Hamilton, and Thomas Lauria, accessory. Messenger Jimmy Brown was shot through the leg.

On November 7, 1865, the Overland stagecoach bound for Carson City was stopped and robbed at midnight as it was passing up Six-Mile Canyon, about a mile below the Gould & Curry Mill. The five highwaymen were led by "a large powerful man," and all the robbers were masked and armed with shotguns. There were nine passengers aboard but none gave any resistance. One passenger contributed $1,000 and two others $250 and $75 respectively, but the other five men had the presence of mind to hide their money when they heard the call to halt and the only lady aboard was not molested. The road agents were pursued but not captured. On October 31, 1866, two coaches of the Pioneer line, each pulled by six horses, were coming by the Donner Lake route from California on their way to Virginia City. At 2:00 A.M. they reached the sharp turn above the Geiger Grade, four miles from their destination, when they were ordered to stop by a band of highwaymen. The five road agents made their appearance from the roadside, brandishing guns in a threatening manner, and were armed with shotguns, pistols and knives. Their faces were blackened and the lower portions were disguised with a dark cloth mask. Both drivers reined in their horses, one coach being immediately behind the other. Fourteen passengers were at once ordered out of the coaches and the robbers told them they were after Wells, Fargo & Company's treasure safe. The road agents were acquainted with some of the passengers and called them by name, but they could not be recognized because of their disguises. The drivers were forced to unhitch their horses and get them out of the way as the treasure safe, which was in the foremost coach, had to be blown open with gunpowder. The passengers were gathered together and a guard placed over them, while two of the robbers worked to open the safe. They first had to cut the large staple for the padlock and loosen the heavy hasp before they could get at the keyhole, but they were well prepared with a hammer and cold chisels. They poured a pound and a half of powder into the safe, leaving behind two empty cans, inserted a piece of fuse, and lit it. The safe soon exploded with a tremendous report and being made of boiler iron it reflected the force of the explosion and the body of the coach was literally torn to pieces and the interior was set afire. The side of the coach was blown out and the top and bottom were badly shattered; in fact, it was so badly wrecked that it could hardly hold together, but the running gear was not damaged. The road agents extinguished the flames and found one end of the safe blown out and the lid was torn off. As soon as the smoke cleared away the booty was secured, consisting of $5,150 in gold coin, $5,000 of which belonged to Wells, Fargo & Company, and they took the express bag which contained letters. After the safe was cleaned out the road agents gave the passengers permission to enter the rear coach but, reneging on their promise to rob only Wells, Fargo, they searched each passenger and robbed them of all valuables. There was one lady among the passengers but she was not molested. The drivers, too, were not robbed and one road agent remarked that they "earned whatever they had, hard enough, and I don't believe they have much anyhow." The drivers were permitted to hitch up their teams and arrived in Virginia City at 3:00 A.M. The coach with the passengers arrived first, soon followed by the wrecked coach. The leader of the road agents was described as a medium-sized, well-built man who spoke in a gruff, evidently disguised, voice. He commanded and directed all the operations and none of the others had much to say. The five robbers were all dressed similarly in linen coats, buttoned up, with pistols and knives in their belts. The leader was an American, well spoken except when he tried to disguise his speech with "non-grammatical words and phrases." Wells, Fargo & Company offered a reward of $4,000 for recovery of the stolen treasure, or a proportionate reward for a part of it, and $1,000 each for the five highwaymen. The Bank of California increased the total reward by $2,500 and Nevada's Governor Henry G. Blasdel added a like sum to the total. Still, the road agents were not identified.

At 11:30 P.M. on June 10, 1868, the incoming Overland stagecoach was stopped and robbed in Six-mile Canyon five miles from Virginia City. Three robbers, armed with double barreled shotguns and completely masked by white cloth tied over their faces, had selected a bridge across the bed of a canyon just beyond Sugar Loaf Mountain. The robbers had been lying in wait where the coach would be going at a slow pace, leaped out, and one of the robbers stood in front of the leaders with his gun leveled at the head of driver Baldy Green, and ordered him to get down from his seat. "Get out," one of the robbers said to the passengers and they got out. The man who did the talking, and appeared to be the leader of the gang, hastily searched all the men for arms and afterwards more leisurely searched the four gentlemen and two ladies for valuables. Meanwhile another road agent threw the mail bags and baggage out of the coach and, retaining three bars of bullion, two of them drove the coach up the canyon. The mails and baggage were not rifled. The remaining robber, the leader of the gang and the only one that spoke a word in the hearing of the passengers, ordered them all to take up their line of march to a nearby ravine. They were driven like sheep from the road up into the hills, a distance of three quarters of a mile, where they were halted and ordered to sit. After standing guard over the party until his two partners had sufficient time to accomplish their work, the leader turned to the passengers and told them they should remain and he would come for them with the coach. After waiting and shivering in the cold for half an hour the party started down the ravine, and it was nearly daylight when the passengers reached Virginia City and told of their unpleasant experience. Wells, Fargo & Company offered a reward of $3,000 in gold for the arrest and conviction of the three robbers and on June 30 Virginia City's police chief arrested three men who were living in Six-mile Canyon—Andrew J. Davis, Benjamin F. Dale, and John H. Squires. A hearing was scheduled for the following afternoon but driver Baldy Green could not say that the voices of these three prisoners matched those of the previous robbers. Davis was released while Squires and Dale were held to answer in the sum of $2,000 each, but they were not indicted for the stagecoach robbery due to a lack of evidence and released, and Dale left the region and was not heard of again. The stolen bars of bullion were discovered in November 1872 and returned to Wells, Fargo & Company.

On August 31, 1870, at 2:15 A.M. the second of Wells, Fargo & Company's two coaches was stopped by two masked highwaymen when it was six miles south of Reno, at the water tank a half mile beyond Huffaker's Station. Here the robbers were prepared with a telegraph pole, the end of which one of them carried around so as to bring it across the road ahead of the lead horses just as the coach drove up. The fellow who did this carried a shotgun in one hand while handling the end of the pole with the other, and the sides of the road were higher than the roadway so the pole served as a bar to the further progress of the team. The second robber then made his appearance from behind the water tank and called upon driver Ned Blair to halt. The coach stopped and one of the robbers leveled his shotgun at the driver and two passengers riding atop while the other robber demanded the treasure-box. The box was thrown down and he smashed it open with an ax, the work of but a moment as he struck only three blows — one on the end and two on the bottom. He took out a sack containing $1,300 in coin and immediately both of the highwaymen prepared to depart. The driver, however, called to them to remove the pole from the road so one of them carried it around out of the way. The coach then drove on as the robbers vanished into the darkness. On Friday, September 16, 1870, at 10:00 P.M. the Wells, Fargo & Company's coach running from Carson City to Reno was stopped at the old Tamarac Mill in Pleasant Valley. The robbers had built a fence across the road at the mill and when the coach came up they leveled their double-barreled shotguns at driver Bill Blackmore. They broke open the treasure-box but thought there was nothing inside so they ordered the dozen passengers to disembark, placed them in a single file line with their backs against the side of the mill, and carefully searched every passenger not relying on them to produce their valuables. In the leather wallet carried in the treasure-box was a bundle of greenbacks and a small amount of coin which the robbers overlooked. Blackmore, during the entire affair, was told to mind his team and was not molested. After they had plundered the passengers they ordered them back into the coach, pulled down the fence, and told Blackmore to proceed. When the coach started one of the robbers fired a salute of one barrel, to hurry it along. Thirteen days later, on September 29, the stagecoach from Carson City to Reno driven by Bill Blackmore was robbed again at the same place — the Tamarac Mill. The road agents took the treasure-box, smashed it open and obtained $600, which seemed to satisfy them so they departed without molesting the passengers. Virginia City's *Enterprise* observed, "The robbers, three in number, were masked and are supposed to have been the same parties that last stopped the coach. These fellows appear to have set up a regular claim to that particular point on the road, which seems to be very well calculated from the lay of the land as a station for the road agency business." Later some of the letters, the box, and the sledge hammer used to demolish it were found and brought in.

John E. Chapman, a school teacher and respectable citizen of Reno, Nevada, met with a group of road agents and devised a plan to capture a train. He chose a place where the train would slow down to allow easy boarding and then the robbers would take control of the engine, tender, express and baggage cars. Chapman was too inexperienced in the ways of road agency so he was sent to San Francisco where he watched for a big shipment. Chapman learned that the code word "Red Coat" meant a big payroll shipment for the Gold Hill mines so, under the alias Joseph Enrique, he sent a ciphered telegram to R. A. "Sol" Jones saying that Central Pacific's Overland Express had pulled out of San Francisco with a payroll of $60,000 in gold aboard. In Nevada six men rode to an abandoned mine in the Peavine Mountains not far from Verdi and eleven miles west of Reno. As the train passed through Verdi just after midnight on November 5, 1870, it slowed and, as it passed a shed, five men in black masks and wearing dusters swung aboard, three men on the "blind baggage" platform between the tender and the combination express-baggage car, and two men on the rear platform of the same car where it was coupled to the remainder of the train. Two of the men at the front of the car climbed over the tender, pistols cocked, and captured engineer Hank Small and his fireman. The third man at the front of the car, seeing that the engine had been secured, climbed over the roof of the express car to the rear platform and informed the two men stationed there of their success in taking control of the train. Conductor D. G. Marshall was working his way toward the engine but when he stepped from the first passenger car onto the rear platform of the express-baggage car he was confronted by three men pointing six-shooters at him, so he retreated and locked the door behind him. The engineer, at that moment, was being forced to "whistle off the brakes" which required brakemen to go to their stations and prepare to bring the train to a halt by mechanically applying the brakes. The engineer gave the required single short blast of his whistle, which also signaled the men at the rear of the express-baggage car to pull the pin to uncouple the rest of the train and cut the bell rope. The engine, tender and express-baggage car continued down the tracks while the rest of the train screeched to a halt several miles east of Verdi. The front part of the train continued to the Lawton Springs gravel quarry where Jones waited with six saddle horses and two pack horses and the engineer was ordered to stop at the barricade of rail ties piled on the tracks. The train was halted at the precise place the robbers intended. The engineer and fireman were herded as a shield to the express car and engineer Small was ordered to knock and ask to be admitted. Central Pacific's express messenger Frank Minch did not arm himself because he recognized Small's voice and opened the sliding door to the express car. He was immediately covered with three sawed-off double-barreled shotguns, one right in his face, and he immediately surrendered. The robbers searched for treasure while Jones brought forward tools to pry off the padlocks on the boxes. It took an hour to search the car and their take was short of the $60,000 they expected, finding only $41,000 in $20 gold pieces, but they left behind over $8,000 in silver bars and coins and overlooked $15,000 in gold bars buried beneath the wood pile. The leader of the gang made a careful inspection of the car to see that no clues were left behind before departing.

The robbers moved some distance away into the quarry and there the loot, weighing close to one hundred fifty pounds, was divided and placed into the saddle bags of the horses, the leader taking about half of the coins and the other five men getting an equal share of the remainder. The six men separated into three parties, each headed in a different direction. Davis left alone, Jones and Tilton Cockrell left together toward Reno while John Squires, E. B. Parsons and James Gilchrist headed northwest toward California. The men had left behind, at the quarry, a crow bar and sawed-off shotgun but these items provided no clues to their identity. Meanwhile D. G. Marshall coordinated the careful release of the brakes on the passenger cars and the train rolled ahead, down a gentle grade, until it reached the engine, tender and express car. He stopped the rear of the train a safe distance back and after the obstruction was removed the train was coupled together and then backed into Verdi, but the telegraph had been disabled so the train proceeded to Reno to report the robbery, arriving at dawn which was about the same time the telegraph lines were repaired. Sheriff Charley Pegg and Undersheriff J. H. Kinkead formed a posse and sixteen men took the field. Wells, Fargo & Company quickly posted a reward of $10,000 and the Central Pacific Railroad and State of Nevada quickly added $15,000 each, bringing the total reward for arrest and conviction of the six robbers to $40,000. Everyone had an interest in the case and all agreed to share manpower and resources and they put F. T. Burke, the most experienced detective, in charge. He examined the scene and found several sets of tracks, one set from a distinctive "gambler's boot," a narrow shoe with an unusually small heel. He followed the track for several hundred yards where it left the hard ground and there he found two other boot tracks, and the place where the three men mounted horses and headed north toward

California. Burke's posse followed the tracks and finally came to Pearson's Tavern where they found the proprietor sitting with his shotgun across his lap, waiting for California lawmen to arrive. Pearson said his wife had discovered that one of their boarders had a large number of gold coins and they suspected he "might be a brigand of some sort," but his two partners had departed the day before. The lawmen approached the room with the greatest stealth and had Mrs. Pearson knock. When the occupant opened the door he looked into the muzzles of several rifles and pistols so he had no opportunity to resist. He was handcuffed and questioned and it was learned his name was James Gilchrist, recognized by some posse members as an unskilled mine laborer from Virginia City. Gilchrist's flippant demeanor suggested he would not break easily so Sheriff Pegg let slip that the people were so outraged by this first robbery of a western train that a large lynch mob was forming. The prisoner weakened and named the others involved in the robbery but he could only say that Parsons and Squires were heading for Loyalton in Sierra Valley, and from there the two men were planning to go on to a hide-out in Grass Valley. He knew nothing of the whereabouts of the other men. Pegg sent a telegram to Reno to have Davis and Chapman arrested as soon as they appeared in town, and the posse then started after Parsons and Squires.

Upon arriving in Loyalton the posse men discovered that there was only one hotel in the tiny town so Burke and Pegg went there to ask about strangers. The proprietor said that there was only one stranger staying there and he was in room 21, but his description did not match the man described by Gilchrist or Mrs. Pearson. Still, they decided they should see the man before they dismissed him as one of the robbers. They found the door to room 21 warped and held shut by a leaning chair so Burke reached inside and moved the chair away carefully. The posse entered with rifles and shot-guns at the ready and found the occupant sleeping soundly. His loaded revolver was removed from beneath his pillow and, upon wakening him, found they had captured E. B. Parsons, a gambler from Virginia City who wore a "gambler's boot." After the prisoner was secured in double-shackles and on his way to the jail at Truckee, Pegg learned that Squires' brother had a ranch a few miles from town so he and his posse rode there before day light. They surrounded the farmhouse to await the appearance of Squires but within a few minutes a man came out to milk the cow and he left the door ajar. The entire posse slipped into the house and found Squires asleep in his bedroll, with eight other men also sleeping on the floor. They captured Squires but nearly had to fight the occupants and neighbors, who all agreed that the posse had no authority to make an arrest in California. However, before the residents of Loyalton could organize and rescue the prisoner the posse was able to obtain a buckboard and spirit away their prisoner. They lodged him in the Truckee jail with Gilchrist and Parsons and only had to wait one day to get their extradition order from Nevada's Governor Henry G. Blasdel who had requisitioned it from California's Governor Henry H. Haight. Before leaving Truckee Gilchrist tried to secure his freedom by agreeing to cooperate fully with the officers and he told them where they had hidden their shares of the gold coins not found in their pockets. Judge T. Plunkett of Truckee City, Captain J. J. Green and Detective James Eddington took Gilchrist to a spot three miles down Honey Lake Road and then some distance down a side canyon. They stopped at a rugged ledge of rocks jutting out into the ravine where there was a natural cleft, and in this chasm the men had poured their gold coins. The party succeeded in pulling out nearly $12,000 that day and returned the following day with the proper tools and recovered the remainder of the plunder, worth more than $750. Gilchrist also told the whereabouts of Davis' stash, though how he would know that is a mystery since he was not with Davis when he hid his share. However, Davis had already given up his gold coins before the Truckee lawmen could go for them. Gilchrist, Parsons, and Squires were returned to Washoe City and lodged in the Washoe county jail.

When Davis appeared in Reno he was closely watched until all was ready and then officer Morrow arrested him. When told that the officers had caught some of the men engaged in the train robbery Davis said, "I'll bet you $2.50 that you haven't." Chief Downey answered, "I'll bet you $2.50 that I have one of them right here in town." Davis asked, "Where?" and Downey pointed his finger at Davis and said, "There!" Davis at first would not believe that any of his men had informed but the officers seemed so confidant and had so many clues that he finally had to admit they knew enough, so he decided he had better cooperate as well. He told the officers he would take them to where a great deal of the plunder was stashed but insisted he had not been involved in the robbery and had only overheard men talking, and that was how he knew of the hiding place. He went with Chief Downey, officer Ben Lackey, and Len Matthews to Hunter's Bridge on the Truckee River. Davis guided them to a place one hundred yards above the bridge and the same distance from the railroad tracks and directed their attention to a clump of four sagebrush, saying the gold was beneath one of them. Downey scuffed his boots in the loose dirt beneath each bush until he kicked up gold coins, so then the tedious process of digging and collecting the coins proceeded until they had recovered nearly all of the $20,000. Davis, Parsons, Gilchrist and Squires were soon joined in the Washoe City jail by Jones, Cockrell, and Roberts who had been tracked to a bordello in Long Valley by a heavily armed posse of twenty-eight men and they were arrested without resistance. Meanwhile Chapman, who had no idea that the scheme had been exposed and that he had been implicated, calmly disembarked from the Oakland-to-Reno stagecoach right into the arms of waiting lawmen.

A grand jury was convened by Judge C. N. Harris of the district court of Washoe County and all eight men were indicted for the train robbery. They were all found guilty but Gilchrist and Roberts were released in consideration of turning state's evidence while the other six men were sentenced to hard labor in the Nevada state penitentiary near Carson City. All the prisoners arrived at the prison between December 17 and 25, 1870. Squires, prisoner No. 66, was sentenced to twenty-three years and was pardoned on April 10, 1882, Cockrell, No. 68, received twenty-two years and was pardoned on July 12, 1882; J. E. Chapman, No. 67, got twenty years and was pardoned on July 13, 1877; E. B. Parsons, No. 69, received eighteen years and, though involved in several escapes including the "Big Break" of 1871, was pardoned on November 7, 1881; A. J. Davis, No. 59, received ten years and was pardoned February 16 1875; and R. A. Jones, No. 62, was sentenced to six years and was pardoned on March 27, 1874. After their release all the train robbers disappeared from Nevada's criminal record except Davis. He had refused to take part in the "Big Break" on September 17, 1871, and even provided assistance to the guards. When Davis came up for his pardon hearing in December 1874, after serving only four years, the board took into consideration his help during the prison riot and recommended favorably for his release, so the Governor pardoned Davis on February 16, 1875.

On the evening of April 14, 1876, the down-stagecoach was nearing Pioche when it was stopped by road agents three miles from its destination. Pat Ryan was driving with Eugene Blair riding as messenger when the command came from one robber to "throw down that box!" Blair slid down into the boot as Ryan threw down the express box, which both men knew was empty. As the robber who had called for the box went to grab the plunder he called out, "Ryan, is that the right one?" Ryan made some reply as Blair took aim and fired one barrel of his shotgun at the robber. The robber seemed to be spun around by the blast, giving Blair the impression that his load of buckshot had struck the robber's side. Ryan immediately whipped up his team to prevent return gun fire and drove the coach a short distance before he stopped again so that Blair could go back and get the box and robber, if still there. The box was lying in the middle of the road but the road agent was nowhere to be found. With nothing taken and no one aboard injured there was no reward posted and therefore no motivation to pursue the road agents. Still, several men went to the site of the robbery and followed the tracks for some distance and noted that here was no blood trail so it was then thought that the robber might not be wounded, and when the trail gave out the search was abandoned.

Davis had met Thomas Lauria and Bob Hamilton while in prison. Lauria was serving two years and Hamilton was serving six years, both for grand larceny, and both were from Lander County. Hamilton had hidden the money he stole and the three men began to plan a stagecoach robbery using Hamilton's cache for their stake. Lauria was released first, then Davis, and finally Hamilton and he recovered his loot. He purchased horses and twenty-seven head of cattle which he herded near Buttes Station on the Pioche Road, where he was joined by Lauria. They sent for Davis, who had been living in Virginia City, and over the next two weeks they obtained arms and supplies, and perfected their plans for the robbery. The three men, with Hamilton's brother Bill, went into Eureka and once they were satisfied with the arrangements they left Lauria in Eureka to watch for a big shipment. When Lauria saw that there were two messengers aboard, indicating a large haul, he hurried to signal Davis and Bob Hamilton. He rode toward Pinto and turned up a canyon and went to the top of Bald Mountain, a high peak that overlooks the whole country to the south. When it was dark he built two large fires which was the signal to Hamilton and Davis that the coach for Tybo was loaded with treasure and had two messengers, but he built the fires too close together and they looked like one fire from that distance. The road agents had set up their camp near Willow's Station, forty miles south of Eureka, and knew that the coach would arrive at the station about 9:00 P.M. Hamilton and Davis rode to Willows Station and captured William Hood, the blacksmith and station keeper, and a rancher visiting the station. The road agents bound and gagged their prisoners and waited for a stagecoach, which they believed carried only one messenger guarding a very large treasure.

The stagecoach from Eureka to Tybo left town on September 3, 1877, carrying two passengers — Professor T. Price and J. M. Haskell, and two messengers with Jack Perry driving. They were on schedule when they arrived at Willows Station and one of the robbers called out, "Eugene Blair, get off that coach and surrender." Blair thought that the men in the station had gotten drunk and were playing a joke at his expense, and the man had remained in the shadows which seemed to confirm his suspicions. When the order came again, however, Blair got down leaving messenger "Shotgun" Jimmy Brown and driver Perry on the seat. He had just reached the ground when two of the three road agents fired their shotguns at him, one from the rear and the other from the corner of the stable in front of him. Both blasts missed though one was so close he felt the heat of the gun powder and he immediately returned fire toward the stable. He was blinded by the first two blasts and the smoke of his own discharge but before he could regain his night vision one of the robbers placed his shotgun against Blair's breast. Blair pushed it aside as the bandit pulled the wrong trigger, and he pushed the bandit away from him. Brown saw his chance and blasted the robber with one barrel of his shotgun, nine buckshot striking the man's back just above the hip. Blair pushed the muzzle of his shotgun into the chest of the robber but seeing that he was badly wounded did not fire. Brown jumped down to join the fight but was immediately wounded in the calf of his left leg. The two remaining robbers then each unloaded their shotguns at the messengers and fired one shot each from their revolvers as they retreated into the darkness. The wounded robber was writhing in agony and begged to be killed but neither Blair nor Brown would accommodate him. They then discovered and untied the station men and examined the preparations made by the robbers — a small fort built beside the stable and the ax kept handy for opening the treasure box. The following day Perry continued on with his passengers while the messengers took the wounded robber to Eureka on the return stagecoach, but he died before reaching town. Every effort was made to secure his name and the names of his associates but he would not inform on them nor identify himself. Before his death the road agent revealed that this was the second time he had exchanged shots with Blair, confirming that he had been the person who fired at him during the stagecoach robbery of April 14, 1876. As soon as the body reached town it was taken to Schwamb's Funeral Parlor and put on display, and a half-dozen men immediately identified the dead man as Andrew J. "Gentleman Jack" Davis. On September 5 Davis was officially identified during the inquest and later that day he was "buried in the county graveyard, not a single mourner attending the funeral."

John N. Thacker, one of Wells, Fargo & Company's best detectives, was on the case and he soon learned that Davis' associates were Thomas Lauria and the Hamilton brothers, Bob and Bill. They were soon arrested by Thacker and Blair, and many of the details of the affair became known. The three men had their examination at Belmont in October and were held for the grand jury, indicted, and tried in November. Bob Hamilton and Lauria were convicted of robbery but the jury disagreed on the charge against Bill Hamilton, a man of weak intellect, and he was released. In December the two convicted robbers were each sentenced to serve fourteen years at Nevada's State Prison. Hamilton and Lauria arrived at the prison on December 8, 1877. Lauria was pardoned on June 20, 1882, and Bob Hamilton was pardoned in October 1887.

Carson City News [NV]: February 22, 1913. *Carson Daily Appeal [NV]*: November 8, 1865; November 10, 1865. *Eureka Republican [NV]*: September 5, 1877. *Eureka Sentinel [NV]*: September 5, 1877; September 7, 1877; October 25, 1877; October 28, 1877. *Pioche Record [NV]*: April 15, 1876. *Reno Gazette [NV]*: April 15, 1876. *Territorial Enterprise [Virginia City, NV]*: November 1, 1866; November 4, 1866; June 12, 1868; June 30, 1868; July 1, 1868; July 7, 1868; September 1, 1870; September 16–18, 1870; October 1,1870; November 24, 1870; December 17, 1870; November 17, 1872 September 6, 1877; November 1, 1877; December 2, 1877.

Delaney, Michael—*alias* Mickey Delaney

Nativity, New York; Age, 38 years; Occupation, Laborer; Height, 5 feet 7¾ inches; Complexion, Dark; Color of eyes, Hazel; Color of hair, Brown. Long features, round scar on the forehead near right temple, scar on center of upper lip, 3 vaccine marks left upper arm, scar on inside of right hand near the thumb, round scar on right shoulder; slim built.

Received at the California State Prison, March 13, 1867. First term, No. of commitment, 3493; Crime, burglar; Term, 3 years; County sent from, San Francisco.

Discharged, by expiration of sentence, September 27, 1869.

Received at the California State Prison, July 3, 1871. Second term, No. of commitment, 4906; Crime, burglary and grand larceny; Term, 8 years; County sent from, Napa.

Commuted by Governor William Irwin, May 30, 1876, to 6 years, and *discharged* by expiration of sentence, July 15, 1876.

Burglarized W. F. & Co's office at Newcastle in 1879, but was sent to State Prison for a burglary in Alameda County, being easier case tried.

Received at the California State Prison, August 2, 1879. No. of commitment, 8944; Crime, burglary first degree; Term, 6 years; County sent from, Alameda.
Discharged, upon expiration of sentence, October 2, 1883.
Now in jail, January 1, 1885, awaiting trial for burglarizing W. F. & Co's safe at Drytown, October 16, 1884.

Michael Delaney was not tried for the burglary of Wells, Fargo & Company property in Newcastle, Placer County in 1879 but instead was convicted of a burglary in Alameda County that same year which did not involve Wells, Fargo & Company property. He was sentenced to serve six years, which satisfied Wells, Fargo. He arrived at San Quentin on August 2, 1879, registering as prisoner No. 8944. On October 2, 1883, he was discharged upon expiration of his sentence. On Thursday night, October 16, 1884, burglars stole tools from a blacksmith shop near the store of William Jennings in Drytown, California. They broke into Jennings' store through a window in the rear part of the building, dug through the brick wall into his cellar, and then broke through the floor upward into the room where the safe was located. They drilled a hole in the safe's door and blew it open with blasting powder and removed $2,221—$400 belonging to Wells, Fargo & Company, $600 belonging to Henry Burchell, and the remainder belonging to several parties including Jennings. They fled with the money, leaving the tools behind and although there seemed no clue to the burglars' identities, they had been quite familiar with the store's interior and the location of the safe. A reward of $600 was posted for the arrest and conviction of the burglars and on Sunday, November 2 Sheriff Murray and deputy Glenn arrested two men near Ione, California, and charged them with the Jennings' store burglary. One prisoner gave his name as Phillips and the other as DeLacy but they were well known to lawmen from serving several terms in prison as William Harris [alias Phillips] and Michael Delaney [alias Hackett and DeLacy]. They were lodged in jail and then taken to Drytown for their examination, which lasted two days. Harris was held to answer to the grand jury but a case could not be made against Delaney and he was discharged. Delaney was immediately arrested by a deputy U.S. Marshal for the burglary of a post office, which involved Wells, Fargo & Company property. Delaney was taken to San Francisco, indicted by the U.S. grand jury, tried in the circuit court, convicted and sentenced to serve a four year term at San Quentin as a federal prisoner. He arrived on April 4, 1885, and registered as prisoner No. 11639. He was released, by expiration of sentence, on April 2, 1888.

The Amador County grand jury indicted Harris in January and the superior court called for jurors to report on February 16, 1885. The first case called was that of Harris and a large number of witnesses were called to testify, and the court was filled with spectators interested in the case. The trial lasted until Thursday afternoon even though the evidence against Harris was all circumstantial but, according to the *Amador Dispatch*, "the circumstances were so closely linked together that the jury had little room to doubt his guilt." Harris was convicted of 2nd degree burglary and ordered to return the following Monday for sentencing. However, the sentencing was delayed when his attorney stated that new evidence had been discovered. On Friday, March 6, 1885, the judge heard the motion for a new trial based on the new evidence, found it lacking, and denied the motion before pronouncing sentence — seven years at San Quentin. On Sunday, March 9 Harris was delivered to the prison to serve his sixth term, registering as prisoner No. 11609. Harris was released on December 9, 1889.

Amador Dispatch [San Andreas, CA]: October 18, 1884; October 25, 1884; November 8, 1884; December 13, 1884; February 21, 1885; March 7, 1885; March 14, 1885.

Dollar, James R.

Nativity, North Carolina; Age, 34 years; Occupation, Laborer; Height 5 feet 9½ inches; Complexion, Florid; Color of eyes, Brown; Color of hair, Brown. Square features, wide jaws, small scar on upper lip, scar base of left thumb, large do. near left elbow, mole back of left upper arm; slim built.
Robbed W. F. & Co's Express on 2 stages running between Lakeport and Calistoga, June 12, 1877, with William Russell.
Received at the California State prison, July 3, 1877. No. of commitment, 7653; Crime, robbery — two convictions; Term, 9 years; County sent from, Napa.
Discharged, upon expiration of sentence, June 3, 1883.

On June 12, 1877, after noon the stagecoach from Calistoga in Napa County to Lakeport in Lake County driven by Wash Gwin was seven miles above Calistoga and "toiling up the grade going north" on the St. Helena toll road near Bradford's Station. Suddenly two medium sized, masked and heavily armed road agents appeared. The two men wore over their heads sacks with eye holes cut in them, and the sacks went all the way to their waists where they were tied off with string. One man, wearing blue overalls, was armed with an army musket while the other, who wore brown overalls, carried a double-barreled shotgun. They pointed their weapons at Gwin, ordered him to halt, and then demanded the Wells, Fargo Express treasure box. As soon as the box was handed down the road agents ordered Gwin to continue on. Gwin's coach had been filled with many women and children but none of the passengers were molested. Gwin had only gone one hundred yards when he met the Lower Lake coach bound for Calistoga driven by Budd "Eli" Philpott. That coach had two treasure boxes aboard, one from Lakeport filled with coin and the other from the quicksilver mines which was comparatively light. Wash shouted to Philpott "Look out, I have just been robbed," but the warning came too late for Philpott to turn around as the grade was much too narrow, so he continued on. As Philpott reached the place where Gwin had been robbed the road agents appeared and shouted, "Halt, or we'll blow your brains out!" Philpott reined in his team and when the command to hand out the box came he fumbled about to give himself some time. The robbers became impatient and, as one covered Philpott, the other began to climb up onto the boot so Philpott handed out the light box and the two road agents, being satisfied it was the only one aboard, ordered the coach to proceed. Philpott's coach was filled with Chinese men but the road agents did not bother to go through them either. There seemed no clue to their identities but it was certain, though they were "green at the business," they were familiar with the stagecoach route and schedule and had selected a place where they could rob both stagecoaches within a few minutes and flee. As soon as the down coach arrived at Calistoga Gwin notified the authorities and the lawmen formed a posse. At the scene they found both boxes "bursted open with an ax, which was lying nearby and identified as one stolen at Calistoga," and there was a trail of boot tracks with distinctive nail marks in the heels and soles leading away from the robbery scene.

During the investigation which followed a Mr. Weybright, who lived at the foot of St. Helena mountain, said that two young men had come to his house for breakfast saying they had not eaten for a day, and he provided their description. Meanwhile Mr. Cherry, Rufus Henson and C. Connor, who lived near Calistoga, followed the foot tracks of the two road agents to a wheat field near Kellogg, only five miles from the scene of the robbery. Henson, on horseback, was following the trail which skirted along the edge of the field and saw that the tracks turned into the field. As he looked in that direction he saw one of the road agents pointing a shot-gun at him so he dropped down on the opposite side of his horse and made his way to a nearby house where he borrowed a Henry rifle. He motioned to Cherry and Connor to join him and the three men gave chase. Cherry fired two shots at one of the fleeing fugitives before he surrendered, and the other robber also surrendered immediately when Connor fired one shot at him. They were handcuffed, taken into Calistoga, and lodged in jail. The two men were given an examination and identified themselves as William Russell and James R. Dollar. The shot gun was shown to the court but the musket could not be found and was thought to have been hidden or thrown away. Testimony proved that they had only obtained $25 from both boxes, and $14.50 had been recovered when they were arrested. They had purchased a bottle of whiskey and, when discovered, had just turned into the field to drink their bottle and take a nap. They were held to answer before the grand jury and the night of June 13 they were taken to Napa and jailed there. The *Napa Daily Register* noted, "They are the same parties spoken of in yesterday's edition as being under suspicion, and although they deny their guilt, and the evidence against them is wholly circumstantial, yet there is little doubt of their being the robbers, as they have been traced from Calistoga to the scene of the robbery, and from there to the place where they were captured. They account for their actions in running from their captors by saying that they had stolen two turkeys the night before, and thought the farmers were after them. This was so; the turkeys were found in a sack, but this does not acquit them of the stage robbery."

The men were questioned about their identities and Dollar, a man of medium height with light hair and moustache, about twenty-five years old, said he had a wife in San Francisco and had worked in the Lower Lake school house until it burned down recently; and Russell was of medium height with dark eyes and hair, and about twenty-three years old. The two prisoners were tried at the June session of the Napa County court and each was convicted of two robberies — a separate conviction for each stagecoach. Both men were sentenced to serve nine years at San Quentin and both men arrived on July 3, 1877, where Russell was registered as prisoner No. 7652 and Dollar as prisoner No. 7653. Governor George C. Perkins commuted Russell's sentence to seven and one half years and he was discharged on September 28, 1882. Dollar served out his entire sentence and on June 3, 1883, he was released upon expiration of his sentence.

Napa Daily Register [CA]: June 14–15, 1877.

Downer, Albert

Nativity, Missouri; Age, 34 years; Occupation, Laborer; Height, 5 feet 9¼ inches; Complexion, Florid; Color of eyes, Blue; Color of hair, Light. Round features, eyes deep-set, 3 moles on right cheek-bone, 1 do. on right cheek, 1 do. on chin, 1 scar under left ear, 1 do. right thumb, 1 do. on second and index finger of right hand, several moles on breast and arms; stout built.
Robbed W. F. & Co's Express on stage from Visalia to Tulare, November 29, 1873 — alone.
Received at the California State Prison, March 16, 1874. No. of commitment, 5923; Crime, robbery, Term, 22 years; County sent from, Tulare.
Escaped, October 1, 1878.
Recaptured in Nevada County and returned to prison, December 11, 1878, by G. W. Giffen.
Commuted by Governor George Stoneman, September 12, 1884, to 10½ years, and *discharged*, by expiration of sentence, September 16, 1884.

On Saturday, October 18, 1873, the stagecoach from Visalia left for Tulare on schedule at 9:00 P.M. Winn Thoms was driving with Sam Caruthers riding atop on the left and inside was Caruthers' brother Bob, John Ridgeway with his wife and two small children, a

Mr. Howard, and two other passengers. When the stagecoach had traveled one and one half miles south of Visalia, still in Tulare County, two men suddenly sprang in front of the coach and, with guns in hand, ordered the driver to rein in his team. The appearance of the masked men was so sudden it startled the leaders and they turned into the wheelers, nearly upsetting the coach. The road agents demanded the Wells, Fargo & Company's Express box but before Thoms regained control of his team one of the robbers, "in a savage tone with a cocked revolver near his [Thoms'] person" made a second demand. Thoms complied and the robbers then ordered the passengers to pass out their valuables, under threat they would be removed from the coach, tied, and searched. The passengers, in consideration of the women and children, handed out $85 dollars, bringing the total plunder to $600 when the $515 in the box was added. Thoms was then ordered to continue, and he drove at a rapid pace until he was able to send word back to Visalia. Lawmen rushed to the scene of the robbery but could find no clue to the identity of the road agents. They found the treasure box, broken open and emptied, and returned it to the Wells, Fargo office in Visalia. The Express company then posted a reward of $250 for the arrest and conviction of each road agent and offered a quarter of any part of the plunder recovered. While there was no definite clue to the identity of the robbers lawmen thought it was the same man who had burglarized Frenchy's Cabin near Wagy's Mill shortly before the stagecoach robbery. Lawmen had pursued the burglar to Stockton but he eluded capture and, it was supposed, returned to Visalia to rob the coach. On Saturday, November 22 the stagecoach bound for Tulare left Visalia at 9:00 P.M. When the coach reached the same place it had been robbed six weeks earlier the horses suddenly came to an abrupt stop in the road and a lone road agent leveled his revolver at the driver and demanded the Wells, Fargo & Company's Express box. Driver Thoms delivered the box and, when the robber determined that there was only one female passenger he ordered Thoms to continue. The coach could not proceed, however, until the road agent removed a large rail he had placed across the road, the reason the horses stopped. The box, which contained $67 in coin, was found later at the same place the previous box had been broken open and it was returned to Wells, Fargo.

Officers had, since the burglary and the first stagecoach robbery, been interested in a man who gave his name as John Bell. Later in the evening following the second stagecoach robbery officers found a man loitering about Keener's Stable in the south part of Visalia. They did not recognize him as "John Bell" and he convinced them he was a harmless drunk but soon afterward a horse belonging to a Mr. McCloud was stolen and the horse thief fled toward King's River. A posse was soon on his trail and they recovered the stolen horse, then a mile and a half further along the trail they captured the fugitive. They found in his pockets $67 in coins, in the exact denominations of that stolen from the second coach, and a watch stolen from Frenchy's Cabin when it was burglarized. The prisoner gave his name as Albert Heuse Downen, often misspelled Downer, Downey, or Downing. On Friday, November 28 Downen was arraigned before Judge N. O. Bradley and Winn Thoms identified him as one of the two road agents on October 18 and the lone highway man on November 22. Downen was held to answer to the grand jury, bail set at $5,000, and he was lodged in the county jail. On February 19, 1874, the *Visalia Delta* reported that Downen "has got tired of cell life" and tried to escape through the wooden floor from the second floor jail to the first floor. The walls were lined with iron so he began burning through the wooden flooring, starting the flame by rubbing together two pieces of wood and using lint from his bedding for kindling, and was nearly through when discovered.

Downen was indicted, tried, and on March 4 was found guilty of robbing the stagecoach on October 18, 1873, and of burglarizing Frenchy's Cabin, but the jury could not agree on the second stagecoach robbery charge. On March 19, 1874, the *Visalia Delta* reported, "...and the Court sentenced him to the Penitentiary for 22 years: 20 years for stagecoach robbery and 2 years for house-breaking." Downen arrived at San Quentin Prison on March 16, 1874, and registered as prisoner No. 5923. On October 1, 1878, Downen, who had been doing the laundry for families within the "dead lines" of the prison, passed through the gates with his laundry basket to deliver the clean laundry and when near the Commissary building he changed into a fashionable suit, lit a cigar, and sauntered past six guards. When he arrived at the last guard he stopped to speak of the weather and said, "Well, I've been waiting a long time for this." The guards recognized him but seeing his dress and demeanor thought his time was up and he had been released, and it was an hour before his escape was reported. The warden offered a reward of $50 for his capture and his description was circulated through-out the area. Downen made his way to Nevada County, California, and remained free until he was captured by G. W. Giffen on December 11, 1878. On September 12, 1884, Governor George Stoneman commuted Downen's sentence to ten and one half years and four days later he was discharged by expiration of sentence.

National Police Gazette: December 5, 1896. *San Francisco Chronicle [CA]*: October 3, 1878. *Visalia Weekly Delta [CA]*: October 23, 1873; December 4, 1873; March 12, 1874.

Downey, Charles

Age, 40 years; Occupation, Stage Driver; Height 5 feet 9 or 10 inches; Complexion, Light; Color of eyes, Blue; Color of hair, Light.
Robbed W. F. & Co's Express and U.S. Mail on stage from Boise to Silver City, I. T., November 10, 1875, in company with John Lee, George Bouldin and J. W. Trask.
Received at the United States Prison, near Boise, December 30, 1875. No. of commitment, —; Crime, mail robbery; Term, 2 years; County sent from, Ada.
Discharged, upon expiration of sentence, August 30, 1877.
[*See* Bouldin, George]

Dunkin, Thomas H.

Nativity, Massachusetts; Age, 37 years; Occupation, Blacksmith; Height, 5 feet 6½ inches; Complexion, Light; Color of eyes, Blue; Color of hair, Sandy. Scar outer corner of right eye, scar 3 inches long right side of head near top, end of right little finger disfigured — nail growing over end, deformed nail middle finger right hand, deformed nail second finger left hand, 4 scars inside right leg — above knee.
Robbed W. F. & Co's Express on stage from Elko to Tuscarora, Nevada, March 10, 1883, with Bill Huyck. Huyck was released in consideration of testimony given against Dunkin.
Received at the Nevada State Prison, April 27, 1883. No. of commitment, 252; Crime, robbery; Term, 10 years; County sent from, Elko.
Commuted and *discharged*, upon expiration of sentence, July 13, 1886.

The stagecoach for Tuscarora driven by James Ferguson was stopped by two armed, masked road agents wearing canvas overcoats when it was a few miles from town. A. J. Potter was riding next to the driver and was the only passenger robbed, contributing $16. The Wells, Fargo & Company box was demanded and broken open by one of the robbers. Apparently they expected the miner's payroll, about $10,000 which was normally transported on the 10th of each month, but it had been shipped a day early. The robber who broke open the box exclaimed, "By God, there is nothing here!" and the other robber asked, "Ain't there nothing there Tom?" They did find two silver watches inside and took them but there was no money. The robbers then cut the harness on the lead horses, removed them from the team and had Potter stand with the animals until the coach had gone a short distance, pulled only by the wheelers. The robbers then told Potter to run after the coach. The next day A. J. Banks, a Wells, Fargo messenger, went to the scene of the robbery and found footprints. He followed the tracks of two men to the houses of William H. Huyck and Thomas H. Dunkin, which were situated close to one another. The men were arrested and the track of Huyck was examined and determined to match one of the footprints at the scene of the robbery. Huyck informed on Dunkin, insisted he was not involved, and told deputy sheriff M. Polk that his gun was at the robbery but said that it was in the hands of Dunkin or "Butcher" Jim. He said that, "about a month ago Dunkin made a proposition to go and rob the coach. I told him I would not go and he should give it up. He said he wanted my gun, and I told him that the only way was for him to steal it. Dunkin told Jim where it was and he came and took it the night of the robbery." G. W. Phillips testified at trial that he recognized the gun belonging to Huyck, and Huyck also had a canvas overcoat like that worn by one of the robbers. Phillips said the gun and coat were at Huyck's house the day before the robbery and they were there the day after. As the trial commenced it was clear that the evidence, though entirely circumstantial, was strong against both men. All the testimony was in and it was expected that the prosecution would rest when, at 2:00 P.M. on April 24, 1883, the district attorney surprised everyone when he called Huyck to the witness stand. The co-defendant was asked, "Who were the persons engaged in the robbery of the Tuscarora stage on the 10th of March?" and Huyck replied, "Thomas Dunkin and myself." He then gave the details of the robbery from the first proposition to the conclusion, and the two silver watches which had been recovered by Officer Al Parker in Dunkin's shop were then introduced into evidence. The case was closed, final arguments made, and it was submitted to the jury.

Dunkin, who continued to insist he was innocent, was found guilty of robbing the stagecoach and ordered to return on Wednesday for sentencing. District Attorney J. W. Dorsey, when asked why he would make a deal with Huyck so late in the case, said he was not confident he had enough evidence to convict either man and thought it best to ensure the punishment of at least one of the robbers. A complaint charging perjury was then filed against Huyck but the District Attorney moved that the perjury case be dismissed as the perjured testimony was in the robbery case in which he had immunity. The judge agreed and the perjury case was dismissed. Huyck was released at noon on April 27, 1883, but he was in mortal fear of being mobbed or lynched so he quickly ran into the sagebrush behind town, made his way through the graveyard, and struck out for the railroad to "beat it" out of the country. He was not heard of again in Nevada. Dunkin was sentenced to serve ten years at Nevada's state prison and arrived on April 27, 1883. On July 13, 1886, he was released after serving a little more than three years.

Territorial Enterprise [Virginia City, NV]: March 13, 1883; March 27, 1883; April 6, 1883; April 24, 1886. *Silver State [Winnemucca, NV]:* April 27, 1883.

Dwyer, John

Nativity, Missouri; Age, 23 years; Occupation, laborer; Height, 5 feet 8½ inches; Complexion, Florid; Color of eyes, Blue; Color of hair, Light, Size of foot, 6. Broad full features, high full forehead, heavy eyebrows, thick lips, dimpled chin, small scar top of forehead, large scar on left side, three moles and vaccine mark on left upper arm, scar back of left upper arm, square shoulders, sway-backed; stout built.

Robbed W. F. & Co's Express on stage from Cloverdale to Mendocino, October 9, 1884, with William Corbett.

Escaped from County Jail at Ukiah, November 8, 1884. Recaptured November 13, 1884.

Received at the California State Prison, November 14, 1884; No. of commitment, 11450; Crime, robbery; Term, 5 years; County sent from, Mendocino.

[*See* Corbett, William]

Earl, Sylvester

Nativity, Utah; Age, 19; Occupation, Teamster; Height, 5 feet 8 inches; Complexion, Light; Color of eyes, Gray; Color of hair, Light Brown; Weight, 170 pounds; Size of foot, 7. Number of moles on back of neck and shoulders, several small scars on right index finger; wart on inside of right wrist, small scar above right knee, two scars on right knee cap, scar on right of belly 1½ inches long above navel, does not drink nor use opium, uses tobacco, single.

Attempted to rob Overland Express train from San Francisco to Ogden at Montello, January 22, 1883, in company with Rais Anderson, Francis "Frank" Hawley, Orrin Nay and David Francis.

Received at Nevada State Prison, March 2, 1883. Commitment, —; Crime, assault to commit robbery; Term, 12 years; County sent from, Elko.

[*See* Anderson, Rais]

Earl, William L.

Nativity, California; Age, 31 years; Occupation, Laborer; Height, 5 feet 8½ inches; Complexion, Florid; Color of eyes, Brown; Color of hair, Black. Small features, prominent nose, narrow chin, mole on throat, do. between shoulders; stout built.

Robbed W. F. & Co's Express on stage from Soledad to San Luis Obispo, April 14, 1877, with Jose M. Gil.

Received at the California State Prison, July 13, 1877. No. of commitment, 7661; Crime, grand larceny; Term 4 years; County sent from, Monterey.

Discharged, per Act, July 13, 1880.

On Saturday, April 14, 1877, at 1:30 A.M. the stagecoach from Soledad to San Luis Obispo driven by W. Cambridge was stopped by two masked road agents when it was three quarters of a mile below Jolon in Monterey County. Each man wielded a double-barreled shotgun which they pointed at Cambridge when they ordered him to halt and demanded the Wells, Fargo treasure box. Cambridge threw down the box and the road agents then ordered him to continue on. They did not ask for the mail sacks, nor did they molest the passengers. Cambridge hurried on to the next station and reported the robbery. Posses were soon on the trail of the robbers and it was not long before they were captured and lodged in jail. They gave their names as William L. Earl and Jose M. Gil. At their examination they were held for action by the grand jury and in early July they were indicted on the lesser charge of grand larceny, upon the agreement they would plead guilty and receive a reduced sentence. When brought into court for their arraignment they pled as agreed and in consideration of their cooperation Earl and Gil were sentenced to serve four years at San Quentin. They arrived on July 13, 1877, Earl registering as prisoner No. 7661 and Gil as No. 7662. Both men served out their entire terms, less good time as required under the Goodwin Act, and they were released by expiration of sentence on July 13, 1880.

San Luis Obispo Tribune [CA]: April 21, 1877.

Estrado, Joe

Nativity, California; Age, 35 years; Occupation, none; Height 5 feet 6½ inches; Complexion, Dark; Color of eyes, Black; Color of hair Black; Weight, 149 lbs. Vaccine marks on both upper arms, large mole on right forearm, two scars above left eye, scar on left thigh neat groin — made by bullet, and on back of thigh scar where same bullet came out.

Robbed W. F. & Co's Express on stage from Belleville to Carson, March 6, 1876, with James Wallace and Manuel Sharania.

Received at the Nevada State Prison, April 23, 1876. No. of commitment, 37; Crime, robbery; Term, 25 years; County sent from, Esmeralda.

Pardoned and *released,* July 16, 1890.

On March 13, 1876, three men rode their mules to a ranch near Aurora, Nevada. The men were described as an American five feet nine inches in height and thin, while the other two were described as Mexicans of a much smaller stature. They had come from Belmont in Inyo County, California, and announced that they were planning to rob a stagecoach. They asked the rancher if they could take his mule for a pack animal, promising that if the rancher came to Cerro Gordo they would give him four mules for his one, but they required him to keep their plans secret. The rancher gave them the mule but immediately after their departure reported their plans to a deputy sheriff. The deputy followed them as far as Belleville where they stopped at a camp of Mexicans, again bragging of their plans. One of the three men, a Mexican who was clearly the leader, told the lawman that he would kill him if he did not turn back so the deputy, being outnumbered and outgunned, returned to town for reinforcements. A Mexican from the camp also went into town and told the citizens of the plan to rob a stagecoach and a posse was formed to make an arrest. When the posse arrived at the Mexican camp the three aspiring road agents had left and later it was learned that they had traveled thirty-five miles and camped overnight in the mountains. The following day, March 14, the stagecoach from Columbus to Aurora was stopped by three highwaymen at 10:00 A.M. and robbed of eight bars of bullion from the Northern Belle mine, valued at $14,000. Two of the robbers were hidden behind a bush on one side of the road while the third man took up a position on the opposite side. The were disguised with flannel masks as they stepped out into the road in front of the approaching coach and the American bandit leveled his shotgun at the driver, ordering him to "tumble out the bullion as soon as God will let you." The other two robbers then threatened to shoot the driver if he did not comply immediately. After the bullion was delivered they demanded the treasure box, broke it open, and took out $68. They returned the broken box before the driver was ordered to continue on. The stagecoach continued into Aurora where the driver reported the robbery. The description of the robbers matched that of the three men at the Mexican camp the day before. The sheriff was out of town so a posse of citizens including W. C. Conover, Dennis Thompson, Detective B. F. Lackey, John G. Irwin, and an Indian tracker were dispatched by Wells, Fargo & Company's superintendent J. J. Valentine to trail the robbers. Near the scene they found one sack containing a bar of bullion which the robbers had not carried away and they also found the tracks of four mules. They followed the tracks of the animals and after a quarter mile saw a deep depression where it appeared the mule had slipped. The marks looked suspicious so Thompson dug at the place with his knife and at twelve inches deep found a bar of bullion. They then began to search carefully, using sharp sticks to prod at every place where the ground looked disturbed, and at intervals of fifteen feet along the trail they found six more bars of bullion. They continued to search for the eighth bar but only found the bullion bags some distance down the trail. The posse continued on the trail of the robbers and outfitted at Benton, California, just over the Nevada line, then tracked the three men through Fish and Lida Valleys. The posse grew in size and finally divided with some men going through Death Valley and others heading toward Gold Mountain and on to Lone Pine, California, but the robbers had struck out across the Snow Mountains and went into Darwin.

Darwin's deputy sheriff James Wales had been notified to be on the lookout for the road agents and saw mules in the corral which he suspected were the animals of the fugitives. He devised a plan to identify the owners of the mules but by the time his plan was put into action the mules had disappeared. Wales then followed the mules' tracks to a Mexican camp near Old Coso and there captured the three stagecoach robbers, and also arrested Nehar Felis the Cerro Gordo murderer he had been looking for. The prisoners were lodged in the jail and identified: James Wallace — the American; Joe Estrado, sometimes spelled Estrada — the Mexican; and Manuel Chavarria, sometimes spelled Sharania — a Chilian though often identified as Peruvian. Wallace and Chavarria were ready to turn state's evidence against Estrado, and Wallace was the quickest to inform on his fellow robbers. Wallace disclosed that the missing bar of bullion had fallen off the pack mule and Estrado had gone back to bury it, so only Estrado could say where it was and he would not talk. The three prisoners were returned to Nevada for a preliminary hearing in the Justice Court, where Wallace and Chavarria pled guilty and Estrado pled not guilty. They were held for the grand jury, indicted, and at trial Wallace and Chavarria pled guilty again and the following day they were sentenced to serve ten years each and arrived at Nevada's state prison on April 6, 1876. Estrado's trial was set for April 19 and he was easily convicted based upon the testimony of Wallace and the other evidence. Estrado's failure to cooperate earned him a sentence of twenty-five years and he was delivered to the prison on April 23, 1876, but Estrado later told where the last bar of bullion was buried and it was recovered. Wallace's cooperation earned him an early release and he was pardoned on April 15, 1878. Chavarria served out his entire sentence, less good time, and was released on November 6, 1884, and then, on January 9, 1888, he was granted a full pardon to restore his civil rights. Estrado was pardoned on July 16, 1890, after serving only fourteen years, perhaps because he finally cooperated and disclosed the whereabouts of that last bar of bullion.

Territorial Enterprise [Virginia City, NV]: March 17, 1876; March 23, 1876; March 29, 1876; April 1, 1876; April 8, 1876.

Francis, David

Nativity, Kentucky; Age, 34 years; Occupation, Miner; Height 5 feet 7 inches; Complexion, Dark; Color of eyes, Hazel; Color of hair, Black, Size of foot, 8; Weight, 158 lbs. Knife wound on right and left side of small end of back bone, scar on outside right thigh, two scars right side, front gunshot wound right ankle front, scar above wrist left hand one inch long, scar front of left shin, drinks moderately and uses tobacco, does not use opium.

Robbed W. F. & Co's Express on stage from Kelton, Utah, to Albion, I. T., July 25, 1882, in company with William Adams, Jack King, and Francis "Frank" Hawley.

Robbed W. F. & Co's Express on stage from Albion, I. T., to Kelton, Utah, July 31, 1882, in company with William Adams, Jack King, and Francis Hawley.

Robbed W. F & Co's Express on stage from Humboldt Wells to Cherry Creek, Nev., August 14, 1882, in company with Francis Hawley.

Attempted to rob Overland Express train from San Francisco to Ogden at Montello, January 22, 1883, in company with Rais Anderson, Francis Hawley, Orrin Nay and Sylvester Earl.

Received at Nevada State Prison, March 2, 1883. Commitment, 245; Crime, assault to commit robbery; Term, 14 years; County sent from, Elko.
Escaped from State Prison October 8, 1884.
Recaptured and returned October 15, 1884.

On July 25, 1882, David Francis, Francis Hawley, William "Billy" Adams and Jack King robbed the stagecoach from Kelton in the Utah Territory to Albion in the Idaho Territory. On July 31, 1882, the same four road agents robbed the stagecoach from Albion to Kelton then separated and fled into Nevada. John N. Thacker, a Wells, Fargo detective, was put on the case [*see* Adams, William]. On August 14, 1882, Francis and Hawley robbed Wells, Fargo & Company's Express from Wells to Cherry Creek, Nevada, when the stagecoach was a mile past Spruce Mount Station. There was no messenger aboard and no passengers. The two men suddenly appeared with drawn revolvers and demanded that driver John Hamilton throw down the treasure box. He complied and they immediately broke it open, finding only $40 inside. The men were large and were disguised with one wearing a handkerchief over his entire face with eye holes cut in it and the other wearing a fur hat pulled down over his face. Once the robbers had the loot they ordered Hamilton to drive on and then mounted their horses and rode off at a leisurely pace. Hamilton hurried to the next telegraph and reported the robbery so a posse was soon on the road, and they had a good idea who they were after, but they were unable to intercept the fugitives. On August 24 the up-stagecoach for Wells was robbed by two road agents believed to be the same men who robbed the Cherry Creek coach. The take was again quite small but Thacker got word that these two road agents were in the vicinity of Parker's Station, possibly planning another robbery to fund their escape from Nevada. He believed they were heading for Arizona and he was determined to capture them before they dropped out of sight. He employed the assistance of J. B. "Big Sim" Simpson and Lew Kelly to take the Pioche stagecoach as messengers while he rented a buggy and, with Johnny O'Laughlin, started for Hamilton. At Hamilton they recruited a deputy sheriff and caught up with the stagecoach after it passed Ward. They convinced the only passenger to trade places with them, Thacker and O'Laughlin riding inside and the passenger joining the deputy sheriff in the carriage. At daybreak the coach arrived in Cave Valley, thirty miles south of Ward and a few miles from Parker's station. Within minutes after the coach arrived at the station the men noticed a suspicious character, who matched the description of one road agent, lurking one hundred yards from the barn. Thacker and Simpson got the drop on their man with shotguns and with the assistance of Kelly and O'Laughlin arrested him and took from him three loaded revolvers. After the prisoner was secured the four men went around the barn and there spied another suspicious character, resembling the second road agent, loitering behind a horse being shod. Simpson covered him with his shotgun while Thacker marched up and announced, "Now, my dear fellow, as it has become a fashionable custom to throw up hands, please elevate yours," and he did. Thacker took two fully loaded revolvers from him and searched him finding evidence, which he believed, proved them to be the stagecoach robbers. The two men identified themselves as Jack King and Billy Adams, and they were closely guarded on the trip to Eureka where they were lodged in jail. The two men were to be tried for the stagecoach robbery in Elko County but they confessed to being the Idaho stagecoach robbers and denied any part in the Nevada robberies. Thacker took them back to Idaho where they were indicted, tried and convicted of two stagecoach robberies and sentenced to life terms in the Idaho State Prison at Boise.

Attention then turned to Robert Catterson and Charles Nicholes as they had been ranging throughout the region and had broken into several cabins to steal clothes, arms and other valuables. They were captured at the Six-mile house on the Eureka road and mistakenly thought to be responsible for robbing the Cherry Creek stagecoach, and they were lodged in the Hamilton jail. They quickly escaped by kicking out the wall, which was supposed to be brick but in fact was only a flimsy wooden partition plastered over. Sheriff Raum issued a reward of $200 from his own account and parties were quickly in close pursuit. The two fugitives were captured by J. S. Matson who came across the fugitives while on his way home, and they were turned over to Charles Wray and C. M. Thackston who returned them to the Hamilton jail but immediately transferred to the jail at Eureka, a facility considered more secure. On November 5 the men escaped from the Eureka jail by cutting a hole through the wall after they were locked up for the night and they made their way to the Eureka & Palisade Railroad and took a handcar toward Palisade. They were so tired when one and one-half miles from the summit that they threw the handcar to one side and went to sleep. Had they continued that last short distance to the summit they had a fourteen mile downgrade and could have coasted out of danger of being caught, but when the handcar passed the "12 mile station" the section boss hailed them, but they did not slow. When the passenger train came through a short time later A. C. Ward, a Wells, Fargo messenger and a deputy sheriff, was informed and when the train came to the place where the car was discarded he stopped the train. Ward found the men asleep in the brush and capture them with his shotgun and they said they had stopped because they did not expect a train on Sunday. The fugitives were returned to the jail at Eureka and securely shackled. Wells, Fargo & Company contacted J. B. Simpson at Eureka and asked him to photograph the prisoners. Simpson knew that the men would not be willing subjects so he told them, "Boys, there is a young lady in town who is very anxious to have your portraits. Now if you want to have them taken I will pay for it and will bring the gal in and you can give her one." They agreed so Simpson immediately took them to Monaco's Photo Gallery where the work was done "before they had time to drop on the little racket." The stagecoach robbery case could not be "worked-up" against Catterson and Nicholes but there was ample evidence to convict them on charges of "housebreaking." They were tried and convicted during the final days of November 1882 on the lesser charge, a crime that normally carried a sentence of one to three years, but when they were brought into court for sentencing they were surprised to learn they each would serve a term of nine years at the state's prison. They arrived on December 1, 1882, and both men were pardoned on July 13, 1887.

Francis and Hawley, the real Cherry Creek stagecoach robbers, joined Sylvester Earl, Rais Anderson, and Orrin Nay and tried to rob the Overland Express train from San Francisco to Ogden, Utah, on January 22, 1883. At Montello, a water tank one hundred nine miles east of Elko, the men used a signal of danger ahead which no engineer could ignore so the train stopped and the crew was captured. The robbers locked the trainmen in the lower part of the water tank and then approached the express car, but messenger A. Y. Ross refused to surrender. Though wounded three times Ross fought off the robbers for more than three hours, until daylight, when they fled empty-handed. The robbers were arrested at Deep Creek, Utah, on January 30 during a thrilling shoot-out in which Nay and Hawley were badly wounded. They were brought back to Nevada and tried for train robbery, but Hawley and Francis were never tried for the Idaho and Nevada stagecoach robberies as the law was satisfied when they each received substantial sentences for "assault to commit robbery" [see Anderson, Rais]. Francis, Hawley and Nay received fourteen year prison terms while Earl and Anderson received sentences of twelve years. Anderson and Earl were pardoned on July 13, 1887. Francis, Hawley and Nay were pardoned on January 2, 1893, just two months before their tenth anniversary of imprisonment.

Weekly Elko Independent [NV]: August 20, 1882. *White Pine Daily News [Cherry Creek, NV]*: August 19, 1882; August 26, 1882; September 2, 1882; September 9, 1882; October 7, 1882; November 11, 1882.

Frazier, Charles—*alias* Red

Nativity, Indiana; Age, 33 years; Occupation, Teamster; Height, 5 feet 8 inches; Complexion, Red; Color of eyes, Brown; Color of hair, Red. Square features, high forehead, prominent nose, small scar back of left wrist, do. base of right thumb, scar low down on right side, stout built.

First commitment, 4384. Arrived at California State Prison, February 5, 1870; Crime, grand larceny; Term, 1 year; County sent from, San Bernardino.

Discharged by expiration of sentence, December, 6, 1870.

Convicted of being accessory to the robbery of the Redding stage, November 3, 1876, and the Downieville stage, November 13, 1876, in company with Tom and Joe Brown (brothers) and David Tye.

Escaped from Marysville Jail while awaiting trial, June 1, 1877; recaptured and returned to jail December 9, 1877.

Escaped again from Marysville Jail February 26, 1878; recaptured and returned to jail March 6, 1878.

Received at California State Prison, April 6, 1878; No. of commitment, 8121; Crime, robbery; Term, 17 years; County sent from, Yuba.

Pardoned conditionally by Governor George Stoneman, March 16, 1883.

[*See* Brown, Tom]

Fugate, William—*alias* Billy Fugate

Nativity, Kentucky; Age, 33 years; Occupation, Laborer; Height, 5 feet 8¾ inches; Complexion, Florid; Color of eyes, Blue; Color of hair, Brown. Round features, high forehead, large scar on forehead, do. under and back of right arm; stout built.

Robbed W. F. & Co's Express on stage from Yreka to Red Bluff, August 21, 1871, in company with Milton "Milt" Shepardson, John Grant and Ziska Calmez.

Robbed W. F. & Co's Express on stage from Yreka to Red Bluff, September 26, 1871, in company with Milton "Milt" Shepardson, John Grant and Ziska Calmez.

Plead guilty, September 15, 1874, and

Pardoned while *en route* to State Prison by Governor Newton Booth.

Received at the California State prison, September 30, 1879. No. of commitment, 8824; Crime, assault to murder; Term 7 years; County sent from, Merced.

Taken out for new trial, November 16, 1879.

[*See* Shepardson, Milton]

Gil, Jose M.

Nativity, California; Age, 30 years; Occupation, Vaquero; Height, 5 feet 10 inches; Complexion, Florid; Color of eyes, Black; Color of hair, Black. Large features, high forehead, two moles on left side of head, two moles on back; stout built.

Robbed W. F. & Co's Express on stage from Soledad to San Luis Obispo, April 14, 1877, with William L. Earl.

Received at the California State Prison, July 13, 1877. No. of commitment, 7662; Crime, grand larceny; Term 4 years; County sent from, Monterey.

Discharged, upon expiration of sentence, July 13, 1880.

[*See* Earl, William L.]

Gillett, Frederick

Nativity, New York; Age, 40 years; Occupation, Laborer; Height, 5 feet 3 inches; Complexion, Light; Color of eyes, Blue; Color of hair, Light. Square features, high forehead, nose turned slightly to the right, scar on right jaw, scar on right side of forehead, ink marks back of right hand, mole on back of neck; stout built.

Robbed W. F. & Co's Express on stage from Mojave to Darwin, October 12, 1876 — alone.

Received at the California State Prison, March 12, 1877. No. of commitment, 7442; Crime, Robbery; Term, 10 years; County sent from, Kern.

Removed to Folsom Prison, September 30, 1880.

Attempted to escape.

On October 12, 1876, after the up-stagecoach from Mojave to Darwin passed the Panamint junction it was stopped by a lone highway man, masked and heavily armed. He stepped into the road and ordered the driver to halt, then demanded that he throw down Wells, Fargo's treasure box. Once the box was in the roadway he ordered the coach to continue and the driver hurried to the next station to report the robbery. The scene was investigated but there were no clues reported so the description of the road agent was widely circulated.

On Sunday, October 22 Darwin's ex-deputy sheriff James Wales saw a man whom he recognized as the road agent. Wales tried to make an arrest, but the fugitive went for his revolver and the two men exchanged several shots. Wales was wounded in the leg while the fugitive was wounded in the shoulder and, though neither wound was serious, the shoulder wound was sufficient to incapacitate the robber and he was captured. The prisoner identified himself as Frederick Gillett and he was taken before Judge McManus, who found no cause for the arrest and discharged the defendant. McManus then called for an examination of Wales, charging him with being the assaulting party, but the evidence was insufficient and he was also released.

As soon as Gillett was freed he was re-arrested by James B. Hume, Wells, Fargo & Company's chief detective, and he took his prisoner to Kern County charged with another stagecoach robbery. Sheriff Passmore and defense attorney H. W. Woods accompanied the prisoner to Indian Wells where, following another examination, he was again discharged. Hume re-arrested Gillette and this time took his prisoner to Bakersfield. Hume had another arrest warrant issued after he provided new evidence and in Bakersfield Gillett was held to answer to the grand jury, but the jury was not in session so the prisoner was lodged in jail. On January 2, 1877, the grand jury indicted Gillett for the stagecoach robbery near Panamint junction. On January 5 he pled not guilty and his trial was scheduled to begin on January 11 but on January 10 his case was continued to the first day of the next term of the court. In early March Gillett confessed to the robbery but still pled not guilty. He was tried and convicted of robbing the Mojave to Darwin stagecoach on October 12, 1876, and sentenced to serve ten years at San Quentin Prison. He arrived on March 12, 1877, and registered as prisoner No. 7442. On September 30, 1880, he was removed to Folsom Prison where he registered as prisoner No. 204, and from that "prison without walls" he tried to escape but failed. He forfeited the good time he had earned under the Goodwin Act and was finally released, by expiration of sentence, on March 12, 1887, after serving every day of his ten year sentence.

Courier Californian [Bakersfield, CA]: January 2, 1877; January 5, 1877; January 10, 1877. *Inyo Independent [Independence, CA]*: October 14, 1876; October 28, 1876; November 4, 1876; November 11, 1876; March 17, 1877.

Glover, Edward

Nativity, California; Age, 24 years; Occupation, Laborer; Height, 5 feet 3⅜ inches; Complexion, Dark; Color of eyes, Hazel; Color of hair, Black; Size of foot, 5. Round features, small ears, high, full forehead, broad nostrils, thick lips, heavy eyebrows, small mole top of forehead, scar on right forefinger, small hands, large scar left side of head — back of ear, large mole back of left shoulder, round shouldered; stout built.

Accessory to robbing W. F. & Co's Express on stage from Yreka to Redding, May 8, 1884, by Owen Temple and John Williams.

Received at the California State Prison, June 22, 1884. No. of commitment, 11294; Crime, robbery; Term, 5 years; County sent from, Shasta.

[*See* Temple, Owen]

Grant, J. H.—*alias* Johnnie Grant

Nativity, Kentucky; Age, 39 years, Occupation, Cook; Height 5 feet 8¾ inches; Complexion, Fair; Color of eyes, Brown; Color of hair, Dark. Thin features, turn-up nose, mole on left cheek, scar running from center to right side of chin, mole under right jaw, scar on right side of upper lip, small vaccine marks on right and left arms, three small round raised scars on stomach and belly, stooped shoulders; slender built.

Robbed W. F. & Co's Express on stage from Yreka to Red Bluff, August 21, 1871, in company with Milton "Milt" Shepardson, William Fugate and Ziska Calmez.

Robbed W. F. & Co's Express on stage from Yreka to Red Bluff, September 26, 1871, in company with Milton "Milt" Shepardson, William Fugate and Ziska Calmez.

Received at the California State Prison, April 2, 1872. No. of commitment, 5215; Crime, robbery; Term 7 years; County sent from, Shasta.

Commuted by Governor William Irwin, May 30, 1876, to 5 years.

Discharged, June 20, 1876.

[*See* Shepardson, Milton]

Greeley, Burton

Nativity, North Carolina; Age, 38 years; Occupation, Miner; Height, 5 feet 9⅛ inches; Complexion. Dark; Color of eyes, Blue; Color of hair, Black; Size of foot, 8½. Square features, heavy eyebrows, high full forehead, square chin and jaw, small ears, small scar left side of forehead, small scar right side of forehead, scar base of left thumb inside, star base of thumb, fingers of left hand stiff and crooked, arms hairy, two large vaccine marks right upper arm, square shoulders.

Robbed W. F. & Co's Express on stage from Sonora to Milton, February 26, 1884 — alone.

Received at the California State Prison, April 1, 1884. No. of commitment, 11200; Crime, robbery, Term, 5 years, County sent from, Calaveras.

On Tuesday morning, February 26, 1884, the down-stagecoach from Sonora to Milton driven by Joe Mulligan was stopped by a lone highwayman armed with a shotgun when a half mile before Angel's Creek in Calaveras County. Once the coach was halted the road agent made the driver unhitch the team and then ordered the only passenger, Reverend B. F. Rattray of Alameda, to climb down as well. "Now, you lay down on the ground and don't you move a hand or bat an eye," and the Reverend responded, "But, my kind sir, it is cold and I might be made sick by the exposure." The road agent told Rattray, "Cold be d__d! You get down on that ground or I'll make an angel of you d__d quick, D'ye hear?" Rattray was stubborn and said, "But I am not only a minister of the Gospel, but it is awful cold, and you are blue in the face yourself. Please don't insist on the sacrifice," and then he "clasped his hands as if in prayer and rolled his eyes beseechingly." The robber relented and told the preacher to walk down the road a good distance and stand with his back to the stagecoach. The robber then spent a considerable time trying to break into the iron safe bolted inside the coach but, failing to gain entrance, he broke open the wooden treasure box. There was nothing of value inside so he told Mulligan to hitch up his horses and continue on, picking up his passenger on the way. The coach proceeded to a point two miles beyond Angel's Creek when two more road agents sprang from behind a bush and again halted the stagecoach. They were armed with a rifle and a revolver. These road agents also had Mulligan unhitch the horses and, along with Rattray, take them some distance down the road and await a signal, a whistle, before returning. From their position in the road they could hear the robbers banging on the iron safe for fifteen minutes before giving up and leaving without giving the signal to return. After Mulligan and Rattray tired of waiting, and had heard no sound from the coach for a while, they returned and found that the two road agents had managed to break off the outer lock but had no luck in breaking into the interior of the safe. The stagecoach then continued on its way and Rattray said, "My friend, this is a little bit rough to be stopped twice in one morning," and Mulligan replied, "That is nothing on this road." As soon as they started they passed a man walking along the road and he pulled his hat down and bowed his head as he passed, but Rattray immediately recognized him as the first road agent. They continued on to the first farms and told the men of their experience, and the farmers organized a posse and started after the road agent but did not find him. Sheriff Ben Thorn and Wells, Fargo's detective James Hume struck the trail of the first road agent at Burus' Ferry, where he had crossed the Stanislaus River at 10:00 A.M. on the morning of the robbery, traveling on foot. At the Crimea House they learned he was heading toward Sonora, but they soon lost the trail and Thorn, with Sheriff McQuade, headed south leaving Hume behind to watch for the fugitive. At Chinese Camp they cut his trail again and learned their man had crossed the Tuolumne River at Don Pedro's Bar and headed toward Fresno. When two miles from Enterprise the lawmen learned that the robber was in a store at Fresno Flats so they drove their wagon to the store as quickly as they could, dashed through the front door, and rushed upon the fugitive so quickly that he could make no resistance. The prisoner did not question his arrest until they had already traveled many miles from Fresno Flats, and when told it was for stagecoach robbery he made no attempt to deny the charge. They took their prisoner to Mariposa Creek and spent the night and then took him into Sonora, a trip of some sixty miles, where he was lodged in jail. When the party arrived in Sonora several men came forward to identify the prisoner, Burton Greeley, as the road agent, a man seen about town a few days before the robbery. Mulligan, the driver, identified him as the first of the road agents and the man who had passed him on foot just after the second halting of the stagecoach. A representative of the *Union Democrat* was allowed to interview the prisoner and he reported that Greeley was from South Carolina, thirty-five years of age, medium height, with a muscular and raw-boned build, black hair and eyes. He had been mining at Indian Creek but was returning to his home at Fresno Flats, penniless, when the stagecoach was robbed but claimed he was innocent. On March 14 Sheriff Thorn transferred his prisoner to San Andreas, Calaveras County, for trial and on March 17 Greeley was taken before Justice P. H. Kean and the date for his examination was set for the March 27. Kean bound him over to await action by the grand jury. Greeley, now aware of the overwhelming evidence against him, confessed to the stagecoach robbery and agreed to plead guilty. In consideration of his cooperation and lack of a prison record he was sentenced to serve five years at San Quentin

Prison. He arrived on April 1, 1884, registering as convict No. 11200. Greeley died in the prison hospital on July 20, 1886, possibly from consumption which was epidemic in the prison during those years.

Calaveras Chronicle [CA]: March 1, 1884; March 15, 1884; March 22, 1884, March 29, 1884.

Grimes, Cicero

Nativity, Arkansas; Age, 34 years; Occupation, Photographer; Height, 5 feet 5 inches; Complexion, Light, Color of eyes, Blue; Color of hair, Light Brown. Small round ears, very small feet — wear No. 3. Moles all over small of back, wart on left side of stomach, very hairy breast, vaccine scar left upper arm, scar 1 inch long on left knee, has an earnest, pleasing face, quick and active in motion, inclines to corpulence.

On the 20th of August, 1882, Cicero Grimes, Lafayette Grimes (his brother), and Hawley robbed W. F. & Co's Express on stage from Casa Grande, A. T. to Globe, A. T. of $5,000, killed W. F. & Co's messenger, Andy Hall, and Dr. Vail, a passenger. The three were arrested three days later, confessed their guilt, told where the lost treasure could be found, and Lafayette Grimes and Hawley were thereupon hanged by the citizens of Globe, A. T. Cicero Grimes was not present at the robbery, but pleaded guilty of being an accessory, and owing to the importunities of his wife and family, and the widow of Dr. Vail, his life was spared and he was sent to the Penitentiary for a term of twenty-one years.

Received at the Territorial Prison, Yuma, October 11, 1882. No. of commitment 115; Crime, robbery; Term, 21 years.

Shortly after his arrival at Yuma he began playing the insanity dodge, and July 9, 1883, he was delivered to the Superintendent of the Pacific Asylum at Stockton, California, where the Arizona insane are cared for. During the night of September 9, 1883, he *escaped* from the Asylum, and is still at large.

Curtis B. Hawley was in the wood and charcoal business while Lafayette "Fate" Grimes was a dance instructor in Globe. Cicero Grimes, Lafayette's brother and a husband and father of three, had started up Grimes & Co. at Globe to construct a wagon road from Pinal to Riverside, and the Grimes boys and Hawley planned to build the road together and share in the profits. Cicero had submitted the lowest bid but was having difficulty posting the proper bonds when the Florence *Enterprise* reported:

> Grimes and Company of Globe, who offered to build a wagon road from Riverside to Pinal, have notified the board of supervisors that, owing to a mistake they have not been able to secure the bond required. The board, upon receipt of this notice, granted an extension of time, allowing them to file said bond upon any day between now and April 1st. This is right and proper, but we fear the gentlemen will experience considerable difficulty in securing bondsmen, as their bid is too low. Competent judges declare that the road, over the route proposed and according to the terms of the plans and specifications, cannot be constructed at a less cost than $4,000, whereas the bid of Grimes & Co. is only $1,800. We hope, however, that they may succeed.

When the bonds could not be posted, the Board of Supervisors awarded the contract to the next lowest bidder. Lafayette and Cicero Grimes and Curtis B. Hawley met at Hawley's place to consider putting in a bridge at the lower end of Globe as a new plan to make money. As the conversation progressed Hawley suggested an "Indian racket" to take in the stagecoach and lay blame on the Indians. Cicero spoke up and said, "I think that would be easy to do; no one would be suspicious," so the three men agreed to do the work and made their plans. The "stage" they were contemplating was actually a treasure-and-mail pack train. The men planned to fire at the train but not at the men believing this would scare away the messenger and mail carrier, and then they would shoot the mule carrying the treasure box. On August 19 Lafayette left Globe traveling south along the Pioneer trail to search for a spot to execute the robbery. He found just the right place four and one half miles south from town where there was a bend in the trail, and there he hid a miner's pick and hatchet before returning to Globe. Cicero left Globe early on Saturday to meet the treasure train and en route he cut away fifty feet of wire from the Globe-San Carlos telegraph line and carried it away before continuing on. He arrived in time to help load the treasure box, test its weight, and help tie it onto the mule. Cicero then returned to Globe by way of the Pioneer trail, riding ahead of the train to inform the two robbers in their hiding places that there was sufficient treasure to justify the risk of a robbery. He warned of the arms carried by the messenger and mail carrier — a rifle without cartridges and a six-shooter with the messenger while the mail carrier was unarmed. On Sunday morning, August 20 at 4:00 A.M. Lafayette and Hawley left Globe and went to the Milk ranch, took the right hand canyon and continued to the Pioneer trail. They followed the trail a few hundred yards and took up positions at the point selected by Lafayette where they prepared breastworks to conceal themselves. Hawley took the high post to watch the trail while Lafayette took the lower post, and from there he was to kill the mule and take the treasure. Hawley had an old sixteen shot Henry rifle and Lafayette had a .50 caliber rim-fire rifle.

Andy Hall, Wells, Fargo & Company's messenger, and mail carrier Frank Porter were driving the train in front of them as they came to the bend in the trail. The treasure mule was near the lead of the train ahead of the men and as she came around the bend Lafayette and Hawley fired. Hall came forward to investigate and both robbers emptied their weapons in his direction. Hall then went to the top of a hill to see if there was a way through but could see none. He saw that Porter was ready to bolt and called out, "Frank, I'll stay with you, old boy, don't run," but when he saw there were two shooters he called, "there is more than one, we had better get out of this." Frank Porter made tracks for a nearby ranch house to get a gun while Hall stepped off the trail looking for cover. Lafayette thought that Hall had also fled so after Hawley shot the mule carrying the treasure box Lafayette approached, cut the ropes with the hatchet, and broke open the box. He took out $5,000 belonging to Fisk, Waldridge & Co. and a watch and put them into his saddlebags. He then started toward Globe with Hawley following and when Hawley caught up he scolded Lafayette for leaving the registered mail. Hawley told him to go back but Lafayette said, "We have got enough here, come on." The two robbers went over two ridges and down a ravine and were nearing Bremen's Road when Dr. W. F. Vail came upon them. Vail said he had been fired upon by Indians and thought they should get into town quickly, and the two robbers were certain that the doctor suspected them of the robbery, so they shot him dead. Lafayette and Hawley, now murderers, continued their flight but, tiring, stopped in some oak brush to rest. Soon they saw Hall following their tracks and when he was within forty feet Lafayette took a shot at him but missed. Hall spun around with revolver in hand, ready for a fight, but immediately recognized the two as white men. Lafayette said, "I thought there were more Indians here. I thought you were an Indian," and Hall then showed them a wound in his leg with the ball protruding. The wound was not severe but was crippling enough to slow him but not severe enough to stop his pursuit. The three men went on together but Hall began noticing things such as the heavy load that Lafayette carried in his saddlebags and the effort the boys made to keep one of them behind Hall. After a while he told them he wanted them to walk on each side of him and not behind and they complied, but finally they came to a place about a mile off the Pioneer trail where they could rest and keep watch for Indians. Hall stood up to look over the terrain, and had his six-shooter in hand. Lafayette and Hawley fired at once but Hall had heard something and had spun to face them as both bullets struck him in the chest. Hall returned fire but without effect because of his mortal wounds, and the robbers fired again killing the messenger as he lay on the ground. When found Hall was found lying face down with his six-shooter in his extended hand with all cartridges fired and, when examined it was determined that he had eight .44 caliber bullets in his chest.

Andy Hall was well liked throughout Arizona and was a close friend of U.S. deputy Marshal J. P. Gabriel. Hall had come to the Territory in 1868 with Powell's expedition through the Grand Canyon and had not left the Territory since. He first resided in Prescott and lately had become manager of the Gray Eagle Stables and a messenger for Wells, Fargo & Company. Gabriel was at the Silver King when the robbery occurred and he hurried to Globe to investigate the murder of his friend and the first clue found was a footprint at the scene. It was very small and at first there was speculation that a woman might be involved until one man mentioned that Lafayette Grimes, Globe's dance instructor, had unusually small feet for a man. There were two other men with small feet as well, so Gabriel made further inquiries and asked Captain D. B. Lacey if anyone in Globe was suspicioned. The Captain replied, "Yes, I suspicion young Grimes. He belongs to my company of rangers and during Indian excitements was first to answer the call to arms. But, on this occasion, has kept away, and did not even come to see the bodies when they were brought in." Lacey had loaned Lafayette a new rifle the day before the murders but, when returned, the gun had been fired and had dents in the stock from being struck against rocks. Gabriel, Lacey and Lindsley Lewis went to the gunsmith shop to have the cartridges compared and there the deputy Marshal saw a man who acted very suspicious. When the man left Gabriel said, "he is a guilty one" and asked his name, and upon learning that the man was Lafayette's brother Cicero they decided to arrest Lafayette. Lafayette Grimes was found and arrested by Gabriel, Lacey and Lewis at Mack Morris' Mill. He was questioned and he finally confessed. While returning to Globe with the prisoner Gabriel suggested that they keep Lafayette away from town until the money could be recovered, so he was taken to the Golden Eagle Mill under close guard. Hawley was then arrested at his house in Globe and taken to Saxes' ranch. Gabriel rode to the Golden Eagle Mill, collected Lafayette and headed for Saxes' ranch, but en route Sheriff W. W. "Tip" Lowther overtook them and tried to take the prisoner but Gabriel would have none of it and took his prisoner to the ranch. Lowther followed and the party arrived at 1:00 A.M., and an hour later Lacey arrived with Hawley and the two prisoners were placed in the ranch house together. Lowther continued to insist that the prisoners be turned over and Gabriel stated that he held them as U.S. deputy Marshal and would turn them over only by the use of force, but suggested that he would abide by a finding of Judge McCabe that he should turn them over. He told Lowther he would take the prisoners to the Pinal ranch and wait there until 4:00 P.M. for the judge's decision. At 3:00 P.M. detective John M. Jones rushed up to the ranch, read warrants for the two prisoners, arrested them and took them to Globe in spite of a warning that they would be hung there. Cicero had been arrested Wednesday at the Grimes' home and soon his brother and Hawley joined him in the Globe jail.

At 10:00 P.M. the three men were taken from their cell and marched to Stalla's Hall, where a committee of citizens tried them, found them guilty, and sentenced the two murderers to hang. Cicero's wife and Dr. Vail's widow pleaded for Cicero's life and the committee, which had already determined that he was not present at the killings, returned him to his cell to await trial. Lafayette and Hawley asked for three hours to put their lives in order and in return they offered to divulge the location of the stolen money. With a party of thirty men they went into the foothills and dug up the money, one third in Hawley's cache and two-thirds hidden by Lafayette for himself and his brother. At 2:00 A.M. Thursday, August 24 Lafayette V. Grimes and Curtis B. Hawley were taken to a large sycamore tree at the center of town on Main Street near Pinal Creek. The saloons had closed their doors and not one drunken man was present. The church bell tolled continuously as the men were marched along and while they were being pulled up by their necks, where they dangled until dead. Cicero Grimes was tried, convicted and sentenced to twenty-one years in the Territorial Prison. He arrived at the prison on October 11, 1882, and registered as prisoner No. 115. Shortly after his arrival he began to display bizarre behavior and was determined to be insane. On July 9, 1883, he was transferred to the Pacific Asylum for the Insane at Stockton, California, and two months later he escaped from that institution never to be heard of again. In October 1882 Cicero Grimes' family left Arizona Territory for San Francisco and they were not heard of again in the Territory.

Arizona Gazette [Phoenix, AZ]: August 31, 1882. *Arizona Weekly Enterprise [Florence, AZ]*: February 18, 1882; August 26, 1882; September 2, 1882; September 7, 1882; October 7, 1882; October 14, 1882. *Tombstone Epitaph [AZ]*: August 26, 1882. *Weekly Miner [Prescott, AZ]*: September 1, 1882.

Hamilton, A. P.—*alias* Albert Tarlton, Al Hamilton

Nativity, Ohio; Age 36 years; Occupation, Laborer; Height, 5 feet 6½ inches; Complexion, Light; Color of eyes; Blue; Color of hair, Fair. Round full features, small mole close to the left eyebrow, large round vaccine mark on the left upper arm, several scars on the left forefinger, scar between first and second joints of left thumb, scar on first joint of first finger of right hand, and the finger crooked, two boil marks on the back of neck, several small moles on the back, small mole on the right upper arm, gunshot wound on left upper arm; stout built.

No. of first commitment, 3619. Received at the California State Prison, September 16, 1867; Crime, forgery and grand larceny; Term 6 years; County sent from, Tulare.

Discharged, by expiration of sentence, September 28, 1872.

Robbed W. F. & Co's Express on stage from Santa Clara to Santa Cruz, April 1, 1874, in company with Peter Carr. In resisting arrest received a severe gunshot wound in the arm.

Received at the California State prison, May 26, 1874; No. of commitment, 6020; Crime, robbery; Term, 10 years; County sent from, Santa Clara.

Escaped from State Prison, November 15, 1874.

Robbed W. F. & Co's Express on stage from Grass Valley to Colfax, April 16, 1875.

Robbed W. F. & Co's Express on stage from Ione City to Galt, May 3, 1875.

Rearrested May 19, 1875, in San Francisco, and returned to San Quentin.

Commuted by Governor William Irwin, May 30, 1876, to 8 years.

Discharged upon a writ of *habeas corpus*, December 3, 1879.

Robbed W. F. & Co's Express on stage from San Andreas to Milton, April 29, 1880, in company with Roger O'Meara

Attempted to rob W. F. & Co's Express on stage from Jackson to Ione, exchanging several shots with the guard who was in charge of the Express, May 6, 1880, in company with Roger O'Meara

Robbed W. F. & Co's Express on stage from Georgetown to Placerville, May 24, 1880, in company with Roger O'Meara.

In resisting arrest was shot in the [previously] wounded arm, but *escaped* and is still at large.

Albert P. Hamilton had a fair education as a youth and before he turned eighteen he left his Ohio home for California. The promised opportunities for fame and fortune did not materialize so the disillusioned youth joined the army. After a few months, however, he realized that a military life was not for him and in August 1867 he deserted. He made his way to Tulare County where he "uttered" a false order for goods at a Visalia mercantile, stole a horse, and fled into Inyo County. A tenacious lawman tracked him down, made the arrest, and charged him with grand larceny. Hamilton gave his name as Henry Tarlton when he was taken to the Tulare County jail and, after the army refused to pick up the deserter, he was prosecuted in the district court. Tarlton was easily convicted of the charge and sentenced to serve six years at San Quentin prison, where he disclosed his first name was actually Albert but persisted in using Tarlton for a last name. In prison Hamilton continued his education but of a different nature, and when he was released on September 28, 1872, by expiration of sentence he considered himself a much improved outlaw. Hamilton did not again come to the attention of lawmen for eighteen months, but by late March 1874 he had partnered with Peter Carr to rob a stagecoach. Hamilton took an honest job for a few weeks to earn a stake to support their plan and, after receiving his first paycheck, absconded with his employer's shotgun. The two aspiring road agents selected a steep grade near the summit above Santa Clara Valley in Santa Clara County where the horses would walk slowly and passengers, if any were aboard, might disembark and walk to lighten the load. During the late afternoon of April 1, 1874, the two men stretched a rope across the road as a barrier and hid in the brush. Hamilton wore a mask and carried the shotgun, the only weapon they had, so Carr remained in hiding. The four horse celerity wagon from Santa Clara bound for Santa Cruz driven by J. P. Smith reached the rope barrier just before 3:00 P.M. and Hamilton rose up, pointed his shotgun at Smith, and demanded Well's, Fargo's treasure box. The driver said there was no box aboard and, after a brief argument, threw out two mail pouches. Hamilton refused to molest the U.S. mails and then went through the passengers, ordering them to throw out their money. The occupants began throwing out bills and coins and then Hamilton returned the mail pouches to the driver's boot before ordering Smith to continue on. Once the coach was underway the passengers looked back to see the road agent groveling in the dirt, collecting the bills and coins totaling less than $45. Four weeks later a concord stagecoach driven by W. E. McFarland was stopped again at almost the same place. It was nearly 2:00 P.M. when two masked men, both now armed with shotguns and wearing dark hats pulled down, stepped from the same side of the road and into the path of the team. Once the coach was stopped Hamilton walked to the rear of the coach while Carr held the horses. Hamilton walked to the opposite side before poking his shotgun into the window and demanding that everyone hand out their wallets, but the men began handing him coins so he again demanded their wallets. The horses were becoming restless so Hamilton allowed McFarland to continue on to Santa Cruz after collecting less than $10. In Santa Cruz the driver reported the robbery to Sheriff Bob Orton and several posses were soon in the field.

One posse consisted of deputies Jackson Sylva and Frank Curtis and they followed up a lead which took them to the cabin of "Mountain" Charley McKiernan. He claimed to have seen two men hunting squirrels the previous day, and their descriptions matched the two road agents. McKiernan joined the two lawmen as they searched the area and they discovered the two fugitives hiding in an old barn. They exchanged several shots before McKiernan wounded Hamilton and both men surrendered, and the lawmen recovered the stolen money and took the men to jail. In May they were tried for the April 1, 1874, stagecoach robbery, convicted, and both men were sentenced to serve ten years at San Quentin, and they both arrived on May 26, 1874. Carr was pardoned by Governor William Irwin on

August 15, 1878, but he would commit a burglary in San Francisco in early 1879 and return to prison for another five years, to be released again on September 4, 1882. Hamilton escaped from prison on November 15, 1874, in company with his three cell mates. He hid for five months but on April 16, 1875, the stagecoach from Grass Valley to Colfax in Nevada County, California, was stopped by Hamilton working alone, and he demanded the Wells, Fargo express box. On May 3 the same lone highwayman stopped the stagecoach from Ione in Amador County to Galt in Sacramento County and again took the Wells, Fargo box. On May 19 Hamilton, who hoped to blend into San Francisco's large transient population, was arrested and returned to prison without being tried for the two 1875 stagecoach robberies. On May 30, 1876, his sentence was commuted to eight years and on December 3, 1879, he was released on a writ of *habeas corpus*. While in prison he met Roger O'Meara, who was released one month before Hamilton.

As soon as both men were free Hamilton and O'Meara rendezvoused and began to plan stagecoach robberies in Calaveras County. On April 29, 1880, the two masked, armed road agents stopped the coach from San Andreas to Milton and demanded the Wells, Fargo treasure box. They broke it open, took the contents, and disappeared into the brush. On May 6 they tried to stop the stagecoach from Jackson to Ione in Amador County but the driver whipped up his team as the messenger exchanged shots with the two robbers. On May 26 the same two men stopped the stagecoach from Georgetown to Placerville in El Dorado County and once again they got the Wells, Fargo express box, but in an exchange of gunfire Hamilton was once again seriously wounded in his arm. Both men, now well know and the subjects of an intensive manhunt, fled from California. Hamilton was not heard of again but O'Meara was arrested on a charge of burglary in St. Louis, Missouri and after receiving a stiff sentence was not brought back to California for prosecution.

Mariposa Gazette [CA]: November 28, 1874. *Santa Cruz Sentinel [CA]*: April 4, 1874; May 2, 1874. *Visalia Delta [CA]*: September 11, 1874.

Hamilton, Bob

Nativity, Canada; Age, 36 years; Occupation, Saloon keeper; Height, 5 feet 6¼ inches; Complexion, Dark; Color of eyes, Gray; Color of hair, Black, Weight, 141 lbs. Vaccine mark on left arm, scar on right cheek from a bullet wound, scar on right wrist, scar back of tight ear, scar on middle knuckle of right hand, scar on buttock near middle of back, two scars on left knee, birth mark on left shin.

Attempted to rob W. F. & Co's Express on stage from Eureka to Tybo, September 3, 1877, in company with Jack Davis and John Doe.

Received at the Nevada State Prison, December 8, 1877. No. of commitment, 68; Crime, assault to rob; Term, 14 years; County sent from, Nye.

[*See* Davis, Jack]

Hamilton, George Cates

Nativity, Maine; Age, 30 years; Occupation, Stage Driver; Height, 5 feet 6⅞ inches; Complexion, Florid; Color of eyes, Hazel; Color of hair, Dark Brown. Square features, forehead below the medium, small ears, small lobes attached, rather thin square cut nose, high on the bridge, large long nostrils, slightly arching small mouth, small square cut chin, hair inclined to be a little curly, tolerable large irregular scar on left wrist joint — inside, dim vaccine mark top of left upper arm, black mole about a quarter of an inch to the left of spine between shoulders, small scar middle joint of right index finger, small flesh moles near right arm-pit on breast; medium built.

Burglarized W. F. & Co's Office at Point Arenas, July 19, 1882, in company with Porter Randolph. Randolph confessed, and was released, in consideration of having testified against Hamilton.

Received at the California State Prison, August 16, 1882. No. of commitment, 10511; Crime, burglary; Term, 3 years; County sent from, Mendocino.

Discharged, by expiration of sentence, December 16, 1884.

Between 11:00 P.M. on July 10 and 1:00 A.M. July 11, 1882, two burglars pried open the window to Wells, Fargo's office in Point Arenas, Mendocino County. Once inside the burglars broke open the express boxes from the up and down coaches. The up-coach box had only letters and a package containing $15 while the down-coach box contained $80 in coin and mill orders in the amount of $225, on which payment was immediately stopped so they were of no value to the thieves. Ukiah's agent Linderoos telegraphed Sheriff Donohue and he immediately had suspicions of the identity of the guilty parties. By Thursday, July 27 Sheriff Donohue had arrested a man who gave his name as George Cates and soon afterward he arrested his partner Porter Randolph. Randolph joined Cates [Hamilton] in the Ukiah jail and their examination before Judge Cunningham was set for August 11. Randolph informed on his partner and agreed to turn state's evidence to gain his release. Hamilton was held to answer and convicted at trial in August based upon the testimony of Randolph. Hamilton was sentenced to serve a term of three years at San Quentin while Randolph was released in consideration of his cooperation and testimony. Hamilton arrived at San Quentin Prison on August 16, 1882, and registered as prisoner No. 10511. He served out his entire sentence and was released, by expiration of sentence, on December 16, 1884.

Mendocino Beacon [CA]: July 22, 1882. *Ukiah City Press [CA]*: July 21, 1882; August 4, 1882.

Harker, Francis—*alias* John Burke

Nativity, Texas; Age, 45 years; Occupation, Laborer; Height, 5 feet 10 inches; Complexion; Fair; Color of eyes, Dark; Color of hair, Dark. Sharp features, two scars on right knee, large scar on right leg below knee, light circular scar under left nipple, one upper tooth gone, has an affection [*sic*] of the stomach which occasions frequent vomiting.

Received at the Nevada State Prison, August 12, 1871. No. of commitment, —; Crime, assault to murder; Term 3 years.

Escaped in "Big Break," September 17, 1871.

Recaptured and returned to Prison, October 23, 1871.

Escaped March 1, 1872, from Carson Jail with Frank Clifford and others who were awaiting trial for Prison-breaking. He and Clifford fled to Eureka County, Nev., and robbed W. F. & Co's Express on stage between Eureka and Mineral Hill.

Recaptured and returned to State Prison without trial for the stage robbery.

Discharged, upon expiration of sentence, February 1, 1876.

Robbed W. F. & Co's Express and the U.S. Mail on stage from Salt Lake City, Utah, to Pioche, Nev., May 31, 1876, in company with Ed. Bigelow, alias Willis.

Robbed W. F. & Co's Express and the U.S. Mail on stage from Pioche, Nev., to Salt Lake City, Utah, May 31, 1876, in company with Ed Bigelow, alias Willis.

Arrested June 2, 1876, and placed in the Beaver County Jail, U. T.

Escaped from County Jail a few days later.

Recaptured and taken to Utah Penitentiary for safe keeping.

Escaped, in a few days, from the Penitentiary. Burke [*sic*] was re-captured, taken to Beaver and tried,

convicted, and sentenced to a Life Term for Mail Robbery, in Detroit Prison. While en route made a desperate attempt to escape from U.S. Marshal, who had him in charge.
Receive at the Detroit Prison, October 1877. No. of commitment, —; Crime, mail robbery; Term, life. *Escaped*, on the night of November 2, 1877, and is still at large.

Francis Harker, using his alias John Burke, was first sent to Nevada's state prison on August 12, 1871. He had committed an "assault to murder" and was sentenced to serve three years. A month after Harker arrived, twenty-nine prisoners escaped from the prison in what has been called "the Big Break-out." He went along, was captured in a month, and returned to prison on October 23, 1871, but was soon transferred to the jail at Carson City to await trial for the prison break. Harker escaped from the jail on March 1, 1872, with Frank Clifford and several others [*see* Clifford, Frank] and they robbed a stagecoach between Eureka and Mineral Hill in Eureka County on March 28. Harker, using his alias John Burke, Clifford and George Roth were captured and returned to prison without being tried for the "big break" or for the stagecoach robbery and was discharged upon expiration of sentence on February 1, 1876.

On May 30, 1876, between 10:00 and 11:00 P.M. the Gilmer & Salisbury stagecoach from Salt Lake City, Utah, bound for Pioche, Nevada, driven by John Daniel Whitbeck was halted when three miles north of the Sevier River in Millard County, Utah. Two masked and armed road agents stepped from the side of the road and halted the coach. One of the robbers put his gun to the head of the driver and demanded the Wells, Fargo treasure box, registered mail sack, and two "way" mail sacks. Once they were thrown on the ground the second road agent broke open the box and slashed the three mail sacks to ribbons, took everything of value, and fled. G. Huntsman, Gilmer and Salisbury's agent at Fillmore, and driver Whitbeck with Roy H. McBride went to the scene of the robbery but could not find a clue to the identity of the robbers, though they recovered the broken box, mail sacks, letters and papers. They started on the northbound trail and camped when it grew too dark to follow the trail. The following night, May 31, the southbound stagecoach driven by a Mr. Bird was coming from Salt Lake City to Pioche when it was stopped one mile north of Tidwell's Chicken Creek Hill. They took $25 from the only passenger, M. B. Sowles, but upon being told it was all the money he had they returned $1. They took Sowles' pistol and fired all rounds before returning it, then took the Wells, Fargo Express box and the "way" mail sack. They smashed open the box but it was empty and the mail sack produced nothing. They missed Sowles' gold watch so for their risk they got only $24. They were about to go through the registered mail sack when driver Bird said to them, "You'll have to hurry up this thing, as there's a team coming," causing them to abandon the last mail sack still intact when they fled. After they left Sowles picked up a field glass cover they had dropped. The coach hurried south and as it reached Chicken Creek Hill it met the posse and Bird called out, "Are you going to give up what you've got? They've just gone through me." The coach stopped long enough to give Huntsman the details of the robbery and he examined the broken box and slashed mail sack. The three man posse then followed the road agent's trail, McBride riding on one of the stagecoach horses while Huntsman and Whitbeck rode inside the coach. When McBride reached the summit of a hill he saw the two robbers hiding in the cedars and fired at them as Huntsman and Whitbeck came up and the robbers, upon seeing their pursuers, began firing at them immediately. The party then took positions in the coach and driver Bird drew his pistol while Huntsman and Whitbeck boarded and McBride rode alongside, and they drove past the ambush site and went to Whitbeck's Station. McBride and Whitbeck remained on the robbers' trail while Huntsman went north to Nephi on the stagecoach and secured the services of R. Rollins, E. Sparks and Alfred McCune. The reinforcements went to Kettleman's ranch and saddled fresh horses, one saddle being borrowed and promised to be returned at a certain time. They followed the trail for some distance and finally, as the hour grew late, Huntsman had to return to Kettleman's with the saddle while the other three men went on. Meanwhile McBride and Whitbeck had overhauled the road agents near Church's corral and the two opposing parties opened fire on each other, but on the first firing Whitbeck's gun jammed so McBride answered the gunfire as they retreated and they were obliged to give up the chase. McBride and Whitbeck soon met the three reinforcements and the five men resumed the chase, the trail then heading toward Tintic. After traveling four miles Whitbeck saw the two men crouching in a clump of sagebrush located on the north side of the Sevier River about twenty miles west of the bridge so he pointed in the opposite direction saying he had found the trail. When the other four posse men came up he turned and pointed at the two road agents and one of the robbers rose up with his hands raised, and McBride said, "Your partner must get up too or we'll blow you to pieces." The second road agent arose, they were bound, and taken to Nephi. They identified themselves as Francis Harker, alias John Burke, and Sam Willis, alias Edward Bigelow. They said they had been willing to fight two men but when badly outnumbered by five men with better arms, as they had only one pistol and one Henry rifle between them, they gave up without resistance. When searched the posse found fifty dollars and a field glass, and the field glass cover found by Sowles at the robbery scene matched the field glass found with the prisoners. They were moved to the Beaver County jail and on June 6 they were taken before U.S. Commissioner E. T. Sprague for examination, but the prosecuting witnesses were not present so the examination was postponed to Monday, June 12.

The two road agents managed to escape from the Beaver County Jail but were quickly recaptured and lodged in the penitentiary for safekeeping. On June 22 Willis and six other prisoners managed to escape from the penitentiary at 3:00 P.M. They chose the hour when the guards were at dinner and the prisoners were given access to the yard, with only one guard to watch them. One of the prisoners captured the guard and bound him. They then took a plank with spikes, leaned it against the wall, and easily scaled it to freedom with Willis leading the way. The escaped convicts were pursued for days and finally four were recaptured, but Willis was not among them. He remained at large and managed to flee the region and was never prosecuted for the robbery. The *Salt Lake Tribune* reported on the "Speedy Justice" afforded Harker in their July 1 edition. Harker and Willis were indicted on June 26 by the grand jury in U.S. Circuit court of the First District and his trial commenced on Thursday, June 29. He was easily convicted and sentenced by Judge Emerson to a term of life at Detroit's House of Corrections. Harker was transferred to the prison at Detroit in October 1877 and he made a desperate attempt to escape while en route, but the U.S. Marshal kept his prisoner. Within a month after his arrival Harker managed to escape from the federal prison and was not head of again.

Deseret News [Salt Lake City, UT]: June 7, 1876. *Salt Lake Tribune* [UT]: June 2, 1876; June 6, 1876; June 22–23, 1876; June 25, 1876; June 27, 1876; June 29, 1876; July 1, 1876.

Harniss, T. C.

Nativity, Ireland; Age, 36 years; Height, 5 feet 7⅜ inches; Complexion, Florid; Color of eyes, Brown; Color of hair, Brown; Size of foot, 7. High forehead, scar on left cheek-bone, scar center of forehead, scar right side of forehead, large vaccine mark on left upper arm, mole between shoulders, sloping shoulders; stout built.

Robbed W. F. & Co's Express on stage from Bishop Creek to Bishop Creek R. R. Station, December 29, 1883, in company with A. F. Mairs and Louis Schalten, the driver.

Received at the California State Prison, February 25, 1884. No. of commitment, 11152; Crime, robbery; Term, 2½ years; County sent from, Inyo.

On Thursday night, December 27, 1883, the Express box from the stagecoach traveling between Bishop Creek and the railroad station in Inyo County, driven by Louis "Lew" Schalten, was reportedly stolen by two masked, heavily armed road agents. On board the coach were passengers Arlie F. Mairs and T. C. "Bud" Harniss, a Bishop Creek saloon keeper, but neither man was molested. According to the three men aboard as soon as the robbers had the Express box, which contained $680, they ordered Schalten to continue on. Wells, Fargo's special agent John N. Thacker was put on the case and, with the assistance of messenger Mike Tovey, they began to carefully put together a chain of circumstantial evidence with each link pointing to the driver and two passengers as the robbers, and the two detectives finally swore out complaints against the three men. Sheriff Gregg arrested Schalten and Harniss at Bishop Creek while Undersheriff Crough arrested Mairs at Independence. They were jailed and confronted with an "indisputable chain of circumstances surrounding them, and they 'fell down.'"

On February 14 Schalten provided a detailed confession:

I got up the night the stage was robbed about half past one; there was a light in Bud Harniss' saloon and I called or knocked at the door. One of them got up and let me in. We had a drink, and Bud Harniss says to me, "Is there any money going out in the stage to-night?"

I says, "You heard what Charles Levy said at the supper table to-night," and he says, "I don't remember."

I said that he said that there would be about $900 to-night in the box and he wanted me to act as messenger, I says to Charles Levy, "How much is there in it?" He says, "$3." Bud Harniss says, "We can make more than that out of it," and says, "Arlie, let's take it in."

He (Arlie) says, "Dry up; you don't mean what you say." Bud says, "I am in for it," and says, "Get up and put on your boots." Bud then says to me, "Come on, Lew."

I hesitated, and he says, "What are you afraid of? They can't catch us. We three can swear to the same thing and all hell can't catch us." I says, "Boys, this is a scaly piece of business and we all know the consequences."

We then got to the bar and had another drink, and Bud then says, "Hurry up, as we have not much time to spare." and he said, "Where can we get an ax?"

I says, "If you fellows want to rob the stage you can get an ax at Dunn's wood pile or at George Gill's."

"All right," says Bud; he then says, "You go and get the ax and Arlie and I will go to the barn and hitch up."

I went and got an ax at George Gill's, put it in the wagon and went and helped them. I got out at the office and put the box in. Arlie says, "Let me drive." I let him drive and on the road about 300 yards Bud says, "Lew, you break the box open, as you know how to get into it easier than I do." I got in on the back seat and took the box in between the two seats and smashed her in, took out what money there was in it and put it in my pocket. When we came to the bridge they pulled up and I said, "All right, boys," so I jumped out of the wagon and packed the box about 40 yards from the road, and came back and got in, and drove on to the depot. When we got there Mairs went on to Independence and Bud and I came back to Bishop. We went into the saloon and burned the way pocket and way bills and money sacks. Bud had the handling of the money, some time after he gave me $20 and then $80. That is all that I have received of it. The ax I took back to Geo. Gill's wood pile.

On Friday, February 15, at 2:00 P.M. the prisoners had their examination before the magistrate and within an hour and a half had been held for trial in the Superior Court, an information had been filed, they had pled guilty, submitted their statements to the court, and had their date set for sentencing on Monday, February 18.

The *Inyo Independent* of February 19 reported that Schalten was primarily responsible for the robbery and that the other two men believed the driver's suggestion to take in the coach was just "drunken joshing." The newspaper's editor observed that the driver, the trusted agent of the Express and stagecoach companies, conceived and executed the entire scheme, took and broke open the box, and disposed of the contents. The editor insisted that Harniss and Mairs, long time residents of Bishop Creek, were entirely innocent but had protected Schalten because of their long-time friendship. Schalten took offense to the characterization of his part in the robbery and pointed to his confession, and in response the newspaper published the confession in full on February 23, and also reported on the sentencing of the three men.

The three defendants had been found guilty of grand larceny, rather than robbery, and sentenced by Inyo's Superior Court Judge Hannah to terms of two and one half years in San Quentin Prison. All three men arrived at the prison on February 25, 1884, Harniss registering as prisoner No. 11152, Schalten as prisoner No. 11153, and Mairs as prisoner No. 11154. On February 25, 1886, the three men were discharged after serving their entire sentence, less good time credit awarded under the Goodwin Act.

Inyo Independent [Independence, CA]: December 29, 1883; February 16, 1884, February 23, 1884.

Harrington, James—*alias* William Waverly, J. W. Clark, Emigrant Boy, Alkali Jim

No. of first term, 2735. Received at the California State Prison, May 6, 1864; Crime, grand larceny; Term year; County sent from, El Dorado.
Discharged, by expiration of sentence, March 15, 1865.
No. of second term, 3224. Received at the California State Prison, March 13, 1866; Crime, grand larceny; Term, 2 years; County sent from, San Francisco.
Discharged, by expiration of sentence, November 27, 1867.
No. of third term, 4122. Received at the California State Prison, May 14, 1869; Crime, burglary; Term, 1¼ years; County sent from, San Francisco.
Discharged, by expiration of sentence, June 3, 1870.
No. of fourth term, 4903. Received at the California State Prison, June 28, 1871; Crime, robbery; Term, 10 years; County sent from, Calaveras.
Discharged, by order of the Court, February 9, 1872.
Robbed W. F. & Co's Express on stage from San Andreas to Stockton, January 23, 1871, in company with William "Billy" Miner and Charlie Cooper.
Received at the California State Prison, March 30, 1872; No. of commitment, 5207; Crime, robbery; Term, 13 years; County sent from, Calaveras.
Escaped from State Prison, July 17, 1875, by storing himself in a box that was being taken from San Quentin to San Francisco. Re-captured in St. Louis, Missouri, by special officer W. F. & Co. and returned to Prison, February 14, 1876.
Discharged, upon expiration of sentence, January 28, 1881.
After his release he drifted through Arizona and New Mexico, and back to California.
Died in County Hospital of Colusa County, Cal., April 21, 1884.
[*See* Miner, William]

Harris, George—*alias* Compton

Nativity, Chicago, Ill.; Age, 21 years; Occupation, Farmer; Height, 5 feet 3⅝ inches; Complexion, Florid; Color of eyes, Hazel; Color of hair, Brown. Oval features, pointed chin, medium forehead—rather narrow, large eyes rather deep-set, square cut nose, small nostrils, small round ears and projecting small lobes attached, small round scar on bridge of nose, small mole on lobe of left ear, very small dim vaccine mark left upper arm, two moles about two inches apart back side of left upper arm, mole right side of back of neck near the base, mole below right collar bone near point of shoulder, small mole center of breast, flesh mole about two inches below left nipple, lips a kind of pouting, hair inclined to be curly; medium built.

Attempted to rob stage from Yreka to Redding, June 26, 1882—alone.

Received at the California State Prison, July 8, 1882; No. of commitment, 10475; Crime, assault to rob; Term, 1½ years; County sent from, Shasta.

Discharged, upon expiration of sentence, October 8, 1883.

At 3:00 A.M. Monday, June 26, 1882, the stagecoach from Yreka in Siskiyou County bound for Redding in Shasta County was ascending the grade from Reid's Ferry into Redding when driver Horace Williams heard the command, "Halt!" The masked road agent, armed with a six-shooter, then commanded the driver to "throw down that box," but Williams informed the robber that it was fastened to the stagecoach. The robber made a second demand and would not believe the driver until Williams got down and showed him that the box was firmly riveted to the coach. The road agent, who appeared quite young, then asked if there were any passengers aboard and, upon learning that there was but one, he ordered Williams to continue without molesting the passenger, and he did not ask for the mail sacks. Williams hurried into Redding, reported the robbery, and described the young man in detail, and the robber's description was circulated throughout the region. On Tuesday a young man who gave his name as John Harris was arrested at Redding on suspicion of being the road agent, and taken to Shasta where he was lodged in jail. He said he had recently come from Chicago and had a gun but sold it. At his examination there was enough evidence to hold him for action by the grand jury. He was indicted on the charge of "assault to rob" and when brought into court for arraignment he corrected his name to George Harris and pled guilty, hoping to get a lighter sentence. He was successful and was sentenced to serve only one and one half years at San Quentin Prison. He arrived on July 8, 1882, registering as prisoner No. 10475, and was discharged by expiration of sentence on October 8, 1883, after serving only fifteen months.

Shasta Courier [CA]: July 3, 1882.

Hart, Samuel

Nativity, United States; Age, 32 years; Occupation, Teamster; Height, 5 feet 4¾ inches; Complexion, Dark; Color of eyes, Gray; Color of hair, Black. Long features, scar on first joint of left thumb, do. on right side; stout built.

Robbed W. F. & Co's Express on six different stages in the counties of San Luis Obispo and Santa Barbara on the coast line, in 1876 and 1877, in company with Joe Hendricks.

Losses in each case were nominal, and the apprehension of the robbers was left in the hands of the local officers, who were unsuccessful.

Robbed W. F. & Co's Express on stage from Shasta to Redding, January 22, 1877, in company with Joe Hendricks.

Received at the California State Prison, February, 23, 1877; No. of commitment, 7403; Crime, robbery, Term, 10 years; County sent from, Shasta.

Removed to Folsom Prison, August 23, 1880.
Pardoned by Governor George Stoneman, June 2, 1883.

James B. Hume, Wells, Fargo's chief detective, reported that after some limited success as road agents in San Luis Obispo and Santa Barbara Counties in 1876 and 1877 Samuel Hart and Joe Hendricks moved their operations to Shasta County. There is no explanation given why these men would pull up stakes where they had been successful and travel three hundred fifty miles to resume the same criminal activity, nor do these robberies appear in any newspaper record. On Sunday, January 14, 1877, Hart and Hendricks bought shot and powder at Grotolend's store in Redding and five days later they burglarized Breslauer's store at Redding, where they stole blankets and other items. On January 22 as the Shasta stagecoach was nearing Redding in Shasta County two men covered themselves with blankets in a poncho-like manner and, with handkerchiefs tied over their heads, stepped from the brush onto the roadside while pointing their weapons at the driver and ordered him to stop. One man was armed with what appeared to be a revolver, but this later turned out to be a wooden gun blackened with soot, while the other carried a double barreled shotgun. The next command was to throw down the Wells, Fargo treasure box and the driver tossed out the wooden box immediately, assured that the all the treasure he carried was locked safely in the iron box bolted inside the passenger compartment. The robbers knew there was another box and one of them wanted to bust open or "blow the stuffing" out of the inside box but the other road agent talked him out of it, so they got very little for their risk. The following day Sheriff Hull and special officer Douglas went to the scene and cut the trail of the road agents. They tracked them to Anderson Station where they found the two road agents waiting for the train to the lower country, and they still had with them the property stolen from Breslauer's store. On Wednesday, two days after they robbed the stagecoach, the two men were lodged in the Shasta County jail. Justice was swift as the two men had their examination within days and were held over for action by the grand jury. They were indicted and when brought into court for arraignment they pled guilty. On February 20, 1877, Judge Hopping sentenced each man to serve ten years in San Quentin Prison. They arrived on February 23 and Hendricks registered as prisoner No. 7402 while Hart registered as prisoner No. 7403. Hendricks was only in prison twenty months before he died on October 30, 1878, possibly of consumption [tuberculosis] which was epidemic in such close quarters. Hart was removed to Folsom Prison on August 23, 1880, and was pardoned and released by Governor George Stoneman on June 2, 1883.

Shasta Courier [CA]: January 27, 1877; February 24, 1877.

Hawley, Francis

Nativity, New York; Age, 26 years; Occupation, Teamster; Height, 5 feet 9 inches; Complexion, Dark; Color of eyes, Hazel; Color of hair, Dark Brown; Weight, 161 pounds; Size of foot, 6½; drinks, chews and smokes, large scar right great toe, vaccine scar left upper arm, marks from bed sores on left buttocks, front teeth crowded, scar from gunshot wound on left leg.

Robbed W. F. & Co's Express on stage from Kelton, Utah, to Albion, I. T., July 25, 1882, in company with William Adams, Jack King, and David Francis.

Robbed W. F. & Co's Express on stage from Albion, I. T., to Kelton, Utah, July 31, 1882, in company with William Adams, Jack King, and David Francis.

Robbed W. F & Co's Express on stage from Humboldt Wells to Cherry Creek, Nev., August 14, 1882, in company with Francis Hawley.

Attempted to rob Overland Express train from San Francisco to Ogden at Montello, January 22, 1883, in company with Rais Anderson, David Francis, Orrin Nay and Sylvester Earl.
Received at Nevada State Prison, March 2, 1883. Commitment, 249; Crime, assault to commit robbery; Term, 14 years; County sent from, Elko.
[*See* Anderson, Rais, regarding the Montello train robbery; *see* Adams, William, regarding Idaho stagecoach robberies; *see* Francis, David, regarding the Nevada stagecoach robbery.]

Hays, John—*alias* Shorty Hays

Nativity, Ireland; Age, 41 years; Occupation, Laborer; Height, 5 feet 1¼ inches; Complexion, Light; Color of eyes, Blue; Color of hair, Light. Round features, large scar on right cheek, large ears, round scar inside of left lower arm, large vaccine marks right upper arm, heart in ink on right lower arm; stout built.
No. of first commitment, 3869. Received at the California State Prison, July 18, 1868; Crime, grand larceny; Term, 5 years; County sent from, Yuba.
Discharged, by expiration of sentence, October 31, 1872.
Robbed W. F. & Co's Express on stage from Forest Hill to Auburn, September 12, 1873, in company with John "Jake" Clark and Eddie Lee.
Robbed W. F. & Co's Express on stage from Yreka to Redding, October 10, 1873, in company with John "Jake" Clark, Charlie Thompson and John Doe [*sic*].
Escaped from the Shasta Jail while awaiting trial. Recaptured at Marysville a few day later.
Received at the California State Prison, February 16, 1874; No. of commitment, 5884; Crime, robbery; Term, 21 years; County sent from, Shasta.
Taken out by order of the County Court of Placer County, March 7, 1874, to be tried for the stage robbery of September 12, 1873, and returned to prison March 17, 1874, under a new commitment, and received a new number, 5929; Crime robbery; Term, 30 years; County sent from, Placer.
Escaped from State Prison, May 28, 1876. Recaptured and returned, June 6, 1876.
Commuted by Governor William Irwin, April 23, 1878, to 29 years.
Escaped while employed outside prison walls making bricks, December 13, 1884. Recaptured at Los Angeles, January 1885.
[*See* Clark, John]

Heinsman, W. H.

Nativity, New York; Age, 39; Occupation, Carpenter; Height 5 feet 3 inches; Complexion, Dark; Color of eyes, Brown; Color of hair, Black.
Robbed W. F. & Co's Express on stage from Helena, Montana to Corrine, Utah, July 9, 1871, in company with Donald McLean and George N. Rugg.
Received at the Territorial Prison, Deer Lodge M. T., October 30, 1873; No. of commitment, —; Crime, robbery; Term 10 years; County sent from, Beaverhead, M. T.
Pardoned by Governor Benjamin F. Potts, May 8, 1880.

Just after noon on July 2, 1871, Kirkendall's fast freight team, driven by "Monte," stopped a short distance below Corbett's Station. Suddenly two men rushed out of the willows along the banks of the Snake River and approached the driver with pistols and Bowie knives drawn, and demanded the purses of the passengers. One passenger stated that he had no money but the road agents told him they knew he had a purse of gold and wanted it. This distracted the robbers long enough for Dock Yandle to mount a wild mustang and, even though the horse tried to throw him, he rode several hundred yards to the place where the Kirkendall agent, a Mr. Brady, was standing with a number of men. When told of the robbery in progress Brady grabbed a pitch fork and started for the wagon with six men following, each armed with whatever weapons they could readily lay hands on. Only one man had been robbed when the road agents saw the men coming to the rescue and Monte, seeing his chance, knocked down one road agent with a blow to the head from the butt of his whip and started his team, driving the other passengers out of danger. Another stagecoach robbery occurred a week later and it was supposed these were the same men. On July 8 the Gilmer & Salisbury stagecoach for Corrine, Utah Territory, left Helena, Montana Territory, carrying a Wells, Fargo & Company Express box filled with treasure. The box contained: "one purse containing 94 ounces of gold dust; one gold bar No. 1644, value $7970.50; one gold bar No. 1745, value $2,989.07 — Chas. Rumley, Assayer; one gold bar No. 8574, value $2, 505.41; one gold bar No. 8573, value $1,046.91— S. F. Melitor, Assayor." Three road agents named W. H. Heinsman, Donald McLean, and George N. Rugg were well informed as Heinsman's brother Henry managed the Red Butte Stage Station, and Rugg was the attending stage clerk for Gilmer & Salisbury's stage line. The three men put off the job until the box was heavy, as it was on July 9, and when the stagecoach stopped at Red Butte Station they pulled the smaller Wells, Fargo & Company treasure box from the boot while the driver was having his dinner. They buried it in the bed of the nearby creek and the theft was not discovered until the stagecoach was unloaded at Corrine. On July 12 Wells, Fargo & Company posted a reward of the value of one fourth of the plunder for its return and, while there was no mention of a reward for the capture and conviction of the road agents, the company had a standing reward of $300 per road agent. Men took the field and tried to track the robbers but without results.

The three road agents left the box buried until winter and about Christmas-time 1871 Heinsman dug up the box, divided the easily recognized plunder into smaller portions, and took it to Canada where he disposed of it. He returned in the spring and informed his fellow road agents that he had not gotten as much as he expected, but in the meantime Rugg had disclosed all the details to a man named McCoy and he claimed a full fourth share of the plunder for his silence, and received $1,800 in currency and $600 in coin. Because there was now limited treasure remaining Rugg had to settle for $126 and promises of future riches, which were never delivered. Rugg went to Salt Lake City in November 1872 and from there started for Bannock, Montana but, ironically, he was arrested for the robbery when he arrived at Red Butte Station. Rugg saw the opportunity to reduce his sentence and have revenge on the men who had cheated him so he informed on Heinsman and McLean. They were tracked down and arrested and Rugg, to secure his release, agreed to plead guilty and to testify against them, so Rugg was convicted and immediately pardoned in consideration of his cooperation. Rugg went to Marysville, California, and remained a law abiding citizen for four years but he was determined to become a successful road agent. He found a new partner in E. H. White and they robbed the stagecoach from Marysville to Downieville on July 31, 1877 [*see* Rugg, George N.]. Heinsman and McLean were tried at the fall term of the court, convicted of robbery, and each man was sentenced to serve ten years at the prison at Deer Lodge. Both men arrived on October 30, 1878, and on May 8, 1880, both men were pardoned by Governor Benjamin F. Potts.

Helena Daily Herald [MT]: July 11–12, 1871; July 19, 1871.

Hendricks, Joe

Robbed W. F. & Co's Express on six different stages in the counties of San Luis Obispo and Santa Barbara on the coast line, in 1876 and 1877, in company with Sam Hart.

Losses in each case were nominal, and the apprehension of the robbers was left in the hands of the local officers, who were unsuccessful.

Robbed W. F. & Co's Express on stage from Shasta to Redding, January 22, 1877, in company with Sam Hart.

Received at the California State Prison, February, 23, 1877; No. of commitment, 7402; Crime, robbery and burglary; Term, 10 years; County sent from, Shasta.

Died in prison, October 30, 1878.

[*See* Hart, Sam]

Herbert, John M.

Nativity, Illinois; Age, 20 years; Occupation, Laborer; Height, 5 feet 5 inches; Complexion, Light; Color of eyes, Brown; Color of hair, Brown, Size of foot 5½. Square features, high forehead, heavy eyebrows, eyes deep-set, small ears, long scar left side upper lip, large vaccine scar left upper arm, long scar inside of left wrist extending to palm of hand, broad shoulders, spare waist; stout built.

Robbed stage from Fresno to Yosemite, in company with Harvey H. Lee.

Received at the California State Prison, September 19, 1884; No. of commitment, 11385; Crime, robbery; Term, 20 years; County sent from, Fresno.

The first toll road into Yosemite Valley opened in mid–June 1874 and two other toll roads were in operation within a month, but people had been traveling into the valley for two decades on horseback to take in the beauty of the scenery. Once the roads were in operation stagecoaches began to roll and they carried rich tourists and occasionally an express box. On May 7, 1884, two road agents, masked and heavily armed, stepped out and halted the stagecoach from Fresno to Yosemite when it was still in Fresno County, twenty-three miles from Madera. They went through the passengers but found only a cheap silver watch and a $5 gold coin, though later reports said they found $60 and three watches. They were nervous and ordered the coach to continue without thinking to ask for a treasure box or mail sacks. The two road agents fled to San Jose while the driver hurried into Madera and reported the robbery. The following day Fresno County's deputy sheriff Witthouse went to the scene to investigate after circulating detailed descriptions provided by the driver and passengers. Santa Clara County Sheriff Benjamin Branham, upon receiving the descriptions, started looking for the two men and found Harvey H. Lee early on the morning of June 7, and by that evening John Herbert had joined him in a San Jose jail cell. Branham notified Witthouse and he transferred the prisoners to the Fresno jail on June 1. On June 24 the two prisoners had their examination before Justice of the Peace S. H. Hill and were held over for the grand jury, bail set at $5,000. Their trial commenced in early September and, though they mounted a vigorous defense, they were easily convicted on September 8 by the overwhelming evidence. Lee, it appeared, had stayed out of trouble for a decade before robbing the Yosemite coach. Each man received a sentence of twenty years and on September 19 they arrived at San Quentin Prison. Herbert registered as prisoner No. 11385 and Lee as prisoner No. 11386. Herbert was transferred to Folsom prison on March 1, 1890, and Governor Henry Markham commuted his sentence to ten years on May 12, 1892, and one week later he was discharged. Lee was released, with good time credits, on June 18, 1897.

By August 1897 Lee had found another partner in twenty-three year old Charles Williams. Like many an imprisoned stagecoach robber Lee found that coaches rarely carried treasure by the late 1890s so the two men decided to rob a train, capitalizing on what Lee had learned during his recent years imprisoned with train robbers. They went to Oregon, rented a room at the Hamilton boarding house, and began to make preparations. The robbery took place on September 25, 1897, and it turned into as great a fiasco as Lee's stagecoach robbery. In the end the two men only obtained a watch and chain and $13 before they stood watching the train pulling away from them down the tracks. As soon as the robbery was reported in Portland's *Oregonian*, the Hamiltons knew they had the robbers as tenants and went to the police. The two men were quickly arrested and Lee, using the name George Jackson, and Williams were lodged in jail. They were indicted three days later and on October 8 Lee pled guilty and tried to exonerate Williams in an effort to get a reduced sentence. Lee was ordered to return in a week for sentencing and then Williams' trial began. The young train robber was convicted and when the two men came into court for sentencing they were surprised to receive a total of thirty years, seven months each. After arriving at the prison Lee tried every scheme he could devise to shorten his long sentence and finally on July 16, 1906, he managed a pardon and release. He died in Fresno's County Hospital, penniless, ten years later at the age of sixty-nine, a ward of the county.

Fresno Weekly Expositor [CA]: June 18, 1884. *Fresno Weekly Republican [CA]*: May, 9, 1884. *Mariposa Gazette [CA]*: August 18, 1883; August 25, 1883. *Oregonian [Portland, OR]*: September 26–28, 1897; October 9–10, 1897. *Red Bluff Beacon [OR]*: February 6, 1862. *San Bernardino Guardian [CA]*: October 22, 1870. *San Jose Herald [CA]*: June 12, 1884. *San Jose Mercury [CA]*: December 27, 1866; May 2, 1867; June 8, 1884.

Holden, Henry

Nativity, Chicago, Ill.; Age 32 years; Occupation, Printer; Height, 5 feet 7⅛ inches; Complexion, Sallow; Color of eyes, Brown; Color of hair, Black. Spare features, medium forehead, medium nose, large bushy eyebrows, small ears, large mouth, scar center of upper lip below nose, slight scar left cheek about one inch from corner of mouth, scar base of left thumb near palm, small ink dot do., dim ink marks left forehead, three very dim vaccine marks on left upper arm; medium build.
Burglarized W. F. & Co's office at Downey City, Cal., in company with Fred Morris, January 9, 1881.
Received at the California State Prison, April 1, 1881; No. of commitment, 9863; Crime, burglary; Term, 3 years; County sent from, Los Angeles.
Pardoned by Governor George C. Perkins, October 20, 1881.

On January 9, 1881, after the Downey, CA depot closed for the day, Henry Holden and Fred Morris broke into the building and then into the Wells, Fargo office, cracked open the safe, and removed the contents. It was not long before they were suspected and arrested, and at their examination they denied their guilt, but there was enough evidence to hold them for the grand jury. Both men were lodged in jail for several months as neither man could post bail, and they were indicted on the charges. When brought into court on March 10 for arraignment they pled not guilty and Judge J. Sepulveda set their trial date for April 6. When their trial began they filed a motion to be tried separately and this was granted, so the cases had to be continued with Holden to have his trial begin on April 11 and Morris the following day. Both men were convicted on the evidence and on April 13 Holden was sentenced to serve three years at San Quentin. On April 14 Morris was brought into court and sentenced to serve two and one half years at San Quentin. The court was particularly busy with felonies at that time so the two prisoners were returned to their cells for several days. On April 17 Holden, Morris and several other convicted felons were taken north to the prison and arrived on April 18, 1881. Holden registered as prisoner No. 9863 and Morris registered as prisoner No. 9873. On October 20, 1881, both men were pardoned and released by Governor George C. Perkins after serving only six months.

Los Angeles Express [CA]: April 5, 1881; April 11–14, 1881.

Horrell, W. S.

Nativity, Texas; Age, 21; Occupation, Farmer; Height, 6 feet; Complexion, Fair; Color of eyes, Light Gray; Color of hair, Light Brown. Scar on inside of left foot, small scar inside of each leg between knee and thigh, long narrow scar above left knee-cap, large mole center of back, mole left arm.

Robbed W. F. & Co's Express on stage from Boise City, I. T., to Baker City, Oregon, May 13, 1884, in company with Gus Stanley.

Received at the Oregon State Prison, June __, 1884; No. of commitment, —; Crime, robbery; Term, 5 years; County sent from, Baker, Oregon.

On Tuesday, May 12, 1884, at 1:00 P.M. the stagecoach from Boise City, Idaho Territory, to Baker City, Oregon, driven by Ben Price was halted near Weatherby's Station on the Burnt River. Two highwaymen, one described as slim with light complexion and the other darker and heavier, were masked with red silk handkerchiefs tied over their heads. One pointed a rifle and the other a shotgun at Price and ordered him to rein in his team. They demanded the Wells, Fargo treasure box and it was thrown down, and then they ordered the passengers to throw out their pocketbooks, and they complied. Miss Emma Lewis contributed $2, John Hogan handed out $114 in cash and $400 in checks, Al Butts gave up $5 cash and $250 in notes, and C. J. McDougal contributed $10. They even took $11 from Price even though common practice excused the driver from "pungling." Also in the coach was a family consisting of six children, their mother and father, and their grandmother but they were not molested. The road agents kept the box to open later, and were enriched by $1,000. As soon as the plunder was collected they ordered the coach to continue on and warned all aboard not to look back. However, after the coach had gone a safe distance Price looked back and saw the two men still watching him. He hurried on to the next telegraph and reported the robbery. It was not long before lawmen were on the trail of the two road agents and they had a good idea as to their identity. On Tuesday, May 19 Augustus "Gus" Stanley was arrested in Indian Valley by a posse lying in wait. He was trying to make his way home but, as soon as he was arrested and confronted with the evidence against him, he confessed every detail of the robbery and named W. S. Horrell as his partner in crime. Horrell soon joined him in his cell and they were taken before Judge Ballery for an examination, but they pled guilty and were immediately sentenced to serve terms in Oregon State's Prison at Salem, both receiving five years. They left Baker City for the prison on May 21 and arrived the following day where Horrell registered as prisoner No. 1527 and Stanley as No. 1528. On February 5, 1887, Stanley died of pneumonia while still in prison and on February 24, 1888, Horrell was discharged by expiration of sentence.

Baker County Reveille [Baker City, OR]: May 22, 1884. *Idaho Statesman [Boise, I. T.]*: May 15, 1884; May 20, 1885. *Oregonian [Portland, OR]]*: May 16, 1884.

Howe, Frank—*alias* Frank Thomassen

Nativity, American; Age, 34; Occupation, Laborer; Height, 5 feet 6 inches; Complexion, Light; Color of eyes, Light Blue; Color of hair, Brown and Gray. Face, legs and body badly pock-marked, sight of left eye entirely gone, on left forearm marked in India ink with letter "C. A." above a Maltese cross in a circle, ears grow close to head to extreme tips, long round white scar on right side of buttock.

Robbed W. F. & Co's Express on stage from Prescott to Phoenix, A. T.. October 17, 1884, in company with Oscar White and Frank Weeden.

Received at the Territorial Prison, Yuma, A. T., November 7, 1884; No. of commitment, 268; Crime, robbery, Term, life; County sent from, Maricopa, A. T.

The *Arizona Silver Belt*, on October 25 reported on the robbers still active on the Black Canyon route: "A dispatch to the Tucson Star from Prescott states that the south bound stagecoach was robbed of Wells, Fargo & Co.'s express box on the evening of the 19th inst. two miles south of Bumble Bee by two Americans. Sheriffs were in pursuit." The two men who robbed the stagecoach on October 19 were part of a gang of three and all three robbers were run to ground and arrested. They were convicted and sentenced to terms in the Territorial Prison at Yuma. Frank Howe, alias Thomassen, was thirty-four years old when he arrived at the Yuma Territorial prison to serve a life sentence. He registered as prisoner No. 268 on November 7, 1884, and was described as five feet six inches in height with light complexion and blue eyes, though the sight in his left eye was entirely gone. His brown hair was prematurely graying; and, he had a tattoo on his left forearm of initials "C.A." above a Maltese cross in a circle. His ears grew noticeably close to his head ending in extreme tips. He was pardoned by Governor Zulick on July 25, 1888. Oscar White was thirty-four years old when he arrived at the Yuma Territorial prison to serve a life sentence and he registered as prisoner No. 269 on November 7, 1884. White was five feet seven inches in height with sandy complexion, red hair, and brown eyes. He was pardoned by Governor Zulick on July 25, 1888. The third man was Frank Weeden, who managed to escape while en route to the penitentiary and was never seen nor heard of again in the Territory.

Arizona Silver Belt [Globe, AZ]: October 25, 1884. *Sentinel [Yuma, AZ]*: October 25, 1884.

Ivey, John J.—*alias* James Curry, James Sanders, James Chambers, James Russell, James Ivey

Nativity, Tennessee; Age, 55 years; Occupation, Farmer; Height, 5 feet 10 inches; Complexion, Fair; Color of eyes, Hazel; Color of hair, Dark Brown. Three moles on left side of face, forefinger of left hand disfigured, the 3 adjoining fingers have scars, 2 front teeth on under jaw broken off, mole below right nipple, left eye out; raw-boned and slim built.

No. of first term, 335 as John J. Ivey. Received at the California State Prison, February 20, 1854; Crime, grand larceny; Term, 7 years; County sent from, San Joaquin.

Escaped in break, July 24, 1854, and returned on new charge, as below:

No. of second term, 849 as James Curry. Received at the California State Prison, February 29, 1856; Crime, grand larceny and prison-breaking; Term, 7 years; County sent from, Amador.

Escaped February 26, 1857; returned February 26, 1857.

Escaped August 24, 1857; returned June 20, 1858.

Escaped May 21, 1859; returned on a new charge, as below:

No. of third term, 1686 as James Sanders. Received at the California State Prison; August 16, 1859; Crime, grand larceny; Term, 8 years; County sent from, Stanislaus.

Escaped May 13, 1860; returned on new charge, as below:

No. of fourth term, 2143 as James J. Chambers. Received at the California State Prison, April 18, 1861; Crime, grand larceny; Term, 10 years; County sent from, Napa.

Escaped February 14, 1863; returned on a new charge, as below:

No. of fifth term, 2611 as James Russell. Received at the California State Prison, September 24, 1863; Crime, burglary; Term, 5 years; County sent from, Calaveras.

Discharged, upon expiration of sentence, January 11, 1868.

No. of sixth term, 3841 as James Ivey. Received at the California State Prison, June 15, 1868; Crime burglary; Term, 10 years, County sent from, Santa Clara.

Discharged, upon expiration of sentence, September 2, 1876.

No. of seventh term, 8865 as John J. Ivey. Received at the California State Prison, May 30, 1879; Crime, burglary; Term, 5 years, County sent from, Solano.

Discharged, upon expiration of sentence, December 30, 1882.
Burglarized the Post Office at Healdsburg, May 25, 1883.
Burglarized the store of S. Shocken, in Sonoma, July 10, 1883. Brought the stolen goods to San Francisco, where he was arrested with the property in his possession; was indicted and plead guilty, and sent again, as follows:
No. of eight term, 10900 as James Ivey. Received at the California State Prison, July 23, 1883; Crime, burglary; Term, 9 years; County sent from, San Francisco.

John J. Ivey was not only a habitual criminal but a consistent, and persistent, thief and burglar. His first four commitments to prison were for grand larceny and his next five were for burglary. During his early prison years he engaged in several escape attempts but in later years he became a trusty inmate who was respected by guards and fellow prisoners. Ivey would have never made it into Hume and Thacker's report but for several burglaries late in his career. On May 29, 1879, he burglarized Wells, Fargo & Company's safe at Benicia, Solano County, California. The record shows that the following day he arrived at the prison to serve a five year term, his seventh commitment — swift justice indeed. He was discharged on expiration of sentence on December 30, 1882. On March 22, 1883, he burglarized the Wells, Fargo & Company office at Guerneville and then the Post Office at Healdsburg. Next he burglarized a store, took the plunder to San Francisco and was captured there. The stolen goods were recovered and he was tried in San Francisco County, arriving at San Quentin prison on July 23, 1883. He was discharged on June 23, 1890. Ivey's final trip to prison occurred in 1890 when he was arrested for a burglary in Eliot, San Joaquin County. He was returned to prison, this time Folsom, where he died on July 23, 1894.

Daily Alta California [San Francisco, CA]: May 23, 1859; May 25, 1859; May 29, 1859; June 1, 1859; February 5, 1875; February 14, 1875. *Sacramento Daily Bee*: December 9–11, 1878. *Sacramento Daily Record-Union [CA]*: December 11, 1878; March 1, 1890.

Jackson, Tom

Nativity, Ireland; Age, 50 years; Occupation, Laborer; Height, 5 feet 8 inches; Complexion, Light; Color of eyes, Dark, Color of hair, Dark. High cheek-bones, medium sized nose, wart on right side of neck, three vaccine marks left upper arm, small white spot on right forearm near wrist.
No. of first commitment, 3128. Received at the California State Prison, November 7, 1865; Crime, assault to murder; Term, 2 years; County sent from, El Dorado.
Discharged, by expiration of sentence, February 27, 1867.
No. of second commitment, 3736. Received at the California State Prison, January 21, 1868; Crime, robbery, Term, 8 years, County sent from, Alameda.
Discharged, by expiration of sentence, September 23, 1874.
No. of third commitment, 6441. Received at the California State Prison, March 18, 1875; Crime, burglary; Term, 5 years; County sent from, San Mateo.
Commuted, by Governor William Irwin, May 30, 1876, to 4½ years.
Discharged, by expiration of sentence, July 3, 1878.
Attempted to rob W. F. & Co's Express on stage from Yreka to Shasta (via Trinity Center), September 7, 1878, in company with Martin Tracy and Andy Marsh. Marsh was killed by W. F. & Co's Guard Johnnie Reynolds. Jackson and Tracy fired several shots at the stage, killing one horse, then fled.
Received at the California State Prison, December 31, 1878; No. of fourth commitment, 8607; Crime, assault to commit robbery; Term, 10 years; County sent from, Siskiyou.

Thirty year old Thomas Jackson entered San Quentin on November 7, 1865, convicted of "assault to murder." He served sixteen months before being released by expiration of sentence. In less than a year he was back in prison serving an eight year term, this time for a robbery in Alameda County. Again he received no executive clemency and was released by expiration of sentence on September 23, 1874. Within a few months Jackson committed a burglary in San Mateo County, was captured, convicted, and sentenced to serve five years, arriving at the prison on March 18, 1875. California's Governor William Irwin commuted his sentence to four and one half years and he was released on July 8, 1878. While in prison Jackson met Martin Tracy, a man serving his second term in prison — the first a three year sentence for grand larceny and the second a term of three years for burglary. Once released the two ex-convicts rendezvoused and went on a crime spree. They were planning and preparing to rob a stagecoach when they met Andy Marsh and decided it would be better to use three men for the job. Marsh was also an ex-convict who had learned the shoemaking trade in prison, but after working at his new found trade he was ready for some action and easy money. The trio headed north into Siskiyou County, an area where they were not known, and after they sized up the situation they set up their ambush along the Yreka to Redding stagecoach route, four hundred yards below the summit of the Scott Mountain grade. Here the horses would be walking at a slow pace and would be relatively spent from the hard pull up the steep incline. The stagecoach approached at 3:30 A.M. so the three men pulled over their heads flour sacks with eye holes cut in them. They had with them an "improved" Winchester model 76, a double-barreled shot-gun, and each man had a six-shot revolver. They leaped out in front of the horses, Jackson and Tracy with the rifle and shotgun and Marsh with his revolver, and pointed their weapons at driver Charlie Williams and ordered him to rein in his team. Tracy and Jackson stepped up to the four horse team on each side and grabbed the reins of the leaders while Marsh stepped up to the driver and told him to raise his hands. The driver shifted the whip and reins to his right hand and raised his left, then said to the robber, "lower your pistol, I have no arms." The robber, seeing he had the driver under his control, lowered his pistol. The driver's comment was meant to alert Wells, Fargo & Company's messenger John E. Reynolds, who was riding inside with the treasure box, and give him time to act. Reynolds took but a moment before he pushed his shotgun out the window and shot Marsh in the chest and neck causing gaping wounds which resulted in instant death, though the road agent's gun discharged when he jerked his hand in a death grip. Jackson and Tracy, seeing Marsh killed, began their retreat while firing wildly at the driver and coach. Reynolds could not reload fast enough to shoot at the remaining road agents before they disappeared into the brush and the team, startled by the gunfire, bolted and ran seventy-five yards before the nigh (left rear) wheeler fell dead, peppered with heavy buckshot. James Hume, Wells Fargo's chief detective, asked that the horse not be destroyed or buried until all the shot was removed and saved as evidence. The wheeler was unhitched and the coach continued to the next station with three horses. As soon as the robbery was reported and the description of the robbers circulated a three man posse led by Jack Conant was on the trail of the two fleeing robbers, but the two men with Conant abandoned him. At Sisson's Station Conant hired Indian tracker Sisson Jim, and Dick Hubbell also joined his posse as they headed toward Picayune Lake. They heard a shot after dark and realized it was the two fugitives hunting for food, and at dawn they captured the two men without resistance. Jackson gave his name as Charles Brown while Tracy said he was Charles Mitchell, and the two were taken to Callahan's Stagecoach Station. The posse collected everything the men had with them, including a supply of buckshot. The body of Marsh had also been taken to Callahan's Station but had been buried before the arrival of his two confederates. The two prisoners were taken to Yreka and lodged in jail where Tracy was diagnosed with heart disease and moved from the iron cell to a more comfortable wooden one, but he attempted to escape and was moved back to an iron cell.

Jackson hired Elijah Steele, an attorney of some renown, for his defense but it was all for naught as the evidence against him was conclusive. The trial began on December 17 and Jackson's past prison experiences were read in court. Hume introduced the buckshot removed from the dead stagecoach horse and the buckshot collected when the men were arrested, showing it was the same in size, weight, and appearance — a rudimentary attempt at introducing ballistics evidence. The case went to the jury on December 30, 1878, and it took only five minutes to deliberate and convict Jackson of an attempt to rob a stagecoach. Jackson was sentence to serve ten years in prison and arrived on December 31, 1878. He was released on June 30, 1885, by expiration of sentence. Tracy, seeing the outcome of Jackson's trial, pled guilty to the attempted robbery in January 1879 and, for his cooperation, received a reduced sentence of five years, arriving at the prison on January 19, 1879. He was released by expiration of sentence on August 14, 1882, after serving three years seven months. However, Tracy was not yet finished with his criminal career and three months later he was back in prison serving a fourteen year term, convicted of a first degree burglary in Contra Costa County.

Daily Alta California [San Francisco, CA]: January 3, 1868. *Daily Evening Bulletin [San Francisco, CA]*: January 2, 1868. *Marysville Daily Appeal [CA]*: September 3, 1904. *Oroville Weekly Union Record [CA]*: July 15, 1865. *Redding Independent [CA]*: September 12, 1878. *Shasta Courier [CA]*: September 14, 1878. *Yreka Journal [CA]*: September 11, 1878; September 18, 1878; September 25, 1878; October 9, 1878; November 27, 1878. *Yreka Union [CA]*: September 14, 1878; September 21, 1878; November 30, 1878; December 21, 1878; December 28, 1878.

Johnson, Andrew—*alias* Andy Johnson

Nativity, New York; Age, 37 years; Occupation, Machinist; Height 5 feet 8¾ inches; Complexion, Light, Color of eyes, Light Blue; Color of hair, Dark. Two full wrinkles in forehead, large hands, bony fingers, large nose, Size of foot, 9. Large scar left forehead, large scar near left elbow.
Robbed W. F. & Co's Express on stage from Reno to Virginia City, March 4, 1871, in company with John Doe and Richard Roe.
Received at the Nevada State Prison, April 15, 1871; No. of commitment, 75; Crime, robbery; Term, 12 years; County sent from, Storey, Nev.
Pardoned, November 9, 1878.

On March 4, 1871, shortly before 4:00 A.M. as Wells, Fargo & Company's coaches were coming from Reno to Virginia City the leading coach driven by Billy Hoge was stopped by robbers on the Geiger Grade. He was a short distance beyond the summit when the treasure boxes were taken and plundered. The place where the robbery occurred is at a narrow place in the road at a sharp curve, and just where teamsters going toward Reno stop to put the "shoes and rough locks" upon their wheels. General John E. Winters was an inside passenger and P. Deidisheimer was on the seat with the driver when one of the robbers yelled out "Stop him!" Two men then appeared on the upper side of the road and one on the lower side, all masked and armed with shotguns. The driver halted and one of the men in a disguised voice, speaking hoarsely, said, "Throw that box on the lower side of the road!" Hoge took a survey of the situation and finding the muzzles of two shotguns in close proximity to his and Deidisheimer's heads he complied. There were two fast freight wagons, the other coach, and two or three private carriages only three hundred yards behind and just around the bend, so he delayed as long as he could. He was a long time in getting the box out and when he did throw it down it fell so light that he said, "There is not much in that." The robber screamed, "Throw out that other box!" and Hoge asked "What do you want with that?" The robber said, "Never mind, throw that box out!" Hoge, fumbling about as long as he dared, at last threw it out and as soon as it hit the ground the order came, "Now drive on!" and Hoge complied. Hoge drove into town at a very lively rate, arriving in the city about twenty-eight minutes after the robbery; the distance being over five miles.

As soon as Hoge reached the city he reported the robbery and soon Chief G. W. Downey and other officers were investigating. The rifled treasure boxes were soon found near the scene of the robbery with the letters and papers scattered about. Two officers went through a ravine to the southward of Mount Davidson and got to the west side of the mountain and after traveling some distance they saw a man upon the snow. He saw them at the same moment and made tracks at a lively rate, but he was soon overtaken and one officer dismounted and, by a knock on the head with his revolver, captured him. Going back on his trail they found a sack containing $531.50 in coin and $251.75 in currency. The man arrested was known by the name Andrew Johnson but with several aliases, and he had been arrested some months previous for a safe robbery at Cornell's drug store. Afterwards Chief Downey arrested a man named Ned Dean, well known as a barkeep and restaurant man. He was found at home in bed and the nature of the evidence against him was that he procured the shotgun found in the possession of Johnson from Scholl's gunsmith shop. The third man was never identified. Johnson and Dean were indicted for the stagecoach robbery and tried in early April. Johnson was found guilty but there was not sufficient evidence to incriminate Dean and the jury found him not guilty. On April 15 Andrew Johnson was sentenced to serve twelve years at Nevada's state prison and registered as convict No. 75. He was pardoned November 9, 1878, and was not heard of again on the criminal rolls of Nevada. The other two robbers were never identified.

Territorial Enterprise [Virginia City, NV]: March 5, 1871.

Johnson, Frank

Nativity, Georgia; Age, 51 years; Occupation, Laborer; Height, 5 feet 9 inches; Complexion, medium Fair; Color of eyes, Gray; Color of hair, Brown. Scar on lower end of breast-bone caused by gunshot, right leg much enlarged caused by gunshot wounds, flesh mark on ankle of left leg, face thin, nose sharp and thin; good build.

Robbed W. F. & Co's Express on stage from Baker City to Umatilla, Oregon, in 1874, in company with Milt Shepardson, and Frank Fulford.

Received at the Oregon State Prison, October 23, 1874. No. of commitment, 586; Crime, robbery; Term, 4 years; County sent from, Baker, Oregon.

Discharged, upon expiration of sentence, April 9, 1877.

[*See* Shepardson, Milton]

Johnson, Richard—*alias* McMahon

Nativity, Pennsylvania; Age, 56 years; Occupation, Miner; Height, 5 feet 10⅛ inches; Complexion, Light; Color of eyes, Dark; Color of hair, Dark. Four scars on back, one on neck, badly freckled, round shoulders, ears large and lopping, nose and chin prominent, mouth small and compressed, one upper front tooth gone.

No. of first commitment, 1049. Received at the California State Prison, December 7, 1856; Crime, Grand Larceny; Term, 5 years; County sent from, Calaveras.

Escaped, June 27, 1857. Returned by J. C. Boggs, of Placer County, March 14, 1859.
Discharged, by expiration of sentence, December 4, 1861.
No. of second commitment, 2612. Received at the California State Prison, September 24, 1863; Crime, burglary; Term, 3 years, County sent from, Calaveras.
Discharged, by expiration of sentence, May 5, 1866.
No. of third commitment, 3315. Received at the California State Prison, July 9, 1866; Crime, robbery; Term, 2 years; County sent from, El Dorado.
Discharged, by expiration of sentence, March 20, 1868.
No. of fourth commitment, 3923. Received at the California State Prison, September 29, 1868; Crime, burglary, Term, 6 years, County sent from, El Dorado.
Discharged, by expiration of sentence, October 11, 1873.
Attempted to rob W. F. & Co's Express on stage from Spadra to San Bernardino, August, 29, 1874, in company with B. F. Clark. After arrest Clark got possession of Deputy Sheriff's pistol and shot the Deputy through the thigh in an effort to escape.
No. of fifth commitment, 6200. Received at the California State Prison, October 15, 1874; Crime, attempt to commit robbery; Term 6 years; County sent from, San Bernardino.
Discharged, by expiration of sentence, December 14, 1878.
[*See* Clark, B. F.]

Jones, James—*alias* Texas

Nativity, Kentucky; Age, 60 years; Occupation, Miner; Height, 6 feet 1 inch; Complexion, Light; Color of eyes, Hazel; Color of hair, Black, and mixed with Gray; Weight, 165 lbs. Breast covered with hair, five large moles on back, three bullet scars on left shoulder, vaccine marks on left arm, scar on left knee, scar on left jaw, scar on left cheek, scar under right eye, scar base of left thumb. An honest looking fellow, and does not look like a thief.
Received at the California State prison October 22, 1866. No. of first commitment, —; Crime, robbery and assisting to rob; Term, 25 years; County sent from, Placer.
Discharged by order of Court April 10, 1867, for a new trial. Returned April 7, 1868, under a new commitment, to serve a term of 5 years for assisting to rob.
Discharged, by expiration of sentence, June 29, 1872.
Robbed W. F. & Co's Express on stage from Oroville to Laporte, June 27, 1876, in company with S. A. "Ned" Allen.
Robbed W. F. & Co's Express on stage from Carson City, Nev., to Aurora, October 3, 1876, in company with S. A. "Ned" Allen.
Received at Nevada State Prison, December 20, 1876. No. of commitment, 146. Crime, robbery; Term 5 years; County sent from, Douglass.
Escaped from prison December 1880.
[*See* Allen, S. A. "Ned"]

Jones, R. A.—*alias* Sol Jones

Nativity, Virginia; Age, 43 years; Occupation, Laborer; Height, 5 feet 8 inches; Complexion, Light; Color of eyes, Gray; Color of hair, Black. Scar on left leg.
Robbed Overland Express train from San Francisco [Cal.] to Odgen [U. T.] near Verdi [Nev.], November 6, 1870, with J. E. Chapman, A. J. Davis, John Squires, Tilton P. Cockrell, E. B. Parsons, and James Gilchrist.
Received at the Nevada State Prison, December 17, 1870; No. of commitment, 62; Crime, robbery; Term, 5 years; County sent from, Washoe.
Pardoned, March 27, 1874.
[*See* Davis, A. J.]

Joy, Kit

Age, 25 years; Height, 5 feet 11 inches; Complexion, Light; Color of eyes, Light; Color of hair, Auburn; Size of foot, 7. Large hands, one or two upper front teeth missing, has good English education, pleasant spoken, and polite in deportment.

On November 24, 1883, in company with George W. Cleveland, Mitch Lee and Frank Taggart, ditched and robbed Express train on the Southern Pacific Railroad from San Francisco to Deming, N. M., at a point about four miles east of the Gage Station and 15 miles west of Deming. After wrecking the train they shot and killed T. C. Webster, the engineer, then robbed W. F. & Co's Express, they robbed the Conductor, T. Z. Vail, of $100 in coin and a watch, and R. O. Gaskell, agent for the United States Publishing Co., Chicago, of $155. They then rifled the mail, but took nothing.

The four were arrested about two months later, and while awaiting trial at the Grant County Jail at Silver City, N. M., escaped. Were pursued by Sheriff's posse, and having provided themselves with arms, made a desperate resistance when overtaken, and George W. Cleveland was killed and Frank Taggart and Mitch Lee arrested. During the fight Joseph N. Laffer was instantly killed. He was a worthy citizen of Silver City and one of the Sheriff's posse. His untimely death so exasperated the citizens comprising the Sheriff's posse that they hanged Mitch Lee and Frank Taggart on the spot. Kit Joy for the time made a clean escape, but was pursued unrelentingly, and when taken some two weeks later made a desperate resistance, and received a shot which badly shattered his left leg; was brought into Silver City, had his leg amputated below the knee, and afterwards four inches above the knee; was placed on trial for the murder of T. C. Webster, but on account of his aged father and mother, his youthful sisters and other female relatives, and in consideration of having lost a leg, the jury brought in a verdict of murder in the second degree, November 20, 1884.

Received at the Territorial Prison, Santa Fe, N. M., November 25, 1884.

On November 24, 1883, the eastbound No. 19 Southern Pacific train coming from San Francisco to Deming, New Mexico was four miles west of Gage Station and fifteen miles from Deming when fireman Thomas North yelled out, "My God. There's a hole in the track!" Engineer Theophelus C. Webster set the brakes but it was too late and the engine, tender and the first three cars were derailed. The two trainmen rode the engine until it stopped and then, fearing the boiler would explode, the fireman jumped off with Webster close behind. When the engineer appeared at the door of the engine cab he was shot twice, one bullet piercing his heart killing him instantly and he fell near the tracks right beside his ditched engine. Conductor T. Zach Vail and passenger Gaskell went forward to investigate and see what help they could provide but were met by four unmasked, armed men who robbed Vail of $200 he had collected from late-boarding passengers and his gold watch. From Gaskell, a Chicago publisher, they took $155 but returned his watch when he said it had sentimental value. It was 4:20 P.M. so the robbers were in no rush as they seemed to be waiting for darkness to make their escape. The robbers battered in the door to the express car and the messenger put up no resistance as they searched and found $1,800 in the safe, then went to the mail car but they could find nothing of value. By the time they finished their work the sun had set so they loaded their plunder, mounted their horses, and fled north toward Grant County. Brakeman Tom Scott was sent to Gage Station on foot and he tried to telegraph Deming for help but the lines had been cut, so he telegraphed to San Francisco and they telegraphed through Denver to Deming. By 10:00 P.M. a special train was en route to the scene to transfer the passengers and baggage and in the morning deputy Dan Tucker, with fifty armed men including several excellent trackers, took up the trail. However, after traveling a half dozen miles the trail led onto hard, rocky ground where all sign was lost so the posse gave up the chase. A company of soldiers from Fort Huachuca also took the field but they had no better luck. There were no clues and even the reward of over $2,500 produced no leads so the lawmen had no choice but to wait patiently for a break in the case. A month after the robbery Albert C. Eaton, owner of a hay camp nine miles from Gage Station, contacted Grant County's Sheriff Harvey Whitehill and reported that on November 23 four indigent cowboys named Joy, Taggart, Lee and Cleveland had stopped at his camp. From their peculiar behavior he suspected they were up to something but mistakenly thought they were rustling stock in the area. He questioned them but they were evasive in their answers so he made a point of carefully examining their animals for later identification, and they included three horses and a mule ridden by Cleveland. When Eaton found that there was no rustling going on at that time, and then heard of the train robbery, he suspected the four cowboys. Whitehill personally followed up on the lead and made several discreet inquiries from which he learned that on the day following the robbery Taggart, Lee and Cleveland had been in Silver City, all supposed to be out-of-work cowboys but no longer looking for work. Whitehill knew by sight all four men named by Eaton, especially Joy who had once been an employee on the Sheriff's ranch, and the four men had visited his ranch on November 29. The descriptions were distributed throughout the territory: Cleveland described as, "A large ugly Negro, about six feet in height, as black as Erebus, and has been in this neighborhood for nearly two years"; Mitch Lee described as, "a native Texan, 21 years of age, 5 feet 8 inches tall with black hair and brown eyes, and dark complected"; Frank Taggart described as "26 years old, 5 feet eight inches tall, with light colored hair, blue eyes and a fair complexion, and had dark tobacco stains about his mouth and teeth which were plainly seen when he smiled, which was often"; and Kit Joy described as "born in Burnet County, Texas in 1869, missing several front teeth, nearly blind in his right eye, 5 feet 10 inches tall and weight 140 pounds; light complected with blue eyes and brown hair."

Whitehill told what he had learned to Wells, Fargo & Company's chief detective James Hume, who had been following up every lead after his arrival in New Mexico with fellow detective J. N. Thacker. Hume soon learned that Joy, Lee and Taggart had been loitering about the Duck Creek country before the train wrecking but had disappeared with Cleveland afterwards. The detectives found one of the camps and retrieved a copy of the Placer, California, *Herald* newspaper, which they traced to a saloon in Silver City. The owner remembered the four cowboys making several small purchases and it was supposed they had taken his copy of the *Herald*. Hume sent out inquiries and learned that Cleveland had been seen in Socorro so Whitehill went there and contacted County Sheriff Pedro S. Simpson who agreed to help. On December 28 Whitehill, a large powerful man, approached Cleveland in the lobby of a hotel and offered his right hand in greeting. Cleveland took it and the Sheriff tightened his grip and would not let go until Sheriff Simpson got the drop on Cleveland and they arrested him. They questioned Cleveland but their prisoner would admit to nothing, and they felt certain he would not inform on his fellow robbers, so Whitehill told him that the others were in jail and had confessed. Whitehill told Cleveland that all the other robbers had identified him as the man who shot Webster and this upset Cleveland so thoroughly that he confessed and confirmed the names of the three men who had robbed the train with him; and he insisted that it was Lee who had shot Webster. Cleveland gave such a detailed confession of the robbery that there was no doubt of its truth, so he was taken back to Grant County and jailed and then learned how he had been fooled by Whitehill. Deputy Sheriff John W. Gilmo then learned that Frank Taggart was in La Parte el Frio in Socorro County and on January 6, 1884, Gilmo, with a Mexican guide and a small posse, found Taggart rounding up two hundred head of cattle he had just purchased, presumably with the stolen money. They arrested him saying it was only for horse stealing, to avoid a fight, and Taggart soon joined Cleveland in the Silver City jail. Near the end of January, Joy and Lee stopped at the ranch of the Lyons & Campbell Cattle Company looking for work. The boys had stopped at Horse Springs and were seen by deputy sheriffs Andrew J. Best and Charles C. Perry. They fit the description of two train robbers so, after they left the Springs, Best and Perry caught them on the trail and proposed that they join them in a raid on the Soccoro County jail to free murderer Joel Fowler. The two lawmen said Joy and Lee would be well paid for doing their part in the jail delivery so the two fugitives agreed to help in the jail break and returned to Horse Springs. As soon as Joy and Lee fell asleep they were disarmed, captured, and turned over to Socorro County Sheriff Simpson, who took them to Silver City and lodged them in jail with Taggart and Cleveland.

Sheriff Whitehill had been dismissed soon after Taggart was captured, under charges that he had neglected his duties while chasing the train robbers, and he had been replaced by George M. Smith. Smith's jail policy was that each day the prisoners, four at a time, were given fifteen minutes in the yard for exercise and fresh air. On March 10, 1884, jailor Steve Wilson and another guard were watching four men in the yard and when their exercise time was up he started them for their cells, but the prisoners suddenly turned on the two lawmen and overpowered them. The two officers said later that the struggle lasted for a full ten minutes but their calls for help went unheeded, so the prisoners finally took their weapons and locked them in a cell. The prisoners opened the other cells and invited all the prisoners to join them, but only convicted murderer Carlos Chavez and horse thief Charles Spencer joined them. Cleveland had been locked up separately in a plank house so when they captured the Chinese cook and released Cleveland they locked the cook in there so he could not sound an alarm. The escapees went through the guard room, captured guard Nick Ware who was asleep and put him in the cell with the others, then went into the armory and took six-shooters, one shotgun and one Winchester rifle, all that was there. They also found a hammer and cold chisel and removed their shackles, leaving them on the floor of the guard room before they slipped out of the jail. As they went through the front office they were discovered by deputy sheriff Tom Hall who, unarmed, slammed the door to the rear rooms, locked it behind him and went for his guns. The prisoners fled down Market Street directly to the Elephant Corral, where they got the drop on George Chapman, the owner. They spent only a few moments selecting horses and saddled their mounts. Cleveland chose an unbroken mount which threw him just outside the corral, so he swung aboard behind another man and the party fled north toward the Piños Altos Mountains, their final destination being Mexico.

One of the local citizens, John C. Jackson, realized what was happening and followed the fleeing men from a safe distance while a posse was being formed, which included Joseph N. Lafferr, Frank Andrews, Thomas E. Park and Dan Coomer. The advance posse joined Jackson and a running gun fight continued for five miles, and meanwhile deputy Tom Hall organized a larger posse including deputy U.S. Marshal Louis C. Kennon, deputy sheriff F. C. Cantley, and a large number of citizens. When the reinforcements caught up with the forward posse the fugitives saw that they were in trouble and their horses were tiring. When a shot killed Chavez the rest of the gang dismounted and took refuge in a brushy canyon and the gun battle continued for over an hour as each side fired every time a target presented itself. Cleveland was killed in the shooting and Lee was seriously, but not fatally, wounded. Taggart called out that he was ready to surrender and he was joined by Spencer as they stepped out with arms raised. Lee was incapable of coming out or fighting but he surrendered as well and the posse had to carry him to a wagon which had been brought out from town. There seemed to be no sign of Joy but he was now afoot, so the posse began scouring the hills and ravines to find him. Posse man Lafferr, the widowed father of six children, rode through the brush looking for some sign when Joy suddenly rose up from behind, not ten feet away, and fired both barrels of his shotgun into the man's back, and Lafferr fell to the ground and died within minutes. The rest of the posse took cover again and this allowed Joy to escape through the heavy brush. After an extended period of silence the posse recovered Lafferr's body and again looked for the fugitive but when there was no sign of him they loaded the wagon with the bodies of Lafferr, Chavez and Cleveland, and prisoners Lee, Taggart and Spencer and started for town.

The posse had not gone far before they halted and held a people's court in the middle of the road. They were angry at the killing of Lafferr and were determined to exact justice on their live prisoners, but after some discussion it was decided that Spencer should be returned to his cell while Lee and Taggart would be hanged. While the men looked for an appropriate tree a deputy U.S. Marshal arrived and intervened but the men suggested he continue on to Fort Bayard and ask for directions on what should be done with the prisoners, and he agreed. After the deputy U.S. Marshal left deputy Sheriff Cantley strongly hinted to the men that he could not allow them to continue so long as he was armed so they promptly disarmed him and continued to search for a sturdy limb. They finally found a large Piñon tree suitable for the work and then removed Spencer from the wagon and moved the bodies of Chavez, Cleveland, and Lafferr to one side, pulled the wagon beneath the limb, and had Taggart stand while they held up Lee. The men positioned nooses around the necks of the men and bound the prisoners' feet, their hands already being tied. Lee at that moment knowing his end was near confessed to the killing of Webster and cleared Taggart of the crime, but the posse was angry over the killing of Lafferr, a crime for which both men were innocent, and the posse men whipped up the horses. The team rushed forward and the two men were left dangling. Taggart struggled for some time but finally strangled to death, while Lee died with hardly a quiver due in part to the great loss of blood he had already experienced. After they were dead the bodies were cut down, loaded into the wagon with the other three bodies, Spencer was again put aboard, and the wagon was driven to town. An inquest was held on the bodies of Cleveland, Lee, Taggart and Chavez on March 14 and the jury found, "...that the deceased came to their death by gun-shot wounds and other injuries inflicted by the sheriff's posse while in pursuit and endeavoring to recapture the prisoners after having broken jail by overpowering the guards and attempting to make their escape and committed seven miles north of Silver City, Grant County, New Mexico on the 11th day of March 1884."

Following his narrow escape from the posse, after murdering Lafferr, Joy went to the house of E. Smith at the mouth of Bear Canyon and at the point of his shot gun he demanded food and was supplied. He discussed the end of his fellow robbers with Sam Houston and declared he would never be hanged. He next went down Bear Creek and stole some blankets and other supplies from Pete Jensen's cabin. Joy seemed on good terms with Houston so lawmen asked him to negotiate a surrender and the proposal was presented to Joy, and it was agreed he was to appear on Thursday to be arrested, but Joy did not show. Instead the fugitive went to the home of Allen Fraze and begged for food, was supplied, and then headed for the bottom land near the cabin of Rackety Smith. He was seen by a man named McGuire who, with Smith and Sterling Ashby, formed a posse of three and went after Joy. They suddenly came upon him but they claimed they were following the fresh tracks of a deer as a ploy to get out of range of Joy's shotgun, and when they were at a safe distance they ordered his surrender. Joy had already become suspicious so when the demand came he turned to run and Smith fired one round from his rifle but missed. The next shot, however, struck Joy's left leg and shattered both bones below the knee. Joy collapsed and called out that he surrendered. The three men captured Joy, bound his wound the best they could, and took him to Silver City, arriving at 1:30 A.M. Saturday morning. The delay in getting their prisoner to the city allowed the wound to fester and later that day Joy's leg was amputated below the knee, but this did not resolve the medical problem so soon afterwards he had to undergo another amputation as the stump was taken above the knee. A number of men then claimed a portion of the rewards that had been offered and finally Whitehill, who had spent a substantial amount of his personal funds in the pursuit and lost his job as sheriff, was forced to file a suit. The court resolved the dispute and awarded amounts to eight men: Whitehill received $1,333; Perry, Best and Simpson got $444 each; Park, Andrews, Jackson, and Coomer each got $500.

In July Joy was indicted by the Grant County grand jury but there was little chance for a fair trial there so a change of venue was granted to Kingston, seat for the newly formed Sierra County. Trial was held at the fall term of the court and his aged father and sisters were in court each day, and the defendant had just lost his brother in a terrible mining accident. All this seemed to weigh heavily on the jurors so on November 20, 1884, they returned a verdict of guilty of second degree murder in the killing of engineer Webster and Joy was sentenced to life imprisonment. He was delivered to the territorial penitentiary on January 7, 1885, and on April 6, 1889, Governor E. G. Ross commuted his life sentence to twenty years, and then a six year campaign began in earnest to get him a pardon. On March 4, 1896, the Commissioners recommended that Joy receive his pardon and twelve days later it was granted by Governor W. T. Thornton. Joy, after his release, moved to Arizona where he was suspected of running a still, but was never charged with that offense. He died quietly of natural causes in 1928 at the age of fifty-nine.

Albuquerque Morning Journal [NM]: November 27, 1883. *Lone Star [El Paso, TX]*: November 25, 1883; March 12, 1884; March 22, 1884; February 11, 1885. *New York Times*: November 24, 1883. *Rio Grande Republican [Silver City, NM]*: March 15, 1884. *Silver City Enterprise [N. M.]*: January 4, 1884; January 11–12, 1884; January 18, 1884; January 20, 1884; January 25, 1884; March 14, 1884; May 16, 1884; August 29, 1884; September 12, 1884; December 9, 1884; December 19, 1884. *Socorro Sun [NM]*: January 22, 1884.

Kerby, G. A.

Nativity, New York; Age, 29 years; Occupation, Laborer; Height, 5 feet 11 inches; Complexion, Dark; Color of eyes, Brown; Color of hair, Dark Brown; Weight, 160½ lbs. Two large red scars or moles on left hip, scar on right shoulder, deformed nail on left little finger, wears a truss.

Robbed W. F. & Co's Express on stage from Ash Fork to Prescott, A. T., August 10, 1883, in company with J. S. Owen and Seely Owens.

Received at the Territorial Prison at Yuma, December 19, 1883; No. of commitment, 217; Crime, robbery; Term, 8 years; County sent from, Yavapai, A. T.

Escaped, April 21, 1884. Recaptured and returned, April 25, 1884.

The *Arizona Gazette* of August 16, 1883, reported on a stagecoach robbery on August 10 at Ash Fork in Coconino County, Arizona Territory: "The Ash Fork stage, O. Mercer driver, when out six miles from the railroad en route to Prescott, on Friday evening, was stopped by three masked men and the passengers, three in number—two gentlemen and a lady, invited to alight. The robbers proceeded to relieve the men of their cash, which amounted to about fifty dollars. The lady was not molested. The driver was requested to hand over the treasure box, which was full of emptiness, so the gay knights of the road got but little for their trouble, unless they captured the outgoing stage with Jesus for driver." The governor issued a proclamation covering two stagecoach robberies occurring the same day. The information pertinent to the Ash Fork robbery follows:

> GOVERNOR'S REWARD
> Whereas, Stage robbing is becoming apparently
> a permanent industry of the Territory and
> is one which carries with it the destruction of life and
> always is attended with danger to
> the peaceful traveling public, and
> Whereas, On Friday, the 10th of August, 1883,
> near Ash Fork, in Yavapai county,
> three masked highwaymen did stop and rob
> the coach and passengers and
> Wells, Fargo & Co.'s treasure box of money ...
> Now therefore, I, H. M. Van Arman,
> Acting-Governor of the Territory of Arizona,
> by virtue of the power vested in me,
> do hereby offer a reward of
> TWO HUNDRED DOLLARS
> For the arrest and conviction of each
> of the persons who committed the robberies
> on the Ash Fork road ...
> Should fatal consequences to the robbers
> attend their capture, identification and proof
> that they were guilty parties will be sufficient
> to secure the payment of the reward offered.
> Done at the City of Prescott, the Capital,
> the 13th day of August, A.D., 1883
> H.M. Van Arman
> Acting Governor
> Attest: John S. Furman
> Assistant-Secretary
> Arizona Territory

On September 27 the *Arizona Gazette* reported: "The three highwaymen who robbed passengers and stage last month near Ash Fork made a full confession of the crime today in the county jail, stating the whole amount they obtained was about $21." The robbers were tried, convicted and sentenced to terms at the Territorial Prison near Yuma. George Allen Kerby was received on December 19, 1883, as prisoner No. 217, sentenced to eight years. He was described as twenty-nine years of age, five feet eleven inches tall, with brown eyes and brown hair, and he was illiterate. He escaped on April 20, 1884, but was recaptured the same day. He was pardoned by Governor Zulick on June 21, 1887. Joseph S. Owens, prisoner No. 214, was received on December 19, 1883, to serve a sentence of four years. He was described as twenty-one years of age, five feet eleven inches tall, blue eyes and brown hair, and literate. He was pardoned by Governor Tritle on March 6, 1885. Seely Owens had also been sentenced to a term of eight years and was described as twenty-eight years of age, five feet ten inches in height, one hundred sixty-five pounds, with dark hair and eyes. He had an ugly knife scar on his right wrist which also disfigured a finger on that hand. The *Salt River Herald* reported on Seely Owens' escape: "The 4 o'clock stage for Maricopa yesterday evening carried six prisoners consigned from Yavapai to the Yuma penitentiary. The prisoners were under the charge of a single guard, deputy sheriff Vanderburg, who took his post on top of the stage. Upon arrival at Maricopa a prisoner named Owens, sentenced for stage robbery, was absent having thrown himself from the stage on the way. He is shackled and will doubtless have difficulty in escaping." Owens spoke fluent Spanish so it was believed he fled south of the border and was not seen nor heard of in the Territory again.

Arizona Gazette [Phoenix, AZ]: August 16, 1883; September 27, 1883. *Salt River Herald [Phoenix, AZ]*: December 20, 1883. *Weekly Enterprise [Florence, AZ]*: August 24, 1883.

King, Jack

Nativity, Kentucky; Age, 25 years; Occupation, Laborer; Height, 5 feet 9 inches; Complexion, Light; Color of eyes, Light Blue; Color of hair, Light Brown.

Robbed W. F. & Co's Express on stage from Kelton, U. T., to Albion, I. T., July 25, 1882, in company with William Adams, Dave Francis, and Francis Hawley.

Robbed W. F. & Co's Express on stage from Kelton, U. T., to Albion, I. T., July 30, 1882, in company with King, Francis, and Hawley.

Received at Territorial Prison, Boise, I. T., June 12, 1883. No. of Commitment, 31. Crime, Robbery; Term, life; County sent from, Oneida.

[*See* Adams, William]

Kirkendall, Jefferson

Age, 24 years; Occupation, Cowboy; Height 5 feet 7¼ inches; Complexion, Light; Color of eyes, Blue; Color of hair, Brown. Scar on wrist of right hand, scar on lower joint of third finger left hand.

Attempted to rob W. F. & Co's Express on train No. 102 on A. T. & S. F. R. R. At a point about five miles north of Socorro, N. M. in company with Edward White, J. W. Pointer, P. "Punch" Collins, and Bill Allen.

Received at the Kansas State Prison, November 21, 1884; No. 3398; Crime, assault to rob; Term, 7 years; County sent from, Socorro, N. M.

[*See* Collins, P.]

Larsen, James

Nativity, Denmark; Age, 32 years; Occupation, Blacksmith; Height, 5 feet 10 inches; Complexion, Fair; Color of eyes, Brown; Color of hair, Light Brown. Mole on left side of neck, two moles on left shoulder, scar on right hip, thick lips.

Robbed W. F. & Co's Express on stage from Phoenix to Prescott, A. T., July 1, 1883, in company with Joe Chambers.

Robbed W. F. & Co's Express on stage from Phoenix to Prescott, A. T., July 20, 1883.

Received at the Territorial Prison, Yuma A. T., November 4, 1883; No. of commitment, 192; Crime, robbery; Term, 10 years; County sent from, Maricopa, A. T.

The *Arizona Gazette* of Phoenix on April 19, 1883, reported: "Last week as the stage was coming down the Black Canyon a man was noticed in the road. As Marshal Evans and James Dodson, the City Marshal of Prescott, both well armed, were aboard, they speedily dismounted and ran ahead with the intention of giving the 'rustler' a round. There was a sharp turn in the road, but when the officers got to the spot where the suspicious individual was discerned there was no one to be seen. However, the tracks of two men were followed into the brush. If the men were really robbers, and had undertaken to stop the stage, it would have been the most fatal project that they ever indulged in. It was a 'bad' load of passengers." No one was ever charged with a crime but later two men would be arrested and charged with subsequent robberies in the vicinity of this attempt. There were no other robberies nor robbers active in the vicinity of Gillette during that period suggesting that this was the first attempt made by these two men, and defendant James Larsen would later testify that "Chambers has been with me since about the 4th of April last." At 10:30 P.M. on Wednesday evening, June 27, 1883, Amos Niccolls maneuvered his Gilmer & Salisbury Company stagecoach out of Gillette northbound for Prescott. When the coach was two and one half miles from town two robbers stepped from the left, the side farthest from the driver, and halted the stagecoach. One robber sported a shotgun and the other a Winchester rifle. They were both described as being "not too tall and heavy set," and both men had their faces covered with handkerchiefs. The robber with the rifle pointed it at the driver and did all the talking, first ordering the driver to stop and then ordering him to "throw off the box," and the driver threw down the Wells, Fargo & Company treasure box. The robbers did not ask for the mail sacks nor did they molest Mr. Brown, Miss Burfind or the young boy who were passengers in the coach, before they ordered Niccolls to proceed. The box was broken open about thirty yards from where the stagecoach was stopped and $22.50 was taken, but a shawl in the treasure box was left behind. An investigation followed and all that was learned was that the robbers had walked back to Gillette, partly over the hills and partly on the road, and their identities remained a mystery. On Sunday evening, July 1, 1883, Amos Niccolls drove the Gilmer & Salisbury Company's stagecoach south out of Gillette bound for Bumble Bee Station. At 11:30 P.M. when three miles from Gillette, and just before reaching the Agua Fria river, the coach was stopped by one heavy set man sporting a gun. There was moon light so, even though the driver was not sure whether the robber had a rifle or shotgun, he was sure it was a long barreled weapon and not a pistol pointed at him. The robber ordered the driver to throw down the treasure box, which he did immediately. The mail sacks were not requested nor was the single passenger molested, and the driver was then ordered to continue. The box contained $569.70, one small package valued at $9.00, two waybills, and two metal charms valued at $5.00 each. A description was sent throughout the Territory by telegraph. Suspicion quickly focused upon the blacksmiths at Gillette — James Larsen and Joseph Chambers. They fit the description of the men and had recently acquired a quantity of money they could not explain. Larsen was arrested upon a warrant on July 2, 1883, and he quickly admitted his guilt. He dug up the charms, one a distinctive Masonic emblem, from the floor of his blacksmith shop and gave them to deputy sheriff McDonald, upon the deputy's promise to go easy on him. Based upon Larsen's confession Chambers was arrested on July 3.

The *Gazette* reported on July 21, 1883, that "Larsen and Chambers, the Black Canyon stagecoach robbers have had their examination and have been held in the sum of $5,000 each to await the action of the Grand Jury." The men were indicted on October 15, 1883, and soon afterward tried. Following Larsen's conviction he was sentenced to serve ten years in the Territorial prison near Yuma. Upon his arrival as prisoner No. 192 Larsen, a Dane, was described as thirty-one years of age, five feet ten inches in height with light brown hair and brown eyes, and literate. Larsen, after serving four years of his sentence, was pardoned by Governor Zulick. The pardon was in recognition of his assistance to law enforcement in solving the case and requested by the officers and agents of Wells, Fargo &

Company. The pardon also cited, "by his mechanical skill he has while in prison rendered the Territory extraordinary service, and believing that his punishment has effected a thorough reformation, and the ends of justice fully served, Now therefore I, G. Meyer Zulick, Governor ... hereby grant James Larsen a full and unconditional pardon, restoring to him all the rights of citizenship, and direct that he be forthwith set at liberty." Larsen had distinguished himself by designing a hammer, which won first prize at the Mechanic's Fair in San Francisco in 1884, and numerous other devices and inventions. He was released on July 1, 1887. Chambers received a sentence of six years but obtained a new trial and was acquitted.

On November 14, 1884, a stagecoach was robbed and Thomas Owens informed the *Salt River Herald* that the Yuma bound coach was stopped by two highwaymen at 2:00 P.M. when six miles north of Date Creek station, between Kelsey's and Gilson's Ranches. The road agents took and shook the express box but concluded the sound did not indicate sufficient treasure to warrant the trouble of breaking it open. Learning that no bullion bars were on board they were so disappointed that they ordered the coach to continue on. Mr. Asher and wife were the only passengers on board and they were not disturbed. On November 30 the *Daily Miner* reported that James Hume and Bob Paul, Wells, Fargo & Company detectives, "brought in and lodged in jail yesterday afternoon two strangers whom they charge with stopping the coach near Date Creek on the 12th ... [Hume and Paul] feel quite confident that they are the roosters who made the attempt and that they are young in the business," and one of the men was Joseph Chambers. The detectives scheduled a hearing before Judge A. O. Noyes for Monday, December 2 but it was delayed until Wednesday, and then the *Enterprise* reported: "DISCHARGED—The two men who were arrested last week in Thompson's Valley, by Special Agents Hume and Paul, upon a charge of stopping the coach, were brought before Judge Noyes this morning. District Attorney Paul Weber stated that he had carefully examined the evidence against them and did not consider it sufficient to justify the expense even of an examination and asked that they be discharged, which was done." No additional evidence was forthcoming to implicate the two men brought to court by Hume and Paul so that robbery was never solved, but it apparently put a scare into the road agents as the robberies by these two men ceased.

Arizona Gazette [Phoenix, AZ]: April 19, 1883; July 21, 1883; August 9, 1883; October 11, 1883; October 25, 1883. *Daily Miner [Prescott, AZ]*: November 30, 1884. *Enterprise [Florence, AZ]*: December 2, 1884. *Salt River Herald [Phoenix, AZ]*: November 15, 1884. *Sentinel [Yuma, AZ]*: June 28, 1883; August 30, 1884. *Weekly Arizona Citizen [Tucson, AZ]*: July 6, 1883.

Lauria, Thomas

Nativity, Scotland; Age, 46; Occupation, Stockman; Height 5 feet 7½ inches; Complexion, Light; Color of eyes, Blue; Color of hair, Sandy; Weight, 166 lbs. Cupping marks on right side of abdomen, vaccine marks on left arm, several large moles on back.

Attempted to rob W. F. & Co's Express on stage from Eureka to Tybo, in company with Bob Hamilton and Jack Davis, September 3, 1877.

Received at the Nevada State Prison, December 8, 1877; No. of commitment, 69; Crime, attempted robbery; Term, 14 years; County sent from: Nye, Nev.

Pardoned June 20, 1882 and left next day for the East in company with a brother who came from Washington and procured his pardon.

[*See* Davis, Jack]

Lee, Charles—*alias* James Johnson

Nativity, Maryland; Age, 40 years; Occupation, Sailor; Height, 5 feet 7 inches; Complexion, Light; Color of eyes, Gray; Color of hair, Fair. Slim features, high cheek-bones, face and neck freckled, scar across the right cheek-bone, star on left forearm, do. at the base of left thumb, several spots of ink on left arm and back of left hand, eagle, shield and three stars on breast, two flags, two faces, heart pierced with arrow and anchor, wreath with the word "Love" inside two hearts and spear, a star, two hearts and face right forearm, small boil mark left side of neck; slim built.

No. of first commitment, 3480. Received at the California State Prison, March 8, 1867; Crime, burglary; Term, 2 years; County sent from, San Francisco.

Discharged, by expiration of sentence, November 9, 1868.

No. of second commitment, 4182. Received at the California State Prison, July 21, 1869; Crime, grand larceny; Term, 1 year; County sent from, Yuba.

Discharged, by expiration of sentence, May 23, 1870.

No. of third commitment, 5095. Received at the California State Prison, January 19, 1872; Crime, burglary; Term, 3 years; County sent from, Sonoma.

Discharged, by expiration of sentence, August 8, 1874.

Burglarized W. F. & Co's safe at Suisun, October 25, 1874, in company with Henry Stubbs, Jack Bowen, and Charlie Burch.

Burglarized W, F, & Co's safe at Georgetown, El Dorado County, Cal., November 2, 1874, in company with Stubbs and Burch.

Received at the California State Prison, January 7, 1875; No. of commitment, 6323; Crime, (two commitments) assault to murder and grand larceny; Term, 18 years; County sent from, Solano.

On October 25, 1874, Charles Lee, Henry Stubbs, Jack Bowen and Charles D. Burch burglarized the depot at Suisun in Solano County, broke into Wells, Fargo's safe and stole everything which had been entrusted to the express company and though there were no clues to the guilty parties the investigation continued. On November 2, 1874, Lee, Stubbs and Burch burglarized the depot at Georgetown in El Dorado County, broke open Wells, Fargo's safe and stole everything inside. This time these three well known criminals were suspected and it was not long before they were tracked down and arrested, but Lee and Stubbs resisted arrest and were also charged with assault to commit murder. Soon Jack Bowen joined them behind bars and, knowing he was innocent of the second crime and expecting to gain his release, quickly confessed to the Suisun burglary and agreed to testify against the other prisoners.

Bowen was only able to testify about the Suisun burglary, making that the strongest case, so the prisoners were transferred to Solano County where Lee and Stubbs were also charged with assault to commit murder. Burch, who had no prior prison record but was facing a prison sentence, then also agreed to turn state's evidence. At the examination Bowen and Burch were the primary witnesses against Lee and Stubbs for the Suisun burglary, while Burch testified to the Georgetown burglary and the resistance to the arrest by the two defendants, and in consideration of their cooperation Bowen and Burch were released.

The officers from El Dorado County then testified regarding the assault and the two defendants, hoping for a reduced sentence, agreed to plead guilty to the lesser charge of grand larceny rather than burglary and the assault charge. However, both defendants had extensive records—Lee serving three prior terms and Stubbs four prior terms at San Quentin—so when they were brought into court they were sentenced to two consecutive terms totaling eighteen years each. Stubbs arrived at San Quentin Prison on January 1, 1875, as prisoner No. 6320. He was conditionally pardoned by Governor George C. Perkins on December 20, 1882, which required him to leave the State of California. Lee arrived at San

Quentin Prison on January 7, 1875, as prisoner No. 6323. He was discharged on March 6, 1886.

Stubbs, after his release, violated the conditions of his pardon and burglarized the store of Anthony & Company at San Francisco. He was captured, indicted by the San Francisco County grand jury, tried, convicted, and sentenced to serve twelve years at Folsom prison. He arrived on May 15, 1883, registering as prisoner No. 602 and was released on January 15, 1891.

Bowen had first arrived at San Quentin from San Francisco on August 19, 1853, as prisoner No. 260 serving twenty years for highway robbery. He was released on a writ of *habeas corpus* on August 19, 1863. Bowen stayed out of trouble for more than a decade before the 1874 burglary but then, in June 1876, Burch with James Demerest burglarized a store at Trinity Center and when Constable Bell from Anderson tried to arrest them Burch resisted and was killed.

Lee, Eddie—*alias* Thomas Martin

Nativity, Michigan; Age, 34 years; Occupation, Waiter; Height, 5 feet 5 inches; Complexion, Light; Color of eyes, Hazel; Color of hair, Brown. Pockmarked, sharp features, heavy eyebrows, mole on right and left shoulder, blue spot left lower arm, woman with wreath in ink left lower arm, mole on back, mole on right side of belly; slim built.

First term, 4144. Received at the California State Prison, March 25, 1870; Crime, burglary; Term, 6 years; County sent from, San Francisco.

Pardoned by Governor Newton Booth, February 22, 1872.

Robbed W. F. & Co's Express on stage from Forest Hill to Auburn, September 12, 1873, with John "Jake" Clark, John "Shorty" Hays, and Charlie Thompson [*sic*].

Received at the California State prison, March 24, 1874; No. of commitment, 5933; Crime, robbery; Term, 4 years, County sent from, Placer.

Discharged, by expiration of sentence, August 13, 1877.

Received at the California State Prison, January 22, 1878; No. of commitment, 7972; Crime, grand larceny; Term, 4 years; County sent from, San Francisco.

Discharged, per Act, January 22, 1881.

[*See* Clark, John]

Lee, Milton Harvey

Nativity, Arkansas; Age, 37 years; Occupation, Cabinet-maker; Height, 5 feet 10 inches; Complexion, Florid; Color of eyes, Blue; Color of hair, Gray; Size of foot, 8. Square features, deep-set eyes, heavy eyebrows, large ears, long sharp nose, small scar between eyebrows, square chin and jaw, vaccine mark left upper arm, large hard hands, bald spot top of head, square shoulders; stout built.

No. of first term, 3615. Received at the California State Prison, August 12, 1867; Crime, grand larceny; Term, 2½ years; County sent from, Santa Clara.

Pardoned by Governor H. H. Haight, April 14, 1868.

No. of second term, 4640. Received at the California State Prison, November 28, 1870; Crime, grand larceny; Term, 4 years; County sent from, San Bernardino.

Discharged, by expiration of sentence, April 17, 1874.

Robbed stage from Fresno to Yosemite, in company with John Herbert.

Received at the California State Prison, September 19, 1884; No. of commitment, 11386; Crime, robbery; Term, 20 years; County sent from, Fresno.

[*See* Herbert, John M.]

Lester, George—*alias* George Lane, George Jackson

Nativity, Kentucky; Age, 24 years; Occupation, Cowboy; Height, 5 feet 7½ inches; Complexion, Light; Color of eyes, Blue; Color of hair, Red. Long features, large nose and crooked, face freckled, scar on left cheek, small scar between the eyebrows, vaccine mark on left upper arm, forearms freckled, wart on side under left nipple, back of neck and shoulders freckled, end of left thumb deformed; slim built.

No. of first commitment, 3785. Received at the California State Prison, April 2, 1868; Crime, grand larceny; Term, 5 years; County sent from, San Bernardino.

Discharged, by expiration of sentence, June 7, 1872.

Robbed W. F. & Co's Express on stage from Colfax to Grass Valley, July 27, 1873, in company with Early, Dribblesbeis, and Stover, and James Meyers as an accessory.

Received at the California State Prison, June 5, 1874; No. of commitment, 6031; Crime, robbery, Term, 15 years, County sent from, Nevada.

Discharged, by expiration of sentence, November 5, 1883.

Robbed stage from Forbestown to Oroville, September 11, 1884, with Bob Clements.

No. of third commitment, 11533. Received at the California State Prison as George Jackson; Crime robbery U.S. Mail; Term, 10 years.

[*See* Thompson, Charles, regarding the 1873 stagecoach robbery.]

On Thursday morning, September 11, 1884, the stagecoach from Laporte driven by Fred Morse left Forbestown in Butte County bound for Oroville with three male passengers and one female passenger aboard. At 3:00 P.M. the stagecoach was coming down the grade above Smith Hurles' ranch when a masked road agent armed with a shotgun stepped into the road, which blocked the way for the horses so they stopped. A second road agent, also masked and armed with a shotgun, then stepped out from the side of the road and covered the passengers. The man holding the reins of the lead horses demanded the Wells, Fargo Express box but, upon being told there was none aboard, he ordered the passengers out. The road agent at the side of the coach assisted Mrs. Rollins in stepping down but assured her she needn't be alarmed. The road agents then told the men to hand over their money and they collected $150. Robert Hall also had $80 in coin and $1,000 in checks in his pockets which the robbers did not find. Mr. Chapman tried to "pungle" some silver change but when his hand came out of his pocket he had three $20 gold coins and five singles. When he asked to keep enough to pay his fare and hotel bill three dollars was returned to him. Mr. Williams tried the same dodge of asking to keep $20 to get home to Santa Rosa after producing several twenties but he was told he could borrow the money in Oroville. The two road agents then took the mail bags and ordered the coach to continue on. Morse whipped up his team and hurried into Oroville to report the robbery. The description given by the driver and passengers fit two men suspected of burglarizing Bell's store in Oroville the previous night. Later, on the same night as the stagecoach robbery, Edward Quinton was driving his team up a grade near Miner's Ranch when a masked foot pad, armed with a shotgun, stepped out and robbed him of all he had—$11 he carried in a pocket book. The robber, after removing the money, returned the pocketbook and told Quinton to drive on. Lawmen were soon on the trail of the robbers and it was thought all the work had been done by the same two men. Forbestown's Constable Parks went out on the Laporte coach the next morning and soon returned with the stolen mail bag, but it had been ripped open with a knife and everything was taken except for a bundle of newspapers.

On September 28 George Lester was captured by Sheriff McClellan at Ione, but he gave the name George Jackson, and he was lodged in the county jail to await the arrival of his partner in crime. A dispatch was received on October 24 saying that the second robber was captured in the southern part of the state but it appears they had the wrong man. Lester was tried and convicted under that name, and was sentenced to serve ten years. He was released upon expiration of sentence on July 8, 1891. Bob Clements was never prosecuted for the robbery and did not serve time in prison for that offense.

Oroville Weekly Mercury [CA]: September 12, 1884; September 19, 1884; October 10, 1884; October 24, 1884.

Lugo, Chico—*alias* Santos Sotello

Nativity, California; Age, 34 years; Occupation, Laborer; Height, 5 feet 5½ inches; Complexion, Dark; Color of eyes, Black; Color of hair, Black. Long features, pockmarked, small ears, mole on right cheek-bone, mole on left side of forehead, body covered with venereal scars, mole back of neck; stout built.

Robbed W. F. & Co's Express on stage from Darwin to Mojave, January 6, 1877, in company with Francis Sotello.

Robbed W. F. & Co's Express on stage from Newhall to Ventura, January 20, 1877, with Francis Sotello.

Received at the California State Prison, September 23, 1877; No. of commitment, 7763; Crime, robbery; Term, 15 years; County sent from, Kern.

The Sotello brothers, Santos and Francisco, came from one of the oldest families in California. Both men had been in trouble during their youth and, to spare the family the shame, these "black sheep" adopted aliases, Santos Sotello taking the alias Chico Lugo and Francisco Sotello taking the alias Francisco Olivas. In late 1876 Francisco Olivas was suspected of a first degree murder, a crime which could bring the death penalty. He could not return home even after the posse gave up the search, so he and his brother fled northwest past Mojave into Kern County. In January 1877 when Lugo was just twenty-six years old and Olivas was just nineteen years old the two brothers decided to rob stagecoaches. On January 6 when the coach from Darwin to Mojave was in Red Rock Canyon in Kern County they stepped out, masked and with guns in hand, and robbed the stagecoach of the Wells, Fargo & Company Express box. After receiving the box and going through the passengers the robbers fled into the Tehachapi Mountains, confident that they could not be captured while hiding in that rough terrain. On January 20 Lugo and Olivas, with Jose Tapia, appeared on the stage road between Newhall and Ventura in Los Angeles County and robbed the Ventura bound stagecoach. Again they secured the Wells, Fargo & Company box and then fled to Elizabeth Lake. The two brothers, with Francisco Romero, made their way over the Tehachapi Mountains again and went to Panama, a Mexican settlement near Bakersfield, and stole a small string of horses. Next they robbed a Tulare Lake store of $500 and supplies for the trail, beating the owner into unconsciousness. The men drove the stolen horses south and when recognized they had a running gun battle with men trying to recover the stock. No one was hurt but a large posse was soon on their trail and they had to abandoned the horses. The posse kept on their trail for a week but finally gave up and, on their return to Bakersfield, stopped at the ranch of George Reig, and they found him dead and his house ransacked. Next the outlaw brothers were heard of in San Francisquito Canyon where they bound fourteen Chinese miners and robbed them of $260 in gold dust. The posse, led by ex-Sheriff R. H. "Bob" Paul, grew and kept pressure on the two fugitives until finally a tip came which put the two men in a valley in the San Bernardino Mountains. The posse captured Olivas without resistance, coming upon him so quickly he could not make his fight even though he had two fully loaded six-shooters in his belt. Lugo, at the time of the capture of his brother, was at a celebration in town but being clean-shaven for the first time he was not recognized and escaped. Bob Paul, then the shotgun messenger for Wells, Fargo between Mojave and Lone Pine, lodged Olivas in jail. Friends of Olivas tried various legal maneuvers to gain his release and finally obtained a writ of *habeas corpus*, but driver Briggs appeared and identified Olivas so a warrant was sworn out by Justice Peterson ordering Olivas taken before a Kern County Justice for examination. E. Diaz, to counter this maneuver, arrested Paul for "personating an officer," and his examination was held in Lone Pine where he was acquitted. Paul was then deputized to take Olivas before the Kern County Justice and the prisoner was held to answer to the grand jury.

Soon afterward Romero was captured at Kern and taken to Tulare County while Tapia was captured at Darwin and charged in the Ventura stagecoach robbery. Tapia was held to answer to the grand jury at his examination and at trial Tapia pled guilty to the stagecoach robbery and was sentenced to serve ten years at San Quentin Prison. He arrived on March 21, 1877, and registered as prisoner No. 7463. Tapia's sentence was commuted and he was discharged on December 21, 1881, after serving only four years and nine months. Francisco Olivas (Francisco Sotello) was convicted and also sentenced to serve a term of ten years, arrived at San Quentin Prison on May 29, 1877, and registered as prisoner No. 7602. Olivas was released on November 20, 1883, by expiration of sentence but he would return to prison on a conviction for grand larceny in 1886. Francisco Romero was charged in the Tulare Lake store robbery, convicted, and sentenced to serve five years at San Quentin. He arrived on June 25, 1877, and registered as No. 7647. Romero was discharged, by expiration of sentence, on January 25, 1881.

Chico Lugo (Santos Sotello) once again fled into the Tehachapi Mountains but by July 19 he had been tracked down and captured. A bold young man had come upon the desperado lounging beneath a tree smoking a cigarette and the desperado was immediately recognized. The young man, Rafael Lopez, crept up keeping a tree between himself and the bandit and then, suddenly springing upon him with pistol in hand, he took Lugo prisoner. Lugo was taken into Los Angeles and later transferred to Kern County where he was tried and convicted of robbing the Darwin stagecoach on January 6. Lugo talked freely of his exploits and was easily convicted, receiving a sentence of fifteen years at San Quentin. He arrived at the prison on September 23, 1877, and was discharged from prison in February 1887.

Bakersfield Courier Californian [CA]: March 8, 1877; March 15, 1877; March 22, 1877; May 13, 1877; June 7, 1877; June 27, 1877. *Calaveras Chronicle [CA]*: February 24. 1877. *Kern County Weekly Courier [CA]*: July 19, 1877; *Los Angeles Weekly Star [CA]*: January 17, 1876; April 29, 1877; May 5, 1877. *Los Angeles Daily Star [CA]*: March 15, 1877; June 17, 1877; July 10, 1877. *Los Angeles News [CA]*: November 7, 1877; November 13, 1877. *Daily Alta California [San Francisco, CA]*: July 13, 1877.

Machado, Jose

Nativity, California; Age, 31 years; Occupation, Vaquero; Height, 5 feet 3⅜ inches; Complexion; Dark; Color of eyes, Black; Color of hair, Black. Thin features, scar on upper lip, large ears, scar near right elbow, mole inside of right forearm; slim built.

Robbed W. F. & Co's Express on stage from Marysville to Downieville, July 26, 1877, in company with Trinidad Nunez.

Received at the California State Prison, October 18, 1877; No. of commitment, 7834; Crime, robbery; Term, 14 years; County sent from, Sierra.

On July 26, 1877, the up-coach from Marysville in Yuba County to Downieville in Sierra County driven by Dave Quadlin was halted by three Mexican road agents when four miles north of Camptonville. Onboard were seven passengers, including A. M Crocker of San Francisco and Isaac Elias of Downieville, who rode on top with the driver and inside were Antonio Macon with his wife and two daughters and one Chinese man. The robbers demanded the Wells, Fargo treasure box but there was none aboard. They searched Macon, an Italian, taking $40 and from the Chinese man they took $22. They did not molest the mother and daughters, the driver, nor the passengers riding on top. A posse was soon on their trail and they tracked the three men near San Juan where they captured two while the third road agent made his escape. The two prisoners identified themselves as Jose Machado and Trinidad Nunez, and they were lodged in the Sierra County jail. At their examination they were held to answer to the grand jury. In early October the two defendants were indicted, tried, and found guilty of the robbery after only a half hour of jury deliberations. Sentencing was postponed so that their attorney, F. D. Soward, could argue a motion for a new trial but the motion was denied. Machado, the leader of the road agents, was then sentenced to serve fourteen years while Nunez was sentenced to serve eight years at San Quentin Prison. Both men arrived at the prison on October 18, 1877, Machado registering as prisoner No. 7834 and Nunez registering as prisoner No. 7833. Nunez was discharged by expiration of sentence on February, 17, 1883, while Machado was discharged on August 18, 1886, after serving less than nine years.

The Daily Appeal [Marysville, CA]: July 27, 1877; July 28, 1877; October 10, 1877.

Mairs, A. F.

Nativity, Canada; Age, 29 years; Occupation, Teamster; Height, 5 feet 9¼ inches; Complexion, Dark; Color of eyes, Brown; Color of hair, Dark; Size of foot, 7½. High retreating forehead, eyes deep-set, heavy eyebrows, small scar right side forehead, long scar under right eye, large scar on left little finger, square shoulders; stout built.

Robbed W. F. & Co's Express on stage from Bishop Creek to Bishop Creek R. R. Station, December 29, 1883, in company with T. C. Harniss and Louis Schalten, the driver.

Received at the California State Prison, February 25, 1884. No. of commitment, 11154; Crime, robbery; Term, 2½ years; County sent from, Inyo.

[*See* Harniss, T. C.]

Maria, Jose—*alias* Kokimbo

Nativity, Chili; Age 58 years; Occupation, Laborer; Height, 5 feet 3¾ inches; Complexion; Dark; Color of eyes, Black; Color of hair, Gray. Broad features, flat eyebrows, face wide across cheek bones, 2 scars left cheek, do. right eyebrow, 1 do. breast-bone, mole under left collar-bone, do. under right nipple, do. left do., scar left wrist, do. middle finger of right hand at first joint; stout built.

Robbed W. F. & Co's Express on stage from Laporte to Oroville, August 3, 1875, with Ramon Ruiz, Red Antone, and Isador Pardillo.

Received at the California State Prison, February 17, 1876; No. of commitment, 6889; Crime, robbery; Term, 5 years; County sent from, Butte.

Commuted by Governor William Irwin, April 23, 1878, to 4½ years.

Discharged, per Act, August 12, 1879.

[*See* Ruiz, Ramon]

Marshall, John—*alias* Robinson, Simpson

Nativity, Michigan; Age, 44 years; Occupation, Cabinet-maker; Height, 5 feet 9¾ inches; Complexion, Florid; Color of eyes, Gray; Color of hair, Brown; Size of foot, 8. Two small dim vaccine marks on left upper arm.

No. of first commitment, 6296. Received at the California State Prison, December 18, 1874; Crime, grand larceny; Term, 3 years, County sent from, Placer.

Discharged, by expiration of sentence, July 11, 1877.

No. of second commitment, 8508. Received at the California State Prison, October 31, 1878; Crime, burglary first degree; Term, 6 years; County sent from, Yuba.

Discharged, by expiration of sentence, December 30, 1882.

Robbed W. F. & Co's Express on stage from Sierra Valley to Truckee, August 13, 1883, in company with George B. Saylor.

Robbed W. F. & Co's Express on stage from Sierra Valley to Truckee, October 15, 1883, in company with James Martin.

Received at the California State Prison, November 1, 1883; No. of commitment, 11014; Crime, robbery; Term, 15 years; County sent from, Sierra.

On Monday, August 13, 1883, the stagecoach from Sierra Valley to Truckee driven by G. Q. Buxton, the proprietor of the stage line, was stopped near the Little Truckee River in Sierra County. The two masked road agents demanded the Wells, Fargo treasure box, one pointing a shotgun and the other a revolver at Buxton. He threw out the box and the road agents then went through the passengers, five men and one woman, collecting $60. They kept the box which contained $976 in gold dust and sent Buxton on his way. The two men decided to return to the "states" and visit family, so they went to Omaha where they were arrested "on suspicion" when they tried to sell the dust. After a careful investigation by the Nebraska authorities no charges were filed and they were released. Once their money ran out Marshall returned to California while his partner struck-out for Baltimore, Maryland. On Monday, October 15, 1883, the stagecoach from Sierra Valley to Truckee was stopped by two road agents when it was near Cooley's Station. Both road agents were masked and armed with six-shooters, which they brandished as they demanded the Wells, Fargo treasure box. G. Q. Buxton, again the driver, threw down the box and they required him to get down from his seat and break it open. After they removed the gold dust from the box they went through the passengers, taking their money and jewelry, in all collecting $300. Lawmen were soon on their trail and on Sunday, October 21 the first road agent was captured by Captain Aull at Wadsworth and he gave the name John Marshall. He had on his person some of the gold dust taken from the stagecoach and the jewelry taken from the passengers. Marshall was well known to the lawmen as he had robbed the Forbestown stagecoach in 1874 but James Hume, Wells Fargo's chief detective, made a deal to recover the treasure and the charge was reduced to grand larceny for stealing the shotgun he used to stop the stagecoach, and he was sentenced to serve only three years at San Quentin. Marshall, on the promise from Aull that he would intercede to see he did not get a life sentence, gave a full confession naming George B. Saylor as his partner in the August 13 robbery. The second road agent from the October 15 robbery was soon arrested and he gave the name James Martin, and Martin was new to the business. Marshall and Martin were lodged in the Oroville jail and when taken into court both men pled guilty. Marshall was given a sentence of fifteen years while Martin was sentenced to a term of five years. Both men arrived at San Quentin Prison on November 1, 1883, where Martin registered as prisoner No. 11013 and Marshall registered as prisoner No. 11014. Martin was discharged, by expiration of sentence, on June 1, 1887, and Marshall was discharged on April 1, 1893, after serving ten years.

The search for Saylor continued and on January 19 the *Mountain Messenger* reported, "George B. Saylor was recently arrested in Baltimore, Maryland and will arrive in Colfax on Tuesday on his way to jail in Downieville." The Sheriff of a Pennsylvania County where Saylor's well-to-do father lived was sent to arrest the fugitive but, by mistake, arrested George's brother. George then went to Baltimore, Maryland and prepared to board a ship for Europe but a Baltimore detective arrested him before he could board and started the road agent on the train for California. Saylor, who was then only twenty years old, arrived on Tuesday, January 22, 1884, and freely admitted the crime, but said he was induced by Marshall to rob the stagecoach. He was taken before Judge Howe for his examination where he confessed, pled guilty, and was ordered to return on Monday, January 28 for sentencing. Saylor was given a sentence of seven years and he arrived at the prison on February 2, 1884, registering as prisoner No. 11118. Saylor was discharged on November 3, 1888, after serving only four years, nine months.

Mountain Messenger [Downieville, CA]: August 18, 1883; October 20, 1883; November 3, 1883; January 19, 1884; January 26, 1884; February 2, 1884.

Martin, James

Nativity, Illinois; Age, 37 years; Occupation, Teamster; Height 5 feet 10 inches; Complexion, Florid; Color of eyes, Gray; Color of hair, Brown; Size of foot, 7½. Round features, high forehead, long narrow ears — left more narrow than right, very prominent nose — slightly crooked to right, left index finger slightly deformed, scar outer edge right wrist, large dim vaccine mark left upper arm, tuft of hair between breasts; medium built.

Robbed W. F. & Co's Express on stage from Sierra Valley to Truckee, October 15, 1883, in company with John Marshall.

Received at the California State Prison, November 1, 1883; No. of commitment, 11013; Crime, robbery, Term, 5 years; County sent from, Sierra.

[*See* Marshall, John]

Maxon, J. H.

Nativity, Oregon; Age, 40 years; Occupation, Miner; Height, 6 feet 1 inch; Complexion, Dark; Color of eyes, Blue; Color of hair, Dark. Scar on right cheek-bone caused by a kick from a horse, scar on right leg done with an ax, double scar on left leg below knee from gunshot.

Robbed W. F. & Co.'s Express on stage from Pendleton to Umatilla, Oregon, October 21, 1875, with Benjamin Berry.

Received at Oregon State Prison, May 3, 1876; No. of commitment, 665; Crime, robbery, Term, 10 years; County sent from, Umatilla, Oregon.

Pardoned, August 30, 1878.

[*See* Berry, Benjamin]

Mays, William

Nativity, Missouri; Age, 35 years; Occupation, Laborer; Height 6 feet 1 inch; Complexion, Dark; Color of eyes, Gray; Color of hair, Brown.

Robbed W. F. & Co's Express and the U.S. Mail on stage from Boise, I. T., to Kelton, Utah, November 18, 1879, in company with W. H. Overhoeltz.

Received at the Penitentiary at Boise, I. T., January 22, 1880; No. of commitment, —; Crime robbery; Term, life; County sent from, Ada, I. T.

Transferred to U.S. Prison at Auburn, N. Y., June 4, 1881.

On November 18, 1879, at 10:00 P.M. before the stagecoach from Kelton, Utah, bound for Boise, Idaho Territory, arrived at Pilgrim Hill Station, fourteen miles above Glenn's ferry on the Overland road in Ada County, two road agents suddenly appeared. They took the hostler, the only man at the station, some distance away and bound and blindfolded him and then robbed the station of small items and two rifles before hiding in the barn to await the arrival of the stagecoach. As soon as the coach pulled to a stop the road agents appeared and, at gunpoint, took control of the driver and one passenger, Edward Bluett. The two men were tied and blindfolded and then searched for valuables and the robbers took from the driver one hundred pennies and from Bluett $90. Next they broke open the Wells, Fargo treasure box, but it was empty, and then one of the robbers told Bluett they were disposed to return his money but they had done so poorly with the box they must keep it to "pay their honest debts." They did not molest the mails which contained considerable money but took Bluett's blankets and fled down the Snake River. Soon men were out looking for the two road agents, including Col. Orlando Robbins, and he tracked the two fugitives for more than eight days and, at one time, had not slept for two days and a night but had covered one hundred seventy-five miles on horseback. Once he determined the road agents had not swung up the Brunneau Valley he went into town and procured the assistance of Henry Pierce. They went down the Boise Valley and crossed the Snake River at McDowell's Ferry, went to Willow Creek in Baker County, Oregon, and on Friday, November 28 Robbins and Pierce overtook the two men at the ranch of A. B. Roberts. The two lawmen easily captured the two suspected road agents, who identified themselves as William H. Overholt, sometimes spelled Overhoeltz, and William Mays, sometimes spelled Mayes. Overholt was known to one man who confirmed his identity but Mays had in his pockets papers which showed his true name was Hermann Leissner and showed that he had been a musician in the army during the Civil War, but he persisted in denying that identity. The two prisoners had been driving Oregon cattle to Cheyenne, Wyoming and robbed the stagecoach as they were returning home. The lawmen found in the possession of the two prisoners the blankets belonging to Bluett and a number of fine tools they had just stolen from Roberts. The prisoners had assembled a good outfit including two saddle horses, two pack horses, and a large packet of blankets and clothing, as well as the items stolen from Pilgrim Station. They had seven guns including three needle guns of large caliber, two of which were stolen from Pilgrim Station, and four revolvers.

The prisoners were taken to Boise and their examination was scheduled before U.S. Commissioner Stout on Wednesday, December 3, and then they were lodged at the penitentiary for safekeeping. When the two prisoners were brought into court they discussed their situation with their defense counsel, F. E. Ensign, and waived the examination. Still, Commissioner Stout had the various articles in evidence brought in and identified by the driver and hostler so it would be in evidence. When it came time to set bail the Commissioner said he would place it so high that the prisoners would be sure to be present for the grand jury and he fixed it at $10,000 each. The two prisoners were returned to the penitentiary to await the action of the grand jury. Both men were indicted and in January 1880 they were brought to trial in the Circuit Court and convicted of "robbing the U.S. mails," though they had not gone through the mail bags. Both men were sentenced to serve life terms and arrived at the prison in Boise on January 22, 1880. On June 4, 1881, they were transferred to the U.S. Prison at Albany, New York.

Idaho Statesman [Boise, ID]: November 22, 1879; December 2, 1879; December 4, 1879.

McCabe, John

Nativity, Rhode Island, Age, 23 years; Occupation, Plasterer; Height 5 feet 5 inches; Complexion, Dark; Color of eyes, Gray; Color of hair, Dark. Long features, low forehead, indistinct marks on left forearm, D on left forearm, ballet girl inside right forearm, large mole near left shoulder, vaccine marks left upper arm, scar under right ear; medium built.

Robbed safe in office of W. F. & Co. and R. R. Co. at Madison in Yolo County, June 14, 1884, in company with Charles Baltz.

Received at the California State Prison, Folsom, June 28, 1884; No. of commitment, 889; Crime, burglary; Term, 2 years; County sent from: Yolo.

On Saturday, June 14, 1884, during the daytime John McCabe and Charles Baltz broke into a building belonging to the Vaca Valley & Lilian Lake Railroad Company, the Wells, Fargo & Company, and the Western Union Telegraph Company, which was being used as a depot and office in Madison, Yolo County. The two burglars opened the safe and carried away the contents, money and property amounting to a value of $199. The two men were quickly suspected of the crime and arrested. Baltz confessed and said he was willing to testify against McCabe to avoid punishment, and this was agreed to. However, on June 27 when he was taken before Judge E. R. Bush for his examination he waived the proceeding and pled guilty. There was no reason to delay sentencing so the Judge sentenced McCabe to serve two years at Folsom Prison. He arrived at the prison the following day and registered as prisoner No. 889. McCabe served out his entire sentence and was released, on February 28, 1886.

Yolo Superior Court transcript: The People of the State of California vs. John McCabe; June 17, 1884; June 27, 1884.

McCarty, Dan—*alias* John E. Richards

Nativity, New York; Age, 26 years; Occupation, Laborer; Height, 5 feet 5½ inches; Complexion, Light; Color of eyes, Brown; Color of hair, Brown. Small features, full forehead, mole on throat, mole on right arm near elbow, mole on right side of upper lip, mole on left arm, mole on back of right shoulder; thin built.

Robbed W. F. & Co's Express on stage from Los Baños to Gilroy, May 7, 1877, in company with Eugene Tyler.

Received at the California State Prison, August 16, 1877; No. of commitment, 7714; Crime, robbery; Term, 1 year; County sent from, Merced.

Discharged, upon expiration of sentence, June 15, 1878.

Robbed W. F. & Co's Express on stage from Hills Ferry to Bantas, April 27, 1882, in company with John Weisenstein.

Robbed W. F. & Co's Express on stage from Soledad to San Luis Obispo, May 18, 1882, in company with John Weisenstein.

Escaped from County Jail at Salinas, February 26, 1883. Stole a horse and buggy and fled. Overtaken same day by Sheriff and his party. McCarty had supplied himself with a pistol, and upon attempting to make a fight, was seriously wounded by the Sheriff's posse. Pleaded guilty to last robbery.

Received at Folsom Prison, April 3, 1883; No. of commitment, 572; Crime robbery, Term, 12 years; County sent from, Stanislaus.

On Monday, May 7, 1877, the stagecoach from Los Banos to Gilroy in Merced County driven by Paul Reynard was stopped by two masked road agents when three miles east of the Summit House, or thirty-five miles west of Gilroy. One road agent was white and appeared very young while the other was an older Negro, and the latter directed all the action during the robbery. Each robber was armed with a six-shooter which they pointed at the driver when demanding the treasure box. The driver told them he had no box so they ordered him to disembark, lay face down on the ground, and put his hands behind him. They tied him securely and went through the coach, cutting open the express bag which contained nothing, and went through the U.S. mail pouches tearing apart every letter and package. Still, however, their take was negligible so after forty-five minutes' work they untied Reynard and took from him $2.50, all he had. As soon as the men were through with the robbery they ordered the driver to board and continue on. Reynard whipped up his team and at his first opportunity reported the robbery. The disguises of the road agents had been ineffective and they were immediately recognized by Reynard so it was not long before their descriptions were broadcast throughout the region: "One of them is a colored man, very black, named Eugene Tyler; five feet, eight inches high; weighs 180 pounds; and twenty years old. The other is a white man named D. McCarty; about five feet five inches high; light hair; and about twenty years old. He has been working for Donnelly, Dunne & Co." California's Governor William Irwin and Wells, Fargo & Company posted rewards totaling $600 for the arrest and conviction of each road agent.

On May 18, 1877, Undersheriff Thomas M. Lane and deputy H. L. McCoy arrived in town with two prisoners who had been arrested and charged with being the road agents. Earlier that morning a Mr. Boyd had met Tyler traveling along the rail lines with McCarty and he hurried into town and gave the information to the sheriff's office. Lane and McCoy, with Boyd, hurried to the place where the two fugitives were last seen, each lawman armed with a pocket pistol. The two fugitives had continued on so the lawmen followed them to Hughes & Keys Station near Hills Ferry on the San Joaquin River and, though the station had burned down recently, the two fugitives were found among the rubble. The lawmen started for the fugitives, handing their reins to a bystander, and as McCoy reached into his pocket McCarty leveled his Smith & Wesson six-shooter at him. The two parties then discussed the situation for some time with the lawmen insisting it was their duty to capture the two men "dead or alive" and McCarty insisting he was ready for a fight. Finally Tyler intervened and convinced McCarty to surrender, and both men gave up their weapons, two fine six-shooters, and the two prisoners were lodged in jail. The two men were given their examination and held over for action by the grand jury, they were indicted in August and pled guilty.

The *Gilroy Advocate* reported, "Eugene Tyler, the Negro, and Dan McCarty, the boy, who stopped the stage in the Pacheco Pass, a few months ago, and robbed Paul Reynaud (*sic*), the driver, of $2.50, have acknowledged themselves guilty of highway robbery. They now await the sentence of the court of Merced County." They had hopes of receiving a lighter sentence for their cooperation and this worked as McCarty, because of his youthful appearance, was given a sentence of only one year while Tyler, being considered the bad influence and leader at the robbery scene, was sentenced to serve five years. Both men arrived at San Quentin Prison on August 16, 1877, and McCarty registered as prisoner No. 7714 and Tyler as prisoner No. 7715. McCarty was discharged upon expiration of sentence on June 15, 1878. Tyler was pardoned and released on March 16, 1881, and Tyler does not appear in the Hume report again.

McCarty, after his release from San Quentin, stayed out of trouble or at least was not caught until early 1882 when he met John Weisenstein. McCarty's new acquaintance, seven years his senior, was game to find a way to make quick, easy money. McCarty related his experiences with robbing stagecoaches, emphasizing that he now knew what he had done wrong and knew how to correct it, and he mentioned that when caught the time served was minimal—only one year. For some unknown reason they seemed to figure that stagecoaches on Thursdays carried the heaviest treasure and set their sights on the stagecoach from Hills Ferry to Bantas. On Thursday evening, April 27 they stepped into the road, masked and armed, halted the coach and demanded the Wells, Fargo treasure box. As soon as it was delivered they ordered the driver to continue and he hurried into Bantas to report the robbery, but lawmen responding to the scene could find no clue to the identity of the road agents nor a track to follow. Emboldened by their success in stopping the first stagecoach, but disappointed in the small amount of plunder they had to share, they moved their operation to the Coast Line Stagecoach route between Soledad and San Luis Obispo.

On Thursday, May 18 when at the foot of a mountain four miles from San Luis Obispo the two masked and armed road agents stepped into the road and halted the coach. They demanded, and received, Wells, Fargo's box and then ordered the driver to continue, and he hurried into San Luis Obispo and reported the robbery. Sheriff Oaks was notified of the robbery at 6:00 A.M. and went to the scene but could find no clue to the identity of the road agents, except noting that there were two men involved. Following this second "water haul" McCarty and Weisenstein, early on the morning of Thursday, May 25 tried to stop the same stagecoach when it was about to ascend the small hill near Bean's place. However, two masked men in the road frightened the horses and they took off at a dead run carrying the stagecoach out of danger. Later that same day John Hanson found the treasure box from the robbery of May 18 under a small bridge near his home, where it had been cut open with an axe, and all the contents—a pair of ladies shoes, a pair of boots, and one letter— were lying nearby. From that place there was enough of a trail and other clues to track the road agents and it was not long before McCarty and Weisenstein were lodged in jail. The two men had their examination and the evidence, though mostly circumstantial, was strong enough to hold them for the grand jury. Weisenstein, who had no previous prison record, pled guilty and agreed to turn state's evidence to get a reduced term. He was sentenced to serve five years and was received at Folsom Prison on December 15, 1882, registering as prisoner No. 543.

Weisenstein was taken out on December 21, 1882, to testify against McCarty and he escaped from the Salinas jail with McCarty on February 24, 1883, but he was recaptured and returned to Folsom Prison on March 5, 1883. Weisenstein escaped from Folsom Prison on December 8, 1884, and was not heard of again. McCarty pled not guilty and while awaiting his next court appearance escaped from the Salinas jail with several other prisoners including Weisenstein. McCarty, alone, stole a horse and buggy and armed himself with a six-shooter. When overtaken by the sheriff's posse that same day he attempted to fight them off but was seriously wounded in his right side and had to surrender. He was returned to his jail cell and, being in no condition to escape again, pled guilty to the robbery of the Soledad to San Luis Obispo stagecoach hoping to get a lighter sentence by cooperating. But McCarty had been in prison for robbing a stagecoach in 1877 so he was sentenced to serve twelve years. He arrived at Folsom Prison on April 3, 1883, and registered as prisoner No. 572. He was discharged December 3, 1890, after serving seven years eight months.

Gilroy Advocate [CA]: May 12, 1877; May 26, 1877; August 11, 1877. *San Luis Obispo Tribune [CA]*: May 27, 1882. *The Stanislaus News [CA]*: May 25, 1877.

McComas, Hiram

Nativity, Missouri; Age, 36 years; Occupation, School Teacher; Height, 5 feet 6¾ inches; Complexion, Florid; Color of Eyes, Gray; Color of hair, Brown; Weight, 157 pounds. Scar on thumb of left hand, scar on sole of left foot, drinks moderately.

Robbed W. F. & Co's Express on stage from Boise, I. T., to Winnemucca, Nev., September 15, 1873, in company with J. B. Buckner.

Received at Nevada State Prison, December 15, 1873; No. of commitment, 183; Crime, robbery; Term, 5 years; County sent from, Humboldt, Nev.

Pardoned, July 13, 1877.

[*See* Buckner, J. B.]

McLean, Donald

Nativity, Canada; Age, 39 years; Occupation, Turner; Height, 5 feet 7¾ inches; Complexion, Dark; Color of eyes, Brown; Color of hair Black.

Robbed W. F. & Co's Express on stage from Helena, Montana to Corrine, Utah, July 9, 1871, in company with W. H. Heinsman and George N. Rugg.

Received at the Territorial Prison, Deer Lodge M. T., October 30, 1873; No. of commitment, —; Crime, robbery; Term 10 years; County sent from, Beaverhead, M. T..

Pardoned by Governor B. F. Potts, May 8, 1880.

[*See* Heinsman, W. H.]

Mellville, Clark—*alias* Denver

Nativity, Ohio; Age, 30 years; Occupation, Laborer; Height 5 feet 6½ inches; Complexion, Light; Color of eyes, Blue; Color of hair, Light Brown; Size of foot, 7; Weight, 145 lbs. Black mole on back of neck, round scar on right elbow, two vaccine marks on left arm, thin white scar center of forehead.

Robbed W. F. & Co's Express on stage from Glendale to Redding, August 5, 1883 — alone.

Plead guilty to larceny, and was not prosecuted for stage robbery.

Received at the Oregon State Prison, November 19, 1883; No. of commitment 1450; Crime, larceny; Term, 2 years, County sent from, Jackson, Oregon.

On Friday, August 3, 1883, just after daylight the southbound stagecoach driven by Milman was stopped by two road agents near the summit of Wolf Creek, eight miles south of Glendale. When the coach reached the top of the grade the horses were spent and moving at a slow pace. Suddenly two men, so completely masked that not even their hair was visible, appeared from the bushes on each side of the road. Their hands were also covered and their feet were muffled so they would not leave boot tracks. One man knelt in the roadway right in the path of the horses and took deliberate aim at the driver with a double barreled shotgun. This startled the team and Milman had great difficulty bringing them under control. A barkeeper from the Villard House at Pendleton rode next to the driver and, when the Wells, Fargo treasure box was demanded, he had to dig it out from under the mail sacks and throw it down, as Milman was busy with the horses. The box was smashed open and $2,000 in greenbacks and a few letters were removed. Next the four male passengers were ordered out, lined up in the road, and were relieved of $200 in coin and three watches. The barkeeper argued that his initials were engraved in his watch and so was of no use to the robber but he kept it anyway. There was one lady aboard but she was not molested. Throughout the entire affair the second road agent said nothing but kept his shotgun leveled at the party. The road agents did not request the U.S. mails, so as soon as the passengers had contributed they were ordered aboard and Milman was told to continue on his route. Once the coach was underway the two road agents fled into the heavy timber. It was not long before Clark Mellville was captured, charged as the road agent in charge at the scene of the robbery, and lodged in the county jail. There was strong evidence against him though it was all circumstantial, and all the plunder was recovered and returned to its owners, which set the stage for aggressive plea negotiations. At his examination Mellville was held to answer to the grand jury and in the late fall he was indicted. When the defendant came into court, under an agreement with the prosecution, he was allowed to plead guilty to the lesser charge of larceny even though he had refused to cooperate in naming the second road agent. Mellville was sentenced to serve two years in Oregon's State Prison and arrived on November 19, 1883, registering as prisoner No. 1450. Although there were clearly two road agents involved Hume and Thacker, in their report, stated that Mellville acted alone. Mellville had his sentence commuted by Governor Z. F. Moody and was discharged on February 23, 1885.

Oregonian [Portland, OR]: August 6, 1883; August 9, 1883.

Meyers, James

Accessory to robbery of W. F. & Co's Express on stage from Colfax to Grass Valley, by George Lester, Dribblesbeis, Early, et al, July 27, 1873.
Received at the California State Prison, November 29, 1873; No. of commitment, 5801; Crime, robbery; Term 10 years; County sent from, Nevada.
Discharged, per Act, May 29, 1880.
Died in Grass Valley.
[*See* Thompson, Charles]

Miller, John W.

Age, 30 years; Height, 5 feet 8 inches; Complexion, Dark; Color of eyes, Brown; Color of eyes, Black.
Robbed W. F. & Co's Express on stage from Boise to Silver City, February 2, 1876, in company with Tarlton B. Scott.
Robbed W. F. & Co's Express on stage from Silver City to Boise, April 19, 1876, in company with Tarlton B. Scott.
Received at the Penitentiary near Boise, I. T., December 26, 1876; No. of commitment —; Crime robbery; Term, 5 years; County sent from, Ada, I. T.
Pardoned.

On April 19, 1876, the Silver City stagecoach driven by Charley Downey left Boise at 3:30 A.M., ten minutes behind the Umatilla coach and the same length of time ahead of the Overland coach. The Silver City stagecoach had aboard four passengers including Division Agent Andy Baker, stagecoach driver Ed Paine, and Mrs. Charles Adams inside and outside with the driver was Francisco Soto. It was a bright night and the frost reflected the star light, but the lamps were also lit. When the coach arrived at the first bridge a half mile south from town a man appeared almost in front of the horses with gun in hand and sang out, "Halt!" The team had slowed as the horses were about to step onto the bridge and stopped at the command. At that instant another man appeared in the door of the old vacated ferry house and called out in a guttural tone, an attempt to disguise his voice, "throw out that box." The box was under some luggage in the boot and this delayed the driver so the road agent, apparently anxious at the prospect of the arrival of the Overland coach, called out his command again. The box was thrown off and then the coach was ordered to drive on. The Overland coach passed the spot on schedule but saw nothing and first learned of the robbery when they got to Fruit's Ferry House at the second bridge a quarter mile beyond. Baker and Paine got off the Silver City coach at the ferry house and, with Mr. Fruit, went back to the scene of the robbery but could find no trace of the robbers. Later the scene was examined by W. B. Morris, superintendent of the line, Sheriff Agnew and deputy U.S. Marshal Joseph Pinkham but no trace of the robbers, or any clue at all, could be found. The box was found broken open, the catch of the padlock having been cut off with a cold chisel, but the box had been empty so the robbers got nothing for their trouble. The *Idaho Statesman* announced that this was "the boldest of the three robberies" which had occurred at the same place recently.

On Monday, April 25 just after 3:30 A.M. the same two road agents stopped the Silver City coach a half mile south of town, the same place as before. There had been so many robberies close to one another that a signal had been arranged and if the coach was robbed the driver, as soon as he was over the first bridge and out of danger, was to fire a single shot in the air. He was then to continue on his route while men were assigned to watch for anyone coming into town from the south, and others were assigned to go directly to the scene and try to find evidence and track the robbers. Still, other trusted men were to be awakened and they were to begin a systematic check of certain persons suspected by the lawmen. Billy Ridenbaugh, agent at the stage office, was just buckling the last strap on the boot of the Overland coach when the shot was heard. Tom Morrow and several others were standing about the stage office so Ridenbaugh called to Fred Epstein to watch the office while he started on a run for the bridge, with Morrow close behind. They were at the scene in less than ten minutes and were soon joined by several others who had hitched a ride on the Overland coach; and Mr. Boomer, the general route agent who was on the Umatilla coach when he heard the shot, jumped off and ran back and Mrs. Pinkham, when she heard the shot, woke her husband — the deputy U.S. Marshal. The town was closed up with heavy patrols on the south end so there was no possibility of anyone going in or out without being seen. The men at the first bridge found nothing but the box broken open and the contents rifled, but this box had contained no treasure so the robbers got nothing for their trouble. At daylight Sheriff Agnew, Marshal Pinkham, Undersheriff Joe Oldham, Bill Noyes, Joe Davis and others got onto a trail they believed were the tracks of the robbers and followed them across Tom Davis' orchard, then waded through the slough and, where the wet tracks came out, they followed a clear trail to the road. One man's track was large and the other very small and the robbers showed they sometimes ran as if they thought they were being pursued. They went through John Krall's field and then above the old burying ground, but there the trail went onto hard ground and could not be followed further. It appeared that the two men planned by a circuitous route to circle the town and come in from the north side, but most of the effort at catching a glimpse of them had concentrated on the south side of Boise as it was thought the robbers would take the shortest route into town. The night had been particularly dark and a man could not be distinguished if more than a few rods distant so the few patrols on the north had seen nothing.

On Sunday John W. Miller, strongly suspected to be one of the robbers, was arrested and lodged in the prison. He made a full confession which was written down by A. L. Richardson, clerk of the district court, in the presence of Marshal Pinkham, stage line superintendent Morris, and Judge Hollister. Sheriff Agnew learned from Miller's confession that the other robber was named Tarlton B. Scott, and it was Scott who had done all the active work at the last two robberies. All day Sunday Scott lay hidden away in his camp among the lava rocks within an hour's walk of the city and from this vantage point he watched the officers and citizens who were traversing the plain in every direction. On Sunday night one of the alert searchers saw a fire among the rocks but it was put out before anyone could get close enough to pinpoint the location. On Tuesday hunger and the need to find out what happened to his partner forced Scott to go into town where he hid beneath the Baptist Church awaiting an opportunity to search for Miller. He was discovered on Thursday by a man named Gilman, who was mixed up in the later movements of Scott, and he acted as a decoy to try to get the fugitive to surrender while undersheriff Joe Oldham, deputy sheriff Cutter, and deputy Marshal Pinkham covered the building. Scott did not respond to Gilman's coaxing so Sheriff Agnew called out to Scott to surrender and when he received no answer he called out again, "Come out Scott, I want you." At this urging, which left no doubt that the lawmen knew he was there, the fugitive crawled out and was ordered to throw up his hands. He was bound and relieved of a revolver and knife, then led to the penitentiary. Gilman, in consideration of his cooperation and since he had not been at the scene of the robberies, was released.

The *Statesman* interviewed Scott and learned that he had come from Plattsburgh, Missouri, or at least still had relatives living there, and had received letters from that address at the Boise post office. The editor described Scott as, "a young man of medium size and height, and apparently about twenty-five years old. He is physically as fine a specimen of young manhood as we have ever seen. His features are regular and classic in their outline, presenting a model for the most critical and fastidious artist. A head shaped with all the requisites for the 'dome of thought,' and covered with hair of a rich brown, while his 'goatee' and unshaven beard is of a lighter hue. His eyes are large, somewhat prominent, blue in color ... he is decidedly the handsomest man in Boise City." The newspaper also gave a brief description of Miller as, "a medium sized man with black hair, black eyes and dark complexion. He is rather common-place ... we shall not stop to tell how ugly or homely he is." On Tuesday the two prisoners were taken before Judge Gideon and charged with the robbery of February 2. They waived examination and were held on $3,000 bail to answer at the next term of the grand jury. After Scott was in custody one of his camps was found on the banks of the Boise river and in it were found mufflers for his feet, a brown mask which would cover his head and face, a shot gun heavily loaded with buck shot, a loaded revolver, a good sized hatchet, a knife in its scabbard, and other conveniences including blankets and picket ropes. The camp was found before the river overflowed its banks and the *Statesman* said, "Now that the Boise river has cleansed the scene by washing away the old toll house, thus making future robberies impossible, and other important and satisfactory changes having been made which promise to provide a good supply of State's evidence for the trials...."

In early May Scott obtained a case knife and was sawing away at the iron bars of the trap door above the jail when discovered by Undersheriff Oldham. Scott was then heavily ironed to prevent his escape but he boasted that, "if I could get a few tools I'd soon get out of this wooden box." Apparently he got his tools because on Sunday, July 10 at 7:00 P.M. Scott and Miller made their escape. The prisoners were kept on the lower floor of the building and in the upper floor, separating the prison room from the one above which was occupied by the jailor, there was an iron grating fastened with strong iron bolts. Miller was still unshackled so he stood upon the benches and passing his arm through the grate unscrewed two of the bolts from above, and then tore the grating off by breaking the remaining bolts. In the jailor's room they found a Spencer rifle and shot gun which they took before they fled out of town. The went by way of the alley between Main and Idaho streets, crossed Seventh Street near the Central Hotel and kept in the alley until they reached Lemp's brewery. A posse led by Sheriff Agnew spent Sunday evening in trying to locate the escapees and the men and horses were worn out by noon, but they had Scott and Miller surrounded at the head of Ruby Gulch eight miles northeast of town. Wells, Fargo's agent Morris and Undersheriff Oldham took five men and went there to help the sheriff and they met Baldwin returning to town for supplies, and he gave them all the necessary particulars of the situation. It took two hours to reach the summit in the midst of dense chaparral country and after searching for two hours the group retired to a wood camp for food, but suddenly a shot was heard and the men rushed to the scene. They found Undersheriff Oldham where he had been lying in wait and he had captured Miller and the Spencer rifle. Oldham reported that Scott had gone in the opposite direction when he fired so the men scattered and began to listen for someone breaking through the brush, and systematically searched the area. In half an hour they had surrounded Scott who called out, "Well, boys, you've got me. I've got to give in." They returned to the wood camp, finished their meal, and then took their prisoners back to Boise, arriving in town at 6:00 P.M. The prisoners were taken to the penitentiary while renovations to the jail were completed and by the first week of November they were back in their jail cells awaiting the December term of the district court. On December 6 Sheriff Agnew heard the sounds of men working on the grating door and when he rushed in he found that Scott and three others prisoners had nearly picked and pried off the lock of the door. They had acquired a medium sized ax, a small bar of iron and an old pocket knife. The sheriff believed he knew who had passed these items through the grating to the prisoners and warned, "They had better keep away, as everything goes from this on." On December 19 the grand jury indicted Scott and Miller for stagecoach robbery and trial was set for December 23. The trial took only a few days and the two men were convicted of the charges. Miller was sentenced to serve five years and Scott was sentenced to serve seven years, both at hard labor. The two convicts were familiar with the penitentiary, having spent several weeks there during their time awaiting trial, but now they were delivered there to serve out their terms. Scott arrived on December 20, 1876, but he escaped on May 5, 1877, and was not heard of again. Miller arrived the day after Christmas 1876 and became a model prisoner so he earned an early release and was pardoned.

Idaho Statesman [Boise, ID]: April 20, 1876; April 24–25, 1876; April 29, 1876; May 13, 1876; May 18, 1876; June 2, 1876.

Miller, William A.

Nativity, Iowa; Age, 35 years; Occupation, Farmer; Height 5 feet 11½ inches; Complexion, Florid; Color of eyes, Gray; Color of hair, Light. Small square features, narrow high forehead, rather small thin nose, long nostrils, narrow long ears, small lobes attached, bald headed, slight scar about one and a quarter inches above left eye on forehead, small vaccine mark on left upper arm; slim built.

No. of first term, 5017. Received at the California State Prison, October 30, 1871; Crime, robbery and felony; Term, 6 years; County sent from, Yolo.

Pardoned by Governor Newton Booth, November 27, 1874.

Robbed W. F. & Co's Express on stage from Sonora to Milton, November 27, 1881, in company with William A. Miner, James Crum and S. C. Jones.

Received at the California State Prison, December 21, 1881; No. of commitment, 10190; Crime robbery; Term, 25 years; County sent from; Tuolumne.
Transferred to Folsom Prison, March 11, 1882.
[*See* Miner, William]

Mills, Charles

Nativity, Germany; Age, 25 years; Occupation, Laborer; Height, 5 feet 6 inches; Complexion, Light; Color of eyes, Brown; Color of hair, Brown. Square features, high broad forehead, large prominent nose, long nostrils, rather round pointed ears, small lobes attached, very dim slight vaccine mark left upper arm, anchor base of right thumb, shield and eagle right forearm, slight built.

First commitment, 8237. Received at the California State Prison, May 23, 1878. Crime, burglary first degree; Term, 4 years; County sent from, San Francisco.

Discharged, by expiration of sentence, May 23, 1881.

Burglarized W. F. & Co's Office at Galt, November 18, 1881, in company with Michael Sheehan and John Anderson, but was sent to penitentiary for burglary in Alameda County of a later date.

Received at California State Prison, March 24, 1882. Commitment, 10338. Crime, burglary second degree and prior felony; Term, 10 years; County sent from, Alameda.

[*See* Anderson, John]

Miner, William A.—*alias* Billy Miner [*alias* Old Bill, California Bill]

Nativity, Canada; Age, 32 years; Occupation, Shoemaker; Height, 5 feet 8⅝ inches; Complexion, Florid; Color of eyes, Brown; Color of hair, Dark.

New Description: Spare features, rather long, medium forehead, and rather broad, thin pointed nose, long nostrils, round projecting ears, lobes attached, face pitted, ink marks base of thumb back of left hand, flesh mole left shoulder blade, do. on breast — near point of right shoulder, Dancing Girl on right forearm, mole about two inches below pit of stomach; slim built.

No. of first commitment, 3248. Received at the California State Prison, April 5, 1866; Crime, robbery; Term, 3 years; County sent from, San Joaquin.

Discharged by order of the Court, June 9, 1866.

No. of second commitment, 3313. Received at the California State Prison, July 3, 1866; Crime, grand larceny; Term, 5 years; County sent from, Placer.

Discharged, by expiration of sentence, July 12 1870.

Robbed W. F. & Co's Express on stage from San Andreas to Stockton, January 23, 1871, in company with Charlie Cooper and James Harrington, alias "Alkali Jim." Convicted June 22, 1871.

No. of third commitment, 4902. Received at the California State Prison, June 28, 1871; Crime, robbery; Term, 10 years; County sent from, Calaveras.

New trial granted by Supreme Court and taken out for new trial, February 9, 1872. On March 21, 1872, was again convicted and sentenced to 13 years in the State Prison.

Received at the California State Prison, March 30, 1872; No. of commitment, 5206; Crime, robbery; Term, 13 years; County sent from, Calaveras.

Attempted to escape, May 7, 1874.

Commuted by Governor William Irwin, March 5, 1878, to 12½ years.

Discharged, by expiration of sentence, July 14, 1880, and went to Colorado Springs, Colorado, where he had a sister living.

He returned to California and September 22, 1880, robbed W. F. & Co's Express on stage from Auburn to Forest Hill — alone. Just as he had finished this stage robbery, the Hon. Frank Page came up in a buggy, and he was relieved of a valuable gold watch and $280 coin. He went to Colfax that night and paid a brakeman $5 to stow him away in a box car. At Reno he bought a ticket to Denver. At Denver he pawned Page's watch for $65. Was joined in Denver by Stanton P. Jones, and together they robbed a stage in Sagauche County, Colorado and fled. Were pursued 300 miles by Sheriff Bronaugh, of said county, and Deputy, and after arrest got possession of the Sheriff's pistol, shot the Sheriff, breaking his wrist, and seriously wounded the Deputy and *escaped.*

Went to Silver City, New Mexico, and robbed stage from Deming. Came to California via S. P. R. R., where he and Jones were joined by Jim Crum and Bill Miller.

Robbed W. F. & Co's Express on stage from Sonora to Milton, November 7, 1881, in company with Miller, Crum and Jones.

Convicted and received at the California State Prison, December 21, 1881; No. of commitment, 10191; Crime, robbery; Term, 25 years; County sent from, Tuolumne.

Attempted to escape by placing a dummy in his cell and stowing away in the Door Factory, April 17, 1884.

Ezra William "Old Bill" Miner was soft spoken and gentlemanly, apologizing to his victim's for any undue delay they suffered while robbing them. But crime was his chosen career and when he was free he was always planning or preparing for his next caper, but when he was behind bars or prison walls he had only one thought — escape. Long periods of model prison behavior were a ploy, and a religious awakening a ruse, all designed to foster complacency among his keepers. Miner was born at Bowling Green, Kentucky in 1847 but by 1860 he was living in California. He began his criminal career in late December 1865 when he went to Newcastle, hired a horse, and rode to Auburn. There he outfitted in a fine new suit of clothes but when it came time to pay he drew his pistol and robbed the clerk. He returned to his hometown of Yankee Jim's riding the rented horse, which he never returned, and a week later stole another horse for John Sinclair and they went to San Francisco. The boys sold the stolen horses and went on a spree but were soon without funds. On January 19 they went to Oakland and rented a two horse buggy and team and took it into San Joaquin County where, at gun point, they robbed ranchman Porter of $80. The boys were arrested at Woodbridge the following day and jailed at Stockton. As soon as Miner was behind bars he began planning their escape, but digging through the wall was thwarted by an iron plate behind the bricks. Miner altered the plan and decided that they would lure in the jailer, club him unconscious with a slung shot and make their escape, but the jailor was too cautious and they couldn't gain their freedom. They were tried for the robbery of Porter, convicted and each man was sentenced to three years in California's San Quentin Prison. Miner entered the prison on April 5, 1866, but was soon on his way to Placer County to be tried for stealing two horses, where he received a sentence of one year for each animal bringing his total sentence to five years. He was released on July 12, 1870, and joined up with James "Alkali Jim" Harrington, and they recruited ex-convict Charles Cooper. On January 23, 1871, Miner waved down the stagecoach at Murray's Creek one and one half miles from San Andreas in Calaveras County and asked for a ride into town. Driver Billy Cutler, when he looked forward again, saw two men at the heads of his leaders wielding shotguns and Miner at that moment coined the phrase "Hands up!" which thereafter became a distinctive element of his *modus operandi*. They demanded the Wells, Fargo treasure box and it was delivered. Cutler told them there were no passengers aboard so they went through his pockets and took $5 in coin and his watch, but returned the latter for sentimental reasons. They considered taking the driver's boots but they were too small. After Cutler continued on to San Andreas they broke open the box and took out $200 in coin and $2,400 in gold dust. Miner and Harrington took the loot, skipped-out on Cooper, and started for San Francisco. Miner was caught in San Francisco so Harrington went to Mayfield, but he was captured there. Cooper had been picked up earlier and immediately informed on the other two road agents, turned state's evidence, testified against them, and was released. In mid–June Miner and Harrington were sentenced to serve ten years at San Quentin prison. Their attorney fought for a new trial and this was granted after ten months, but when they got to the San Andreas jail it was found that Harrington had a saw sewn into his pants. They were closely watched, retried and sentenced to thirteen years imprisonment. Miner escaped from the prison on May 7, 1874, but was captured within hours. He was disciplined several times during his eight year stay but his good time credits were restored and he was released on July 14, 1880.

Hume reported that on September 22, 1880, Miner robbed Wells, Fargo & Company's Express from the coach between Auburn and Forest Hill. The road agent acted alone which would have been quite a departure from Miner's usual methods. Just as this road agent finished robbing the stagecoach the Hon. Frank Page came up in a buggy and he was relieved of a valuable gold watch and $280 coin. The robber went to Colfax that night and paid a brakeman $5 to stow him away in a box car, and at Reno the same man bought a ticket to Denver and there pawned Page's watch for $65. Hume then reports that on September 23 Miner and Stanton P. Jones robbed a coach near Ohio City in Sagauche County, Colorado and fled. They were pursued three hundred miles by Sheriff Bronaugh and a deputy but after their arrest they got possession of the sheriff's pistol, shot the sheriff breaking his wrist, and seriously wounded the deputy before escaping. It seems unlikely that both robberies could have involved Miner as the robbery in Colorado occurred only one day after the Auburn to Forest Hill robbery, and his Colorado road agent activities with Jones came at a much later date.

Miner is next reported in New Mexico but Hume reported that the fugitive found no opportunities so he went to Colorado, arriving sometime between late July and early September 1880. There he met Arthur Pond who adopted the alias Billy Leroy and the two men teamed up to rob the Barlow & Sanderson stagecoach near Ohio City on September 23, 1880, but they got only $50. With pickings slim they robbed another stagecoach near Slum Gullion Pass on October 7, 1880, but got only $100. A week later they stopped the Alamosa to Del Norte stagecoach near Banshee Station and this time found nearly $4000. LeRoy had assumed command which irked Miner so they split their take and ended their relationship. Miner went to Michigan while Pond began spending lavishly in Chicago. When broke Pond returned to Denver and was soon arrested, convicted, and on his way to a federal prison. He cut his shackles and escaped from the train, then returned to Denver where his brother Silas joined him. The brothers robbed the Del Norte stagecoach again and were quickly captured, and this time the outraged citizens of Del Norte intervened and lynched the two boys.

In Michigan Miner spent freely for several months but soon his funds were running low so he returned to Colorado and partnered with Stanton P. Jones and Charles Dingman. On February 4, 1881, they robbed the Del Norte stagecoach but found nothing aboard. The boys were pursued and Dingman was captured, while Miner and Stanton fled. On April 28 the two fugitives were captured in the company of their new partner Jim East while riding three stolen horses. The lawmen searched the prisoners but failed to find a .32 caliber pistol in Miner's boot, so at 1:00 A.M. he and Jones made their escape by wounding two of the officers. Fearing the same fate as the Pond brothers if caught in Colorado, Miner and Jones fled to California in the fall of 1881. The two road agents recruited Bill Miller and Jim Crum and on November 7, 1881, they stopped the Sonora to Milton stagecoach driven by Clark Stringham. The coach was near Angel's Camp in Calaveras County and was toiling up a steep grade when Miner, again in control, called out numbers for his men and they took up assigned positions. One covered the driver while another took control of three passengers who were ordered out. Two wooden Wells, Fargo boxes were delivered on demand and they, along with the iron safe bolted inside, were broken open with a sledge hammer. The robbers took $3,300 from the box and a little more than $500 from the passengers before Stringham asked if he could leave as "I do not want to miss my connection with the train at Milton," and Miner waved him on saying, "Ta, Ta, my boy." A massive manhunt ensued and Miner, Crum and Miller were tracked to Miller's ranch in Yolo County. As lawmen surrounded the ranch house the three fugitives made a run for it and Crum was captured, but Miner and Miller got away. Miner and Miller were seen the following day near Sacramento and after a thrilling chase they were captured and lodged in the jail at Sacramento, but Jones managed to elude captured. They were tried, convicted, and on December 17, 1881, Miller and Miner were sentenced to serve terms of twenty-five years in San Quentin prison, while Crum received a sentence of twelve years. In 1884 Miner made a feeble attempt to escape by having his cell mate put a dummy in his bed while he hid in one of the shops, planning to scale the wall after dark, but the plan was discovered and he was found. In November 1892 he again tried to escape, this time with J. Marshall, but the guards learned of the plan and set up an ambush. Marshall was killed by a shot-gun blast and Miner, badly wounded, managed to crawl back into his cell. Miner was released on June 17, 1901, after serving nearly twenty years.

While Miner was in prison much had changed for the career criminal as stagecoaches rarely carried great treasure anymore, but he had the benefit of the constant arrival of new prisoners who taught him the art of train robbery, and Miner began searching for an opportunity and found it in Oregon. He partnered with Charles "Kid" Hoehn and Jeplan Guy Harshman, a fellow convict from San Quentin who had been released in 1892. On September 23, 1903, the three aspiring train robbers went to Troutdale where Miner and Harshman planned to board the Oregon Railroad & Navigation Company's No. 6 Express from Portland en route to Chicago. Hoehn went three miles up-track and waited with a lantern to signal the two robbers. The chosen site was on a curve near mile post 21 just west of the Corbett tunnel where Hoehn had stashed a boat on the Columbia river, not far from the tracks, and this was to be their means of escape. The train arrived at Troutdale on schedule just before 9:00 P.M. where Miner and Harshman climbed aboard the dark platform in front of the express car called the "blind baggage." Once the train was underway the two robbers climbed over the tender and into the cab of the engine and covered Engineer Ollie L. Barret and Fireman H. F. Stevenson with six-shooters. The man in charge, Miner, politely told the two men that if they followed orders they would not be harmed and they complied. When the train stopped at the 21 mile post Hoehn came out of the brush with two long willow poles, each having dynamite tied to one end. The trainmen were ushered to the express car and they first called to the express man to open the door, but when there was no answer they were each handed one stick and at gunpoint told to hold the explosives against the express car door. The fuses were lit and the explosion opened a large hole in the side door, the express portion of the car with the baggage compartment to the rear. The inside of the express car was dark because, when the train had slowed and stopped at an irregular location, express messenger Fred A. Korner suspected that something was amiss. He turned off the lanterns, armed himself with his short barreled shot gun, and he and assistant Solomon Glick waited. Several shots were fired along the face of the train to keep the passengers inside while Harshman, in the lead with Barret as a shield and Miner following with Stevenson in front of him, started for the forward door to the express car. Korner carefully slid open the rear baggage area door, leaned out and fired one barrel of his shot gun. Harshman was but twenty yards away and one heavy pellet went through Harshman's chest and another struck him in the head, while one of these pellets passed through and wounded Barret in the shoulder. Barret called for Korner to cease fire as Harshman collapsed to the ground and Barret fell against the side of the car. Miner and Hoehn saw the futility in continuing their assault and fled toward the river. Korner got down and fired his second barrel at them but they were too distant for the short barreled weapon to have any effect. Barret was taken aboard and the train was backed into Corbett where telegrams were sent to Portland relating the details of the robbery attempt. Pinkerton's local superintendent James P. Nevins took charge of the case and with Multnomah county Sheriff W. A. Storey, and his posse, arrived at the scene three hours later. Harshman, though badly wounded, was alive when found near the tracks and he was rushed to Portland for treatment. A search by lantern light produced no clues but at daybreak tracks showed that the men had fled to the river, and it was concluded they had made their escape by boat. Meanwhile in Portland Harshman, who identified himself as Jim Conners, refused to answer questions though interrogated numerous times over the next several days. Harshman, a counterfeiter and seasoned convict, finally decided to talk in the hope of getting a lighter sentence and identified Miner and Hoehn as the other two robbers. The railroad posted a reward of $500 for each of the fugitives, the Pacific Express Company added $300 to each reward and the state matched that amount, bringing the total to $1,100 for each fugitive. This encouraged many false sightings but Hoehn was finally arrested at Everett, Washington only a week after the robbery attempt. Hoehn told them that after he and Miner had left the train they drifted downstream to Kalama, Washington and hid in the woods for two days. They separated and agreed to meet at Puget Sound but Hoehn said Miner never showed and he never saw him again. Harshman and Hoehn were tried, convicted, and on November 15, 1903, the ex-convict received a sentence of twelve years while Hoehn was sentenced to serve ten years.

Miner had not gone to Puget Sound but instead fled into Canada and settled at Princeton, one hundred seventy-five miles east of Vancouver in British Columbia. He had adopted the alias George Edwards and had chosen that area to hide because his brother, living under the alias Jack Budd, had lived there since the mid–1880s. Miner boarded with the Schisler family until late September 1904 when he moved in with Budd. Over the years, probably during his stay in prison, Miner had mastered the fiddle and his animated musical talent made him a favorite among the locals. Miner was a good judge of bad men and he sized-up William "Shorty" Dunn as soon as they met. He took on Dunn as his new partner in crime and they recruited "Cowboy Jake" Terry. Train robbery had remained a uniquely American enterprise until September 10, 1904, when three aspiring train robbers climbed aboard the "blind baggage" platform of the westbound Canadian Pacific Railway train when the train was stopped at Mission Junction, forty miles east of Vancouver. As soon as the train was underway the robbers climbed over the coal tender and got the drop on the engineer and fireman with six-shooters and a rifle. They ordered the trainmen to stop the train after traveling five miles and then uncoupled the express car from the rest of the train and had the engineer pull forward one mile where they threatened to blow up the express car. The doors were opened and the three robbers took out $6,000 in gold dust, $1,000 in currency, $50,000 in U.S. bonds and $250,000 in Australian bonds. The men returned to Princeton and resumed their quiet life style, never suspected of being involved in Canada's first train robbery. On October 2, 1905, a Great Northern train was held up by three men near Raymond's brickyard outside of Seattle, Washington and the old man who led the robbers was polite and gentlemanly, and Pinkerton's Seattle agent P. K. Ahearn reopened the file on Bill Miner. The three robbers got away with $36,000 but no trace of them could be found south of the Canadian border. Miner and Dunn soon returned to Princeton but Terry, with his share, left the trio. When Miner thought it was safe to rob another train he recruited Louis Colquhoun as the third man. On May 8, 1906, Miner and Dunn, carefully masked, swung aboard the "blind baggage" platform of the westbound Canadian Pacific Railway's Imperial Limited when it stopped at Ducks. After the train was underway the two robbers climbed over the coal tender and pointed their six-shooters at engineer J. Callin and fireman A. Radcliffe. The soft spoken robber assured them that they would not be harmed and ordered them to stop the train at mile post 116. They arrived at 11:30 P.M. and Colquhoun, unmasked, ran up with a bundle of dynamite wrapped in newspaper. The fireman was ordered to uncouple the first car from the remainder of the train and pull forward to the flume. The engineer and fireman were pushed in front as the five men approached the express car and ordered clerks A. L. McQuarrie and W. M. Thornburn to open the door, and the explosives were not needed when they complied. Miner and Dunn kept McQuarrie in the car while they searched. Dunn blurted out, "This is the baggage car, not the express car," and the leader turned so suddenly that his masked dropped below his chin. McQuarrie had a good look at Miner's features before he told the robbers that they had stopped the first of two trains running an hour apart, the second bringing along the express car. Miner and Dunn could only find $15.50 and a container of catarrh pills but Miner, in his haste, passed over two obscure packages containing $40,000 in currency. They ordered the engineer to board and pull the engine forward to mile post 120 where Miner waved them back to the train with, "Good-night, boys. Take care of yourselves." The next day the pursuit began and the posse followed three sets of distinctive boot tracks, one slender and smooth and the other two of hob nailed boots. Once again the Seattle office of the Pinkerton Agency was certain that Miner was involved and they sent agents to help in the pursuit. The robbers' camp and several horses were found and it was determined that the men had been unable to find their animals and had left on foot, leaving behind most of their supplies. The lawmen followed the tracks for three days but finally lost them during a heavy downpour, which obliterated the trail. Constable Fernie chose one of several directions taken by the pursuers and persisted until on May 14 he saw three men seated together. He circled back to find their trail and saw their distinctive tracks so he went into Chapperon Lake and raised a posse. They overtook the fugitives at 1:00 P.M. but the men were so cool that they nearly bluffed their way through until Dunn lost his nerve, pulled his revolver, and ran for the brush. He was wounded and the three robbers were arrested, but Miner continued to assert that he was George Edwards from Princeton. However, when the description of Miner arrived and the officers matched tattoos they believed they had the notorious robber Bill Miner. When his photo arrived they were certain.

The three defendants were tried twice and following the second trial, which began June 1, they were convicted. All three men were sentenced to life in prison at the notorious New Westminister penitentiary near the western coast of Canada. Upon hearing his sentence Miner announced, "No prison walls can hold me," and two days later they were on their way to their new home by train. While the prison was a grim place it was not very substantial, being surrounded only by two dilapidated wooden fences. Miner became a model prisoner and soon his keen intellect and quick wit attracted the attention of deputy

Warden Bourke's daughter Katherine. He claimed a religious awakening and promised her he would reform and she visited almost daily for conversation and supplied him with religious reading matter. He seemed such a changed man that, at the urging of Katherine, he was given the freedom of the brickyard to exercise his crippled feet and he was excused from having his hair shorn to the scalp. On August 8, 1907, Miner was at work wheeling bricks from the yard to the drying kiln. He stopped each time to rest against the fence and the guards took little note of an old man taking a moment's respite from the heavy work. Each time the convict stopped he used his feet to dig at the dirt. Soon three other convicts joined in the effort and they managed to dig a hole under the inner fence. When the tower guard went into his shack for a smoke the four men quickly slipped under the fence, went to a storage shed between the fences where a ladder was stored, and used it to scale the outer fence. The other three convicts were soon captured but Miner disappeared from Canada. Miner assumed the alias George Anderson, fled to the east coast of the United States, and took a job in a sawmill in Pennsylvania. He soon found a partner in fellow employee Charles Hunter and in 1910 they left their jobs and went to Virginia, where they enlisted George Handsford as their third man. They continued to Lula, Georgia and took work at a sawmill near the main line of the Southern Express. On February 22, 1911, three masked men, well armed, flagged the New Orleans to New York Southern Express at Sulphur Springs near Gainesville, Georgia and used dynamite to blow open the small safe from which they took $1,000, but the larger safe which contained $65,000 resisted three explosions. After dividing the plunder Miner went south while the other two men headed north. Two days later the posse came upon an old man in poor health living in a deserted cabin and they didn't believe he could have been involved in the train robbery, but Miner could not bluff himself free. The posse took their prisoner to jail to prove their diligence in searching for the robbers and on February 26 a Pinkerton's detective arrived in Gainesville and recognized Miner. Hansford and Hunter had been captured on the road and in mid–March the three men were tried but Miner's partners, to get a reduced sentence, confessed, pled guilty, and testified against Miner. They received sentences of fifteen years while Miner was sentenced to twenty years imprisonment. The old man was at first put on the chain gang but he was so feeble he was soon moved to the state prison farm at Milledgeville. Georgia refused to return their prisoner to Canada, doubting the authorities there could prevent him from escaping again. On October 18, just seven months after arriving at the prison farm, Miner and fellow convict Tom Moore overpowered a guard and escaped. Moore contracted swamp fever but with Miner's help they continued on toward Moore's hometown of St. Clair. Seventeen days later they stumbled out of the swamp and hid in a boxcar but they had been seen, the police surrounded the fugitives and a gunfight followed, but when Moore was shot dead Miner immediately surrendered. Back in Milledgeville, Miner was fitted with a ball and chain and was still weighted down with these shackles when, on June 29, 1912, he managed to cut himself free, saw the bars from a window, and with two other convicts escape during a raging thunderstorm. They stole a boat and were floating down river when the boat overturned and one of the escapees drowned. The two surviving convicts made their way into the swamp and managed to fight their way through poisonous snakes and alligators, without food or water, wading through filthy water in sweltering heat, but when Miner's feet and age slowed him the other man left him behind. Miner came out of the swamp near McIntyre where a posse was waiting for him. This ordeal was too much for "Old Man" Miner and he never recovered his health. On September 2, 1913, he died in prison and the local newspaper called it his third and final escape from the Milledgeville prison farm.

Daily Alta California [San Francisco, CA]: August 7, 1863. *Daily Evening Bulletin [San Francisco, CA]*: February 4, 1871; February 6, 1871; February 11, 1871; November 11, 1871. *Daily Evening Herald [Stockton, CA]*: January 24, 1866; February 22, 1866; March 12, 1866; January 23, 1871. *Daily Independent [Stockton, CA]*: February 7, 1871. *Daily Patriot [San Jose, CA]*: January 27, 1871; February 1, 1871; February 27, 1871. *Denver Republican [CO]*: June 7, 1881. *San Francisco Chronicle [CA]*: September 18, 1879; November 8, 1881. *San Francisco Examiner [CA]*: May 21, 1892; November 30, 1892. *San Juan Prospector [Del Norte, CO]*: May 28, 1881. *Rocky Mountain News [Denver, CO]*: October 15, 1880. *Weekly News [Milledgeville, GA]*: September 5, 1913.

Mitchell, Henry B.

Robbed W. F. & Co's Express on stage from Petaluma to Cloverdale, December 25, 1871 — alone.
Received at the California State Prison, January 19, 1872; No. of commitment, 5096; Crime, robbery; Term 1 year; County sent from, Sonoma.
Discharged, upon expiration of sentence, November 25, 1872.
Served two terms subsequently of one year each from Mendocino County, and *died* in prison, July 27, 1878.

Late on December 25, 1871, when the stagecoach from Petaluma to Cloverdale was just below Geyserville in Sonoma County, and about one hundred fifty yards from William Ellis' ranch, a boy of about sixteen years stepped from behind a tree with gun in hand and signaled for driver "Doc" Curtis to halt. Curtis did not see the gun at first and thought it was someone wanting a ride into town, but when Curtis asked what he wanted the boy waved his pistol and told him "throw out that box." This was immediately done and Curtis was ordered to continue. There was one passenger aboard but he was not molested. As soon as the stagecoach reached Healdsburg Curtis reported the robbery to deputy sheriff William Reynolds who, with his brother Hedge, accompanied Curtis to the scene. They found the box thirty steps from where it had been dropped and it had been cut open. It was too dark to track the robber so the lawman took the box back to town and found that the letter pouch, which had been inside the box, had not been molested though one letter not in the pouch, and addressed to Sheriff Potter, was torn open. There was no money nor valuables in the box so the road agent had made a "water haul." The next morning a small posse went to the scene and carefully circled the area for several miles but could not find a track of man nor horse. The morning of December 26 the boy, an Indian giving the name Harvey Bell, went to the ranch of Daniel Sink and there told a worker that he had robbed the stagecoach. The employee told Sink what the boy said and Sink went to Cloverdale and had a warrant issued by the Justice of the Peace. A Mr. Crawford was deputized to make the arrest, as the boy had at times lived with Sink and he declined to arrest him. The two men returned to the Sink ranch and Crawford arrested Bell. On the way to town the boy confessed that he had done the work alone and had no gun but had pointed, as if it were a gun, a redwood picket he tore from a fence. He said he got the notion to rob a stagecoach because he had heard the Brown brothers, with whom he had lived recently until they were jailed, talking about several stagecoaches they had robbed. He then offered to take Crawford to a certain place in a canyon where one of the express boxes had been cut open and the valueless contents, including a box of type for the Mendocino *Press*, was scattered about. He also said that when another stagecoach was robbed below Truett's ranch one of the road agents, whom he knew as "Rattle Jack," was mortally wounded and he offered to show the grave. He told Crawford that the Browns had said it was Truett's shot which killed Rattle Jack. Bell, once he was in jail, disclosed that his true name was Harry B. Mitchell. He was indicted and tried in early January 1872 and found guilty. On January 15 he was sentenced to serve one year in prison. The light sentence was probably due to his youth, willingness to confess, and his cooperation with the lawmen. He arrived at San Quentin Prison on January 19, 1872, and was released by expiration of sentence on November 25, 1872, just eleven months after holding up the stagecoach. Mitchell would serve two more terms in San Quentin before he died of consumption on July 27, 1878, while serving his final term.

Sonoma Democrat [CA]: December 30, 1871; January 13, 1872.

Morgan, William A.—*alias* Dave Jenkins, Dave Williams

Nativity, Wales, England; Age, 47 years; Occupation, Brick-maker; Height, 5 feet 11¼ inches; Complexion, Light; Color of eyes, Blue; Color of hair, Sandy and Gray; Weight 155 or 160 lbs.

Robbed W. F. & Co's Express on stage from Prescott to Maricopa, A. T., November 19, 1879, with Thomas Francis. Francis was killed while resisting arrest.

Received at the Territorial Prison, Yuma, A. T., December 15, 1879; No. of commitment, 47; Crime, robbery; Term, life; County sent from, Yavapai, A. T.

On November 20, 1879, Prescott's *Daily Miner* reported: "The outgoing coach of Gilmer, Salisbury & Co., Billy Osborne, driver, was stopped about fourteen miles west of Prescott and four miles east of Dixon's station Wednesday evening by two highwaymen. There were on board, besides the driver, two passengers, Mr. Rothchilds of San Francisco and Mr. Walters of Phenix. The passengers were not molested and nothing was taken from the coach except W. F. & Co.'s express box, which contained about $250. The robbers were armed with shotgun and rifle, which they brought into direct line with the persons of the driver and passengers, commanding them to 'throw up.' The order was obeyed, the treasure box delivered and the coach allowed to pass on much to the relief of Billy Osborne, one of the best drivers on the route, who felt a little sea sick while looking down the large chambers of the shot gun." Within a week officers knew who the robbers were and on November 28 Prescott's *Weekly Miner* reported "STAGE ROBBERS CAPTURED!; One Killed, the Other Alive—Good Work.":

> Sheriff Joseph R. Walker received information on Saturday last that satisfied him beyond doubt that the two men who robbed the outgoing stage on Wednesday night of last week near Skull Valley, were living at the lower end of Thompson valley, and immediately set about for their capture. He secured the services of Marshal Dodson, Tom Simmons and Al Seiber, three of the best men in the county, and about noon Sunday left for Thompson valley where they arrived that night. They remained at the residence of Mr. Alred until Monday afternoon when the robbers came up from their cabin to see Mr. Alred about driving cattle to Phoenix. The sheriff and his *posse* immediately commanded the two men, Thos. Francis, *alias* Wilcox and David Williams, *alias* Jenkins, to surrender. As quick as thought Francis started to run his horse, trying to pull a revolver at the same time, but before he could accomplish either was shot and fell from his horse dead. Williams taking in the situation concluded to surrender and slowly raised his hands heavenward, and allowed the sheriff to disarm him. He was ornamented with jail jewelry and brought to town and lodged in prison at 2 o'clock this morning. There is no doubt about these gents being the right ones, and the authorities who went out and captured the "birds" deserve much credit. In twenty-seven hours after the sheriff and party left here Francis was dead and Williams in irons and on his way to Yavapai county jail.
>
> R. H. Paul, Wells Fargo & Co.'s detective is here and will render all the assistance possible toward convicting the surviving knight of the road. Stage robbers in this Territory have been

unfortunate indeed, for in nearly every instance they have either been captured or killed, just as they should be. Men who go out on the highway and stop stages, poke shot guns and revolvers in the faces of passengers, open mail bags, smash up express boxes, etc., deserve death and nothing short of it. Hurrah for Walker, Seiber, Dodson and Simmons.

At the hearing David Williams, alias David Jenkins, disclosed that his true name was William Morgan. He was tried at the November term and convicted. Judge Silent said, in passing sentence, "It is the intention of this Court to stop the practice of highway robbery, so far as it is in its power so to do. You have been found guilty of that crime and this Court will impose the full penalty of the law. The sentence of this Court is that you be confined in the Territorial prison of Arizona for and during the time of your natural life." William Morgan registered as prisoner No. 47 when admitted to the Territorial Prison near Yuma on December 15, 1879. Morgan, a bricklayer by trade, was a Welshman aged forty years, five feet eleven inches in height with blue eyes and sandy hair. His sentence was listed in the prison record as "life until death" but he was pardoned by Governor Frederick A Tritle on August 7, 1885, upon recommendation of the Prison Board of Commissioners.

Daily Miner [Prescott, AZ]: November 20, 1879; November 25, 1879. *Salt River Herald [Phoenix, AZ]*: November 20, 1879; November 25, 1879; *Sentinel [Yuma, AZ]*: November 22, 1879; November 29, 1879. *Weekly Miner [Prescott, AZ]*: November 21, 1879; November 28, 1879.

Morris, Fred

Nativity, New York; Age, 23 years; Occupation, Laborer; Height, 5 feet 7¾ inches; Complexion, Florid; Color of eyes, Blue; Color of hair, Light. Round oval features, high broad forehead, long slim nose, large nostrils, curly hair, small ears, dim scar outer corner of left eye, long scar on thumb and left hand — extending from thumb down towards the wrist, small mole neat spine above small of back, right arm slightly deformed from a break, several circular scars back of right hand, large mole about 4 inches above right nipple; stout built; is very quiet.

Burglarized W. F. & Co's office at Downey City, Cal., in company with Henry Holden, January 19, 1881.

Received at the California State Prison, April 18, 1881; No. of commitment, 9873; Crime, burglary; Term, 2½ years; County sent from, Los Angeles.

Pardoned by Governor George C. Perkins, October 20, 1881.

[*See* Holden, Henry]

Morton, Leander

Robbed Overland Express Train from San Francisco [Cal.] to Odgen [U. T.] near Pequop [Nev.], November 7, 1870, with Daniel Boone Baker and Daniel F. Taylor.

Received at Nevada State Prison, January 19, 1871; Commitment, 72; Crime, robbery; Term, 30 years.

Escaped September 17, 1871, in big break, and in company with Charles Jones, J. B. Roberts, Tilton P. Cockrell, John Burke, and Moses Black; separated from the other twenty-three escapees, and fled in a southerly direction through Esmeralda County. On the twentieth they were unexpectedly met by William A. Poor, a boy carrying the mail on horseback between Aurora and Carson City, and fearing this meeting would lead to their pursuit and recapture, they murdered the boy, piled brush on the body, set fire to it, and fled — Black, Morton and Roberts pursuing a southerly direction toward Benton. The whole country was aroused at the atrocious murder of young Poor, and near Benton the convicts were overtaken by a pursuing party. They made a desperate resistance, and during the fight Robert Morrison, W. F. & Co's Agent at Benton, and Mono Jim, an

Indian, of the Sheriff's posse were shot and killed, and Roberts seriously wounded. The three outlaws were captured, and returned to the locality where the boy had been murdered. Morton and Black were hung by citizens of Aurora, but Robert's life was spared on account of his youth, wounds, and the disclosures he made.
[See Baker, Daniel Boone]

Murphy, Eugene

Nativity, California; Age, 23 years; Occupation, Clerk; Height, 5 feet 8¾ inches; Complexion, Florid; Color of eyes, Gray; Color of hair, Brown, Size of foot, 8. Square features, high broad forehead, high cheek-bones, wide jaws, small mouth and chin, slightly Roman nose, small round ears, small mole inside left eyebrow, long slender hands, small scar back of head, scar right side of back of neck, square shouldered; stout built.

Robbed W. F. & Co's Express on stage from Grayson to Bantas, October 23, 1884, in company with Peter Smith and James Casey

Received at California State Prison, October 29, 1884; No. of commitment, 11435, Crime, robbery; Term, five years; County sent from, San Joaquin.
[See Casey, James]

Nay, Orrin

Nativity, Iowa; Age, 35 years; Occupation, Teamster; Height, 5 feet 6 inches; Complexion, Dark; Color of eyes, Hazel; Color of hair, Black, Weight, 152 pounds, Size of foot, 7. Drinks, smokes and chews, several scars from bed sores on back, dark mole and scar on right hip, teeth full and regular, about five inches of the upper portion of the humorus has been removed, leaving scar from incision made about 7 inches long, scar from bullet wound 2½ inches below right shoulder blade, scar from bullet front of left thigh.

Attempted to rob Overland Express train from San Francisco to Ogden at Montello, January 22, 1883, in company with Rais Anderson, Sylvester Earl, Francis "Frank" Hawley, and David Francis.

Received at Nevada State Prison, March 2, 1883. Commitment, 248. Crime, assault to rob; Term, 14 years; County sent from, Elko, Nev.
[See Anderson, Rais]

Nelson, John W.

Nativity, Missouri; Age, 33 years; Occupation, Teamster; Height 5 feet 5½ inches; Complexion, Light; Color of eyes, Gray; Color of hair, Light Brown; Weight, 154 lbs. Vaccine mark on left arm, scar on knuckle of first finger left hand, mole and two scars on back of neck, scar on left elbow, scar on left side of back at waist, two scars on left hip, scar on right knee cap; stout built.

Robbed W. F. & Co's Express on stage from Wells to Cherry Creek, July 2, 1875 — alone.

Received at the Nevada State Prison, March 23, 1876; No. of commitment, 34; Crime, robbery; Term, 11 years; County sent from, Elko, Nev.

Escaped from prison, October 29, 1877. Recaptured same day.

Pardoned, July 14, 1884.

Shortly after leaving Wells, Nevada, on July 2, 1875, Woodruff & Ennor's stagecoach bound for Sprucemount, with its final destination being Cherry Creek, was stopped by a lone highwayman, masked and wielding a shotgun. He demanded the mail sack and express box and got nothing from the mails, but from the box he took a watch, other jewelry, and a few trinkets valued at $34; and from the passengers he took $4 in coin, $20 in currency, and National Bank gold notes of various denominations making his total take $131. Detective Ed Alexander was put on the case and within a few days the detective had tracked down the man he thought was the road agent, who gave his name as John W. Nelson, but Nelson had none of the plunder when arrested. Alexander took Nelson before Justice R. H. Taylor for an examination and he pled not guilty, but there was enough evidence to hold him for the grand jury so his bail was fixed at $3,000 and he was lodged in jail. On October 23, 1875, Nelson was indicted but his trial did not begin until March 6, 1876, nearly nine months after his arrest. He was taken into court but the proceedings had to be postponed for ten days to await the arrival of witnesses from the east who were coming by train. When everything was ready he was brought into court again and on March 16 he was easily convicted in one day, including the taking of testimony, closing arguments, and jury deliberations. The prosecution called a dozen witnesses and linked together a chain of evidence that proved Nelson was the road agent. Still Judge J. H. Flack, when it came time for deliberations, instructed the jury, "The evidence in this case consists almost entirely of that kind of evidence known as circumstantial. You are instructed that if this evidence, in this case, is not only consistent with the guilt of the defendant, but inconsistent with any other rational conclusion, the law makes it your duty to convict." The jury deliberation was brief and they found that Nelson was "guilty as charged in the indictment." On March 22 Nelson returned to court and was sentenced to serve eleven years in Nevada's state prison. Nelson arrived at the prison the following day and was registered as prisoner No. 34. Nelson managed to escape on October 29, 1877, but was recaptured the same day and returned to prison to complete his sentence. He was pardoned on July 14, 1884, and did not appear in Nevada's criminal history again.

Elko Independent [NV]: July 10, 1875. *Territorial Enterprise [Virginia City, NV]*: July 11, 1875; March 18, 1876; March 22, 1876.

Norton, Henry—*alias* Liverpool

Nativity, England; Age, 34 years; Occupation, Sailor; Height, 5 feet 10 inches; Complexion, Light; Color of eyes, Blue; Color of hair, Dark. Heavy eyebrows, scar on forehead, do. on left jaw, three vaccine marks on left arm, body free from marks; stout built.

No. of first commitment, 5099. Received at the California State prison, January 20, 1872; Crime, attempt at burglary; Term, 3 years; County sent from, San Francisco.

Discharged, by expiration of sentence, August 12, 1874.

Robbed W. F. & Co's Express on stage from Laporte to Oroville, June 20, 1876, in company with John Doe.

Robbed W. F. & Co's Express on stage from Downieville to Marysville, June 21, 1876, in company with John Doe.

W. F. & Co's Guard G. W. Hackett, "stood him off" and arrested him.

Received at the California State Prison, July 15, 1876; No. of commitment, 7072; Crime, robbery; Term, 15 years; County sent from, Yuba.

Escaped, August 10, 1878. Recaptured, August 12, 1878. Transferred to Folsom Prison, September 16, 1880.

On Monday, June 20, 1876, the stagecoach from Laporte to Oroville was stopped and robbed by two masked road agents when at the junction of the Marysville and Laporte Road, thirteen miles from Oroville in Butte County, California. Wells, Fargo & Company's treasure box was demanded and thrown down. It was broken open and, though at first reported to contain only $20, it actually contained between $600 and $800. The stagecoach driver was then ordered to continue into Oroville. The following day Johnny Sharp was driving the stagecoach from Downieville to Marysville and at 2:00 P.M. reached the foot of Stanfield Hill in Yuba County, a short distance below Charley Smith's place, when he saw two men one hundred yards from the coach on his right coming toward the road and they were partially unclothed and disguised. George Hackett, the company's messenger, was on Sharp's left and the driver drew the guard's attention to the two men so Hackett immediately raised his rifle and the two men, seeing the movement, started to run away. Hackett dismounted and took up the pursuit which lasted several hundred yards before they got away, but he came upon their clothes where they had been left when they disrobed and donned their disguises. He also found a carpet sack which contained the package of gold dust taken from the Laporte coach valued at $640. The men had disappeared into a thicket of underbrush and the guard could not keep them in view so he gathered their clothing and carpet sack and returned to the coach. When he searched the clothing Hackett found two gold watches and a considerable amount of coin so he gave the articles to the driver to be brought into Marysville and he started after the robbers, with a volunteer passenger joining him. Sharp hurried into town and reported the robbery and soon the Sheriff had organized a posse and was also on their trail. Hackett and his volunteer, thinking that the road agents would return for their clothes and plunder, hid in the underbrush to watch for them and within twenty minutes they saw a man in the nearby underbrush heading for the place Hackett had found the clothes. The man had a pistol in his hand but he was covered and made to drop it and surrender, and then he was taken to a nearby farmhouse. James Hume, Wells, Fargo's chief detective, had been in the area investigating the robbery of the Laporte coach and upon learning of the arrest he went to the farmhouse and took Hackett and the prisoner into Marysville, arriving 2:00 A.M. Thursday. The robber was well known to lawmen throughout the region as "Liverpool" and it was soon known that his partner was "Doc" Johnson, alias "snapping Andy." Posses from Butte and Yuba county were out looking for Johnson but he had fled the area and was not heard of again.

"Liverpool" was soon was identified as Henry Norton, had his picture taken, and then was lodged in jail to await his examination. Norton was held to answer to the grand jury and in July he was indicted. Norton was brought into court on July 13 and he pled guilty and was sentenced to serve fifteen years at San Quentin Prison. He arrived at the California State Prison on July 15, 1876, and registered as prisoner No. 7072. He managed to escape from prison on August 10, 1878, but was recaptured in two days. On September 6, 1880, Norton was transferred to the more secure facility at Folsom Prison where he registered as convict No. 130. In late December 1885 Governor George Stoneman commuted his sentence and he was discharged on December 23, 1885.

The Weekly Appeal [Marysville, CA]: June 30, 1876; July 14, 1876; July 21, 1876.

Nunez, Trinidad

Nativity, Mexico; Age, 27 years; Occupation, Laborer; Height 5 feet 6½ inches; Complexion, Dark; Color of eyes, Black; Color of hair, Black. Round features, flat cheeks, large nose, scar on left forefinger; medium built.

Robbed W. F. & Co's Express on stage from Marysville to Downieville, July 26, 1877, in company with Jose Machado.

Received at the California State Prison, October 18, 1877; No. of commitment, 7833; Crime, robbery; Term, 8 years; County sent from, Sierra.

Discharged, by expiration of sentence, February 17, 1883.
[*See* Machado, Jose]

Olivas, Francisco—*alias* Francisco Sotello

Nativity, California; Age, 27 years; Occupation, Laborer; Height, 5 feet 9 inches; Complexion, Dark; Color of eyes, Black; Color of hair, Black. Square features, wide jaws, slightly pock-marked, small scar under lip, small mole on left shoulder, do. left breast, scar back of left forearm, do. right elbow; stout built.

Robbed W. F. & Co's Express and U.S. Mail on stage from Newhall to Ventura, January 20, 1877, with Francis Sotello [*sic*].

Received at the California State Prison, May 29, 1877; No. of commitment, 7602; Crime, robbery; Term, 10 years; County sent from, Los Angeles.

Discharged, by expiration of sentence, November 29, 1883.
[*See* Lugo, Chico]

Overhoeltz, William H.

Nativity, California; Age, 22 years; Occupation, Laborer; Height, 5 feet 6 inches; Complexion, Light; Color of eyes, Brown.

Robbed W. F. & Co's Express and the U.S. Mail on stage from Boise, I. T., to Kelton, Utah, November 18, 1879, in company with William Mays.

Received at the Penitentiary at Boise, I. T., January 22, 1880; No. of commitment, —; Crime robbery; Term, life; County sent from, Ada, I. T.

Transferred to U.S. Prison at Auburn, N. Y., June 4, 1881.
[*See* Mays, William]

Owens, J. S.

Nativity, Utah; Age, 24 years; Occupation, Laborer; Height, 5 feet 11 inches; Complexion, Fair; Color of eyes, Light Blue; Color of hair, Light Brown; Weight, 174 lbs. Large red mark on right elbow, long scar on left knee, scar on calf of left leg, little finger of right hand crooked, full cheeks, round face, large ears.

Robbed W. F. & Co's Express on stage from Ash Fork to Prescott, A. T., August 10, 1883, in company with G. A. Kerby and Seely Owens.

Received at the Territorial Prison at Yuma, December 19, 1883; Crime, robbery; Term, 4 years; County sent from, Yavapai, A. T.
[*See* Kerby, G. A.]

Owens, Seely

Age, is about 28 years old; Height, 5 feet 10 inches; Color of hair, Dark; Weight, 165 lbs. Piercing eyes, has a large ugly scar on right wrist—apparently from a knife wound—which also disfigures the little finger on same hand, has scar on instep of right foot, speaks Spanish fluently.

Robbed W. F. & Co's Express on stage from Ash Fork to Prescott, A. T., August 10, 1883, in company with G. A. Kerby and J. S. Owens.

The three pleaded guilty, and Kerby and Seely Owens were sentenced to eight years and J. S. Owens to four years, in the Penitentiary at Yuma, A. T.

While en route to prison Seely Owens *escaped* from Jacob Hinkle, Sheriff of Yavapai County, and is still at large, January 1, 1885.

Sheriff Hinkle offers a liberal reward for his arrest and detention.
[*See* Kerby, G. A.]

Palmer, James

Nativity, California; Age, 26 years; Occupation, Laborer; Height, 5 feet 6⅛ inches; Complexion, Florid; Color of eyes, Blue; Color of hair, Sandy. Long features, high forehead, vaccine mark left upper arm, scar on each wrist—close to hands, large mole on left shoulder blade, small scar back of neck, left foot deformed; stout built.
Robbed W. F. & Co's Express on stage from San Luis Obispo to Soledad, March 30, 1880—alone.
Received at the California State Prison, April 26, 1880; No. of commitment, 9248; Crime, robbery; Term, 7 years; County sent from, Monterey, Cal.

On Tuesday night, March 30, 1880, the Coast Line stagecoach from San Luis Obispo driven by Jim Meyers was nearing its destination when a masked youth, sporting a shotgun, stepped into the road and ordered the driver to rein in his team. The road agent next demanded the Wells, Fargo treasure box and it was thrown down. Meyers was then told to continue into town and he immediately whipped up his team. Meyers reported the robbery to Sheriff C. Franks who dispatched a deputy to the scene, the same place the stagecoach had been robbed six months earlier, and he took up the robber's trail. At daylight the box was found on the bank of the river, broken open and rifled of its contents. Sheriff Franks then took up the trail and followed the road agent into Tulare County. He was on the trail five days, the same time it took to capture the previous road agent, and he captured this robber as well. The prisoner gave the name James Palmer and claimed he was only nineteen years old, and he was taken to Salinas and lodged in jail. Franks had earned a $600 reward by the capture, $300 from the state and $300 from Wells, Fargo & Company, and he still had $600 due for his previous capture of a stagecoach robber. Palmer had his examination and was held to answer to the grand jury, was indicted in early April, and within a month of the robbery he had his trial, was convicted, and sentenced to serve a term of seven years at San Quentin Prison. Palmer arrived at the prison April 26, 1880, and registered as prisoner No. 9248. He was released, by expiration of sentence, on January 26, 1885.

San Luis Obispo Tribune [CA]: April 10, 1880; May 8, 1880.

Pardillo, Isidor

Robbed W. F. & Co's Express on stage from Laporte to Oroville, August 3, 1875, in company with Ramon Ruiz, Red Antone, and Kokimbo.
Robbed W. F. & Co's Express on stage from Marysville to Downieville, October 5, 1875, in company with Red Antone, Kokimbo, Ramon Ruiz and Jose Lenaris.
Received at the California State Prison, November 23, 1876; No. of commitment, 7262; Crime, robbery; Term 20 years; County sent from, Yuba.
Died in Prison, May 7, 1877.
[*See* Ruiz, Ramon]

Parks, Daniel—*alias* Dave Parks

Nativity, Indiana; Age, 48 years; Occupation, Miner; Height 5 feet 8 inches; Complexion, Light; Color of eyes, Blue; Color of hair, Light. Broad high forehead, regular features, large prominent eyes, two warts—one under each shoulder blade, two scars on right leg from stabs, on thigh and right side of knee-pan, dimpled chin, well built.

First term, 2683. Received at the California State Prison, February 18, 1864; Crime, robbery; Term, 10 years; County sent from, Calaveras.

Pardoned by Gov. Newton Booth, May 1, 1872.

Robbed W. F. & Co's Express on stage from Milton to Sonora, August 3, 1879, in company with John Benson and Ab. Bryant [*sic*]. Fled to Missouri, but was overtaken there and brought back to Calaveras County by W. F. & Co's Special Officer.

Received at California State Prison, April 29, 1878; Commitment, 8188; Crime, robbery; Term, 18 years; County sent from, Calaveras.

[*See* Benson, James]

Parsons, E. B.

Nativity, New Hampshire; Age, 44 years; Occupation, Miner; Height, 5 feet 8¾ inches; Complexion, Fair; Color of eyes, Blue; Color of hair, Dark Brown; Weight, 170 lbs. Bullet mark on left side of spine, 2 large and 3 small moles on right shoulder, mole at right corner of upper lip, mole on right cheek near corner of eye, scar on third joint of left forefinger.

Robbed Overland Express train from San Francisco [Cal.] to Odgen [U. T.] near Verdi [Nev.], November 6, 1870, with J. E. Chapman, A. J. Davis, John Squires, R. A. Jones, Tilton P. Cockrell, and James Gilchrist.

Received at the Nevada State Prison, December 25, 1870; No. of commitment, 68; Crime, robbery; Term, 20 years; County sent from, Washoe, Nev.

Escaped in "Big Break" of September 17, 1871; recaptured and returned to prison, September 28, 1871.

Taken to Carson Jail, March 5, 1872, to be tried for Prison-breaking.

Escaped from Jail, 1872.

Returned to State Prison, November 18, 1876.

Pardoned, November 7, 1881.

Startling abuse of the pardoning power.

[*See* Davis, A. J.]

Paul, Thomas

Nativity, Kentucky; Age, 23 years; Occupation, School Teacher; Height, 5 feet 6⅛ inches; Complexion, Light; Color of eyes, Gray; Color of hair, Brown. Square features, high forehead, nose turned to the left, small scar back of left hand, small scar right side of neck, scar near first joint of right thumb; medium built.

Robbed W. F. & Co's Express on stage from Ukiah to Eureka, October 11, 1879—alone.

Fled to Oregon, and was arrested on a requisition from Governor George C. Perkins.

Escaped from arresting officer, January 31, 1880.

Recaptured, February 2, 1880.

Received at the California State Prison, May 1, 1880; No. of commitment 9256; Crime, robbery; Term, 5 years; County sent from, Mendocino.

Removed to Folsom Prison, July 26, 1880.

Escaped from Folsom Prison, 1880; recaptured and returned 1880.

Pardoned by Governor Perkins, January 8, 1883.

At noon on Saturday, October 11, 1879, the stagecoach bound for Eureka from Ukiah, by way of Little Lake, had only traveled three and one half miles and was near Cal's English when a road agent called out to driver Tom Forse, "Hand out that box, quick!" Tom was startled and asked, "What did you say?" The masked road agent then repeated his demand from concealment and emphasized the urgency with the twin barrels of his shotgun. The box was thrown out and the road agent next commanded, "Drive on seven miles before you stop to speak to anyone." Forse drove on and shortly came to a group of people traveling in the opposite direction and he warned them of the road agent ahead, but they continued anyway and when they came to the scene of the robbery they were not molested. Forse hurried on to the next station and reported the robbery to Wells, Fargo's agent Wheeler and Sheriff James R. Moore. Wheeler and Moore organized a small posse and went to the scene but could find no trace nor a clue to the identity of the lone robber, described only as a masked man heavily armed and of average size. On Sunday the posse discovered the broken treasure box and papers scattered about a bush not far from the scene. The box had contained $942 in gold and silver coins but was now empty. They also found the leg from some knit drawers with eye holes cut in it, which had served as the robber's mask. Wells, Fargo & Company posted a reward of $600 for the arrest and conviction of the road agent and dispatched detective James B. Hume to Ukiah to investigate. There were other outlaws active in the area and they had murdered two men and Hume was able, from their descriptions, to identify them as ex-convicts well known to him and recently released from San Quentin Prison.

However, Hume was not concerned with that case and concentrated his efforts on the stagecoach robbery case, and soon had identified his man as Thomas Paul. Hume circulated Paul's description and in January 1880 the highwayman was captured by Oregon lawmen, and Governor George Perkins issued a requisition. The arresting officers were en route to Mendocino County when Paul managed to escape and remain free for three days before being recaptured on February 2. Not willing to take any more chances of an escape Hume went to Oregon to bring back Paul arriving in Ukiah on Thursday, February 12, and he was lodged in jail. Paul hired, as his defense counsel J. T. Rogers, for his examination but the evidence was sufficient to hold him over for action by the grand jury. In late February a man came forward and surrendered property stolen during the robbery stating he had received it from Paul. In April Paul was indicted and, when brought into court, he pled guilty hoping for a lighter sentence, and his strategy worked as he received a sentence of only five years. Paul arrived at San Quentin Prison on May 1, 1880, and registered as prisoner No. 9256. He was transferred to Folsom Prison on July 26, 1880, where he registered as prisoner No. 37. Folsom was not a secure facility and in late November 1882 Paul managed to escape and remain free for several weeks. Freedom as a fugitive did not suit Paul so he turned himself in to a county officer and asked to be returned to prison. An application was filed for a pardon and the accompanying letter, dated December 20, 1882, mentioned that he had voluntarily surrendered to authorities to complete his term. This swayed the state executive and Paul was pardoned by Governor George C. Perkins on January 8, 1883, after serving only two years eight months.

Daily Humboldt Times [CA]: October 21, 1879. *Mendocino Democrat [CA]*: February 14, 1880; February 21, 1880. *Mendocino Weekly Dispatch [CA]*: October 18, 1879; February 13, 1880; March 1, 1880; April 30, 1880. *Ukiah City Press [CA]*: October 17, 1879.

Pearson, Jesse

Nativity, Kentucky; Age, 37 years; Occupation, Teamster; Height 5 feet 6¼ inches; Complexion, Florid; Color of eyes, Hazel; Color of hair, Iron Gray; Size of foot, 5½; Weight, 136 lbs. Small India ink mark on right forearm, scar on point of left elbow, scar on right shin, vaccine mark left

arm, scar on left shin, scar on outside and inside of left knee, D in blue India ink on left hip, scar in front of left thigh.
Robbed W. F. & Co's Express on stage from Bodie to Monmouth [sic], September 27, 1880—alone.
Robbed W. F. & Co's Express on stage from Belleville to Hawthorne, December 15, 1881, in company with Hank Rogers and John Doe.
Received at the California State Prison, May 29, 1882; No. of commitment, 223; Crime, robbery, Term 6 years; County sent from, Esmeralda, Nev.

On November 14, 1881, the northbound Bodie to Carson City stagecoach, after leaving Belleville and when in the canyon a few miles beyond town, was stopped by three masked highwaymen. The road agents stepped out from the brush and one of the robbers fired a shot into the driver's boot of the coach as he yelled, "Halt, you s__s of b__s!" The shot missed everyone aboard and the same robber then commanded, "Tell that messenger to step out," but he was informed there was no messenger. While his two companions covered the driver with their guns the same man then ordered the four passengers to come out and line up on the road. The passengers included Dr. F. R. Waggoner of Reno, Brooks McLane of the Garfield mining district, and the "Swisher sisters of Red Oak, Iowa," who were actually members of Belleville's demimonde. The highwaymen went through the passengers and the leader of the road agents, who was "half-drunk," struck the men with his pistol as he robbed them. He took $13 from McLane and $40 from each of the girls, but the doctor had no money to contribute. The robbers next demanded that the Wells, Fargo & Company box be thrown down and as soon as they had the box they ordered the passenger to board and the coach to continue on.

It was later reported in Bodie's *Free Press* that the box contained $500.

The driver whipped up his team and as soon as he reached the next telegraph he sent the details back to Belleville. A search was conducted and the broken box was found three miles below the lower mill in the canyon. When the "Swisher sisters" arrived in Carson City they reported that they knew the men who had perpetrated the robbery, men well known to them in their profession at Belleville, and named Jesse Pierce (*sic*), Hank Rogers, sometimes spelled Rodgers, and man named Wilson as the three road agents. The girls were detained at Carson City while an investigation was conducted and would later testify at the hearings and at trial. On November 19 Sheriff David J. Robb arrived in Belleville and arrested Pearson and had Rogers and other parties were under surveillance, and Rogers soon joined Pearson in jail.

There was a great deal of interest in the case and the state's attorney general arrived to give the matter his personal attention. Wilson, seeing the jig was up, fled and was not heard of again, so thereafter is referred to as "John Doe" in all matters pertaining to the robbery. On December 3 Pearson and Rogers had their examination and were held to answer to the grand jury with bail set at $9,000 each, and A. W. Crocker was appointed to represent the defendants. On May 6, 1882, according to Candalaria's *True Fissure*, indictments were returned against Jesse Pearson and Hank Rogers by the grand jury at Aurora. They were taken into Judge William M. Seawell's Third Judicial District Court where Pearson pled guilty while Rogers pled not guilty. Pearson was returned to his cell to await sentencing while Rogers trial was set to begin on Wednesday, May 17. Rogers was tried twice and, when the jury could not agree a second time, he was released. Pearson arrived at the prison on May 29, 1882. He served his full six year sentence, less good time credits, and was released on November 29, 1886.

Reno Evening Gazette [NV]: November 16, 1881. *Territorial Enterprise [Virginia City, NV]*: October 2, 1880; November 19, 1881; November 20, 1881. *True Fissure [Candalaria, NV]*: May 16, 1882.

Perkins, Richard—*alias* Dick Fellows, G. Brett Lytle

Nativity, Kentucky; Age, 37 years; Occupation, Farmer; Height 5 feet 7⅝ inches; Complexion, Florid; Color of eyes, Blue; Color of hair, Light. Broad features, high forehead, long pointed nose, high cheek-bones, scar on left cheek-bone, scar on left cheek near corner of mouth, slight scar over left eye, dim vaccine mark upper right arm, mole on right shoulder; stout built.

No. of first commitment, 4378. Received at the California State Prison, January 31, 1870; Crime, robbery and assault to murder; Term, 8 years; County sent from, Los Angeles.

Pardoned by Governor Newton Booth, April 4, 1874.

Robbed W. F. & Co's Express on stage from Los Angeles to Bakersfield, December 4, 1875.

Received his sentence January 9, 1876, and *escaped* from Jail same night.

Recaptured and returned to Jail, January 14, 1876.

Received at the California State Prison, January 16, 1876; No. of commitment, 6834; Crime, robbery, Term, 8 years; County sent from, Kern.

Discharged, by expiration of sentence, May 16, 1881.

Robbed W. F. & Co's Express on stage from San Luis Obispo to Soledad, July 19, 1881.

Robbed W. F. & Co's Express on stage from Duncan's Mill to Fort Ross, August 1, 1881.

Robbed W. F. & Co's Express on stage from Santa Barbara to San Luis Obispo, August 25, 1881.

Robbed W. F. & Co's Express on stage from Santa Barbara to San Luis Obispo, December 29, 1881.

Attempted to rob W. F. & Co's Express on stage from San Luis Obispo to Santa Barbara, January 2, 1882. Fired several shots at the driver.

Robbed W. F. & Co's Express on stage from San Luis Obispo to Santa Barbara, January 8, 1882. Robbed the driver, also.

Robbed W. F. & Co's Express on stage from San Luis Obispo to Soledad, January 13, 1882.

Arrested January 27, 1882, in Santa Clara County and taken to San Jose, and *escaped* from the officer having him in charge, just before reaching the Jail.

Recaptured February 4, 1882, and taken to Santa Barbara County for trial for robbery of January 8, 1882.

March 27, 1882, was tried and convicted, and on March 30 was sentenced to imprisonment for the term of his natural life.

On March 31 he overpowered the jailer, took his pistol, and *escaped*. Recaptured same day.

Received at the California State Prison at Folsom as Dick Fellows, April 6, 1882; No. of commitment, 470; Crime, robbery; Term life; County sent from, Santa Barbara, Cal.

After robbing a lone rider near Los Angeles Richard Perkins, whose real name was G. Brett Lytle, moved north and in 1869 he stopped the Coast Line stagecoach when it neared Santa Barbara. The lone road agent was soon tracked down, arrested, and said his name was Dick Fellows. Perkins, as Fellows, was tried for the stagecoach robbery in Santa Barbara County, convicted, and sentenced to serve eight years at California's San Quentin Prison. He arrived on January 31, 1870, and registered as prisoner No. 4378. As soon as Perkins arrived behind the prison's walls he began a campaign to gain an early release and represented himself as being well-educated, and then convinced the prison officials to place him in the library, an "elevated trusty" position given only to those favored by the staff. In this position he was in contact with a majority of prisoners so he next established bible study classes and positioned himself as the religious spokesman for all the convicts. All these efforts convinced the warden and other officials that he had been thoroughly reformed by their influence and by the prison experience and they recommended an early pardon, so on April 4, 1874, Governor Newton Booth granted an unconditional pardon, which restored all his rights. Perkins (Fellows) had served less than half of his original sentence and for the next twenty months he managed to stay out of trouble, or at least was not caught for any crimes he committed. Perkins, still using the name Dick Fellows, learned that a large shipment of gold coin totaling $240,000 would be carried by stagecoach from end-of-track at the rail depot in Caliente to save a failing bank in Los Angeles, a trip that took an entire day and night. The stagecoach was scheduled to make the trip through Kern County on December 4, 1875, so Perkins devised a plan to rob the coach and recruited another desperado to assist him. While this aspiring road agent remained unnamed he was probably one of the many ex-convict hard cases seen in the vicinity at that time. The train carrying three Wells, Fargo boxes of gold coins arrived at the Caliente depot at 7:00 A.M. on December 4 guarded by S. D. Brastow, Division Superintendent for Wells, Fargo & Company, and Jerome Meyers, Stockton's Chief of Police. James B. Hume, chief detective for Wells, Fargo met the train and within an hour the gold was transferred to the stagecoach and the three men boarded, Brastow and Meyers riding inside and the heavily-armed Hume atop with the driver, and the stagecoach made the trip and delivered its gold shipment without incident. Perkins had sent his companion ahead to the spot where they planned to stop the stagecoach while Perkins, who wanted to avoid any premature pursuit that might be started if he stole an animal, went to a nearby livery and rented a horse. However, shortly after leaving town the horse threw Perkins and galloped off so Perkins picked himself up and walked back into town, where he found that the mare had returned to her stall. The pair of road agents missed the stagecoach and Perkins' companion, when his partner failed to arrive, abandoned the scheme to rob the heavily guarded stagecoach. Perkins had wasted many hours and night was rapidly approaching but, since he was again in the business of robbing stagecoaches, he decided to stop the incoming coach. He stole a likely looking animal which was tied to a hitching post and rode a mile and a half from town. At 9:00 P.M. he halted the northbound stagecoach from Los Angeles by pulling his pistol and ordering driver Duggan to halt. He demanded the Wells, Fargo treasure box and as soon as it was thrown down he motioned the driver to continue. He had not brought any tools to open the box so he decided to tie it on the saddle and carry it to a secluded spot where he could work on it at his leisure. However, lifting the box onto the saddle spooked the horse causing it to run off so Perkins was again afoot and dragging the stolen box. It was very dark as he carried the box toward the rail construction site nearby, but he suddenly fell headlong into a deep ditch breaking his left foot and ankle. Still determined he managed to pull himself out of the ditch and, crawling, pushed the box in front of him until he found a place to bury it, after removing more than half of the $1,800 inside. He made his way to a farm where he stole another horse but this animal had a peculiar temporary shoe, a mule's shoe on one hoof, and left a track easily followed. By the following morning a well-mounted and well-rested posse caught the injured road agent hiding in a barn and he was lodged in the Kern County jail at Bakersfield. Perkins was tried for the robbery, convicted, and on June 8, 1876, he was sentenced to serve eight years at San Quentin. The following day Perkins managed to chop through the wooden plank walls of the makeshift, temporary jail and, using a pair of crutches provided by Kern County, escaped. For two days he hid in the willows along the Kern River before slipping into a farmer's corral. Using a bit of rope he tied the only horse to a rail while he went into the barn to steal a saddle, but the horse broke loose and ran away leaving Perkins to limp away. A $300 reward had been posted and without a mount to help him escape Perkins was arrested the next afternoon and returned to jail. The prisoner was put under a constant guard until he could be transferred to prison on June 16, 1876, where he registered as prisoner No. 6834. Perkins was released by expiration of sentence on May 16, 1881.

In late May the ex-convict registered at a Santa Cruz hotel, and a few days later found a job as an advertising solicitor for the Santa Cruz *Daily Echo*. He declined monetary payment for his services and instead placed an ad using his real name: "G. BRETT LYTLE, PROFESSOR OF LANGUAGES, SEEKING PUPILS IN SPANISH." However, after his recent imprisonment Perkins made only a token effort at rehabilitation. At noon on July 19, 1881, the Coast Line Stage Company's northbound coach from San Luis Obispo to Soledad was robbed near Gonzales in the Salinas Valley. The coach, driven by John Walker with four passengers aboard, was stopped by a lone highwayman a mile beyond R. R. Harris' place near the junction of the new roads over the Cuesta Mountains, just five miles from San Luis Obispo. The first the driver knew of the road agent was his voice from behind a sycamore tree, in Spanish, ordering Walker to halt and throw down the box. As soon as Wells, Fargo's treasure box was in the road the driver was ordered to continue. The mails were not requested and the passengers were not molested, and the robber got only $10 in coin and a package containing $8. Perkins [Lytle] was in the area, but not the road agent, and he telegraphed a detailed account to the *Daily Echo*. On August 25, 1881, Perkins, possibly encouraged by that July 19 road agent adventure in which he took no part, robbed the Coast Line stagecoach from San Luis Obispo to San Jose when it was three miles south of San Luis Obispo. He took only the treasure box which contained $268 in coins but did not request the mail nor molest the passengers. He did not appear on the road for four months but on December 11, 1881, at 8:00 P.M. he stopped the coach from San Luis Obispo to Soledad when it was a mile from its destination. He wore a white mask as he demanded the treasure box and profited by only $60 before ordering the driver to continue. On December 29, 1881, Perkins closed out the year by stopping the stagecoach from Santa Barbara to San Luis Obispo driven by Townsend when seven miles from Arroyo Grande. This time he was wearing a handkerchief for a mask and brandishing a six-shooter as he commanded the driver to halt and throw out the treasure box, which contained only $46.50. On Monday, January 2, 1882, Perkins attempted to stop and rob the Telegraph Stage Company's coach going from San Luis Obispo to Santa Barbara when at the old adobe house two miles beyond Los Alamos as driver George Richmond drove near the old house to avoid dead sheep along the roadway. He was trying to make up time and the horses were at a trot when a voice from the house shouted, "Stop! Box!" and a shot was fired. One passenger, a blacksmith named Dorsey riding atop, said the bullet whizzed within inches of their heads as Richmond applied the whip and, after two more shots were fired at them, he drove the coach out of danger and into Los Alamos. The two passengers riding inside were not harmed. A posse went to the scene but could find no clue to the robber's identity nor a clear track to follow. On Sunday, January 8 Perkins succeeded in stopping the same coach from San Luis Obispo bound for Santa Barbara when five miles from Los Alamos, and he took the Wells, Fargo treasure box. Driver Richmond saw a horseman in the road acting suspiciously, making a complete circuit of the coach and inspecting the passengers, before he rode up and brandished his six-shooter. The robber, masked by a gunny sack with eye holes, ordered Richmond to halt, then dismounted and tied his horse to a tree. He demanded the treasure box and told Richmond, "The next time I order you to stop, I guess you'll mind. G__ d__ you!" Richmond threw out the box and Perkins continued, "I understand that you carry a pretty good watch. Just drop it out in the sand. I want it to time you by, you ___." Richmond dropped his gold, hunting-case watch valued at $250 and was then ordered to continue. There were two passengers aboard, one man and one woman, but they were not molested. A party went to the scene and found the box where the road agent had burned a hole in one corner, but the box had been empty. There was no clue to the robber's identity or a clear track to follow.

On January 9, 1882, Wells, Fargo & Company dispatched detective Charles Aull to capture the road agent who had been so active on the roads of Santa Barbara County. He started his investigation in the city of Santa Barbara and, from the descriptions, knew that it was Dick Fellows (Perkins, Lytle) as Aull had been a turnkey at San Quentin for several years and knew Perkins, as Fellows, quite well. He sent out dispatches and tried to track his quarry but he had no clues until Monday, January 23 following the robbery of a stagecoach ten days earlier. On Friday evening, January 13, 1882, the Coast Line stagecoach coming towards Soledad had been stopped between the Oak Grove Hotel and the Salinas River by a road agent masked with a gunny sack. There had been several passengers aboard but they were afraid the coach would be robbed and laid over at the hotel. Driver James Meyers was stopped when he was a mile from Soledad and ordered to throw out the treasure box, and the robber then took the hatchet from the coach, broke it open, and took out $41. He told Meyers he would leave the hatchet where he could find it the following day and ordered him to continue. Aull learned that Perkins had first gone to Santa Cruz and stayed at Pescadero overnight of January 24, and on Wednesday he went to San Mateo. Aull was joined by several more detectives but before they could take action Perkins was captured at 4:00 P.M. by C. van Duren on Couts' Ranch on the road to Mayfield in Santa Clara County. Van Duren surrendered his prisoner to Constable Burke of Santa Clara and on Friday, January 27 Burke telegraphed that he was taking his prisoner to San Jose by buggy, but at Mountain View he boarded the train and arrived at San Jose at 6:35 P.M. The detectives were watching for a buggy and were not at the railroad depot, so Burke decided to take the street car to St. Johns and Market Streets where he disembarked with his prisoner and started for the jail. Perkins was a congenial sort and as the two men passed the I. X. L. Saloon the prisoner invited the lawman to have a drink, and in they went. As soon as Perkins downed his drink he started for the door at a run with Burke in pursuit, but Perkins was too fleet-afoot and escaped. Burke fired at him but missed and the barkeep, Thomas Farrel, joined the chase and briefly gained on Perkins but, not knowing the gravity of his crime, refrained from shooting the fleeing fugitive. Perkins was spotted several times over the next twenty-four hours but no capture was made so the sheriff formed a posse to join in the search but by January 28 they had given up and a posse of twenty private citizens then took up the chase.

On February 3 at 5:00 P.M. Dr. W. F. Gunckel found a man hiding on the second floor of his barn on Stockton Avenue. The doctor went to the second floor to throw down hay to feed his horse but smelled a strong odor like bad whiskey-breath and believed a drunk or tramp was hiding there. He found the man bedded down behind bales of hay and ordered him out. The doctor summoned a neighbor and, when Perkins came down, he kept both hands in his pockets. The neighbor then gave him a hat and, while he was putting it on, the doctor's wife came out and remarked that she thought it was Perkins as the man fit the description of the fugitive. After Perkins left the doctor searched behind the hay stacks and found empty bottles of porter, food taken from his cellar, a hatchet, and he discovered that his file was missing. Lawmen were summoned and the area was searched for hours but Perkins could not found, but was later captured in San Jose. He managed to escape from that jail and was finally captured by a posse deep in the Santa Cruz Mountains near Boulder Creek while he was trying to make his way to the coast. He was taken to Santa Barbara, tried and on March 27, 1882, convicted of a number of robbery charges. On March 30 the judge sentenced Perkins to a life term in Folsom Prison but Perkins had one last chance for freedom and on April 2, 1882, he escaped from the Santa Barbara jail before he could be taken to the prison. He ran several blocks and found a horse staked out in a vacant lot, quickly mounted, and tried to ride off. However, the horse bucked him off and left him lying in the dirt, stunned by the fall, and he was returned to his cell. Perkins arrived at Folsom Prison on April 6, 1882, registered as prisoner No. 470, and after serving twenty-two years he was pardoned on March 8, 1904.

Daily Herald [San Jose, CA]: January 28, 1882; February 3, 1882. *Los Angeles Daily News* [CA]: December 10, 1869; December 24, 1869. *Los Angeles Star [CA]*: December 11, 1869; January 22, 1870. *Kern County Weekly Courier [CA]*: December 4, 1875; December 11, 1875; January 15, 1876; January 22, 1876. *San Jose Herald [CA]*: January 28, 1882, January 29, 1882; February 3–5, 1882; April 2, 1882; April 22, 1882. *San Luis Obispo Tribune [CA]*: July 23, 1881; August 6, 1881; August 20, 1881; August 26, 1881; September 3, 1881; October 1, 1881; January 7, 1882; January 14, 1882; January 21, 1882; February 4, 1882; February 11, 1882; April 8, 1882. *San Jose Mercury [CA]*: January 28, 1882; January 29, 1882; February 3–5, 1882; April 2, 1882; April 22, 1882. *San Francisco Examiner [CA]*: June 24, 1894.

Pointer, J. W.

Nativity, Iowa; Age, 23 years; Occupation, Cowboy; Height, 5 feet 8¼ inches; Complexion, Sallow; Color of eyes, Dark Brown; Color of hair, Brown (dark). Semi-circular scar over joint of thumb of left hand seven-eights of an inch long, scar on wrist of right hand.

Attempted to rob W. F. & Co's Express on train No. 102 on A. T. & S. F. R. R. at a point about five miles north of Socorro, N. M. in company with Jefferson Kirkendall, Edward [sic] White, P. "Punch" Collins, and Bill Allen.

Received at the Kansas State Prison, November 21, 1884; No. 3397; Crime, assault to rob; Term, 7 years; County sent from, Socorro, N. M.

[*See* Collins, P.]

Pratt, Charles—*alias* Charlie Pratt the Shoemaker

No. of first commitment, 2070. Received at the California State Prison, January 7, 1861; Crime, grand larceny; Term 4 years; County sent from, Solano.

Discharged, by expiration of sentence, November 1, 1864.

No. of second commitment, 3197. Received at the California State Prison, January 24, 1866; Crime, house-breaking; Term, 1½ years; County sent from, Alameda.

Discharged, by expiration of sentence, February 13, 1867.

No. of third commitment, 3654. Received at the California State Prison, October 10, 1867; Crime, grand larceny; Term, 2 years; County sent from, Alameda.

Discharged, by expiration of sentence, June 24, 1869.

No. of fourth commitment, 4283. Received at the California State Prison, November 29, 1869; Crime, grand larceny; Term, 3 years; County sent from, Santa Clara.

Discharged, by expiration of sentence, June 20, 1872.

No. of fifth commitment, 5531. Received at the California State Prison, March 15, 1873; Crime, grand larceny; Term, 3 years; County sent from, San Joaquin.

Discharged, by expiration of sentence, October 6, 1875.

Robbed W, F. & Co's Express on stage from Fiddletown to Latrobe, in company with "Old Jim" Smith, and George Wilson, alias "Texas," January 10, 1876.

Robbed W. F. & Co's Express on stage from Georgetown to Auburn, in company with "Old Jim" Smith, and George Wilson, alias "Texas," January 17, 1876.

Received at the California State Prison, June 15, 1876; No. of commitment, 7055; Crime, robbery; Term, 12 years; County sent from, El Dorado.

Commuted by Governor William Irwin, April 23, 1878, to 11½ years.

Died in Prison, March 22, 1883.

On January 10, 1876, the stagecoach from Fiddletown bound for Latrobe, when it was near Plymouth in Amador County, was halted by three men, masked and armed with six-shooters. They took the Wells, Fargo treasure box but did not ask for the mails. On January 17 the stagecoach from Georgetown bound for Auburn was halted when it was near Greenwood in El Dorado County. The only male passenger was robbed but two females were not molested, and the three road agents shared $105 from Wells, Fargo's treasure box. The description of the three road agents matched the three road agents who had robbed the Fiddletown to Latrobe coach a week earlier. Miss Ella Marlett of Grass Valley, one of the passengers on the Auburn coach, was riding atop with the driver and reported "the pistols used by the robbers looked very large." James B. Hume, Wells, Fargo's chief detective, recognized the description of the men who were well known to him from many terms in prison, and who had recently been released, and he called upon the renowned road agent killer Stephen Venard to join him in a search for Charles "the Shoemaker" Pratt, James P. "Old Jim" Smith, and George "Texas" Wilson. Pratt had been in San Quentin five times, Smith three times, and Wilson twice so Hume knew them well and thought they would be quite desperate. He enlisted the help of Len Harris, a Sacramento lawman, and after ten days they located the robbers hiding in a house near Folsom. Folsom's Constable I. W. Kimble joined the posse and they had a warrant of arrest issued on January 27 and the following day, early in the morning, they surrounded the house. Hume and Harris went through the back door but Smith and Wilson heard them coming, grabbed their revolvers, and fled out the front door. They were met by the cocked revolvers of Venard and Kimble and were about to make their fight when Hume and Harris came up behind them. Seeing they had no chance they surrendered without further resistance. They were taken to Placerville in El Dorado County and charged with the Greenwood stagecoach robbery. The defendants were tried together, convicted, and sentenced to serve twelve years in San Quentin Prison. Smith arrived at the prison on February 25, 1876, and registered as prisoner No. 6903. He was removed to the state insane asylum at Napa on October 7, 1884. Wilson also arrived on February 25, 1876, and registered as prisoner No. 6904. Following a commutation of his sentence to ten and one half years he was discharged on September 19, 1883, by expiration of sentence. Pratt was not at the house when his two partners were captured but he was soon run to ground and arrested in February. He was tried at Placerville in El Dorado County for the Greenwood stagecoach robbery and also received a twelve year sentence. He arrived at San Quentin Prison on June 15, 1876, and registered as prisoner No. 7055. On April 28, 1878, his sentence was commuted to ten and one half years, but before he could be released he died in prison on March 22, 1883.

Amador Dispatch [Jackson, CA]: January 29, 1876; February 5, 1876; February 24, 1876. *Amador Ledger [Jackson, CA]:* February 5, 1876. *Folsom Telegraph [CA]:* February 5, 1876. *Placer Herald [Auburn, CA]:* January 22, 1876; February 5, 1876. *Sacramento Daily Record Union [CA]:* January 29, 1876.

Priest, Al

Robbed W. F. & Co's Express on stage from Baker City, Oregon, to Boise, I. T., October 2, 1871, in company with John Black.
Received at the Territorial Prison, Boise, December 19, 1871; No. of commitment —; Crime, robbery; Term, 15 years.
Escaped, April 25, 1872. Stole some horses, was overtaken by the owners, and killed.
[*See* Black, John]

Ragsdale, J. L.

Nativity, California; Age, 20 years; Occupation, Hunter; Height, 5 feet 9⅝ inches; Complexion, Florid; Color of eyes, Blue; Color of hair, Red. Oval features, high forehead, thick nose, round nostrils, large ears, lobes detached, flesh mole one-half inch from left nostril, "J. L. R. 1864" on outer edge of left arm, two vaccine marks left upper arm, broad shoulders; stout built.

Robbed W. F. & Co's Express on stage from Yreka to Redding, May 24, 1882 — alone.

Received at the California State Prison, June 9, 1882; No. of commitment 10445; Crime, robbery, Term, 4 years; County sent from, Shasta.

Attempted to escape by stowing away under a pile of straw while employed at work outside the prison walls, August 30, 1883.

At noon on Wednesday, May 24, 1882, the stagecoach from Yreka to Redding driven by Horace Williams was crossing over Bass' Hill in Shasta County, fourteen miles from its destination. Suddenly a lone highwayman, masked and armed with a rifle, stepped in front of the leaders and commanded, "Halt! Throw out that box!" Once the box struck the roadway the command came for the driver to throw down the mail sacks and Williams was then ordered to continue. The box and letter sacks were later found only a few feet from the roadway, carefully gone through for valuables. Williams whipped up his team and hurried into Redding where he reported the robbery, and a posse was soon on the trail of the road agent. They returned empty-handed and then circulated a description of the robber. On Sunday, May 28 Anderson's constable Elmore arrested a man who gave the name J. L. Ragsdale, whom Elmore believed to be the road agent, and he took his prisoner to Shasta where he was lodged in jail. The man's mask and gun were found in the bushes near Anderson and brought in for evidence, and the prisoner had a diary in which he was detailing his adventures. He documented the purchase of a gun and commented about writing to his girlfriend and telling her, "I am robbing for a living now, and doing pretty well." The editor of the *Shasta Courier* thought he was "too green to be allowed to run free" and speculated that he would plead guilty to receive a lighter sentence. It seems he was correct as on Wednesday, June 7 Ragsdale, along with stagecoach robber Stonewall Jackson Arthur, were taken to San Quentin Prison by Undersheriff Kennedy. Ragsdale had been sentenced to serve only four years and registered as prisoner No. 10445 when he arrived on June 9, 1882. On August 30, 1883, Ragsdale tried to escape from prison by hiding under a pile of straw while employed outside the walls, but the ploy failed and he was quickly secured behind the prison's walls. Ragsdale forfeited twelve months of his good time credit, awarded under the Goodwin Act, and though the record does not state the reason it was almost certainly for his escape attempt. He was discharged on June 9, 1886, after serving his entire four year sentence.

Shasta Courier [CA]: May 27, 1882; June 3, 1882; June 10, 1882.

Ratovich, Mitchell — *alias* Big Mitch

Nativity, Austria; Age, 45 years; Occupation, Mining; Height, 5 feet 10 inches; Complexion, Light; Color of eyes, Hazel; Color of hair, Brown. Large long features, high forehead, large nose, hairy breast, two small moles on throat, three moles left upper arm, two small scars left thumb, two small scars base of right thumb; stout built.

Robbed W. F. & Co's Express on stage from Sonora to Milton, November 2, 1874, in company with "Little Mitch," Ramon Ruiz, and Old Joaquin.

Robbed W. F. & Co's Express on stage from Mokelumne Hill to Lodi, March 1, 1875, in company with "Little Mitch."

Robbed W. F. & Co's Express on stage from Sonora to Milton, March 23, 1875, in company with Ramon Ruiz, Antone Savage alias Old Joaquin, and "Little Mitch."

Attempted to rob W. F. & Co's Express on stage from Sonora to Milton, October 25, 1875, in company with Ramon Ruiz, Antone Savage alias Old Joaquin, and "Little Mitch."

Received at the California State Prison, May 5, 1876; No. of commitment, 7009; Crime, robbery; Term, 15 years, County sent from, Calaveras.

Commuted by Governor William Irwin, April 23, 1878, to 14¾ years.

[*See* Ruiz, Ramon]

Rhodes, James

Nativity, Michigan; Age, 57 years; Occupation, Laborer; Height, 5 feet 10¼ inches; Complexion, Fair; Color of eyes, Blue; Color of hair, Light Brown; Weight, 190 lbs. Light brown eyebrows and large ears. Speaks Mexican well, and is rather a fluent talker, with an off-hand address; stout built, with a slight stoop while walking. Claims to be a F. & A. Mason.

Received at the Nevada State Prison, August 19, 1871; Crime, arson; Term, 8 years; County sent from, Esmeralda.

Pardoned, December 29, 1874.

Robbed W. F. & Co's Express on stage from Wickenburg, A. T., April 19, 1878, in company with Mullen and Rhodapouch.

Robbed U.S. Mail on same stage.

Received at the Territorial Prison, Yuma, A. T., November 16, 1878; No. of commitment, 25; Crime, mail robbery; Term, 9½ years; County sent from, Yuma, A. T.

Removed to Detroit Prison.

Under the headline "Another Stage Robbed" Yuma's *Sentinel* announced that a telegram had been received in Yuma from Phoenix stating that the westbound stagecoach had been robbed by Mexicans about twenty miles west of Maricopa Wells on Monday, September 2. The robbers reportedly "took three bars of bullion, plundered the passengers and mails." Communications were delayed nearly a week because the telegraph lines had been down but Mr. J. H. Onstott, who was a passenger on the coach, related the facts of that event:

> Barney Lee was driving and besides Onstott there were on the stage a Chinaman, a blacksmith, and a stock tender, the two latter being employees of the stage company. About nine o'clock P.M. when near the Chimules, the stage was stopped by three armed Mexicans, one of whom spoke very fair English. The passengers were made to get out and to hold up their hands until these could be tied behind them. All hands and the stage were then taken a short distance from the road. The men were carefully searched, but not stripped. Onstott had a pocketbook with $70 and some checks in his vest pocket: this he managed to take out and throw into a bush while marching from the road with his hands tied. From him the robbers took $8, a silver watch and his blankets; from the Chinaman they got $196; and from the stock tender $26. They broke the express box open with an axe, but got nothing. They cut open the mail bags and scattered their contents. There was a bright moon: Onstott watched them closely and says he saw them pocket nothing from the mails. They took three bars of silver bullion, the stage horses, and started South. The driver and passengers walked to Happy Camp and had to wait there two days until another stage came along. A party of thirty Papago Indians was put on the robbers' track the next morning, properly stimulated by cash in hand and offer of contingent rewards. The tracks followed were of six horses and one mule being of three ridden by the robbers and of the four taken from the stage. They were followed to a camp, from there part of the tracks continued to the southwest and part turned off to the northwest. The pursuing party was divided in two, and we shall no doubt get good news from one or both of them.

U.S. deputy Marshal Joseph W. Evans followed the trail heading southwest into Mexico. The *Enterprise* reported on September 28: ... Mr. Evans is considerably bronzed from his recent trip through Mexico and Southern Arizona. He penetrated about 250 miles into Mexico and for eighteen days was in rapid pursuit of the robbers, at one time being within a few miles of them, when a heavy rain obliterated their trail. He was assisted in his endeavors by the Prefect of the northern district of Altar, who furnished him with a detachment of cavalry. Mr. Evans cannot be too highly commended for his untiring energy in this matter. He has subjected himself to numerous hardships, made incredibly long rides, and done everything possible in connection with this case as well as former ones.

Immediately after Evans returned from Mexico he was put on the trail of "the 'Mexican' who spoke very fair English." That set of northwesterly tracks were made by James F. Rhodes. Evans arrested Rhodes in late September for robbing the stagecoach on September 2 and then learned from his prisoner that he, with two others his prisoner identified as Louis Rodepouch and John Mullen, were responsible for the April 19, 1878, theft of U.S. mail near Wickenburg. The *Arizona Sentinel* on September 28 published the following account of the pursuit and arrest of Rhodes under the headline "Jugged Robber":

> John S. Stout, alias Rhodes and other names, was lodged in Yuma jail last Saturday by Deputy Marshal Evans and Special Mail Agent Mahoney, who are entitled to great credit for the perseverance with which they have followed his trail. Stout is charged with having robbed stage, passengers, and mails on the Maricopa desert on the night of Sept. 2d, an account of which was published in the SENTINEL. The above named officers first heard of his having been at Rio Miembres, New Mexico after committing the robbery and of his having probably left there for Arizona. Evans went over there, while Mahoney remained in Arizona to follow any clues telegraphed by Evans. The latter followed traces of Stout over to Silver City, to Fort Cummings, toward Clifton, and back toward Pueblo Viejo, and finally to a point 15 miles above Camp Thomas on the Gila River, where the arrest was made. Mahoney had started for Camp Thomas, but was met by Evans with the prisoner at Point of Mountain: owing to wires being down Evan's telegram from Silver City had not reached him in time to enable him to be present at the capture. Stout had broken up his share of the stolen silver bullion and had sold the pieces at various points, thus scattering sure traces of his course. When captured he was driving a herd of cattle for Van Smith. Evans rode up to the herd, asked for Stout, who was pointed out to him, and said, "Good morning." Then quickly covering him he made him alight, threw him a pair of hand-cuffs, made him put them on, mount his horse again, and trot down the road toward Camp Thomas before any of the other herders had an opportunity to know what was going on. That morning Stout's back had hurt him, and he had taken off his pistols and left them in the mess wagon. At Tucson Stout waived examination and was committed by U.S. Commissioner Neugass to await action of Grand Jury. The robbery having been committed in the Second Judicial District, Stout will be tried at Yuma next November. He is a large, athletic man who must be over forty, though looking much younger. Parties here knew him many years ago in California, at which time his reputation was not bad. Other parties recognize him as a resident of this Territory for the past ten years or more, and give him a bad name. But this usually occurs when a man has been arrested for crime....

James F. Rhodes had come to the Arizona Territory shortly after his release from the Nevada State Penitentiary in December 1874. By February 1878 Rhodes was working at the ranch of John William 'Jack' Swilling north of Gillette. Swilling was one of the Arizona Territory's most active pioneers and he often employed men who seemed down on their luck, as Rhodes had been when he approached Swilling, but Swilling soon learned of Rhodes' bad character, dismissed him, and ordered him off the ranch. Swilling later explained that he had been suspicious of Rhodes for some time, explaining, "it was generally supposed that Rhodes and others were up to something. They were figuring around there, and Rhodes had got a gun of mine and he was armed."

Trinidad, Swilling's wife, wanted him to get away from the saloons in Gillette and convinced him to go out and recover the remains of Jacob Snively for a Christian burial. Another old Hassayamper named George Monroe and a new comer to the territory named Andrew Kirby agreed to accompany him. The party of three left at mid-day April 18 and traveled several days, arriving at Snivley's Holes about 4:00 P.M. and soon took up the remains. A camp was set up near the grave, but it commenced to rain during the night so the men arose to get an early start. On rising Jack noticed three sets of foot tracks passing very near where they had slept and later remarked, "...I told Monroe 'There is some devilment going on in this section and if there is any develment done they will blame me—you and I and Andy Kirby for it because this [our] track is similar to this.' They passed as close to us as that [eight feet] and they did not wake us up."

Rhodes' party had followed the Swilling party to ensure they did not turn back and after confirming that the Swilling party was in camp at the Holes, the party of robbers traveled fourteen miles northwest to the hogback which lay four miles west of Wickenburg and there awaited the arrival of the evening coach. On November 15 seven witnesses were brought before the grand jury to testify against Rhodes and these included William Reed, the stagecoach driver who was robbed; Joseph W. Evans, the U.S. deputy Marshal who had arrested Rhodes; W. Whipple; Charles Evans; Andrew Kirby; Pablo Salsido; and Thomas Napper. Possibly because he had cooperated in exposing the truth about the April 19 robbery James F. Rhodes, alias John S. Stout, was allowed to plead guilty to robbery of the mail, a lesser offense than robbing it by jeopardizing the life of the carrier. On November 16 Rhodes was sentenced to nine and a half years at hard labor and the following day he became the twenty-fifth prisoner delivered to the Territorial Prison. Rhodes was held at the prison outside Yuma, rather than being transferred to Detroit, at the suggestion of Evans and the U.S. District Attorney "as it is more likely that he will be needed to testify against his accomplices." However, after three years at the Territorial Prison Rhodes was transferred to the Detroit House of Corrections. He arrived there on December 18, 1881, at which time he was fifty-seven years old and in poor health. On June 30, 1884, he was pardoned and nothing more is heard of James F. Rhodes.

Meanwhile, acting Governor John J. Gosper had become anxious to put an end to robberies in the Territory, which seemed to be increasing in frequency and boldness. He issued a "Proclamation" offering a reward for the capture of Rodepouch and Mullen and on November 15 the *Weekly Miner* reported:

> $500 Reward — Governor J. C. Fremont has caused to be printed 250 handbills offering a reward of $500 for the arrest of Louis Rondepouch [*sic*] and John Mullen, who were partners with Rhodes, now in confinement at Yuma, for robbing the United States mails near Wickenburg on the 19th of April last, or $250 for the arrest of either of the robbers. The Governor has put his foot down and intends to stop mail robbing in this Territory, or at least see that the thieves are caught and punished, though he bankrupt the Government in the attempt. This is a proper move, and we sincerely hope that the *whole* gang implicated in the Wickenburg affair may be shown up in the proper light. There is something back, which if properly worked up will astonish more than a few, and be the means hereafter of making stage robbing less frequent.

On November 16 the two fugitives were indicted *in absentia* for "robbing the United States mail by putting the life of the carrier in jeopardy on April 19, 1878." It was reported on November 22 that, "Rodapouch and Mullens, are yet at large," and on December 20, 1878, the *Arizona Weekly Miner* reported that officers, especially Marshal Dake, had been actively sending "circulars descriptive of the above named mail thieves." The circulars, or handbills, had brought reports of several sightings and in the same issue of the *Miner* was a story that Marshal Dake had received a telegram from Olympia, Washington informing him that Rodepouch and Mullen had been taken into custody there. On the following day the *Miner* had news of Rodepouch, but not of Mullen, in Topeka, Kansas: "...Rodepouch, another hard case, who has been in many nasty scrapes such as shooting, robbing, black mailing, etc., and who took the stagecoach together with about $1,900 in gold bullion from Wells, Fargo & Co. has been captured, it is believed, at Topeka, Kansas, and J. W. Evans, a detective of W. F. & Co. has gone to that place for the purpose of identifying this bad, bold highway robber, who values the life of a human being in about the same light that a cat does that of a mouse." Evans went to Topeka but determined that the man in custody was not Louis Rodepouch. His adventure in Kansas the day after Christmas was reported in the *Topeka Blade*:

> INNOCENT— It will be remembered by readers of the BLADE that the officers of this city arrested and lodged in the county jail a man by the name of F. M. Chambers, on the description of a man by the name of Ronderpouch (*sic*) from the Governor of Arizona and Wells, Fargo & Co.'s Express Company, San Francisco, for the robbery, last spring, of the United States Mail in Arizona. Deputy United States Marshal Evans, of California, arrived yesterday to identify Chambers as being the man.
>
> This morning in company with Maj. Simpson, Officer Sherman and Sheriff Evans went to the jail, looked at Chambers said the man filled the description almost exactly, but was not Ronderpouch [*sic*]. Chambers was immediately taken before Justice Searle and discharged.
>
> Mr. Evans received a telegram this morning that both the robbers for which the reward had been offered were captured in Washington territory....

Evans handled several other matters before proceeding to Olympia, Washington, perhaps hoping to avoid the rough winter weather typical in the Pacific northwest. Unfortunately he arrived too late and the *Sentinel* printed on April 5, 1879: "Major J. W. Evans, U.S. Detective, returned from Olympia, Washington Territory where he has been after Rodepouch and Mullen, accused of stagecoach robbery in this Territory. Before Mr. Evans reached Olympia, however, the men had made their escape from the Jail in which they were confined and are now at large, so the journey was fruitless." Neither Louis Rodepouch nor John Mullen were ever tried for robbing the stagecoach and U.S. mails on April 19, 1878.

Arizona Citizen [Tucson, AZ]: September 14, 1878; December 21, 1878. *Arizona Silver Belt [Globe, AZ]*: November 28, 1878. *Arizona Star [Tucson, AZ]*: November 28, 1878. *Daily Miner [Prescott, AZ]*: August 20, 1878; September 2, 1878; September 5, 1878; November 19, 1878; December 17, 1878; December 20, 1878. *Salt River Herald [Phoenix, AZ]*: March 9, 1878; September 28, 1878; November 30, 1878; December 7, 1878. *Sentinel [Yuma, AZ]*: September 7, 1878; September 9, 1878; November 16, 1878; December 7, 1878. *Topeka Blade [KS]*: December 26, 1878. *Weekly Miner [Prescott, AZ]*: September 14, 1878; December 21, 1878.

Rogers, William—*alias* William Root, W. H. Rote, Big-Foot

Nativity, Pennsylvania; Age, 27 years; Occupation, Blacksmith; Height, 6 feet; Complexion, Light; Color of eyes, Gray; Color of hair, Brown, Size of foot, 11. Square features, heavy eyebrows, high square forehead, wide jaws, high cheek-bones, large rough bony hands, small black mole on top of right shoulder, small scar back of head, mole right side of back — low down; large heavy bones; stout built.

No. of first commitment, as William Root, 8100. Received at the California State Prison, March 25, 1878; Crime burglary; Term, 1½ years; County sent from, Tehama.

Discharged, by expiration of sentence, June 25, 1879.

No. of second commitment, as W. H. Rote, 9153. Received at the California State Prison, December 18, 1879; Crime, burglary; Term, 2 years; County sent from, Calaveras

Discharged, by expiration of sentence, August 18, 1881.

Robbed W. F. & Co's Express on stage from Cloverdale to Lakeport, November 29, 1884. Plead guilty.

No. of third commitment, as William Rogers, 11539. Received at the California State Prison, January 15, 1885; Crime, robbery, Term, 30 years; County sent from, Lake.

On the afternoon of Saturday, November 30, 1884, the Sanderson & Company stagecoach from Cloverdale in Sonoma County northbound for Lakeport in Lake County, when near Tyler's Station was halted by a lone highwayman, masked and armed. He demanded the express box and mail sacks and the driver had no choice but to deliver them, and the robber then gestured for the driver to continue. As soon as the driver reached Lakeport he reported the robbery and within the hour posses were in the field from Cloverdale and Lakeport. However, they were not able to capture the road agent. It was later learned that the mails had contained nothing and the box contained only $1.50, but still progress was being made to capture the bold, ineffective road agent and these efforts were joined by James B. Hume, Wells, Fargo & Company's chief detective and his fellow detective Captain Aull. The detectives happened to be in the area looking for John "Shorty" Hays, a stagecoach robber who had escaped from San Quentin Prison on December 13, and he had been seen in the vicinity of Guerneville but Hays was captured at Los Angeles on January 1, 1885, so the two detectives joined the search for the Lake County road agent. The fugitive was soon captured and he turned out to be William Rogers, well known to prison officials and lawmen as William Root, W. H. Rote, and "Bigfoot." He had previously served two terms in San Quentin: first in 1878 from Tehama County for burglary; and again in 1879 from Calaveras County, again for burglary. Rogers was captured in early January and when taken before the Justice of the Peace for his examination he entered a plea of guilty expecting to get a reduced sentence. However, when he was brought before the judge and again pled guilty he was surprised when he was sentenced to serve a term of thirty years at San Quentin Prison. Rogers arrived at the prison on January 15, 1885, and registered as prisoner No. 11539. He was released on March 15, 1903, after serving more than eighteen years.

Cloverdale Reveille [Santa Rosa, CA]: December 6, 1884; January 3, 1885.

Rolfe, Frank II.

Nativity, New York; Age 41 years; Occupation, Cooper; Height, 5 feet 9 inches; Complexion, Florid; Color of eyes, Gray; Color of hair, Light Brown. Square features, tolerably high broad forehead, long ears and rather narrow, tolerably large lobes detached, square-cut thickset prominent nose, tolerably long nostrils, eyes rather deep-set, square cut chin, two small scars just below bridge of nose, small star back of left wrist, larger one outside of left forearm, do. inside of do., dim outline of flag, anchor and man inside of do., two small lumps left upper arm, cup marks left side about four inches from small of back, slight scar center of back of neck, do. right side of neck, star outside and inside right wrist, dim outline of flag and staff also anchor right forearm, full breasted; stout built.

No. of first commitment, 3730. Received at the California State Prison, January 30, 1868; Crime, grand larceny; Term, 5 years; County sent from, Tulare.
Discharged, by expiration of sentence, April 8, 1872.
No. of second commitment, 5969. Received at the California State Prison, April 27, 1874; Crime, house-breaking; Term, 5 years, County sent from, San Bernardino.
Taken out by order of the County Court of San Mateo County to be tried on an additional charge, June 22, 1875.
Returned under a commitment from San Mateo County, under the name of Frank Rollins, June 26, 1875; Crime, assault to murder; Term, 10 years.
Discharged, by expiration of sentence, December 26, 1881.
Robbed W. F. & Co's Express on stage from Sonora to Milton, February 2, 1882, in company with Calvin Bragg.
Escaped from Sonora Jail, April 1882. Recaptured same day.
Received at the California State Prison, April 8, 1882; No. of commitment, 10363; Crime, robbery, Term, life; County sent from, Tuolumne, Cal.
[*See* Bragg, Calvin]

Rugg, George N.

Took W. F. & Co's box from stage at Red Butte Station, Idaho, July 9, 1871, turned State's evidence against his accomplices [W. H. Heinsman and Donald McLean] and escaped punishment.
Robbed W. F. & Co's Express on stage from Marysville to Downieville, July 31, 1877, in company with Eph. H. White.
Received at the California State Prison, November 8, 1877; No. of commitment, 7867; Crime, robbery; Term, 6 years; County sent from, Yuba.
Died in prison, July 26, 1880.

On July 2, 1871, Kirkendall's fast freight team was halted at a point below Corbett's Station and one of many passengers was robbed before help arrived and scared off the road agents. On July 9 a treasure box was removed from the stagecoach coming from Helena, Montana Territory bound for Corrine, Utah Territory. The investigation was going nowhere until Rugg was arrested and he informed on W. H. Heinsman and Donald McLean. Rugg, to secure his release, testified against them at trial, pled guilty, was convicted, immediately pardoned, and released [*see* Heinsman, W. H.].

Rugg went to Marysville, California, and led a law abiding life for four years but he was determined to be a road agent so he joined forces with E. H. "Eph." White. On July 31, 1877, the stagecoach bound for Downieville from Marysville in Yuba County driven by Johnny Sharp had only traveled a mile and a half from town on the lower road, about one hundred fifty yards from H. L. McCoy's place near a wooden bridge, when two road agents, one armed with a shotgun and the other with a Colt's revolver and a shotgun, stopped the coach. One robber told the passengers to disembark saying, "every one of you to the last man." Once everyone was standing in the road the robber with the pistol ordered Sharp to deliver the Wells, Fargo Express box, but Sharp replied that it was empty. The robber then told him again to throw out the box and he did. The robber took an ax and broke open the box, spilled the contents, and kicked the items about until he finally picked up one item but there seemed little of value inside. He went through the passengers taking everything of value including a silver "5 groschen" German coin carried by G. Schottler as a "good luck pocket piece." The passengers, which included Schottler, B. P. Hugg, J. H. Hart, Pat Elmore, Lawrence "Irish Jimmy" McCarrell, Samuel D. Johns, G. Shotier, and a Mr. Lyons, were ordered aboard and Sharp was told to continue. The coach hurried into town and

Sharp reported the robbery. Officer H. L. McCoy and George Hackett, a Wells, Fargo messenger, started for the scene and found two sets of boot tracks, one set of tracks for two men coming from town and the other set of two going in the direction of town. Both tracks were quite distinctive because of the pattern of nails and tacks in the heels and defects in the soles. They followed the tracks to the wooden bridge and from there into a levee coming from town, and then into town as far as Eleventh Street. It was clear that one set of two tracks were made after the coach passed as they were on top of the wheel ruts and the other before the coach passed as the ruts obliterated those two sets of tracks, and McCoy recorded the design of the boot tracks for later evidence. The investigation continued and evidence began to point to White and Rugg as both men had been seen on the road several times in the days before the robbery, apparently reconnoitering a place to commit the robbery. Finally on August 3 McCoy arrested White in Trickle's Saloon and soon afterward arrested Rugg, who was then working as a driver for the competing stage line from Marysville to Colusa. McCoy took their boots and matched the design with the tracks at the robbery scene and found they were identical. He also took their property and found in Rugg's pocket a silver "five groschen" coin." Their examination was set for August 16 and among those who testified were E. Brow who had made the boots for White and Rugg a week before the robbery, Albert Metz who had sold each man a shotgun, several men who had seen the two road agents looking over the road just days before the robbery, and driver Sharp who identified them by size and appearance. Along with a number of other witnesses and the physical evidence there was enough to hold them for the grand jury and Judge C. M. Gorham set their bail at $5,000 each.

On the first Sunday in October Rugg and prisoner Juan Sancho, another robber, tried to escape from the jail. The prisoners had braided a twenty-five foot rope from their woolen blankets which they were going to use to scale the outer wall, and they made a pole from several broom handles to throw up to secure the rope. The prisoners were turned out of their cells into the yard at 8:00 A.M. so the cells could be cleaned and the deputies, as was the practice, absented themselves from the yard as the wall was believed to be unscalable. However, the sheriff had word of the escape attempt and had his men take up positions for observation and posted several men outside the wall. As soon as the guards were out of the yard Rugg and Sancho went to work. They tried several times to toss the pole up on the northeast corner and then the southeast corner of the wall to secure the rope and climb out but every effort failed. Finally the officers had seen enough and returned to lock the prisoners in their cells and confiscate the escape equipment. Rugg and White were convicted of robbery in Yuba County, California, and sentenced to serve six years at San Quentin. Rugg arrived at the prison on November 8, 1877, and registered as prisoner No. 7868. Rugg died in the prison hospital, possibly of consumption, on July 26, 1880. White arrived at San Quentin Prison on November 12, 1877, and registered as prisoner No. 7874. He was released by expiration of sentence on January 12, 1882. It may be worthwhile to note that the Wells Fargo report has erroneous information regarding Eph. White, showing him sentenced to fifteen years, arriving on February 8, 1882, and registering as convict No. 10263, with the "county sent from" listed as Alameda, Cal.; but the prisoner number and information is accredited to convict John Wright and the date of transfer to Folsom prison listed is for William Miner; and Rugg's number in the report, No. 7867, is actually No. 7868.

Daily Appeal [Marysville, CA]: October 11, 1877. *Helena Daily Herald [MT]*: July 11–12, 1871; July 19, 1871. *Weekly Appeal [Marysville, CA]*: August 10, 1877; August 17, 1877.

Ruibal, Juan

Robbed W. F. & Co's Express on stage from Prescott to Yuma, A. T., October 6, 1878, in company with Jesus Moreno [*sic*].
Received at the Territorial Prison, Yuma, A. T., June 26, 1879; No. of commitment, 38; Crime, robbery; Term, 10 years.
Died in Yuma Prison, March 27, 1883.

The buckboard stagecoach left Prescott for Yuma on Sunday evening carrying only one passenger. At 8:00 P.M., as the coach reached a point nine miles west of the sink of Date Creek, it was stopped by two road agents. Lieutenant P. G. Wood was the only passenger and he was robbed of $585 and a watch, and the thieves were mean ones taking even a ten-cent piece out of his pocket, pen-knives and tobacco from him and from the driver, and refusing to give him back even a few dollars for meals. Wood had curled up on the seat and had just gone to sleep when he was awakened by a rough voice and prevented from "foolish demonstrations" by a gun pointed at him. He and the driver were blindfolded and made to sit down beside the road while the robbers gathered the plunder together. The robbers got three bars of silver bullion and the treasure box, which had little of value in it, but they did not disturb the mails. While sitting blindfolded Lieutenant Wood and the driver were made exceedingly nervous by the discharge of one of the robbers' guns, but it was an accidental discharge caused by nervousness and caused no harm. The Lieutenant described in detail the property stolen from him: "the watch was bought from Morgan the jeweler at Prescott, who has the number; a .36 caliber Smith and Wesson six-shooter, nickel plated with black handle; a pen knife and an old buckskin wallet." Wood also described the horse ridden by the younger robber as a light bay mare and was certain he could identify the robbers if seen again. On October 12 the *Salt River Herald* reported on the bullion stolen: "...Three bars of bullion from the Peck mine, valued at $5116 were also taken. This is said to be the first instance where silver bullion has been taken on this road, and the second in the Territory." The *Daily Miner* expressed concern over the most recent innovation in stagecoach robberies:

> ROBBERY RAMPANT— The stage robbing business now assuming a more serious aspect than heretofore. Silver bullion, the principal product of Arizona, has hitherto been considered safe from attack of robbers, owing to the weight of the bars and small worth as compared with gold or greenbacks, but on two recent occasions, at least, the freebooters have concluded to try the experiment of getting away with silver bullion, and so far as appears, at least, with temporary success. What the final result will be, of course, remains to be seen.... The recent robbing near Date Creek seems to have been one of the most daring yet perpetrated and is perhaps but a foretaste of what may be expected unless the most vigorous measures are adopted to catch and kill the guilty.

The Governor immediately offered a reward of $500 for each of the two coach robbers, Wells, Fargo & Company had a standing reward of $300 each, and Marshal Dake gave his assurance that "any extra expenses reasonably incurred in their capture, [he would] use his best endeavors to have put by the Department of the Government." There was no delay to starting in pursuit of the robbers and Eugene Whitcomb, stagecoach driver, brought word that Henry Adams with three men and William Gilson with two men "started from Date Creek on good horses and well armed ... intending to pursue and capture the robbers if possible." Several day later it was reported that Marshal Dake had sent men in all directions and that a party of Indian scouts was then en route to the scene of the robbery to act as trailers and trackers, and to try to find the bullion if hidden. William Gilson later reported that it was impossible to track the robbers as they had calculated coolly and prepared to elude their pursuers. He said that the point chosen for the robbery was one where bands of horses, mares and colts are running at large and making tens of thousands of tracks in all directions and the robbers intentionally were riding barefoot horses so that it was impossible to differentiate their tracks from the others. U.S. deputy Marshal Joseph W. Evans happened to be at Date Creek and he also took the field in pursuit of the robbers, and Dan O'Leary went out with a group of Wallapai Indians and "scoured very rough country without, however, doing more than satisfying himself that the coach was robbed by two Mexicans."

In February 1879 U.S. Marshal Dake received new information on the robbers and, with deputy R. H. Walker and J. N. Thacker of Nevada, a Wells, Fargo detective, was again on their trail. Dake and Thacker went by way of Wickenburg and Rawhide, always just behind their prey. By the time they arrived at the town of Signal Deputy R. H. Walker, who had arrived in town just in time to grab the two fugitives, had the two men jailed. The three lawmen took the robbers back to Prescott, arriving on the evening of the February 26, and on March 9, 1879, the *Weekly Miner* reported: "WAIVED EXAMINATION— The two Mexicans who were brought here a few days since, from Signal, on a charge of having robbed the stage, near Date Creek, on the 6th of October in which Lieutenant Woods lost his watch and about $500 in money and the Wells, Fargo & Co., three bars of bullion, were taken before Judge Cate on the 27th of February for examination. They waived examination and were held to answer before the next Grand Jury, one in the sum of $10,000 and the other $3000. Juan Ruibal had been arrested with Nicanora Rodrigues, a well-known Nevada badman. Testimony revealed that Jesus Molino had been Ruibal's partner in the robbery and that Rodrigues had only assisted in selling the bullion, but had not taken any part in the robbery. Only one bar of the bullion, valued at $2,000, was recovered by Wells Fargo and Co. detective J. B. Hume." The grand jury indicted Juan Ruibal and upon being arraigned he pled guilty and, "had divulged many things and made the officers but little trouble since being arrested," so the District Attorney asked the court to make the sentence as light as the enormity of the offense would permit. The court agreed and sentenced Ruibal to serve ten years at the Territorial Prison near Yuma. Efforts continued to bring Jesus Molino to jail and the authorities received word of the fugitive in the eastern portion of the Territory. "Messrs. Walker and Pierce were sent to capture him. They traveled over 800 miles, but the lead was false and they came back without their man." The *Miner* then reported, "The information that was given here in regard to Molino being in that section was altogether hearsay, and the parties alluded to were found to bear good names." Molino was never tried for the robbery and was not heard of again in the Territory.

Daily Miner [Prescott, AZ]: October 8–10, 1878; October 28, 1878; February 27, 1879; March 15, 1879; March 31, 1879. *Enterprise [Prescott, AZ]*: October 12, 1878; October 26, 1878. *Salt River Herald [Phoenix, AZ]*: March 15, 1879; June 25, 1879; June 27–28, 1879; October 12, 1879. *Sentinel [Yuma, AZ]*: October 12, 1878. *Weekly Miner [Prescott, AZ]*: March 7, 1879; March 21, 1879.

Ruiz, Ramon

Nativity, California; Age, 48 years; Occupation, Laborer; Height, 5 feet 5 inches; Complexion, Yellow; Color of eyes, Dark; Color of hair, Black. Flat large nose, mole on left cheek-bone, mole right side of nose, number of small moles right side of neck and breast, scar on left thumb, several scars on left forefinger, right and left little fingers crooked.

No. of first commitment, 1243. Received at the California State Prison, October 27, 1857; Crime, assault with deadly weapon; Term, 1 year; County sent from, Los Angeles.
Discharged, by expiration of sentence, October 22, 1858.
No. of second commitment, 2165. Received at the California State Prison, May 11, 1861; Crime, manslaughter; Term, 3 years 2 months; County sent from, Contra Costa.
Discharged, by expiration of sentence, June 1, 1864.
No. of third commitment, 3683. Received at the California State Prison, November 15, 1867; Crime, grand larceny; Term, 5½ years; County sent from, Contra Costa.
Discharged, by expiration of sentence, July 2, 1872.
Robbed W. F. & Co's Express on stage from Laporte to Oroville, August 3, 1875, with Red Antone, Jose Lenaris, and Isador Pardillo.
Attempted to rob W. F. & Co's Express on stage from Sonora to Milton, October 12, 1875, in company with "Old Joaquin," and "Big Mitch" and "Little Mitch."
Robbed W. F. & Co's Express on stage from Chinese Camp to Copperopolis, December 1, 1875 — alone.
No. of fourth commitment, 7083. Received at the California State Prison, July 25, 1876; Crime, robbery; Term, 4 years; County sent from, Calaveras.
Discharged, by expiration of sentence, July 25, 1879.
No. of fifth commitment, 9034. Received at the California State Prison, October 14, 1879; Crime, robbery; Term, 2 years; County sent from, Tuolumne.
Discharged, June 14, 1881.

Ramon Ruiz began his career as a horse thief and would return to that profession several times but, as he became popular in the saloons and gambling dens of old California, his reputation also grew to include assaults and killings. After serving several terms at San Quentin Prison he joined a gang led by Isador, or Ysidro, Pardillo, sometimes spelled Padillo. Pardillo divided his gang into two parties and put Joaquin Olivera in charge of the second band. They divided their territory with Pardillo headquartering near Doty's Flat and Olivera's party quartering at Jackson in Amador County. During the two year period of 1874–1875 a number of stagecoach robberies were attributed to one party or the other but there was no hard evidence to implicate any of the members. In November 1874 they stopped the coach from Sonora in Tuolumne County to Milton in Calaveras County and on March 23, 1875, they stopped the same coach again. On August 3, 1875, Ruiz, in the company of Pardillo, Jose Lenaris and Joaquin Olivera robbed the Laporte, Plumas County to Oroville, Butte County stagecoach and on October 5 they stopped the same coach. On October 12, 1875, Ruiz, with Antone "Old Joaquin" Savage, Mitchell "big Mitch" Ratovich, and Mitchell "little Mitch" Brown stopped the coach from Sonora to Milton. The driver told them the express box would be coming on the coach which was following at some distance and the robbers waved him on. They waited for quite a while before they realized there was but one coach on the route that day. On December 1, 1875, Ruiz, alone, stopped the coach from Sonora to Copperopolis by way of Chinese Camp in Tuolumne County and demanded the express box. This time Ruiz would accept no excuses and the box was delivered, he broke it open, and took out $600 in gold coin and dust. Ruiz did not cover his face and driver Jack Gibbons gave a detailed description to Tuolumne County Sheriff Ben K. Thorn. Thorn went to the scene and tracked Ruiz to a cabin near Telegraph City in Calaveras County and on December 9, 1875, the lawman broke in on Ruiz and surprised the unarmed bandit before he could get hold of his pistols. Ruiz informed on the gang and soon all of the members were either killed or captured. Pardillo died in prison on May 7, 1877; Joaquin Olivera was discharged from prison on November 17, 1882; Mitchell "big Mitch" Ratovich was discharged from prison on April 23, 1878; Mitchell "little Mitch"

Brown was discharged from prison on October 5, 1885. The losses to Wells, Fargo were so great and the inability of lawmen to find and arrest the road agents that the company in December 1875 temporarily suspended express operations in the area. In April 1876 Ruiz was convicted of the October 12, 1875, robbery and sentenced to serve only four years, in consideration of his cooperation with lawmen. He arrived at San Quentin prison on July 25, 1876, and was released on July 25, 1879, upon expiration of his sentence, with time off for good behavior. As Ruiz exited the prison he was arrested by Tuolumne Sheriff Tyron M. Yancey for the December 1, 1875, stagecoach robbery. He was tried, convicted, and received another two year sentence, arriving at the prison on October 14, 1879, and being released on June 14, 1881. After his release Ruiz tried horse stealing again and managed to elude capture. In November the Sonora to Milton stagecoach was robbed and Ruiz was arrested and questioned but he proved an alibi and was released. He again tried horse stealing and ended in prison once more, this time for a four year term. When he was released he went to Baja, California, and opened a butcher shop, but it soon became apparent he was selling more beef than he bought legally so, when a mob of ranchers came to put an end to the rustling, Ruiz fled. Narrowly missing a lynching seemed to have quite an effect on Ruiz, and he "went straight" and became a tamale vendor in the Angel's Camp area. In the summer of 1899 he caught a serious chest infection and, medical knowledge and skill being primitive in those days, he was able to do little to cure the malady. On August 31, 1899, Ramon Ruiz suddenly collapsed in the street of Angel's Camp and died.

Calaveras Prospect, [CA]: September 2, 1899. *Calaveras Weekly Citizen [CA]*: October 13, 1875; September 2, 1899. *Morning Tribune [San Luis Obispo, CA]*: December 13, 1873. *Union Democrat [Sonora, CA]*: December 4, 1875; June 13, 1997.

Russell, William

Nativity, Scotland; Age 40 years; Occupation, Carpenter; Height, 5 feet 7¼ inches; Complexion, Florid; Color of eyes, Blue; Color of hair, Brown. Long full features, high forehead, Goddess of Art inside of left forearm, scar base of left thumb, British coat of arms inside right forearm; stout built.

Robbed W. F. & Co's Express on 2 stages running between Lakeport and Calistoga, June 12, 1877, with James R. Dollar.

Received at the California State prison, July 3, 1877. No. of commitment, 7652; Crime, robbery — two commitments; Term, 9 years; County sent from, Napa.

Commuted by Governor George C. Perkins, July 28, 1882, to 7½ years, and *discharged*, September 28, 1882.

[*See* Dollar, James R.]

Rutherford, John

Nativity, Missouri; Age, 36 years; Occupation, Laborer; Height 5 feet 6¾ inches; Complexion, Florid; Color of eyes, Brown; Color of hair, Brown; Size of foot, 6. Long features, small ears, hair very thin on top of head, nearly bald, sharp nose slightly turned to one side, vaccine mark on left upper arm, heavy black eyebrows, small chin, small mole low down on back, small mole on top of left shoulder, square shouldered; stout built.

Robbed W. F. & Co's Express on stage from Santa Maria to Guadalupe, September 23, 1884, in company with James Thompson.

Received at the California State Prison, December 16, 1884; No. of commitment, 11494; Crime, robbery; Term, 12 years; County sent from, Santa Barbara.

The stagecoach for Guadalupe in Santa Barbara County, driven by seventeen year old Wesley Froom, left the rail depot at Santa Maria at 7:15 P.M., Monday night September 22, 1884. The coach was moving at a slow pace due to heavy fog and as they approached the graveyard near Guadalupe at 7:45 P.M. Froom heard two shots fired in quick succession followed by the command "Halt!" Next came the order "Throw out the treasure box," but Froom replied that he could not as it was too heavy. He was then commanded to exert himself and, if needed, get the aid of a passenger though there was only one passenger, a drummer, aboard. He glanced toward the voice and saw two horses and behind each was a man with a pistol pointed in his direction. He then applied himself and managed to get the box over the edge of the boot and let it tumble to the ground. As soon as the box was on the road one robber ordered him to continue on, and "not look back under pain of death." Froom whipped up his team and hurried into Guadalupe to report the robbery. The town became quite excited and within minutes there were several bands of armed men scouring the surrounding country-side. C. W. Merrit, acting agent for Wells, Fargo & Company at Guadalupe, with deputy sheriff T. C. Nance and constable Lierly hurried to Santa Maria. At 9:15 P.M. two riderless horses came into town and fifteen minutes later two men walked in from the east and went directly to Graves' Saloon. These men were already suspected as they had been making daily trips to the stage depot in Santa Maria and their absence at the time of the robbery added to the suspicion. Nance and Lierly, after deputizing Merrit and a man named Cook, arrested the two men without incident and they gave their names as James Thompson and John Rutherford. In Santa Maria on the night of the robbery James Thompson had been so intent on watching the loading of the box that he was conspicuous, and Rutherford stood nearby leaning on a rail. They saw that the box, when loaded on the coach at Santa Maria, was very heavy. Immediately after the box was loaded the two men were looked for in Santa Maria and missed and the horses belonging to the Tunnell brothers, James and Henry, also went missing, and these were the two riderless horses which came into town an hour and a half after the robbery. The saddles showed wear and had "blue paint marks similar to the color of the treasure boxes" on one saddle. Lawmen were sure that the road agents had taken the box some distance from the scene of the robbery and hidden it so on Tuesday morning, September 23 parties were sent out to look for the treasure box. Two men saw where a fence had been cut recently and followed two sets of horse tracks to a field of haystacks. Late in the afternoon Lark Thornburgh and J. B. Darden found the box in one of the haystacks within two hundred yards of the place where the robbery occurred. The box was taken into town, opened, and all of its contents were found intact including $1,860.

The two prisoners had their examination on Tuesday, September 30 and they claimed to have an alibi and could prove they were at the "disreputable house" when the robbery occurred. However, at the hearing Louis Hertz said he was responsible for delivering the box at the depot and he saw both defendants there after he checked the waybill and contents and locked the box, and while he was delivering it to the stagecoach. After the box was recovered it showed signs of hard use and it was entered into evidence. Stagecoach driver Froom testified that, "on the road near the graveyard two men stopped me, they had cut through the field and when I turned the corner they were in front of me. I saw that one had a light roan and the other a darker horse, but I could not see the men." James Tunnell then said he had hitched his dark roan to the rail and when he returned the horse was gone. When it returned it was very tired, the saddle was cut and worn, and there was blue paint, like the treasure box, on the saddle; and Henry Clay Tunnell said about the same of his light roan horse and saddle. Hugh Graves testified that the defendants were in the habit of spending their evening in his saloon but did not arrive on the night of the robbery until 9:30 P.M.; they had lunch and then were arrested. Deputy sheriff Nance said he had taken one pistol from each man and each pistol had one round fired recently. N. H. Rose then testified to boot tracks and matched them to Rutherford's boots. Charles De Witt testified that he was on the road ahead of the coach and saw Rutherford and another man he did not recognize riding hard for Guadalupe just before the robbery. After several recesses, and motions to dismiss, the defendants were held over for trial with bail set at $6,000. The two men were tried in the Superior Court and convicted of the stagecoach robbery in December 1884. Rutherford was sentenced to serve twelve years and Thompson was sentenced to ten years, and both men arrived at the prison on December 16, 1884. Thompson was released, by expiration of sentence, on June 16, 1891. Rutherford was released, by expiration of sentence, on August 16, 1892.

Santa Maria Times [CA]: September 27, 1884; October 4, 1884. *Territorial Enterprise [Virginia City, NV]*: September 28, 1884.

Sansome, John

Nativity, Missouri; Age, 46 years; Occupation, Laborer; Height 5 feet 7 inches; Complexion, Fair; Color of eyes, Gray; Color of hair, Brown. Three small scars on left cheek, small mole on left side of chin, numerous warts on both hands, good looking, well built.

No. of first commitment, 2505. Received at the California State Prison, February 13, 1863; Crime, grand larceny; Term 1 year; County sent from, San Joaquin.

Discharged by expiration of sentence, February 11, 1864.

No. of second term, 2800. Received at the California State Prison, July 30, 1864; Crime, grand larceny; Term, 3 years; County sent from, San Francisco.

Escaped, January 14, 1866.

No. of third term, 3259. Received at the California State Prison, April 17, 1866; Crime, burglary; Term, 3 years; County sent from, Contra Costa.

Discharged by expiration of sentence, November 6, 1868.

No. of fourth term, 4873. Received at California State Prison, May 11, 1871. Crime, burglary and grand larceny; Term, 18 years; County sent from, Sutter.

Escaped, December 3, 1872, and recaptured January 14, 1874. Taken out on a writ of *habeas corpus*, by order of the Supreme Court and *discharged*.

Burglarized W. F. & Co's office at Quincey May 24, 1875, in company with Frank Barker.

Received at California State Prison, October 7, 1875; No. of commitment, 6707; Crime, burglary; Term, 15 years; County sent from, Plumas.

Transferred to Folsom Prison, December 4, 1880.

Escaped December 27, 1881; *recaptured*, January 10, 1882.

[See Barker, Frank, regarding W. F. & Co. burglary of May 24, 1875.]

Savage, Antone—*alias* Old Joaquin

Nativity, Portugal; Age, 75 years; Occupation, Laborer; Height, 5 feet 9½ inches; Complexion, Dark; Color of eyes, Hazel; Color of hair, Gray. Long spare features, face pock-marked, head bald, thick protruding lips, scar between the chin and lower lip, several small scars on the left jaw-bone, 2 small flesh moles on the lower part of neck — left side, 2 warts under left ear, scar between second and third joints of middle finger of left hand, 2 scars on the back of right hand, several small moles on right breast, flesh moles on point of right shoulder, do. on the back do., shoulders hairy, large veins on the temples; slim built.

No. of first commitment, 3655. Received at the California State Prison, October 10, 1867; Crime, grand larceny; Term, 2 years, County sent from, Alameda.
Discharged, by expiration of sentence, June 23, 1869.
Robbed W. F. & Co's Express on stage from Sonora to Milton, March 23, 1875, in company with "Big Mitch" and "Little Mitch."
Attempted to rob W. F. & Co's Express on stage from Sonora to Milton, October 12, 1875.
Received at the California State Prison, May 17, 1876; No. of commitment, 7029; Crime, robbery; Term, 10 years; County sent from Calaveras.
Discharged, per Act, November 17, 1882.
[*See* Ruiz, Ramon]

Saylor, George B.

Nativity, Pennsylvania; Age, 21 years; Occupation, Cigar-maker; Height, 5 feet 8¾ inches; Complexion, Light; Color of eyes, Blue; Color of hair, Brown; Size of foot, 8. Spare features, big forehead, long thin nose, small chin, two small moles on right breast, two small moles between shoulders, vaccine mark on left upper arm, small scar back of right hand, small scar inside right forearm, sloping shoulders; slim built.
Robbed W. F. & Co's Express on stage from Sierra Valley to Truckee, August 13, 1883, in company with John Marshall. Fled the country; was arrested in Baltimore, Md., and brought back for trial by W. F. & Co. special officers.
Received at the California State Prison, February 2, 1884; No. of commitment, 11118; Crime, robbery; Term, 7 years; County sent from, Sierra.
[*See* Marshall, John]

Schalten, L.

Nativity, Idaho; Age, 24 years; Occupation, Saddler; Height, 5 feet 7¼ inches; Complexion, Florid; Color of eyes, Brown; Color of hair, Brown; Size of foot, 8½. Long features, broad forehead, projecting chin, large scar on left cheek, Large scar on breast, large scar on breast under left nipple, large scar on second joint of left thumb, mole on tight side of head, mole on top of left shoulder, mole under left elbow; slim built.
Robbed W. F. & Co's Express on stage from Bishop Creek to Bishop Creek R. R. Station, December 29, 1883, in company with T. C. Harniss and A. F. Mairs.
Received at the California State Prison, February 25, 1884. No. of commitment, 11153; Crime, robbery; Term, 2½ years; County sent from, Inyo.
[*See* Harniss, T. C.]

Scott, Tarlton B.—*alias* Scotty

Age, 35 years; Height, 5 feet 8 inches; Complexion, Sandy; Color of eyes, Blue; Color of hair, Sandy.
Robbed W. F. & Co's Express on stage from Boise to Silver City, February 2, 1876, in company with John W. Miller.
Robbed W. F. & Co's Express on stage from Silver City to Boise, April 19, 1876, in company with John W. Miller.
Received at the Penitentiary near Boise, December 20, 1876; No. of commitment —; Crime robbery; Term, 7 years; County sent from, Ada, I. T.
Escaped from Prison, May 5, 1877.
[*See* Miller, John W.]

Sharania, Manuel—*alias* Manuel Chavarria

Nativity, Chile; Age 54 years, Occupation, Tailor, Height 5 feet 7½ inches; Complexion, Dark; Color of eyes, Black; Color of hair, Dark Brown. High forehead, thin bony features, woman under wreath over left nipple, eagle with cactus and flag crossed over a breast-plate, "Tomas Busta" in large letters, Buenos Ayres [*sic*] and Chilian flag over woman, "M. C." in large letters and bracelet on left arm in ink, scar from cupping on left shoulder.

Robbed W. F. & Co's Express on stage from Belleville to Carson, March 6, 1876, with Joe Estrado and James Wallace.

Received at the Nevada State Prison, April 6, 1876. No. of commitment, —; Crime, robbery; Term, 10 years; County sent from, Esmeralda.

Discharged, upon expiration of sentence, November 6, 1884.

[*See* Estrado, Joe]

Sharp, M. A.

Nativity, Missouri; Age, 39 years; Occupation, Laborer; Height, 5 feet 6 inches; Complexion, Dark; Color of eyes, Dark Brown; Color of hair, Dark Brown; Weight, 161 lbs. Large Roman nose, scar over right eye, scar on back of head, scar across right forearm, scar on first finger of right hand, scar on back of neck, two scars on right knee-cap; does not smoke, chew, swear, nor gamble.

Robbed W, F. & Co's Express on stage from Forest Hill to Auburn [Calif.] May 15, 1880, in company with W. C. Jones, alias Frank Dow.

Robbed W, F. & Co's Express on stage from Carson City to Bodie, June 8, 1880, with Jones, alias Dow.

Robbed W, F. & Co's Express on stage from Carson to Bodie, June 15, 1880, with Jones, alias Dow.

Robbed W, F. & Co's Express on stage from Auburn to Forest Hill [Calif.], August 6, 1880, with Jones.

Robbed W, F. & Co's Express on stage from Carson City to Bodie, September 4, 1880, in company with Jones.

Robbed W, F. & Co's Express on stage from Bodie to Carson the morning of September 5. At the time of halting the stage Jones fired two shots, killing one of the stage horses. Mike Tovey, W. F. & Co's guard, then fired, killing Jones. Sharp then fired, seriously wounding Tovey in the right arm. Tovey being disabled, started for a neighboring farm-house to have his arm dressed, when Sharp returned to the stage, demanded the box from the driver, and robbed it of $700, while Jones was lying dead in the road, and the stage being detained by the dead horse still attached to the team.

On October 30, 1880, Sharp was convicted of the robbery of September 4, 1880.

Escaped from the Aurora jail, November 8, 1880.

Recaptured and returned to the Aurora jail, November 8, 1880.

Received at the Nevada State Prison, November 12, 1880; No. of commitment, 158; Crime, robbery; Term, 20 years; County sent from, Esmeralda, Nev.

Milton Anthony Sharp's mother Elisabeth managed to raise her family of eight, four brothers and four sisters, near Lee's Summit, Missouri without the assistance of their father. She was determined that her children receive at least a moderate education and after Milton completed his schooling he helped support the family until he left home in 1866 at the age of twenty-six. He made his way to California and Nevada where he worked as a miner over the next dozen years. He had a penchant for investing in questionable mining stocks but never managed to strike it rich. In 1879 after going broke once again Sharp was working on the farm of Peter Ahart on the outskirts of Auburn, California, when he met William C. Jones, alias Frank Dow. Jones had just been released from prison and took a menial job on the Ahart farm, but the ex-convict still had a desire to find the perfect opportunity to make a "big haul." Jones managed to convinced Sharp to join him in a stagecoach robbing scheme and assured his thirty-nine year old "green" partner that he had learned the business well. The two aspiring road agents worked at the Ahart farm a while longer, accumulating a stake, and then disappeared. They stocked a deserted cabin and laid low for months expecting to be forgotten. On May 15, 1880, the two men suddenly appeared on the road between Forest Hill, California, and Auburn Station, less than one mile from the latter place, and stopped the down coach. They made the passengers line up along the road and searched them and the driver, taking $150 dollars and several valuable watches, and then quickly made their escape into Nevada.

On June 8 Jones and Sharp stopped the Carson City to Aurora coach driven by Cambridge, and carrying seven passengers, when it was in the vicinity of Dalzell's station between Sulphur Springs and Sweetwater. On board when the coach left Carson City were Edward B. Shaw, Mr. Rowe, Mr. Kinssendorf, J. F. Nugent, Mrs. Cass, John O'Donnell and S. Gambriner but two of the men got off at some way station along the route. Both road agents were masked and held shotguns on the driver while they ordered him to throw out the treasure box, which he did immediately. The passengers who were still aboard were ordered out and told to line-up and place their hands on their heads. One of the robbers held his shotgun on the passengers while the other searched them for valuables. Nugent said that when the coach was stopped he took his gold watch chain and a gold ring and put them in the hollow of his palm, and in that way saved them from the robbers, but his silver watch and $14 dollars were collected. Shaw of Cutting & Company was relieved of a gold watch and chain and $12, but the robbers overlooked $100 in a side pocket. Mrs. Cass was robbed of $9, all she had, and Kinssendorf was forced to give up his lunch but saved $37 by dropping it between his pants and drawers. Kinssendorf was asked if he had any money and he answered that he had none so one of the robbers remarked he would give him a half dollar coin, but never handed it over. They even went through the driver taking his watch but promised to return it "when next we meet." The road agents delayed the coach for over an hour while working on the express box and finally took out $3000 dollars before telling the driver to continue on his route, and it was estimated that the aggregate take was over $4,000. The driver hurried into Aurora to report the robbery and Wells Fargo's agent at Carson City, H. L. Tickner, took a shotgun messenger and went to the scene to investigate but could find no trace or clue. On June 15 the duo stopped the up-coach on the Carson City to Bodie run eighteen miles beyond Wellington's station near Dalzell's station, the same place they stopped the coach on June 8. Cambridge was again driving and just as they came to a bend in the road which required the driver to slow his team passenger John Cameron, riding next to the driver, asked, "Wasn't the stage robbed some where along here?" Cambridge answered, "This is the very spot," and in that moment the same two road agents stepped onto the road and covered the men with shotguns. The coach stopped and the box was thrown out when the order was given, but this time it carried only $300. The robbers did not molest the driver or Cameron, nor the inside passengers which included Mrs. R. Crown, Mrs. McBride and child, I. Stead, and I. W. Smith. An hour later the down coach loaded with bullion passed the same location but passed safely, probably because there were three shotgun messengers aboard. The *Carson Daily Appeal* on June 17 had an opportunity to reflect on the frequency of the robberies on the Carson City to Bodie route:

> ROBBERS BEHIND TIME— There was no attempt made yesterday to rob the Bodie stage. When the stage reached the spot where the robberies generally occur the horses stopped as usual and remained at a dead standstill for about fifteen minutes from force of habit. No

robbers appeared, and then they jogged on. It is supposed that the foot pads over slept themselves. The robbers who do business along the Bodie line should be up and stirring with the lark or else they are liable to get left. The stage from Carson is a fast concern and can't bother to wait for road agents who are not promptly on hand. Business is business with us every time.

On June 22 the *Appeal* remarked that they had recently published a "foot pad map" to guide parties in pursuing the road agents and Virginia City's *Territorial Enterprise* said, "In the history of journalism in this country there has probably never been so marked an instance of appreciation of enterprise as that displayed by the entire press of the land for work performed by the Carson Appeal in publishing a map of the route taken by the Bodie stage robbers, for the guidance of Indians in pursuit of the highwaymen. It is true the Indians have not caught the robbers yet, but that is the fault of the Indians, not the map." Jones and Sharp wrote to the editor of the *Appeal* and said:

Sweetwater, June 19, 1880

Editor Appeal: We pause a few moments on our route south to state that we have just received a copy of your map marking our movements since we robbed the Bodie stage. In our opinion your meddlesome interference is wholly without the province of journalism. The map is correct as far as it goes but it will never do the State any service. We have already ordered a fresh lot printed at the Bodie *News* office (never heard of the paper — Ed.) and when the Indians get hold of them they will be thrown completely off the scent. If in future you will devote yourself to the business of instructing the Republican party of Ormsby county and let our business take care of itself we have every reason to believe that your paper will give much better satisfaction in Nevada.

Yours,
Slim Jim
Club-foot Jack

The standing reward of $300 per robber had been posted by Wells, Fargo for the capture and conviction of the two road agents so several posses were soon in the field. A large force of Indians was also pursuing the robbers and Wells, Fargo's chief detective James B. Hume was brought out of Utah and put on the case. It was getting too hot for Jones and Sharp in Nevada so, with several good hauls to split between them, they decided to lay low for a while and crossed over into California. On August 6 the two masked road agents took up their positions a short distance from the Grizzly Bear House, two miles from Auburn, and at 6:30 P.M. they stopped the up-stagecoach from Auburn to Forest Hill as it was climbing the North Fork hill. They ordered the passengers to get out and line up and one of the robbers held a shot gun on them while the second robber tried to open the treasure safe bolted inside the passenger compartment. He could not get it open so the robbers had the passengers board, the road agent with the shotgun boarding with them, and the other taking a seat next to the driver and ordered him to steer his team a quarter mile off the road. Once again they lined up the passengers and then managed to break the safe free from the coach. When it was on the ground they opened the iron box with a hammer and cold chisel and found $1,500 inside. Next they went through the two passengers and from John McAllis they took $100, but he was able to drop his valuable gold watch into his boot; from Father Cassidy, a Catholic priest from Oakland, they took $80 and a gold watch valued at $250. The Father pleaded for them to return the watch saying it had been given to him by friends, but they refused. The robbers then ordered everyone to board and told the driver to return to the road and continue on his way. The driver, the same man who was driving the California coach which had been robbed on May 15, said later he was certain these were the same men.

The robbers returned to Nevada and on Monday, August 30, 1880, the stagecoach from Belleville to Candelaria was stopped by two road agents near Coal Valley Station and driver G. Finley was ordered to halt. Finley ignored the order and one of the road agents fired at him, the bullet passing between him and a passenger. The sound of the pistol startled the team and they took off on a dead run, urged on by Finley's whip, and the road agents were identified as the same two men who had been working the road from Aurora to Carson City. On September 2, 1880, the stagecoach from Bodie, California, to Mammoth City, Nevada, which was located on the road between Aurora and Carson City near the Mammoth Ledge, was robbed. When Wells, Fargo & Company's chief detective James B. Hume reported the event in his famed report of 1885 he laid blame upon Jesse Pearson, sometimes spelled Pierce or Pierson. Hume mistakenly reported the date as September 27, 1880, and the destination of the coach as "Monmouth." However, by the end of August 1880 mining operations had ceased at Mammoth City and Wells, Fargo & Company closed their office the week previous to the robbery, so this was the last shipment of money sent to Mammoth City by way of Wells, Fargo Express. The Bodie newspapers reported on October 10, 1880: "On Saturday afternoon, as the coach hence for Mammoth City, was a mile or two this side of King's Ranch, a man whose face was blackened and tarred after the most improved Digger style, stepped boldly up, rifle in hand, and demanded the express box. His demand was complied with, when he commanded the chief engineer of the buckboard to "move on," and this command was also obeyed. The stolen express box contained $800 in coin. There was no clue to the perpetrator of the robbery." By November 1881 Genoa's *Weekly Courier* reported, "Mammoth City is now almost deserted, the only business house there being P. A. Wagner's store and the brewery. The Mammoth Mill is being torn down and ... shipped to Bodie...." The September 2 encounter was brief and, as will be seen in the robbery of September 4, the robbers were using masks made of black oil cloth such as that used to make buggy tops. This shiny black material was mistaken for a tar coating to disguise the face of the robber — either Jones or Sharp — while the other road agent remained concealed. It was Sharp and Jones, not Pearson, who were active on the road eastward from Bodie at that time. On September 3 at 9:00 P.M. the two men stopped the Bodie to Carson City coach near the forks of Hall and Simpson's road nine miles south of Wellington's Station, but they were interrupted and fled without getting anything. At 2:30 A.M. the return coach was five miles from the place where the previous robberies had occurred when shot gun guard Mike Tovey, who rode next to the driver, saw footprints in the roadway traveling in the same direction as the coach. He ordered the driver to stop, lit a lantern and got down to investigate, and then about every half mile he repeated the process. When they reached the place the coach had been stopped the night before Tovey got down and, as before, he bent over to examine the tracks next to the near leader of the team. Just then Jones and Sharp appeared out of the darkness and Jones covered Tovey with a rifle and ordered, "Throw up your hands, you ___." Sharp was behind Jones and said, "You are trying to sneak up on us, are you?"

Tovey straightened up and, throwing up his hands, said, "Don't shoot; I'll go back and get the box," and Jones replied, "Go back, you whelp, and if you make a move we'll murder every mother's son of you." As Jones spoke Sharp, also armed with a rifle, stepped around his partner and fired a single shot toward Tovey but the bullet went into the chest of the nigh leader. The horse lunged forward several times and then sank to the ground, dead. The others horses began to lunge and rear but they could not run away because the dead horse held them in place. This distracted the robbers long enough for Tovey to make his way behind the stagecoach, so he was now behind the lamps in darkness while both robbers were at the dim edge of the light coming from the coach lamps. Tovey whispered to J. Billings, the division agent who was also riding guard on the box, "Hand down that gun," and Billings passed down Tovey's double barreled shotgun. Tovey crouched behind the coach and rested the barrel of his shotgun on the rear wheel, then waited patiently for the robbers to advance on the coach. Sharp moved to the right to flank the coach while Jones came straight forward saying, "Don't move or I'll murder every last ___." Tovey shouted out, "Who's moving?" which covered the sound of cocking his shot gun. Tovey then continued in a tone simulating fear, "You've got the drop on us. Come and get what you want." Tovey's voice must have convinced Jones that he had the upper hand because he lowered his rifle and advanced into the full glare of the lamps. Tovey then said loudly to the driver, "Throw down the box, quick, and let's get out of this." Jones again muttered something about murdering everybody, moved forward again until he was next to the fallen leader and said, "Your heads are level." These were the last words he spoke as Tovey opened up with the right barrel of his shotgun and the load of heavy buckshot struck Jones in the face killing him instantly. The dead man fell under the horses and one of the swingers, a middle horse in a six-up, began to rear and lunge stomping Jones' legs to mush. Within a few seconds Billings had retrieved his weapon and fired several rounds at Sharp while Tom Woodruff, the messenger riding inside the coach, pulled his six-shooter and also fired at the second robber. Sharp was returning fire when Tovey ran to the rear of the coach and came face-to-face with Sharp not twenty yards away. Tovey fired one barrel without effect and the road agent returned fire striking Tovey in the right arm, which shattered one of the bones between his wrist and elbow. Tovey dropped his shotgun causing the second barrel, which he had reloaded after shooting Jones, to discharge harmlessly. Tovey next managed to pull his revolver with his left hand and fire after the fleeing robber twice but being right-handed his shots missed. Tovey examined his wound and saw that he was bleeding profusely so he called to Billings and Woodruff to take him to Hall and Simpson's house not far off the road. Woodruff, who had pursued Sharp into a stand of willows but lost him there, returned and they took Tovey to the farm house where the bleeding was stopped and the wound bandaged. As soon as the three guards were out of sight the driver heard a voice say, "Throw down that box," and he looked back to find Sharp covering him with a Henry rifle. The driver, who was unarmed, threw down the box and Sharp cut it open with a hatchet. He pocketed the few hundred dollars it held but in his haste missed a package of $800 in coin. The robber next asked the driver which way his partner had gone, as Sharp was behind the coach and could not see Jones lying in the road between the horses. The driver, who was afraid to speak the truth, said he did not know. Sharp then walked off into the darkness while calling to his partner several times as he made his way into the brush. The messengers came back in a short time and were surprised to hear that the foot pad had been so brazen as to come back after the treasure. The guards examined the dead robber and saw that the buckshot had struck him in the lower part of his face, taking out the lower jaw; one buckshot had taken out an eye; and there was blood oozing from several neck wounds. The deceased was tall, dark complected, with a black moustache and probably a goatee, as there were some remnants of a beard on the lower part of the neck which remained. The deceased was dressed in dark clothes but there seemed little else to determine his identity. The body was carried a short distance off the road and buried deep enough to protect it from scavengers, and the grave was marked so it could be easily found later.

Detective Hume was still investigating this series of stagecoach robberies so he went to the scene and exhumed the dead robber's remains. He returned to Carson on September 10 and told the editor of the *Daily Appeal* that he had cleaned up the face of the corpse and took a long look but could not identify the remains, though he had expected to recognize him as a road agent from lower California. He had gone through the deceased's pockets for clues and collected the mask he wore, which was made of black glazed oil cloth of the type used in carriage tops, and Hume left for California on the next stagecoach. Hume had found a bank deposit book in the robber's pocket but kept this a secret, and from it he learned that the dead road agent shared a room in a Minna Street boarding house in San Francisco. The book also showed that both men had made substantial deposits in the Savings Union on the same day and that the deceased robber was named W. C. Jones, while the fugitive was M. A. Sharp. Hume coordinated his efforts with the police in San Francisco and Chief Crowley detailed detectives to examine the fugitive's room. Detectives Coffey and Jones found, in a valise, the watch and chain belonging to E. B. Shaw, another stolen watch and ring, and material resembling the dead robber's mask. The two detectives remained in the room waiting for Sharp to return and finally he arrived, telling the landlady he had come for his valise. The officers sprang from the room and covered Sharp with pistols, threw their prisoner to the floor, took a new Colt's six-shooter from his belt, and put on the handcuffs. Their prisoner had been carrying a roll of blankets when he entered the house and it contained another six-shooter and a Bowie knife, which the officers collected. Sharp was then searched thoroughly and the detectives found $1,600 in a money belt tied around his waist and $800 sewn into his coat lining. Sharp gave his correct name but denied knowing anyone named W. C. Jones. He said he had only come to get his property to move to another house and claimed a partner named Frank Keith, but could not say where he was. The landlady was then given the description of Jones and she confirmed that Jones was the man who shared the room with Sharp. Hume took custody of the prisoner and returned him to Carson City on September 18. By October 1 the prisoner was lodged in the Aurora jail and his bail had been set at $10,000. The grand jury had returned seven indictments: four for robberies from Wells, Fargo & Company, one for robbing driver Cambridge, one for robbing Ed Shaw, and one for attempting to kill Mike Tovey. On October 24 Sharp escaped from the jail by making a hole in the east side of the courthouse through a wall three bricks thick, but the streets were crowded so a large posse was soon raised and they began scouring the hills. Sharp was soon captured and his trial, set for October 27, was not delayed. He was convicted on the second robbery indictment on October 30 and trial on indictments three through seven were postponed. He was sentenced to twenty years in prison on the first conviction so the other charges were dropped and on November 12 Sharp was delivered to the Nevada State Prison where he registered as prisoner No. 158.

Sharp, through model behavior, earned trusty status which gave him the opportunity to escape from prison, which he accomplished on August 15, 1889. Sharp remained free for several years taking work at menial jobs in California to remain unnoticed. On the evening of June 15, 1893, Mike Tovey was shot and killed while riding messenger on the Ione to Jackson stagecoach. The robber made no effort to rob the coach after the killing which raised strong suspicion that it had been a murder for revenge committed by Sharp. This renewed the effort to find the escapee and on September 28, 1893, he was recognized and arrested. Sharp gave a detailed account of his whereabouts for the years after he escaped from prison and, consequently, was cleared of the murder of Tovey. Sharp was returned to the Nevada State Prison but was paroled, on the recommendation of Hume and other influential men, on July 10, 1894.

Free Press [Bodie, CA]: October 10, 1880. *Carson Daily Appeal [NV]*: June 16–17, 1880; June 22, 1880; September 5, 1880; September 9, 1880; September 11, 1880, September 14, 1880. *Carson Tribune [NV]*: June 9, 1880; September 6, 1880. *Belmont Courier [NV]*: September 11, 1880. *Genoa Weekly Courier [NV]*: November 18, 1881. *Nevada City Transcript [CA]*: August 10, 1880. *San Francisco Daily Morning Call [CA]*: September 14, 1880; February 5, 1885; August 17, 1889. *Territorial Enterprise [Virginia City, NV]*: May 16, 1880; June 15, 1880; August 10, 1880; September 7, 1880; September 15, 1880; September 19, 1880; September 21, 1880; September 23, 1880; October 1, 1880; October 26, 1880; November 2, 1880.

Sheehan, Michael

Nativity, New York; Age, 26 years; Occupation, Gardner; Height 5 feet 4 inches; Complexion, Florid; Color of eyes, Hazel, Color of hair, Brown. Square features, high forehead, mole inside of right elbow, two vaccine marks on right upper arm, stout built.

No. of commitment 8166. Received at the California State Prison, April 24, 1878. Crime, assault to rob; Term 4 years. County sent from, San Francisco.

Removed to Folsom Prison September 6, 1880, and discharged, by expiration of sentence, April 24, 1881.

Burglarized W. F. & Co's office at Galt, November 18, 1881, in company with Charles Mills and John Anderson.

Received at California State Prison March 24, 1882. No. of commitment, 10339; Crime, burglary, second degree and prior felony; Term 10 years; County sent from, Alameda.

[*See* Anderson, John]

Shepardson, Milton—*alias* Milt Shepardson

Nativity, Kentucky; Age, 53 years; Occupation, Miner; Height 5 feet 8 inches; Complexion, Dark; Color of eyes, Black; Color of hair, Black. Scar on right side—right eye, tooth out.

Robbed W. F. & Co's Express on stage from Yreka to Red Bluff, August 21, 1871, in company with Ziska Calmez, Billy Fugate and Johnny Grant.

Robbed W. F. & Co's Express on stage from Yreka to Red Bluff, September 26, 1871, in company with Calmez, Fugate, Grant, and Billy Cullen.

Was arrested in Baker County, Oregon, and brought to Shasta jail, September 9, 1872. Gave bonds, returned to Oregon, and robbed W. F. & Co's Express on stage from Baker City to Umatilla, July 12, 1873, in company with Frank Fulford and Frank Johnson.

Was convicted March 7, 1884, in Shasta County for the Shasta robbery of September 26, 1871, and sentenced for a term of 7 years.

New trial granted by the Supreme Court.

September 16, 1874, was again convicted on same indictment, and sentenced to a term of 8 years.

New trial granted by the Supreme Court.

November 6, 1875, the third trial resulted in a verdict of acquittal.

Was taken to Oregon upon a requisition from the Governor of that State, and in November, 1876, was tried and convicted of the robbery of the Baker City stage in 1873.

Received at the Oregon State Prison, November 15, 1876. No. of commitment, 693; Crime, robbery; Term, 10 years; County sent from, Baker, Oregon.

Discharged, upon expiration of sentence, August 23, 1883.

On August 21, 1871, four masked road agents, three armed with Henry rifles, stepped out of the brush twenty miles north of Red Bluff in Tehama County and ordered stagecoach driver Ed Lynch to "hold, and hand down the Wells Fargo treasure boxes!" The horses could not proceed because the men had stretched a rope across the road so the driver had no choice but to comply. The driver had the presence of mind to hand down the smaller box but then the other boxes were demanded. When Lynch said there were no others one robber said, "You are a d___d liar," and climbed up on the wheel. He pulled out the other boxes and threw them down on the road. There was one passenger aboard but he was not molested, and the driver was ordered to continue on. The coach hurried into Red Bluff and reported the robbery. Lawmen hurried to the scene and found boot and mule tracks where the plunder had been packed on a mule and carried away, but the trail was lost and the robbers were not captured. The road agents laid low for a month but on September 26, 1871, they reappeared at the same place along the road to Red Bluff and Lynch was again driving. They took $60 from the Wells, Fargo box sent to Yreka and $240 from the box for Shasta. The amount was so small that they went through the passengers and collected $160. After this second robbery Wells, Fargo & Company offered a reward of $500 for the arrest and conviction of each robber. A posse was able to track the men but three of five made a clean getaway. The lawmen captured Billy Cullen and Johnny Grant as well as five horses, the pack mule, four Henry rifles, and a camping outfit. Those that escaped included Milton Shepardson, Billy Fugate and Ziska Calmez. Cullen and Grant were tried, convicted, and sentenced to serve seven year sentences at San Quentin Prison. As soon as Fugate was captured he informed on the other two men and pled guilty on September 15, 1874. He had been promised an early release and while he was being transported to prison Governor Newton Booth granted a full pardon. He was released when he arrived at the prison, in consideration of his cooperation but in September 1879 he would return to prison for a seven year term for a conviction of "assault to murder." He would be granted a new trial in November and acquitted.

On Friday, July 12, 1872, C. N. Thornbury and two companions were traveling by buggy through Antelope Canyon going toward The Dalles in northern Oregon. They were five miles from the Tompkins spread, a few miles past H. Moppin's place, and still five miles from Ward's Stagecoach Station when Thornbury saw two men standing not far off the trail. Each man was armed with a long barreled weapon, a rifle or shot-gun, but no horses were seen. Anticipating trouble the three travelers took out their pistols and laid them close at hand but they passed by the suspicious looking foot-pads without incident and had almost forgotten them until the stagecoach caught up with the Thornbury party at Ward's Station. The topless stagecoach wagon from Canyon City to The Dalles driven by Ad Edgar was thirty minutes behind the Thornbury party and five miles from T. M. Ward's Station, or about sixty-five miles from The Dalles and about the same from Canyon City, when it reached Antelope Canyon at 6:30 P.M., a half hour before sunset. Antelope Canyon is a deep hollow a mile long, very rocky throughout with heavy brush at some places, but the country around the canyon was prairie and comparatively flat. The sides of the canyon were very steep and the road through the canyon was quite steep in places. The coach was traveling up one of the steep grades with three of the passengers walking closely behind, to relieve the horses of the extra weight, and this party consisted of two men and a boy while teacher Mary Morrison, who had boarded with her son at the Burnt Ranch Station thirty-six miles previous, and Miss Lizzie Franklin, granddaughter of H. Moppin, rode inside. Captain Fearing was sitting next to Edgar on the driver's seat when suddenly three men, thoroughly disguised with masks of blue cloth, stepped out of the brush on the right side. There were two men six feet tall and one medium-sized man and the smaller man shouted, "Halt! Throw up your hands." Mrs. Morrison cried out, "My God, we are all murdered," and Edgar said, "Hello! Oh my God!" The medium-sized man responded, "Mr. Edgar, we will not hurt you, we only want the mail." The two tall men passed around the front of the coach, one taking the reins of the leaders while the other tall man covered the passengers with his shotgun. The leader of the gang was holding a short-barreled Henry rifle, the robber at the reins was armed with a Henry rifle of a standard barrel length, and the third man held a double-barreled shotgun. Once the road agents were in position the robber-leader demanded that the mail and express be thrown out but Edgar kept hold of the reins and let Captain Fearing do the work. Miss Franklin was sobbing the entire time but Mrs. Morrison disembarked when the coach stopped and took her boy behind the coach for protection, in case shooting started. George Knisley and a passenger named Jack, the men afoot, were not molested and after the sacks were thrown down the leader of the road agents ordered the driver to continue on. Mrs. Morrison then asked the robbers to allow her and the boy to board the coach and the leader replied, "get in babies" and they quickly climbed aboard. Edgar took special note of a distinctive pearl handled revolver in the belt of the leader and Miss Franklin said much later, after considerable prompting by her grandfather, that she had noticed red hair showing from beneath the mask of one of the robbers and freckles on his hands, and said he had blue eyes. All heard the voice of the leader, but there was little else to help identify the robbers.

The coach continued to Ward's Station and from there hurried on to The Dalles, arriving on Saturday evening. Sheriff Schurz of Wasco County, with deputy Joseph Cunningham, started the next morning for the scene and they arrived at Ward's Station on Sunday night. It was too dark to begin their investigation so they stayed the night and left for the scene at daybreak Monday. On the way they met Moppin, whose house was about one mile from the mouth of the canyon on the Canyon City side and less than three miles from Tompkins' ranch, and he had with him John Attleberry and Billy Cantrell. Moppin said that he and C. Adams had gone to the scene of the robbery the previous morning and searched for tracks, and found several trails of foot tracks and horse tracks. Moppin directed the search for the Sheriff's party and pointed out the foot tracks, including a very distinctive boot print, and then after traveling about three miles found where the horses had been tied. He pointed out one hoof print which was long and slender as of a mule, sometimes called a "hoof bound," and another distinctive print which was the large round track of a shod American horse. The five men searched the area and found trails leading to and away from the scene and the party then traveled the road in both directions thirty miles and, though they were not able to find any place where the robbers had left the road, Moppin found several masks made from a saddle blanket which he gave to the sheriff with much ceremony. He then said he suspected Frank Tompkins and they went to his ranch, where Moppin almost immediately selected several horses from a herd grazing nearby, whose tracks matched exactly those of the tracks at the robbery scene. One was an iron-gray horse about the size of a cayuse horse and the source of the small, narrow shoe print while the other was a bay mare which made a large round shoe print. They removed one of the shoes from the iron gray horse for a comparison and found it matched exactly the tracks they had followed from the scene. They next made a careful search of Tompkins' ranch and found in a barn half a saddle blanket, and the two masks found near the scene fit exactly with the torn blanket. They also found a pair of boots in Tompkins' loft and the left boot was an exact match for the boot prints they found near the scene of the robbery, and they determined that the boots belonged to William Bramlette.

Moppin later claimed that he had been deputized to arrest Bramlette, so he had gone to Coleman's on Trout Creek with Attleberry, Cantrell, and his son Garret, and made the arrest. After traveling four miles Moppin sent Cantrell and his son ahead while he and Attleberry took Bramlette off the road three hundred yards from the creek to a level bench on the side of the mountain where there was a large juniper tree. The two men said they told their prisoner that he was running with bad people and that he [Moppin] was going to hang them as quickly as he could catch them. Moppin said he scared Bramlette so thoroughly that the prisoner agreed to confess and said he always looked upon Moppin, the man who had just threatened to hang him, as his father. According to Moppin, Bramlette then provided a detailed confession of every detail of the robbery implicating Tompkins, Hanson and White, but Moppin never mentioned strangling their prisoner to extort the confession nor demanding answers to leading questions which required only a nod or a "yes" answer. Bramlette had been "pulled up a tree" at least three times and held aloft until he was unconscious before being dropped. Before the fourth hanging he was threatened with being tied off and left to strangle to death. The two men claimed their prisoner provided a description of the horses used and, conveniently, they were the exact animals that Moppin had identified when the sheriff's party went to Tompkins' pasture. Once Bramlette was safe in the house, with others present, he recanted his confession. On Friday Moppin, Attleberry, Cantrell, Samuel Porter, William Quinn, and W. C. Hale went to Grater's one room log cabin on Trout creek. They tied their horses one hundred yards from the house and crept up, where they found Tompkins tying his horse to a wagon. He was surrounded, covered with arms, and arrested. When told the charge of robbing the stagecoach Tompkins said, "I am clear of that charge, and can prove myself clear by Hanson and White, and by my wife." Moppin said that Hanson and White would not be competent witnesses as he was going to arrest them also, so Tompkins said, "If that is all, it don't amount to much." Moppin then told Tompkins that he had Bramlette and told of his confession, and Tompkins reportedly replied that Bramlette was scared or crazy. The prisoner was taken to Moppin's place by Porter while Moppin and the others went on to Tompkins' place where they arrested Ed Hanson. He said White had gone to the valley to look for horses so Moppin sent Quinn and Attleberry after White, and they returned with their prisoner in two hours, and the entire party went to Moppin's to await the return of Sheriff Shurz.

Sheriff Shurz had gone to The Dalles to swear out warrants for the arrest of Tompkins, White, Bramlette and Hanson and on his way he met deputy U.S. Marshal Williams and they went to Antelope Canyon together. When the sheriff arrived he learned of the arrests of the suspected robbers and of the detailed confession of Bramlette, the particulars being recorded by Moppin and Attleberry who had forced the confession from Bramlette. Sheriff Shurz did not have room to take in four prisoners in his buggy so he took custody of White, Hanson, and Tompkins and took his three prisoners to The Dalles where he lodged them in the county jail. Bramlette was left under guard at Ward's Station and brought down by Joseph Cunningham on The Dalles boat two days later. The U.S. grand jury met and indicted all four men on a single true bill charging them with putting the life of the mail carrier in jeopardy when robbing the mails, a charge which was punishable by life imprisonment. The legal maneuver of a single indictment prevented Mrs. Tompkins from testifying and corroborating the alibis of White, Bramlette and Hanson. It was the strategy of the defense that once these three defendants were exonerated by her testimony they could testify for Tompkins and clear him of the charges, but when Tompkins' wife was prohibited from testifying the men were left with no alibi, excepting their self-serving claim of innocence. The defendants were brought to trial in Judge M. P. Deady's Circuit Court on Monday, August 20, 1872. The trial lasted six days, their alibi testimony was dismissed by the jury, and the four men were convicted entirely on circumstantial evidence. Much of the testimony of Moppin and the other men interested in the rewards was refuted by disinterested parties, but their testimony must have been disregarded as well, and several decisions by the Judge appeared quite prejudicial against the defendants. The jury was only in deliberations for fifteen minutes and upon rendering their guilty verdicts a motion was filed for a new trial. Judge Deady denied the motion and sentenced the four defendants to terms of life imprisonment at hard labor in the State Prison at Salem. However Ad Edgar, the driver, Sheriff J. M. Boyd of Baker County and Wells, Fargo & Company's agent H. C. Page were certain the four men were innocent and kept a watch for any clue that would lead them to the guilty parties. One strong factor in their belief was that when the four men were arrested none had a pearl handled revolver, and it was proved that none of the four men had ever owned one. Tompkins had used nearly all his property and wealth in defending the case and when he was delivered to the prison his wife became a charity case.

Frank Johnson, alias Fulford, was serving a term at the Oregon penitentiary on another charge when he encountered Sheriff Boyd, who was at the prison on other business several years later. He told the lawman that a man named Homily, whose real name was Milton Shepardson, along with T. D. Phelps and Charles Darnell were the men who had robbed the Canyon City stagecoach on July 12, 1872. He said that he was going to participate but his wife would not allow it so he withdrew. He did, however, know enough of the details to convince Boyd that he was telling the truth. He said that Shepardson and Darnell met the Gem Town blacksmith named Phelps and tried to convince him to take Johnson's place, as they wanted three men to do the work. Phelps declined until Shepardson returned in a few days and described the plan. Shepardson said he had picked the spot and described the role each man would play and it seemed foolproof so Phelps agreed to take part. Johnson said that after the mail sacks were thrown out, and the stagecoach ordered to drive on, the robbers loaded the matter on a pack animal and rode all night. They went into camp at daylight and searched all the matter, burning everything with no value, then divided the plunder. Shepardson went to Lewiston, Phelps went to his ranch near Dayton in Walla Walla County, Washington, and Darnell went to Iowa Hill, Placer County, California. Boyd was soon on their trail, arrested Darnell, and took him to Portland. He next went after Phelps but, realizing he would need substantially more evidence to get a conviction and secure the release of four innocent men, he hinted that Shepardson was in jail and was about to inform on his confederates. Phelps then made a detailed confession and would later turn state's evidence in court to gain his release. Meanwhile Shepardson was arrested by Baker County, Oregon, deputy sheriff William Harper at Sparta, Oregon, and the deputy took from him a derringer and a distinctive pearl handled revolver. He was charged with the robbery of a Shasta County, California, stagecoach on the night of August 21, 1871, when five road agents shared $4,300 in gold bullion and coin. Shepardson was not charged in the September 26, 1871, robbery of the same stagecoach at the same place where the same five men only shared $160, but it was after that second robbery that two members of the gang were captured and Shepardson fled to Oregon. Shepardson posted $2,400 bail on the Shasta County charge and was released but returned for his trial in March 1872. His defense was that he was in Oregon during a long period before, during, and after the robbery and proved his alibi through false testimony. He was convicted but granted a new trial based on an error. At his second trial he was again convicted and again granted a new trial on an error. Following the third trial he was acquitted, the jury finding him "guilty, but not proven," and he was released. On January 26, 1876, deputy U.S. Marshal Boyd arrested Shepardson in his Colusa, California, hotel room. Shepardson had been working on his brother's farm thirteen miles from town but had come into Colusa that day. The warrant had been issued for an alias he was then using, Mathews, and Shepardson denied he was the wanted man but Boyd had the forethought to include a "John Doe" on the warrant and Shepardson was taken into custody under that name. He was taken to Portland on the steamer *Ajax*, Boyd being assisted by deputy U.S. Marshal Malarkey. Shepardson's trial was called in the U.S. Circuit Court on June 21, 1876, and he was confronted with his alibi testimony in the California case, where he had proved he was in Oregon at the time of the Canyon City stagecoach robbery. He was tried by Judge M. P. Deady and there was strong evidence of his guilt, but the judge directed the jury to return a verdict of not guilty because conviction was barred by the statute of limitations. Still, the evidence was sufficient to gain the release of the four innocent men then in prison. President Grant signed a full pardon for the four men and they were released on November 6, 1876, after serving nearly four years of their life sentences. Shepardson was immediately arrested on another charge of stagecoach robbery in Baker County, Oregon, which occurred in 1873 and this crime was not barred by the statute of limitations. He was convicted and sentenced to serve ten years in the Oregon State Penitentiary. He was admitted on November 13, 1876, and registered as prisoner No. 693. He served his time as a model prisoner and was released on August 23, 1883, and then lived a law abiding life thereafter, or at least was never again convicted of a crime, and he died at his home in Peanut, California, on November 14, 1915.

In 1872 Tompkins was a well-to-do cattle man in the vicinity of Antelope Canyon and, possibly because he was a major land owner and a powerful force in the community, had a number of neighbors who were envious and desired his downfall. It was clear afterwards that Moppin and others gave perjured testimony and manufactured physical evidence in a conspiracy to incriminate four innocent men. During the trial Moppin testified that he had known Tompkins for many years and in several places and had good relations until Jack Mount was killed at the Tompkins place. Soon after that killing Moppin was sued by the French & Gilman Company and he blamed Tompkins for instigating the action against him, saying he did not ask Tompkins to be his security on that note, but Tompkins had signed for his neighbor. Moppin later denied that he said of Tompkins when at The Dalles, "I will send him to Hell if I get the chance." Moppin had testified that when Tompkins was arrested the prisoner said that he had always treated his captor well, and Moppin responded, "You played me a mean trick in the matter with French. French never refused to trust me for goods, for I was always good on my contracts; my property always made me good." It was clearly a matter of revenge but Moppin and his conspirators were never prosecuted for their crimes.

Daily Oregonian [Portland, OR]: July 16, 1872; July 22–23, 1872; July 25, 1872; July 27, 1872; August 21–24, 1872; August 26, 1872; February 7, 1876. *Gold Hill Daily News [NV]*: January 15, 1874. *Idaho Statesman [Boise, ID]*: November 16, 1872; February 8, 1876; February 10, 1876. *Shasta Courier [CA]*: April 10, 1875; May 22, 1875; February 12, 1876; April 1, 1876; July 8, 1876; September 23, 1876.

Shinn, George H.

Nativity, Michigan; Age, 35 years; Occupation, Teamster; Height, 5 feet 6⅜ inches; Complexion, Florid; Color of eyes, Gray; Color of hair, Sandy. Oval features, medium forehead, tolerably long narrow ears, tolerably large lobes partially detached, rather small square cut nose, small elongated nostrils, very small thin vaccine mark and hair mole alongside on left upper arm, patch of long hair small of back, large irregular scar slightly to right of center of breast; medium built.

Attempted to rob Overland Express Train from San Francisco to Ogden at Cape Horn Mills, August 31, 1881, in company with Steinagal, Mason, Frazier, and Rogers.

Received at the California State prison, July 19, 1882; No. of commitment, 10487; Term, 12 years, 8 months, 10 days; County sent from, Placer.

George H. Shinn was a gambler who was known to cheat at cards and frequent brothels. He fell in with Ed Steinegal, a gold miner determined to find his fortune and, if he could not find mineral wealth in the ground, then he would take it from others who had been successful. In the late summer of 1881 the two men enlisted the help of three men, as the work they planned could not be done by just two. The first man they involved was Ruben Rogers, a gold miner who lived at Pickering Bar on the north fork of the American River. From the Rogers' cabin there was a trail to the Cape Horn Mills five miles from Colfax in Placer County near the tracks of the Central Pacific Railroad. Henry Frazier, the second recruit, was also a gold miner and well acquainted with the explosives used by miners, Hercules giant powder cartridges. The third recruit was John Mason, a teamster working at Iowa Hill. They told the three new recruits that they had a scheme which would make them all rich and the men, who had not become wealthy in their lines of work, were interested. On August 30, 1881, Steinegal, Shinn and Mason met Frazier at Rogers cabin at 2:00 P.M. and the two leaders laid out their plans. Steinegal had a gun on his shoulder and another in a sack and the two men told the new recruits that they had hidden tools nearby in the brush. They had stocked the cabin with four days' provisions which they had taken from the Aurora blacksmith shop. The tools were retrieved and the two leaders displayed two picks, two shovels, several axes, a wrench, a hatchet, a sledge hammer, two pairs of boots, eight pounds of nails, and giant powder cartridges, fuse and caps. It was decided that after dark on the following night the men would take all the tools to the tracks at Cape Horn and remove a rail. On the night of August 31 Steinegal, Shinn and Mason showed at the cabin but Rogers and Frazier were not there so the men went to the spring near the railway cut and sat down near the tracks to wait. Rogers appeared at 9:00 P.M. and he had brought a shot gun and a six-shooter, the sack containing twenty-four cartridges of giant powder, fuse and caps, a wrench, and several bottles of whiskey to fortify their resolve. He carried a lantern but it was not yet lit. When Rogers got to the spring all the men had a drink of water and some whiskey and Rogers laid down his monkey wrench, which he left there when they later fled.

Steinegal, Shinn, Rogers and Mason went down to the tracks and met Frazier on the way. Frazier was to make an iron bar to pry up the rail and, if he had not, then the affair would have to be postponed. But Frazier had made the bar so the party of five went into the bushes and loaded two guns, then went to the tracks which were on a grade, and used the bar to take up the right hand rail. They pulled the higher point out and the lower part of the rail they pressed into the dirt, thinking this would disguise it so the engineer could not see it was tampered with. It was a difficult task removing the rail and the bar broke once during the operation, but finally the rail was loosened by Mason and Shinn while Steinegal and Rogers went on the tracks as lookouts. The men then went to a place near the telegraph poles and put on their masks, took several large drinks of whiskey and smashed the bottles, then hunkered down to await the arrival of the train. A few minutes after midnight the eastbound Central Pacific No. 1 train pulled by two engines came slowly up the grade at 11:47 P.M. As it came around a gentle curve both locomotives were thrown off the tracks, followed by the tender, a fruit car, and the express and baggage coaches. Once the train came to a halt fireman Fred Boyd jumped free but was immediately captured by one of the robbers holding a shotgun. The robber threatened to blow his head off if he moved but Boyd ignored the threat and fled along the side of the train. Wells, Fargo's messenger

N. M. Chadwick slid open his door to see what had happened and was met by John Mason, who pointed his gun at Chadwick and yelled, "You s__ of a b___, fall out of there!" Chadwick slammed and locked the door, extinguished the lantern, drew his six-shooter and prepared for the fight he was sure would soon follow. However, the five robbers turned their attention to the mail car and confronted U.S. mail agent Louis Tripp with their firearms and ordered him to raise his hands. Tripp also ignored the robbers and refused to move, but by then curious passengers were starting to disembark to see what had happened to their train. One of the robbers called out, "This is a freight train!" and Mason noticed that Shinn and Frazier were standing motionless looking down the tracks, so he yelled for them to get busy with the work. Frazier replied that he saw soldiers coming off the train, thinking the large number of passengers were soldiers, and Steinegal yelled, "It's too big to take!" Mason replied, "Well if we are going, we had better go quick." At that the five men ran into the brush leaving behind their tools and a note which read, "Sacramento, May 20. Dick, will be at Stump's Ret's, Ne City, Monday. Everything O. K. 349." After they had run some distance Frazier said, "We have done enough now. We better go home," and they separated. Rogers went to his home in Gold Run while the rest went to Rogers' cabin.

As soon as the robbers fled conductor Charles Allen walked back to Colfax and telegraphed Auburn and Sacramento and a special train was dispatched to bring in the passengers and baggage and a crew was sent to put the train back on the tracks, and it took eight hours to get the No. 1 underway again. At dawn Sheriff John Boggs took his posse to the scene and began his investigation. They began to inventory all the equipment they found including twenty-four Hercules giant powder cartridges and fuses, all the tools, masks, and the note. Boggs new that Stump's Restaurant in Nevada City was a hangout for every sort of criminal type and thought that the robbery might have been planned and staged from there. Rewards of $2,000 were offered and the detectives of each concerned company rushed to the scene by special train, including James Hume and John Thacker from Wells Fargo & Company; Fred Burke, Len Harris, and Bill Hickey from the railroad; and San Francisco Police Department's Captain A. W. Stone. They began running down every clue and sighting and soon learned that the note was a plant to steer them in the wrong direction. They made a few arrests but the men were proved innocent of this crime and released. Boggs was certain that the robbers were local miners, made inquiries, and learned that Ed Steinegal had recently purchased a large number of Hercules giant powder cartridges and fuse so, with Jim Hume, he rode to the cabin at Pickering Bar on September 9. He found Mason and Steinegal there and they insisted that they were miners even though they had no tools. The lawmen searched the cabin and found material which matched the masks found by the tracks. They next found shovels and picks, with the handles cut off, sunk in the river. The men were closely questioned but Steinegal was firm. Mason, however, was convinced that he could only save his neck if he informed on his fellow robbers and Boggs convinced him that they had a good case against them, so he confessed and named the other four men. He would later draw a map showing every movement of the men at the tracks. Lawmen began searching for the robbers and arrested Henry Frazier the following day. They learned from Frazier that Rogers had just eloped with Mary Sullivan from Iowa Hill. They tracked them to the Union Hotel in Nevada City where the newlywed couple was spending their honeymoon night, and Hume sent a telegram to City Marshal Erastus Baldridge asking him to arrest Rogers. Baldridge arrested Rogers at daybreak when the couple came down to breakfast. All four of the robbers were brought into Auburn and lodged in the county jail, but Mason was soon moved to Sacramento to protect him from the other prisoners. The search for Shinn continued and on October 27 Fred Burke, the railroad detective who played such a major role in the arrest of the Verdi train robbers, captured Shinn when the fugitive stopped at the Doolin Ranch in Antelope Valley, eighteen miles west of Maxwell in Colusa County. Shinn was taken back to Auburn and lodged in jail with the other three robbers. The four prisoners hired several of the best attorneys in California so Wells, Fargo and the Central Pacific railroad hired two special prosecutors to assist district attorney Bill Lardner. This strategy would backfire on the prosecution as the trial was costing the citizens a great deal of their tax dollars and, conveniently, the public learned that the railroad had refused to pay its taxes for several years and was $90,000 in arrears. This gave the appearance that the railroad wanted the people to subsidize the trial.

Steinegal's trial began on November 11, 1881, and took twenty-one days because each side called fifty witnesses, and the number of prosecution witnesses gave credence to the belief that the defendants were being persecuted by the railroad. One of the strongest pieces of evidence was the note which matched the handwriting of letters sent from the jail by Steinegal, and were intercepted by deputies. There was no analysis of the handwriting permitted by the court but a simple comparison of the handwriting by jurors was allowed, as it was believed that each man's handwriting was unique. They saw clearly that it was Steinegal's handwriting but still the jury could not bring in a verdict, so Steinegal was retried three months later. This time he was convicted of attempted robbery and sentenced to serve thirteen years at San Quentin Prison. Shinn was the next to be tried and his case began on June 26, 1882. Now the public concern for the cost had escalated, fueled by newspaper reports, but Shinn was also convicted and on July 18 he was sentenced to serve twelve years eight months at San Quentin Prison. John Mason had testified against each man and had remained free in consideration of turning state's evidence.

On September 11, 1882, Rogers' and Frazier's trial began and by then both Steinegal and Shinn were at the prison and had confessed, corroborating Mason's story. Steinegal agreed to return to Auburn and repeat his confession on the stand, which the prosecution decided would strengthen the testimony of Mason. With the trial already underway Sheriff Boggs went to San Quentin Prison and took Steinegal back to Auburn. On September 13 Boggs was met at the depot by his twenty-one year old son John when the train arrived at 10:00 P.M. The train had been filled with passengers returning home from the state fair and as they disembarked the streets quickly became crowded. Steinegal was handcuffed but his ankles were not shackled, as he had to walk from the train to the courthouse where the jail was located. When they neared their destination the prisoner saw his opportunity and jumped in front of two girls, ran quickly into a dark alley and disappeared. Both lawmen drew their pistols but could not fire for fear of hitting an innocent bystander. The lawmen called for everyone to get down and once their field of fire was cleared they each fired several rounds but without effect, and Steinegal escaped. The following morning a posse led by Boggs followed the trail to a creek bed six miles north of town where they found the handcuffs, which Steinegal had managed to break off. They lost the trail there and the fugitive was never recaptured, even though the state offered a reward of $300 dollars. Now with only Mason to testify against Frazier and Rogers, and the ill feelings toward the railroad and their prosecutors, some of the jurors accepted the alibi of Rogers and could not arrive at a verdict. The two defendants were retried in December and two days before Christmas the jury returned a unanimous verdict acquitting both men.

Mason was freed in consideration of his turning state's evidence, Steinegal had escaped and was never heard of again, and Rogers and Frazier were acquitted, so Shinn was the only train wrecker still in prison. He served his time as a model prisoner and earned a position as an outside trusty. He was allowed to leave the prison unsupervised so there was little concern when, on a rainy December 1, 1887, he drove a horse drawn cart out of the front gates. Unknown to the guards who remained indoors he had Charles Dorsey hidden in the cart and both men escaped. They remained at large until 1890 when someone notified authorities where they could be found. Wells, Fargo & Company sent Hume to Chicago and, with a force of men from the Pinkerton detective agency, he arrested the two fugitives. Hume learned that the two men had been traveling west periodically to commit all sorts of crimes, including stagecoach robberies. Shinn was returned to California in late October 1890 but he was sent to Folsom to separate him from his partner in the escape, who was returned to San Quentin. They were never prosecuted for the rash of crimes committed while they were fugitives but Shinn spent another nine years in prison on his original charge and was released in 1899. He then disappeared from the criminal rolls of California.

Los Angeles Times [CA]: September 2, 1881. *Nevada City Transcript* [CA]: September 13, 1881. *Placer Herald [CA]*: September 3, 1881; September 17, 1881; October 1, 1881; September 16, 1882; October 7, 1882. *Sacramento Bee [CA]*: September 1, 1881; September 12, 1881; September 14, 1881; October 28, 1881. *Sacramento Record-Union [CA]*: September 12, 1881; September 28–29, 1881. *San Diego Union [CA]*: September 2, 1881. *San Francisco Alta [CA]*: September 2–3, 1881; September 29, 1881. *San Francisco Chronicle* [CA]: September 2, 1881. *Territorial Enterprise [Virginia City, NV]*: September 2, 1881.

Sloan, William—*alias* Idaho Bill

Robbed W. F. & Co's Express on stage from Leeds, U. T., to Pioche, Nev., December 13, 1875 — alone.
Received at Utah Territorial Prison, —; No. of commitment, —; Crime, robbery; Term, 10 years.
Escaped, September 4, 1877.
Was afterward *killed* in Wyoming.

On September 11, 1857, the Fancher party was massacred at Mountain Meadows, Utah. Seventeen children thought too young to remember the details of the heinous crime were allowed to live, and one of them was five year old Charley Fancher. The children were distributed among Mormon families to be raised but they were finally rescued and taken east to relatives in Arkansas. In the early 1870s a young man who gave his name as William Sloan appeared in the Idaho Territory and established a horse stealing enterprise. Sloan soon became better known as "Idaho Bill" but he was believed by those who came to know him to be little Charley Fancher. Sloan decided to rob the stagecoach traveling between Leeds, Utah Territory, and Pioche, Nevada, and on December 13, 1875, acting alone, he put his plan into action. He went to Desert Station, a home station on the Salt Lake Road, stopped the coach bound for Pioche, took the treasure box, and ordered the driver to continue. The box was broken open and the contents taken. Sloan was soon arrested, indicted, convicted, and sentenced to serve ten years in Utah's state prison. On September 4, 1877, Sloan escaped and made his way to Evanston, Wyoming. There he met the Glasscock family, Stephen R. and his wife Matilda, who had recently moved there with their thirteen year old daughter Lillie and a two year old son. Sloan impressed Lillie and, against her father's wishes, she married Sloan and they moved away. Glasscock, being a desperado himself, saw the bad in Sloan so after a short period of married life, which completely disillusioned Lillie, her father convinced her to leave Sloan and return home. After a time Sloan, who felt that his failure to act earlier might be construed as abandonment of his Lillie, decided he must have his wife back and obtained passage on a westbound emigrant railroad train passing through Cheyenne, his destination being Evanston. On July 13, 1881, he arrived at the Glasscock farm five miles from town and demanded his wife, then threatened to murder the entire family if she was not surrendered to him. He pulled his pistol and chased Lillie's father around the house several times until Stephen picked up a pitman, a connecting rod from a mowing machine, and struck three blows. One of the blows fractured Sloan's head so severely that brain matter oozed out of the wound. Glasscock rushed to Evanston with his injured son-in-law and surrendered to the authorities. Dr. Hocker, with the assistance of several other town doctors, examined Sloan and pronounced the case hopeless, and Sloan died at 6:00 P.M. Glasscock appeared before the coroner's jury and, with corroborating testimony, the death was determined to be self-defense and he was released.

Pioche Record [NV]: December 15, 1875. *Ogden Pilot [UT]*: July 12, 1881.

Smith, Austin N.

No. of first commitment, 4357. Received at the California State Prison, January 18, 1870; Crime, grand larceny; Term, 3 years; County sent from, Yuba.
Pardoned by Governor Newton Booth, April 3, 1872.
No. of second commitment, 5725. Received at the California State Prison, September 1, 1873; Crime, grand larceny; Term, 1 year; County sent from, Solano.
Discharged, by expiration of sentence, July 24, 1874.
Robbed W. F. & Co's Express on stage from Downieville to Marysville, April 14, 1875 — alone.
Received at the California State Prison, May 10, 1875; No. of commitment, 6522; Crime, robbery; Term, 18 years; County sent from, Yuba, Cal.
Commuted by Governor William Irwin, May 30, 1876, to 17 years.
Killed in prison yard by a fellow prisoner, Peter Gibson, on the morning of September 17, 1879.

At 10:30 A.M. on April 14, 1875, the stagecoach from Camptonville to Marysville driven by Johnny Sharp was three and one half miles northeast of the Fountain House ascending the Oregon Hill in Yuba County, which required the horses to walk at a slow pace. On the upper side of the road was a grove of mountain spruces and from this stand of timber a road agent suddenly appeared. He wore no coat nor boots but was masked with a handkerchief with eye holes cut in it, and pulled over his head to hide his hair. He stepped off the steep embankment onto the road and leveled his double barreled shotgun at the head of Sharp and ordered him to rein in his team. He demanded the Wells, Fargo treasure box adding, "Throw it out d__d quick, as I am in a hurry!" Sharp responded, "Don't hurry, you'll get it presently." The road agent kept his shotgun pointed at the driver while he awaited delivery of the box and at one point called out to imaginary confederates, "keep back there, I need no assistance." Inside were ten passengers, Mrs. William Edgar and Mrs. David E. Williams with her two daughters and six males, and they were fidgeting about for fear that at any moment they would lose their driver or be ordered to "pungle" for their valuables, but none could give aid as they were unarmed. The men began to scramble about hiding their purses and Mrs. Williams' oldest daughter advised her to cover her gold necklace with her shawl but at that moment one of the women, overcome with fright, screamed. The road agent then assured them, "Don't fear ladies, no harm will be done you." Within a moment the treasure box struck the ground and Sharp was ordered to continue on to

Marysville, but the road agent kept the coach covered with his shotgun until it reached a sharp turn sixty yards ahead. Just before the coach passed out of sight of the robbery scene Sharp turned and saw the road agent grab the box and scramble up the embankment in the direction from which he had come. The road agent went thirty yards, broke the box open with a hatchet, and removed the contents. The box was found by Sharp two days later with two packages of letters, an empty watch box, the way bills still inside, and the hatchet used to break open the box lay nearby, and these items were all gathered up and taken to Marysville, but the $6,000 from the box was missing.

Rewards were posted for the arrest and conviction of the road agent and also offered one fourth of the value of the treasure recovered. The promise of substantial rewards put many men on the trail of the road agent but it was the jealousy of a Chico man over his "woman of ill repute" that was this robber's undoing. The road agent had told a soiled dove that he "had a stage robbery put up, and I will make my big strike," and they made plans to leave Chico together once he had the treasure. The jealous rival called upon U.S. Marshal Mart Casad and gave him the details. Casad went to the bordello and captured his man — a well-known San Quentin ex-convict named Austin N. Smith. Smith had arrived in Chico on April 17, had been courting his soiled dove, and had been flashing a purse filled with gold, and evidence began to accumulate against Smith. First came Herman Thomas, the owner of the hatchet, who identified the tool and Smith as the man who had taken it. The hatchet seemed to worry the prisoner and he told officers, "Don't you suppose that if I had committed the robbery I would take the precaution to put that hatchet out of the way?" Next the clothes Smith wore during the robbery, and described by Mrs. Williams' daughter, were found and brought in for evidence. A man named George Williams, not related to the women passengers, said that Smith had approached him on March 12 to join in a robbery of the Downieville stagecoach in company with John Clark, a San Quentin escapee, but Williams declined to take part. Smith's examination was held on April 29 and 30 and Smith blamed John Clark, denying any part in the robbery, but Clark was too tall and did not fit the general description of the robber, while Smith was the exact size and shape. The large number of witnesses included Herman Thomas, George Williams, driver Johnny Sharp, and several passengers. He was held to answer to the grand jury which easily returned an indictment. During the first week of May 1875, on the advice of his attorney, Smith pled guilty and turned in the plunder. Smith said of his plea, "Mr. Murphy advised me to compromise the case as the evidence was sure to convict me, and told me I wouldn't get over four years as he, Murphy, was assured by the Court. [The defendant] adopted the suggestion and directed officers to the place where the treasure was concealed on condition that one-fourth [the reward for recovery] should be turned over ... to [his attorney] as a fee." However, when Smith came into court he was sentenced to serve eighteen years in California's state prison and only then did he learned that his attorney had no understanding with the court. The reward money was being held in trust for the convicted robber so he turned it over to Wells, Fargo on the understanding that his attorney would get no part of it. On May 10 Smith was taken across San Francisco Bay to San Quentin Prison and registered as prisoner No. 6522. On May 30, 1876, Governor William Irwin commuted his sentence to seventeen years, something which suggested that his long term of imprisonment would be further shortened at a later date. However, on the morning of September 17, 1879, Smith was killed by fellow prisoner Peter Gibson while in the prison yard.

The Weekly Appeal [Marysville, CA]: April 23, 1875; April 30, 1875; May 14, 1875.

Smith, James P.—*alias* Old Jim Smith

Nativity, Prussia; Age, 54 years; Occupation, Laborer. Ink mark on right arm—"F. K. T. P." underneath, woman with Black Flag on left arm, Crucifix and Anchor underneath, Ship on right thigh, scar on right side.

No. of first commitment, 497. Received at the California State Prison, September 11, 1851; Crime, grand larceny; Term, 2 years; County sent from, Sacramento.
Escaped, December 27, 1854. Recaptured same day.
Escaped, April 11, 1855. Recaptured May 18, 1856 [*sic*].
Discharged, by expiration of sentence, February 29, 1855 [*sic*].
No. of second commitment, 1014. Received at the California State Prison, October 12, 1856; Crime, robbery; Term, 11 years; County sent from, Amador.
Escaped, May 14, 1860. Recaptured, July 31, 1860.
Discharged, by expiration of sentence, March 16, 1867.
No. of third commitment, 3849. Received at the California State Prison, July 9, 1868; Crime, robbery, Term, 9 years; County sent from, Placer.
Discharged, by expiration of sentence, December 16, 1875.
Robbed W. F. & Co's Express on stage from Fiddletown to Latrobe, January 10, 1876, in company with George Wilson and Charlie Pratt.
Robbed W. F. & Co's Express on stage from Georgetown to Auburn, January 17, 1876, in company with George Wilson and Charlie Pratt.
Received at the California State Prison, February 25, 1876; No. of commitment, 6903; Crime, robbery; Term, 12 years; County sent from, El Dorado.
Pardoned conditionally by Governor William Irwin, September 10, 1879.
No. of fifth commitment, 9172. Received at the California State Prison, December 30, 1879; Crime, robbery and prior conviction; Term, life; County sent from, El Dorado, Cal.
Removed to the State Insane Asylum at Napa, October 7, 1884.
[*See* Pratt, Charlie]

Smith, Peter

Nativity, Massachusetts; Age, 24 years; Occupation, Laborer; Height, 5 feet 8 inches; Complexion, Light; Color of eyes, Gray; Color of hair, Brown; Size of foot 5½. Full fat features, eyes deep-set, large ears, broad full forehead, scar in right eyebrow, female figure inside and outside left forearm, blue dot back of left hand, female figure inside and outside right forearm, large mole left shoulder-blade, round shouldered; stout built.
Robbed W. F. & Co's Express on stage from Grayson to Banta, October 23, 1884, in company with James Casey and Eugene Murphy.
Received at California State Prison, October 29, 1884; No. of commitment, 11436, Crime, robbery; Term, five years; County sent from, San Joaquin.
[*See* Casey, James]

Smith, William—*alias* C. P. Weibusch

Nativity, Germany; Age, 26 years; Occupation, Clerk; Height, 5 feet 5⅜ inches; Complexion, Florid; Color of eyes, Gray; Color of hair, Light. Round features, medium forehead, short square cut nose, large nostrils, nose crooked to the left, small flesh mole above inner corner of left eye about a quarter inch from eyebrow, small ears slightly projecting, ears pierced, mole back part of upper left arm, mole left shoulder blade about three inches from spine, small mole left side of small of back about two inches from spine, two moles right upper arm, one of them towards the arm pit, and the other about three inches below the point of shoulder, two moles about a half an inch apart on outer edge of right forearm; medium built.

About the first of November 1879, he selected a position on the road from Carson City to Aurora for the purpose of robbing the stage. As the stage approached he discovered a carriage a few hundred yards in the rear of the stage. The former he allowed to pass unmolested, but stopped the carriage and robbed the occupant, Mr. Kilgore, of a valuable gold watch and a sum of money. He was afterwards arrested and convicted, under the name Charles P. Weibush.

Received at the Nevada State prison, December 17, 1879; No. of commitment, 117, Crime, robbery; Term, 5 years; County sent from, Douglass.

Pardoned, April 12, 1881.

Robbed W. F. & Co's Express on stage from Sierraville to Truckee, June 29, 1881—alone.

While waiting in ambush for the arrival of the stage from Sierraville, Sol Rousseau appeared with a light wagon and six passengers. The robber stood them all up out of sight of the road for one and a half hours, until the stage from Sierra Valley arrived. This contained four passengers, all of whom were compelled to get down, except G. Q. Buxton, the driver, who was obliged to break open the W. F. & Co. box and hand out the contents. While this was going on two other vehicles approached, and the driver in each was compelled to get down and mingle with the "audience." At the close of the afternoon's performance he had thirteen men, sixteen horses, and four vehicles under the control of his "little shot-gun."

Robbed W. F. & Co's Express on stage from Sierraville to Truckee, with same driver, and in same locality, August 15, 1881. As on previous occasion, he compelled the driver to break open the box and deliver the contents.

Robbed W. F. & Co's Express on stage from Milton to Sonora, December 29, 1881. Also, robbed the U.S. Mail. In this instance he held the stage one and a half hours, endeavoring to break open the iron box. During this time one passenger from Sonora and two from Milton appeared, all three of whom he compelled to halt while he was working on the box.

Arrested and convicted of the robbery of December 29, 1881.

Received at the California State prison, June 27, 1882; No. of commitment, 10220; Crime, robbery; Term, 5 years; County sent from, Calaveras.

On December 29, 1881, the stagecoach from Milton to Sonora, driven by Clark Stringham, was approaching the top of a steep hill, the steepest on the road and about four miles beyond Copperopolis, when a lone road agent, wearing a black mask and armed with a breech-loading shotgun, stepped out and ordered the driver to rein in his team. The robber then demanded the Wells, Fargo treasure boxes. The horses were exhausted from the climb, and Stringham has no choice but to comply. As soon as the coach halted, the passengers were ordered out, and these included Madeline Cuno, an Italian lady from San Francisco, and H. S. Cohn, a "Jew peddler" whom the coach had stopped to pick up along the road. The road agent ordered the driver to open the box, offering a hatchet he had brought along, but Stringham refused saying he had to care for the horses. The road agent then broke open the boxes, removed the valuables, and then went for the mail bags. He cut open all but one bag and mutilated the letters, the one bag containing a large sum of money was not molested because the sound of a wagon's wheels were heard, and the road agent dodged behind a large rock. The wagon was driven by Dick Martin of Copperopolis, who was "sparking" his girlfriend, and the robber got the drop on him. He then ordered Stringham to break open the iron safe. Stringham again refused and said there was nothing in the box and he couldn't open it anyway. The road agent then threatened to shoot him, and he replied, "Shoot and be d__d. I'll not open the box." The road agent hacked away at the box until his hatchet gave out, and he gave up. He next went through two trunks, but when he found nothing, left the remainder of the baggage unmolested. He ordered Stringham to "pungle," and the driver dropped his money in the mud, where the robber left it. Stringham and his passengers were ordered aboard and the driver was told to continue on. Dick

Martin and his sweetheart were not molested and they followed the stage from the scene. The entire robbery took nearly two hours.

Stringham hurried into Sonora and sounded the alarm. Sheriff Ben K. Thorn went to the scene the following day and found the tracks of the robber and his horse. The animal's hoof prints were peculiar and this gave Thorn an opportunity to follow the trail to Milton. There he enlisted the help of Constable Devin Henderson and they continued on to Linden before night fell. The next day the trail was lost so they went to Stockton and reported the matter to Sheriff Thomas Cunningham and Deputy Sheriff Oscar F. Atwood. Thorn and Cunningham went north and Henderson and Atwood went south. Cunningham and Atwood cut the trail at French Camp and followed it into Lathrop. At the livery in Lathrop, Atwood found the robber's horse, and soon found the road agent having a meal at the Shannon House. Atwood went in while Henderson covered the exit and, with his pistol drawn, captured the road agent without resistance. The prisoner was handcuffed and the deputy took from him two revolvers, a Bowie knife, a black mask, and a very sharp chisel. He said he had discarded the shotgun along the trail. The prisoner was taken to Stockton and lodged in jail. His eye was blackened, which he said was from a fall from his horse, but the officers believed it was from his hatchet bounding back when he tried to break open the iron safe. The twenty-three-year-old German gave his name as William Smith, and the horse he was riding had been stolen from Martin Duffy of Comanche on Christmas day, but not being familiar with the animal, he had not noticed the peculiar track, which led to his arrest.

Sheriff Thorn took Smith to San Andreas and lodged him in the Calaveras County jail. The prisoner admitted guilt for the December 29 robbery and waived examination. He was held for the grand jury, which convened in June, and he was indicted. When brought into court he pled guilty and was sentenced to serve 5 years at San Quentin Prison. He arrived on June 27, 1882, and registered as prisoner No. 10220. He was released, by expiration of sentence, on August 17, 1885.

Daily Evening Herald [Stockton, CA]: December 30, 1881; January 6, 1882. *San Francisco Examiner [CA]*: August 18, 1885.

Spratt, John

Nativity, Missouri; Age, 41 years; Occupation, Blacksmith; Height, 5 feet 8 inches; Complexion, Florid; Color of eyes, Gray; Color of hair, Brown, Size of foot; 7; Weight. 185 lbs. Round fat face, high forehead, heavy eyebrows, small scar on left side upper lip, "J. S." on inside of right forearm, small vaccine mark left upper arm, large gunshot wound on right hip, large scar above left knee; stout built.

Robbed private conveyance from Kernville to Caliente, October 13, 1883, in company with the two Burton boys.

Received at the California State Prison, January 20, 1884; No. of commitment, 11108; Crime, robbery; Term, 10 years; County sent from, Kern.

His connection with depredations on Wells, Fargo & Company Express has failed to receive a place in State criminal records, but is nevertheless real. He robbed W. F. & Co's Express of $3,000 in gold coin on stage from Mojave to Panamint, December 8, 1879 — alone. He then lived with the Indians, and the robbery having been committed in a sparsely settled community, evidence was considered insufficient to warrant his arrest, though there is no doubt of his guilt.

On October 12, 1883, Michels & Co., mine owners, made their regular clean-up of the Sumner Mine, at Kernville, Cal. It is their custom, at the time of these clean-ups to convey the bullion to

Caliente by their own conveyance, if it so happened that they themselves can attend it; otherwise it is shipped by W. F. & Co's Express. The community is generally cognizant of these shipments and upon this occasion Spratt conceived the plan of securing the bullion, and inveigled the two Burton boys into his service. They concealed themselves near the stage road, about three miles from Kernville, while Spratt remained in town to ascertain whether the bullion was to be taken to Caliente by private conveyance, or shipped by W, F & Co's Express. The shipment was made by Express, on the 13th of October, 1883, but the agent disposed of the bullion in the stage so adroitly as to mislead the vigilant Spratt, who concluded that the mine owners themselves would carry it, and mounting his horse, rode rapidly to the ambush, passing the stage, and directing the Burton boys not to molest it, as the bullion was coming on the private conveyance. This they did; and when, an hour later, the mine owners reached this point, they were stopped by the Burtons, who instituted a thorough but unsuccessful search for the bullion. The three were shortly afterwards arrested, and the Burton boys, confessing their guilt, were used as witnesses against Spratt, who was convicted as above while they escaped punishment. *Spratt is bad.*

At 9:00 A.M. on Monday, December 8, 1879, John Spratt, acting alone, robbed Wells, Fargo & Company's Express of $3,831 in gold coin consigned to Darwin, being carried on the stagecoach leaving Mojave for Independence by way of Panamint. The masked, armed road agent selected a place on the desert seven miles beyond Indian Wells and as he "rose out of the earth" he pointed his six-shooter at driver Miller. He commanded, "Throw down that box!" and then immediately after the box was thrown down commanded, "drive on." There were no passengers aboard and the U.S. mail bags were not requested. Miller hurried on to the next station and reported the robbery, and he described the road agent as a very small man.

The Wells, Fargo & Company agent at Mojave did not broadcast any information about the robbery for several days and by the time a posse arrived the trail was cold. Spratt took the treasure box two and a half miles toward the Slate mountain range, broke it open, and removed everything inside. He then lived with the Indians and, though there seemed no doubt of his guilt, the robbery had been committed in a sparsely settled community and evidence was considered insufficient to warrant his arrest. On October 12, 1883, the mine owners of Michels & Co. made their regular clean-up of the Sumner Mine near Kernville, California, and it was their custom to deliver the bullion to Caliente by their own conveyance, if it so happened that they themselves could attend to it, but otherwise it was shipped by Wells, Fargo & Company's Express. The community knew of these shipments and upon this occasion Spratt conceived a plan for stealing the bullion and recruited the two Burton boys into his service. The Burton boys concealed themselves near the stage road three miles from Kernville while Spratt remained in town to determine whether the bullion was to be taken to Caliente by private conveyance or shipped by Wells, Fargo & Company's Express. The shipment was made by Express on October 13, 1883, but the express agent hid the bullion in the coach so adroitly that he misled Spratt, who was carefully watching the loading of the stagecoach. Spratt concluded that the mine owners themselves would carry the bullion and, mounting his horse, rode to the ambush scene passing the coach on the road. He directed the Burton boys to let the stagecoach pass as the bullion was coming by private conveyance, and the Burtons let the stagecoach pass by and an hour later, when the mine owners reached this point, they were stopped by the Burtons. The two masked, armed road agents searched for the bullion but found nothing. All three road agents were shortly afterwards arrested, the Burton boys confessed their guilt, implicated Spratt, and were then employed as witnesses against him. The Burton brothers, because they had cooperated in turning state's evidence and testifying against Spratt, were released. John Spratt was indicted, tried, convicted, and sentenced to serve a term of ten years at San Quentin Prison. He was received at the prison on January 20, 1884, and registered as prisoner No. 11108. Spratt was discharged, by expiration of sentence, on July 20, 1890.

Inyo Independent [CA]: December 13, 1879.

Squires, John

Nativity, Connecticut; Age, 52 years; Occupation, Miner; Height, 5 feet 8 inches; Complexion, Dark; Color of eyes, Brown; Color of hair, Brown; Weight, 136 lbs. Sharp nose, high forehead, enlargement on left eye, mole on left shoulder blade, scar above left knee, heavy mustache and full long beard.

Robbed Overland Express train from San Francisco [Cal.] to Odgen [U. T.] near Verdi [Nev.], November 6, 1870, with J. E. Chapman, A. J. Davis, Tilton P. Cockrell, R. A. Jones, E. B. Parsons, and James Gilchrist.

Received at the Nevada State Prison, December 25, 1870; No. of commitment, 69; Crime, robbery; Term, 23 years; County sent from, Washoe, Nev.

Escaped in "Big Break" of September 17, 1871; recaptured and returned to prison, September 27, 1871.

Pardoned, April 10 1882.

[*See* Davis, A. J.]

Stanley, Gus

Nativity, Texas; Age, 24 years; Occupation, Farmer; Height 5 feet 9½ inches; Complexion, Fair; Color of eyes, Gray; Color of hair, Light Brown. Small scar on instep of each foot, small scar on right hip, scar in center of back from bullet wound, scar on right knee — extending up the leg inclining toward inside.

Robbed W. F. & Co's Express on stage from Boise City, I. T., to Baker City, Oregon, May 13, 1884, in company with W. S. Horrell.

Received at the Oregon State Prison, June __, 1884; No. of commitment, —; Crime, robbery; Term, 5 years; County sent from, Baker, Oregon.

[*See* Horrel, W. S.]

Steinagal, Edward

Nativity, California; Age, 31 years; Occupation, Laborer; Height, 5 feet 8⅝ inches; Complexion, Florid; Color of eyes, Hazel; Color of hair, Dark. Rather long square features, full square cut forehead, thick set prominent nose, long nostrils, long ears, large lobes attached, point of left thumb slightly deformed — scarred, large irregular scar top of left forearm, black mole midway left shoulder, one very large black mole about half an inch to right of spine, two small moles on spine about half an inch apart — near base of neck, skin slightly discolored around left nipple, slight flesh mole right cheek; stout built.

Attempted to rob Overland Express Train from San Francisco to Ogden at Cape Horn Mills, August 31, 1881, in company with George H. Shinn, J. K. Mason, Henry Frazier, and R. A. Rogers.

Received at the California State prison, March 29, 1882; No. of commitment, 10351; Term, 13 years; County sent from, Placer.

Escaped from Sheriff Boggs at Auburn, Calif., September 14, 1882, while *en route* to testify against Rogers and Frazier.

[*See* Shinn, George H.]

Stover, N. C.

Robbed W. F. & Co's Express on stage from Colfax to Grass Valley, July 27, 1873, in company with Dribblebeis, Early, and George Lester.
Received at the California State Prison, November 29, 1873; No. of commitment, 5802; Crime, robbery; Term, 10 years; County sent from, Nevada.
Died in prison, August 20, 1879.
[*See* Thompson, Charles]

Stubbs, Henry

Nativity, Missouri; Age, 43 years; Occupation, Laborer; Height, 5 feet 6 inches; Complexion, Florid; Color of eyes, Gray; Color of hair, Brown, Broad full features, flat face, long scar at base of left forefinger; do. on thumb, do. on ball of left thumb, scar from burn on palm of right hand, two scars on third and fourth fingers of right hand, right lower leg crippled and deformed; stout built.
No. of first commitment, 2784. Received at the California State Prison, July 22, 1864; Crime, grand larceny; Term, 1½ years; County sent from, Colusa.
Discharged, by expiration of sentence, November 8, 1865.
No. of second commitment, 3260. Received at the California State Prison, April 17, 1866; Crime burglary; Term, 3 years; County sent from, Contra Costa.
Discharged, by expiration of sentence, November 6, 1868.
No. of third commitment, 4057. Received at the California State Prison, March 10, 1869; Crime, burglary; Term, 1½ years; County sent from, Napa.
Discharged, by expiration of sentence, June 27, 1870.
No. of fourth commitment, 5248. Received at the California State Prison, May 9, 1872; Crime, burglary; Term, 3 years; County sent from, San Francisco.
Discharged, by expiration of sentence, November 30, 1874.
Burglarized W. F. & Co's office at Suisun, October 25, 1874, in company with Jack Bowen, Charles Lee and Charlie Burch.
Burglarized W. F. & Co's office at Georgetown, El Dorado County, November 2, 1874, in company with Lee and Burch.
Received at the California State Prison, January 1, 1875; No. of commitment, 6320; Crime, assault to murder and grand larceny (two commitments); Term, 18 years; County sent from, Solano.
Pardoned conditionally by Governor George C. Perkins, December 20, 1882.
Now serving a term of 12 years in Folsom Prison for burglarizing the store of Anthony & Co., money brokers in San Francisco.
[*See* Lee, Charles]

Tadman, Charles—*alias* Gumboot Charlie

Nativity, Mexico; Age, 38 years; Occupation, Laborer; Height, 5 feet 11¾ inches; Complexion, Light; Color of eyes, Blue; Color of hair, Brown. Square features, broad jaws, small scar on left cheekbone, do. top of forehead, do. base of left thumb, do. back of left forearm; stout built.
Robbed W. F. & Co's Express on stage from Jackson to Latrobe, September 11, 1876, in company with Charles Thompson.
Received at the California State Prison, December 26, 1876; No. of commitment, 7319; Crime, robbery; Term, 4 years; County sent from, Amador.
Commuted by Governor William Irwin, April 23, 1878, to 3 years 10 months.
Discharged, per Act, and *pardoned*, November 15, 1879.

On September 11, 1876, the stagecoach of the William Hamilton line, bound for Latrobe in El Dorado County, left Jackson in Amador County with Edward Smith driving. There were passengers aboard as well as U.S. mail and two Wells, Fargo treasure boxes. When the stagecoach reached Finn's Ranch two road agents stepped out, masked and armed, and ordered Smith to halt. Smith reined in his team and then, on demand, threw down the two treasure boxes. There was no demand made for the mail sacks nor were the passengers molested. As soon as the boxes were delivered the road agents told Smith to continue, and he hurried into Latrobe to report the robbery. Lawmen went to the scene and recovered the battered boxes, which had contained $195 — $145 in gold and silver coins and $45 in gold notes — then found a trail and tracked the robbers until the trail gave out. A description of the two men was circulated and a man fitting the description of one of the road agents, who gave the name Charles Tadman but was better known as "Gumboot Charley," was soon arrested at Jackson by Constable Hopkins and he was lodged in jail. It was not long before he was joined by Charles Thompson and their examination was scheduled for September 18 before Justice of the Peace H. Goldner. After hearing the evidence, a positive identification by the driver and passengers, and the testimony of co-defendant Thompson, Goldner held the two men for action by the grand jury with bail set in the sum of $2,000. Tadman, it seems, had been known to the lawmen as he was suspected of "having got up a job some three or four years since to rob the Volcano and Jackson stage," according to Virginia City's *Enterprise*. The grand jury indicted the two prisoners and they were brought into court for trial in early December. Thompson was again the principal witness against Tadman and both men were found guilty as charged. On December 22, 1876, Tadman was sentenced to serve four years in the state penitentiary. He arrived the day after Christmas and was registered as prisoner No. 7319. He served out nearly all of his sentence, with only two months being commuted, and he was released on November 15, 1879. Thompson arrived at the prison on January 27, 1877, and, in consideration of his cooperation with lawmen and his testimony against Tadman, he had received a sentence of only one year. Thompson was registered as prisoner No. 7358. He was discharged, by expiration of sentence, on December 7, 1877, and pardoned to restore all his rights.

People of the State of California vs. Charles Tadman and Charles Thompson: Justice Court Records, County of Amador — September 18–19, 1876; County Court Records, County of Amador — December 5–6, 1876; County Court Records, County of Amador — December 22–23, 1876. *Territorial Enterprise [Virginia City, NV]*: September 19, 1876.

Taylor, Dan F.

Nativity, Virginia; Age, 50 years; Occupation, None; Height, 6 feet; Complexion, Dark; Color of eyes, Dark; Color of hair, Black.
Robbed Overland Express Train from San Francisco to Ogden near Pequop [Nev.], November 7, 1870, in company with Leander Morton and Daniel Boone Baker.
Received at Nevada State Prison, January 19, 1871. No. of commitment, 71; Term, 30 years; County sent from, Elko, Nev.
Pardoned, January 15, 1878.
[*See* Baker, Daniel Boone]

Temple, Owen

Nativity, California; Age, 18 years; Occupation, Miner; Height, 5 feet 5½ inches; Complexion, Light; Color of eyes, Gray; Color of hair, Brown; Size of foot, 6½. Small features, high forehead eyes deep-set, small mouth, sharp nose, mole on right side of forehead, two moles on right side of neck, mole on left upper arm, mole on right upper arm, long scar on inside of right arm, square shoulders; stout built.

Robbed W. F. & Co's Express on stage from Yreka to Redding, May 8, 1884, in company with John Williams and Edward Glover (half-breed).

Received at the California State Prison, June 22, 1884. No. of commitment, 11495; Crime, robbery; Term, 6 years; County sent from, Shasta, Cal.

On Thursday, May 8, 1884, at 2:00 P.M. the down stagecoach from Yreka to Redding driven by Dave Curtis was near Buckeye in Shasta County when it was stopped by two masked road agents armed with a pistol and a shotgun. They demanded the Wells, Fargo treasure box and then went through the passengers, but got very little for their risk. The coach continued on to Redding to report the robbery and the sheriff quickly organized a posse of lawmen and volunteers to track the robbers. They were not successful in finding the road agents but their descriptions were circulated and several lawmen were certain they knew the identities of the road agents. After the robbery Owen Temple and John Williams camped along the river while Edward Glover stole a boat from Indian Frank and took them supplies for their escape. Afterwards Glover, with his share of the plunder, returned to Redding where he had been boarding at the Pennsylvania House for three weeks, while Temple and Williams floated down river to Red Bluff. There they abandoned the boat and took to the rails, Williams disembarking at Marysville and Temple continuing on to Rocklin. In mid–May Undersheriff John Reynolds arrested Owen Temple at Rocklin and as soon as he was behind bars he confessed his part in the robbery and informed on his fellow robbers, naming John Williams and Edward Glover. Williams was arrested in Marysville when he tried to pawn a stolen watch and was brought back to Shasta, and he also confessed. Glover, who was from Junction City in Trinity County and well known through-out the region, was soon arrested at Redding and joined his crime partners in the Shasta County jail. During the week of June 7 the three men had their examination before Justice Knox and they were held over for action by the grand jury. They were indicted on a charge of robbery, with Glover's trial scheduled first, and on June 16 he was tried and found guilty of robbery. The following day Temple and Williams, seeing the outcome for Glover, pled guilty in the hope of getting a lighter sentence, but Glover was sentenced to serve five years while Temple and Williams were sentenced to serve six years. All three men arrived at San Quentin Prison on June 22, 1884: Glover registering as prisoner No. 11294; Temple registering as prisoner No. 11295; and Williams registering as prisoner No. 11296. Glover's prison record notes he was discharged on September 9, 1886, but lists the reason for his release as "Died." Temple and Williams were both discharged by expiration of sentence on August 22, 1888.

Republican Free Press [Redding, CA]: May 24, 1884. *Shasta Courier [CA]:* May 10, 1884; May 31, 1884; June 7, 1884; June 21, 1884; June 28, 1884.

Thayer, Eugene—*alias* Josh

Nativity, New York; Age, 47 years; Occupation, Printer; Height, 5 feet 9⅝ inches; Complexion, Florid; Color of eyes, Blue; Color of hair, Brown. Long features, high forehead, scar on right upper arm, mole between shoulders; stout built.

Robbed W. F. & Co's Express on stage from Sonora to Milton, January 16, 1878, with Pedro Ybarra, Dick Bolter, and Charles Barnwell.

Received at the California State Prison, June 5, 1878; No. of commitment, 8296; Crime, robbery; Term, 8 years; County sent from, Tuolumne, Cal.

Pardoned by Governor George C Perkins, January 6, 1883, and
Discharged, January 10, 1883.

During the latter part of 1877 Wells, Fargo & Company suffered so many losses along stagecoach routes in Tuolumne County, California, that they stood nearly $20,000 in the red. They threatened to discontinue service in the county but had not taken any action as 1878 began, perhaps hoping that lawmen would now be motivated to put an end to the highway robberies to keep the company operating in their county. On January 16, 1878, after 4:00 P.M. four masked, armed road agents halted the stagecoach from Sonora to Milton when it was near Columbia in Tuolumne County. They demanded the Wells, Fargo treasure box and it was thrown down. The men took $4,600 out of the box and then ordered the driver to continue, and he hurried into Milton to report the robbery. Soon three men were jailed for the crime: Jack White, Newt Taylor, and Jesus Rendone; but detective James B. Hume believed these men were innocent. Hume was put in charge of the investigation and with the assistance of Calaveras County Sheriff Ben K. Thorn they soon had a new suspect identified—Pedro Ybarra—but they lacked the evidence to make an arrest. They continued investigating and their perseverance paid off when they interviewed Fabiana Soto, a soiled dove whose paramour was Josh Thayer. She confided to the lawmen that Thayer and Ybarra had committed the stagecoach robbery in the company of Dick Bolter and Charles Barnwell. She also directed them to the place behind her house where the men had buried $1,200, and then told them where $2,000 had been buried under the front steps of Ybarra's house; but the remaining $1,400 was never recovered. The four men were arrested and lodged in the jail at Sonora. Under close questioning Bolter informed on his friends, giving all the details of the robbery, and Barnwell agreed to testify against Thayer and Ybarra in return for his release. When the road agents came to trial Bolter and Barnwell both testified against Thayer and Ybarra and, in consideration of turning state's evidence, they were released as promised. The two defendants were tried at Sonora in Tuolumne County in late May and Thayer and Ybarra were found guilty as charged in the indictments. Thayer was sentenced to serve eight years at the San Quentin prison, arrived on June 5, 1878, and registered as prisoner No. 8296. Thayer was pardoned by Governor George C. Perkins on January 6, 1883, and discharged four days later. Ybarra was sentenced to serve a life term and he also arrived at San Quentin on June 5, 1878, registering as prisoner No. 8297. He was pardoned by Governor George Stoneman on February 27, 1884, and was discharged on March 3, 1884, after serving less than six years.

Tuolumne Independent [Sonora, CA]: February 2, 1878. *Calaveras Chronicle [CA]*: February 2, 1878.

Thompson, Charles

Nativity, Louisiana; Age, 29 years; Occupation, Sailmaker; Height, 5 feet 5½ inches; Complexion, Florid; Color of eyes, Gray; Color of hair, Dark. Large nose, dim scar on right cheek, Heart, American Coat of Arms, Anchor, Woman, "Faith, Hope and Charity" in ink on left lower arm, Anchor on left wrist, Woman in ink right upper arm, Crucifix in ink on inside of right lower arm, Woman and M. A. in ink right lower arm.
No. of first commitment, 4298; Crime, robbery; Term, 3 years; County sent from, Nevada.
Date of arrival, December 7, 1869.
Date of *discharge*, June 22, 1872.
Robbed W. F. & Co's Express on stage from Red Bluffs to Shasta [*sic*] (actually Yreka to Redding), October 10, 1873, in company with John "Shorty" Hays and John "Jake" Clark.

Escaped from Shasta County Jail with Shorty Hays while awaiting trial. Recaptured and returned same day.

Received at the California State Prison, February 16, 1874; No. of commitment, 5885; Crime, robbery, Term, 21 years; County sent from, Shasta, Cal.

Commuted and restored by Governor George C. Perkins, September 24, 1881.

[*See* Clark, John]

Thompson, Charles—*alias* Bill Early, Thurman

Nativity, Kentucky; Age, 57 years; Occupation, Laborer; Height, 5 feet 7¼ inches; Complexion, Light; Color of eyes, Gray; Color of hair, Light. Small scar just above navel, mole on left shoulder, scar on right ankle, small scar on right hip.

No. of first commitment, 975. Received at the California State Prison, August 24, 1856; Crime, grand larceny; Term, 1 year; County sent from, El Dorado.

Escaped, September 4, 1856, and returned as below:

No. of second commitment, 1321. Received at the California State Prison, January 12, 1858; Crime, grand larceny; Term, 2 years; County sent from, Solano.

Escaped, July 3, 1859. Recaptured, September 14, 1859.

Discharged, by expiration of sentence, February 26, 1860.

No. of third commitment, 2281. Received at the California State Prison, November 22, 1861; Crime, grand larceny; Term, 2 years; County sent from, Colusa.

The foregoing conviction was for robbing W. F. & Co's Express on Coulterville stage with Charlie Boyle, alias "Stiffy."

After arrest escaped from the Sheriff of Mariposa County, and was recaptured in El Dorado County some months later.

Discharged, by expiration of sentence, November 16, 1863.

No. of fourth commitment, 2994. Received at the California State Prison, April 8, 1865; Crime, robbery; Term, 10 years; County sent from, Mariposa.

Murdered Frederick Eagles [*sic*], a fellow prisoner, May 20, 1865.

(All witnesses to the crime were convicts, who at that time were not allowed under the law to testify in the courts, and so he escaped a well-merited punishment for the murder.)

Discharged, by expiration of sentence, June 9, 1873.

Robbed W. F. & Co's Express on stage from Colfax to Grass Valley, July 27, 1873, in company with Dribblesbeis, Stover, and Lane.

Received at the California State Prison, March 5, 1874; No. of fifth commitment, 5903; Term, 15 years; County sent from, Nevada.

Discharged, by expiration of sentence, August 5, 1883.

Now (January 1, 1885) in jail at Jackson, Amador County, awaiting trial for burglarizing W. F. & Co's safe at Drytown, October 16, 1884.

Charles Thompson, alias Bill Early and Ormstead Thurman, had served two terms in San Quentin Prison before 1860: he arrived at the prison on March 7, 1855, to serve a four year term for grand larceny but was free by the end of 1857; but he was soon convicted of grand larceny again and arrived at the prison on January 12, 1858, for a two year term. In July 1861 Thompson, with Charlie "Stiffy" Boyle and several others, robbed the Coulterville stagecoach. Ten days later Thompson, using his alias Bill Early, was arrested at Coulterville. Thompson, a man without means or prospects, had gone to Sonora and gambled away a large sum which raised suspicions he might be one of the road agents. He was lodged in jail and the lawmen found that his revolver was inscribed with the name of one of the stagecoach passengers, who had surrendered it to a road agent while covered with a shotgun. Thompson quickly confessed and informed on his fellow road agents. He said that they had closely watched for the treasure being shipped from the McAlpin vein and thought it was aboard the stagecoach when they demanded the express box. However, the box was light so the men fled toward Moccasin Creek without even breaking it open. They went toward Chinese Camp expecting to intercept the mine's owner but they missed their chance and only managed to stop a guard returning to Coulterville. They tied him to a tree and took $20, and the guard might have died if a Chinese man had not come by and cut the ropes. The Monday following Thompson's arrest a Tuolumne County deputy sheriff was taking the prisoner and two others to the county seat for trial but Thompson escaped and went to the Colorado River. He broke into a cabin and stole a shotgun, then used it to rob John Clark at the Horse Shoe Bend. Next he burglarized the McKewen and Scott house in Coulterville and within a week he broke into a cabin and stole another shotgun and blankets, but was closely pursued and threw down the plunder to make his escape. He fled to El Dorado County where he was arrested in late October and returned to Colusa County, tried, convicted of grand larceny and sentenced to serve two years in San Quentin. He arrived on November 22, 1861, and was released by expiration of sentence on November 16, 1863. In March 1865 Thompson committed another robbery in Mariposa County but this time he was sentenced to serve ten years. He was discharged by expiration of sentence on June 9, 1873. During this term he murdered Frederick Engles, a fellow prisoner, but the only witnesses were convicts who, by law, could not testify so he was not tried for the killing.

Two weeks after Thompson's release from prison the regular stagecoach driven by Johnny Sharp left Downieville at 3:00 A.M. bound for Marysville in Yuba County. There were four passengers aboard: Daniel Kime, Mrs. Ashcraft, W. T. Day, and a little girl. The coach was carrying a Wells, Fargo treasure box containing $2,800 in gold coin and dust and a gold bar. At 1:00 P.M. the coach was twenty-one miles east of it destination when three men slide down an embankment and took their places in front of the horses. The men were masked, their feet muffled, and they were armed with shotguns which they pointed at Sharp as they ordered him to halt. The driver had no choice but to rein his team and then the demand for the treasure box was made. One of the passengers, Daniel Kime, was riding on top and while Sharp handled the team Kime threw down the box. One of the road agents told the passengers, who seemed agitated, "Don't be frightened, we will not disturb you." Sharp wanted to start out again as soon as the box was delivered but one of the robbers said, "Hold on where you are!" Two of the men covered Sharp with their guns as the horses became restive and the third robber broke open the box with three blows from a large rock. The contents were removed and the broken box returned to the coach before Sharp was ordered to continue on. Kime and Sharp were certain one of the robbers was Dreibelbis, a local desperado, so as soon as the road agents let them continue they hurried into Marysville and reported the robbery. Wells, Fargo offered a reward of $500 for each road agent and one fourth of any treasure recovered and a posse went out in search of the robbers, but no arrests followed. James Hume, Wells, Fargo's chief detective, was assigned to the case.

On July 27, 1873, at 7:30 P.M. the Telegraph Stage Company's coach from Colfax driven by Bob Scott was on the stage road five miles below Grass Valley in Nevada County when it was stopped by road agents. The place chosen was at the top of the grade above Morrison's Station near Bear River, where the horses would be tired and walking at a very slow pace. Usually two coaches ran over that route but there were only twelve passengers that day so the other driver, George Britton, was riding along. The coach came to a bend in the road at the lower end of Sheet's Ranch about dusk when four masked and well-disguised men, three with muffled feet, stepped through a gate in front of the horses. They were armed with three shotguns and a revolver, and these were trained on Scott and the passengers. The horses stopped of their own accord but nothing was said until Scott asked, "What do you want?" Passenger E. B. Ryan, riding atop, asked, "Yes Boys! What does this mean?" After a long pause one of the road agents finally responded, "We want that treasure box," and Scott told him it was on the other coach. There was another long pause until one robber said, "Well, we'll keep you till the stage comes up." After some arguing Scott finally admitted, "It's no use fooling, this is the only stage tonight," and one road agent replied, "That's what we thought." Two road agents began unhitching the horses but Scott told them he could do it better, and he and Britton unhitched the team and tied them to the fence twenty yards away. Next the passengers were ordered to disembark and they were escorted thirty paces ahead of the coach where they were guarded by two of the men with shotguns while the other two robbers went through the baggage. The safe, made of sheet iron, was bolted inside the coach and had an outer and an inner lock. The robbers easily removed the outer lock with a pick and then packed giant powder into the inner lock. They lit the fuse and stepped away and it seemed to take a long time, which led several passengers to think they had made several attempts to blow the safe, but the slow burning fuse finally ignited the powder with a loud report. The contents of the safe amounting to $7,578 was removed and the four men retreated through the same gate from which they had first appeared.

The passengers returned to the coach and found that the coach had been shattered by the blast. The lock was torn to pieces, the plate bent nearly double, and the back portion of the top of the coach was blown to pieces, a hole being made clear through nearly eight inches in diameter, and fragments of the lock were driven through the iron safe and the bottom of the coach. The lining and padding was ripped off all around the inside, the back part being almost gutted. The sides of the coach box were blown out and the wood badly broken. However, the running gear was still intact so the horses were hitched, the passengers boarded, and the coach hurried into Grass Valley. As soon as the robbery was reported Sheriff Joseph Perrin formed a posse, went to the scene, and began tracking the robbers. They found footprints and carefully measured them, then followed them for half a mile where they found masks, giant powder, and other items used by the road agents. At a nearby cabin they arrested two men who were taken into Grass Valley and lodged in jail. On Monday night a third person was arrested and his examination was set for Friday, August 1. At the examination before Judge Davidson a variety of passengers, lawmen and the stagecoach driver testified and Thompson was identified, partly by his deep-set eyes and his clothing. The prisoner was held to answer to the grand jury with bail set at $2,000. There were many delays but Thompson was finally indicted and tried in late February 1874 and the testimony of Dreibelbis sealed his fate. Following his conviction he was sentenced to serve fifteen years and delivered to San Quentin prison on March 5, 1874. Thompson remained in prison for more than nine years and was released on August 5, 1883.

A number of men were suspected of being the other road agents and arrested but each one had an alibi and was released. James Hume, Wells, Fargo's chief detective, captured a man in Coloma whom he believed was one of the road agents. He had in his possession a small bar of gold bullion from the June 23 robbery and gold coins which were powder burned, taken in the robbery of the Downieville coach on July 27. Seeing the case against him was made he admitted to being Louis J. Dreibelbis, confessed to both robberies, and informed on his men including Ormstead Thurman [Thompson], Nat Stover, and George Lane, whose real name was George Lester, and also named James Meyers as an accessory. He testified against the four men in separate trials and in consideration of turning state's evidence he was released. Dreibelbis had a long criminal history in California as he had served six years of a twelve year sentence in San Quentin Prison for a stagecoach robbery in August 1865, so it was stipulated that he would leave the state and he returned to Illinois. Stover was captured after being named by Dreibelbis, indicted and tried in November 1873. On November 29 he arrived at San Quentin to serve a five year term. However, less than four years later he died in prison.

James Meyers was arrested and tried in November, convicted of being an accessory, and sentenced to serve a term of ten years. He was released on May 29, 1880, and later died in Grass Valley.

The last man named by Dreibelbis, George Lane, was arrested and charged with the July 27 robbery under the name George Lester. He was convicted primarily on the testimony of Dreibelbis and sentenced to serve a term of fifteen years. He arrived at the prison on June 5, 1874, and served his entire term before he was released on November 5, 1883. Lester, if he learned anything in prison, it wasn't reform as on September 11, 1884, he robbed the coach from Forbestown to Oroville in company with Bob Clement. He was captured, tried, convicted, and sentenced to serve a term of ten years at San Quentin Prison, this time for the federal charge of robbing the U.S. mail [*see* Lester, George, for robbery of September 11, 1884].

Downieville Messenger [CA]: June 28, 1873. *Marysville Daily Appeal* [CA]: September 12, 1865; September 16, 1865; September 23, 1865. *Grass Valley Daily Union [CA]*: June 25–27, 1873; July 3, 1873; August 2–3, 1873; August 8, 1873; August 14–15, 1873; August 17, 1873; August 19, 1873; August 27, 1873. *Sacramento Daily Record Union [CA]*: April 6, 1889. *San Francisco Police Gazette [CA]*: August 19, 1865; October 14, 1865, September 16, 1865.

Thompson, Charles C.

Nativity, Chili; Age, 29 years; Occupation, Book-keeper; Height, 5 feet 4¼ inches; Complexion, Dark; Color of eyes, Dark; Color of hair, Black. Long features, high forehead, scar on top of do., large do. top of head; slim built.

Robbed W. F. & Co's Express on stage from Jackson to Latrobe, September 11, 1876, in company with Charles Tadman.

Received at the California State Prison, January 27, 1877; No. of commitment, 7358; Crime, robbery; Term, 1 year; County sent from, Amador.

Discharged, per Act, and *pardoned*, December 7, 1877.

[*See* Tadman, Charles]

Thompson, Dave—*alias* Major Thompson

Nativity, Ireland; Age, 53 years; Occupation, Laborer; Height, 5 feet 8 inches; Complexion, Dark; Color of eyes, Blue; Color of hair, Dark. Long features, high forehead, prominent nose, mole and dim scar on right cheek, mole under left eye, scar over left temple, 2 moles left cheek, bracelet in Red and Blue ink left wrist, "H B: with "C" above and "F" below and Star left upper arm, 2 moles left side of neck, wart top of right shoulder, 2 do. small of back—left side, American Coat of Arms right forearm, ink line around right wrist, large scar right side of belly, black mole right collar bone, 2 do. on left breast, wart left side of belly; medium built.

No. of first commitment, 1758. Received at the California State prison, December 14, 1859; Crime, grand larceny; Term, 1 year; County sent from, Calaveras.
Discharged, by expiration of sentence, December 14, 1860.
No. of second commitment, 2380. Received at the California State Prison, June 4, 1862; Crime, grand larceny; Term, 3 years; County sent from, Tuolumne.
Discharged, by expiration of sentence, March 20, 1865.
No. of third commitment, 5128. Received at the California State Prison, February 2, 1872; Crime, burglary; Term, 6 years; County sent from, Los Angeles.
Discharged, by expiration of sentence, February 9, 1877.
Robbed W. F. & Co's Express on stage from Murphy's to San Andreas, May 24, 1880 — alone.
No. of fourth commitment, 9381. Received at the California State Prison, June 15, 1880; Crime, robbery; Term, 5 years; County sent from, Calaveras.
Discharged, by expiration of sentence, January 15, 1884.

Dave Thompson was no stranger at San Quentin Prison. He had served three terms there: two for grand larceny and one for burglary. In 1880 after being free for three years Thompson was staying at the home of Patrick McCoffery but not doing well in adjusting to the life of a law-abiding citizen. About the middle of May he told several people that he was "going to make a raise or go back to my old quarters." At sunrise of May 24, 1880, the stagecoach from Murphy's to Milton in Calaveras County driven by "Colonel" Lovelace was stopped by a masked road agent armed with a shotgun. He ordered Lovelace to throw down the Wells, Fargo & Company treasure box and while under the threat of being shot to pieces the driver did so immediately. As soon as the box was on the ground the road agent ordered Lovelace to "move on." Thompson broke open the box after the stagecoach was out of sight and removed all the money inside — $3. Lovelace hurried into Angels and told Constable J. B. Meyers of the robbery and his description of the road agent matched Thompson. Meyers went to the McCoffery house and arrested Thompson without resistance and the prisoner quickly confessed every detail of the robbery. He was taken into Angels and examined by Justice Tait who held him over for action by the grand jury. Thompson was anxious to return to San Quentin and did not want to wait for the grand jury to convene so, on May 26, by agreement he was arraigned on an information and pled guilty to the robbery. Judge C. V. Gottschalk ordered Thompson to return to court on June 3 and just ten days after stopping the stagecoach Thompson was sentenced to serve five years in prison. Thompson arrived at the prison on June 15 and registered as prisoner No. 9381. He served out his entire term and was released by expiration of sentence on January 15, 1884.

Calaveras Chronicle [CA]: May 29, 1880; June 5, 1880.

Thompson, James

Nativity, Ireland; Age, 28 years; Occupation, Shoemaker; Height, 5 feet 10¾ inches; Complexion, Light; Color of eyes, Blue; Color of hair, Black; Size of foot, 6. Long large features, eyes deep-set, heavy eye-brows, low full forehead, large ears — stand out well from head, thick nose, square chin, small mole below left nipple, scar center of breast — low down, broad shouldered, large boned; stout built.
Robbed W. F. & Co's Express on stage from Santa Maria to Guadalupe, September 23, 1884, in company with John Rutherford.
Received at the California State Prison, December 16, 1884; No. of commitment, 11495; Crime, robbery; Term, 10 years; County sent from, Santa Barbara.
[*See* Rutherford, John]

Todd, J. R.

Nativity, Kentucky; Age, 41 years; Occupation, Laborer; Height, 5 feet 10 inches; Complexion, Florid; Color of eyes, Blue; Color of hair, Auburn; Size of foot, 9; Weight, 147 lbs. Two large scars from knife on top of right shoulder, lump or knot between the scars, scar three inches long above right elbow, scar four inches long on right side of body, round white scar size of half dollar on inside of right leg below knee, gunshot wound six inches above right knee.
Robbed W. F. & Co's Express and U.S. Mail on stage from Glendale to Jacksonville, Ore., July 25, 1883 — alone.
Received at the Oregon State Prison, November 14, 1883; No. of commitment, 1444; Term, life.

The southbound stagecoach on the Oregon to California route left Glendale, Oregon, Monday night, July 22, 1883, at 11:00. After it had traveled only eight miles and was near Wolf Creek it was halted by a lone road agent, though first reports said there were three — one large and two medium-sized men. The lone highwayman was standing in the road and pointed his shotgun at the driver when he ordered him to "hold up." When the coach stopped the robber asked if there was a messenger aboard while pointing his shotgun at a Portland drummer seated beside the driver. The passenger threw up his hands and shouted, "I am no messenger." The road agent then demanded Wells, Fargo's Express box, the U.S. mails, and the passengers' baggage, and assured the passengers inside they would not be molested. When the baggage was thrown down one passenger, an old Frenchman, poked his head out and said, "wait, that luggage is mine," but he pulled his head in just as quickly when told he would be scalped. After the express box, three mail sacks, and all the luggage was on the ground the driver was ordered to continue. He hurried to the next station and tried to telegraph for help but the telegraphers were on strike and there was a delay in reporting the robbery. A posse finally went to the scene and found the treasure box smashed with a rock, the mail sacks slit to pieces, and their contents scattered about. Valuable papers had been torn and left behind, apparently out of frustration, in that they were worthless to the robber and these included a check for $64,000 and another for $37,000. The posse followed a trail and found a bundle of bonds hidden under a log a half-mile away, and nearby they found the shotgun used by the road agent. Eugene Shelby represented Wells, Fargo & Company at the scene and he gathered up the box, letters, bonds, shotgun, and other materials and took them into Glendale. By Friday, July 26 ex-Sheriff P. F. Hogan had tracked the road agent to "Doc" Shortwell's ranch eight miles east of Eugene. In the morning the road agent was washing for breakfast when Hogan stepped up behind him and covered him with a pistol. Todd said the ex-sheriff's hand was trembling and he was afraid he might accidentally shoot, so he raised his hands and surrendered without resistance. Hogan arrested him and the prisoner gave the name James R. Todd. When searched he had in his pockets an amount of money corresponding to the plunder from the stagecoach — $1,571.50, less $40 which Todd had paid for a horse and saddle. The money, Todd's pistol, horse, bridle, and saddle were turned over to Colonel Dudley Evans to be held for evidence and the prisoner was placed in a buggy and taken into Riddles. Hogan and Todd had breakfast at 9:00 A.M. and then took a slow freight into Roseburg, and afterwards went on to Portland by passenger train. Todd was lodged in the county jail and all the while he insisted he was innocent. He gave an *Oregonian* reporter a detailed itinerary of his whereabouts for days before the robbery and assured the newsman he would be cleared of the charge. On Monday, July 30 the three mail sacks and three hundred letters arrived in Portland and Captain B. B. Tuttle overhauled many of the torn and damaged letters and, along with those undamaged, sent them on to their destinations. On August 1 lawmen took their prisoner and the coins he had on him when arrested to a Chinese firm located at the front of the O & C Railroad. The firm had shipped a large package of coins and they wanted to determine if there was any way the accountant could identify the company's money. It happened that one $20 coin had been treated with mercury and had distinctive markings and discoloration, and appeared bogus so they had taken it to the bank to confirm it was genuine. That coin, which had been shipped on the coach, was among the coins found on Todd when arrested. A Montana man, who Todd knew when in that territory, said that Todd had pawned a pistol for $2.50 several days before the robbery and then tried to induce him to recover the pistol and join him in robbing a stagecoach. On Friday, August 3 the man from Montana and another witness, who would testify that Todd had bought a shotgun in Eugene just before the robbery, arrived in Portland for Todd's examination. The robber's shotgun had also been sent to Portland to be entered as evidence against Todd and it was assumed by the *Oregonian* it could be proven it was the weapon the defendant had recently purchased. The hearing commenced at 10:00 A.M. and Todd was held to answer to the federal grand jury on a charge of robbing the U.S. mails. He was indicted and tried at the fall term of the Circuit Court and on November 10, 1883, the *Oregonian* announced, "Found Guilty — James R. Todd, the Glendale highwayman, was yesterday found guilty of robbing the United States mail." Three days after his conviction Todd was ordered to return to court for sentencing, but when U.S. Marshal Frost went to the jail to bring the prisoner to court he found him *in puris naturalibus*, and all his clothing was missing. They could not take a naked man to court so it was necessary to purchase a suit of clothes and require the prisoner to dress before he was taken before the judge, and he was sentenced to serve a life term at Oregon's state prison in Salem. Todd arrived at the prison on November 14, 1883, and registered as prisoner No. 1444. On November 12, 1905, Todd was removed to the federal prison on McNeil Island to complete his sentence.

Oregonian [Portland, OR]: July 26, 1883; July 27, 1883; July 31, 1883; August 1, 1883; August 3, 1883; November 11, 1883; November 13–14, 1883.

Toney, John A.

Nativity, Kentucky; Age, 60 years; Occupation, Brickmaker; Height, 5 feet 7 inches; Complexion, Light; Color of eyes, Gray; Color of hair, Dark. Round full face, medium features, stout, built, small round white spot on left side of forehead, small scar on left side of upper lip, two moles near left nipple, long scar on back of left hand, small do. left wrist, do. point of third finger of left hand, vaccine mark on right arm, several small moles left side of neck, flesh mole on back of neck, several scars do.

No. of first commitment, 3173. Received at California State Prison, December 14, 1865. Crime, grand larceny; Term 12 years. County sent from, Colusa.

Pardoned by Governor Newton Booth, October 18, 1872.

No. of second commitment 5788. Received at California State Prison, November 17, 1873. Crime, assault to rob; Term 2 years. County sent from, Yuba.

Discharged by expiration of sentence, August 6, 1875.

Robbed W. F. & Co's Express on stage from Shasta to Redding, November 6, 1876, in company with John Allen and Frank Chapman.

Robbed W. F. & Co's Express on stage from Shasta to Redding, November 8, 1876, in company with John Allen and Frank Chapman.

Robbed W. F. & Co's Express on stage from Yreka to Redding, November 11, 1876, in company with John Allen and Frank Chapman.

Received at California State Prison, December 25, 1876. No. of commitment, 7312. Crime, Robbery; Term, 21 years, on three convictions. County sent from, Shasta, Cal.
[*See* Allen, John]

Tracy, Martin

Nativity, New York; Age, 33 years; Occupation, Laborer; Height 5 feet 10 inches; Complexion, Fair, Color of eyes, Blue; Color of hair, Black. Scar on right eyebrow, do. on the left, little finger of left hand crooked, vaccine mark left upper arm; stout built.

No. of first commitment, 4982. Received at the California State Prison, September 26, 1871; Crime, grand larceny; Term, 3 years; County sent from, San Francisco.

Discharged, by expiration of sentence, April 16, 1874.

No. of second commitment, 6606. Received at the California State prison, August 2, 1875; Crime, burglary; Term, 3 years; County sent from, San Francisco, Cal.

Discharged, by expiration of sentence, February 23, 1878.

Attempted to rob W. F. & Co's Express on stage from Yreka to Shasta (via Trinity Center), September 7, 1878, in company with Tom Jackson and John Doe [Andy Marsh].

Received at the California State Prison, January 14, 1879; No. of third commitment, 8617; Crime, attempt to commit robbery; Term, 5 years; County sent from, Siskiyou, Cal.

Discharged, per Act, August 14, 1882.

No. of fourth commitment, —. Received at the California State Prison, November 28, 1882; Crime, burglary, first degree; Term, 14 years; County sent from, Contra Costa.

[*See* Jackson, Tom]

Tracy, Thomas

Nativity, Illinois; Age, 28 years; Occupation, Laborer; Height, 5 feet 5¼ inches; Complexion, Florid; Color of eyes, Gray; Color of hair, Dark. Rather narrow, square features, deep-set eyes, rather thick nose, small round ears, lobes attached, initial H inside left forearm, small vaccine mark left upper arm, small black mole right shoulder blade, small perpendicular scar right side of center of back of neck, hair mole center of belly — about 3 inches above navel, mole left side of neck; medium built.

Robbed W. F. & Co's Express on stage from Dutch Flat R. R. Depot to office, May 27, 1881, in company with Charles Wilson, alias "Schwartzwalter."

Received at the California State Prison, June 29, 1881; No. of commitment, 9967; Crime, robbery; Term, 15 years; County sent from, Placer, Cal.

On May 27, 1881, the Dutch Flat stagecoach was returning from the Dutch Flat Rail Station when two masked, well armed road agents stepped out and ordered the coach to halt. They demanded the Wells, Fargo treasure box and as soon as it was delivered they sent the driver on his way, and he hurried into town and reported the robbery. The two road agents smashed open the box and took out less than $25, then fled leaving behind an old pistol and their masks. Lawmen could find no clue to the identity of the robbers, and so little was stolen that no reward was posted and there was little motivation to pursue the robbers. On Saturday morning, June 11 the pay wagon for the New York Hill mine was ascending Massachusetts Hill just beyond the Black Lead hoisting works when two road agents appeared and ordered the driver to halt. Both men wore flowing black masks which concealed their features and one sported a double barreled shotgun. At first the two men aboard the wagon were incredulous as they were so close to town and the mine with several residences nearby, but they soon realized the demand was in earnest and reined in their team. Once stopped one of the robbers positioned himself at the head of the horses while the other went around and lifted out a sack of coins which had been made up at Campbell's store and contained $8,000. Obviously he was aware of the money aboard as he went directly to it, and then he waved his gun indicating the driver should continue. No words were spoken after the initial order to halt and the wagon hurried to the mine to report the robbery. George Johnson, mine superintendent, immediately dispatched men to intercept the robbers if they went south while another man went to Boston Ravine and another to town to summon authorities. Within an hour deputy sheriff William Reynolds and constable Peters, with a posse of citizens, took the field and later that day the famed road-agent-killer Steve Venard arrived to join the pursuit. Some arrests were made but these proved to be the wrong men so rewards totaling $2,000 were posted. Two men, who identified themselves as Thomas Tracy and "Smith" were arrested at San Juan Ridge and taken into Grass Valley for an examination and they proved an alibi, but as soon as they were released they were rearrested by Constable Peters for the Dutch Flat stagecoach robbery. Tracy soon confessed his part, clearing Smith, and informed on his partner Charles Wilson, alias Schwartz or Schwartzwalter. Railroad Detective Len Harris then worked up a case against the prisoners for recent robberies of several stagecoaches in the area and believed that Tracy and Smith, when arrested, were on their way to Camptonville in Yuba County to rob another stagecoach. They were turned over to Sheriff John C. Boggs of Placer County and lodged in the county jail at Auburn. On Tuesday, June 21 Wilson was arrested between Colfax and Dutch Flat and he joined Tracy in jail but Smith, who up to that time was thought to be one of the robbers and a well known San Quentin resident, was cleared and released. The case against Tracy and Wilson, though mostly circumstantial, was strengthened by several admissions and the two men when brought into court for their examination pled guilty hoping to get a lighter sentence. However, when the prisoners returned to court in late June they were each sentenced to serve fifteen years at San Quentin Prison and both men arrived at the prison on June 29, 1881. Tracy was registered as prisoner No. 9967 and Wilson as No. 9968. Tracy was released by expiration of his sentence on November 29, 1892, after two years of good time credit was forfeited for bad behavior. Wilson was released on July 9, 1891, after forfeiting seven months twenty days of good time credit.

Placer County Herald [CA]: June 4, 1881; June 18, 1881; June 25, 1881; July 2, 1881.

Tye, David

Nativity, Connecticut; Age, 34 years; Occupation, Laborer; Height, 5 feet 4 inches; Complexion, Florid; Color of eyes, Blue; Color of hair, Black. Long features, scar right side of neck, long nose, mole on right breast, third finger right hand off at first joint, mole left side of neck, medium built.

Robbed W. F. & Co's Express on stage from Yreka to Redding, November 3, 1876, in company with Tom Brown and Joe Brown, brothers.

Received at California State Prison, March 8, 1877; No. of commitment, 7431; Crime, robbing U.S. Mail; Term, 7 years; County sent from, San Francisco, Cal.

Discharged per Act and *Pardoned*, December 5, 1881.

[*See* Brown, Tom]

Tyler, Eugene

Nativity, Honolulu, S. I.; Age, 32 years; Occupation, Laborer; Height, 5 feet 7⅝ inches; Complexion, Negro; Color of eyes, Negro; Color of hair, Negro. Long features, flat nose, thick lips, three small scars on left upper arm, scar left side of back low down; stout built.

Robbed W. F. & Co's Express on stage from Los Baños to Gilroy, May 7, 1877, in company with Dan McCarty.

Received at the California State Prison, August 16, 1877; No. of commitment, 7715; Crime, robbery; Term, 5 years; County sent from, Merced, Cal.

Discharged, per Act, and pardoned, March 16, 1881.

[*See* McCarty, Dan]

Valacca, Antone—*alias* Red Antone

Nativity, California; Age, 44 years; Occupation, Farmer; Height, 5 feet 6 inches; Complexion, Sallow; Color of eyes, Brown; Color of hair, Brown. High cheek-bones, eyes sunken, face freckled, breast covered with moles, scar on right shoulder; stout built.

No. of first commitment, 5026. Received at the California State Prison, November 7, 1871; Crime, grand larceny; Term, 4 years; County sent from, Yuba, Cal.

Discharged, by expiration of sentence, March 29, 1875.

Robbed W. F. & Co's Express on stage from Laporte to Oroville, August 3, 1875, with Ramon Ruiz, Jose Maria, alias Kokimbo, and Isador Pardillo.

Received at the California State Prison, May 24, 1876; No. of commitment, 7042; Crime, robbery; Term, 10 years; County sent from, Butte, Cal.

Commuted by Governor William Irwin, March 5, 1877, to 9½ years.

Discharged, per Act, August 8, 1882.

[*See* Ruiz, Ramon]

Wallace, James

Nativity, Louisiana; Age, 32 years; Occupation, —; Height, 5 feet, 8¼ inches; Complexion, Light; Color of eyes, Blue; Color of hair, Light Brown; Weight, 158 lbs. Very light colored mustache, vaccine mark on left upper arm.

Robbed W. F. & Co's Express on stage from Columbus to Carson, March 16, 1876, with Joe Estrado and Manuel Charania [*sic*].

Received at the Nevada State Prison, April 6, 1876. No. of commitment, —; Crime, robbery; Term, 10 years; County sent from, Esmeralda, Nev.

Pardoned and *released*, April, 15, 1878.

[*See* Estrado, Joe]

Watkins, E. G.—*alias* Kentuck

Nativity, Kentucky; Age, 44 years; Occupation, Shoemaker; Height, 5 feet 9¼ inches; Complexion, Fair; Color of eyes, Gray; Color of hair, Brown. Square boney features, mole right side of forehead near hair, two moles left side of face, strawberry mark on right shoulder, wart on right breast, two small scars on left upper arm, hole on inside of right thumb, and thumb enlarged, sharp nose; stout built.

Robbed W. F. & Co's Express on stage from Georgetown to Auburn, January __, 1872 — alone.

Received at the California State Prison, April 10, 1872; No. of commitment, 5231; Crime, robbery; Term, 4 years; County sent from, El Dorado.

Pardoned and restored by Governor Romualdo Pacheco, May 6, 1875.

No. of second commitment, 8116. Received at the California State Prison, April, 4, 1878; Crime, embezzlement; Term, 3 years; County sent from, Merced, Cal.

Discharged, by expiration of sentence, August 4, 1880.

On Tuesday, November 28, 1871, the stagecoach from Georgetown in El Dorado County to Auburn in Placer County driven by William H. Hill was stopped by a lone highwayman when halfway between Georgetown and Greenwood, about three miles from each place. The road agent piled brush in the roadway and this stopped the horses long enough for him to step out and demand the Wells, Fargo treasure box. Hill thought it was someone in disguise playing a joke and he replied, "You go to the devil!" However, the masked robber pointed his revolver at Hill and again demanded the treasure box and it was thrown down. He then motioned for Hill to continue and the driver wasted no time in whipping up his team. He hurried into Greenwood and reported the robbery and by 3:00 P.M. the stage line owner, Frank Page, and Sheriff James B. Hume left Placerville for the scene. For their trouble they only managed to recover the empty treasure box, found broken open one hundred yards from the road. The contents, $1,000 in gold dust and $60 in coin, were taken. They followed tracks for some distance but a storm obliterated the trail and they lost it and returned to town Thursday evening. Hume took charge of the investigation and published a story that the lawmen had not a single clue to the identity of the robber. In fact the stolen gold dust, or at least a portion of it, was quite distinct so he sent letters to thirty Wells, Fargo agents asking them to contact all gold buyers in their region to watch for the plunder but say nothing of the affair, and Hume made it appear that all his efforts were abandoned. Nothing surfaced until late February when the stolen gold dust was sold at Michigan Bluff in Placer County. As soon as Hume received the telegram he sent a deputy to Michigan Bluff with several men who could identify the gold dust. They got a good description of the man who had sold it and learned that the man known as James "E. G." Watkins had fled into Nevada. A case could not yet be made against Watkins for stagecoach robbery so a California warrant was issued charging the fugitive with "the crime of feloniously receiving, having, concealing, and keeping, money and property obtained by robbery." Governor Newton Booth issued a requisition to have Watkins returned to California and sent it, with Sheriff James B, Hume, to Carson City to be delivered to Governor Lewis R. Bradley. Upon receipt of the requisition in early March 1872 the order was issued for the arrest of Watkins and Nevada lawmen soon had him behind bars. The prisoner was delivered to Hume who took him to El Dorado County and lodged him in the county jail on March 20. Watkins was then identified as the road agent and had his examination, where he pled not guilty. However, he was held over for action by the grand jury on the new charge of being the road agent, rather than just receiving the stolen property. He was indicted on March 23 and when brought into court on April 4 he withdrew his not guilty plea and entered a plea of guilty, supposing he would get a reduced sentence for his cooperation. He was correct and Watkins was sentenced to serve a term of only four years at San Quentin. He arrived at the prison on April 10, 1872, and registered as prisoner No. 5231. Watkins, after serving a little more than three years, was pardoned by Governor Romualdo Pacheco with all rights restored and he was discharged on May 6, 1875. Three years later Watkins would return to prison for a three year term for an embezzlement in Merced County, but not from Wells, Fargo & Company. This time he would serve-out his entire sentence and be released on August 4, 1880.

Mountain Democrat [Placerville, CA]: December 2, 1871; February 24, 1872; March 30, 1872; April 6, 1872.

Weisenstein, John

Nativity, Germany; Age, 33 years; Occupation, Teamster; Height, 5 feet 7½ inches; Complexion, Dark; Color of eyes, Hazel; Color of hair, Black, Weight, 160 lbs. A fluent talker and an inveterate smoker.

Robbed W. F. & Co's Express on stage from Hills Ferry to Bantas, April 27, 1882, in company with Dan McCarty.

Robbed W. F. & Co's Express on stage from Soledad to San Luis Obispo, May 18, 1882, in company with Dan McCarty.

Received at the California State Prison at Folsom, December 15, 1882; No. of commitment, 543; Crime robbery, Term, 5 years; County sent from, Stanislaus, Cal.

Escaped, December 8, 1884.

[*See* McCarty, Dan]

White, E. H.—*alias* Eph. White

Nativity; Iowa; Age 30 years; Occupation, Moulder; Height, 5 feet 7¼ inches; Complexion, Florid; Color of eyes, Brown; Color of hair, Black; Weight, 161½ lbs. Long features, high forehead, scar on breast, scar below left shoulder-blade, vaccine mark left upper arm, flesh mole about midway of back—about one inch to right of spine, large prominent nose—slightly Roman, scar on top of right shoulder, scar on right leg, scar on right side of head, scar on right elbow, mole on left cheek, ruptured on right side.

No. of first commitment, 7874. Received at the California State Prison, November 12, 1877; Crime, robbery; Term 6 years; County sent from, Yuba.

Discharged, by expiration of sentence, January 12, 1882.

Robbed W. F. & Co's Express on stage from Marysville to Downieville, July 31, 1877, with George N. Rugg.

Received at the California State Prison, February 8, 1882; No. of commitment, 10263; Crime, robbery; Term, 15 years; County sent from, Alameda, Cal.

Removed to Folsom Prison, March 11, 1882.

[*See* Rugg, George N.]

White, Edwin

Nativity, Texas; Age, 24 years; Occupation, Cowboy; Height, 5 feet 10¼ inches; Complexion, Light; Color of eyes, Blue; Color of hair, Auburn. Small scar in middle of forehead.

Attempted to rob W. F. & Co's Express on train No. 102 on A. T. & S. F. R. R. At a point about five miles north of Socorro, N. M. in company with P. "Punch" Collins, J. W. Pointer, Jefferson Kirkendall, and Bill Allen.

Received at the Kansas State Prison, December 1, 1884; No. 3407; Crime, assault to rob; Term, 5 years; County sent from, Socorro, N. M.

[*See* Collins, P.]

White, Oscar

Nativity, American; Age, 34; Occupation, Teamster; Height, 5 feet 7½ inches; Complexion, Sandy; Color of eyes, Light Brown; Color of hair, Red and Sandy. Two large dark blotches on small of back, scar an inch long on right side of forehead near right eyebrow.

Robbed W. F. & Co's Express on stage from Prescott to Phoenix, A. T.. October 17, 1884, in company with Frank Howe and Frank Weeden.

Received at the Territorial Prison, Yuma, A. T., November 7, 1884; No. of commitment, 269; Crime, robbery, Term, life; County sent from, Maricopa, A. T.

[*See* Howe, Frank]

Williams, John

Nativity, Iowa; Age, 42 years; Occupation, Carpenter; Height, 5 feet 7¾ inches; Complexion, Florid; Color of eyes, Brown; Color of hair. Bald; Size of foot, 7. Small square features, large ears, retreating forehead, long nose, small scar over left eye, small scar on back of left wrist; same on inside right upper arm, vaccine mark right upper arm, small scar back of right thumb, long scar on palm of right hand, small scar back of neck, square shoulders; stout built.

Robbed W. F. & Co's Express on stage from Yreka to Redding, May 8, 1884, in company with Owen Temple and Edward Glover.

Received at the California State Prison, June 22, 1884. No. of commitment, 11296; Crime, robbery; Term, 6 years; County sent from, Shasta, Cal.

[*See* Temple, Owen]

Williams, John—*alias* John Mack, Mayfield, Mansfield

Nativity, Illinois; Age, 39 years; Occupation, Laborer; Height, 5 feet 9 inches; Complexion, Light; Color of eyes, Blue; Color of hair, Brown; Weight 161½ lbs. Scar on top of right shoulder, scar on right leg, scar on right side of head, scar on right elbow, mole on left cheek, ruptured on right side.

Robbed W. F. & Co's Express on stage from Hamilton to Pioche, February 25, 1876—alone.

Received at the Nevada State Prison, August 8, 1876; No. of commitment, 42; Crime, robbery; Term, 5 years; County sent from, Lincoln, Nev.

Discharged, by expiration of sentence, November 6, 1880.

On May 11, 1876, just as it turned dark the stagecoach from Eureka to Pioche via Hamilton reached a point six miles from the "Sheep Ranch," about eighty miles before Pioche and sixty-five miles past Hamilton. The road ahead was "very swampy and miry" so shotgun guard Philip Barnhart dismounted to examine the road ahead and find a place to cross. While he was searching a man sprang from the sagebrush and demanded that the driver "throw down that box!" Barnhart did not hear the order but upon his return to the stagecoach he saw the figure of the man and called out, "Say, stranger, where is a good place to cross?" The man immediately whirled around and ran whereupon Barnhart "smelling a large-sized mice, blazed away at the flying figure." The box was returned to the stagecoach and they turned back to the previous station. The next morning they took the road again, stopped at the scene of the attempted robbery to make an investigation and found the tracks of the robber, clear in the wet earth, which showed he was running hard and apparently not wounded by the shotgun blast. The *Territorial Enterprise* of May 17 then incorrectly reported, "The next morning the dead body of the robber was found, riddled with bullets on the spot where he stood at the time the weapon was discharged." With nothing stolen and no one injured on the stagecoach there was no reward offered and no motivation to pursue the road agent. However, on May 25, 1876, the *White Pine Daily News* reported "George Mayfield, the man who was reported to have been shot, killed and buried, was arrested last Sunday at Blackburn's ranch on the Hamilton and Pioche Road by Eugene Blair, Wells, Fargo & Company's messenger, and brought to this place [Pioche] and lodged in jail. Mayfield is suspected of being the party who ordered the driver to 'throw off that box' four miles north of the Sheep Ranch on the night of the 12th instant." Mayfield, whose real name was John Williams, used several aliases including George or John Mayfield but when he had his examination on July 1 he used his true name and was held over for the grand jury. Williams, when brought into court at 10:00 A.M. on July 24, 1876, was indicted, arraigned, and then pled guilty to robbing the stagecoach on February 25, 1876, but he would not confess to robbing the stagecoaches of April 14 or May 11. He was brought back to court at 3:00 P.M. and sentenced to serve a term of five years in the state prison. He arrived at the prison on August 8 and was registered as prisoner No. 42. He served out his entire term, less good time, and was released upon the expiration of his sentence on November 6, 1880.

Territorial Enterprise [Virginia City, NV]: May 17–18, 1876. *White Pine Daily News [Hamilton, NV]*: May 19, 1876.

Williamson, Charles—*alias* Charlie Cooper, George Robertson

Nativity, New Jersey; Age, 38 years; Occupation, Laborer; Height, 5 feet 10 inches; Complexion, light; Color of eyes, Gray; Color of hair, Brown; Crooked teeth, dim mark left lower arm, two small moles back of neck, one small mole front of neck, one small mole left shoulder, one small mole left breast, slim built.

No. of first commitment 4301. Received at the California State prison December 14, 1869. Crime, robbery; Term, 1 year; County sent from, Sacramento, Cal.

Discharged by expiration of sentence, October 20, 1870.

Robbed W. F. & Co's Express on stage from Lone Pine to Bakersfield, January 15, 1875, with Ned Allen.

Received at California State Prison March 13, 1875. No. of commitment 6430; Crime, robbery; Term, 10 years; County sent from, Kern, Cal.

Commuted by Gov. William Irwin April 23, 1878, to 7½ years.

Discharged by expiration of sentence, August 6, 1881.

No. of third Commitment, 10051. Received at California State Prison, September 19, 1881. Crime, grand larceny; Term 4 years; County sent from, San Francisco, Cal.

Discharged by expiration of sentence September 19, 1884.

[*See* Allen, S. A. "Ned"]

Wilson, Charles—*alias* Otto Schwartzwalter, Charles Hall, Charles Bell

Nativity, Wisconsin; Age, 36 years; Occupation, Door-maker; Height, 5 feet 9⅛ inches; Complexion, Florid; Color of eyes, Gray; Color of hair, Sandy. Square features, large nose, scar below right corner of mouth, two scars above right wrist, mole on left shoulder blade, fingers of left hand having been broken — middle and third finger badly deformed, large vaccine mark left upper arm, two moles between shoulders, round shouldered; stout built.

No. of first commitment, 6551, as Otto Schwartzwalter. Received at the California State Prison, June 3, 1875; Crime, robbery, Term, 4 years; County received from, Nevada.

Pardoned by Governor Romualdo Pacheco, November 24, 1875.

No. of second commitment, 7222, as Charles Hall. Received at the California State Prison, October 11, 1876; Crime, grand larceny; Term, 2 years; County sent from, Sonoma.

Discharged, by expiration of sentence, June 20, 1878.

No. of third commitment, 8640, as Charles Bell. Received at the California State Prison, June 21, 1879; Crime, grand larceny; Term, 1 year; County sent from, Shasta.

Discharged, November 21, 1879.

Robbed W. F. & Co's Express on stage from Dutch Flats R. R. Depot to office May 27, 1881, with Thomas Tracy.

Received at the California State Prison, July 29, 1881; No. of commitment, 9968; Crime, robbery; Term, 15 years; County sent from, Placer, Cal.

[*See* Tracy, Thomas]

Wilson, George

Nativity, Boston, Massachusetts; Age, 35 years; Occupation, Barber; Height, 5 feet 7½ inches; Complexion, Dark; Color of eyes, Blue; Color of hair, Brown.

Tried at Carson, Nev., in U.S. Circuit Court for mail robbery, W. F. & Co. furnishing assistant counsel in prosecution, &c.

Robbed W. F. & Co's Express and U.S. Mail on stage from Wells to Cherry Creek, Nev., November 21, 1877, with W. T. Bell and Felix Donnelly.

Received at Albany Prison, February 3, 1882; Commitment —; Crime, Mail Robbery; Term, Life.

[*See* Bell, W. T.]

Wilson, George—*alias* Texas

Nativity, Missouri; Age, 52 years; Occupation, Laborer; Height, 5 feet 9 inches; Complexion, Light; Color of eyes, Dark Brown; Color of hair, Black. Sharp features, nose turned up, face smooth and boyish looking, scar on first finger of right hand near the point, scar on second knuckle of middle finger right hand, eyebrows black, hair straight.

No. of first commitment, 1937. Received at the California State prison, July 24, 1860; Crime, having dies for counterfeiting coin; Term, 3 years; County sent from, Calaveras, Cal.

Discharged, by expiration of sentence, July 24, 1863.

No. of second commitment, 3850. Received at the California State prison, July 9, 1868; Crime, robbery; Term, 9 years; County sent from, Placer, Cal.

Discharged, by expiration of sentence, December 16, 1875.

Robbed W. F. & Co's Express on stage from Fiddletown to Latrobe, January 10, 1876, in company with James P. "Old Jim" Smith and Charlie Pratt.

Robbed W. F. & Co's Express on stage from Georgetown to Auburn, January 17, 1876, in company with James P. "Old Jim" Smith and Charlie Pratt.

Received at the California State Prison, February 25, 1876; No. of commitment, 6904; Crime, robbery; Term, 12 years; County sent from, El Dorado, Cal.

Commuted by Governor William Irwin, April 28, 1878, to 11½ years.

Discharged, by expiration of sentence, September 19, 1883.

[*See* Pratt, Charlie]

Wixon, Shephard L.—*alias* Shep

Nativity, New York; Age, 53 years; Occupation, Harness-maker; Height, 5 feet 9¼ inches; Complexion, Light; Color of eyes, Gray; Color of hair, Light; Married. Small scar on right knee, scar on big toe of left foot, scar on inside of left shin, large mole between shoulders.

Robbed W. F. & Co's Express on stage from Battle Mountain to Austin, October 22, 1873—alone.

Robbed W. F. & Co's Express on stage from Battle Mountain to Austin, October 27, 1873—alone.

Robbed W. F. & Co's Express on stage from Battle Mountain to Austin, November 1, 1873—alone.

Received at the Nevada State Prison, January 19, 1874; No. of commitment, 19, crime, robbery; Term, 10 years.

Discharged, by expiration of sentence, September 30, 1882.

Virginia City's *Territorial Enterprise* noted in their October 7, 1873, edition that "stage robberies have become so common in Eastern Nevada that they are scarcely worth noticing." However, a series of five stagecoach robberies did get attention from the *Enterprise* as they involved the same three road agents: one tall, one medium-sized and one short robber. On Saturday, September 27, 1873, at 10:30 P.M. Woodruff & Ennor's up-stagecoach was traveling through a canyon leading up to Vick's Station when a man stepped out and put the muzzle of his Henry rifle near the cheek of driver Eugene Burnett. The road agent called out "Halt!" and Burnett reined in his team. Two other road agents then appeared, one armed with a shotgun and one with a revolving six-shooter, and their heads were covered with masks made from barley sacks with eye holes cut out. There were two passengers inside including Mrs. Soule of Virginia City and Charles Sutherland of Palisade. When Mrs. Soule said she thought they were being robbed Sutherland said he wanted to see what a road agent looked like and lifted the curtain, but his gaze was obstructed by the double barrels of a shotgun and this was accompanied with a harsh order to, "Drop that curtain!" He immediately complied and did not see the man who held the shotgun as the passengers were not molested. The shortest road agent was in command and he ordered driver Burnett to "hand down that box." The medium-sized robber broke it open with a hatchet and removed every package which appeared to contain money or valuables, about $200 in all. The shorter robber asked if there was another box aboard and, when told there was not, he returned the broken box and ordered the driver to continue. The stagecoach arrived in town and Sheriff John Emery was at once on the trail, but he returned without finding a trace or a clue. On October 1 Woodruff & Ennor's stagecoach from Palisade driven by S. P. Sampson was stopped by the same three men when one stepped in front of the horses and brought them to a halt by pointing his rifle at the driver. The other two robbers appeared on the driver's side and both pointed their weapons, a shotgun and a revolving six-shooter, at Sampson and the passenger riding atop. The Wells, Fargo & Company treasure box was demanded and this time it was taken a short distance from the road before being broken open. The box was not returned to the coach and the driver was ordered to drive on, but he and the passenger were covered with arms until a quarter of a mile distant. This time the box was empty so it was expected that the robbers would strike again soon to recover from their "water haul." The road agents waited four weeks and on October 26 two of the same road agents stepped onto the road near the crossing of Reese River on the Battle Mountain stagecoach route. They commanded driver Bill Monk to stop but he was unable to get control of his startled team and the horses carried him some distance beyond. Messenger Lew Faurot, sometimes spelled Ferot, called to the road agents to come up if they wanted anything but this suggestion made them cautious and they simply disappeared into the brush.

The leader of the road agent was gathering confidence as he had acted with three men on September 27 and October 1, with two men on October 26 and now, on October 27, a single road agent stopped the stagecoach just at the crossing of the Reese River. The coach was two miles from Vick's Station and Eugene Burnett was again driving when he saw one man afoot in the middle of the road pointing a double barreled shotgun at him. The man shouted, "Stop! Hand down that box!" The box was handed down as J. Strain, a passenger riding next to Burnett, tried to engage the robber in conversation saying, "Doctor, you stopped us in a good place." The robber replied, rather curtly, "Drive on." Burnett drove a short distance and stopped, hoping to recover the broken box after the man was finished with it, but the robber shouted, "Drive on!" Burnett replied, "Yes sir," and then, seeing that the road agent meant to keep the box, he drove on. There were six passengers aboard, one atop and five inside, but they were not molested and there was no request for the U.S. mails. As soon as the stagecoach reached town Sheriff Emery with tracker Indian Dick took the trail but once again he returned empty-handed. The amount taken from Wells, Fargo & Company's treasure box was not disclosed but it was thought to be a very small amount so it was expected that the road agent would strike again soon. On Saturday night, November 1 one half mile from the place of the last robbery the lone road agent built a barricade of sagebrush across the road and spread a blanket over it to give it the appearance of solidity to the horses. Mike Kehoe was driving with "Major" Stonehill and Road Superintendent W. Addington riding on top. When the horses came to the barricade they shied and would not continue on, and Addington said, "I guess we're in for it." Just at that moment the road agent stepped out, with gun in hand, and called out, "Hand out that box!" and the men noted that the robber had a decided "Yankee accent," something not previously reported. The box was handed down and the robber order Kehoe to drive on but the driver asked, "won't you remove your blockade?" The road agent replied "certainly," and while he was pulling down the brush barricade Addington asked, "Will you give us back the box?" The robber shouted, "Drive on!" Addington then requested, "Leave it where the down stage can get it," and the robber replied, "All right, drive on." The road agent did as requested and the box was returned to town the next morning. There was nothing of value among the contents of the box so and everything was still in the box when recovered, though it had been thoroughly rifled through. It was then reported of the robber that "he is playing in bad luck; stopped the stage three times and didn't get a cent." Still, Wells, Fargo & Company offered a reward of $500 for the capture of the road agents who robbed the stagecoaches on "October 22, October 26, and November 1, respectively."

Shephard "Shep" Wixon, sometimes misspelled Wixom, was seen in Battle Mountain wearing a rather distinctive coat and it fit the description of a coat sent from a tailor in San Francisco to Allen A. Curtis of the Manhattan S. M. Company at Battle Mountain. The coat had been stolen from the treasure box during one of the earlier robberies and Allen had immediately sent an order for an identical coat to be made. When the two coats were compared, according to Sheriff Emery, "they were as like as two eggs." Wixon then told several conflicting stories regarding the coat, first saying he had bought it in Salt Lake City for his wedding and then said that it had been given to him as a gift. He was arrested and lodged in the county jail. Wixon was no stranger to Nevada lawmen. He had been arrested in 1871 for stealing horses and, while in jail, became acquainted with Hattie Frank, alias Kate Forest who was charged with murdering her husband. Wixon was acquitted of the horse stealing charge and then set about helping with the escape of Hattie Frank. He smuggled in men's clothing and Frank managed to walk out of the jail unmolested. She hid out for a while but soon surrendered, was tried and acquitted. Wixon was convicted of aiding in a prisoner's escape and sentenced to serve three years but was released in less than one year due to ill health. He was not heard of again until his arrest on November 7. In mid–January, 1874 Wixon was tried for his part in the stagecoach robberies. He would not inform on his fellow robbers so he stood trial alone and justice was swift as, on Monday, January 12 the jury was empaneled at 5 P.M., witnesses examined, the case submitted to the jury who deliberated fifteen minutes, and a guilty charge returned, all in one evening, and he was ordered to return on Thursday for sentencing. After returning to his cell he asked to see the judge and asked him to hang him rather than send him to prison, but the judge declined. Wixon then tried to strangle himself with his socks, which failed, and then he insisted he would starve himself to death rather than go to prison. When he was brought to court for sentencing he made no remarks when the judge gave him ten years at hard labor, and upon his return to his cell he was served hash which he ate ravenously for over an hour. On January 19, 1874, Wixon was received at the Nevada State Prison and registered as prisoner No. 82. He served out his entire sentence, less good time accredited according to the Goodwin Act, and he was released on September 30, 1882. Wixon was not heard of again in Nevada's criminal courts.

Eureka Sentinel [NV]: October 2, 1873. *Reese River Reveille [Austin, NV]*: October 2, 1873; October 26, 1873; October 28, 1873; November 3, 1873; November 7–8, 1873; January 13, 1874. *Territorial Enterprise [Virginia City, NV]*: October 31, 1873; January 21, 1874. *Virginia City Chronicle [NV]*: January 22, 1874.

Wright, J. A.—*alias* John A. Garvin

Nativity, Ohio; Age, 44 years; Occupation, Laborer; Height, 5 feet 10¾ inches; Complexion, Florid; Color of eyes, Brown; Color of hair, Black. Square features, high forehead, prominent nose, eyes deep-set, large ears, mole left side of neck, mole and scar right of center of neck, slim built.
Robbed W. F. & Co's Express on stage from Angels to Milton, December, 28, 1876 — alone.
Robbed W. F. & Co's Express on stage from San Juan to Marysville, January 16, 1877 — alone.
Robbed W. F. & Co's Express on stage from Murphy's to Milton, February 2, 1877 — alone.
Robbed W. F. & Co's Express on stage from Jackson to Ione, February 5, 1877 — alone.
Robbed W. F. & Co's Express on stage from Sonora to Milton, February 24, 1877 — alone.
Received at the California State Prison, May 1, 1877; No. of commitment, 7550; Crime, robbery; Term, 15 years; County sent from, Calaveras, Cal.
Removed to Folsom Prison, September 30, 1880.

On December 28, 1876, the down stagecoach from Murphy's to Milton driven by McConnell was stopped at dawn when it neared Altaville in Calaveras County. The lone road agent was masked and wielding a shotgun as he stepped into the road in front of the horses, pointed his weapon at the driver, and demanded the Wells, Fargo treasure box. The road agent's sudden appearance startled the team and one of the leaders became "fractious," and then the entire team became unruly, but McConnell gained control and halted the coach. The box was handed down but unknown to the robber it contained only letters and waybills, as the treasure was safely locked in an iron safe bolted to the floor of the coach's interior. As soon as the box was on the ground he ordered the coach to continue. There was one passenger riding inside and the robber, according to the driver, acted as if he was concerned the passenger might shoot him. On January 16, 1878, the stagecoach from San Juan to Marysville driven by M. Hogan was three quarters of a mile below the South Yuba River bridge in Bridgeport township, Nevada County, at 9:30 A.M. Suddenly a lone highwayman, masked and armed with a six shooter, appeared and halted the coach. He ordered Hogan to get down from the driver's box and enter the coach where the Wells, Fargo Express box was stored on that trip, and ordered him to throw it out onto the road. Hogan threw out the wooden box but the road agent demanded the iron safe. The safe was bolted into the body of the coach and Hogan told the robber he could not comply. The road agent accepted the explanation and ordered Hogan to drive on adding, "you will find your box in the road when you come this way again." The robber removed a $5 coin and a watch worth $20, all that was in the box, and left the box in the road before he fled. Hogan drove a short distance but returned and found the box broke open with a small ax, such as those used by a boy, and it had been left behind. It was an old ax with a new helve and had been recently ground to a sharp edge. The box and ax were brought into Marysville and turned over to lawmen, who formed a posse and went to the scene but could find no clue. On February 2, 1877, the down stagecoach from Murphy's to Milton was robbed by the same road agent at the same place, and the robbery followed the identical pattern to the one on December 28, 1876. Again the robber got very little for his risk so he moved to the route from Mokelumne Hill to Ione.

On February 5 at 8:30 A.M. the stagecoach driven by Clark Stringham had reached a point south of the Spring Mountain House in Amador County when a man, wearing a silk mask as ladies wear at a masquerade, stepped out of the brush and pointed a revolver at the driver's head. Stringham reined in his team and upon command threw down the Wells, Fargo treasure box, the lighter of two aboard. The road agent then threatened, "throw out that other box or I will blow your brains out." Stringham complied and the road agent then went to the window of the coach and demanded that the six passengers surrender their money. One man contributed $12 but when the next offered $2 he waved it aside and looked to a third man, who said he had several hundred dollars but had no intention of giving it up and reached toward his "pistol pocket." The road agent stepped back and ordered Stringham to continue. In all the robber, described as an American of average height and slim build, got $141. The coach hurried on to the next telegraph and the sheriff of Amador County was soon on the trail. On the morning of February 24, 1877, the stagecoach from Sonora to Milton was ascending the Reynold's Ferry Hill Grade south of Stanislaus when a lone, masked road agent stepped out of the brush and pointed his revolver at the head of the driver. The coach halted and the demand was made for the treasure box. The driver told him there was nothing in the box but he threw it down, and then the road agent ordered the passengers to deliver their money. He stuck his pistol close to the face of one passenger but the passenger grabbed the muzzle and tried to wrest it from the robber. The robber won the tussle and passenger Milo Hoadley then surrendered his purse containing $83. The road agent ordered the coach to continue on, deciding it best not to molest the other passengers, and from the box he got $81 bringing his total plunder to about $160. In the afternoon hours of the same day a man walked across the field to the ranch of Jackson Eproson, five miles from Milton, and asked for food. He acted very uneasy and when the food was ready he refused to go into the house to eat but asked that the meal be brought to him. After he ate he left and soon afterward a horse was missed. Eproson rode into Milton and reported the missing horse to Constable H. G. Davis and his description of the man fit exactly the road agent. The lawman formed a posse and they rode hard to Farmington in San Joaquin County, expecting to overtake the fugitive on the way. At Farmington the posse was just sitting down to breakfast when the man they were after, who later gave the name J. A. Wright, walked in but as soon as he saw Eproson he turned and tried to leave but Davis got the drop on him. Wright first reached for his pistol but then surrendered without a fight, was arrested, and on Sunday he was taken to San Andreas and lodged in jail. The prisoner was searched and found to have the exact amount of money taken in the robbery but was allowed to retain it. On Monday, February 26 he had his examination before Justice Reddick and, with Hoadley positively identifying him, he was held to answer to the grand jury. His trial was set for April 17 before Judge Ira H. Reed. The jury was empaneled on the morning of the April 18 and he was tried, convicted, and ordered to return on April 25 at 10:00 A.M. for sentencing. The motion to set aside the verdict and grant a new trial was denied and Wright was sentenced to serve fifteen years at San Quentin Prison. He arrived at the prison on May 1, 1877, and registered as prisoner No. 7550. On September 30, 1880, he was transferred to Folsom Prison where he registered as prisoner No. 195. On October 1, 1886, Wright was discharged from Folsom after serving nine years and five months.

Milo Hoadley applied for the return of the stolen money and for reimbursement for three trips to Calaveras County to testify, a total of nine hundred sixty miles of travel as well as accommodations. It appears that most of the money found on Wright when arrested went to his attorney, a small portion was spent for clean undergarments, and $30 was given to the district attorney, by law. Hoadley's claim was refused and he was instructed that he had to seek a remedy in civil court against Wright, but that the time for such a claim had passed.

Calaveras Chronicle [CA]: December 30, 1876; January 6, 1877; February 2, 1877; February 10, 1877; March 3, 1877; April 21, 1877; April 28, 1877; May 12, 1877. *Weekly Appeal [Marysville, CA]*: January 19, 1877.

Ybarra, Pedro

Nativity, Mexico; Age, 54 years; Occupation, Laborer; Height, 5 feet 6⅛ inches; Complexion, Dark; Color of eyes, Brown; Color of hair, Black. Long features, high forehead, Large ears, large scar on right side of neck, do. on left wrist and thumb, do. inside of left forearm, right forearm crooked; stout built.

Robbed W. F. & Co's Express on stage from Sonora to Milton, January 16, 1878, with Eugene Thayer, Dick Bolter, and Charles Barnwell.

Received at the California State Prison, June 5, 1878; No. of commitment, 8297; Crime, robbery; Term, life; County sent from, Tuolumne, Cal.

Pardoned by Governor George Stoneman, February 27, 1884, and

Discharged, March 3, 1884.

[*See* Thayer, Eugene]

Appendix: Additional Robbers and Their Crimes

These robbers were only listed in the summary pages of the original report. Following are the details of their crimes.

Almer, Jack

The editor of Florence's *Enterprise* was a friend of the man murdered during the robbery of the stagecoach at Riverside on August 10, 1883, and he took a personal interest in the capture of all those concerned with the crime. The *Enterprise* of August 18 published the first report of developments and then diligently followed up on all phases of the case:

> The stage was taken in at the foot of the hill leading out of the Gila Valley about one and a half miles above Riverside. The robbers had stationed themselves behind bushes on either side of the road and when the stage passed between them, opened fire on the messenger and driver without a single word of warning. The messenger, Johnny Collins, was killed dead at the first fire, a charge of buckshot entering his chins and neck, but the cowardly assassins continued shooting at him till the driver called out, "For God's sake stop shooting; you have killed one man, what more do you want?" They then shot one of the lead and one of the wheel horses, after which they ceased firing and proceeded to examine the stage. They discovered Felix Le Blanc inside the coach and ordered him to step out and drop his money into road. As soon as he had obeyed this command they ordered him to throw the express box out the boot. He made an effort to do so but the box was very heavy and the dead messenger was lying on top of it. Seeing that Felix could not remove the box alone the robbers ordered Humphrey, the driver, to assist him. The latter asked permission to remove the body of the murdered man from the boot, but the assassins replied, "Let him lie where he is and get that box out at once or we'll put holes through you s–s of b–h." By an almost super-human effort the two men dragged the box from the boot and threw it onto the ground. The robbers then handed Le Blanc a new hatchet and ordered him to break open the box. As soon he had accomplished that work they ordered both Le Blanc and Humphrey to march up the road in the direction of Cane Springs and accompanied the order with a threat of assassination should they attempt to return. The robbers then took from the box $2,000 in silver and $500 in gold and "packed" it on one of the stage horses. They left in the box $620 in currency, having overlooked it in their haste. They also dropped, where their horses were hitched, a pair of leather saddle bags, a belt full of Winchester cartridges, a package of tea, loaf of bread, and an old-fashioned dirk knife evidently made by some blacksmith.
>
> Le Blanc and Humphrey continued up the road till they met the down-stage at Cane Springs, about three miles from the scene of the robbery. There were several passengers aboard and McKenny was driving. When Le Blanc and Humphrey recited the tragic experience through which they had passed, McKenny and the passengers concluded to camp at Cane Springs till daylight and, to make sure that they would be safe, climbed up the side of the

mountain some distance above the road. At daylight they hitched up and drove to the scene of the robbery and murder. The dead messenger was still lying on the boot face down and his gun lay in the road a few steps in the rear of the stage, where it had dropped from his lap when the fatal charge of buck-shot struck him. McKenny turned the broken express box over and found under it $12 of the money the robbers had made LeBlanc drop on the ground.

The Plan of the Robbery

The robbers had laid their plans carefully. They sent one of their confederates, known under the aliases of Jack Averill, Jack Elmer, Red Jack and Boreman to Florence to watch the stage and see when the treasure box had the appearance of being well filled. This man of many names remained here nearly one week and was looked upon as a hard character. Fred Adams had seen him in suspicious circumstances a month or so previous. But there was no evidence at hand to warrant officers in arresting him. He had sold his horses and claimed that he was going to Riverside to obtain work in the mines. He was observed at the stage office every day when the agent was loading the Globe stage and Friday, when he saw that it required two men to lift the treasure box into the boot, he suddenly concluded that he must go to Riverside on that stage. He paid his passage and informed the agent that he would get aboard the wagon farther down the street, as he would have to go down that way to get a saddle he had to take with him. In the meantime the two men who were to murder the messenger and capture the treasure had established a camp in the mountains near Riverside, where they could watch the road and see who was aboard the stage. They were seen Friday afternoon near the road in the large wash just this side of Evan's station. They were under a large mesquite tree, one of them sitting and the other lying down. Against the tree leaned their rifle and shot-gun and their horses were hitched near by. When the stage passed by this point Jack commenced to sing for the purpose, we presume, of assisting his partners to recognize him. His presence on the stage was the signal that the treasure box was full. As soon as the stage passed the assassins mounted and followed at a distance till twilight came, then they pressed on and were only a few yards behind the stage when the driver pulled up at Evans & LeBlanc's station to change horses and afford his passengers an opportunity to take supper. As the robbers came up they made a careful survey of the stage to make sure that Jack was aboard. They rode by the station a short distance then turned out of the road towards the river and rode along the river bank to avoid being seen at Riverside. Having reached the ford a hundred yards above Riverside station they crossed the river and rode on a mile and a half to the point they had selected for the robbery and murder. They had evidently inspected and prepared the place for the robbery sometime during the previous week, for the branches on the bush behind which one of them stood, were carefully parted and tied back so as to give the robber full command of the road toward Riverside without exposing himself to view.

The Trail

After accomplishing their dastardly work the robbers took a trail circling to the right from the place of the robbery and leading over the hills to the San Pedro road at a point about two miles above Riverside. When they came to the San Pedro road they stopped and the tracks would indicate that they did so for the purpose of dividing the treasure into two packs and strapping it on to the stage horse which they had taken with them for that purpose. At this point they dropped a nickel-plated shot-gun shell, number 12 Winchester fire. From here they followed the San Pedro road and passed Dudleyville at a full gallop, one leading the pack horse and the other riding behind and whipping up the almost exhausted animal. Each man held a revolver in his right hand and both men were as silent as a tomb. The boys in front of the Dudleyville store hallooed to them and demanded the reason for their hurry, but they made no reply. About five miles above Dudleyville the robbers turned out of the road into the timber and their tracks could not be followed owing to the fact that the ground was covered with a thick growth of summer grass. They probably killed the stage horse in this timber and buried the money. This view of the case is sustained by the fact that when the robbers passed Mesaville, five miles further on, they did not have any pack animal with them. At five o'clock Saturday morning the robbers passed Mr. Perdue's place and were noticed by both Mrs. Perdue and

Mrs. Pearson, who was a guest at the house. They were still riding at a high rate of speed. They could not be traced above Redfield's.

THE PURSUIT

The news of the robbery did not reach Florence till about 10 o'clock Saturday morning, thus giving the robbers a good start. As soon as possible after receiving the news Sheriff Doran, who was at Pinal and telegraphed that he would meet the posse at Riverside. Under Sheriff Scanland and Fred Adams left for the scene of the tragedy. Upon arriving on the ground Under Sheriff Scanland and Adams took the track of the fugitives with orders to follow it as long as a trace remained. In the meantime Mr. J.P. Gabriel, who was at Riverside on mining business, commenced an investigation and learned that Red Jack had got off the stage at Evans and Le Blanc's station and inquired if two men had left a horse for him there, and that upon being answered in the negative had raved about their treachery and asserted that he would make it warm for them if they should fail to keep their agreement. He learned further that Jack had brought with him on the stage a saddle and bridle and that he had started up the river on foot, leaving the saddle at the station and taking the bridle with him. These facts convinced Mr. Gabriel that Jack was a party to the robbery and he determined to follow up and capture him. The editor of the *ENTERPRISE* had arrived at Riverside, on his return from Globe, an hour previous to the discovery of this information by Mr. Gabriel and accidentally meeting him he informed us of his purpose and extended us an invitation to join him in the expedition. No proposition could have suited us better, as the dead messenger had been our friend. Going to Putnam's to secure a horse and arms we found Sheriff Doran, who had just returned from inspecting the robber's camp in the mountains, and informed him of the purpose of Mr. Gabriel and ourself. Mr. Doran saddled up his animal while Mr. Putnam was having a jack saddled for us (the only available saddle-animal he had that night) and joined us. At ten o'clock we were off in the direction of the San Pedro. Some time after midnight we reached Dudleyville, where we ascertained that Jack had given one of Mr. Finch's sons $15 to take him as far up river as Captain Cage's and that he had said to the boy during the journey that he must reach Redfield's that night if he had to steal a horse to accomplish the journey. This information confirmed us in the belief that Jack was a party to the robbery and borrowing two Winchester rifles and a six-shooter from our young friend Alex L. Pam, of the Dudleyville store, we pushed on with all speed possible. Just before daylight we arrived at Mesaville where we found Messrs. Scanland, Adams and Harrington, who had spent the night there. They came out from under their blankets promptly, saddled their horses and joined our party. We arrived at the ranch of Messrs. Woods & Brown in time for breakfast. Our party was treated to a royal meal. Mr. Brown furnished us with fresh horses and we pushed on to Captain Cage's where we ascertained that Red Jack had paid a young man by the name of Huntley $10 to take him on to Redfield's. We pressed on to G. M. William's where we secured another change of horses. Noon found us at Frank Shield's residence where we found Frank Bernard in charge. Frank prepared us a superb dinner and on an order from Mr. Williams furnished us with fresh horses. While we were waiting for dinner young Huntley came up and said that he was the man who had started to take Red Jack to Redfield's. When questioned he said that Frank Carpenter had met himself and Jack about one half mile above Shield's place and that Frank and Jack had got off their horses and gone out to one side where they had a very confidential talk. After finishing their talk they returned to Huntley, and Frank gave Jack ten dollars with which to pay Huntley. Then Frank gave Jack his horse, the latter went on to Redfield's and the former came on down to Mesaville. We learned subsequently that Frank had agreed to meet Jack with a horse. Dinner over we mounted our fresh horses, divided our party — three taking one side and three the other side of the river — and pushed on to Redfield's. We reached the ranch about seven o'clock and swooped down upon the occupants unexpectedly. Two of our men were in sight and three suspicious looking strangers were camped in front of the house. But Red Jack had passed on at one o'clock that afternoon. We had anticipated a lively fight at this ranch, but were agreeably disappointed. Both Tuttle and Redfield were meek as doves and shook from head to foot. We unsaddled our horses and went into camp, keeping our guards through the night to see that our birds did not take wing or attempt to take our scalps. Next morning Sheriff Doran placed both Tuttle and Redfield under arrest and then made a careful search of the premises. He found a number of suspicious articles, among other things a United States mail sack. After the arrests it was decided that Mr. J. P. Gabriel would continue the pursuit of Red Jack, while the rest of the party should return to Florence with the prisoners and take in on the way Frank Carpenter. Carpenter was found at Mesaville and arrested. On the way down we found at the mouth of the Arivaipa a portion of the stage harness reins lost by the robbers. At Dudleyville Carpenter, who is a nephew of Redfield, gave the latter completely away, as the saying goes. Mr. Scanland had on his saddle the saddle-bags found at the scene of the robbery, and as soon as Carpenter saw them he turned to Len Redfield and said:

"Len, these fellow have got your saddle-bags."

"Shut up!" replied Len.

Carpenter evidently did not know that the saddle-bags had been lost.

The investigation revealed that Tuttle was one of the robbers while Len Redfield and Frank Carpenter were accessories. Another principal, Charles Hensley, was known but not named in the August 18 article. The robbers and their accessories were believed to be part of an organized gang of criminals who made their headquarters at Redfield's. The *Citizen* reported that "for years Redfield's place had been a rendezvous for horse-thieves and robbers who could always go there and get fresh horses and leave their old and broken down ones in place of them, or secrete their booty. There are men in Benson who saw Curly Bill [Brocius] at Redfield's when he was plying his vocation in and about Tombstone, also men who saw Murphy and Gibson there last spring. Parties in this town told the Redfields more than two years ago that they were harboring thieves and robbers; that their neighbors both above and below them thought hard of them and that they had better rid themselves of such men or they would get into trouble. They did not thank the men who gave him (*sic*) this advice, and as good as told them that they had better attend to their own business."

The governor issued a reward proclamation:

GOVERNOR'S REWARD
Whereas, Stage robbing is becoming apparently
a permanent industry of the Territory and
is one which carries with it the destruction of life and
always is attended with danger to
the peaceful traveling public, and
Whereas, ... highwaymen did stop
the coach on the Florence road,
killing W. F. & Co.'s messenger, and
wounding the driver of said coach,
Now therefore, I, H. M. Van Arman,
Acting-Governor of the Territory of Arizona,
by virtue of the power vested in me,
do hereby offer a reward ...
For the arrest and conviction of
the murderers on the Florence road,
ONE THOUSAND DOLLARS
Should fatal consequences to the robbers
attend their capture, identification and proof
that they were guilty parties will be sufficient
to secure the payment of the reward offered.

> Done at the City of Prescott, the Capital,
> the 13th day of August, A.D., 1883
> H.M. Van Arman
> Acting Governor
> Attest: John S. Furman
> Assistant-Secretary
> Arizona Territory

In addition to the rewards offered by the Territory, Pinal County offered $200 and Wells, Fargo & Company had a standing reward of $300 for each robber, though these additional rewards were for arrest and conviction. This brought the total reward for each robber to $1,500. Public sentiment was feverish and the editor of the *Enterprise* wrote, "...and it has already been decided that as soon as it shall be positively known that the prisoners are the guilty ones they shall be taken out, given a fair trial before a citizen's committee, and promptly executed. There is no other way to put an end to these atrocious murders. The administration of justice through our courts is too uncertain. We have seen this truth illustrated here in several instances. The so-called strong arm of the law has proven to be very feeble when raised against criminals in this section, and the people have concluded to take the matter into their own hands in extreme cases like the one now under discussion." Joe Tuttle provided two confessions and in each he implicated the principals and the accessories. He insisted that he had only fired one shot while Hensley had fired seven times. His statement also suggested that a man named Hartzell might have had knowledge of the robbery before it occurred, and that he had given them assistance afterwards. Tuttle said that the robbery was first proposed to him by Hensley and Almer in Johnsonville, in the presence of Hartzell. Their preliminary hearing was scheduled for Monday, August 27 and the defendants were held to answer and remanded to the sheriff, who lodged them in the county jail. The following Monday morning U.S. deputy Marshal J. W. Evans, accompanied by a posse of seven men, arrived at Florence with a writ of *habeas corpus* for Len G. Redfield. The town's people had been informed that among the posse was a close friend of Len Redfield named Bullis and Len's brother Hank. The writ issued by Judge Daniel H. Pinney had been based upon affidavits setting forth that the life of Len Redfield was in danger from mob violence. As soon as Evans arrived he served the writ on deputy sheriff Lou Scanland and placed his guards around the jail. Evans planned to smuggle the prisoner out of town before dawn but deputy Scanland asked that Redfield be kept there until 7:00 A.M. to give him an opportunity to telegraph Sheriff Doran for instructions, and Evans agreed to cooperate. District Attorney Jesse Hardesty discovered Evans' guards at the jail and immediately protested against the procedure. Scanland then informed Evans that his guards must be withdrawn as the U. S. Marshal had no authority to guard a county jail. Evans assented and withdrew his guards. Hardesty then telegraphed Judge Pinney asking him to suspend his order and informed the judge that the town was arming and that any attempt to remove Redfield from the jurisdiction of the sheriff could result in his lynching, but Judge Pinney did not reply.

Once Evans' presence and purpose became known the citizens became aroused to the highest pitch of indignation and assembled. The presence of Len's brother and a friend "armed to the teeth" gave the impression that the posse would, at the first opportunity, overpower Evans and set the murderer free. It was finally determined after much debate that Len Redfield would not be permitted to leave town alive. Evans attempted to counter the rising bitterness by sending Hank Redfield and Bullis back to Tucson and by announcing that he would summon every citizen in town as his posse to assist in removing Len Redfield from the jail and taking him to Tucson. Upon hearing this deputy sheriff Scanland summoned every able bodied man as his posse to guard the jail against any unauthorized actions by the U. S. deputy Marshal, and the *Enterprise* later reported on the events which followed:

> Guards were stationed around the court house and jail on the outside to repel any attack that might be made by the Marshal's party and the main body of the citizens' force, numbering nearly one hundred, filed into the jail yard, took Mr. Scanland and Mr. McKane prisoner, and placed them under guard. The Deputy and his assistant were then searched for the jail keys and the key to the outside door was found in Mr. McKane's pocket. A search of the Sheriff's office was then made and the key to the inside lock was found. The jail was opened and Joe Tuttle and Len Redfield were quietly taken out into the corridor and hanged. The ropes were thrown over the braces between the joist. Although strangled they both died without a struggle. Redfield was game. When the men went into the cell to bring him out he cooly looked around and said, "Who is the leader of this gang," and as the rope was placed around his neck he remarked, "Well, boys, I guess my time has come." Tuttle broke down completely when the men entered his cell. He placed his hands over his face and sobbed, "Let me talk; give me time to talk." "You didn't give poor Collins time to talk and we will serve you the same way," replied one of the men. This ended it. After the two men were hanged young Carpenter was bought out of his cell and told to look at his uncle and Tuttle and take warning by their fate, that he was young yet and could turn from his course and make a man of himself. He was pale as a ghost when brought from his cell but recovered when assured that he would not be hanged....
>
> The crowd guarded the hanging men till a physician pronounced them dead, then the committee disbanded and went about their business as though nothing happened.

The newspaper reported that not one of the hundred men involved in the lynching was under the influence of liquor and that the work went efficiently and as quietly as possible. It was recorded that not a harsh word was spoken by anyone and the men guarding the outside perimeter had no idea that a hanging had taken place within the jail. One man who arrived late stood about the jail yard for half an hour unaware that the prisoners had already been hung and finally marched off complaining, "Damned if I'm going to wait here any longer. They ain't going to do anything; they ain't got enough sand to hang anybody." Thus it seems apparent that the body of men who had done the deed were not predisposed to discuss it but stood about the jail yard quietly and solemnly contemplating their work. As soon as news reached the population hundreds of curious Mexican men and women flocked to the jail to see the dead bandits and verify that they had been hung. An inquest soon followed conducted by Judge Thomas, coroner Schoshusen being absent, and a verdict found that the two men had been hung by persons unknown. The remains of Tuttle were buried just after sundown in the town's cemetery. Evans telegraphed Hank Redfield at Tucson informing him of the fate of his brother and asked for instructions on what disposition should be made of the body. The answer was to send it to Tucson and on Monday evening it was sent in one of Eugene Cabott's wagons.

The *Enterprise* charged that the lynching of Len Redfield and Tuttle had been instigated by the actions of Len's brother and said, "Mr. Bullis and Mr. Redfield could not have committed a more fatal mistake than that of coming here with an armed posse to take Len Redfield from the jail after all the talk that had been made about rescuing the prisoners, and in direct violation to the written agreement signed by the attorney by both sides. If no effort to remove Redfield from the county and release him on a writ of *habeas corpus*, and no threats of retaliation in case of lynching had been made, the prisoners would not have been lynched." The newspaper also responded to criticism of the hanging of Redfield who was "only an accessory" by quoting from the Territorial law, "(243) Sec. 11. An accessory is he or she who stands by and aids, abets or assists: or who, not present aiding, abetting, or assisting, hath advised and encouraged the perpetration of the crime. He or she who thus aids, abets or assists, advises or encourages, shall be deemed and considered as principal, and punished accordingly." However, the *Gazette* blamed U. S. deputy Marshal Evans with instigating the lynching, reporting, "He threatened to place Pinal County under martial law, suspend every officer in it, and arrest Deputy Scanland ... this is a specimen of the bulldozing game attempted to effect the release of Len Redfield. Further I have ascertained that it was one of the marshal's party who made the threat that forty cowboys could be found to take Len out of jail." On September 7 Wells, Fargo & Company paid Sheriff Doran the $600 reward for the capture of Redfield and Tuttle.

The pursuit of "Red Jack" Almer and Charles Hensley continued but, meanwhile, Sheriff Doran had been put on the trail of another accomplice by Tuttle's confessions. On Wednesday, September 5 he arrived at Florence with Hartzell, whom he had arrested at Russellville on the charge of being an accessory to the murder of Collins. At first Hartzell denied all knowledge of the gang but upon being confronted with information in the possession of Wells, Fargo Detective John N. Thacker he admitted that Hensley had his gun and that he had carried provisions and taken fresh horses to the murderers since the robbery. He related many facts of the robbery as told him by Red Jack and Hensley. Hartzell was examined by the court at Florence and discharged. While Hartzell was being questioned at Florence by Sheriff Doran, Red Jack and Hensley traveled to a spring near King's ranch and then went on to a miner's cabin belonging to Hartzell and Dan Dougherty, which was located in the Rincon Mountains thirty-five miles from Redfield's ranch. Hensley gave Dougherty ten dollars to go into Benson and buy ammunition and told him they would return the next day. Dougherty went in and while in Benson told his business. Sheriff Paul was notified so he took Mr. Davis of Benson and followed Dougherty back to the cabin. There they contacted Dougherty and explained their purpose, and Dougherty told them that the boys would be there the next day for the ammunition and fresh horses. One horse, Dougherty explained, was being shoed by an old man who had stopped at the cabin. The Sheriff and Davis prepared to camp the night as the old man went out to burn charcoal to heat the shoes, but he soon came rushing back howling in fright and said that Hensley had suddenly appeared and leveled a pistol at him. Paul and Davis hurried in the direction from which the old man had come and saw Hensley running up a gulch. Although he was about two hundred yards away they fired several shots after him, but missed. Red Jack was further up the gulch lying under a cliff and a third man, whom they did not recognize, was with him. When Red Jack and the unknown man heard the shots and saw Hensley running they got up and ran also. Paul and Davis followed them into the rocks where the trail was lost, and they returned to the fugitives' camp to inventory the articles captured which included Hensley's coat, Red Jack's hat with a copy of the reward notice in it, seventy-five Winchester cartridges, an ample supply of provisions, and one horse.

On Monday, September 24, Pete Mathews, a prospector in the Rincon Mountains, went down to Pantano and telegraphed Sheriff Paul that he had seen Red Jack and Hensley in camp the previous day in a canyon a mile and a half from Page's ranch. The lawmen struck the camp at first light on Tuesday and drove the men out of their blankets. The fugitives managed to flee a second time but again were forced to abandon all their provisions and equipment. Red Jack and Hensley then headed for a Mexican ranch eighteen miles above Redfield's, with Sheriff Paul and J. P Gabriel close on their trail. It was supposed that if they succeeded in eluding capture again they would strike for Sonora so there was great motivation to take them this time. On Tuesday, October 2 news was received of the whereabouts of the fugitives so George Martin, the Wells, Fargo & Company's agent in Tucson, notified Sheriff Paul and hired a locomotive to carry the posse to Willcox. The sheriff took with him deputies Alfredo Carrillo, T. D. Casanega and George McClarty. The sheriff on October 6 related the details of the events of October 3 and 4 for Tucson's *Citizen*:

> We went first to Hooker's ranch and got there between 12 and 1 o'clock that night. It is 22 miles northwest from Willcox. The next morning I sent Carrillo to Camp Grant, twelve miles distant, to prospect for information and come back to the Percy brother's ranch ten miles [northwest of Willcox]. There I got information that led me to believe they might come there that night. It was storming very hard.
>
> I waited and did not send for the men. I took Jim Percy, John McCluskey and John Laird as a posse. Red Jack and Hensley were to come and get provisions from the wagon trains. There were two strings of wagons near Percy's house. Four wagons were in one train. Alongside was another train of four more wagons. The trains were about thirty feet apart. They were to get their provisions from the tail board of one of the wagons. I put Laird and McCluskey under one train and Percy and myself were underneath the other. It was another dark and stormy night. A little after nine o'clock Red Jack and Hensley approached the tail-board and I halloed "stop." They started to run back and commenced shooting. The whole posse fired a volley in the dark and the men were heard to fall. Red Jack fell within twenty feet of the wagon; Hensley fell twenty-five yards from the wagons. Then we kept shooting at their flashes. We shot till I told the boys to get out of the way. I was satisfied that both were mortally wounded. Just then Laird got shot in the calf of the right leg. The bullet went right through the boot-leg and made a wound two inches long. About an hour after, McCluskey and a man named Moore went around where they had left their horses tied to the telegraph poles. They got their horses and were coming back when they heard Hensley going off.
>
> Then I sent after the boys, Carrillo, Casanega and McClarty. They got in camp about 2 o'clock in the morning. We started at daylight on Hensley's trail and followed it about eight miles. He took along the telegraph poles toward Willcox three miles and then turned off into the mountains. He stuck into a canyon and went over a ridge, and down on the other side into another canyon and followed it down about three-quarters of a mile. He had followed right down in the bed. I told the boys to trail, while I kept a lookout ahead. I was ahead on the right hand side of the canyon as we went down in. I saw Hensley's horse with bridle and saddle on standing between us and a pile of rocks. I helloed to the boys to circle around on the other side of the canyon.
>
> Casanega and McCluskey staid with me, Carrillo, McClarty and Otto Moore were on the left hand side. A vaquero of Hooker's called Jimmie was with them. I think Hensley heard me when I helloed, I thought he was in the rocks and was watching them.
>
> The first I knew of his whereabouts was his shot about sixty yards from me. He was behind a scrub oak, I could only see the smoke of his gun. He was down on the side of the gulch on my side, laying on his belly, and shooting right up the hill toward us. The boys on the other side could see him plainly. The shooting became general; Hensley shot till a bullet went through his brain.
>
> The posse on the other side ran right down to where he was. Carrillo halloed to me, "Don't shoot, he's deader'n hades." I replied, "Don't go near him, he might shoot you." Carrillo then took his gun away. He was shot right in the center of the breast. There was a shot in the left groin and clotted blood. I think it was a wound received the night before. I left two men with him and returned to Willcox and notified the authorities.
>
> Red Jack crawled about twenty yards. He received a charge of buckshot from McCluskey's gun in the pit of the stomach. He also had a rifle ball through the right cheek-bone just under the eye....
>
> We could hear him groaning for five hours. The next morning we found him dead. An

empty pistol was by his head. Hensley had a .44 model of '73. The cock had been shot off and it was partly broken in the night fight. Then Hensley took Jack's gun and crawled off on his hands and knees four hundred yards, and got to his horse. Jack's gun had a shot right through the butt, and the wood part was covered with dry blood.

When Hensley first shot I jumped off my horse who was frightened and kept bucking, and to get a steady aim on my knees. The horse was between Hensley and myself, about three feet from me. He was shot in the belly; just a flesh wound, but it made him jump around lively for awhile.

Carrillo stated that as Hensley fired at Sheriff Paul the sheriff cooly called out his orders and began firing back. When he [Carrillo] got to Hensley the man was lying on his belly and when rolled over was "perfectly white, there being no blood left in him." He said it appeared that, had they not found him, Hensley would have died of his wounds in a short time and was certain that if Hensley had his usual strength several of the men in the posse would have been killed. He estimated that the pair had fired more than thirty shots during the wagon train battle and Hensley had emptied Red Jack's Winchester rifle in the canyon fight. When searched Red Jack had no money and Hensley had fifty-five cents in his pockets. It was later learned that Hensley and Red Jack had, only three nights previous, declared to "a certain party" that they were determined never to be taken alive and would fight to the death, and they kept their promise. Judge Nichols sent out a wagon and brought the bodies to Willcox for an inquest, and the judge reported that the two fugitives had been "riddled with bullets." The *Enterprise* editorialized on the implications of the chase and shooting of the murderers: "It will have a wholesome effect by proving to that gentry that the law abiding citizens have at last resolved to make life and property secure in this section, and to resort to the severest measures to accomplish their purpose."

Frank Carpenter, last living member of the gang, apparently took the advice of the vigilantes too seriously. On November 22, 1883, the *Gazette* reported on Carpenter's death: "Frank Carpenter, who was recently admitted to bail in Florence on the charge of being an accessory to the Riverside stage robbery, and has been living on his ranch some twenty miles from Benson, died on Tuesday last from nervousness and fear. The hanging of Redfield and Tuttle has so worked on him that he imagined every person he met was going to hang him, which so affected his mind that he died of fright." With all the principals and accessories dead all that remained was to collect the reward. Sheriff Paul went into Florence in August 1884 and laid before the Board of Supervisors his claim for $600 for the capture of Red Jack and Charles Hensley and they paid him accordingly.

Arizona Gazette [Phoenix, AZ]: August 16, 1883; August 23, 1883; August 30, 1883; September 6, 1883; September 13, 1883; October 4, 1883; November 22, 1883; August 2, 1884. *Arizona Weekly Citizen [Tucson, AZ]*: August 11, 1883; August 18, 1883; September 8, 1883; September 15, 1883; September 29, 1883; October 4, 1883; October 13, 1883; November 1, 1883. *Weekly Enterprise [Florence, AZ]*: August 18, 1883; September 8, 1883; October 6, 1883.

Blankenship, Wm.

On July 12, 1879, the *Phoenix Herald* reported "Another Stage Robbery; The Messenger is Badly Wounded by the Highwaymen":

> The southbound stage that left here last night at nine o'clock was robbed by two men at a point seven miles below Phoenix and about three miles from two former robberies of May 5 and June

20. Besides the driver William Blankenship, who was acting as messenger, and one passenger, William. S. Head of Verde, were on board. The robbery took place on the open plain, the highwaymen being concealed by a fallen tree that lay parallel with the road. Blankenship was riding with the driver, with a short express shot-gun lying across his knees. He saw something in advance of the stage, which he took to be men, thus putting him on his guard. As the stage got opposite the tree, two men arose and the leader ordered a halt. No sooner had he spoken than Blankenship fired at him but unfortunately missed. The robber immediately returned the fire and was followed by his companion. They succeeded in putting four buckshot in his hands — two in his right and two in his left. Another grazed his cheek and still another went through his hair over his left ear. With four shot in his hands Blankenship raised his gun and fired a second time and is confident he hit one, as a loud oath was uttered with the firing of the charge. The robbers having disabled the messenger gained the battle, they ordered the driver to throw down the mail and express box, which was done and the stage then ordered on. Upon meeting the up stage, Blankenship returned to town for treatment. The express box contained several hundred dollars. Officers are out after the highwaymen.

The day following the robbery the *Sentinel* reported, "The driver is reported as saying he saw but two robbers, Mr. Head saw but one, and Blankenship asserts there were three. This is the third time the stage has been robbed at almost the same place." The undersheriff rode to the scene that evening and followed foot tracks for one hundred yards where he found the express box and mail bags. The robbers had a rough time getting the box open, first trying to crush in the side and finally chiseling open a third of the top. The mail sacks had been cut open and the mail scattered about the area where the robbers' horses had been tied. Two miles further west another mail sack was found, so all the mail was gathered up and returned to Prescott. The *Daily Miner* announced, "Persons who sent mail matter out in the stage that was 'taken in' south of Phoenix can procure their checks, etc., by giving proper proof to Postmaster Otis." The total plunder from the robbery included $724 consisting of 275 Mexican dollars, $100 in gold coin, a pair of buckles valued at $40, a $35 check, and the remainder in currency. There was also $25,000 in checks and drafts but on July 25 these were reportedly recovered. A few days after the robbery the *Miner* reported under the headline "News by Telegraph: Special to the Miner: Under Sheriff McDonald has returned from his pursuit after the robbers of last night's stage. He has in charge two young men well known here, who he is confident are the right parties. They were tracked from their home to the scene of the robbery and back. They have not yet been searched. The wounded messenger getting along finely." The *Miner* then continued in another article with news from Phoenix that the two men captured were not brothers: "Price Hickey and Frank Mayhew are the names of the two boys charged with robbing the stage July 11th. They were held in $5,000 bail, hearing tomorrow morning." The examination before Judge Warfield occupied seven days and District Attorney Lemon was assisted by J. H. Mahoney, special agent for the Post Office and Wells Fargo detective Bob Paul. Testimony revealed that neighbors had seen the two boys, Price Hickey and Frank Mayhew, go to the pasture for their horses and ride toward the scene a short time before the robbery. One witness noted that the horses were a grey and a dark horse but not black — Mayhew rode the roan and Hickey rode a grey. One robber's horse had a distinctive defect in the left front hoof and the track of Hickey's grey was identical. Hickey and Mayhew were held to answer but released on bail of $1,000 and $500 respectively. In October the grand jury considered all the testimony and evidence presented at the examination and listened to additional testimony, much of which contradicted the incriminating evidence. On November 1, 1879, the grand jury announced that they had dismissed the charges against Mayhew and Hickey, finding insufficient evidence to support an indictment, and no one was ever prosecuted for the assault and robbery.

Citizen [Tucson, AZ]: July 25, 1879; July 30, 1879. *Daily Miner [Prescott, AZ]*: July 11, 1879; July 14, 1879. *Phoenix Herald [AZ]*: May 5, 1879; June 21, 1879; June 28, 1879; July 12, 1879; July 16, 1879; July 19, 1879; July 23, 1879; November 1, 1879. *Sentinel [Yuma, AZ]*: May 10, 1879; June 20, 1879; July 12, 1879. *Weekly Miner [Prescott, AZ]*: July 17, 1879; July 25, 1879.

Brazelton, John

William Whitney "Brazen Bill" Brazelton, mistakenly reported as John Brazelton by Hume and Thacker, seemed to "burst upon the road agent scene" in Arizona in late September 1877. A California-bound stagecoach left Prescott on Thursday morning September 27, 1877, at 6:00 A.M. Twelve hours later it was stopped by a lone highwayman eight miles beyond Antelope Station just where the road leaves the mesa going South and enters the wash. The lone bandit demanded the Express box and U. S. mail. The coach had on board: Hon. E. G. Peck with his wife, his children, and his father and mother; D. C. Thorne; and Gus Ellis. As the robbing was done in broad daylight the passengers were able to see that the robber was masked with black gauze in such a way as to entirely hide his features but reported that he was stout built, about five feet ten, dressed in laborer's garb, and quite prompt in his manner. His first motion was to command the driver to stop and get down from the box and then hold the leaders by the bits and the driver complied to avoid receiving the contents of a double-barreled shotgun. His next command was for passenger Dan Thorne to throw out the express box and break it open with an axe, which was at hand, and hand the contents to the robber. The contents of the express box included one package of gold dust and bars valued at $1,300, one package of small bars valued at $470, a letter valued at $100, and other letters and papers valued at $150. Ellis was then ordered to throw out the mail bags and Ellis and Thorne were required to cut them open, sort through, and give him the letters and packages of value. There was $600 in the mails belonging to the P.O. department but the value of the remainder of the mail was not immediately known. Peck, meanwhile, was inside the coach with his elderly parents and his wife and child, the driver was off the box, and the team was a fractious one so that his hands were kept busy. Had he shot at the robber the chances were that the team would have been frightened at the report of the pistol and ran away with the coach endangering the lives of his passengers. The consequence was that he kept as quiet as possible. Ellis, Thorne, and the driver were covered with a shotgun and the robber got away with the booty but, inexplicably two bars of Peck bullion, worth between three and four thousand dollars, were returned to the coach. The editor of Yuma's *Sentinel* newspaper reasoned that the bars were not taken because of their great weight. As soon as the coach reached Wickenburg the stagecoach agent contacted the authorities and Wells, Fargo & Company and the usual rewards were offered. Pursuits were begun but without results and the *Enterprise* commented on the lone highwayman, "...showing it, in one respect at least, to have been a remarkable job for one 'agent'—as it is certain one did the 'business' alone." It seemed a new robber had started into the business but one with experience, and the editor was right as Brazelton had previously plied his trade in New Mexico and may have been responsible for as many as a half dozen stagecoach robberies. On August 2, 1878, the editor of Tucson's *Arizona Citizen* wrote of another "Bold Stage Robbery" by a lone highwayman northwest of Tucson:

This editor has frequently read of the daring deeds of fierce highwaymen and several times within the last six months it has been necessary for us to describe the bold operations of these desperadoes, but never until day before yesterday have we had the good fortune to witness the *modus operandi* by which these members of the shotgun gentry extract the valuables from a stage coach and passengers by the simple but magical persuasive power of cold lead.

The stage left Tucson on Wednesday at 2 o'clock P.M., the usual hour. Arthur Hill was driver and Veterinary Surgeon Wheatly, J. P. Clum and one Chinaman were passengers. The ranch at Point of Mountain, eighteen miles [northwest] from Tucson, was reached at about 5 P.M., a light rain was falling and our party was correspondingly happy. About ten minutes later we struck the sand at the Point of the Mountain and our horses took a slow walk. Suddenly some one accosted the driver in rather harsh tones to which he made some reply and stopped the coach, but before we could imagine the cause or suspect anything serious a tall form in mask appeared at the left side of the coach and covering us with a Spencer rifle and a six-shooter commanded us not to move at the peril of our lives. THE CITIZEN reporter had a pistol but it lay on the floor of the coach. Mr. Wheatly had one also, but it was on the seat under a blanket. The attack was in open daylight and so unexpected that we were wholly unprepared, and once under the cover of his arms we were quite willing to obey his commands.... After the collection had been taken the robber remarked that some one in our party 'looked like a sick man.' No doubt he was correct, whoever he intended to address. After scanning the coach for a moment he ordered us to drive on, which order we found it quite convenient to obey and just as we started, this persuasive wayfarer extended a very polite invitation for us to come back and fight him as soon as we felt disposed to do so.... We learn from dispatches from Tucson that the express box was empty and there was nothing of great value in the mails, hence as he only obtained $37 from the passengers his booty was small and he will no doubt feel it necessary to rob another coach soon, passengers, and officers should be correspondingly careful.

The newspaper continued and described the robber in a separate article, and tied him to one of the New Mexico robberies:

So near as we remember the man who robbed the stage on Wednesday afternoon, was about six feet high and well built. He had his pants in his boots and wore small brass spurs such as are used by the army. His face was covered with a muslin mask having opening for his eyes only. His weapons were a Spencer carbine and a Colt's army size six-shooter. When making the attack he held his gun to his shoulder all the time and his pistol leveled in the fingers of the left hand closed close to the gun-barrel and parallel with it which gave it the appearance of being fastened to the Carbine. Our readers will remember the man who robbed the stage east of Silver City, New Mexico about three months ago. Colonel Willard and Lieut. West were on the coach. This robbery was committed in the night and the report stated that the robber "had a pistol strapped to his gun." This leads us to believe that the two robberies were committed by the same man.

A second robbery by the same lone highwayman occurred two weeks later, on August 14, and the *Citizen* reported the details under the headline "Here We Are Again":

Once more the stage from Tucson has been stopped by a single highwayman. The stage left Tucson last Thursday with two passengers, and as it happened Arthur Hill was again the driver. Mr. John Miller, one of the passengers, was sitting on the outside and as they neared Point of Mountain he asked Mr. Hill to show him just the place where the coach was robbed on July 31st. Mr. Hill replied that it was only a short distance ahead and he would point out the spot. They reached the place, "There," said Mr. Hill, "the robber was hid behind that bush;" Mr. Miller nodded, "and there he is again," shouted the driver with the same breath, as the same masked robber sprang from behind the same bush and pranced before the horses shouting, "yes, here I am again. Throw up your hands," &c. The surprise of the gentlemen on the box can easily be imagined. In fact there is a decidedly ludicrous side to this "stage of the game," or game of the stage, or the game stage robber, or — but more serious incidents follow. The mail sacks and express box were thrown out, the man on the inside lost only about $8; but Mr. Miller was more unfortunate, he was obliged to give up his pocketbook which contained about $226. Mr. Miller is a poor man with a large family and can ill afford the loss. He has the earnest sympathy of his many friends. The stage arrived at Desert Station just about dark and parties left for Tucson immediately to notify the authorities. We understand that the Sheriff's posse, while on their way to the scene met a lone horseman with whom they conversed but did not arrest. This shows a want of judgement or courage, or both. The next morning the posse took the robber's track and trailed it directly back to the place where they met the lone horseman.

The strangest bit of evidence from these last two robberies was that the tracks of two horses left Tucson toward the scene of the crime but none returned. Finally a tracker named Juan Elias determined that he would solve the mystery and it happened on this second occasion that the robber's horse threw a shoe, creating the odd impression of an animal with three hoofs traveling in one direction and the fourth unshod hoof traveling in the opposite direction. Elias back-tracked the hoof prints to their source and found the robber's horse in the corral of David Nemitz. On examination Elias found that the robber had developed a way to turn the horse's shoes around and had made the shoes especially for this purpose with four nail holes on each side of each shoe so accurately spaced that when the shoes were reversed nails could be pushed through the ready-made holes in the horse's hoof. All that remained was to turn the nails down and cut the clinchers. Nemitz was arrested and bail set at $2500 but Nemitz was known to be an honest man and he expressed an interest in telling all if he could be protected from Bill Brazelton. He admitted that the road agent obtained his supplies of food and water and kept his horse at Nemitz' home, but explained how he had become involved with stagecoach robber William Whitney Brazelton: "Brazelton called one day and merely asked a couple of questions and went away; returned next day or two and asked for a confidential conversation which was granted. First day I did not recognize the man nor did I the second time until informed, and then I saw before me a former fellow-laborer in the corral when Mr. Leatherwood owned it. I says, "You look like a hard game," and the reply was, "you bet I'm a hard game," and then he told all about his robberies. I was then in the power of a man who placed little value on his own or any one's life. I felt obliged to obey the robber's commands. Owing to the facts in connection with my own arrest and the search going on, I feared Brazelton would suspect me and kill me. If the Sheriff's posse failed to kill the robber, my own death would soon follow, and I warned the Sheriff that the man would not be taken alive unless by artful strategy. No other man could have had a stronger desire to have Brazelton killed than myself." From all that Nemitz told Pima County Sheriff Charles A. Shibell the sheriff deemed it necessary to shoot Bill on sight and so instructed his deputies. Shibell summoned Marshall Buttner, R. N. Leatherwood, Charles O. Brown, Charles T. Etchells, Jim Lee and Ika O. Brokaw as his posse to capture Brazelton. The plan was for posse members to sneak out of town and assemble near the mesquite log where Bill was to meet Nemitz, who was supposed to provide Bill with supplies for the evening's work. Brazelton, Nemitz had disclosed, was preparing to commit another robbery that night and would be loaded down with all his arms.

When Brazelton arrived at the log he had upon his person two belts full of cartridges, two six-shooters and a Spencer rifle. Brazelton approached the log cautiously and gave the signal, a cough which was returned by a posse member, and then he placed his hat on the log to signal Nemitz to come to him. Something alarmed Brazelton and he leaned over the log as if to look on the other side, where one of the posse members was concealed, and the silence was broken by the blast from a shotgun. A fusillade of pistol shots followed immediately and Brazelton exclaimed, "You Son of a Bitch," as he fell and as he lay there in the darkness the posse heard him gasp, "I die brave; my God, I'll pray till I die," but all he managed aloud was a rasping wheeze. The posse remained silent, listening in the dark for any sign that there was fight left in Brazelton's body. Finally they lit matches and counted ten holes they had deposited in the road agent's chest between his shoulders in the area of his heart and lungs. The ambush had been so sudden that Brazelton had been captured and mortally wounded without the opportunity to fire a single shot at his captors. The Sheriff searched the body and discovered that Bill had in his possession the hood described in previous robberies and in his pockets was some of the loot, including a pair of distinctive earrings and a gold watch. The remainder of the plunder, particularly all the money, was believed to be buried somewhere south of town but was never recovered. Ika Brokaw went to town and procured a wagon. 'Brazen' Bill Brazelton's body was then taken into Tucson, tied upright in a chair and displayed at the courthouse until the inquest and burial the following afternoon.

Arizona Enterprise [Prescott, AZ]: August 21, 1878. *Arizona Sentinel [Yuma, AZ]*: May 19 1878; August 10, 1878; August 17, 1878; August 24, 1878. *Daily Citizen [Tucson, AZ]*: May 5, 1877; October 6, 1877; August 2, 1878; August 8, 1878; August 16, 1878; August 23, 1878. *Daily Miner [Prescott, AZ]*: June 4, 1878, August 20–21, 1878; August 30, 1878. *Salt River Herald [Prescott, AZ]*: August 3, 1878.

Collins, John H. [see Almer, Jack]

Crane, Jim

The *Arizona Citizen* reported on March 16, 1882, the robbery of the Tombstone to Benson stagecoach eight miles from Contention under the headline "Road Agents at Work."

A telegraph dispatch received in Tucson last night gives the particulars of an attempted robbery, which occurred about two hundred yards this side of Drew's Station, last night. The robbers fired into the coach and the driver, Budd Philpott, was killed, and one passenger O. E. Oertig (*sic*), mortally wounded. The coach was going up a small incline when a man stepped out on each side of the road and called "hold." At the same instant one fired. Wells, Fargo & Co.'s messenger, R. H. Paul, emptied two barrels at the robbers, at the same time the driver fell forward and down between the wheels — supposed to be killed. The horses jumped into a dead run on the first fire, the reins falling from the driver's hands. They ran nearly a mile before they could be stopped; this saved the coach from the robbery, and saved Wells, Fargo & Co.'s treasure. Paul brought the coach on to Benson, with the wounded man, who has since died. It is not known yet whether the robbers are shot. Detective Paul has returned to the scene of the robbery. There were eight or nine passengers on the coach; but none others were injured. Great praise is due to Paul for his coolness and bravery in saving the coach and passengers.

Later accounts state that Mr. Paul was on the box with the driver, and when the robbers appeared and called "hold," Mr. Paul replied, "I don't hold for anybody," at the same time bringing his gun to his shoulder and firing. The shots by Paul and the robber were nearly simultaneous and that it was difficult to tell who shot first. The driver who received the bullet intended for Paul fell forward in front of the stage and the horses, badly frightened, started on a run. Mr. Paul gathered up the reins as soon as possible, and on reaching a place where he could turn the stage and treasure box over to some parties, returned with assistance to the scene of the encounter to hunt up the perpetrators. Mr. Paul has been the terror of road agents and it is thought his recognition on the stage prompted the robbers to attempt his life. His coolness and bravery is theme of much comment among his man friends in Tucson today, and they anxiously await further tidings of his search for the villains. Only $26.00 was in the express box, and no one knows how much the passengers may have had. Parties who returned to Tombstone last night are reportedly closely watched, and we await developments anxiously.

The passenger killed was Peter Roerig and the *Gazette* followed up on March 28 with a report that Detective Paul had, that morning, telegraphed from Tres Alamos to Mr. van Vict, Wells, Fargo & Company's agent that he had tracked the stagecoach robbers to that place the previous night and would take the trail again in the morning, and that the time of his return would depend on circumstances. The newspaper said, "Mr. Paul is following them like a sleuth hound, and when he overtakes the fugitives there will be a short reckoning unless the robbers discretely surrender."

Wyatt Earp and Sheriff John Behan arrested Luther King four days after the robbery on suspicion of being one of the robbers. King submitted to arrest peaceably even though he had a Winchester, two six-shooters and twenty boxes of cartridges with him. King, before he escaped from jail, insisted that he had only held the horses and revealed that his accomplices in robbing the stagecoach were the notorious cowboys Billy Leonard, Jim Crane, and Harry "the Kid" Head. Leonard, Head and Crane hid out in the vicinity of Eureka, New Mexico Territory but by June 1881 their funds had dwindled and they needed a new stake. Leonard, Head, Crane with other members of the Clanton gang decided to rob the store of Bill and Ike Haslett. However, instead of surrendering their cash the Hasletts went for their pistols, which they kept strategically placed under the counter, and during the gunfight Head was killed and Leonard mortally wounded. As he bled to death Leonard named Crane as the stage robber who had killed Budd Philpott. Unaware that Leonard had identified him as the murderer Crane felt obligated to exact revenge on the Hasletts for killing his friends. He approached Curly Bill Brocius who gathered a small army of gang members, which probably included Frank Stillwell, Pony Deal, Pete Spence, Jim Crane and at least five other men, to assist in killing the storekeeper-brothers. In the running gun battle that erupted in Eureka in July two obscure members of Curly Bill's party were killed and three wounded before the Hasletts were murdered, and then Crane fled into Mexico. In August 1881 Newman H. "old man" Clanton went to Mexico on a cattle rustling venture. Stagecoach robber Jim Crane joined up with Clanton and Charlie Snow, Dick Gray, Bill Byers, Harry Earnshaw, and Bill Lang and the rustlers, with their stolen cattle, crossed the international border into the United States and camped in Guadalupe Canyon. Mexican Commandant Filipe Neri, knowing of the old Apache trail used by northbound American rustlers and southbound Mexican smugglers, sent troops onto American soil where they ambushed the gang and recovered the cattle. Crane along with Clanton, Snow and Gray were killed. Bill Byers, Harry Earnshaw and Bill Lang survived the attack, but Lang was mortally wounded and died a short time later.

After Luther King escaped from Sheriff Behan's jail a reward for "arrest and conviction" was posted and the search continued, but Luther King was never heard of again in the Arizona Territory. However, a desperado working under the sobriquet "Sandy" King appeared in the southwest section of the New Mexico Territory and in the fall of 1881 King tried to "take the town" of Shakespeare and was jailed. He was soon joined by "Russian Bill" Tattenbaum who was captured with a stolen horse. A group which called itself the Law and Order Committee were determined to rid their town of the bad element so they took the two men from jail and suspended them from a ceiling beam in the banquet hall of the Grant House. Perhaps a claim for Luther King's reward would have been made if the offer had been "dead or alive."

Arizona Citizen [Tucson, AZ]: March 16, 1881; August 17, 1881; August 21, 1881. *Arizona Gazette [Phoenix, AZ]*: March 21, 1881; March 28, 1881; June 20, 1881; March 23, 1882. *Arizona Silver Belt [Globe, AZ]*: February 16, 1881. *Daily Miner [Prescott, AZ]*: April 6, 1881; October 17, 1881. *Herald [Phoenix, AZ]*: June 23, 1881. *Tombstone Nugget [AZ]*: March 19, 1881. *Weekly Star [Tucson, AZ]*: March 24, 1881.

Culverhouse, Jerry

Barlow & Sanderson's mail stagecoach left Shasta for Redding, Calaveras County, every evening at 7:00 and returned at 2:00 A.M. On February 16, 1875, the stagecoach driven by Jerry Culverhouse rushed back into Shasta at 8:00 P.M., now driven by passenger Charlie Fife, and stopped in front of the Empire Hotel. On board were the U. S. mails, the Wells, Fargo & Company Express box and several passengers who reported that an attempt had been made to stop the coach. They said that just as the coach was descending the grade below Lower Springs three masked road agents jumped onto the road from behind a bush and pointed their weapons, including at least one double-barreled shotgun, and ordered Culverhouse to halt. The coach was nearly abreast of the robbers when they appeared so Culverhouse whipped up his team and drove past them, then turned to look back just as the man with the shotgun fired both barrels. The buckshot struck the coach and Culverhouse's head, face and back but instead of causing the coach to halt the explosion frightened the horses and they "struck out at high speed." Culverhouse, though severely wounded, kept control and reined in his team after they were out of danger from the road agents. He let passenger Fife, who had been riding inside, take the reins and drive back into Shasta. The sheriff was summoned and he organized a posse and they rushed to the scene to investigate before taking the trail of the three robbers. Eight buckshot were removed from Culverhouse and the reporter for the *Shasta Courier* counted forty-three shot in the canvas cover just behind the driver's seat. He said, "it is evident that the shot which struck there glanced upward, striking Culverhouse after their force was partly spent." Had the load struck him directly the driver would have been killed. One buckshot struck the driver's right eye and it was thought it might have penetrated his eyeball so on February 27 he started for San Francisco to consult an oculist.

By February 20 officers arrested Charles D. Burch, a man who had served a term at San Quentin Prison for a burglary in El Dorado County. Burch proved an alibi and, within a month, two more men were behind bars charged with the robbery attempt, one named William Chandler but better known as "Wild Bill," and the other named H. S. Hunt. Both men were examined and held for action by the grand jury, but there was not enough evidence to bring an indictment so they were released. However, it was generally believed that it was Hunt who fired the load that wounded Culverhouse. On April 17 the *Courier* welcomed Culverhouse's return to Shasta and remarked that "we are glad to see him well and hearty" and observed that he had "undergone a severe operation" on his eye. The following year Culverhouse was working as a deputy sheriff and operating his own stage line between Yreka and Shasta via Scott Valley when he announced on March 18 that he was going to operate an express from Trinity Center to Cinnabar. He hired H. L. Tickner to run the operation and P. G. Strickland as Yreka's agent. In June 1876 Charles D. Burch and James Demerest committed a store burglary at Trinity Center and, when Constable Bell from Anderson Station tried to arrest them, they resisted and Burch was killed. H. S. Hunt met the same fate on October 24, 1876, when he was shot during another stagecoach robbery [see Appendix: H. S. Hunt].

Shasta Courier [CA]: February 20, 1875; February 27, 1875; April 17, 1875; March 18, 1876; July 1, 1876; October 21, 1876; October 28, 1876.

Hackett, George W.

The stagecoach from Laporte in Plumas County bound for Oroville in Butte County, California, driven by H. Helms was on the down grade into Strawberry Valley when a lone road agent, masked and armed, stepped from the side of the road. The robber took up a position in front of the horses blocking the road and bringing them to a halt. Messenger George Hackett immediately fired one load from his double-barreled shotgun at the robber who then tried to conceal himself behind one of the leaders, but one arm stuck out and Hackett took careful aim and shot at the exposed arm. The robber then started to run away but fell after going only a few feet. He quickly got up and went on but again he fell before reaching the bushes on the side the road, rose and scrambled into the brush. Hackett dismounted and recovered the robber's hat, which he had dropped, and it showed several buckshot holes so Hackett was certain he had hit his mark. Helms and Hackett were concerned that the man might have confederates nearby so Helms whipped up the team and took the coach at top speed into Strawberry Valley where they telephoned Laporte with the news. There were no passengers aboard but Wells, Fargo was shipping more than $30,000 in treasure on that trip, so it appeared the robber was well informed. From Laporte a posse was organized and headed for the scene of the robbery but, though it was almost certain the robber had been wounded, he could not be found. The stagecoach continued on toward Oroville and when it was two miles above Boston Ranch Hackett saw a coat fluttering from behind a tree and almost at the same instant saw the glistening from a gun barrel. Looking closer he saw a masked man standing nearly behind the tree so he raised his shotgun and fired the load from one barrel. The robber fired his shotgun at the same moment and two of the robber's buckshot struck Hackett in the face, causing minor wounds. The robber then ran out across the road and up a hill while Hackett took careful aim. However, when he tried to fire his second load the shell misfired and he missed a sure chance to dispatch the aspiring road agent. This robber was never identified.

Weekly Mercury [Oroville, CA]: July 14, 1882.

Head, Harry [*see* Appendix—Crane, Jim]

Hensley, Charles [*see* Appendix—Almer, Jack]

Hunt, H. S.

The stagecoach from Weaver to Shasta in Shasta County was coming down the mountain thirteen miles from its destination shortly after noon, and coming around a short curve when a lone road agent jumped from behind a bush and covered John McNemar with a Spencer rifle before the messenger could pick up his shot gun. He demanded the treasure box and it was thrown down. The robber ordered the driver to continue and he started for the side of the road with the treasure box but McNemar, as soon as they were out of sight of the road agent, stopped the coach, got down, and returned to the scene of the robbery. Just as he arrived the road agent was finishing his work, having easily opened the box with a pick. He had taken $6,800 in gold from the box and had it in his hands as he looked up and saw McNemar. The messenger fired one barrel from his shotgun and this knocked the robber down, but he sprang up and started to run. The road agent was about to pass over a ridge fifty yards distant, which would have concealed him, when McNemar fired his second load and killed his man. The messenger gathered up the deceased, the box and treasure and carried it to the coach. The stagecoach then continued on to the Tower House where he left the body and continued on to Shasta. Shasta County's coroner William P. Hartman went to the Tower House with an inquest jury to "inquire into the death of an unknown person found dead in the woods, ... by gun shot wounds, said shots being delivered from a gun in the hand of John McNemar, (Wells, Fargo & Co's Messenger)" and concluded that the death was justified. The description of the dead road agent was circulated and it was soon determined that he was H. S. Hunt, the man believed to be responsible for the shooting of driver Jerry Culverhouse in the robbery of October 21, 1876.

Shasta Courier [CA]: October 21, 1876; October 28, 1876.

Leonard, Bill [*see* Appendix — Crane, Jim]

Lloyd, John T.

On February 10 the stagecoach from Mojave to Darwin in Inyo County, California, driven by Billy Balch was attacked by several masked Mexicans at daybreak, but the messenger managed to arrest one of the party and saved the treasure. On February 14 at daybreak the same coach again driven by Billy Balch was approaching the same location twelve miles south of Darwin with passenger John T. "Jack" Lloyd riding on top next to the driver. It was the day for a messenger and the treasure box to be aboard, and Lloyd's position next to the driver gave the impression he was the messenger and confirmed for the road agents that there was heavy treasure on board. In fact, there was no treasure nor messenger aboard.

One road agent, without warning or command, fired at Lloyd just as the coach passed and nearly the entire load took effect in the back of Lloyd's head killing him instantly. Lloyd slumped forward but did not fall off the stagecoach and Balch, who had one buckshot pellet pass through his coat sleeve, again whipped up his team and took it into Darwin. The local deputy sheriff organized several posses and led the main force to the scene of the killing to take up the trail of the murderers, but to no avail. The remains of Lloyd were turned over to the Odd Fellows Lodge at Darwin for burial and his lodge at Palisade was notified by mail.

Silver State [Winnemucca, NV]: February 19, 1877.

Mann, Billy

The stagecoach from Hamilton was bound for Pioche when it was stopped by road agents ten miles from its destination. It was just passing over the summit of a steep grade when three men disguised with barley sacks for masks, feet muffled with sacks, and painted as Indians suddenly sprang from behind rocks onto the road. They ordered the coach to stop and one of the robbers, to emphasize their determination, leveled his shotgun at driver William Mann. The driver pulled up the team and Frank Sanderson, a passenger riding next to the driver, handed down Wells, Fargo & Company's treasure box upon demand, but the mail sacks were not requested. As the box was being delivered the shotgun of one robber accidentally discharged, one buckshot pellet striking Mann in the right hand and ranging along the lower part of the thumb, passing through the arm between the elbow and shoulder, and severing an artery. The four passengers riding inside were then assured that they would not be molested. The leader of the road agents broke open the box and, after securing the contents, ordered the coach to drive on. Sanderson took the reins from the wounded driver and when the stagecoach was a quarter mile from the scene of the robbery it was stopped and Mann was examined. It was concluded that he was dying from loss of blood and Sanderson was determined to whip up the horses and hurry to the next station but within a few moments, before the station was reached, Mann died. J. T. Parker, a passenger on his way to Pioche, brought Mann's body back to Hamilton in a light wagon while Sanderson continued on to Pioche with the stagecoach. An inquest was held at Hamilton and the jury found that: "The deceased was named William Mann, was a native of Wisconsin, aged about 35 or 40 years, that he came to his death on the 27th day of April, A.D. 1873 in the county of Nye, from a gunshot wound, the gun being fired in the hands of a person to the jury unknown." Passenger Joe Parker described the road agents for the lawmen: "The leader was a large man with a prominent nose, full face, squarely built, evidently a Dutchman, and done all the talking. The second one was evidently a young man of light, slim build. The third one who shot Mann was taller than the others, of light build." While the inquest was being held men were already organizing and soon a posse was on the trail of the murderers, under the direction of deputy sheriff Jacob M. Bellrude. Parties of Shoshone Indian trackers also took to the field to search for the trail of the robbers. Soon a man named John Peters was arrested for the robbery but he does not appear on any later rolls in Nevada's criminal record. No other persons were arrested for the murder or robbery.

Carson Daily Appeal [NV]: April 30, 1873. *Territorial Enterprise [Virginia City, NV]*: May 20, 1873. *White Pine News [Hamilton, NV]*: May 3, 1873, May 31, 1873.

Phelps, Charlie

On Wednesday, July 16, 1873, Charlie Phelps was driving the Gilmer & Salisbury stagecoach from Corrine, Utah to Helena, Montana. In the evening hours, when he reached Black Rock Station in Port Neuf Canyon, road agents attacked the stagecoach and shot Phelps. He was seriously wounded and lingered for a day before he died of his wounds. Phelps, who was fifty years old, had come to Montana from western New York, and had been working for the stage line for several years before his death. He was buried at Malad City on July 18. Wells, Fargo posted a reward of $500 for the capture and conviction of each road agent and dispatched their detectives to search the roads and surrounding area for the murderers. Gilmer & Salisbury also dispatched several detectives to pursue the robbers, but they could not be found.

Corrine Reporter [UT]: July 18, 1873.

Philpott, Budd (Eli) [see Appendix—Crane, Jim]

Redfield, Len [see Appendix—Almer, Jack]

Richards, Richard

The leading six horse coach driven by Jimmy Harrington, followed by the bullion wagon driven by Richard "Whistling Dick" Richards, had just left Malcolm's water station, the last house on the road to Contention and only four miles from Tombstone. They were moving along at a rapid gait when the order to "Halt" was given from the roadside and simultaneously a volley was fired into them from both sides of the road. The off-leader [front right horse] of the coach was struck in the neck and all the horses became unmanageable. Richards, in the rear wagon, was hit in the calf of the leg, receiving a painful flesh wound, but kept his seat and his wagon right side up. The horses ran about half a mile before the wounded horse weakened and fell from loss of blood. John Clum, mayor and editor of Tombstone's *Epitaph* newspaper with the assistance of other passengers, cut the leaders loose and on they went, it being the general impression that all the passengers were aboard. Clum had been riding on the inside and he was missed but it was supposed by his fellow passengers that he had taken a seat on top, so his absence was not detected until the arrival of the coach at Contention. Sheriff John Behan and C. D. Reppy started out at 3 A.M. to search for the missing mayor and arrived at Contention after 4:00 A.M. where they learned from a passenger the particulars of the affair. Behan and Reppy then started for Tombstone and, upon arriving at the place where the attack was made, examined the locality carefully but found no trace of the missing man. In the meantime a second party which left Tombstone at 4 A.M. arrived at Malcolm's Station and learned that two teamsters, in camp with their wagons near the point of the attack, had not only heard the noise of the shooting but could distinctly see the flashes, the attack having been made about the apex of the first rise beyond. The party continued down the road about a half mile beyond the attacking point and by lighting a match found two large pools of blood on the right where the off leader had given out, and after wandering several hundred rods to the right of the road marking his trail by his ebbing life had already fallen prey to the skulking coyotes. They could not discover any trail for Clum so the party proceeded to Contention where they heard that Clum had been heard of at the Grand Central Mill, so they went there and learned that the mayor had taken the ore road to the mill and after resting had gone by horseback to Benson, arriving between 7 and 8 o'clock. When it was light the scene of the attack was searched again and it was found that there were no rifle cartridge shells on the ground, though all parties claim that there were from fifteen to twenty shots fired in quick succession. From one of the teamsters it was learned that the would-be murderers had probably fled up the gulch to the northeast just above Malcolm's as about one hundred yards from the road there was evidence of the repeated hitching of horses in the thick brush, and shortly after the shooting the sound of fleeing hoofs came from that direction. The road agents were never identified.

Daily Epitaph [Tombstone, AZ]: December 14, 1881. *Weekly Epitaph [Tombstone, AZ]*:December 19, 1881.

Roerig, Peter [see Appendix—Crane, Jim]

Romero, Senor

On the night of June 19, 1884, W. Thompson, agent for Wells, Fargo & Company in Leone, Mexico, went to the depot of the Mexican Central Railroad, which was three miles from the office. It had become a habit for the agent to take a wagon to meet the through-train at 6:06 P.M. and then await the arrival of the local train, which arrived at 7:55 P.M. He would deliver any passengers, mail and express for the trains and pick-up passengers, mail and express for Leon. Alberto Romero, clerk for Thompson, sometimes worked as his driver and porter Antonio rode along on that evening. The local authorities provided one man from the mounted police (gendarmes) to serve as a messenger on every trip and he climbed into the wagon bed. They arrived without incident and, there being no passengers nor mail, loaded the treasure box and started for the office a little after 8:00 P.M. The roads between the office and depot were very narrow and the houses in many parts were separated by fields. The wagon came by way of the Calle de la Pieata Parada into an area where Thompson usually prepared his shotgun, but Romero forgot to put the shotgun in the wagon boot before they started for the depot that evening. As they arrived at the Calle Honda, a lonely watercourse crossing the Calle de la Pieata Parada, a dozen men opened fire on the wagon and its occupants. The mules bolted just as Romero cried out that he had been shot, and Thompson pulled Romero's pistol from its scabbard just before the driver fell from the wagon. Thompson returned fire until he was out of ammunition and at the same time the gendarme stood up and fired one shot, then fell into the wagon bed wounded. Seeing their predicament porter Antonio ran away. The wagon was still moving forward so one of the road agents ran out of his hiding place and grabbed the lead mules and then turned the wagon into the first house on the left while firing his pistol at Thompson. A policeman who had been lighting street lamps at the corner of the Calle Conquista, the next large cross-street, ran toward the wagon and fired at the man holding the mules but when two yards distant the road agent returned fire and wounded the policeman. Thompson jumped down and ran onto the Calle Conquista but as soon as he thought it safe he started back for the wagon and treasure box. He met the wounded policeman and Antonio and the three men returned to the scene. Romero lay in the roadway where he fell, dead from his wounds, but the wagon was gone. The laws of the country prohibited the touching of any dead person until seen by the police and a judge so Thompson was obliged to go to town and bring them back. By the time he returned the wagon had been found on a nearby street and brought up. The treasure box was gone and by 10:00 P.M. Romero's body was lifted into the wagon bed and taken into Leone. There were five bullet holes in the wagon, one through the lantern, and two in Romero but Thompson estimated that there were more than twenty-five shots fired at them. The loss to Wells, Fargo was the treasure box with $100 inside, a buffalo robe worth $15, a roll of blankets and clothing, and one pistol belonging to the company.

Wells, Fargo & Company received a great deal of sympathy and support from the local authorities and they were soon on the track of the road agents, but there were many undesirable characters in the vicinity of Leone at the time and all were of interest to the police. J. J. Valentine, General Manager for Wells, Fargo, sent detective John Thacker to Leone to investigate and he wrote back of the progress. He said that the police had arrested every bad character they could find and had shipped twenty-five men to the Yucatan, a place where "the climate is slow death to the natives of this table land," and the life expectancy of a worker was about one year. This group did not include the two leaders of the band of men involved in the attack—Ciriaco Isas and Dolores Zaragoza—but they were being sought and several other gang members were known by name. The 7th Military District was given orders to arrest any undesirable characters within their jurisdiction, which included the regions of Guanajuato, Queretaro and Morelia, and detachments of troops took to the field. The 4th Cavalry took up the search as well and by July 16 fourteen more "undesirable" men had been arrested and were being prepared for their journey to the Yucatan, bringing the total to thirty-nine men. Thacker was certain that several of the road agents were among this later group and reported that within a few days all the road agents would be arrested, and those identified as taking part in the attack would probably be sent to the penitentiary for long terms, or to the Yucatan to be worked to death.

Wells Fargo Historical Services—Wells Fargo Bank, N. A.: letter from W. Thompson to E. M. Cooper, June 23, 1884; letter from J. N. Thacker to J. J. Valentine, July 17, 1884.

Smith, George H.

The stagecoach from Anaheim arrived in San Diego on March 10, 1877, carrying the mail from the north and the driver reported that the stagecoach had been stopped on the previous night by highwayman and the driver on the San Juan division wounded. One of the through passengers, C. F. Lutgen, then gave the details to the reporter for the *San Diego Union Tribune*. Lutgen reported that at 9:15 P.M. the coach was nineteen miles south of Anaheim in Orange County, four miles north of Rawson's Ranch and fourteen miles north of San Juan Capistrano where there was deep sand on the road which required the coach to move quite slowly. Lutgen was riding on top next to driver George H. Smith and just as the coach turned a curve a man appeared from behind some bushes on the left side of the road and hailed the driver, saying, "Hold on, hold on!" Lutgen said he had been drowsy but the command to stop awoke him fully and he thought that the man only wanted a ride. Smith began to rein in his team just as the man came into clear view and they saw that he was masked. Smith asked, "What do you want?" and the road agent demanded, "Hand down that box!" as he pointed his six-shooter at Smith to emphasize the command. The driver's question had been intended to distract the robber and Smith instantly raised his whip, and in the same moment the road agent fired one round at him. The ball grazed Lutgen's knee and struck Smith in the left hand, the hand in which he held the reins. Smith applied the lash and held the reins firmly in his wounded hand while Lutgen fired twice at the road agent. The coach lurched forward fifteen yards and the horses were already moving at a fast gait, and this ruined the aim of Lutgen so he missed his man. After driving for three or four minutes Lutgen asked Smith, "Are you wounded?" and Smith replied, "Yes, Sir. I'm shot through the hand; can you drive?" Lutgen answered, "not four horses," and Smith said, "well then, I must go on so." Smith "plied the whip and kept the animals at a 12-mile gait for at least ten minutes, all the while holding the reins with his bleeding and shattered hand, determined to get the coach and treasure box beyond the reach of the highwayman." At last Smith could not hold on any longer so Judge Egan, a passenger riding inside, was called to the driver's boot while the coach was still in motion and he took the reins. Egan drove to Rawson's Ranch where Lutgen dressed Smith's wound. The journey was then continued to San Juan Capistrano, Egan driving, Lutgen and Smith atop, and there a surgeon took charge of the wounded driver and treated Smith's wound. A new driver was put aboard and the coach continued on to San Diego. Lutgen was certain there was more than one road agent but this conjecture was based solely on the brazen behavior of the man, as neither Lutgen nor Smith saw other road agents. The man seen was described as medium height; with whiskers but carefully masked; wearing a light colored hat and coat. He spoke in a "clear, ringing voice and was unquestionably an American." Lutgen then spoke "in terms of the highest praise of the cool, steady courage and fortitude of the driver, to whom is due the protection of the passengers and the safety of the treasure box." There were no clues and, without anything stolen, there was no reward posted for the arrest of the road agent, and he was never identified.

San Diego Union Tribune [CA]: March 11, 1877.

Tuttle, Joe [*see* Appendix—**Almer, Jack**]

Bibliography

Block, Eugene B. *Great Stagecoach Robberies of the West.* Garden City, NY: Doubleday, 1962.

Boessenecker, John. *Badge and Buckshot: Lawlessness in Old California.* Norman: University of Oklahoma Press, 1988.

Breakenridge, William M. *Helldorado: Bringing Law to the Mesquite.* Lincoln: University of Nebraska Press, 1982.

Franklin, Philip L. *Stagecoach: Wells Fargo and the American West.* New York: Free, 1997.

Hoag, Maury. *Stagecoaching on the California Coast: The Coast Line Stage from Los Angeles to San Juan.* McKinleyville, CA: Fithian, 2001.

Jackson, Joseph H. *Tintypes in Gold: Four Studies in Robbery.* New York: Macmillan, 1939.

Kansas State Prison Records: convict nos. 3396, 3397, 3398, and 3407.

Moody, Ralph. *Stagecoach West.* Lincoln: University of Nebraska Press, 1998.

New Mexico State Prison Records: Convict nos. 107, 108, 109, 110, 111.

Oregon Historical Society scrapbook, 132, p. 229.

Oregon Historical Quarterly, v. 58, 1957; v. 99, 1998.

Oregon Journal, October 20, 1946.

Ormsby, Waterman L. *The Butterfield Overland Mail.* San Marino, CA: Huntington Library, 1968.

Patterson, Richard. *The Train Robbery Era.* Boulder, CO: Pruett, 1991.

People of the State of California vs. John McCabe: Yolo Superior Court transcript, June 17, 1884; June 27, 1884.

People of the State of California vs. Charles Tadman and Charles Thompson: Justice Court Records, County of Amador, September 18–19, 1876; County Court Records, County of Amador, December 5–6, 1876; County Court Records, County of Amador, December 22–23, 1876.

Pinkerton, Robert. *The First Overland Mail.* New York: Random House, 1953.

Secrest, William B. *California Badmen: Mean Men with Guns.* Sanger, CA: World Dancer, 2007.

_____. *California Desperadoes: Stories of Early California Outlaws in Their Own Words.* Clovis, CA: World Dancer, 2000.

_____. *Dangerous Trails: Five Desperadoes of the Old West Coast.* Stillwater, OK: Barbed Wire, 1995.

_____. *Perilous Trails, Dangerous Men.* Clovis, CA: Quill Driver, 2002.

Wells Fargo Historical Services, Wells Fargo Bank, N. A. Letter from W. Thompson to E.M. Cooper, June 23, 1884; letter from J.N. Thacker to J.J. Valentine, July 17, 1884.

Winther, Oscar O. *Via Western Express & Stagecoach.* Stanford, CA: Stanford University Press, 1947.

Newspapers

Albuquerque Morning Journal [NM]
Alta California [San Francisco, CA]
Amador Dispatch [Jackson, CA]
Amador Dispatch [San Andreas, CA]
Amador Ledger [Jackson, CA]
Appeal [Marysville, CA]
Arizona Citizen [Tucson]
Arizona Enterprise [Florence]
Arizona Enterprise [Prescott]
Arizona Gazette [Phoenix]
Arizona Silver Belt [Globe]
Arizona Sentinel [Yuma]
Arizona Star [Tucson]
Baker County Reveille [Baker City, OR]
Bakersfield Courier Californian [CA]
Belmont Courier [NV]
Calaveras Chronicle [CA]
Calaveras Citizen [CA]
Calaveras Prospect [CA]
Carson City News [NV]
Carson Daily Appeal [NV]
Carson Tribune [NV]
Chicago Tribune [IL]
Cloverdale Reveille [Santa Rosa, CA]
Corrine Reporter [UT]
Courier Californian [Bakersfield, CA]

Daily Herald [San Jose, CA]
Daily Humboldt Times [CA]
Daily Patriot [San Jose, CA]
Democratic Times [Jacksonville, OR]
Denver Republican [CO]
Deseret News [Salt Lake City, UT]
Downieville Messenger [CA]
Elko Independent [NV]
Epitaph [Tombstone, AZ]
Eureka Republican [NV]
Eureka Sentinel [NV]
Evening Bulletin [San Francisco, CA]
Evening Expositor [Fresno, CA]
Evening Herald [Stockton, CA]
Evening Mail [Stockton, CA]
Folsom Telegraph [CA]
Free Press [Bodie, CA]
Fresno Weekly Republican [CA]
Fresno Weekly Expositor [CA]
Genoa Weekly Courier [NV]
Gilroy Advocate [CA]
Gold Hill Daily News [NV]
Grass Valley Daily Union [CA]
Helena Daily Herald [MT]
Humboldt Register [NV]
Idaho Statesman [Boise]
Independent [Stockton, CA]
Inyo Independent [Independence, CA]
Kern County Weekly Courier [Bakersfield, CA]
Las Vegas Daily Optic [NM]
Lone Star [El Paso, TX]
Los Angeles Express [CA]
Los Angeles News [CA]
Los Angeles Star [CA]
Los Angeles Times [CA]
Marin County Journal [CA]
Mariposa Gazette [CA]
Marysville Daily Appeal [CA]
Mendocino Beacon [CA]
Mendocino Democrat [Ukiah, CA]
Mendocino Dispatch [Ukiah, CA]
Mendocino Dispatch-Democrat [Ukiah, CA]
Mendocino Press [Ukiah, CA]
Miner [Prescott, AZ]
Morning Tribune [San Luis Obispo, CA]
Morning Call [San Francisco, CA]
Mountain Messenger [Downieville, CA]
Mountain Messenger [Sierra County, CA]
Mountain Democrat [Placerville, CA]
Napa Daily Register [CA]
Nevada City Transcript [CA]
Nevada State Journal [Reno]
New York Herald
New York Times
Ogden Pilot [UT]
Oregonian [Portland, OR]
Oroville Union Record [CA]
Oroville Mercury [CA]

Osage County Chronicle [Burlingame, KS]
Phoenix Herald [AZ]
Pioche Record [NV]
Placer Herald [Auburn, CA]
Plumas National [Quincy, CA]
Red Bluff Beacon [OR]
Redding Independent [CA]
Reese River Reveille [Austin, NV]
Reno Evening Gazette [NV]
Republican Free Press [Redding, CA]
Rio Grande Republican [Silver City, NM]
Rocky Mountain News [Denver, CO]
Russian River Flag [Healdsburg, CA]
Sacramento Record [CA]
Sacramento Daily Record-Union [CA]
Sacramento Bee [CA]
Salinas City Index [CA]
Salt River Herald [Phoenix, AZ]
Salt Lake City Tribune [UT]
San Bernardino Guardian [CA]
San Diego Union [CA]
San Diego Union-Tribune [CA]
San Francisco Alta [CA]
San Francisco Call [CA]
San Francisco Chronicle [CA]
San Francisco Examiner [CA]
San Francisco Police Gazette [CA]
San Jose Mercury [CA]
San Juan Prospector [Del Norte, CO]
San Luis Obispo Tribune [CA]
Santa Cruz Sentinel [CA]
Santa Maria Times [CA]
Sentinel [Yuma, AZ]
Shasta Courier [CA]
Silver City Enterprise [NM]
Silver State [Winnemucca, NV]
Socorro Sun [NM]
Sonoma Democrat [CA]
Stanislaus News [CA]
State Record [Reno, NV]
Stockton Daily Independent [CA]
Territorial Enterprise [Virginia City, NV]
Tombstone Epitaph [AZ]
Tombstone Nugget [AZ]
Topeka Blade [KS]
Transcript [Nevada City, CA]
True Fissure [Candalaria, NV]
Tuolumne Independent [Sonora, CA]
Ukiah City Press [CA]
Union Democrat [Sonora, CA]
Virginia City Chronicle [NV]
Visalia Delta [CA]
Weekly News [Milledgeville, GA]
White Pine Daily News [Cherry Creek, NV]
White Pine News [Hamilton, NV]
Yreka Journal [CA]
Yreka Union [CA]

Index

Adams, A.C. (driver) 44
Adams, C. 201
Adams, Fred 242–243
Adams, George 13–14
Adams, William 13, 97–98, 116, 134
Adams Express Company 3
Addington, W. 236
Agnew, __ (sheriff) 51, 151–154
Alamosa, CO 156
Albany, NY 35–36, 145, 234
Albion, I.T. 13, 97–98, 116, 134
Alexander, Ed (det.) 165
Allen, Charles 206
Allen, John 15–17, 64, 226
Allen, S.A. "Ned" 17–18, 127, 233
Allen, William "Bill" 72–74, 134, 176, 231
Almer, Jack 11, 241–249
Altaville, CA 237
Alturas, CA 24, 42, 45
Ames, Charles G. 69
Anaheim, CA 11, 262
Anderson, John 18–19, 154, 199
Anderson, Rais 19–21, 95, 99–100, 117, 164
Anderson, CA 54, 75, 138, 178
Anderson (stagecoach) Station 116, 256
Anderson Valley, CA 26
Andrews, Frank 130, 132
Andrews, Tom 69
Andrus, W. Elisha 21–24, 55
Angel's (creek) Camp, CA 48, 102, 156, 159, 224, 237
Antelope Canyon, OR 200
Antelope (stagecoach) Station 251
Antonio 261–262
Arcata, CA 42, 44
Arroyo Grande, CA 174
Arthur, Stonewall J. 24–25, 174
Arthur, Thomas C. 24–25
Ash Fork, A.T. 132–134, 167
Ashby, Sterling 131–132
Ashland, OR 57
Attleberry, John 201–202
Atwood, Oscar F. (deputy) 213
Auburn, CA 66–68, 117, 138, 154–156, 176–177, 193–195, 205–207, 211, 215, 228–230, 234
Aull, Charles "Captain" (det.) 51–52, 54, 143, 175, 183
Aurora, NV 11, 17–18, 29, 96, 127, 163, 171, 193, 198, 212
Austin, NV 70, 79–80, 234–236
Ayers, J.Y. 4

Baker, Charles 25–27
Baker, Daniel B. 27–30, 163, 217
Baker City, OR 40–41, 121, 177, 199, 215
Bakersfield, CA 17, 52, 61–62, 101, 140, 172, 233
Balch, Billy (driver) 258
Bald Mountain, NV 87
Baldridge, Erastus (city marshal) 206
Baltimore, MD 143–144, 192
Baltz, Charles 146
Banks, A.J. 94
Banshee (stagecoach) Station 156
Banta(s), CA 60, 146–148, 164, 211, 231
Barber, William 30–31
Barker, Frank 32–33, 191
Barnhart, Philip (messenger) 232
Barnwell, Charles 218–219, 239
Barret, Ollie L. 157
Barry, Dan (driver) 44
Bartlett, Gov. Washington 37
Bassett, Charles 34–35, 53
Battle Mountain, NV 234–236
Baugh, William (constable) 27
Beatty, W.H. (judge) 69
Behan, John (sheriff) 255, 260
Bell, __ (constable) 138, 256
Bell, W.T. 35–36, 234
Belleville, NV 96, 171, 193, 196
Bellevue, I.T. 63
Bellrude, Jacob M. (deputy) 259
Belmont, CA 96
Belmont, NV 88
Benicia, CA 123
Benson, A.T. 10–11, 249, 254
Benson, James 36–38
Benson, John 36–38, 169
Benson, Patrick 36

Benton, Henry P. 11, 22–23
Benton, CA 26, 97, 163
Bernard, A.P. (driver) 52
Berry, Benjamin 38–39, 144
Berry Creek Sawmill 44
Best, Andrew J. (deputy) 130, 132
Bickford, L.D. 16
Big Pinoche, CA 51–52
Bigelow, Ed 110
Billings, J. 197
Bird, __ (driver) 111
Bishop, Dr. A.C. 79
Bishop Creek, CA 113–114, 142, 192
Bixler, John S. 39–40
Black, John S. 40–41, 177
Black, Moses 29–30, 163
Black Bart *see* Bolton, Charles E.
Black Rock (stagecoach) Station 259
Blackmore, Bill (driver) 83
Blair, Eugene (messenger) 11, 75–76, 86–88, 232
Blair, Ned (driver) 83
Blanchard, Joe 11
Blanchard, William 30–31
Blankenship, William (messenger) 10, 249–251
Blasdel, Gov. Henry G. 82, 85
Bludworth, H. (deputy) 17
Bluett, Edward 145
Bodie, CA 10–11, 29–30, 171, 193, 196
Boggs, John C. (sheriff) 206, 215, 228
Boise, I.T. 40–41, 50, 58, 62–63, 93, 121, 144–145, 149–153, 167, 177, 192, 215
Boles, C.E. *see* Bolton, Charles E.
Bolter, Dick 218–219, 239
Bolton, Charles E. 41–50
Boomer, A.H. 63, 151
Booneville, GA 74
Booth, Gov. Newton 100, 138, 153, 172, 200, 226, 230
Bouldin, George 50–51, 93
Bourke, Katherine 160
Bowen, Jack 137–138, 216
Bowes, __ (sheriff) 17

Boyd, __ 147
Boyd, Frank 205
Boyd, J.M. (sheriff) 203–204
Boyle, Charlie 220
Brackett, Edward (driver) 24–25
Bradford's (stagecoach) Station 90
Bradley, Gov. Lewis R. 230
Brady, __ 117
Bragg, Calvin 51–52, 184
Bramlette, William 201–204
Branham, Benjamin (sheriff) 119
Brannan, John M. 52–53
Brastow, S.D. (messenger) 173
Brazelton, William W. 11, 251–254
Brently, John 21
Brewster, Lewis (driver) 46
Briggs, __ 141
Brighton, CA 59
Briscoe, William 34–35, 53
Bristol, NV 76
Britton, George (driver) 221–222
Brocius, Curly Bill 255
Brokaw, Ika O. (deputy) 253–254
Bronaugh, __ (sheriff) 155–156
Brown, Charles O. (deputy) 253–254
Brown, Jack 11
Brown, Jimmy (messenger) 10–11, 81, 87–88
Brown, Joe 11, 56–58, 100, 228
Brown, John 53–55
Brown, Johnny 22–24
Brown, Lodi 21–24, 55
Brown, Mitchell 55–56, 178–179, 188–189, 192
Brown, Tom 56–58, 74, 100, 228
Bruton, Wes 73
Bryan, Ab 36–38, 169
Bryon, __ (sheriff) 40
Buckeye, CA 15, 45–46, 67, 218
Buckner, J.B. 58–59, 149
Buffalo Springs, NV 58
Bullis, __ 245
Bumble Bee (stagecoach) Station 122
Burch, Charles D. 137–138, 216, 256
Burke, __ (constable) 175
Burke, Fred T. (det.) 84–85, 206–207
Burke, John see Harker, Francis
Burnett, Eugene (driver) 235
Burnt River, OR 121
Burton, __ 213–214
Bush, E.R. (judge) 146
Bushyhead, Ned 39
Buttes (stagecoach) Station 87
Buttner, Marshall (deputy) 253–254
Buxton, G.Q. (driver) 143, 212
Byers, Bill 255

Cady, C.L. 3
Caliente, CA 173, 213–214
Calistoga, CA 90–91, 189
Callahan, Dr. J.J. 79
Callahan's (stagecoach) Station 124
Callin, J. 159
Calmez, Ziska 100, 102
Cambridge, W. 95, 194, 199
Camp Halleck, NV 27–29
Campbell, Z.T. 59–60
Camptonville, CA 142, 209, 228
Candelaria, NV 196
Cane Springs, A.T. 241
Canebreak (stagecoach) Station 62
Cantley, F.C. (deputy) 130–131
Cantrell, Billy 201–202
Canyon City, OR 200–204
Cape Horn Mills, CA 204, 215
Carbondale, KS 59
Carlo, John 11, 75–76
Carpenter, Frank 243–249
Carr, Edward 27
Carr, Peter 60, 107–109
Carrillo, Alfredo (deputy) 248–249
Carroll, Charles 31
Carson City, NV 10–11, 17–18, 21, 29–30, 36, 69, 81, 83, 86, 96, 127, 163, 171, 193, 198, 212, 229
Casa Grande A.T. 104
Casad, Mart (marshal) 210
Casanega, T.D. (deputy) 248–249
Casey, James 60–61, 164, 211
Castle, Charles 61–62
Castle Rock (stagecoach) Station 34
Catterson, Robert 98–99
Chadwick, N.M. (messenger) 206
Chambers, Charles 62–64
Chambers, Joseph 134–136
Chandler, William 256
Chaperon Lake, Canada 159
Chapman, Frank 15–17, 64, 226
Chapman, J.E. 64, 71, 83–87, 127, 169, 215
Chase, George (driver) 46
Chavarria, Manuel see Sharania, Manuel
Chavez, Carlos 130–131
Cherry, __ 90–91
Cherry Creek, NV 35–36, 69, 97–100, 116, 164, 234
Chicken Creek Hill, U.T. 111
Chico, CA 16, 57, 210
Chimules, A.T. 179
Chinese Camp, CA 51, 103, 188–189, 221
Clanton, Newman H. 255
Clark, B.F. 65–66, 127
Clark, John 66–68, 117, 138, 210, 219
Clements, Bob 139, 223
Cleveland, George W. 11, 128–132

Clifford, Frank 68–71, 110–111
Cline, P. 62
Cloverdale, CA 11, 22–23, 26, 42, 47, 55, 74–75, 95, 161, 183
Clum, John 260
Coal Valley (stagecoach) Station 196
Cockrell, Tilton P. 29–30, 64, 71, 81–87, 127, 163, 169, 215
Coffey, __ (det.) 198
Coffman, B.S. 11, 22–23
Colfax, CA 107, 109, 139, 144, 156, 205–206, 216, 220–223, 228
Collins, George 71–72
Collins, John H. (messenger) 10, 241, 254
Collins, Punch 72–74, 134, 176, 231
Coloma, CA 222
Colquhoun, Louis 159
Columbus, NV 96, 229
Colusa, CA 203
Conant, Jack 124
Conger, __ 54
Connibeck, Bill (driver) 47
Connor, C. 90–91
Connor, Thomas 57, 74
Conover, W.C. 76, 96
Contention, A.T. 254, 260
Cook, __ (deputy) 190
Cooley's (stagecoach) Station 143
Coomer, Dan 130, 132
Cooper, Charlie 17, 114, 154–155
Copperopolis, CA 36, 43, 48, 51, 188–189, 212
Corbett, William 74–75, 95
Corbett, OR 157–158
Corbett's (stagecoach) Station 117, 184
Corrine, U.T. 10, 117–118, 149, 259
Corvallis, OR 30
Cottonwood, CA 44
Coulterville, CA 220–221
Covello, CA 42, 45
Coyote Holes (stagecoach) Station 62
Crane, Jim 11, 254–256
Crawford, __ (deputy) 161
Crawford, Dick (driver) 47
Crawford, James 75–76
Creamer, Charley (driver) 45
Cromer, Mr. and Mrs. __ 70–71
Crough, __ (undersheriff) 113
Crowley, __ (chief of police) 198
Crum, James 77, 153–156
Cullen, William 199–200
Culverhouse, Jerry (driver) 11, 256, 258
Cummings, James H. 77–78
Cunningham, Joseph (deputy) 201
Cunningham, Thomas (sheriff) 61, 213
Curran, John 78–80

Curtis, Allen A. 236
Curtis, Billy 22–24
Curtis, Dave (driver) 218
Curtis, "Doc" (driver) 161
Curtis, Frank (deputy) 108
Cutler, Billy (driver) 155
Cutter, __ (deputy) 152

Dake, Crowley P. (U.S. marshal) 182, 186
Dale, Benjamin F. 82
Dalzell's (stagecoach) Station 194
Danskin, John 63
Darden, J.B. 190
Darnell, Charles 203
Darwin, CA 11, 26, 97, 101, 140–141, 214, 258
Date Creek (stagecoach) Station 136, 186–187
Davis, __ 247
Davis, A.J. 11, 64, 71, 81–88, 109, 127, 136, 169, 215
Davis, H.G. (constable) 238
Davis, L.C. 52
Day, John 54–55
Deady, M.P. (judge) 202, 204
Deal, Dr. Daniel L. 79
Dean, Ned 126
Deep Creek, U.T. 20–21, 28, 99
Deep Holes Springs, NV 57
Deidisheimer, P. 125
Delaney, Michael 88–89
Del Norte, CO 9, 156
Demars, Joe 69
Demerest, James 138, 256
Deming, NM 128, 155
Denver, CO 154, 156
Desert (stagecoach) Station 208
Detroit House of Corrections 14, 71, 111–112, 181
Devil's Gate, NV 79
Diamond Wells, NV 78
Dingman, Charles 156
Dixon's (stagecoach) Station 162
Dodson, James (city marshal) 134, 162–163
Dollar, James R. 90–91, 189
Dolliver, Alonzo (deputy) 57
Donnelly, Felix 35–36, 234
Donohue, __ (sheriff) 110
Doran, Andrew (sheriff) 243–247
Dorsey, Charles 208
Doty's Flat, CA 188
Dougherty, Dan 247
Douglas, __ (spec. officer) 116
Downer, Albert 91–93
Downey, Charles (driver) 50–51, 93, 150–153
Downey, G.W. (chief of police) 86, 126
Downey, CA 120, 163
Downieville, CA 11, 42, 46, 56, 100, 118, 141–142, 144, 165–166, 168, 184–185, 209, 221, 231

Dreibelbis, Louis J. 139, 150, 216, 220–223
Dry Creek, CA 23
Drytown, CA 89, 220
Ducks, Canada 159
Dudleyville, A.T. 242
Duggan, __ (driver) 172
Duncan's Mills, CA 42, 44–45, 172
Dunham, Warren 54
Dunkin, Thomas H. 93–94
Dunn, William 158–159
Dustan, __ (det.) 59
Dutch Flat, CA 227–228, 233
Dwyer, John 74–75, 94–95
Dwyer, Capt. T. 77–78

Earl, Sylvester 19–21, 95, 99–100, 117, 164
Earl, William L. 95, 100
Early, Bill *see* Thompson, Charles
Earnshaw, Harry 255
Earp, Wyatt 255
East, Jim 156
Eaton, Albert C. 129
Ebi, David 58–59
Eckles, __ (constable) 16
Eddings, Nort (driver) 46
Eddington, James (det.) 85
Edgar, Ad (driver) 200–201, 203
Egan, "Judge" 262
Elias, Juan 253
Eliot, CA 123
Ellis, Gus 251
Elko, NV 19–21, 93–94
Elmore, __ (constable) 178
Emerson, __ (judge) 112
Emery, John (sheriff) 79, 235–236
Engles, Frederick 220–221
Eproson, Jackson 238
Estrado, Joe 96–97, 193, 229
Etchells, Charles T. (deputy) 253–254
Eugene, OR 225
Eureka, NV 10–11, 68, 70, 78–80, 87, 99, 109–111, 136, 169–170
Evans, Joseph W. (deputy) 134, 180–182, 187, 245–247
Evans & Le Blanc (stagecoach) Station 242–243
Evanston, WY 208–209
Everett, WA 158

Fancher, Charley 208
Fargo, William G. 3–4
Farmington, CA 238
Farrel, Thomas 175
Faurot, Lew (messenger) 235
Fellows, Dick *see* Perkins, Richard
Ferguson, James (driver) 93
Fernie, __ (constable) 159
Ferrin, John 62–64
Fiddletown, CA 176–177, 211, 234

Fife, A. (sheriff) 80
Finch, __ (constable) 61
Finley, G. (driver) 196
Fitch, J.B. (sheriff) 28
Flack, J.H. (judge) 165
Florence, A.T. 10–11, 242
Forbestown, CA 45, 54, 139, 143, 223
Forest Hill, CA 66–68, 117, 138, 154–156, 193–195
Forse, Harry (driver) 47
Forse, Thomas (driver) 47
Fort Ross, CA 172
Fowler, Alex (driver) 44
Francis, David 13–14, 19–21, 95, 97–100, 116–117, 134, 164
Francis, Thomas 11, 162–163
Franklin, Harry J. (deputy) 73
Franks, C. (sheriff) 13, 168
Frazier, Charles 56, 100
Frazier, Henry 204–208, 215
Freemont, Gov. J.C. 181
French Camp, CA 213
Fresno, CA 51, 119, 138
Fresno Flats, CA 103
Froom, Wesley (driver) 190
Fugate, William 100, 102, 199–200
Fulford, Frank 199, 203
Fulkerth, __ (deputy) 61
Funk Hill, CA 43, 48–49

Gabriel, J.P. (deputy) 106–107, 243–247
Gage, Watt (driver) 54
Gage (rail) Station 128–129
Galt, CA 18–19, 107, 109, 154, 199
Garvey, __ (undersheriff) 37
Gaskell, R.O. 128
Geiger Grade, NV 125
Genoa, NV 17–18
Georgetown, CA 107, 109, 137, 176–177, 211, 216, 229–230, 234
Geyserville, CA 167
Gibbons, Jack D. (driver) 37, 188
Gibson, Peter 209–210
Giddings, Ab (driver) 34
Giffen, G.W. 93
Gil, Jose M. 95, 100
Gilchrist, James 64, 71, 81–87, 127, 169, 215
Gillett, A.T. 135–136
Gillett, Frederick 101
Gilman, __ 152
Gilmer, Jack 76
Gilmo, John W. (deputy) 129–130
Gilroy, CA 68, 146–147, 229
Glendale, OR 149, 225
Glenn, __ (deputy) 89
Glasscock, Lillie 208–209
Glasscock, Stephen R. 208–209
Glick, Gov. George W. 59
Glick, Solomon 157

Globe, A.T. 10–11, 104–107, 242–243
Glover, Edward 102, 218, 232
Gonzales, CA 174
Goshen, CA 17
Gosper, A/Gov. John J. 181
Gottschalk, C.V. (judge) 49, 224
Graham, Bartholomew 44
Grant, John H. 100, 102, 199–200
Grant, Pres. U.S. 204
Grants Pass, OR 34, 53
Grass, Valley, CA 107, 109, 139, 220–223, 228
Gray, Dick 255
Grayson, CA 60, 164, 211
Greeley, Burton 102–104
Green, Baldy (driver) 82
Green, J.J. 85
Greenwood, CA 177, 230
Gregg, __ (sheriff) 113
Gregory & Company Express 3
Grimes, Cicero 104–107
Grimes, Frank (driver) 60
Grimes, Lafayette 11, 104–107
Guadalupe, CA 189–190
Guadalupe Canyon, A.T. 255
Guerneville, CA 123, 183
Gunckel, W.F. 175
Gundlack, John D. 15
Gwin, Wash (driver) 90

Hackett, George W. (messenger) 10, 47, 165–166, 185, 257
Haight, Gov. Henry H. 85, 138
Hailey, __ 63
Hall, Andy (messenger) 10, 104–107
Hall, Tom (deputy) 130–131
Halleck, John (deputy) 44
Hallsted, P.L. 32
Hamilton, Albert P. 60, 107–109
Hamilton, Bill 87–88
Hamilton, Bob 87–88, 109, 136
Hamilton, George C. 109–110
Hamilton, John (driver) 98
Hamilton, NV 10, 75, 98–99, 232, 258–259
Handsford, George 160
Hannah, __ (judge) 114
Hanson, Ed 202–204
Hanson, John 148
Hardesty, Jesse 245
Harker, Francis 29–30, 68–70, 110–112, 163
Harniss, T.C. 112–114, 142, 192
Harper, William (deputy) 203
Harrington, D. 69
Harrington, James 114, 154–155
Harrington, Jimmy 260
Harris, C.N. (judge) 86
Harris, George 115
Harris, Len (det.) 177, 228
Harshman, Jeplan G. 157–158
Hart, Samuel 115–116, 118–119

Hartman, Dr. William P. 258
Hartzell, __ 245
Harvey, William H. 28–29
Haslett, Bill 255
Haslett, Ike 255
Havilah, CA 17
Hawley, Curtis B. 11, 104–107
Hawley, Francis 13–14, 19–21, 95, 97–100, 116–117, 134, 164
Hawthorne, NV 171
Hay Ranch (stagecoach) Station 70
Hays, John 66–68, 117, 138, 183, 219
Head, Harry 11, 254–257
Healdsburg, CA 22, 123, 161
Hedrick, J.D. 72–73
Heinsman, W.H. 117–118, 149, 184–185
Helena, MT 117–118, 149, 259
Helm, George (driver) 47
Helms, H. (driver) 257
Henderson, Devin (constable) 213
Henderson, Steve J. 51
Hendricks, Joe 115–116, 118–119
Hendricks, John (deputy) 31, 57
Hendricks, William (deputy) 51
Hennerson, __ (constable) 35
Hensley, Charles 11, 243–244, 257
Henson, Rufus 90–91
Herbert, John M. 119–120, 138
Hercules Gap, NV 70–71
Hereford, Hugh 75
Hickey, Bill (det.) 206
Hickey, Price 250–251
Hill, Arthur (driver) 252
Hill, William H. (driver) 229
Hill's Ferry 146–148, 231
Hilosa, NM 73
Hinkle, Jacob (sheriff) 167
Hoadley, Milo 238
Hoehn, Charles 157–158
Hogan, __ (det.) 34
Hogan, Mike (driver) 43, 237
Hogan, P.F. (sheriff) 225
Hoge, Billy (driver) 125
Holden, Henry 120, 163
Holladay Overland Mail & Express Company 5
Hollister, __ (judge) 41
Hollister, CA 51–52
Hood, William 87
Hopkins, __ (constable) 217
Hopping, __ (judge) 116
Horrell, W.S. 121, 215
Horse Springs, NM 130
Houx, John "Brown" 21–24, 55
Howard, Frank 34
Howe, Frank 121–122, 231
Hubbard, Richard 31
Hubbell, Dick 124
Huffaker's (stagecoach) Station 82
Hughes & Keys (rail) Station 147
Hull, __ (sheriff) 55, 116
Hume, James B. (sheriff/det./messenger) 1, 5–6, 9, 12, 14, 18, 31, 33, 36–37, 46–49, 54–55, 57, 80, 101, 103, 116, 124–125, 136, 143 166, 170 173, 177, 183, 187, 195, 197–198, 206–208, 219, 221–222, 230
Humphrey, __ (driver) 241
Hunt, H.S. 11, 256–258
Hunter, Charles 160
Hunter & Company Express 3
Huntsman, G. 111
Huston, Tom (driver) 51
Huyck, William H. 93–94

Igo, CA 54
Independence, CA 113, 214
Indian Charley 31
Indian Dick 235
Indian Jim 31
Indian Valley, OR 121
Indian Wells, CA 101
Ingram, John 75
Ione, CA 42, 47, 89, 107, 109, 139, 198, 237
Irwin, John G. 96
Irwin, Gov. William 17–18, 22, 24, 32–33, 60, 77, 88, 102, 107–108, 117, 123–124, 142, 147, 154, 176–177, 179, 209–211, 216, 217, 229, 233–234
Isas, Ciriaco 262
Ivey, John J. 122–123

Jackson, John C. 130–132
Jackson, Tom 123–125, 227
Jackson, CA 17–18, 42, 47, 107, 109, 188, 198, 216–217, 220, 223, 237
Jacksonville, OR 34–35, 53, 225
Jacobs, __ (sheriff) 34
Jarrett, John M. 34–35
"Jimmy" (deputy) 248
Johnson, Andrew 125–126
Johnson, Frank 126–127, 199
Johnson, Richard 65–66
Johnson, Trav (deputy) 63
Jolon, CA 95
Jones, __ (det.) 198
Jones, Charley 29–30, 163
Jones, E.K. 75
Jones, James 17–18, 127
Jones, John M. (det.) 106
Jones, R.A. 64, 71, 81–87, 169, 215
Jones, Stanton C. 77, 153–156
Jones, Thad 54
Jones, Tom 22–24
Jones, W.C. 11, 193–199
Joy, Kit 128–132
Judd, Riley 29
Junction, CA 36

Kalama, WA 158
Kaufman, A. *see* Coffman, B.S.

Index

Kaulback, C.T. 32–33
Keeton, Charles W. 34–35, 53
Kehoe, Mike (driver) 236
Kellog, CA 90
Kelly, Lew 98
Kelton, U.T. 13, 62–63, 97–98, 116, 134, 144–145, 167
Kennedy, R. 16
Kerby, G.A. 132–134, 167
Kernville, CA 213–214
Kilgore, __ 212
Kilgore's (stagecoach) Station 18
Kimball, H.P. 29
Kime, Daniel 221
Kimble, I.W. (constable) 177
King, Jack 13–14, 97–98, 116, 134
King, Luther 255
Kingston, NM 132
Kinkead, J.H. (undersheriff) 84
Kirby, Andrew 181
Kirkendall, Jefferson 72–74, 176, 231
Knowlton, J.L. 29
Korner, Fred A. (messenger) 157–158

Lacey, D.B. 106
Lackey, Ben F. (officer) 86, 96
Ladd, W.J. (driver) 62
Lafferr, Joseph N. 128, 130–131
Laird, John (deputy) 248–249
Lakeport, CA 47, 53–54, 90, 168, 183, 189
Lakeview, CA 42, 46
Lambert, John 79
Lander, Eugene (deputy) 65
Lane, George see Lester, George
Lane, Thomas M. (undersheriff) 37, 147
Lang, Bill 255
La Parte el Frio, NM 129
Laporte, CA 10, 17–18, 42, 44–45, 47, 127, 142, 165–166, 188, 229, 257
Larsen, James 134–136
Last Chance (stagecoach) Station 45
Latrobe, CA 176, 211, 216–217, 223, 234
Lauria, Thomas 87–88, 136
Lawton Springs, NV 84
Leatherwood, L.N. (deputy) 253–254
Le Blanc, Felix 241
Lee, Barney (driver) 179
Lee, Charles 137–138, 216
Lee, Eddie 66–68, 117, 138
Lee, George 29–30
Lee, Jim (deputy) 253–254
Lee, John 50–51, 93
Lee, Milton Harvey 119–120, 138
Lee, Mitch 11, 128–132
Leeds, U.T. 208
Lenaris, Jose 168, 188–189

Leonard, Bill 11, 254–256, 258
Leone, MX 10, 261–262
Leroy, Billy see Pond, Arthur
Lester, George 139–140, 150, 216, 220–223
Lewis, Lindsley 106
Lierly, __ (constable) 190
Linderoos, __ 110
Little Lake, CA 42, 47, 169
Livermore, Lot 39
Lloyd, John T. 11, 258
Lodi, CA 56, 178
Lone Pine, CA 17, 233
Long Valley, NV 86
Lopez, Rafael 141
Los Alamos, CA 174
Los Angeles, CA 117, 141, 172–173, 183
Los Banos, CA 146–147, 229
Lovelace, "Colonel" (driver) 224
Lovelock, NV 80
Lowther, W.W. (sheriff) 106
Loyalton, CA 85
Lugo, Chico 140–141, 167
Lula, GA 160
Lupton, J.C. (deputy) 37
Lutgen, C.F. 262
Lynch, Ed (driver) 199–200
Lynch, John 62–64
Lytle, G. Brett see Perkins, Richard

Machado, Jose 141–142, 166
Madera, CA 119
Madison, CA 146
Magee, Thomas (messenger) 36
Mahoney, J.H. (U.S. mail agent) 180
Mairs, A.F. 113–114, 142, 192
Malarkey, __ (deputy) 204
Malcom's Water Station 260
Mammoth City, CA 171, 196
Mann, Billy (driver) 10, 258–259
Manning, Charles 26–27
Maria, Jose 142, 168, 229
Maricopa, A.T. 10, 162, 179
Markham, Gov. Henry 119
Marsh, Andy 11, 123–125, 227
Marshall, D.G. 84
Marshall, John 143–144, 192
Martin, George 248
Martin, James 143–144
Martin, Thomas 48–49
Marysville, CA 11, 42–43, 46, 56–57, 67, 77, 100, 117–118, 141–142, 165–166, 168, 184–185, 209, 218, 221, 231, 237
Mason, Joe (driver) 46
Mason, John K. 204–208, 215
Massachusetts Hill, CA 227–228
Mathews, Pete 247
Matson, J.S. 99
Matthews, Len 86
Maxon, J.H. 38–39, 144

Mayfield, __ (sheriff) 65
Mayfield, John or George see Williams, John
Mayhew, Frank 250–251
Mays, William 144–145, 167
McBride, Roy H. 111
McCabe, John 146
McCarty, Dan 146–148, 229, 231
McClarty, George (deputy) 248–249
McClennan, __ (sheriff) 139
McClennan, Martin (driver) 45
McCluskey, John (deputy) 248
McComas, Hiram 58–59, 149
McComber, __ (constable) 24–25
McConnell, Reason E. (driver) 48–49, 237
McCoy, H.L. (deputy) 147, 184–185
McCune, Alfred 112
McDonald, __ (deputy) 135
McDonald, Jack 80
McFarland, W.E. (driver) 108
McGrath, Tim 24
McGuire, __ 131–132
McKenny, __ (driver) 241–242
McKiernan, Charley 108
McLean, Donald 117, 149, 184–185
McNemar, John (messenger) 11, 15, 257–258
McQuade, __ (sheriff) 103
McQuarrie, A.L. 159
Meacham, OR 38–39
Mellville, Clark 149–150
Mendocino, CA 74, 95
Mercer, O. (driver) 132
Merrit, C.W. 190
Mesaville, A.T. 244
Meyers, James 139, 150, 223
Meyers, J.B. (constable) 224
Meyers, Jerome (chief of police/messenger) 173
Meyers, Jim (driver) 168
Michigan Bluff, CA 230
Milledgeville, GA 160
Miller, __ (driver) 214
Miller, James (messenger) 10, 78
Miller, John W. 150–153, 192
Miller, William A. 77, 153–156
Mills, Charles 18–19, 154, 199
Millville, CA 25
Milman, __ (driver) 149
Milton, CA 36–38, 42, 48, 51, 56, 77, 102–103, 107–108, 153–154, 156, 169, 178–179, 184, 188–189, 192, 212, 218–219, 237–239
Minch, Frank (messenger) 28, 84
Miner, William A. 77, 114, 153–161
Mineral Hill, NV 68, 110–111
Mitchell, Henry B. 161–162

Mojave, CA 11, 101, 140–141, 213–214, 258
Mokelumne Hill, CA 56, 178, 237
Molino, Jesus 186–187
Monk, Bill (driver) 235
Mono Jim 30, 163
Monroe, George 181
Montello, NV 14, 19–21, 99–100, 117, 164
Moody, Gov. Z.F. 150
Moore, James 54–55
Moore, James R. (sheriff) 44, 170
Moore, John 69
Moore, Otto (deputy) 248–249
Moore, Tom 160
Moppin, Garret 210–202
Moppin, H. 200–204
Morgan, William A. 162–163
Morley's (stagecoach) Station 24
Morris, Fred 120, 163
Morris, W.B. 151–152
Morrison, Robert 30, 163
Morrison's (stagecoach) Station 221
Morrow, __ (officer) 86
Morrow, Tom 151
Morse, Fred 139
Morse, Harry (det.) 48–49
Morton, Leander 11, 27–30, 163, 217
Mount Davidson, NV 126
Mountain Meadows, U.T. 208
Mullen, John 179–182
Mulligan, Joe (driver) 102–103
Murphy, __ (officer) 62–64
Murphy, Eugene 60–61, 164, 211
Murphy's, CA 224, 237
Murray, __ (sheriff) 89
Murray's Creek, CA 155
Myers, Martin 57

Nance, T.C. (deputy) 190–191
Napa, CA 177, 211
Nay, Orrin 19–21, 95, 99–100, 117, 164
Nelson, John W. 164–165
Nemitz, David 253
Nephi, U.T. 111
Neri, Commandant Filipe 255
Nevada City, CA 206
Newcastle, CA 88–89, 155
Newhall, CA 39–40, 140, 167
Niccolls, Amos 135
Nicholes, Charles 98–99
Nicholson, John (deputy) 70
Norco, CA 57
North, Thomas 128
Norton, Henry 165–166
Nunez, Trinidad 141–142, 166–167

Oakland, CA 155
Oaks, __ (sheriff) 148
Ogden, U.T. 10, 14, 19–21, 27, 71, 99–100, 117, 127, 163, 169, 204, 215, 217
Ohio City, CO 156
O'Laughlin, Johnny 98
Oldham, Joe (undersheriff) 151–153
Old's Ferry 40
Olivas, Francisco 140–141, 167
Olivera, Joaquin 188
Olympia, WA 182
O'Meara, Roger 107–108
Onstott, J.H. 179–180
Oreana, NV 80
Ornbaum, Nute 75
Oroville, CA 10, 17–18, 42, 44–45, 47, 53–54, 127, 139, 142, 165–166, 168, 188, 223, 229, 257
Orton, Bob (sheriff) 108
Osborne, Billy (driver) 162
Overhoeltz, William H. 144–145, 167
Owens, Joseph S. 132–134, 167
Owens, Seely 132–134, 167

Pacheco, Gov. Romualdo 229–230, 233
Packard, Mart 79–80
Page, Frank 154–156, 230
Page, H.C. 39, 203
Palisade, NV 10, 70, 78, 99
Palmer, James 168
Panama, CA 140
Panamint, CA 61–62, 101, 213–214
Pardillo, Isidor 142, 168, 188–189, 229
Park, Thomas E. 130, 132
Parker, Al (officer) 94
Parker, J.T. 259
Parker's (stagecoach) Station 98
Parks, __ (constable) 139
Parks, Daniel 36–37, 168–169
Parsons, E.B. 64, 70–71, 81–87, 127, 169, 215
Passmore, __ (sheriff) 101
Paul, Robert H. (sheriff/det./messenger) 136, 140–141, 162, 247–250, 254–255
Paul, Thomas 169–170
Payne, Ed (driver) 45
Pearson, Jesse 170–171
Pegg, Charlie (sheriff) 84–85
Pendleton, OR 38–39, 144
Pequop, NV 27–28, 30, 217
Percy, Jim (deputy) 248–249
Perkins, Gov. George C. (Gov.) 15–16, 52–53, 68, 120, 137, 163, 169–170, 189, 216, 219–220
Perkins, Richard 172–176
Perrin, Joseph (sheriff) 222
Perry, Charles C. (deputy) 130, 132

Perry, Jack (driver) 87
Pescadero, CA 175
Petaluma, CA 11, 22–23, 55, 161
Peters, __ (constable) 228
Peters, Tommy (driver) 65–66
Phelps, Charlie (driver) 10, 259
Phelps, T.D. 203
Philpott, Budd "Eli" (driver) 10, 90, 254–255, 260
Phoenix, A.T. 10, 121–122, 134–135, 231
Picayune Lake, CA 124
Pierce, Henry 145
Pike, J.M. (det.) 43
Pilgrim Hill (stagecoach) Station 145
Pilot's Knob, CA 68
Pinkham, Joseph (U.S. marshal) 41, 51, 151–154
Pinney, Daniel H. (judge) 245
Pinos Altos Mountains, NM 130
Pioche, NV 10, 68–69, 71, 75–76, 78–80, 86, 98, 110–111, 208, 232, 258–259
Pioneer Stage Line 5
Pixley, Matt 30
Placerville, CA 5, 107, 109, 177, 230
Plunckett, T. 85
Plymouth, CA 177
Point Arenas, CA 42, 44–45, 110
Point of Mountain, A.T. 252
Pointer, J.W. 72–74, 134, 176, 231
Polk, M. (sheriff) 94
Pond, Arthur 156
Pond, Silas 156
Poor, William 29–30, 163
Porter, __ 155
Porter, Frank 105
Porter, Samuel 202
Portland, OR 203–204, 225–226
Potts, Gov. Benjamin F. 117–118, 149
Pratt, Charles 176–177, 211, 234
Prescott, A.T. 121–122, 132–135, 162, 167, 187, 231, 251
Price, Ben (driver) 121
Priest, Al 40–41, 177
Prince, Gov. L. Bradford 74
Princeton, Canada 158

Quadlin, Dave (driver) 45, 142
Quincey, CA 32, 42, 44, 101
Quinton, Edward (driver) 139

Radcliff, A. 159
Radcliff, Clint (driver) 48
Ragsdale, J.L. 178
Randolph, Porter 110
Ratovich, Mitchell 56, 178–179, 188–189, 192
Rattray, B.F. 102–103
Raum, __ (sheriff) 99
Rawhide, A.T. 187

Rector, Charles 75
Red Bluff, CA 67, 100, 102, 199, 218–219
Red Butte (stagecoach) Station 118, 184
Red Rock Canyon, CA 140
Redding, CA 11, 15–16, 24–25, 30–31, 42, 45–47, 56–57, 64, 66–67, 100, 102, 115–117, 119, 124, 149, 178, 218–219, 226, 228, 256
Redfield, Hank 245
Redfield, Len 11, 243–247, 260
Reed, Ira H. (judge) 37, 238
Reed, William (driver) 181
Reid's Ferry 15
Reig, George 140
Reno, NV 27, 31, 48, 81–87, 125–126, 154, 156
Reppy, C.D. 260
Reynard, Paul (driver) 146–147
Reynolds, Hedge 22–23, 161
Reynolds, John 57
Reynolds, John (undersheriff) 218
Reynolds, Johnnie E. (messenger) 11, 123–124
Reynolds, William B. (deputy) 22–23, 25, 161, 228
Reynold's Ferry 48, 238
Rhodes, James 179–182
Richards, Richard (driver) 11, 260
Richmond, George (driver) 174
Riddles, OR 225
Ridenbaugh, Billy 151
Rio Pecos, NM 74
Rising River, CA 16
Riverside, A.T. 241–244
Robb, David J. (sheriff) 171
Robbins, __ (city marshal) 63
Robbins, Orlando 145
Roberts, J. Bedford 29–30, 163
Rock Creek, I.T. 41
Rocklin, CA 218
Rockman, Dr. M. 76
Rodepouch, Louis 179–182
Rodrigues, Nicanora 187
Roerig, Peter 11, 254–255, 261
Rogers, Hank 171
Rogers, Ruben A. 204–208, 215
Rogers, William 182–183
Rolfe, Frank H. 51–52, 183
Rolleri, James 48
Rollins, R. 112
Romero, "Senor" Alberto (driver) 10, 261–262
Romero, Francisco 140–141
Rose, __ (deputy) 73
Roseburg, OR 42, 44–46, 57, 225
Ross, Aaron Y. (messenger/driver) 10, 19–21, 99–100
Ross, Gov. Edmund G. 74, 132
Roth, George 69–70, 111
Round Mountain, CA 24, 46
Round Valley, NV 30

Ruby Gulch, I.T. 153
Rugg, George N. 117, 149, 184–185, 231
Ruibal, Juan 186–187
Ruiz, Ramon 56, 142, 168, 178–179, 187–189, 229
Russ' (stagecoach) Station 16
Russell, James (constable) 39–40
Russell, William 90–91, 189
Rutherford, John 189–191, 224
Ryan, Pat (driver) 86
Rynearson, __ 41

Sacramento, CA 48, 59, 67, 206
St. Louis, MO 37, 59, 114
Salinas, CA 13, 146–148, 168
Salt Lake City, U.T. 27, 71, 110–111, 118
Sampson, S.P. (driver) 235
San Andreas, CA 36–37, 103, 107–108, 114, 154–155, 213, 224, 238
San Bernardino, CA 65–66, 127
Sanderson, Frank 259
San Diego, CA 11, 39–40, 262–263
San Francisco, CA 3–6, 10, 13–14, 18–19, 27, 48, 52, 67, 71–72, 83, 89, 99–100, 107, 109, 117, 123, 127–128, 138, 155, 163–164, 169, 204, 215–217
San Jose, CA 58, 119, 172, 174–175
San Juan, CA 42–43, 47, 142, 228, 237
San Juan Capistrano, CA 262–263
San Luis Obispo, CA 95, 100, 115–116, 118, 146–148, 168, 172, 174, 231
San Mateo, CA 175
Sansome, John 32–33, 191
Santa Barbara, CA 115–116, 118, 172, 174–175
Santa Clara, CA 60, 107–108
Santa Cruz, CA 60, 107–108, 173, 175
Santa Maria, CA 189–190, 224
Santa Rosa, CA 24
Saunders, Jim 50–51
Savage, Antone 56, 178–179, 188–189, 191–192
Saylor, George B. 143–144, 192
Scammon, Henry 11, 56–57
Scanland, Lou (undersheriff) 243
Schalten, Louis (driver) 113–114, 142, 192
Schottler, G. 184
Schurz, __ (sheriff) 201–203
Schwartzwalter, Otto see Wilson, Charles
Scott, Bob (driver) 221–222
Scott, Tarlton B. 150–153, 192
Scott, Tom 128
Seattle, WA 159
Seawell, __ (undersheriff) 75

Seawell, William M. (judge) 171
Seiber, Al 162–163
Sharania, Manuel 96–97, 193, 229
Sharp, Johnny (driver) 166, 184, 209, 221
Sharp, M.A. 193–199
Sharpe, George (driver) 46
Shasta, CA 11, 15–16, 25, 64, 74, 115–116, 119, 123–124, 199, 218–219, 226–227, 256
Shaw, Edward B. 194, 198
Shaw, Frank (driver) 39–40
Sheehan, Michael 18–19, 154, 199
Shelby, Eugene 225
Shepardson, Milton 100, 102, 199–204
Shibell, Charles A. (sheriff) 253–254
Shine, John (driver) 43
Shinn, George H. 204–208, 215
Sierra Valley, CA 143–144, 192
Sierraville, CA 212
Signal, A.T. 187
Silent, Charles (judge) 163
Silver City, I.T. 50, 93, 150–151, 192
Silver City, NM 11, 128–132
Simmons, Tom 162–163
Simpson, J.B. 98–99
Simpson, Pedro S. (sheriff) 73, 129–130, 132
Sinclair, John 155
Sink, Daniel 161
Sisson Jim 124
Sisson's (stagecoach) Station 31, 124
Skinner, __ (constable) 35
Skuse, James 72–73
Sloan, William 208–209
Slum Gullion Pass, CO 156
Small, George 80
Small, Hank 84
Smartville, CA 42–43, 47
Smiley, J.W. (sheriff) 54–55
Smith, Austin N. 209–210
Smith, Edward (driver) 216–217
Smith, George H. (driver) 11, 262–263
Smith, George M. (sheriff) 130
Smith, J.P. (driver) 108
Smith, James P. 176–177, 211, 234
Smith, Peter 60–61, 164, 211
Smith, Rachety 131–132
Smith, Sam (driver) 36
Smith, William 211–213
Smithson, James (driver) 45
Snow, Charlie 255
Socorro, NM 72–73, 134, 176, 231
Soda Springs, CA 31
Soledad, CA 13, 39–40, 95, 100, 146–148, 168, 172, 174–175, 231
Sonoma, CA 123
Sonora, CA 36–38, 42, 48,

51–52, 56, 77, 102–103, 153–154, 156, 169, 178–179, 184, 188–189, 192, 212, 218–219, 237–239
Souder, John 50
Sowles, M.B. 111
Spadra, CA 65–66, 127
Sparks, E. 112
Sparta, OR 203
Spencer, Charles 130–131
Sprague, __ (sheriff) 54
Spratt, John 213–215
Spruce Mount (stagecoach) Station 98, 164
Squires, John 64, 71, 81–87, 127, 169, 215
Standley, J. (sheriff) 26–27, 75
Stanfield, __ 76
Stanley, Augustus "Gus" 121, 215
Stark's (stagecoach) Station 17
Steinagal, Edward 204–208, 215
Stevenson, H.F. 157–158
Stockton, CA 49, 61, 104, 107, 114, 154, 155, 213
Stone, Appleton W. (police captain) 49–50, 206
Stoneman, Gov. George 36–37, 57, 77, 91, 93, 116, 219, 239
Storey, W.A. (sheriff) 158
Stover, Nat C. 139, 216, 220–223
Strawberry, CA 47
Strickland, P.G. 256
Stringham, Clark (driver) 156–157, 212, 237
Stubbs, Henry 137–138, 216
Suisun, CA 137, 216
Sullaway, John (driver) 46
Sullivan, C.J. (constable) 35
Sullivan, John D. (sheriff) 79
Sulphur Springs, GA 160
Sumner, CA 52
Susanville, CA 57
Sutherland, Charles 235
Sweeney, J.J. 60–61
Swilling, John W. 180–181
"Swisher sisters" 171
Sylva, Jackson (deputy) 108

Tadman, Charles 216–217, 223
Taggart, Frank 11, 128–132
Tamarac Mill 83
Tapia, Jose 140
Tattenbaum, Bill 255
Taylor, Dan F. 27–30, 163, 217
Telegraph City, CA 188
Telegraph (stagecoach) Station 69
Temple, Owen 102, 217–218, 232
Terry, "Cowboy Jake" 158–159
Thacker, John N. (det.) 1, 5–6, 9, 12, 34, 46, 49–50, 61, 88, 98, 113, 129, 187, 206, 247, 261–262
Thackston, C.M. 99
Thayer, Eugene 218–219, 239

Thompson, Charles 139–140, 150, 216, 220–223
Thompson, Charles C. 216–217, 223
Thompson, Charlie 66–68, 117, 138, 219
Thompson, Dave 223–224
Thompson, Dennis 96
Thompson, James 189–191, 224
Thompson, W. 261–262
Thoms, Winn (driver) 91–92
Thorn, Benjamin K. (sheriff) 36, 43, 48–49, 51, 58, 103, 188, 213, 219–220
Thornburgh, Lark 190
Thornburn, W.M. 159
Thorne, D.C. 251
Thornton, Gov. W.T. 132
Tickner, H.L. 194
Tintic, U.T. 112
Toano, NV 20, 28
Todd, J.R. 225–226
Todd Reynold's & Company Express 3
Tombstone, A.T. 10–11, 260
Tomkins, Frank 200–204
Toney, John A. 15–17, 64, 226–227
Topeka, KS 182
Tovey, Mike (messenger) 10–11, 113, 193, 196–198
Townsend, __ (driver) 173
Tracy, Martin 123–125, 227
Tracy, Thomas 227–228, 233
Trask, James W. 50–51, 93
Tres Pinos Canyon, CA 52
Trinity Center, CA 31, 123, 138, 256
Tripp, Louis (U.S. mail agent) 206
Trittle, Gov. Frederick A. 133, 163
Troutdale, OR 157
Truckee, CA 85–87, 143–144, 192, 212
Truett, Myers F. 22
Tucker, Dan (deputy) 128
Tucson, A.T. 246–254
Tulare, CA 91–92
Tunnell, Henry L. 190–191
Tunnell, James 190–191
Tuscarora, NV 93–94
Tuttle, Joe 11, 243–247, 263
Tybo, NV 10–11, 87, 109, 136
Tye, David 56–58, 100, 228
Tyler, Eugene 146–147, 228–229
Tyler's (stagecoach) Station 183
Tyndall, Tom (driver) 31

Ukiah, CA 22, 24, 26, 42, 44–45, 47, 74–75, 95, 110, 169–170
Umatilla, OR 38–40, 50, 144, 199
Upton, Charles D. (messenger) 22

Vail, T. Zach 128
Vail, W.T. 11, 104–107

Valacca, Antone 142, 168, 188–189, 229
Valentine, John J. 28, 96, 261
Van, Ira (driver) 78–79
van Arman, A/Gov. H.M. 133, 244–245
Vanderburg, __ (deputy) 134
van Duren, C. 175
van Vict, __ 255
Venard, Stephen 23–24, 177, 228
Ventura, CA 140, 167
Verdi, NV 28, 83–87
Vick's (stagecoach) Station 234–235
Virginia City, NV 81–82, 87, 125–126
Visalia, CA 17, 91–92, 108
Volcano, CA 217

Wadsworth, CA 143
Wales, James (deputy) 97, 101
Walker, John (driver) 173
Walker, Joseph R. (sheriff) 162–163
Walker, R.H. (deputy) 187
Walla Walla, WA 38
Wallace, James 96–97, 193, 227
Waltrip, Nathan (driver) 45
Ward, A.C. (deputy) 99
Ward, Frank, 63
Ward, NV 11, 75–76
Ward's (stagecoach) Station 200–201
Ware, Nick (deputy) 130
Ware, Thomas 48–49
Warren, D. 69
Washoe City, NV 86
Watkins, E.G. 229–230
Watkins, Mose 36
Weatherby's (stagecoach) Station 121
Weaver, CA 11
Weaverville, CA 16, 42, 45, 55
Webster, __ (judge) 35
Webster, Theophelus C. 128–132
Weeden, Frank 121–122, 231
Weibusch, C.P. see Smith, William
Weisenstein, John 146–148, 230–231
Wellington's (stagecoach) Station 194, 196
Wellock, James 61–62
Wells, Henry 3–4
Wells, NV 35–36, 98–100, 116, 164, 234
Wesson, G.F. 36
Weston, OR 38
Wheeler, __ 170
Whitbeck, John D. (driver) 111
Whitcomb, Eugene (driver) 188
White, __ 202–204
White, Edwin 72–74, 134, 176, 231

White, Eph. H. 118, 184–185, 231
White, Oscar 121–122, 231
Whitehill, Harvey (sheriff) 129–132
Whiting, __ (deputy) 16
Whitlock, __ (deputy) 51
Wickenburg, A.T. 179, 181, 187, 251
Wilkinson, Ash (driver) 44
Willcox, A.T. 249
Williams, Charles 119–120
Williams, Charlie (driver) 124
Williams, Horace (driver) 46–47, 115, 178
Williams, John 232–233
Williams, John 102, 218, 232
Williams, Dr. W.B. 79
Williamson, Charles 17–18, 127, 233
Willits, CA 47
Willow Creek, OR 145
Willows (stagecoach) Station 87
Wilson, __ 171
Wilson, Charles 57, 227–228, 233
Wilson, George 35–36, 176–177, 211, 234
Wines, Les 69
Winnemucca, NV 58, 149
Witt, J.R.V. 40
Witthouse, __ (deputy) 119
Wixon, Shephard L. 234–237
Wolf Creek, OR 149, 225
Wood, P.G. 186
Woodbridge, CA 155
Woodruff, Tom (messenger) 197
Woodworth, L.C. (driver) 11, 22
Wray, Charles 99
Wright, J.A. 237–239

Yager, __ (deputy) 65–66
Yancey, Tyron M. (sheriff) 189
Yandle, Dock 117
Yaney, __ (sheriff) 51
Yankee Jim's, CA 155
Ybarra, Pedro 218–219, 239
Yeates, James H. (sheriff) 44–45
Yosemite, CA 119, 138
Yreka, CA 11, 15–16, 30–31, 42, 44–47, 56–57, 64, 66–67, 74, 100, 102, 115, 117, 123–124, 178, 199, 218–219, 226–228, 256
Yucatan, MX 262

Zaragosa, Dolores 262
Zulick, Gov. G. Meyer 122, 133, 136

www.ingramcontent.com/pod-product-compliance
Lightning Source LLC
Chambersburg PA
CBHW081545300426
44116CB00015B/2764